TECHNIQUES OF COUNSELING

Guidance, Counseling, and Student Personnel in Education
Walter F. Johnson, *Consulting Editor*

BAILARD AND STRANG   *Parent-Teacher Conferences*

BENNETT   *Guidance and Counseling in Groups*

BERDIE   *Testing in Guidance and Counseling*

BERNHARDT   *Discipline and Child Guidance*

DETJEN AND DETJEN   *Elementary School Guidance*

HOPPOCK   *Occupational Information*

JOHNSON, STEFFLRE, AND EDELFELT   *Pupil Personnel and Guidance Services*

JONES   *Principles of Guidance*

STEFFLER   *Theories of Counseling*

WARTERS   *Techniques of Counseling*

TECHNIQUES OF COUNSELING

SECOND EDITION

Jane Warters

University of Southern California

McGraw-Hill Book Company

New York   San Francisco   Toronto   London

Techniques of Counseling

Library of Congress Catalog Card Number 63-22529

6 7 – M P – 9

68381

Preface

Any technique, procedure, or method that contributes to a better understanding of the individual—understanding by himself and others —and thus contributes to his better development is a counseling tool. Among the instruments important in the performance of the counseling functions are tests, inventories, observation reports, self-reports, cumulative personnel records, interviews, case studies, and case conferences. These are the subjects considered in this volume under the general title of *Techniques of Counseling*. The effectiveness with which these techniques are used depends upon the practitioner's skill acquired through study and experience, his ingenuity in adapting an instrument or method to the requirements of a particular situation, and his general understanding and appreciation of counseling as both an art and a science.

In order that it may serve as a means to more flexible class procedures and richer course content, the book covers almost all the commonly used counseling techniques, apart from the placement and some group procedures. Not many college teachers, perhaps, will attempt to cover through class discussions in a single course all the techniques considered here; but all, no doubt, will wish students to read on a variety of techniques. Even though the book deals largely with counseling in secondary schools, it has practical value for counselors at all levels because the counseling functions and variety of techniques are basically the same at all levels.

The major sources of the contents for the second edition, as for the first, are the professional literature, reports from counselors in the field, and the author's own experience as a counselor and teacher of counselor education courses. Three new chapters have been added to the second edition. The chapters retained from the first edition have been completely rewritten, although the general outline remains the same for some.

In the preparation of this book valuable suggestions were received from too many persons for acknowledgments to be made here to all of them. The author wishes, however, to acknowledge her special indebtedness to certain leaders in the fields of education and psychology who gave detailed, constructive criticisms of parts of the manuscripts for the first and/or second editions. She is grateful for the valuable help received from Mr. Donald E. Kitch of the California State Department of Education; Dr. Bruce V. Moore of the University of Miami; the late Dr. S. A. Hamrin of Northwestern University, who appraised portions of the first-edition manuscript; and Dr. Lawrence H. Stewart of the University of California at Berkeley, who reviewed several chapters of the second edition. The author is under special obligation to Dr. Henry B. McDaniel of Stanford University; Dr. Donald E. Super of Teachers College, Columbia University; and Dr. C. Gilbert Wrenn of the University of Minnesota, who reviewed sections of the manuscripts for both the first and second editions of this volume.

Jane Warters

Contents

PREFACE   vii

1. THE STARTING POINT   1

   The Situation. Some Basic Principles. A Means, Not an End. Quality of Relationship an Important Factor. Summary. References.

2. OBSERVATION: ANECDOTAL RECORDS   20

   Types of Anecdotal Records. Some Common Questions. The Good Anecdotal Record. Organizing and Interpreting Anecdotal Data. The Good Observer. Uses, Advantages, and Disadvantages. Summary. References.

3. OBSERVATION: RATING SCALES AND BEHAVIOR DESCRIPTIONS   42

   Scoring Methods. The Ranking Method. Graphic Rating Scales. Check Lists and Behavior Descriptions. Some Obstacles to Effective Use. Some Improvement Procedures. Development of a Rating Scale for Use in a Particular School. Summary. References.

4. TESTS: SOME BASIC CONSIDERATIONS   63

   Some Advantages. Some Limitations. Some Pitfalls. Factors Important in Test Selection. Development of the Test Program. Norms. Some Ethical Responsibilities. Summary. Major Test Publishers. References.

5. TESTS OF ABILITY AND ACHIEVEMENT   91

   Tests of Scholastic Ability. Multifactor Test Batteries. Measurement of Other Special Aptitudes. Achievement Tests. Summary. References.

6. MEASURES OF INTEREST AND PERSONALITY   113

   Vocational Interest and Its Assessment. Personality Measurement. Summary. References.

7. REPORTING AND INTERPRETING TEST DATA   134

   Precise Interpretation Rarely Possible. Some Graphic Aids. Interpreting Test Data to Students. Two Examples. Summary. References.

8. SELF–REPORTS: PERSONAL DATA AND EVALUATION QUESTIONNAIRES   169

   Personal Data Blank. Improvement of the Personal Data Form. The Evaluation Questionnaire. Summary. References.

9. SELF–REPORTS: FOLLOW–UP STUDIES   194

Purposes and Values. Follow-up Studies of Graduates. Survey Studies of Dropouts. Identification and Retention of Potential Dropouts. Summary. References.

10. SELF–REPORTS: SELF–APPRAISAL AND AUTOBIOGRAPHICAL MATERIAL   223

Self-analysis. Autobiographies. The Daily Record. Some Other Writings. Summary. References.

11. ANALYSIS OF THE INDIVIDUAL'S POSITION AND STATUS WITHIN THE GROUP   241

The Sociometric Test. Sociometric Patterns. Sociometric Grouping. Some Related Procedures. Summary. References.

12. CUMULATIVE PERSONNEL RECORDS   264

Development of the Modern Cumulative Record. Uses and Usefulness. Record Contents. Two Trends and Some Examples. Development and Revision of Record Forms. Maintenance and Use of Cumulative Records. Transfer of Cumulative Records. The Cumulative Record as a Counseling Tool. Student-kept Cumulative Records. Summary. References.

13. THE CASE STUDY   293

Uses and Usefulness. The Method. An Example. Summary. References.

14. THE CASE CONFERENCE   313

The Guidance Staff Conference. Case Conference for Nonspecialists: The Problem of Time, Initiating the Case Conference, General Procedures in the Case Conference, Some Possible Outcomes, Some Cautions. The Student-Parent-Counselor Conference. Summary. References.

15. WORKING WITH THE EMOTIONALLY HANDICAPPED   333

Mental Health Criteria and Maladjustment Signs. Prevention through Promotion of Mental Health. Some Means for Special Assistance. Manipulating the Environment. Teacher Development. Summary. References.

16. USING NONSCHOOL COMMUNITY RESOURCES   361

Types of Community Agencies. Some of the Needs. Organized Information Needed. The Referral Process. Family Group Therapy. Interagency Cooperation. Summary. References.

17. BACKGROUND TO THE COUNSELING INTERVIEW   383

Some Changing Concepts. Theoretical Framework: Psychoanalytic Theories, Field Theory, Organismic Theory, Phenomenological Theory, Stimulus-response Theories, Some Similarities. Professional Standards. Summary. References.

18. THE INTERVIEW AS A COUNSELING TOOL   409

Purposes and Advantages. The Counseling Relationship. The Interview a Learning Experience. Getting Started. Some Aids to Success. Conditions of the Interview. Summary. References.

19. THREE APPROACHES TO THE COUNSELING INTERVIEW   432

The Directive Approach. Example of Directive Counseling Interview. Client-centered Counseling. Example of Client-centered Counseling Interview. Eclectic Counseling. Examples of the Eclectic Counseling Interview. The Trend? Summary. References.

NAME INDEX   469

SUBJECT INDEX   475

1

The Starting Point

Most counselors find that the first steps in their professional education include building a set of concepts and becoming familiar with the most
useful instruments and techniques. From this starting point they move
forward to develop a guiding philosophy or theoretical framework and
to gain skill in applying principles and using techniques. This book is intended to help counselors who are at or near the starting point.

It deals largely with procedures and instruments useful in gathering, synthesizing, interpreting, and using information on individual students. It does not cover techniques that require clinical training and experience of an advanced nature. It gives only limited attention to the
procedures of environmental treatment and group work and none at all
to those used in giving placement service and in providing exploratory
experiences. The limitations of space do not permit discussion of all
important counseling techniques. The tools of the counselor are too many
for all to fit into one kit.

THE SITUATION

Back in the 1920s when student personnel work was a young movement
in education, certain workers who helped to direct it forward could not
agree regarding the part that teachers should have in the program. A few
declared that teachers should take only a very small part, if any at all;
that the work at its best could be done only by professionally trained
specialists. Some others said that the specialists were really not needed,
that the teachers could do the work very well alone. Between these two
groups and standing at various points from the extremes were others who
asserted with varying degrees of emphasis that, to be successful, student
personnel programs must be directed by specialists but, to function effectively, they must involve as many interested and capable teachers as possible and, to work smoothly, the services of the teachers and the specialists
must be closely related.

In the wake of the theorists have come the practitioners. More
often than not they have given the guidance work to the teachers, and
very often the work has been done only on paper. There are, however,
many schools in which good programs have been started, programs that

have steadily gained strength. Such schools are frequently visited by workers from other schools. Some visitors come to gaze. Others come also to ponder. They would know the genesis of a good counseling program, believing that such knowledge may enable them to start another good one.

The inquirers usually learn that the starting point was some dream or hope or plan stubbornly held to by some enterprising man or woman. Anything concrete, the inquirers know, usually has an abstract beginning. It is, however, the concrete beginning that they would know. They would know also why some programs that began well and went so far now seem unable to go farther. These programs had a starting point, then a stopping point. The inquirers ponder, and some find the problem very confusing. Others, as they wander through the maze in their thinking, begin to see the elements in the answer clearly—a qualified leader, enough willing, trained workers, and sufficient time in which to do the work well. Simple and easy, but not cheap. It is the last point regarding time that seems most difficult to provide, and it is failure to include this point that has caused some good programs first to slow up and then to stop. Providing the time needed may mark a new starting point.

The Requirements. No matter how good a plan for guidance and counseling may look on paper, the program has little chance at lasting success if proper provision is not made for three basic requirements: (1) leadership by a professionally trained, competent counselor, (2) an adequate number of interested and trained counselors, and (3) sufficient time in which to do the work. All three are essential. The foundation for the program is a three-prop affair. To omit any one of the three supports seriously weakens the program and may cause its collapse.

Any school that seeks to offer an organized systematic counseling program needs the services of professionally trained counselors who are able to provide the leadership needed, to coordinate the program, and to extend its scope by providing the services that many teachers cannot offer or cannot offer at the desired level of specialization. Unless proper provision is made both for leadership and for counseling of a specialized nature, the chances are slight that the program will progress steadily and grow strong. Moreover, if the services of professionally trained counselors are not available, much that may be done in the name of guidance may be of limited value or even useless. Some of it may actually prove harmful to the recipients.

The leader must be not only someone who has professional knowledge and technical skill but also someone who has skill in human relations, someone who can foster participation and exchange. He should be the type of leader described by Lloyd-Jones [1] as the "chain-reaction leader"—a leader who can stimulate and cultivate growth in others and

<hr/>

[1] Esther Lloyd-Jones, "Leadership as Guidance," *Teachers College Record,* 1952, 53:361.

does it in such a way that he not only helps to release the energies of others by stimulating interest in guidance but also helps others to grow in their capacities to take responsibility, exercise initiative, be creative, and become finer, stronger people.

For every student there needs to be someone with the education, skill, and interest needed for counseling him as a unique person and for interpreting his needs, problems, and potentialities to others so that the conditions important to his good development may be known, provided, and maintained. Satisfactory provision of "guidance for *all* students" cannot be made merely by assigning a certain number of students to each teacher or to a certain number of teachers. To give a teacher a certain number of students and to inform him that thereafter he is responsible for their counseling and guidance may not ensure the students' receiving service of even an inferior quality. Those who serve as counselors need to be carefully selected and prepared for their functions through preservice and inservice education, not through inservice education alone.

As much of the guidance work as possible should be done by class teachers so that guidance and instruction may be closely related. Guidance and instruction are not, however, the same; and while much guidance may be provided through teaching, much of it must be provided apart from teaching. To expect a teacher to provide all the guidance services needed by all his counselees, or to expect him to fulfill all his functions as a counselor while fulfilling his functions as a teacher, is to expect too much—no less than a miracle.

The teacher is often expected to be as versatile, resourceful, and willing as the overburdened, long-suffering mother who is much extolled in public speeches. The mother, we are told, cleans house, cooks, does the laundry, looks after a number of children, and does many other things—all at the same time. Were the mother to make the speech, she might explain that there are times when each of these tasks requires her undivided attention and that there are some tasks, such as ironing and sewing, which she has never been able to do at the same time; that, when she does not have time to do both tasks, she does one and lets the other go undone.

Likewise the teacher: he does as much as he can at one time, but there are times when he must do one thing and let another go undone. It is usually the teaching that he does and the counseling that he lets go undone. He may do so because he considers instruction more important than counseling or, more likely, because he understands instruction better than counseling and, therefore, enjoys doing it more. Or he may do so because he is afraid that, if he does otherwise, he may help to precipitate another lay outbreak against the neglect of the three R's. Hence, he believes that, if he must neglect either the student or the subject, the student should be the one neglected.

As a result, in many communities the easiest way for some young people to obtain counseling is for them to become juvenile delinquents—

to get caught and be committed to the state youth authority. At a reception center (often called a "guidance center") for delinquent boys or girls they will find trained counselors who will give hours, days, and even weeks, if necessary, to studying their cases and providing the counseling needed for helping them to work out their problems and to plan for the future. These boys and girls find that they may spend as much time with their counselors as they wish and that the counselors are ready to help them at almost any time. Could these young people receive the same attention in their schools and receive only a fraction of the guidance *on an individual basis* that they receive at the guidance centers for delinquent youth, many would probably never become wards of the state or need assistance as extensive as that received at the reception centers. The state would be saved considerable money, and some youth would be saved considerable sorrow if all boys and girls could receive at their schools counseling and other guidance services in keeping with their real need, which is often much more extensive than their assumed need for such services.

The Time Problem. In giving special attention here to the time problem, the intention is not to imply that the time requirement is the most important. If any requirement has to be given priority, that one no doubt should be the one with respect to leadership by a professionally trained counselor. Since, however, all three requirements are essential, there is little point in trying to decide which is the most important. Special attention is being given to the time requirement only because it seems the one currently least well provided for. Inadequate provision is seriously limiting the effectiveness of the counselors' work even in many schools in which the programs are carried out by trained, competent workers under the leadership of specialists. There are many high schools in which well-trained counselors are working very hard but are not achieving their goals because they have too much to do in the time available. Their case loads are much too heavy for them to give sufficient time to many cases.

Some school administrators with limited education in student personnel work fail to understand the amount of time needed for a good counseling program. They assign the counselors more students than they can possibly serve well. Some writers who are well trained in guidance and who know the specialized, time-consuming nature of the work help to foster this practice by advocating too high a number of students per counselor, a number that they seem able to defend on paper but which proves definitely not sound in practice. Some writers, for example, state that a counselor can serve 100 students or more for each period that he is released from teaching for work in counseling. These writers apparently do not consider instruction and counseling of equal importance. It is hardly possible that anyone is of the opinion that a class teacher should have as many as 100 students or more per period.

While the national ratio of counselors to students has greatly improved, it is still not good. The standard recommended by the Commission on Guidance in American Schools[2] is a ratio of at least 1 qualified counselor to every 300 students. In 1960 a U.S. Office of Education report[3] showed that some 20,000 more counselors were needed in the secondary schools to raise the national ratio from 1 counselor to more than 600 students to a ratio of 1 to 300. Actually, this ratio is considered by many people to be inadequate. Conant,[4] for example, sets a ratio of 1 to 250–300 in the junior and senior high schools. Furthermore, he recommends that counselors be permitted to give "virtually full time" to counseling. At the 1960 White House Conference[5] it was recommended that in the high schools the number of students per counselor "be reduced from the present ratio of 625 to 1, to 250 to 1." In order that counselors may give virtually all their time to counseling, one state board of education[6] has recommended that counselors receive clerical service to the amount of one hour of service for every 100 to 150 students and that there be a minimum of one guidance secretary in every school.

Even the ratio of 1 to 300 is inadequate in terms of the standards commonly set for instruction. Also, to advocate that counselors have as many as 300 counselees or more may be to ignore certain facts of human nature. A person cannot absorb more than a certain number of human relations. Moreno, in reporting research regarding the limits of emotional interest, stresses that, while emotional expansiveness is subjectable to training, "no individual can be thrown beyond what appears to be his organic limit." The overloaded counselor may show the same reaction as the overloaded housemother in Moreno's[7] example:

A housemother can embrace with her given emotional energy only a certain number of children. If the number of girls she embraces surpasses a certain limit, a process of selectivity sets in. She will develop a one-sided interest towards those to whom she is spontaneously "drawn"; the rest will fall on the sideline. This limit of expansiveness has, thus, an effect upon

[2] C. Gilbert Wrenn, *The Counselor in a Changing World*, p. 156. Washington, D.C.: American Personnel and Guidance Association, 1962.

[3] H. M. Smith, "Pupil Personnel Services: What and How," *School Life*, 1961, 45(9):17.

[4] James B. Conant, *The American High School Today*, p. 44. New York: McGraw-Hill Book Company, Inc., 1959; *A Memorandum to School Boards: Recommendations for Education in the Junior High School Years*, p. 27. Princeton, N.J.: Educational Testing Service, 1960.

[5] Golden Anniversary White House Conference on Children and Youth, *Recommendations: Composite Report of Forum Findings*, p. 26. Washington, D.C.: Government Printing Office, 1960.

[6] "Recommended Standards for Local Guidance Programs," *California Guidance Newsletter*, 1961, 15(4):3.

[7] J. L. Moreno, *Who Shall Survive?* rev. ed., p. 286. Beacon, N.Y.: Beacon House, Inc., 1953.

the organization of the group through producing a number of girls isolated from the housemother either because there are too many in the cottage or because of "faulty" assignments.

The counselor who is assigned more than 300 counselees can establish a relationship with most of them only en masse. He cannot feel or express a genuine interest in each student as a unique individual. He is fortunate if he recognizes his counselees when he meets them in the corridors, on the school grounds, in the streets, or elsewhere. Like the housemother, he will be "drawn" to some and will leave others on the sidelines.

Solution Possible. There is little likelihood of proper provision being made for counseling in schools and colleges until guidance is put on the same time basis as instruction. In many high schools and colleges faculty members who serve as counselors are scheduled for the same number of class hours as the ones who do not. In some states the tax-supported schools and colleges may feel forced to follow this practice because state funds are allocated on the basis of class periods and class enrollments. This situation may continue until members of state departments of education or state legislatures equate guidance or counseling and instruction in their thinking.

There is some evidence of a trend in this direction. In most states, for example, a person may not teach a particular subject unless he is certificated to do so. Now in some states a person may not function as a counselor for even one period of the day unless he holds a certificate showing him to be properly qualified through professional education to function as a counselor. And funds are being allocated specifically for counseling as well as for instruction.

When a group of counselees of the size of the average class group is considered equivalent to a class group and financial provision is made accordingly by legislation or ruling of the state department of education, when counselors are assigned counseling groups *instead of class groups and not in addition to a full class load,* and when counselors give as much time to counseling groups as to class groups, then perhaps proper provision can be made for counseling—provided, of course, that the persons who serve as counselors are properly qualified for their work. Under this plan, if a person is named counselor to 30 students and assigned one class less than he would be given otherwise, he has for counseling the five class periods a week (if the class meets daily) plus the time that he ordinarily gives for one class in grading papers, holding conferences with students about their classwork, assembling materials, and doing other such things.

Ordinarily a student should have the same counselor throughout his stay in the school. Should, however, the assignment of any student to a particular counselor prove "faulty," a change in counselor should be permitted for the same reason that Moreno [8] advocates correction of "faulty" assignments made to housemothers:

> The effort the latter has to make to reach the child is out of proportion to what she has available for her. And if two or three such individuals are assigned to the housemother, problems to her but easily reachable to others, she becomes, if she takes her duty seriously, more exhausted through dealing with them than through efforts made for a dozen other children. Eventually she becomes indifferent and she tries to mask her undoing.

The counselor is not expected to meet all his counselees each day. He spends much of his time conferring with teachers and parents, as well as with individual students. He may wish to have regular group contacts with all or some of his counselees, particularly the ones who are new to the school, so that they may become acquainted with him and learn how he can be of service to them.

In some schools counselors serve as teachers of group guidance classes. This arrangement may not prove satisfactory where such classes are taught in a traditional manner, examinations are given, and marks are assigned. Some students find it difficult to "use" the same person as teacher and counselor, and some counselors find it difficult to play the two roles with the same student. When, however, "orientation," "junior problems," "social living," "human relations," and other such courses are designed as much for group guidance as for information-giving purposes, and when the class procedures resemble as far as possible those of group counseling, then desirably the teacher is a counselor. Certainly he should be someone with more than the basic training in guidance.

In many schools (probably most) all counselees assigned to a counselor are at the same grade level. All are freshmen or sophomores or juniors or seniors. In some other schools a counselor's case load includes students at each grade level. This plan for mixed groups or vertical grouping has important advantages over the horizontal grouping or single-grade plan. For one thing, it fosters teamwork. Under this plan counselors are less likely to focus their attention on matters of special importance at one grade level while giving too little thought to matters of special concern to students at other grade levels. When counselors have counselees from all grades, they are concerned with both the common and the special problems of students at all grade levels. Hence, they tend to pool their efforts.

Furthermore, the use of mixed groups makes for a better distribution of the extra work involved in helping students at special decision points in their school careers. If, for example, a counselor has this year only seniors for his counselees and next year will have a new group of the incoming students, he may find it difficult to meet his present group's need for extra counseling help with their problems of graduation and

[8] *Ibid.*

post-high school plans, and still have enough time for conferring with his next year's counselees and their parents while these students are still in the lower school. To help his counselees of next year make an easy and smooth transition from the lower school to the new one, he should be working with them and their parents now. But he finds this difficult to do without neglecting the seniors. When all counselors are involved in the special work with seniors and the new students of next term, none may find the work so heavy that he has to neglect one group for the other.

The basis on which incoming students are assigned to a counselor is relatively unimportant. If a counselor is to teach one section of a group guidance class, then the students assigned to that section can be also assigned to him as counselees. If the class is more a group guidance than a subject-matter class, such an arrangement can help to relate group work and counseling as well as to broaden the scope of the counselor's relations with his counselees. Also, he can provide valuable precounseling orientation through the group guidance class.

This plan is not likely to work, however, in some adulterated form, such as the homeroom plan, whereby a teacher-counselor is assigned some thirty students whom he meets every day for less than half an hour and once or twice a week for about fifty minutes. Most of the short homeroom period is ordinarily used for administrative purposes (checking attendance, reading announcements, etc.). Nearly all homeroom members are present during the long period, which makes it very difficult for the teacher-counselor to give his undivided attention to individual students. It also makes it difficult for some students to talk freely with the counselor even though the other students cannot hear what he says.

Teacher-Counselors versus Full-time Counselors. One evidence of improvement in the counseling situation at the secondary school level is the trend toward decreased use of teacher-counselors and increased use of full-time counselors. The term "teacher-counselor" is generally used to describe the student personnel worker who is released from teaching on a part-time basis for the purpose of counseling or who provides counseling as an adjunct to teaching without released time for this purpose.

Some teacher-counselors are well prepared through preservice education for their counseling functions. Too often, however, they are appointed teacher-counselors primarily on the basis of their strong interest in the work or their ability to relate well with students. These are important assets; but, unless combined with professional education, they are not enough. As stated above, the use of well-qualified teacher-counselors does not always prove satisfactory because some teachers and some students find it difficult to establish a satisfying counselor-counselee relationship with persons with whom they are already involved in a teacher-student relationship.

The teacher-counselor (with or without released time for counseling) is not to be confused with the part-time counselor. The term "part-time counselor," as used here, refers to the counselor who serves as teacher or leader for group guidance classes which are relatively unstructured, which are student-centered and problem-centered, and in which the teaching method is group discussion more often than the lecture. The part-time counselor's relationship to the class members is more that of a group counselor than the traditional one of teacher.

In some schools the full-time counselors are no better qualified for their counseling functions than are the teacher-counselors. When full-time counselors are required to meet special certification requirements, the average full-time counselor is probably better prepared than the average teacher-counselor. To prevent evasion of certification requirements through use of teacher-counselors, some states require the counselor's certificate of anyone who functions as a counselor if only for a small part of the day.

While examination of the literature on the subject does not show all writers in agreement, it does show majority opinion definitely in favor of full-time counselors as opposed to teacher-counselors. Full-time counselors are recommended by individuals, such as Conant,[9] and by such groups as the Commission on Guidance in American Schools.[10] The recommendation of the Commission is as follows:

> That the professional job description of a school counselor specify that he perform four major functions: (a) counsel with students; (b) consult with teachers, administrators, and parents as they in turn deal with students; (c) study the changing facts about the student population and interpret what is found to school committees and administrators; (d) coordinate counseling resources in school and between school and community. From two-thirds to three-fourths of the counselor's time, in either elementary or high school, should be committed to the first two of these functions. Activities [such as the teaching of academic courses] that do not fall into one of these four areas neither should be expected nor encouraged as part of the counselor's regular working schedule.

Research studies reported by Caravello,[11] Thomson,[12] and others indicate that students also consider full-time counselors preferable to teacher-counselors. In Caravello's study less than 10 per cent of the students in both the experimental and the control groups reported teacher-counselors more helpful than the "guidance specialist," whose only function was that of counseling.

[9] Conant, *op. cit.*

[10] Wrenn, *op. cit.*, p. 137.

[11] Santo J. Caravello, "Effectiveness of High School Guidance Services," *Personnel and Guidance Journal*, 1958, 36:323–325.

[12] G. Muriel Thomson, "Comparisons of Students' Evaluations of Guidance Services under Varying Plans of Organization," unpublished doctor's dissertation. Los Angeles: University of Southern California, 1960.

In Thomson's study more than two thousand seniors rated the "guidance help" which they had received on a five-point scale ranging from "not helpful" to "very helpful." These seniors were enrolled in schools that tended to provide counseling according to one of three patterns of organization: (1) full-time counselors, (2) teachers with released time for counseling, (3) teachers counseling without released time for this purpose. The students with full-time counselors gave the most favorable ratings to the "guidance help received."

Even when there is adequate provision for professionally trained full-time counselors, not all the counseling offered in a school is to be provided by them. There are levels of counseling ranging from the casual, conversation type offered by teachers through the advisory or information-giving service given by homeroom teachers, registrars, and the like, to the specialized counseling offered by counselors and psychologists—and in some schools to the psychotherapy provided by psychiatrists. In this book we are concerned with the techniques of counseling at all levels below that of psychotherapy. Hence, attention is given to the techniques of the nonspecialist, as well as to those of the specialist.

SOME BASIC PRINCIPLES

The basic philosophy underlying counseling and guidance is essentially that of democracy. Frequently referred to as "the student personnel point of view," its principal tenets include the following:

1. *Counseling is concerned with the individual as a group member.* When a counselor ceases to think in terms of aiding individuals, it is doubtful that his work should be called "counseling." To employ tests, for example, in order to determine group tendencies is an administrative or a research procedure rather than a counseling technique. Only when the findings are used to help the individuals tested can testing be considered a part of counseling.

In working with the individual, however, the counselor does not overlook the fact that the individual, as a member of a number of groups, always functions in a social setting. Therefore he considers the contemporary social setting and the social demands imposed upon the individual as well as the individual's needs, interests, and abilities. He considers himself responsible for helping the individual to gain the experiences needed for learning how to establish and maintain good relations with others and for gaining self-understanding through increased understanding of other people.

The primary focus is on the individual. It is on his growth and welfare rather than, for example, on the economic needs of the nation. The counselor may help the student to analyze the manpower factors influencing careers, but he does not impose choices or decisions upon the student. As stressed in one report of the Educational Policies Commission,[13] the nation's manpower needs can best be met by "enabling each individual to discover his own abilities and to develop them fully."

2. *Counseling is concerned with the whole student.* The emphasis is upon the unity of personality and the unitary nature of the counseling process. The counselor knows that a student's intellectual development is helped or hindered by the state of his mental and physical health and that his social adjustment is closely related to his emotional development. He knows that he cannot counsel a student regarding occupational choice, for example, apart from consideration of such other matters as personality, educational achievement, strong interests, health, interpersonal relations, and the like. To separate vocational problems from the educational, social, or personal may block adequate solution to any.

3. *Counseling is for all students.* It is not just for "problem students" and the gifted. It is provided for developmental and preventive purposes, as well as for adjustive and remedial purposes. Moreover, since most students are "normal," the bulk of the counseling offered in the schools and colleges should be primarily developmental in nature.

In some schools counselors do not find it easy to use some techniques, such as the case study and the case conference, with all students. However, when they employ these techniques with average students as well as with the gifted, the slow learners, and the "discipline cases," they apply this principle in practice better than do those who limit use of such techniques to work with exceptional students.

4. *Individual differences should be determined and provided for as far as possible.* In our country this principle is given an interpretation very different from that given it in some other countries where individual differences are considered chiefly for purposes of selection and placement in keeping with the welfare of "the state." In a democracy individual differences have a significance beyond group interests. They are perceived as being important to individual development and are considered in education so that the individual may become a happy, well-developed man or woman, as well as a good citizen.

Provision for individual differences in terms of needs, backgrounds, abilities, personality traits, and interests is possible in our schools and colleges to a far greater extent than many school people are willing to admit. In some schools much more is being done in this respect than is being done in some others that are much better equipped for doing so.

5. *Counseling is directed toward helping the individual to become progressively more self-understanding and self-directing.* It is focused largely on helping students to reach intelligent decisions in all areas of life. When a student is permitted to share in the study of his abilities, interests, goals, and values, he has a much better chance to achieve self-understanding, self-acceptance, and self-direction than when others make

[13] Educational Policies Commission, *Manpower and Education,* chap. 6. Washington, D.C.: National Education Association, 1956.

most of his important choices and decisions for him. As stressed by the Commission on Guidance in American Schools,[14] the major goal of counseling is "increased self-responsibility and an increased maturity in decision-making on the part of the student."

6. *Counseling does not deprive the individual of the right of choice.* For example, three courses of action may be open to a student. Available information indicates that the first has more to offer than the other two and that on the whole the third is quite undesirable. The counselor helps the student explore these three choices. Eventually the student decides to follow the third course of action. Does the counselor take steps to close this course to the student or do all that he can to force him to follow the first course? He does not.

The first course of action may seem more in harmony with the student's pattern of abilities, but interest and effort are also needed for success. Lacking the interest required for putting forth effort, the student might fail in the first course should he decide under pressure to follow it. It is in the third course that he has strong interest. His interest may be sufficiently strong to make him willing to put out the extra effort needed to compensate for any limitations in ability.

More often than some counselors care to admit, a student's "poor choice" does not turn out so poorly as expected. Even when it does, the student may gain more than he loses from the experience. It may prove a valuable experience in terms of self-understanding. To deprive a student of the right to make bad decisions may hamper him in his growing up.

(It is true that at times a student personnel worker has to take from a student the right of decision because of the student's lack of experience or maturity or because of legal requirements. Such action, however, should not be labeled "counseling" or "guidance" but should be called by its proper name of "prescription" or "compulsion.")

The counselor tries to help the student see the need for or importance of certain decisions but refrains from making them for him. Sometimes he must help a student perceive the need for making a decision, as well as help him make a sound one. The choice of a curriculum or the selection of electives, for example, cannot be postponed any longer. Or a student is about to graduate, to withdraw from school, or to seek work and so cannot delay making a particular decision any longer.

In some other cases the counselor may need to help the student put off making a decision. The student may be responding too much to the pressures brought to bear on him by his family, friends, or his own insecurities. He may need to delay decision making until he is less pressured and able to appraise the possible choices in terms of his own needs, wants, and values. In Mathewson's [15] words:

[14] Wrenn, *op. cit.,* p. 109.

[15] Robert H. Mathewson, *Guidance Policy and Practice,* 3d ed., p. 174. New York: Harper & Row, Publishers, Incorporated, 1962.

Individual plans and choices shall be based primarily upon individual values, needs, and interests—not those of parents, not those of current social urgency. This is not to say that either the concerns of parents or the needs of society—long-term or short-term—will be neglected. Both must be taken very seriously into account by the individual and by the counselor. But in so doing the counselor cannot attempt to sway the counselee in a direction contrary to his own inclinations in planning, nor can he recruit the counselee for some sector in the socioeconomic front.

7. *Counseling is a continuous process.* To have developmental and preventive value, counseling and guidance must be a process, not an act. Counseling, as pointed out above, deals with choices and adjustments that cannot always be made within a short space of time. The making of some decisions is a developmental process involving a series of decisions and spanning many years. Hence, counseling needs to be available to students at all points throughout their school careers rather than just at the entry and exit points.

Counseling has to be more than an initial push. It needs to be a continuous, systematic service. In too many schools the service is available only or primarily at certain times, such as at time of entry into a new school, the work world, or military service, or just before the opening of a new term. Because too many students are interviewed in a short period of time and too many matters are taken up during one interview, some students find themselves more confused than aided by such service. Their comments regarding the value of the help received frequently testify to their need for counseling offered in an unhurried fashion throughout the school years rather than at the beginning of a term or at the end of the last year in a particular school.

8. *To function well, counselors need the knowledge, skills, and understandings that are best attained through professional education.* Sympathetic interest in students, common sense, and intuition are needed; but they are not in themselves a sufficiently strong basis for effective performance. Wrenn's [16] review of studies of the counselor's role shows that the counselor needs professional education that will qualify him as a generalist in a number of functions and as a specialist in at least one type of service. His "skills should include not only those necessary for the individual counseling relationship but those essential to working effectively with groups." In addition to students, his clients include parents, teachers, and administrators. To meet the varied expectations of these clients, the counselor "must have a fairly high level of psychological sophistication in his professional education."

9. *Organization is needed for the counseling program to be effective.* Long-range planning is needed. Responsibility has to be fixed for performance of specific functions. Efforts need to be coordinated, and provision must be made for systematic use of available resources. Planned,

[16] C. Gilbert Wrenn, "Status and Role of the School Counselor," *Personnel and Guidance Journal,* 1957, 36:178–179.

cooperative, coordinated action cannot be taken for granted and left to chance; but it will be unless adequate provision is made for suitable organization and proper administration of the counseling program.

The director or leader should be someone with professional education in student personnel work. As brought out in the report of the Commission on Guidance in the American School,[17] "since the work of the counselor deliberately covers the total school program and the total school population, more frequently than not he will be given responsibility for this coordination. The primary consideration is that this is professional leadership by a professional person."

A MEANS, NOT AN END

All counseling and guidance techniques should serve primarily as means to helping individual students. None should be permitted to become an end in itself. Yet this does happen at times. When, for example, case studies are carefully made, filed, and only brought forth to be displayed as examples of good records or of the counselor's skill, and the subjects of the case studies continue on their ways relatively unaffected by the careful studies made of them, then making case studies has become an end in itself.

When detailed cumulative records are made on students and kept locked in a central file, and the information in them is not used because not shared with others, then keeping records is a noneducational or nonguidance objective as far as the students are concerned. When tests are administered and the results are never used as a basis for modifying instructional methods, for providing appropriate curricula and counseling, for changing school routine and regulations, and for doing other such things, then testing is an end in itself rather than a means to the end of helping individual students to achieve optimum personal development as group members—the end that should govern the use of any counseling technique.

In studying and assisting students, the counselor soon finds that rarely can he rely upon the use of one technique alone. He finds that he needs to become skilled in the use of as many techniques as possible. While he learns that some are better than others, he also learns that the best one used with others is usually better than the best one used alone. Furthermore, the best technique in one situation is not the best one in all situations because the one that is best will vary with counselors, students, and situations. One counselor, for example, may be especially skilled in the use of tests, but not all students are equally responsive to tests. Another may ordinarily be very successful in using the interview to secure the information needed for placing students in part-time employment, but he may not be equally successful in using the interview for helping

[17] Wrenn, *The Counselor in a Changing World*, p. 155.

students to find a place in the activity program. Furthermore, he finds that with some applicants for part-time jobs the interview yields little of the information he needs; and so he may use a questionnaire or some other procedure with these students.

No one technique can produce all the information needed. A test may show a student to be superior in scholastic aptitude, but it does not show whether his scholastic success is correspondingly high. Another instrument, such as the cumulative personnel record, may yield this information. Records of observation on another student may give the picture of a passive, indifferent girl but give no clues as to the reason, whereas a case study made of this girl may show that she is usually tired and sleepy and may disclose why she is not getting the rest needed for being as alert and active as she could be under other conditions. A questionnaire or an autobiography may show that a certain boy considers being able to get along well with others exceedingly important and that he wants very much to be popular, but the sociograms on his class group may show him usually unchosen by others.

The information obtained through the use of a particular technique at one time may not be so accurate as that obtained through the use of the same technique or of a different procedure at another time. The findings from one technique may help to disclose the accuracies and inaccuracies in the findings from another. A boy's responses on an interest inventory, for example, indicate that he has a very high interest in the sciences; but the interview data, anecdotal reports, and other material in his cumulative record folder indicate that he may be only professing an interest in science in order to live up to his father's expectations. The data from a reading test show another boy to be low in reading skills, but scholastic aptitude test results and reports by his teachers show him superior in linguistic ability. Also, his cumulative record shows consistently high achievement in some areas in which reading skill is closely related to success.

Such examples show that items of information obtained through the use of different techniques supplement, contradict, and confirm one another. They also underline the importance of a counselor's regarding his hypotheses and conclusions as tentative and of the need for his being flexible and willing to check the reliability of inferences through use of other resources.

Through professional education and practice a counselor gains skill in detecting the significance of different items and different combinations of items. He learns that each must be considered in the light of others and that no important decision can be made on the basis of one item alone and rarely on the findings from use of one technique alone. One item and one technique are not enough when the goal is optimum personal development of individual students.

QUALITY OF RELATIONSHIP AN IMPORTANT FACTOR

The ability to establish and maintain the right kind of relationship with students largely determines the extent to which a counselor is able to apply the personnel point of view in practice. In working with students, he takes care to be cordial, friendly, warmly responsive, and sympathetically understanding. At the same time he tries to be sufficiently objective to maintain proper perspective on a student's problems. To be objective, he need not, however, appear to be cold, indifferent, or uninterested. Nor should he be.

The counselor's interest is personal inasmuch as he is interested in students as individuals and stands ready to help them as best he can with personal matters, as well as with matters primarily educational and vocational. His relationship is not personal, however, in the sense of being intimate or of his becoming too involved emotionally in a student's affairs. Some nonspecialists in counseling err in establishing a relationship that is too intimate or emotional. They do so perhaps largely because of a misconception of student personnel work. Confusing it with sentimentality, they establish a relationship that is undesirably personal. They try, as they may explain, to be like a father or a mother to their counselees. Most students, however, find the parent type of counselor more a handicap than a help. This type of counselor too often fails to develop a professional interest in students as distinct personalities. Interest frequently stems from a desire to run other people's lives or from a thwarted need for attention and affection.

Unfortunately, some men and women enter school work, and counseling in particular, because they hope to gain through relations with students satisfaction of certain personal needs which they find frustrated in their relations with family and others. Unable to satisfy sufficiently elsewhere their desire to love and to be loved, they seek satisfaction in their work with students and, by so doing, harm some. These counselors tend to pull certain students close to them by showing them special consideration. They support these favorites against others—teachers and students —and encourage them to cry on their shoulders. They cannot bear to see their adopted children hurt; and so they try to shield them from disappointment, criticism, and failure. In return they expect full payment in terms of appreciation and gratitude. Consequently, they often deprive their counselees of the right of choice, but not by ordering and forbidding. They use the base technique of blackmailing with love. The average student will not be such an ingrate as to go against the wishes of a devoted, loving counselor. One does not act that way, he thinks, with a loving parent; neither, he feels, should one behave so with a parent surrogate. Such teachers should not be teachers. Never should they be named counselors.

Although the counselor will need to give some students more time and assistance than he gives others, he will not differentiate such students from others through the quality of his relationship with them. He should be friendly with all but ordinarily the bosom friend of none. When a counselee is seriously frustrated in his need to love and to be loved, the counselor may find it necessary to supply the emotional response wanted and needed. But, properly objective, he does not encourage the student to be dependent upon him. He knows that he cannot be a continuing active force in the life of this student and so strives to be an assisting force. He does not withhold support. For a while he may have to permit the student to lean upon him, but he does not foster dependence. He tries to help the student to be on his own as soon as possible and to find friendship and affection among his peers. Before long, he hopes, the student will be able to make and keep friends and through his friendship relations find adequate satisfaction of his social and ego-integrative needs.

This caution against becoming too involved emotionally with students is not to be interpreted as meaning that the counselor should not have feelings or should not show them. It means only that he should seek to understand them and not to satisfy his own emotional needs at the students' expense. Few students are attracted to a colorless, poker-faced counselor. Enthusiasm and vivacity are as much assets in counseling as in teaching. Dynamic personalities attract people, both young and old. Nor is the statement that the counselor will not be a continuing active force in the life of the student to be interpreted as meaning that he should not or will not have a lasting influence. The influence of a good counselor may last throughout the lives of those he counsels.

Objectivity in counseling students certainly does not involve detachment or dehumanization. Nor does it rule out enthusiasm, strong interest, sympathy, and kindness. Instead, it strengthens them by conserving and channeling their force in the right direction. Any counselor would do well to borrow from Wrenn's [18] creed and periodically remind himself that in carrying out his counseling functions he "must have heart, brains, and self-control."

SUMMARY

Professional leadership, a sufficient number of trained, competent counselors, and adequate counseling time are the three basic requirements for a strong counseling program in schools and colleges. The national ratio of counselors to students is improving but is still not satisfactory. The standard currently recommended for high schools is one qualified counselor to every 250 to 300 students. Research indicates that full-time counselors are to be preferred to part-time counselors.

[18] C. Gilbert Wrenn, "Trends and Predictions in Vocational Guidance," *Occupations,* 1947, 23:213.

Certain basic principles underlie the program: The focus is on helping individual students in a social setting. Counseling is concerned with the whole student and is for all students. It is directed toward helping the student to become progressively more self-understanding and self-directing. It is available to him throughout his school years and not at just the major transition and decision points. It is provided systematically under professional leadership by counselors prepared for their functions through professional education in counseling.

In seeking to help students achieve optimal development, the counselor uses a variety of techniques. Rarely does he rely on one alone. Effective use of any technique depends in a large measure upon the quality of his relationship with students. Desirably, it is a relationship that is characterized by sympathy, empathic understanding, and a sincere desire to help. The counselor takes care not to use the relationship as a means for meeting his own ego needs.

REFERENCES

Arbuckle, Dugald S.: "Counseling: Philosophy or Science," *Personnel and Guidance Journal,* 1960, 39:11–14.

Barry, Ruth, and Beverly Wolf: *Modern Issues in Guidance and Personnel Work.* New York: Bureau of Publications, Teachers College, Columbia University, 1957.

Berdie, Ralph F.: "The Counselor and His Manpower Responsibilities," *Personnel and Guidance Journal,* 1960, 38:458–463.

Bowles, Frank H.: "The Nature of Guidance," *Personnel and Guidance Journal,* 1959, 38:112–119.

Carle, Richard F., et al. (eds.): "Guidance: An Examination," *Harvard Educational Review,* 1962, 32:373–519.

Farwell, Gail F.: "Need for a Developmental Approach to Continuity in the Guidance Program," *Educational Leadership,* 1961, 18:358–362.

Henry, Nelson B. (ed.): *Personnel Services in Education,* Fifty-eighth Yearbook of the National Society for the Study of Education, part II. Chicago: The University of Chicago Press, 1959.

Hill, George E.: "The Selection of School Counselors," *Personnel and Guidance Journal,* 1961, 39:355–360.

Hutson, Percival W.: "The Rationale of Guidance," *Bulletin of the National Association of Secondary-school Principals,* 1958, 42(236):121–128.

Malcolm, David D.: "Every Teacher a Counselor, but...." *Education,* 1960, 81:195–197.

———: "The Image of the Future Secondary School Guidance Program," *Journal of Secondary Education,* 1961, 36:72–78.

Mathewson, Robert H.: *Guidance Policy and Practice,* 3d ed. New York: Harper & Row, Publishers, Incorporated, 1962.

Miller, Carrol H.: *Foundations of Guidance.* New York: Harper & Row, Publishers, Incorporated, 1961.

Murphy, Gardner: "The Cultural Context of Guidance," *Personnel and Guidance Journal,* 1958, 37:129–135.

Pierson, George A., and Claude W. Grant: "The Road Ahead for the School Counselor," *Personnel and Guidance Journal,* 1959, 38:207–210.

Rogers, Carl R.: "The Characteristics of a Helping Relationship," *Personnel and Guidance Journal,* 1958, 37:6–16.

Stewart, James A.: "Factors Influencing Teacher Attitudes toward and Participation in Guidance Services," *Personnel and Guidance Journal,* 1961, 39:729–734.

Tennyson, Willard W.: "Time: The Counselor's Dilemma!" *Personnel and Guidance Journal,* 1958, 37:129–133.

Warters, Jane: *High School Personnel Work Today,* 2d ed., part I. New York: McGraw-Hill Book Company, Inc., 1956.

Wilkins, William D., and Barbara J. Perlmutter: "The Philosophical Foundations of Guidance and Personnel Work," *Review of Educational Research,* 1960, 30(2):97–104.

Wolfe, Dael L.: "Guidance and Educational Strategy," *Personnel and Guidance Journal,* 1958, 37:17–25.

Wrenn, C. Gilbert: *The Counselor in a Changing World.* Washington, D.C.: American Personnel and Guidance Association, 1962.

2

Observation: Anecdotal Records

The techniques most commonly used in schools and colleges in appraising personality are tests (usually in the form of inventories) and reports on observation (usually in the forms of ratings and anecdotal records). Observation is the basic technique in studying the individual. It is the most direct and logical way to study a student's typical behavior in naturally recurring situations. It is a technique used by both the specialist and the nonspecialist. Systematic, scientific use of observation, however, ordinarily requires professional education. Many teachers are now obtaining some such education through participation in child-study groups and other similar inservice education activities.

Until the early 1930s observation reports in forms other than ratings, such as behavior descriptions and anecdotal reports, were used more by specialists and for research purposes than by teachers or for guidance purposes. Since the 1930s, however, much attention has been given to educating teachers in observation procedures and in the writing of behavior descriptions and anecdotal records. It is the systematic use of observation rather than the technique itself that is an innovation for the nonspecialists, because teachers have always employed observation. Many elementary school teachers, for example, make it a daily practice to observe their students more or less systematically for symptoms of ill health. Such practices are not, however, usually followed by teachers at the secondary and college levels. Furthermore, high school and college teachers probably make less use of observations in general than do elementary school teachers, and probably because they have had less supervised preservice education in the use of observation as a classroom procedure.

Observation is a technique that can be easily applied to the natural situations of school life. It is best used for studying aspects of behavior that cannot be studied through more objective and accurate methods. Standardized tests and work products, for example, are better than observation for appraising a student's scholastic aptitude, educational achievement, and creative ability. On the other hand, the student's social functioning and his ways of coping with personal problems can be better appraised through observation than through tests and questionnaires.

TYPES OF ANECDOTAL RECORDS

The use of the term "anecdotal record" apparently originated in 1931 at the Rochester Athenaeum and Mechanics Institute (now the Rochester Institute of Technology), where this form of report was adopted as an "administrative substitute for an improvement upon the rating scale." [1] The current rather widespread use of anecdotal records stems, however, largely from the experimental work of the Commission on Teacher Education of the American Council on Education and the child-study programs sponsored by the Institute for Child Study of the University of Maryland, under the leadership of Daniel A. Prescott.

The experimental project conducted by the Commission on Teacher Education [2] between 1939 and 1945 was designed to help teachers gain increased scientific knowledge of human behavior and development through systematic study of individual students. By learning to see behavior clearly, to record observations descriptively, and to interpret the records objectively, many teachers came to understand the motivations and needs underlying a student's behavior and some of the complex forces influencing his life. In 1937 the Institute for Child Study was established at the University of Maryland to continue this work of helping teachers to study individual boys and girls so that they might better understand students as developing individuals. [3]

The explanation of the anecdotal record offered in 1936 by Randall, then president of the Rochester Athenaeum, is still more or less accepted as the standard definition. According to Randall: [4]

> [The anecdotal report] is a record of some significant item of conduct, a record of an episode in the life of a student; a word picture of the student in action; the teacher's best effort at taking a word snapshot at the moment of the incident; any narrative of events in which the student takes such a part as to reveal something which may be significant about his personality.

Randall's Classification. Randall described the four types of anecdotal records used at the Athenaeum: (1) objective description of a specific incident; (2) description of the incident followed by interpretation; (3) description of the incident followed by, first, interpretation and, second, recommendation; and (4) a running account in which description and interpretation are intermixed.

[1] John A. Randall, "The Anecdotal Behavior Journal," *Progressive Education,* 1936, 13(1):22.
[2] Commission on Teacher Education, *Helping Teachers Understand Children.* Washington, D.C.: American Council on Education, 1945.
[3] For a description of procedures and some results see Daniel A. Prescott, *The Child in the Educative Process.* New York: McGraw-Hill Book Company, Inc., 1957.
[4] Randall, *op. cit.*

Because too many anecdotal records tend to be more reports on the teachers' reactions than reports on their observations, some writers believe that the only acceptable or the most acceptable form is the first type, i.e., that a record should be limited to objective description of the incident observed. Others recognize that certain advantages may be gained from the inclusion of interpretation and recommendation but urge that they be separated from objective description. Preferably, interpretive comments and recommendations are reported on the reverse side of the record sheet. If given on the same side, they should be clearly apart from the anecdote itself.

The fourth type of record—a mixture of observations and comments—is the type that teachers tend to write when free to report as they please. It is the type generally frowned upon by the authorities, but at times it may have special value because of the inclusion of comments, or it may have definite significance in spite of the comments. This type of record was held acceptable by Randall [5] because

> ... in many such cases, the insight disclosed in the record as received is so keen that a guidance officer can use it effectively even though it has not been written down strictly in accordance with a logical form. The risk of spoiling the intangible qualities of the record is too great to warrant asking that it be rewritten in a more objective and analytical manner.

The use of a form sheet that provides for the reporting of explanations, interpretations, and recommendations apart from description of the incident can help a teacher to make his report on the incident objective and specific. The record form used in an experimental project at Plainfield, N.J., is shown in Figure 1. In this experiment inclusion of explanatory comments was often found to be not only helpful but also necessary at times for the record to be meaningful. Traxler [6] brings out this point in appraising some of the anecdotes submitted to him by the Plainfield teachers for his evaluation:

> For example, in one of Miss A's anecdotes concerning Tom Smith, the objective description states that "Tom informed me before class that he has finished his library book, The Story of David Livingstone, which I helped him select last Friday." This incident in itself does not seem very important, but in the light of the comment on the back of the sheet to the effect that Tom has the lowest score of any freshman on the Iowa test and that he usually labors through a book, if he finishes it at all, the reading of a book in one weekend becomes an outstanding achievement for this boy and one that is well worth reporting. The teachers should be encouraged to continue the making of comments where such explanatory material will help one to understand the incident reported.

[5] Ibid.
[6] Arthur E. Traxler (ed.), Guidance in Public Secondary Schools, p. 193. New York: Educational Records Bureau, 1939.

Some of the anecdotes described as excellent in one report of the ACE experimentation [7] are of Randall's fourth type, but the directors did not find helpful the teachers' intermixing behavior description and personal comments in statements such as, "Olga came in today upset," or "Sam showed a decided preference for Dora and offered to show her how to operate the machine." The staff found that the helpfulness of such remarks "really depends upon their soundness and validity. If the teach-

PLAINFIELD HIGH SCHOOL

Anecdotal Record

Name of pupil observed   Date

Observer   Place

Objective description:

Anecdotal Record
(Reverse side)

Comment, generalization, diagnosis, remedial measures proposed, action taken, etc.

FIGURE 1   *Plainfield High School anecdotal record.* (A. E. Traxler [ed.], *Guidance in Public Secondary Schools,* p. 192. New York: Educational Records Bureau, 1939. Reproduced by permission of the publisher.)

[7] Commission on Teacher Education, *op. cit.,* pp. 39–40.

ers' diagnoses are correct, then, coming as they do at the beginning of the report, the comments direct the teacher's attention to the significance of what is to follow." It is because diagnosis is seldom as relatively easy as it seems that the staff warns against "cultivating the habit of including too many interpretive statements." In short, the teachers' remarks often suggest important hypotheses; and so inclusion of comments should not be discouraged; but the separation of objective description and comments is strongly urged.

The ACE Classification. The ACE project staff found that teachers who are untrained or unskilled in the writing of anecdotes tend to report how they feel about a student rather than what they observe about him. On the basis of their experience with the teachers cooperating in the child-study program, the directors classified teachers' anecdotal reports into four types, which are not wholly unlike the four types described by Randall. According to the ACE classification, anecdotes of the first type are those that describe a student's behavior as good or bad or as acceptable or unacceptable. Two examples of this type are given below. For both of them the setting happens to be the same—a class in physical education. The records, however, are about different girls and made by teachers in different schools. The behavior reported in the first is obviously judged "bad" by the writer and that of the second "good."

> Throughout the period Alice would not do the activity of the rest of the class. During roll call she would not stay in line with the others. She went to a bench and read "True Romances" although she previously was requested not to bring the magazine to class. She refused to buy the school paper. She admitted it was not lack of money. The rest of the class gave a penny each and paid for her subscription. The class treasurer gave her her receipt which she tore up.

> Joanne was noticeably more cooperative today. She checked out towels for me and went ahead with the records. Her personal appearance was improved. Her hair was neat; her clothes were clean, well pressed and in good taste. Her voice and actions were those becoming a lady today.

Both these records include factual material: Alice read a magazine during roll call, did not participate in class activity, did not subscribe to the school paper, and tore up the receipt for payment given her by a classmate. Joanne checked out towels and helped with the records. The factual record, however, is overshadowed by the teachers' evaluation of the girls' behavior as good or bad. That the evaluation would be held correct by others seems assumed. It would probably never occur to the writer of the first anecdote that some others might see Alice's tearing up the receipt more as evidence of strength than as evidence of weakness. It is clear that the teacher considers Alice's not subscribing to the paper uncooperative behavior. Were the account of the incident confined to objective description and the girl's words quoted as accurately as possible, others might interpret the incident differently. There is a possibility that Alice is opposed to 100 per cent movements because she has noted the hardships that they impose on others less able financially than she is to support them. If so and if this is shown in her answer to the request that she pay her subscription, the report would have a very different meaning than it has in its present form. On the other hand, if the reporter would let Alice tell the story by reporting just what Alice did say, it might appear that she did not display a very cooperative attitude. As it is, it is impossible to judge the girl's behavior because the teacher has revealed her own attitudes better than she has Alice's.

The second type of record described in the ACE report accounts for or explains the student's behavior on the basis of a single fact or thesis. This type—the "interpretive record"—is illustrated by the following anecdote:

> Bill was back in school today after a two-day illness. He lacks interest in his schoolwork and so becomes lazy. He would like to quit school to take a job, but his father will not let him. I believe that his two days of illness is sort of a flight from conflict.

Before reporting his conclusion that the student is lazy, giving the explanation as lack of interest, and offering the hypothesis regarding the use of illness as an escape from conflict, the reporter needs to present more facts than he gives. Hypotheses and explanations should not be offered until enough facts are marshaled to indicate the psychological principles involved.

In the third type of anecdotal record the writer describes the student's behavior in general terms and reports it as occurring frequently or as being characteristic of the student. An example of the generalized descriptive record is given in the following:

> Charles is lively, enthusiastic, and alert. Today he ran into the classroom noisily, greeting other pupils by name. When the bell rang, he continued conversation with others from his seat until asked to stop. Several times he talked out during class when someone else was speaking. He was very much interested in the new work and caught on quickly. He continually volunteered answers whether called on or not. Today as usual he was full of energy.

The fourth type is the desired kind of record—"specific description." It describes an incident specifically and accurately, telling exactly what was said and done by the persons involved. The following report on observation of a sixth-grade boy in a "free play" situation, taken from a report of the California Adolescent Growth Study,[8] illustrates this type:

> John and Allen are working at an easel. John is intent on a picture of an Indian chief. Allen is talking and singing in a high-pitched voice, mix-

---

[8] From *Development in Adolescence* by Harold E. Jones, p. 47. Copyright, 1943. D. Appleton-Century Co., Inc. Reprinted by permission of the publisher.

ing conversation with snatches of song and dramatic imitations. Allen draws a picture of a boy and girl kissing. . . . "Maybe that will be me some day."

Allen: "Now I'm going to do one of the modest artist"—(draws an artist painting at easel). To John: "Mix your paint up; it will be better!"

John: "I like mine just as it is. . . ."

Allen (sings): "Tomatoes are cheaper (etc.); now is the time to fall in love. . . ." Remarks, "They say we're coming up here four times a year . . . what do we do this for?"

John (turning to observer): "So you will be able to tell others how we grow, isn't it—how others grow?"

Each of the four types of anecdotes described by Randall is held acceptable, whereas only one of the four types described in the ACE report is considered generally acceptable—specific, objective description. The directors of the ACE experiment admitted, however, that examination of the anecdotes written by the cooperating teachers showed certain advantages to be gained through not limiting them entirely to specific description. Some of the generalized descriptions provided good pictures of students in action, and "some of the interpretations made on the spur of the moment captured the moods of interacting children in a fashion that would have been well-nigh impossible by straightforward description."

The staff of the ACE project found that anecdotes of the not-always-desirable types—evaluative, interpretive, and generalized descriptive statements—showed certain common criteria in the teachers' judgments about students to be (1) the student's success or failure in schoolwork, (2) the student's being a helping or a disturbing element in carrying out school routine, (3) the standing of the student's family in the community and relation to the teacher's social status, and (4) the student's being personally attractive or unattractive in terms of the teacher's experience, personal needs, and values. Each of the following anecdotes [9] shows one or more of these influences, and all indicate that the teachers who wrote them may be in the habit of dealing with students largely on the level of subjective judgment and personal bias.

> The algebra period found Ellen completely organized and ready to get to work. She gave excellent attention during the explanation of work to be done. She finished her work in half the required time. The appearance of the paper displeased her. She copied it taking the rest of the period, carefully writing the numbers, spacing the problems, and erasing all smudges. She did not turn around to see the cause of a disturbance at the back of the room. Social studies period found her ready with all needed materials on her desk.

> This morning Frank came to class six minutes late. The class was quietly getting ready for the morning exercises (flag salute, etc.). Frank stamped

[9] These illustrations are anecdotes actually written by teachers but not by teachers participating in the ACE program. Similar examples are found in the ACE reports.

his feet noisily as he walked across the front of the room. The entire class observed him. No one said a word, not even the teacher. Frank sat down but immediately turned to poke the boy sitting behind him.

Richard made no attempt to work or to study today. He disturbed the class by laughing and talking to the boys seated near him. When spoken to by the teacher, he became angry and sullen. He subsided for some minutes but soon began talking again. This happened three times.

This morning Betty brought some little cakes that her mother sent for the class Christmas party. Her mother is very active in civic groups and the PTA. Her father is a professional man and active in church work. He is also a scout director.

Ed was absent from school half the day. Upon entering the room with his excuse, he seemed to deliberately step on the foot of the nearest boy. His clothes were dirty and torn. He looked as though he needed a bath. I soon noticed that he was sitting with his hand in mouth and told him to remember our health habits.

Anecdotal reports increase in diagnostic value as they become clear word pictures free of language which suggests that any specific trait or combination of traits is to be associated with the behavior described. Many teachers develop skill in writing this type of record. The teachers who participated in the ACE, Plainfield, and certain other projects were able to progress in their writing of anecdotes from generalized to specific description. As they became more objective both in observing and in reporting, they acquired deeper insights and became increasingly aware of the need for verifying information.

SOME COMMON QUESTIONS

How Many? Ideally teachers should regularly write anecdotal reports on all their students, but such a plan has not proved practical. At the Rochester Athenaeum, for example, it was to be standard practice for each teacher to turn in every week not less than one anecdotal record for every student in his classes along with supplemental reports on out-of-class observations. Very soon this practice had to be modified for the teachers of large classes. Likewise in other schools, according to Jarvie,[10] the number of anecdotes reported decreased with increase in class size.

The democratic practice of permitting teachers to contribute anecdotal reports on a purely voluntary basis has not proved satisfactory either. This practice was followed in the Plainfield experiment.[11] The project directors reported that a few teachers turned in many reports; some, none at all; and many, only a few. Some teachers who were at first enthusiastic later became bored. As the experiment progressed, there was a significant

[10] L. L. Jarvie, "Quantitative Study of Behavior Records," in *Official Report of the American Educational Research Association*, pp. 106–111. Washington, D.C.: American Educational Research Association, 1939.

[11] Traxler, *op. cit.*, pp. 200–201.

decline in both the number and the quality of some teachers' reports. Consequently, the directors concluded that were it possible to initiate the experiment again, the number of anecdotal reports required would be set "arbitrarily at first and diminished or increased as practice warranted a more sound judgment as to what was a reasonable number." Yet to require all teachers to turn in a specified number of records can create antagonism. Anecdotes written reluctantly or unwillingly may have little more value than records written not at all.

In the ACE project the plan was for the teachers to ask themselves at the end of each school day, "What do I remember about individual students today?" and then write notes on two or more students. "It was thought that fifteen or twenty minutes of writing would be sufficient. The expectation was that all children would be mentioned in these reports from time to time in the natural course of events." [12] The teachers, however, in an effort to include anecdotes on all students reduced considerably the length of their anecdotes. The directors found these short reports not sufficiently descriptive of the situations in which episodes occurred and weak in showing the interaction among children. As a result, they gave up the attempt to have anecdotal records kept on all students and, instead, advocated the practice of keeping extensive anecdotal records on one or two students. While a series of anecdotes was not to be kept on more than one or two students by each teacher, occasional anecdotes were to be written for all students and included in their cumulative record files. The instructions for the occasional anecdotes were as follows:

> Only enough anecdotes need be included in a child's record to illustrate his characteristic patterns of behavior, to show his progress toward accomplishing particular developmental tasks, to reveal the adjustment problems that he faces, and to record his reaction to crises and other events of special significance to him. An anecdote or two a month will suffice to document these matters for most children in a class.

When the practice adopted is that of writing many anecdotes about a few students and a few anecdotes about many students, the scarcity of anecdotes written about some students may actually prove helpful by serving to focus attention on the apparently little-noticed students. Hamalainen,[13] for instance, found that the summaries of anecdotes reported on some students became general-impression statements because of the scarcity of anecdotes recorded. He reported that these summaries are likely to be written on the shy, quiet child who often is unnoticed in the classroom. He concluded that the mere absence of anecdotes may provide the starting point from which direction can be given to help the child to become a part of the group in a more normal manner.

[12] Commission on Teacher Education, *op. cit.*, pp. 434–436.

[13] A. E. Hamalainen, *An Appraisal of Anecdotal Records*, p. 57. New York: Bureau of Publications, Teachers College, Columbia University, 1943.

Which Students? The decision regarding which student to make the subject of an extensive series of anecdotal reports may be made for many different reasons: The student is readily observed. He seems to be a good example of the "average student" or is typical of his group. He is a leader. He does not seem accepted by the other students. He is a student about whom very little is known. He is not achieving in keeping with his ability. He seems unhappy.

When the writing of a series of anecdotes is undertaken largely for the purpose of gaining skill in collecting and interpreting data on student behavior, it is probably not wise for a teacher to select as his first subject a student who is so maladjusted that the teacher may find it difficult to interpret the data collected. On the other hand, if the record is being made primarily to collect personality data that are not easily obtained from other sources, the anecdotal record kept by a teacher on a maladjusted student may reveal the type of special assistance needed. It can supply important information for the counselor or other specialist to whom the student may be referred. If the teacher includes in his reports statements regarding interpretation, diagnosis, or recommended treatment, the specialist is not bound by them. If the statements are not sound, they may show the type of professional information that the counselor needs to share with the teacher.

Which Situations? To obtain records that reveal the student's characteristic behavior, the reporter observes him in a variety of situations—in class and out of class, at work, at play, alone, and with others. Any situation serves as a good beginning point for a series of anecdotal records. As the series continues, it indicates what the student thinks about by telling what he talks about, writes about, draws, paints, and constructs. It indicates what others think of him and how he gets along with others by showing him in interaction with teachers, peers, and others. By disclosing him in many different kinds of situations, it reveals his outstanding interests and typical behavior patterns. Observations made at frequent intervals may reveal significant transitory modes of behavior and thereby provide a useful basis for estimating characteristic tendencies.

The anecdotal reports made on a particular student during one school year may run from five or six pages to fifty or sixty. The extensive series is not supposed to be a case study, but like the case study it may give a "full view" of the student. While a long series gives a more comprehensive picture than a short one, the short record can yield significant information and lead to important insights regarding the student. Any incident included in a series, long or short, should be worth reporting. That is, it should represent behavior that is either characteristic of the subject or strikingly unusual. If unusual, this fact should be noted apart from description of the incident.

THE GOOD ANECDOTAL RECORD

A good anecdotal record has such characteristics as the following:

1. *The record provides adequate background information.* The setting for each incident is clearly indicated through information regarding date, place, time, and persons involved. The records included in an extensive series should be preceded by a general background or introductory statement in which the reporter gives the subject's name, age, and grade placement; the relationship of the observer to the subject (teacher, coach, nurse, relative, etc.); and the situation in which the subject is most frequently observed.

The introductory statement may include also information as to why the student was selected for special study, description of his appearance, and the general impression he makes upon the observer. As the reporter adds anecdote after anecdote to the collection, he will come to see the student more clearly because he understands him better than when he began the record. When he is ready to summarize the series, he may reject the description that he first wrote and use a new one which differs greatly from the first. Based on many observations of the subject in many different kinds of situations, the new description is very likely less general, more specific, and more accurate or representative than the first one. The observer now sees his subject differently and so now gives a different description of him.

2. *The incidents are described objectively.* This is the most important characteristic of the good anecdotal record. Ideally each report is objective to a degree approximating that of an X-ray photograph. In writing the report, the observer remembers that he is taking the picture and so is not expected to be in it. He keeps out of it by not reporting his thoughts or feelings. He gets into the record only when he belongs there as one of the persons involved in the incident. He tries to report as objectively on himself as he does on his subject. He records what he did and said and not what, he remembers later, he should have done or said. He does not strengthen, soften, or in any other way modify his part in the incident. He tries to give a clear, exact reproduction rather than a touched-up picture.

If the record is objective, it does not show the observer's personal likes and dislikes, biases and prejudices. The reader cannot tell whether the reporter approved or disapproved or was indifferent regarding the behavior recorded. As stated above, opinion is most frequently injected into anecdotal reports through the use of generalized description, as in this example:

> Charles was moody and said little today. When the teacher inquired about the assigned work, he replied that he was busy and didn't know if he would have time for it or not. He spent most of the period looking out of the window. He did not attempt to talk to anyone in class today. This is unusual.

The information that the boy's behavior is unusual is helpful, but it should be given apart from the report on the episode rather than made a part of it. Furthermore, in stating that "Charles was moody," the teacher is giving his opinion. This statement should be omitted or given at the bottom or on the reverse side of the sheet along with any other comments. Not enough facts are given in the report to indicate that the conclusion is correct. The observer should report his evidence (things seen and heard) rather than his reaction or conclusion. The following report made on Charles by the same teacher at another time is better than the preceding one because it is more objective and is free of generalized description.

> Charles was talking to two other students when the teacher entered the room. He left the students and approached the teacher to ask for an appointment to discuss an original project in drama. Several times during the period he brought up the subject of the project even though other matters were under discussion. When asked to delay the questions until later, he sat quietly for about ten minutes. Then he turned and started talking to his nearest classmate. The conversation continued until the teacher asked him to stop. When Charles left the room, he stopped by the teacher's desk to remind her of his appointment for the next day.

It is not likely that any observer can achieve complete objectivity in his descriptions. Nor is there any clear-cut dichotomy, as Newman [14] says, between "objective" and "interpretive" reports. Nevertheless, it is possible to distinguish statements based on objective observation from those based largely on subjective inferences. The contrast is clear in the following excerpts [15] from the records of observations on an adolescent boy made by three observers during the same observation period. The reports of B and C are obviously more inferential than that of A.

> *Observer A:* Upon entering the yard Dave was one of the first to get a play wagon. He kept up a constant chatter with Albert and Dick. Suggested making a steep runway for the wagons by setting boards at an incline against the top of the "jungle gym." He was the only one who tried to ride down this runway.... Later he was an active member of the group playing basketball.

> *Observer B:* Dave pretends to grouse and to misbehave, but actually seems to be just playing—partly for attention, partly as a mischievous, little-boy sort of teasing, with a mixture of self-expression for its own sake....

> *Observer C:* Dave seems more responsible and independent than previously—shows more directed concentration on activities such as basketball throwing; was the only one to attempt going down the steeply inclined planks on a wagon; was not resistant to leaving yard at end of hour; engaged in less horseplay than the others; ... was more communica-

[14] Frances Burks Newman, with an introduction by Harold E. Jones, *The Adolescent in Social Groups,* Applied Psychology Monographs no. 9, p. 47. Stanford, Calif.: Stanford University Press, 1946.

[15] *Ibid.*

tive with adults. . . . Not altogether sure of himself—his facial expressions are occasionally anxious and self-conscious, and he brings out rather bad puns in a somewhat hesitant, though slightly proud manner.

An observer may reveal lack of objectivity in his selection of incidents to report. If he is biased in favor of the subject, all his reports may show the subject at his best. If he is biased against the subject, the reports may show him always at his worst. If an observer suspects that bias is determining his sampling, he can control it by deciding to report whatever he observes his subject doing at a particular time in the future. He may decide, for example, to report whatever his subject may be doing during the first five or ten minutes of the noon recess or at two o'clock in the afternoon.

One child-study group member whose anecdotal reports invariably showed the subject in some act of hostile aggression was questioned by the other members regarding his feelings toward the student. The reporter admitted that he did not "care for" the student, was aware of his feelings, wanted to understand the boy, and had selected him as his subject for this reason. Upon the advice of the others he decided to follow the practice of setting in advance the time for his special observation of the student. No one in the group was more surprised than he at the contrast between the behavior reported in the subsequent reports and that pictured in the previous ones. At times the reports showed the boy engaged in acts of hostility, but the majority showed him more friendly than hostile toward others. Almost all showed him well accepted by his peers.

3. *The good anecdotal record is selective.* Pertinent incidents are the ones recorded—incidents that are meaningful because relevant to the student's development. Inconsequential details and irrelevant incidents are not reported. The following anecdote is one of six made on a fourteen-year-old girl by her teacher. The other five are very similar. Inclusion of many items like this one is not very helpful.

> Sarah entered the room with the other students. She was wearing a blue skirt and a white blouse. She took her seat and opened her book. She read the assignment written on the board, then took out a tablet and pencil from the desk, and began writing. From time to time she referred to the book. She wrote for the next ten minutes.

It is not undesirable to have some such items in a collection of anecdotes on a particular student. This incident, for example, does yield information on Sarah's work habits. It is not desirable that all or most incidents recorded be minor ones. Irrelevant details should be omitted. The information about Sarah's dress adds little of importance. Yet the report is not insignificant. It shows that the girl can follow class routine without special instructions or prodding; that she concentrates on her work and is not easily distracted.

As the record grows, the observer forms tentative hypotheses regard ing the subject's trend of development, his special concerns, the reasons for some behavior patterns and their meaning to the subject, and his involvement in the life of his school, peer group, and family. To check the correctness of his hypotheses, the reporter seeks more data through more observations and through information gained from others. If he is professional in his work and objective in his observations, he will find that some hypotheses must be discarded or modified. If he is not, then his records may show the "I knew it" or "I told you so" attitude which Jarvie [16] reported encountering in some teachers. The teachers formed an a priori judgment and then collected information to support the judgment. These teachers were undesirably selective. They tended to select incidents that supported their hypotheses rather than incidents that were relevant to the students' development. Their records, although selective, were definitely not good.

4. *The good anecdotal record includes specific action, direct quotation, and a fairly complete sequence of events.* Description of the episode is sufficiently comprehensive or extensive to provide, in Prescott's [17] words, "a little vignette of a behavioral moment" in the life of the subject. Reporting the subject's voice tones, facial expressions, body postures, and gestures gives cues to his thoughts and feelings. Reporting what the subject actually says is better than summarizing his conversation. It is not always easy, however, to remember exactly what was said and done. Many reports have to be written an hour or more after the incident occurred. Making a few notes immediately after the event aids later recall of the main facts and the sequence of events.

A record is made dynamic by giving the exact wording and showing the native quality of an individual's speech. The two following examples selected from Bieker's [18] presentation show how records are strengthened by acute listening and careful reporting of conversation:

"We done bought us a better house."

"Yea, it used to be a old store," said Tom.

"Yea, but it sure is a good house. We paid $650 for it."

"Gollee, that old man was high on that ol' place," replied Tom.

"Yea, but it's got four acres around it."

"Who's all them little bitty girls around there?" asked Tom.

"Them's my sisters and they ain't 'all them.' Ain't but three of them. I got one big sister and two little ones and a little brother.... If the weather is pretty this weekend we're gonna git our house papered. Our yard is full of old stumps and stuff. I've dug up a whole bunch of them."

[16] L. L. Jarvie, "Anecdotal Records as a Means of Understanding Students," *Institute for Administrative Officers of Higher Institutions, Proceedings*, 1940, 12:26.

[17] Prescott, *op. cit.*, p. 154.

[18] Helen Bieker, "Using Anecdotal Records to Know the Child," in Caroline M. Tryon (ed.), *Fostering Mental Health in Our Schools*, pp. 190–191, 193. Washington, D.C.: National Education Association, 1950.

"What are you going to do, Jackie, plant grass?" I asked.

"No'm, flowers. Mamma's always got to have lots of flowers."

Jackie said, "One time I'se in swimmin' with George. I played like I'se drownin' an' George he got so skeered he run home 'thou't no clothes on. Mamma she come a-runnin' and she was so skeered she got right sick. Papa he whupped up on me plenty."

"Jackie, if you get whipped for swimming, why do you do it?"

"I let my daddy take his fun out in whuppin' and I take mine out in swimmin'."

5. *To be of much value, an anecdotal record must be one of many on the student.* Only when a number of anecdotes are given can the subject be seen as a many-sided person and the place and meaning of one type of behavior in his total behavior pattern be understood. When considered alone, for instance, the second of the two anecdotes given above may lead the reader to conclude that Jackie is indifferent to his father's wishes and commands, that the father treats the boy harshly, and that, on the whole, the father-son relationship is not a very good one. When, however, the anecdote is read with others in the series on Jackie, the reader sees that such conclusions are not correct and that in Jackie's home the family relationships are happy ones. The true quality of the family life is partly indicated in the first of the two anecdotes given above. When combined with others, such as the two given below, they show that Jackie does appreciate and respect his father.[19]

We were talking about good manners. Maxine said: "My folks make me say 'Thanks for the biscuits,' instead of just, 'I want a biscuit.' "

Jackie said: "My papa said he was going to slap me if I didn't quit reaching across the table. He make me say 'please,' too."

Some of the children are bringing samples of handwriting. Bill commented that he "didn't see no use in writin' good."

Jackie said, "My daddy can't read and he can't write nothing but his name, and he can git a job anywhere he wants to."

The value of these anecdotes on Jackie is increased by the teacher's letting the boy tell his story. The same information given through a summary statement would be less significant than when given through direct quotations. Stating, for example, that Jackie spoke freely and directly and in the dialect of his social class would provide a much less clear and vivid picture of the boy than is given by showing through direct quotation his style of speech, his manner of relating his thoughts, and his freedom and directness of expression. Moreover, the picture of Jackie is less likely to be distorted through direct quotation than through a summary statement. Also, in giving Jackie's actual words, the teacher helps to reveal the boy's values and attitudes. In summarizing Jackie's conversations and present-

---

[19] *Ibid.,* pp. 189–190.

ing them in her own words rather than in Jackie's the teacher would probably show her own values and attitudes and might even reveal hers more clearly than Jackie's. It should be noted that in these records the talk and actions of the other persons involved are reported as carefully as are those of Jackie.

6. *A good collection of anecdotes gives many different views of the subject.* As the record grows, the observer begins to seek information that he may have previously not considered very important. He finds opportunities to observe the subject in new situations and to observe him with others, such as the parents, who are close to him.

Some investigators, such as Hamalainen,[20] find that material relating to home background, such as type of home, family relationships, and the like "will generally not be included in the anecdotes." Collection of this type of information was, however, a major objective in the ACE experiment. One report [21] states that at the beginning the teachers knew relatively little about their students' homes. They knew the extent to which the parents were cooperative with the school but very little about the home interpersonal and cultural factors influencing the students' development. When the teachers realized the importance of such factors, they began to seek and to report information about them. They recorded the students' talk about homelife. They visited the homes and encouraged the parents to visit the school. They wrote reports about these visits. They learned that not to include home background information in the records is to omit some very important aspects of the students' lives.

ORGANIZING AND INTERPRETING ANECDOTAL DATA

The anecdotes accumulated on a particular student are of limited value until interpreted, and they cannot be interpreted easily or correctly until organized in some way. The facts presented in all the anecdotes must be sifted and arranged so that they may be studied in relation to one another. Contradictions need to be detected and studied to see whether they indicate errors on the part of the reporter or inconsistent and contradictory patterns of behavior on the part of the student. Unique and recurring situations and unusual and repeated behavior patterns need to be studied to see what they indicate regarding the student's principal problems, behavior tendencies, and personality characteristics.

After the facts have been searched out and arranged, clues to their meaning are more easily detected than when the anecdotes are read serially. If adequate and accurate observations have been made and the observation material is arranged in some orderly fashion, the interpretations offered by different persons qualified to give interpretations should be substantially in agreement.

[20] Hamalainen, *op. cit.,* p. 80.
[21] Commission on Teacher Education, *op. cit.,* pp. 42–66.

When sufficient anecdotal material has been gathered to warrant the making of tentative hypotheses, a summary is prepared that presents the facts, interpretations, hypotheses, and recommendations. More anecdotes may be collected to fill in information gaps revealed by the summary and to test further the hypotheses. In due course the material will be again summarized, after which the recording of anecdotes may be resumed. The frequency with which summaries are prepared depends largely upon the amount of material gathered. In all cases the anecdotes should probably be summarized at least once a year. In many cases they should be summarized at least once a semester because of the large number of anecdotes recorded and the great amount of information contained in the reports.

When considerable information has been obtained on a subject, it is well to summarize it and begin a new record on a new subject. Study of the first subject continues, but more informally and less systematically than before. As a teacher or counselor repeats the experience of observing and reporting and of formulating, testing, and revising hypotheses, he finds that he is presenting a better picture of the second subject and is making more valid interpretations than he did with the first one.

There is no standard plan for summarizing anecdotal data. The material found in different anecdotal records varies too much for the data in all to be organized in the same way. One of the simplest ways to present the material is to sift the facts and sort them according to the student's assets and liabilities or handicaps. The beginner may find this simple procedure a good one to follow; but eventually he should try to organize the data to show the student's status and progress in certain large aspects of growth, such as physical, social, and emotional.

Sometimes teachers are instructed to make school objectives the basis for their observations. When this plan is followed, the material may well be organized or summarized according to the objectives. Using, for example, one well-known statement of objectives,[22] the material may be organized according to such classifications as (1) self-realization (health, recreation, aesthetic interests, intellectual interests, inquiring mind, etc.); (2) human relationships (friendships, cooperation, courtesy, home relations, etc.); (3) economic efficiency (vocational interests, occupational information, occupational choice, personal economics, etc.); and (4) civic responsibility (social understanding, critical judgment, tolerance, law observance, etc.). There are definite advantages in making and summarizing observations with reference to the school's professed objectives. If some are stressed and others are neglected or almost wholly overlooked, no doubt the summary will reveal this unbalanced situation.

Participants in the study programs sponsored by the Institute for Child Study are encouraged to use an organizational framework that has

---

[22] Educational Policies Commission, *The Purpose of Education in American Democracy*. Washington, D.C.: National Education Association, 1938.

six major headings: (1) "physical factors and processes," (2) family and other "love relationships and related processes," (3) "cultural background and socialization processes," (4) "peer-group status and processes," (5) "self-developmental factors and processes," and (6) "self-adjustive factors and processes." [23]

As a rule, items are not transferred from anecdotal records to the cumulative record unless used to illustrate typical behavior or change in behavior patterns. This raises the question of who receives and summarizes the reports. The summarizing of reports written on the same student by different teachers is more than a clerical task. It should be done by someone who knows the student and who is qualified to organize and interpret the material. In the secondary schools this may be the person specifically responsible for the counseling of the student. The teacher or counselor who makes an extensive series of anecdotal records on a particular student is ordinarily the one to summarize those reports.

A copy of the summary report should be included in the central cumulative record folder, if such a folder is maintained. A copy should be given to the student's counselor if the person who makes the summary is not the counselor. After the summary report is filed, the teacher or counselor may wish to destroy the individual anecdotal reports. In some schools, however, they are kept as long as the student is enrolled in the school.

THE GOOD OBSERVER

Good sensory equipment and a high degree of objectivity are two requirements for a good observer. Even more important than these two, however, is a third—professional knowledge. Unless a person has sufficient knowledge of what he observes—person, thing, or process—he may understand little of what he sees. A person, for instance, who understands very little about mechanics and machines may closely observe a mechanic at work for an hour or longer and then report his observations. Because the report reflects the observer's lack of understanding, it is of limited value. The judgments expressed in it are likely to be wrong because based on ignorance rather than knowledge.

Another example: Three men go together to visit a fish hatchery. One man is a zoologist who is especially interested in marine life. One is a country dweller whose favorite recreation is fishing. One is a city dweller who would like to go fishing sometime but so far has not had an opportunity to do so. The three men observe the fish with equal interest, perhaps, but not with equal understanding. If asked to report and explain their observations, the country man would, no doubt, give a better explanation than the city man. Undoubtedly the zoologist would offer the best explanation of the three. Some teachers' observations and explana-

[23] Prescott, *op. cit.*, chap. 7.

tions are superior to those of many laymen mainly for the same reason that the country man's explanations are superior to those of the city man —greater opportunity to observe—whereas they should be superior for the same reason that the zoologist's explanation is superior—professional knowledge, as well as extensive experience.

The teachers who participated in the ACE child-study program found that gathering extensive, vital information about students did not "guarantee or even imply sound judgments, objective attitudes, or wise policies in dealing" with students. The report states [24] that there remained to be accomplished certain crucial learnings of scientific methodology and the acquiring of some new mental habits and attitudes consistent with that methodology.

USES, ADVANTAGES, AND DISADVANTAGES

Uses. When the writing of anecdotal records is undertaken largely to increase understanding of student behavior, fulfillment of the purpose is aided considerably by organizing informal study groups. When, for example, teachers meet together to read and discuss their anecdotal reports and summaries, group interest stimulates individual interest. By sharing in the discussions, individual members learn to apply concepts and principles to specific cases. Further gains in skill and knowledge can be expected when a group expands its program to include professional reading and discussion of the subjects covered in the reading. Ideally the program should be further expanded to include the services of a consultant who can help the group members acquire skill in using scientific principles as bases for judgments and can help them avoid use of such criteria as their own preferences, purposes, and cultural standards.

The purposes for which anecdotal data may be used are the same as for data from other sources—to help the school workers see the student as a many-sided changing individual and to throw light on the various aspects of his growth, to supply information useful in helping the student to understand himself and useful in interpreting the student to his teachers, parents, prospective employers, and others.

Many anecdotes are snapshots that show glimpses of growth and indicate what the teachers can do to aid optimal growth. They often show how school life can help counteract unwholesome influences in a student's out-of-school life.

Advantages. The most important advantage of anecdotal records is, no doubt, this usefulness for helping teachers to gain perspective on students and to deepen their understanding of student behavior. They help the teacher to view behavior in its total context and to recognize the importance of the peer culture and family standards in determining at-school behavior.

[24] Commission on Teacher Education, *op. cit.*, pp. 187–188.

Anecdotal records serve as an important source of personality data. In the California Adolescent Growth Study,[25] for example, the principal means employed for gathering information about personality were anecdotes, ratings, and narrative summaries. The Plainfield experiment was undertaken largely because the type of information supplied by personality inventories was "acceptable only with reservations." Anecdotal records proved to be a more helpful source of personality data.

Anecdotal records provide valuable supplementary information. This advantage is well illustrated in Hamalainen's study,[26] which shows that the material gathered through an interest inventory and the material gathered through anecdotal records were of a complementary nature. Hamalainen found that many of the students' interests were recorded in both the inventory and the anecdotes, but some were recorded in the anecdotes and not in the inventories. Moreover, the anecdotal records made a unique contribution by showing the gradual growth or disappearance of an interest, a type of information which is not readily secured through an interest inventory. The inventory gave only the statement of an interest at a particular time, whereas it was sometimes possible to trace through the anecdotes the trend of certain interests, to note their cessation, or to get a definite conception of the variety of interests.

Other studies have shown that anecdotes are especially useful for providing supplementary information about the student as a group member. They show how well he is accepted by others and whom he accepts and rejects. In this way they often indicate both the quality and the quantity of a student's social relationships.

Disadvantages. The principal disadvantages of anecdotal records have been brought out in the preceding pages, and so only a brief summary is added here. The main weaknesses are the following: (1) difficulty in securing objective reports—teachers tend to report their reactions rather than their observations; (2) difficulty in securing reports on many students —the amount of work involved and the large student load make it difficult for most teachers to write the desired number of anecdotal reports; (3) difficulty in organizing and summarizing in some usable form the information contained in the anecdotal reports; and (4) difficulty in securing anecdotal reports that give a fair sampling of a student's behavior—teachers tend to report unfavorable and not-typical behavior more often than they report favorable and typical behavior.

SUMMARY

Lifelike pictures of students are provided by anecdotal records that provide a representative sample of the students' behavior. There are various types of anecdotal records. The preferred type gives objective description

[25] Jones, *op. cit.;* Newman, *op. cit.*
[26] Hamalainen, *op. cit.,* p. 45.

of a specific pertinent incident. When explanations, interpretations, and recommendations are reported, they are given apart from description of the incident. The report is written as soon as possible after the observation so that errors of recall may be reduced or eliminated.

A good anecdotal record gives the background information needed for the report to be meaningful. It is free of personal bias and is selective in that the incident is worth reporting, i.e., provides evidence regarding the student's personal and social development. It gives many different views of the student by picturing him in a variety of situations. It uses direct quotation when possible.

Anecdotal records are most useful for studying aspects of behavior not easily studied through more objective techniques, such as standardized tests. They are valuable sources of information regarding social adjustment and emotional development. If good use is to be made of the data contained in the records, they have to be summarized periodically. The summary needs to be more than a listing of items. The material needs to be organized to reveal status and progress in broad areas of growth.

Preparing anecdotal records helps teachers to deepen their understanding of students as developing individuals and to explain scientifically the facts they gather on them. The usefulness of the technique is limited, however, by certain difficulties: difficulty in securing objective reports, difficulty in obtaining enough reports on many students, difficulty in getting the material in the records organized or summarized, and difficulty in securing reports that give a representative sampling of the subject's behavior.

REFERENCES

Almy, Millie, from materials prepared by Ruth Cunningham and Associates: *Ways of Studying Children,* chap. 2. New York: Bureau of Publications, Teachers College, Columbia University, 1959.

Bales, Robert F.: *Interaction Process Analysis: A Method for the Study of Small Groups.* Reading, Mass.: Addison-Wesley Publishing Company, Inc., 1950.

Bass, Bernard M.: "The Leaderless Group Discussion," *Psychological Bulletin,* 1954, 51:465–592.

Bieker, Helen: "Using Anecdotal Records to Know the Child," in Caroline M. Tryon (ed.), *Fostering Mental Health in Our Schools,* chap. 12. Washington, D.C.: National Education Association, 1950.

Froehlich, Clifford P., and Kenneth B. Hoyt: *Guidance Testing,* chaps. 11–12. Chicago: Science Research Associates, Inc., 1959.

Jarvie, L. L., and Mark Ellington: *Handbook on the Anecdotal Behavior Journal.* Chicago: The University of Chicago Press, 1940.

Jones, H. E.: "The Adolescent Growth Study: V. Observational Methods in the Study of Individual Development," *Journal of Consulting Psychology,* 1940, 4:234–238.

———: *Development in Adolescence*. New York: Appleton-Century-Crofts, Inc., 1943.

Lippitt, Ronald, and Ralph White: "The Social Climate of Children's Groups," in R. G. Barker (ed.), *Child Behavior and Development*, chap. 28. New York: McGraw-Hill Book Company, Inc., 1943.

Newcomb, Theodore M.: *The Consistency of Certain Extrovert-Introvert Behavior Patterns in 51 Problem Boys*. New York: Bureau of Publications, Teachers College, Columbia University, 1929.

Newman, Frances B., with an introduction by H. E. Jones: *The Adolescent in Social Groups*. Stanford, Calif.: Stanford University Press, 1946.

Prescott, Daniel A.: *The Child in the Educative Process*. New York: McGraw-Hill Book Company, Inc., 1957.

Randall, John A.: "The Anecdotal Behavior Journal," *Progressive Education*, 1936, 13:21–26.

Thorndike, Robert L., and Elizabeth Hagen: *Measurement and Evaluation in Psychology and Education*, 2d ed., chap. 14. New York: John Wiley & Sons, Inc., 1961.

Traxler, Arthur E.: *Techniques of Guidance*, rev. ed., pp. 125–140. New York: Harper & Row, Publishers, Incorporated, 1957.

3

Observation: Rating Scales and Behavior Descriptions

Rating scales are another form of observation reports. In making an anecdotal record, the observer reports an incident of observation that reveals some significant aspect of the subject's behavior. In using a rating scale, he reports his general estimate (supposedly on the basis of observation) of an individual's relative strengths and weaknesses with respect to the characteristics named on the scale.

In high schools and colleges rating scales are probably used most frequently for collecting personality data to be reported to prospective employers or to colleges and other training agencies. Ratings are obtained most often just before the students graduate. In some schools, however, they are obtained periodically, and the information is used in studying the development of individual students and as a basis for counseling.

Rating scales, like anecdotal records, are probably best used for helping teachers to become observant of student behavior and sensitive to trends in the growth of students and for helping them to refine their judgments of student behavior. Identification of problems and detection of high potentialities are major objectives in the study of individuals. Teachers use rating scales specifically for such purposes when they rate only the students whom they consider to be at either extreme (high or low) with respect to any characteristic named on the scale. Some scales are specifically designed for helping teachers identify behavior problems in particular areas.

Rating scales may be roughly classed as scoring methods, ranking methods, graphic scales, and check lists or behavior descriptions. These categories are not mutually exclusive. Some scales combine two or more types. Some, for example, are a combination of the graphic and check-list types. And a scoring system can be imposed upon all of them. The classification used here is arbitrary and only suggestive.

SCORING METHODS

The Man-to-man Scale. Certain types of rating scales have been developed for use in industry, clinics, and the Armed Forces that are, on the whole, not practical for use in schools because of the amount of work involved in using them or because of the special training needed by the user. An example is the man-to-man scale developed by Scott in 1917 and adopted in 1918 for rating many United States Army officers. Because the scale has certain advantages and is frequently referred to in the literature, it is considered here.

When the man-to-man method is used, each rater builds his own scale in terms of actual persons. The Army Rating Scale of this type included five traits: physical qualities, intelligence, leadership, personal qualities, and general value to the service. An officer selected as examples of each trait five men of his rank with whom he was well acquainted. He included in his list of examples for each trait officers whom he considered very poor as well as ones whom he considered very good. He listed the names in rank order from highest to lowest in the spaces provided on the scale form. The scores assigned the five intervals were the same for all five traits. For example, the items for intelligence were shown as follows: [1]

Intelligence

Accuracy, ease in learning, ability to grasp quickly the point of view of commanding officer, to issue clear and intelligent orders, to estimate a new situation, and to arrive at a sensible decision in a crisis.	Highest	15
	High	12
	Middle	9
	Low	6
	Lowest	3

In rating subordinates, the officer made a man-to-man comparison with the men named on his scale. Only after he had made concrete comparisons did he consider the numerical scores. If he considered the position of the man being rated to be between the positions of two officers named on his scale, he assigned him a numerical rating accordingly. If, for example, he assigned him a position between the low man and the middle man, he gave him a score of 7, 7½, or 8 in accordance with his estimate of the man's nearness to the middle or the low man.

Some research studies have shown that the man-to-man rating method has a definite advantage in helping to reduce the "generosity error"—the tendency to overestimate favorable qualities. The method has, however, a serious weakness in that each rater's scale is different and may not be closely related to the scales used in rating either the same person or other persons. Moreover, as its authors [2] once stated, it is a relatively cumbersome method and, hence, not generally applicable.

[1] Committee on Classification of Personnel, Adjutant General's Department, *The Personnel Manual*, p. 260. Washington, D.C.: Government Printing Office, 1919. Reproduced by permission of the Department of the Army.

[2] W. D. Scott and R. C. Clothier, *Personnel Management*, p. 207. New York: McGraw-Hill Book Company, Inc., 1923. In the later editions of this book no mention is made of the man-to-man scale, and less attention is given to this rating method than in the 1923 edition.

Simple Analytic Form. The simplest illustration of the scoring type of rating scale used in the schools is the analytic form whereon the two extremes of the traits being considered are listed with intervening possible score points. The following example is an adaptation of a scale used in the California Adolescent Growth Study.[3] Encircling the number nearest either extreme (1 or 5) indicates a maximum rating in terms of the extreme. Encircling the next nearest number (2 or 4) indicates an above- or below-average rating; and encircling the middle number, an average rating.

Self-expressiveness

Talkative	1	2	3	4	5	Silent
Active	1	2	3	4	5	Stationary
Peppy	1	2	3	4	5	Indifferent
Busy	1	2	3	4	5	Idle
Animated (face, etc.)	1	2	3	4	5	Stolid
Eager	1	2	3	4	5	Listless

Haggerty-Olson-Wickman Scales. Perhaps one of the best examples of the scoring type of rating scale is the Haggerty-Olson-Wickman Behavior Rating Schedules, which are more in the nature of measurements than is any other scale discussed in this chapter. They are scoring procedures designed for detection and study of problem behavior and problem tendencies among students and include two schedules printed in one folder.

Schedule A is a behavior-problem record on which the rater indicates his estimate of the frequency of occurrence of 15 types of behavior problems, such as cheating, lying, and speech difficulties. The two following items are taken from Schedule A: [4]

Behavior problem . .	Has never occurred	Has occurred once or twice but no more	Occasional occurrence	Frequent occurrence	Score
Lying	0	4	6	7	
Bullying	0	8	12	14	

In using Schedule A, the teacher, disregarding the numbers used in scoring, indicates how frequently the behavior has occurred in his experience with the student by placing a cross in the appropriate column after each item.

Schedule B is a behavior-rating scale that contains 35 questions regarding intellectual, physical, social, and emotional traits. Brief de-

[3] Frances B. Newman, with an introduction by H. E. Jones, *The Adolescent in Social Groups: Studies in Observation of Personality*, p. 19. Stanford, Calif.: Stanford University Press, 1946.

[4] M. E. Haggerty et al., *Haggerty-Olson-Wickman Behavior Rating Schedules.* New York: World Book Company, 1930. Items reproduced by special permission.

scriptions are given at five points beneath the lines, and the numbers used
in scoring are given beneath the descriptions. The following illustrates the
items contained in Schedule B:

20. How does he accept authority?

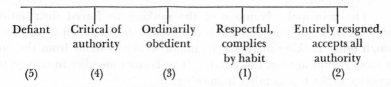

Defiant	Critical of authority	Ordinarily obedient	Respectful, complies by habit	Entirely resigned, accepts all authority
(5)	(4)	(3)	(1)	(2)

THE RANKING METHOD

Ranking scales are used in rating members of the same group for the
purpose of intragroup comparison. The names of the group members are
arranged in serial order from highest to lowest in keeping with the members' status for some characteristic. The rank of 1 is assigned to the top or
best individual, of 2 to the next highest, and so forth. This order of merit
method is frequently used in schools for showing the students' standings
in scholastic achievement, but it is rarely used with personality traits.

It is common practice to show on a student's high school record his
rank in class at the time of graduation and to record this information on
the report to a college. For example, the transcript for John Doe may
show that he ranked 5 in a class of 293. For the information to be very
meaningful, the size of the class must be given. The rank of 288, for instance, has one meaning if the class size is 288 and another if the class size
is 588. It is true that a student who ranks 5 in a class of 12 may be more
able than John Doe who ranks 5 in a class of 293, but a rank of 5 in a
class of 293 is ordinarily more readily accepted as evidence of scholastic
strength than is the rank of 5 in a class of 12.

The ranking method may be employed by a faculty in selecting
the student to receive an honor for which some requirements are intangible. The honor, for example, is to go to the "best all-round student"
in terms of scholastic achievement, citizenship, leadership, service to the
school, and the like. The teachers may agree that certain students should
be given serious consideration, but they may fail to agree regarding the
one to receive the honor. The decision may be reached by having all
teachers rank the candidates and then deciding the winner on the basis
of the ratings given.

It is obviously much easier to rank individuals on the basis of some
quantitative measurement, such as grade point average, than according
to some intangible characteristic that cannot be appraised objectively,
such as citizenship or emotional stability. For that reason raters may be
instructed to rate first the individuals near the extremes and then to work
toward the middle. It is easier to differentiate the individuals near the

extremes than it is to differentiate those in the middle of the range. If the group is large, the rater may not be asked to make a complete ranking but, instead, to sort the members into subgroups, such as the top 5 per cent, the next 20 per cent, the middle 50 per cent, the next 20 per cent, and the bottom 5 per cent.

The principal advantage of the ranking or forced distribution method is that it often yields a better differentiation than is obtained through other ranking methods. Its major weakness stems from the fact that most groups are not comparable. The bottom member in one group is superior to the top member in another.

GRAPHIC RATING SCALES

The most widely used type of rating scale is probably the graphic scale. The rater places a check on a continuous line at the point between the two extremes that, he believes, best indicates the degree to which the ratee possesses the characteristic named. This type of scale is frequently used on transcript forms used by high schools in reporting to colleges and placement offices.

The rating scale is strengthened when the intervals are defined through descriptive phrases. It then becomes a "descriptive graphic scale." In the following example, taken from Freeman,[5] the intervals are defined in terms of quality and frequency.

Attitude toward others

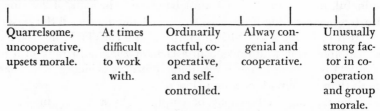

| Quarrelsome, uncooperative, upsets morale. | At times difficult to work with. | Ordinarily tactful, cooperative, and self-controlled. | Alway congenial and cooperative. | Unusually strong factor in cooperation and group morale. |

When the arrangement is a horizontal one, as in this example and in the Haggerty-Olson-Wickman items shown above, the descriptions are ordinarily placed beneath the line. If a vertical line is used, as in Figure 2, they ordinarily come to the left. The vertical arrangement is relatively little used. According to Carpenter's [6] study, the two arrangements yield significantly different results. He found that, on the whole, the horizontal ratings assume a more nearly normal distribution than the vertical ratings.

In some graphic scales the line is unbroken; in others it is divided

[5] Frank S. Freeman, *Theory and Practice of Psychological Testing*, rev. ed., p. 457. New York: Holt, Rinehart and Winston, Inc., 1955. Reproduced by special permission.

[6] James H. Carpenter, "An Experimental Study Investigating the Relation between Vertical and Horizontal Graphic Rating Scales," unpublished master's thesis, pp. 28–37. Los Angeles: University of Southern California, 1950.

into steps or intervals. When the line is divided, the rater is expected to indicate the ratee's position within the interval or to mark at an intermediate point if he does not consider a description wholly suitable. When the line is unmarked, the rater may place his check anywhere along the line between the two extremes. Carpenter [7] found, however, that, when the line is unbroken, raters do not make fine discriminations. They tend to treat the line as if it were divided into thirds or fourths.

Opinions differ regarding the optimum number of intervals for the divided line. The range for most scales is from two to nine with five and seven being used most frequently. Symonds [8] computed that seven is the average optimum number for rating human traits but found, however, that under certain conditions a smaller number is justified. More than three or four are inexpedient when the trait named is an obscure one or when the raters are only moderately interested in the rating task.

The Personality Record. Although asserted not to be a rating scale, the Personality Record [9] developed by the National Association of Secondary-school Principals is a graphic scale, as is shown in the two items reproduced below.

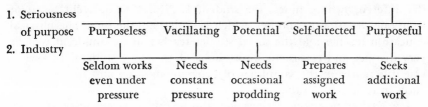

| 1. Seriousness of purpose | Purposeless | Vacillating | Potential | Self-directed | Purposeful |
| 2. Industry | Seldom works even under pressure | Needs constant pressure | Needs occasional prodding | Prepares assigned work | Seeks additional work |

The instructions for use of this scale are clearly designed, however, to prevent the use of scoring or of summary statements in terms of average ratings. According to the instructions, the most common or the modal rating for each characteristic is to be indicated on a student's cumulative record by the letter M followed by a number in parentheses that shows the number of teachers who assign him this rating. The number of teachers who assign other ratings to the student is to be indicated by numbers placed at the proper points along the line. If, for example, five of the eight teachers who appraise a student for "seriousness of purpose" rate him as "potential," two as "purposeful," and one as "vacillating," M (5) is written above the word "potential," 2 above "purposeful," and 1 above "vacillating." In this way both the modal rating and the variations in the ratings are shown for each characteristic listed on the form. This procedure provides much more significant information about the student than can be obtained from recording average ratings only.

[7] *Ibid.,* p. 48.

[8] P. M. Symonds, *Diagnosing Personality and Conduct,* p. 79. New York: Appleton-Century-Crofts, Inc., 1931.

[9] National Association of Secondary-school Principals, *The Personality Record.* Washington, D.C.: National Education Association, 1941.

Recording the Results. It is not easy to show on most graphic scales the ratings received by a student each year over a period of time. It can be done on the "cumulative record copy" of some instruments by drawing a line to separate the record for one year from that of another or by distinguishing the results for one year from those of other years by the color of the ink used. In many cases, however, the result is very likely to be a badly crowded record, one not easy to read. To simplify recording of cumulative results, in some schools a scoring system is imposed upon the scale by assigning numerical values to the various scale intervals, and the results are recorded in terms of average ratings only.

The meaningfulness of average ratings is dependent upon the reliability of ratings by individual teachers. If variations among judgments are large because the ratings are unreliable, using an average of the ratings without regard to their variations might be, as Freeman [10] says, misleading or even absurd. "For example, if, on a seven-point scale, two judges rated an individual at −3, two at +3, and two at zero, the mean rating would be zero (or average level), whereas the probability is that he is not average at all in view of the wide disparity of judgments."

If the ratings are very reliable, there will be slight variations in the different ratings unless the student is displaying different behavior from one situation to another, which is sometimes the case. The physical education teacher and the social studies teacher, for example, may have very distinct and consistent impressions of the same student. In such a case differences in the samplings of behavior may account for the differences in ratings given the student by the two teachers.

Variations among ratings may also be due to a student's displaying unstable or contradictory patterns of behavior or to his displaying characteristics which impress different observers in different ways. In such cases to record the average judgment can be misleading. Note this example from a report on the Adolescent Growth Study: [11]

> On the item "sensitivity to other's opinions" the average rating for John by four judges was consistently close to the mean for the group. Most of the senior high school period, however, practically all of the judgments were either at one extreme or at the other; not one was at the mean. Several other items showed similar discrepancies between averages and single ratings.

The average of several ratings does not give a valid picture of *individual* behavior. The average often conceals rather than reveals specific modes of conduct and may even represent, in Newman's words, "behavior unlike that seen by any rater." For counseling purposes, recording the

[10] Freeman, *op. cit.,* pp. 457–458.

[11] Frances Burks Newman, *The Adolescent in Social Groups: Studies in Observation of Personality,* p. 34. Reprinted with the permission of the publishers, Stanford University Press. Copyright 1946 by the Board of Trustees of the Leland Stanford Junior University.

variations in ratings received by a student for each year is more significant than reporting cumulative numerical ratings in terms of averages.

CHECK LISTS AND BEHAVIOR DESCRIPTIONS

Classified Lists. A check list developed by Hartshorne [12] and his coworkers was one of the earliest scales of this type developed for use by teachers. The list included 80 pairs of antonyms arranged in two columns with positive and negative words intermixed. In using the scale, the teacher checked every word that described the student being rated. He could check as many words as he thought applied, or he could check none at all if he thought none applied. By subtracting the number of negative words from the number of positive words, a score of −1, 0, or +1 was obtained.

Most scales of the check-list type used in the schools today do not provide for scoring. The chief purpose behind the use of such instruments is to ascertain the teachers' opinions regarding the behaviors most characteristic of the students rated rather than to measure the extent to which the students are characterized by certain traits or to compare one student with the others. The emphasis is upon describing behavior rather than upon evaluating it.

Some writers provide check lists to help teachers learn what to observe and how to record their observations in an accurate, methodical manner. Torgerson,[13] for example, offers an inventory or check list that is designed, like the Haggerty-Olson-Wickman scales, to help teachers detect behavior problems, problem tendencies, and sources of problems. Unlike the Haggerty-Olson-Wickman scales, this check list is not scored. It contains some two hundred items that describe undesirable behavior manifestations frequently found among students. The items are classified under the headings of scholarship, reading, spelling, arithmetic, vision, hearing, health, speech, and social behavior.[14]

Multiple-choice Items. Some check lists contain items that resemble the subheads of descriptive graphic scales like the ones discussed above. A good example of this type of check list is the American Council on Education Personality Report, reproduced in Figure 2. In its original form and first revision the ACE instrument was a graphic descriptive scale. However, because raters generally failed to take advantage of the opportunity to make fine discriminations by checking between the descriptions along the line, the check-on-the-line arrangement was discarded. The second revision is a vertical arrangement of five questions with multiple-

[12] Hugh Hartshorne et al., *Studies in Service and Self-control,* pp. 91–93. New York: The Macmillan Company, 1929.

[13] Theodore L. Torgerson, *Studying Children: Diagnostic and Remedial Procedures in Teaching,* chap. 5. New York: Holt, Rinehart and Winston, Inc., 1947.

[14] The 50 items for social behavior are reproduced in Chap. 15 of this book.

Name of student...

A—How are you and others affected by his appearance and manner?	☐ Sought by others ☐ Well liked by others ☐ Liked by others ☐ Tolerated by others ☐ Avoided by others ☐ No opportunity to observe	Please record here instances on which you base your judgment.
B—Does he need frequent prodding or does he go ahead without being told?	☐ Seeks and sets for himself additional tasks ☐ Completes suggested supplementary work ☐ Does ordinary assignments of his own accord ☐ Needs occasional prodding ☐ Needs much prodding in doing ordinary assignments ☐ No opportunity to observe	Please record here instances on which you base your judgment.
C—Does he get others to do what he wishes?	☐ Displays marked ability to lead his fellows; makes things go ☐ Sometimes leads in important affairs ☐ Sometimes leads in minor affairs ☐ Lets other take lead ☐ Probably unable to lead his fellows ☐ No opportunity to observe	Please record here instances on which you base your judgment.
D—How does he control his emotions?	☐ Unusual balance of responsiveness and control ☐ Well balanced ☐ Usually well balanced ☐ Tends to be unresponsive ☐ Tends to be over emotional ☐ Unresponsive, apathetic ☐ Too easily depressed, irritated or elated ☐ No opportunity to observe	Please record here instances on which you base your judgment.
E—Has he a program with definite purposes in terms of which he distributes his time and energy?	☐ Engrossed in realizing well-formulated objectives ☐ Directs energies effectively with fairly definite program ☐ Has vaguely formed objectives ☐ Aims just to "get by" ☐ Aimless trifler ☐ No opportunity to observe	Please record here instances on which you base your judgment.

FIGURE 2   *The ACE Personality Report, Form B.* (Washington, D.C.: American Council on Education, 1929. Reproduced by permission of the publisher.)

choice answers. The rater checks one of five possible answers or indicates that he has not had an opportunity to observe the type of behavior covered by the question.

This scale has several important advantages: (1) Questions, instead of descriptive phrases, are used for designating the qualities covered by the scale. The question helps the rater to define the quality for which an individual is to be rated. (2) Judges are not required to rate an individual for every trait. An effort is made to raise the validity and the reliability of the scale by having the judges rate an individual for only the qualities that have been evident to them. (3) Judgments are to be made on the basis of observation evidence, and the evidence is to be reported.

The ACE Personality Report has been well received and apparently is widely used. With minor modifications it is used in graphic descriptive form on the transcript blanks used by many California high schools in reporting to colleges. The multiple-choice check-list form, also with minor modifications, has been adopted by the National League of Nursing Education, for use in schools of nursing.

The PEA Behavior Description. One of the most important developments in the check-list type of scale is an instrument developed by a subcommittee on records and reports of the Eight Year Study of the Progressive Education Association.[15] Entitled Behavior Description, this scale includes description of complex intellectual activities as well as of the personality characteristics commonly included in rating scales.

The items in the Behavior Description were selected, after extensive experimentation, on the basis of four criteria: (1) importance— they throw light on the student; (2) observability—at least some teachers will have an opportunity to observe significant behavior in relation to them; (3) completeness—they give a reasonably complete picture of the student; and (4) differentness—the terms are independent enough for teachers to distinguish between them. The items are classified as follows: (1) responsibility-dependability, (2) creativeness and imagination, (3) influence, (4) inquiring mind, (5) openmindedness, (6) power and habit of analysis: habit of reaching conclusions on the basis of valid evidence, (7) emotional responsiveness, (8) serious purpose, (9) social adjustability, and (10) work habits. The explanatory heading for the instrument and one complete item in the social adjustability category are reproduced in Figure 3.

Four other characteristics are listed on the form for which check lists are not given: (1) physical energy, (2) assurance, (3) self-reliance, and (4) emotional control. For these four the teachers indicate only whether the characteristic is present or absent to a marked degree. The form also provides spaces in which the teachers record their judgments of the stu-

[15] E. R. Smith, R. W. Tyler, and the evaluation staff, *Appraising and Recording Student Progress*, pp. 470–487. New York: Harper & Row, Publishers, Incorporated, 1942.

dent's success in four broad fields: (1) abstract ideas and symbols, (2) people, (3) planning and management, and (4) things and manipulation. The committee felt that any information obtained on marked differences in success in these four areas would be valuable in helping a student to plan for the future.

_____BEHAVIOR DESCRIPTION [1]_____

Last name   First   Middle   (Experimental Form)   School

This report describes the characteristic behavior of the student in a number of important areas. *It should not be interpreted as a rating.* Instead one should read the descriptions and attempt to get from them an understanding of the person described, and of his fitness for particular opportunities and understandings.

Directions:
(1) In general the initials of subject or activity fields are used in the recording in order to identify the relations between the observers and the student. A complete key is given at the top of the folded over sheet.
(2) The spaces from left to right, being chronological, show the changes or continuity in behavior during the period covered by the record.
(3) While agreements in description may show a student's most common behavior, they may not be more important than an isolated judgment, which often has great significance because of a better basis for judgment, or because it indicates a response to some particular condition, field, or personality.

SOCIAL CONCERN	Type	Grade 7	Grade 8	Grade 9	Grade 10	Grade 11	Grade 12
Generally Concerned: Shows an altruistic and general social concern and interprets this in action to the extent of his abilities and opportunities	1						
Selectively Concerned: Shows concern by attitude and action about certain social conditions but seems unable to appreciate the importance of other such problems	2						
Personal: Is not strongly concerned about the welfare of others and responds to social problems only when he recognizes some intimate personal relationship to the problem or group in question	3						
Inactive: Seems aware of social problems, and may profess concern about them, but does nothing	4						
Unconcerned: Does not show any genuine concern for the common good	5						
EMOTIONAL RESPONSIVENESS							
To Ideas: Is emotionally stirred by becoming aware of challenging ideas	1						
To Difficulty: Responds emotionally to a situation or problem challenging to him because of the possibility of overcoming difficulties	2						
To Ideals: Responds emotionally to what is characterized primarily by its personal or social idealism	3						
To Beauty: Responds emotionally to beauty as found in nature and the arts	4						
To Order: Responds emotionally to perfection of functioning as it is seen in organization, mechanical operation or logical completeness	5						

[1] *Used by special permission of the publisher.*

FIGURE 3   *Behavior Description: heading and one complete item.* (Arthur J. Jones, *Principles of Guidance,* 5th ed., p. 90. New York: McGraw-Hill Book Company, Inc., 1962.)

The subitems do not represent named points with equal intervals between them. Nor can they be said, according to the report,[16] to define orders of excellence, in that there is no certainty that the first subhead is better than the others that follow it. Also there is no certainty that any behavior described is the "best for all kinds of people under all kinds of conditions." The emphasis is upon describing behavior patterns, not upon labeling them "desirable" or "undesirable" or upon comparing one student with another.

[16] *Ibid.,* pp. 484–485.

The PEA Behavior Description is now out of print, but in modified form it is still used in a number of schools. Some have incorporated it in their cumulative records. With minor modifications and one important addition it is included in the revised ACE cumulative record folder (described in Chap. 12). The addition is provision of space for a summarization of observation evidence. Figure 4 shows a simplified version that was used in one of the high schools that cooperated in the Wisconsin Study.

Rothney studied the relationships between teachers' descriptions of students and the marks they give these students to determine whether the descriptions are simply indicators of the students' class achievement. He found that the descriptions could not be predicted accurately on the basis of the marks assigned the students concerned.[17]

Q-sort Technique. Stephenson's [18] Q technique is one of the most recent developments in ratings. Descriptive statements are written on separate slips or cards. The rater is asked to sort them into a given number of piles, putting a prescribed number into each pile. He sorts them so that the ones least descriptive of the subject are at one end, the ones most descriptive of him are at the opposite end, and the ones the rater is uncertain about are around the middle. The rater, for instance, might be told to sort 100 statements into nine piles with a distribution like the following:

	Least Characteristic					Most Characteristic			
Pile no.	1	2	3	4	5	6	7	8	9
No. of cards	1	4	11	21	26	21	11	4	1

The procedure of sorting into a normal distribution is not always required. Forced sorting leads to finer differentiation than uncontrolled sorting, but it can be sufficiently burdensome to lead to fatigue and carelessness. In schools and colleges the Q technique is used more often with students for self-ratings than by teachers and counselors in rating students. It is too complex and time-consuming a technique to use in rating a large group of students, but it is very valuable in the intensive study of individuals. It yields a more comprehensive and less biased picture than is ordinarily obtained through other rating procedures. And it is a very useful research method.

SOME OBSTACLES TO EFFECTIVE USE

A Subjective Technique. A scientific method requires a high degree of validity and reliability attained through strict adherence to objective observation. The criteria commonly used for rating scales are, however, subjective judgments. Widely accepted objective criteria are not available

[17] John W. M. Rothney and B. A. Roens, *Counseling the Individual Student,* pp. 99–102. New York: Holt, Rinehart and Winston, Inc., 1949.

[18] William Stephenson, *The Study of Behavior: Q-technique and Its Methodology.* Chicago: The University of Chicago Press, 1953.

Name of Student __JESSIE_____ Teacher __SMITH____

City __WESTOWNE_____ Grade __11__ Subject __ENGLISH__

   Please describe this student by checking the statements which best characterize him. Write additional comments if you think they will help us to understand him.

RESPONSIBILITY

_____ Does even more than he is required to do in assignments.

_____ Does without prodding what he is told to do but no more.

_____ Needs prodding except on special assignments.
        Which ones?_____

___✔___ Needs some prodding on all assignments.

_____ Needs constant prodding to get anything done.

_____ Doesn't do his assignments even when he is prodded.

INFLUENCE

_____ Habitually controls the activities of other students.

_____ A leader but will accept group decisions.

_____ Doesn't control but does strongly influence the activities of others.

___✔___ In certain groups he influences others. Which groups?_____

_____ Is carried along by nearest or strongest influence.

ADJUSTABILITY

___✔___ Appears to feel secure in group situations.

_____ Seems anxious about his standing in groups, but others accept him.

_____ Other students reject him. Why?_____

_____ He withdraws from the group.

CONCERN FOR OTHERS

_____ Shows balance in considering the welfare of himself and others.

_____ Certain problems of group welfare seem to interest him.
        Which? _____

___✔___ Is not interested about welfare of others unless what they do affects him.

_____ Talks about welfare of others but does nothing about it.

_____ Shows no concern for welfare of others.

Comments: __Jessie is not too reliable when assignments are__
__expected to be in on time. She is absent a good deal__
__because of trips, colds, etc.__

FIGURE 4 *Sample of the behavior descriptions used in the Wisconsin Counseling Study.* (John W. M. Rothney et al., *Guidance Practices and Results*, p. 96. New York: Harper & Row, Publishers, Incorporated, 1958. Reproduced by permission of the author and the publisher.)

for the intangible qualities listed in many rating scales. Lacking appropriate criteria, raters often fail to base their judgments on objective observation instead of subjective opinion. Hence, it is not surprising that in general, rating scales have proved disappointingly low in validity and reliability.

Some raters are more reliable than others. An accurate rater will repeat his ratings with a high degree of consistency, but so will a biased one. The validity and reliability of any scale are lowered by errors made consistently or systematically because of misinterpretation of terms or disagreement regarding their meanings, leniency errors, halo effect, and/or limited information about the ratee(s).

Ambiguity. Both the trait name and the interval descriptions or subheads given in a scale may mean different things to different raters. To one teacher "good citizenship" may mean helping others; to another it may mean tending strictly to one's own business. To one counselor the "leader" may mean the student who gets others to do what he wants them to do; to another it may mean the student who helps others find a way to do what they want to do.

As is to be expected, the greatest variations in judgments occur in the rating of covert or intangible qualities. It is much easier to rate an overt characteristic, such as talkativeness or voice quality, than it is to rate some inner quality or private aspect of personality, such as emotional stability or self-confidence. Considerable disagreement is found, however, in the rating of qualities that are easily observed and that, one might believe, could be evaluated uniformly. Greene [19] illustrates the point with material from the California Adolescent Growth Study which shows that the judges agreed very consistently in their ratings for "social responsibility," "popularity," and "self-assertion" but disagreed considerably in their ratings of "appearance" and "grooming." Yet these two items are characteristics that are supposedly easy to define on a rating scale.

The fact that the judges showed great lack of agreement indicates that the judgments were not made on the basis of objective criteria. They were made, no doubt, in terms of the subjective values of the raters—their own standards, perhaps, for appearance and grooming, which varied with the raters' backgrounds, own problems with respect to appearance and grooming, general experience, and the like. Carefully defining the characteristics for which an individual is to be rated contributes to the reliability and the validity of a scale, but it does not guarantee them.

Raters who regularly see the same subjects in the same situations may consistently disagree in rating them. Newman, for example, found that one boy studied in the Adolescent Growth Study was consistently rated differently by two observers throughout his high school years. Fig-

---

[19] Edward B. Greene, *Measurements of Human Behavior,* rev. ed., pp. 459–460. New York: The Odyssey Press, Inc., 1952.

ure 5 shows that one constantly rated him "more talkative" and "free from anxiety" than did the other. According to Newman: [20]

> These judgments together with those on other items in the scales offer or imply two rather distinct and consistent impressions of John. Rater A considered him to be "self-assertive" and "irritable," "unsociable" and "insensitive to others' opinions." Rater B consistently judged him as lacking in ability to assert himself, but at the same time as "good-natured," "sociable," and "highly sensitive to others' opinions."
>
> In unusual cases, such as John's, wherein raters consistently disagreed on certain items over a period of years, it is improbable that different samplings of behavior can account for all the differences noted. It is also unlikely that differing interpretations of item definitions could have been the primary source of disagreement in this case, since differences occurred in a considerable number of variables, and since a consistent pattern of behavior seemed to be pictured within each observer's ratings.

Leniency Errors. Many (most?) raters tend to overrate (positive leniency) or to underrate (negative leniency) persons in whose favor or against

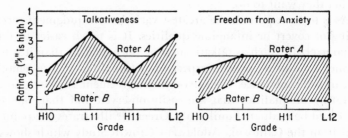

FIGURE 5 *Example of persistent differences in the ratings of same person by different observers.* (Reprinted from *The Adolescent in Social Groups: Studies in Observation of Personality* by Frances Burks Newman with the permission of the publisher, Stanford University Press. Copyright 1946 by the Board of Trustees of the Leland Stanford Junior University.)

whom they are prejudiced. The generosity error is most likely to occur in the rating of persons whom the rater knows well or with whom he is ego-involved. A counselor, for example, in rating applicants for a scholarship, may rate his own counselees more favorably than he rates others who are equally well qualified. He may do so because he identifies with the counselee. If the counselee does not receive the award, the counselor may view it as a reflection on the adequacy of his counseling. If he does receive the award, the counselor may feel that he shares in the honor. It is frequently assumed that the sons and daughters of school principals and

---

[20] Frances Burks Newman, *The Adolescent in Social Groups: Studies in Observation of Personality*, pp. 33–34. Reprinted with the permission of the publishers, Stanford University Press. Copyright 1946 by the Board of Trustees of the Leland Stanford Junior University.

superintendents are overrated by their teachers and counselors. Some raters, however, not wishing to seem to show such favoritism, lean over backwards in rating the children of their colleagues, friends, and superiors. They show a constant tendency toward the error of negative leniency.

So many raters tend toward overestimation that ratings often pile up at the favorable end of a scale until "good" comes to mean "average" and anything less than "good" means "poor." This has been well illustrated in the rating of Army personnel. In some situations commanding officers, in rating junior officers, used only the two top steps of a five-interval scale. Similarly many teachers and counselors overrate their students and counselees and probably for similar reasons: They feel kindly toward students. They don't want to hurt any student's chance at getting the job he wants, of being admitted to the college of his choice, of receiving a scholarship or college loan, etc. They don't want to have to justify or explain a rating less than "good" or "excellent." They find it easier to give everyone a favorable rating than to try to differentiate the strong from the not-strong.

The Halo Effect. The tendency to rate a person for specific traits on the basis of an overall impression of him results in what Thorndike [21] described as the "halo effect." The rater tends to think of the person generally as rather good or rather inferior and to color the judgments of specific qualities by this general finding. Since rating scales are used primarily for obtaining information on the relative strengths and weaknesses of an individual, the halo effect decreases, if it does not destroy, the usefulness of the instrument. Symonds gives an example from Rugg, who tells of a certain "Captain X" who was used by 13 officers in 20 subordinate scales as "the poorest man I ever knew": [22]

> Yet this same Captain X stood first on three different psychological tests among 151 officers. He had been a Rhodes scholar from a Middle Western State university, and at Oxford he had made such a record that he was excused from certain examinations. Comments of eight of the thirteen officers who had judged him so severely showed that their estimates of his intelligence, his physical qualities, and his leadership were dominated by their opinions of his personal qualities. They were unanimous in saying that it was impossible "to live with him." He was a "rotter," or "yellow," or a "knocker," or "conceited."

Acquaintance Factor. Ratings are not likely to be valid if based upon inadequate acquaintance with the ratees. On the other hand, too close a re-

[21] E. L. Thorndike, "A Constant Error in Psychological Rating," *Journal of Applied Psychology,* 1920, 4:25.

[22] From *Diagnosing Personality and Conduct,* pp. 111–112, by Percival M. Symonds. Copyright, 1931. The Century Company, Inc. Used by permission of the publisher.

lationship with the person rated may also lead to inaccurate ratings. As a rule, raters tend to be overgenerous with the persons whom they like, have known for a long time, or are closely associated with. Similarly, they tend to underestimate the strengths and to overestimate the defects and deficiences of the persons whom they dislike.

Wide acquaintance with people in general may help to raise the quality of ratings on particular individuals. Raters who have had broad experience with a variety of people have a better basis for their judgments of human behavior and are likely to rate other persons more accurately than are raters who have had a limited acquaintance with people.

SOME IMPROVEMENT PROCEDURES

Various procedures have been developed for increasing the validity and reliability of rating scales and behavior descriptions. Increased effective·ness has been reported as the result of careful selection and training of raters, of refinement of format, of controlled distribution, and of forced-choice methods.

Selection and Training of Raters. Valid ratings depend largely upon selection of impartial raters who are well acquainted with the ratees and are adequately trained in the technique. Providing raters careful instructions and explanations and training them through practice sessions and group discussions help to minimize errors. Instructing raters, for example, to rate one trait at a time for all ratees helps to counteract the halo effect. Informed regarding the common sources of errors, the raters may try to avoid them.

In some schools all teachers are asked to rate all their students, the assumption being that the combined ratings of a number of ap·proximately equally competent judges are better than those of one or a few, that errors will tend to cancel one another. Research supports this assumption. Research and experience also show, however, that the judg-ment of one expert is ordinarily better than the combined judgments of a number of nonexperts.

Format. A procedure frequently recommended for counteracting the halo effect is to vary the arrangements of the subheads listed for each trait or characteristic. Ordinarily the not-desirable items are listed first in a vertical arrangement or to the left on a horizontal scale. If, however, the subheads are arranged irregularly, the rater will not be able to go down the page checking for each trait in approximately the same place. Varying the arrangement forces him to slow up, to read the items more thought-fully, and to mark them more carefully than he might do otherwise.

Limiting the number of traits to be rated and carefully defining them in simple, objective, unambiguous terms also help to reduce the halo effect. Only items essential to the purposes involved should be included in the scale, and as much as possible they should be defined in operational terms. Arranging items in random fashion also seems a step toward improvement. Disparate traits are put close together, and similar traits are placed far apart to reduce what Guilford [23] terms the "proximity error." The fact that certain studies show that "adjacent traits on a rating form tend to intercorrelate higher than remote ones" indicates that raters assume their degrees of actual similarity to be equal.

Providing space on the rating form for summarization of observation evidence is another useful refinement. Including questions regarding extent of the rater's acquaintance with the ratee and the types of situations in which he has been observed may not improve the instrument but may show whether the rater is sufficiently acquainted with the subject to give a valid rating.

Controlled Distributions and Forced Choices. The piling of ratings at the favorable end of the scale may be avoided or minimized through prescribing a normal distribution by specifying the percentage of ratees to be placed in each category. This procedure is probably most effective when the number of ratees is large.

Some rating forms instruct the rater to select from a pair of items the one that is more descriptive or less descriptive of the subject than the other. Both items usually appear equally favorable or unfavorable, but one member of the pair is more valid than the other for predicting some total quality. A scale used in rating candidates for a college scholarship, for example, might instruct the rater to select from the following four items the one that is most descriptive and the one that is least descriptive of the subject.

a. Follows work schedule carefully.
b. Is serious-minded.
c. Is careless in work.
d. Is inclined to gripe about assignments.

To the average rater the first two items may seem equally favorable and the last two equally unfavorable. On the basis of their research findings, however, the authors of the scale may know that *b* is a better predictor of college success than *a*, and that *c*, better than *d*, differentiates high-grade-point-average students from low-grade-point-average ones.

A number of different forced-choice patterns may be used. The scale may contain single pairs of items (both favorable or unfavorable), four-choice items (all favorable or all unfavorable), five-choice items (two favorable, two unfavorable, and one neutral) or other combinations. Considerable use has been made of the forced-choice method in

[23] J. P. Guilford, *Psychometric Methods*, 2d ed., p. 280. New York: McGraw-Hill Book Company, Inc., 1954.

rating military and industrial personnel, but relatively little use is reported in the rating of students. Construction of this type of scale involves careful research work to determine which items are valid or invalid for predicting a particular criterion. The method has proved effective for controlling personal bias and reducing errors of leniency, but in general it has been poorly received by raters. Cronbach [24] summarizes the situation as follows:

> Raters are generally antagonistic to forced-choice techniques. They want to know how their reports will be interpreted and want to be free to give an entirely favorable impression. Whether a forced-choice scale can be used in a given situation depends upon the cooperation the data gatherer can anticipate or upon the authority he can bring to bear. The Army, after developing the technique and establishing its validity, concluded that resistance from officers was too great to justify continued use of forced-choice scales in efficiency reports.

There is probably little need to disguise the purpose of items or to control the distribution of ratings when the raters are reliable, have the needed information, and are willing to try to rate accurately. Hence, selection and training of raters, and providing them ample opportunity to become acquainted with the subjects, may be the best methods for removing the obstacles to effective use of rating scales and behavior description forms.

DEVELOPMENT OF A RATING SCALE FOR USE IN A PARTICULAR SCHOOL

In view of the technical knowledge needed and the amount of experimentation required to produce a good rating scale, and in view of the number of good standard scales now available, it may be no more desirable for a faculty to try to develop the rating scales than it is for them to try to produce the intelligence tests to be used in their school. If, however, it is decided that some faculty member or committee should develop a rating scale for use in the school, the following guiding principles may be helpful.

1. The faculty decide first what data are needed for giving a better understanding of individual students and then sort out the various ways in which these data may be obtained. Some may be obtained better through some other procedure than through a rating scale.

2. Only observable traits or characteristics are included in the scale. More reliable ratings can be obtained for overt characteristics than for inner qualities.

---

[24] Lee J. Cronbach, *Essentials of Psychological Testing*, 2d ed., pp. 513–514. New York: Harper & Row, Publishers, Incorporated, 1960.

3. General terms are avoided. The traits selected and the terms used in defining them are clearly and specifically explained. Otherwise, different raters may interpret the terms differently, and disagreement may cause considerable variation in the ratings. As pointed out above, for ratings to be valid, variations in judgments must be small.

4. Specific instructions are provided on the rating-scale form and include such cautions as the following:

   a. Make judgments independently without consulting others.

   b. Rate all students for one trait before rating any student for the next trait listed in the scale.

   c. Rate on the basis of actual experience with the student.

   d. Do not guess or infer anything which you cannot determine through observation. In brief, be reasonably sure of your judgment. If you are uncertain, do not give a rating.

   e. Make your ratings as honestly as possible. Try to avoid the influence of gossip, prestige factors, personal likes and dislikes.

5. Use of the scale is preceded by a period of training and practice in its use.

6. The data obtained through use of the rating scale are applied in actual school practice. Practice should include providing students experiences rich in preventive and developmental value as well as experiences of therapeutic value.

These principles should be observed in selecting and using standard rating scales as well as in developing and using teacher-made scales.

SUMMARY

Rating scales can be broadly classed as scoring methods, ranking methods, graphic scales, and check lists or behavior descriptions. The judgments expressed through these instruments are presumably based on sufficiently extensive observation of the ratees. Rating scales are easily administered. Partly for that reason, perhaps, they are widely used for gathering personality data.

Although the validity and reliability of rating scales are not high, they often yield valuable data. Their effectiveness is reduced by the raters' indifference and carelessness, disagreement regarding the meanings of the terms used in the scales, limited information regarding ratees, leniency errors, and the halo effect. Methods contributing to increased effectiveness include careful selection and training of raters, refinements in the rating form, variations in item arrangements, controlled distribution, and forced-choice techniques.

Some guidelines are recommended for use in developing rating scales for use in a particular school. They also apply in the selection of published scales.

REFERENCES

Cronbach, Lee J.: *Essentials of Psychological Testing*, 2d ed., chap. 17. New York: Harper & Row, Publishers, Incorporated, 1960.

Freeman, Frank S.: *Theory and Practice of Psychological Testing*, rev. ed., chap. 17. New York: Holt, Rinehart and Winston, Inc., 1955.

Froehlich, Clifford P., and Kenneth B. Hoyt: *Guidance Testing*, chap. 12. Chicago: Science Research Associates, 1959.

Greene, Edward B.: *Measurements of Human Behavior*, rev. ed., chap. 16. New York: The Odyssey Press, Inc., 1952.

Guilford, J. P.: *Psychometric Methods*, 2d ed., chap. 11. New York: McGraw-Hill Book Company, Inc., 1954.

Newman, Frances B., with introduction by H. E. Jones: *The Adolescent in Social Groups: Studies in Observation of Personality*. Stanford, Calif.: Stanford University Press, 1946.

Rothney, J. W. M., and B. A. Roens: *Counseling the Individual Student*, chap. 3. New York: Holt, Rinehart and Winston, Inc., 1949.

Sisson, E. D.: "Forced Choice: The New Army Rating," *Personnel Psychology*, 1948, 1:365–381.

Smith, Eugene R., Ralph W. Tyler, and the evaluation staff: *Appraising and Recording Student Progress*, chap. 10. New York: Harper & Row, Publishers, Incorporated, 1942.

Strang, Ruth: *Counseling Technics in College and Secondary School*, rev. ed., chap. 3. New York: Harper & Row, Publishers, Incorporated, 1949.

Symonds, Percival M.: *Diagnosing Personality and Conduct*, chap. 3. New York: Appleton-Century-Crofts, Inc., 1931.

Thorndike, Robert L., and Elizabeth Hagen: *Measurement and Evaluation in Psychology and Education*, 2d ed., chap. 13. New York: John Wiley & Sons, Inc., 1961.

Torgerson, Theodore L.: *Studying Children: Diagnostic and Remedial Procedures in Teaching*, chap. 3. New York: Holt, Rinehart and Winston, Inc., 1947.

Traxler, Arthur E.: *Techniques of Guidance*, rev. ed., chap. 8. New York: Harper & Row, Publishers, Incorporated, 1957.

4

Tests: Some Basic Considerations

In this and the next three chapters we are concerned only with standardized tests, although teacher-made tests constitute an important part of a school's testing program. The use of standardized tests is an important counseling technique. It is probably the most commonly used specialized technique, and in many schools it is the only one used to any great extent. During the past decade use has been greatly stimulated by national scholarship programs and by the National Defense Education Act.

The large-scale testing programs sponsored by the College Entrance Examination Board, the American College Testing Service, the National Merit Scholarship program, the independent schools, and other agencies have given a tremendous impetus to testing for the purpose of identifying talented and gifted high school students. In 1958 the National Defense Education Act provided funds for testing programs "in secondary schools to identify students with outstanding aptitudes and abilities." [1] This law, no doubt, has helped to increase the number of statewide testing programs. Since its passage, for example, testing programs have become mandatory in all school districts in California. Some of the tests used must be selected from an approved list.[2]

It would be most unfortunate if NDEA and the national scholarship programs should lead to an overconcern with talented youth and to failure to stimulate students at all ability levels to seek full development of their aptitudes. Happily, many people are aware of this danger, and some are sounding cautions against it. For example, a report of the Rockefeller Brothers Fund,[3] which was published the same year that NDEA was enacted, points out that, while we have given too little attention in the past to individuals of unusual potentialities, "it would serve no purpose to replace our neglect of the gifted by neglect of everyone

---

[1] *Public Law 85–864*, 85th Cong.; H.R. 13,247, Sept. 2, 1958.
[2] *California Education Code*, sec. 12820–12825.
[3] Rockefeller Brothers Fund, *The Pursuit of Excellence: Education and the Future of America*, pp. 15–17. Garden City, N.Y.: Doubleday & Company, Inc., 1958.

else." Wasted skills and misapplied abilities at all levels are "a threat to the capacity of a free people to survive." Moreover, as the report reminds us, "judgments of differences in talent are not judgments of differences in human worth."

SOME ADVANTAGES

In counseling, the primary purpose in using any diagnostic instrument is to obtain information that can be useful in helping students to understand themselves, so that they may select and plan wisely, and useful in helping the faculty to determine provisions and modifications needed in the interest of students' optimal development. Appropriate tests properly used contribute to the achievement of this basic purpose and have some important advantages, which are listed below.

1. *Tests yield certain types of information more economically than most other procedures.* For this reason they are particularly useful in providing objective estimates of a student's abilities when he transfers from school to school or from school to college or from school to business world. A student, for example, reports to enroll in a junior high school in his new hometown. He does not bring a copy of his record from the previous school, and it may be weeks or even months before one can be obtained. The information secured from the boy leaves the counselor in doubt as to whether he should be placed in the seventh or eighth grade. He decides to put him in the eighth grade. Some weeks later he finds, on the basis of the teachers' reports, that he should have placed him in the seventh grade and changes him accordingly.

This procedure of trying the student out in the eighth grade is costly for the student in terms of time and morale. The time spent in the eighth grade could have been better invested in the seventh grade—in participating in the curricular and cocurricular experiences offered there and in adjusting to the other students, the teachers, and the classroom environment. Furthermore, if the boy sees the change as a demotion, he suffers a loss in self-esteem as well as a loss in time and learning. To prevent or to reduce any loss in morale, the worker may try through counseling to help the student to understand and to accept the situation and even, perhaps, to decide himself to make the change. While providing counseling is highly desirable, having to provide it for such purposes further increases the cost of the trial-and-error method.

It would be much more economical of the student's and the teachers' time to administer aptitude and achievement tests to the boy at the time of entrance. Counseling time can then be used to help the boy understand the purpose of the testing and to gain his interest and cooperation. A counseling interview designed to help orient a student and to protect his ego usually contributes more to understanding and morale than one undertaken to repair any damage already done to his self-esteem. Testing a student may require from three to four hours, but the use of three or four hours to determine grade placement is more economical than the use of three or four weeks or even of three or four days.

2. *Objective tests yield more accurate information than subjective techniques,* such as the interview, questionnaire, and observation, because they are relatively free of extraneous factors. The test situation is controlled and is practically the same for all participants. The sample of behavior tested is also the same, and the performance of all subjects is judged by the same standard. Appraisal of performance is not dependent upon the examiner's memory or the scorer's likes and dislikes, biases and preferences.

Judgments made on the basis of test data are likely to be superior to judgments based on teachers' reports, because they are usually more accurate. At times tests show a teacher's judgment to be wholly false. For example, the teacher of a sixth-grade class, used in establishing norms for a listening comprehension test, told the research worker administering the test that she knew a certain pupil would make the lowest score, because he never bothered to listen when she explained anything, no matter how many times she made the explanation or how interesting she tried to make it. But the boy she named earned the highest score. Apparently he usually understood her the first time and through his apparent indifference revealed his boredom with the repetitions. Similarly, a standardized test of intelligence or achievement may show a quiet, withdrawing student not to be the dull child his teachers think him to be but instead to be very bright. Conversely, the tests may show a bright-appearing lad not to be so bright as some of his teachers think. His good marks may be due more to personal charm than to scholastic ability or mastery of subject matter.

3. *Tests provide information in meaningful terms through quantitative description of the data.* Describing a student as very bright or reporting that he does well in school is not so definite or so significant as saying that, according to his performance on certain tests, he has an IQ of about 130 or that his performance on the achievement test places him in a percentile range of the 90th to the 95th.

4. *Tests aid in the classification and placement of students.* It is more efficient, for example, to place students in remedial reading groups on the basis of reading test data than solely on the basis of teacher judgment or classroom performance at a particular time. Other tests are useful for identifying students in need of remedial assistance in other areas. And the systematic use of ability tests improves the selection of students to be included in the special programs for the gifted.

5. *Tests facilitate evaluation of treatment and the study of growth or change.* A test administered at the beginning of a remedial reading program helps to show the strengths and weaknesses of individual students. Another form of the same test or a similar test administered later

shows the gains made by each one in correcting his weaknesses and improving his strengths. Likewise, a test administered to students at the beginning of a term may provide the data needed for establishing two comparable groups to be taught by widely different methods. The same test or a comparable form administered at the end of the experiment will help to reveal whether the members of one group made greater progress than the members of the other group. The test data may also reveal which types of students in each group profited most or least from the particular learning experiences and environment provided for each group.

SOME LIMITATIONS

Like other measuring devices, tests are subject to errors resulting from limitations in the technique, in the instrument, and in the user of the instrument. The better a worker's understanding of the technique and the greater his skills in the use of the instrument, the fewer will be his errors. Also, the more likely he is to heed such limitations as the following:

1. *Tests are not refined tools that give exact measurement.* The best tests are crude instruments that yield approximations rather than exact estimates. Some provide only rough estimates because in some areas, such as personality assessment, our tests are, as Super and Crites [4] have said, still in the embryonic stages.

2. *Tests do not provide comprehensive measurement.* Achievement tests, for example, commonly measure information possessed. They less often measure ability to apply information. Rarely do they yield evidence regarding appreciation and critical discrimination. A vocabulary test may measure a student's ability to recognize synonyms but not give any real information about his functioning vocabulary. Similarly a paper-and-pencil test of mechanical aptitude may measure a student's knowledge of the names of certain tools and of the purposes for which these tools can be used but may not test his ability to use any tool for achieving its purposes. And, finally, intelligence is such a complex concept and involves so many factors that it would be very difficult to develop a truly comprehensive test of general intelligence. Were such attempted, the resulting test would most likely omit assessment of some important factors, such as foresight and creativity or originality.

3. *The test yields a score, the numerical indication of the student's performance; but it does not show why he made the score.* It does not show, among other things, whether the student's performance was affected by such factors as motivation, visual acuity, physical energy, anxiety, excitement, reading skill, cultural background, desire to make a good im-

4 Donald E. Super and John O. Crites, *Appraising Vocational Fitness by Means of Psychological Tests*, rev. ed., p. 8. New York: Harper & Row, Publishers, Incorporated, 1962.

pression, and the like. In the light of such information, the meaning of the scores may be altered considerably.

4. *The test may show what a student can do in a test situation; but it does not show what he will do under other conditions, especially in complex educational and vocational situations.* It is not, for instance, uncommon for a student to do much better in his schoolwork than some others who received higher scores than he on a scholastic aptitude test. More highly motivated and better organized than the others, he puts forth greater effort and achieves at a higher level than do some of his more able classmates. Scholastic aptitude tests supply very little evidence regarding interest, planning, and effort, which, as well as ability, are required for success. The combination of test scores and of information regarding the student's past achievement, emotional balance, social acceptance, and the like can offer a better basis for predicting success than test scores alone. Judgments based on test scores alone, however, are very likely to be superior to judgments based on subjective data alone.

SOME PITFALLS

Inept users of tests have done much to nullify the work done by authors of good tests. Better results are obtained from the use of tests when the users are wary of such pitfalls as the following:

1. *Failure to choose measurements in keeping with the specific purposes to be served.* If, for example, the objective is to test a student's ability to construct a good sentence, to compose unified thoughtful paragraphs, and to assemble paragraphs into an acceptable composition, the type of measurement to be used is not an English test that measures mainly a student's ability to recognize right and wrong forms and to organize or reorganize material written by others. In this case, the test should be in the form of an essay examination; that is, the student should be instructed to write a composition about some assigned topic or one of his own choosing. On the other hand, if the objective is to test the student's power to recognize correct English forms, then the use of a test like the one first referred to seems appropriate.

2. *Use of tests for purposes not intended.* The use that some teacher-counselors make of vocational interest tests well illustrates this error. Most vocational interest tests give scores representing *interest* in broad fields of interest, such as artistic or mechanical. They do not give information concerning a student's *ability* and *opportunity* to enter a specific occupation in the field of professed interest, but some student personnel workers use them as though they did and counsel students accordingly.

3. *Overenthusiastic support of tests and failure to recognize their imperfections.* As indicated above, the experts among the test makers and

users know that their tests do not supply an exact estimate of the traits they purport to measure. Many less expert test users, however, treat test data as though they were the product of some fine, exact instrument. This type of error is often made with personality inventories. The complex structure of personality cannot be measured by any paper-and-pencil inventory currently available to nonclinical workers. Nevertheless, data from such instruments are being used in many schools as the chief basis for diagnosis and treatment of maladjustment.

Yet it is wrong to go to the opposite extreme and refuse to recognize virtue in any test because all tests are to some degree imperfect. Instead of making good use of the tests available, some people foolishly refuse to use them at all. Many tests designed for use in school and college counseling programs are well constructed and, when properly used for the purposes intended, do much to help change counseling from artful guesswork to a scientific art.

4. *Failure to remember that a score represents a range rather than a point on the scale.* We cannot view a student's psychological test score with the same confidence with which we might accept a report on his weight. An individual's test score may vary considerably from one trial to another; so no one score can be accepted as his true score. If we were to test him many times on equivalent forms of the test, we could then determine the average amount of variation in his scores. We do not have to do this, however, because a calculated estimate of this amount may be obtained statistically. This statistic is termed a "standard error."

If a student were tested on a large number of comparable forms, about 68 per cent of his obtained scores would fall within one standard error of his true score; and about 95 per cent would lie within two standard errors of his true score. The counselor should view a test score as symbolizing a band that stretches from a point one standard error above the obtained score to a point one standard error below it. He is on safer ground if he assumes that the student's true score lies at some point within this band than if he says that it lies at a certain point.

When raw scores are translated into percentile ranks, bands near the middle of the distribution may be so wide that they have very little meaning. Because in such cases we cannot know in which direction chance errors have influenced a student's score, we cannot tell whether he is average, above average, or below average in the ability or the trait measured. This is particularly true when the test is of only moderate reliability.

To help counselors think of test scores as ranges instead of points, the authors of some tests, such as the School and College Ability Tests and the Sequential Tests of Educational Development, report norms in terms of ranges or bands rather than single scores. See Figure 11.

5. *Too strong generalizations from group tendencies.* Some college admission officers note that most students who score below a certain score on the admission test do not succeed in the college concerned, and so they

rule that no student earning a score below the critical point may be admitted. Some such students, however, gain admission to other colleges and make good. Others who are admitted to college primarily on the basis of high admission test scores fail in their studies.

Because, as Cronbach [5] emphasizes, "*almost never are psychological tests so valid that a prediction about a single case is certainly true,*" counselors must be cautious in generalizing from group tendencies. In interpreting test data to a student, a counselor might well tell him that most students with scores as low as his, for example, in verbal and abstract reasoning encounter considerable difficulty in succeeding in law school. But he should not, on the basis of the group tendencies, predict certain failure in law school for this student.

6. *Neglect of data that cannot be obtained through tests.* Super and Crites have pointed out that counselors need two types of data for diagnosis—psychological data on aptitudes, skills, interests, and personality traits, and social data on environment, influences, resources, and the like. Counselors, in keeping with their training, tend to neglect one type or the other. "The fact that many psychological characteristics are best judged by means of tests which require special study and have the appearance of objectivity and concreteness has often led to the relative neglect of social factors in counseling by those trained to use tests, and to the neglect of important psychological factors by those not trained to use tests." [6]

7. *Making the part the whole.* Counselors stumble into this pitfall in many ways. Some do it by concentrating on diagnosis and neglecting or wholly overlooking other counseling functions. They believe in follow-up work, for example, but have no time for such time-consuming tasks. Some who narrow the work to the diagnostic service sin even further by making tests the whole of this service. They overlook practically all other diagnostic methods, such as exploratory activities and role playing or sociodrama.

FACTORS IMPORTANT IN TEST SELECTION

A good test possesses three qualities to a high degree—validity, reliability, and practicability or usability. Adequate information on these points is not always provided in test manuals. Hence, selection of a good test is not always easy even though there may be hundreds of tests available for the particular purposes to be served through testing.

Validity. Validity indicates how well a test measures that which it is supposed to measure. Even though the title of a test should tell what it is

[5] Lee J. Cronbach, *Essentials of Psychological Testing,* 2d ed., p. 286. New York: Harper & Row, Publishers, Incorporated, 1960. Italics in the original.

[6] Super and Crites, *op. cit.,* p. 6.

expected to measure, its validity cannot be assumed from its title. Naming a test of mechanical vocabulary a test of mechanical aptitude does not make it one. After the testing objective is determined, validity of the test is the first thing to be considered in selecting a test. Without sufficient validity the test is worthless.

There are two methods of judging the validity of a test. One is subjective—the use of logic or opinion. The other is objective—the use of quantitative or statistical procedures. To examine the contents of a standardized algebra test and to appraise the degree to which it is a true measure of the objectives of an algebra course is to use the subjective method. To select some variable as the criterion of that which is to be measured and then to compute the coefficient of correlation to discover the degree of relationship between the test scores and the criterion data is to use the statistical or quantitative method. For example, the criterion selected for validating a scholastic aptitude test for college freshmen might be the average grades made by the tested students during their freshman year in college.

None of the available criteria is wholly satisfactory because none is sufficiently relevant or reliable. Research studies, for example, repeatedly show school marks to be of low reliability and so not as good a criterion as is desired against which to validate tests of scholastic aptitude.

Validity is not an absolute quality. A test may be useful in making one type of decision but not very useful in making another. Consequently, information may be needed on more than one type of validity—on content, construct, concurrent, and/or predictive validity.[7]

A test has content validity to the extent that it covers a representative sample of the behavior to be measured. This type of validity is especially important in achievement tests, whereas in personality and aptitude tests it may be relatively unimportant. As Anastasi [8] says, "the content of the aptitude and personality tests can do little more than reveal the hypotheses that led the test constructor to choose a certain type of content for measuring a specific trait. Such hypotheses need to be empirically confirmed to establish the validity of the test."

Construct validation involves experimentally confirming or testing the hypotheses that led to selection of a certain type of content for measuring or assessing a particular trait. The test maker may hypothesize, for example, that his test measures a trait that increases with training. If the subjects in his experimental study do better on a retest after a period of training than on the test administered before training, the test apparently

    [7] American Psychological Association, "Technical Recommendations for Psychological Tests and Diagnostic Techniques," Supplement to *Psychological Bulletin*, 1954, 2(2):1–38.
    [8] Anne Anastasi, *Psychological Testing*, 2d ed., p. 137. New York: The Macmillan Company, 1961.

has construct validity. Should the test maker also hypothesize that test performance improves with increase in age, and the older subjects perform better on the test than the younger subjects, the hypothesis seems confirmed.

Concurrent validity indicates how well the test scores correspond to other indicators of the trait that the test is designed to measure. The criterion indices are obtained at about the same time that the test scores are. The scores made by secretarial students on a typing test, for example, may be correlated with their grade point averages in typing obtained at the time of testing.

The future rather than the present is the time reference for predictive validity. This type of validity shows the relation between the test scores and criterion data obtained at some later time. Predictive validity is particularly important in tests used for selection purposes, such as college admission. The scores earned by college students on a preadmission test may be correlated with the grade point averages attained by these students during one or more years at college. As stated above, it may be difficult to find a reliable criterion. Teachers' marks, we know, are not always reliable. Also, selection of a good criterion may be complicated by the fact that the one selected may have good validity as an immediate criterion but not as an ultimate one. Super [9] illustrates as follows:

> If grades in medical school, for example, are used as an index of success, some men with good academic ability but poor social adjustment will be rated as more successful than certain other students with somewhat less academic ability but superior social adjustment, whereas if an ultimate criterion of success in the practice of medicine can be utilized, the latter may prove to be more successful than the former.

Criteria such as earnings, output, grades, and ratings provide external evidence of validity. Some test manuals report only internal evidence of validity, which means that the test has been validated through item analysis, instead of through comparison with some external standard. The evidence may indicate, for example, that each test item or subtest has a high correlation with the total score. If the total score, however, is of low validity, a high correlation of the subordinate parts with it may mean only that they are also of low validity. Such evidence of consistency is not an acceptable substitute for external evidence—the only type considered by most authorities as providing an adequate basis for judging the validity of a test.

The relation between the test scores and the criterion data is expressed in the form of a correlation coefficient. If there is perfect agreement with the criterion, the coefficient is 1.00. If there is no consistent relationship, it is .00. Some idea of the meaning of correlation coefficients can be gained from the following table:

[9] Super and Crites, *op. cit.*, p. 34.

Assuming large enough numbers and low enough probable errors, correlation coefficients are generally defined in the following terms:

.80 and up: very high correlation
.50 to .80: substantial correlation
.30 to .50: some correlation
.20 to .30: slight correlation
.00 to .20: practically no correlation

Because of the low reliability of the criteria commonly found usable, the validity coefficient is not likely to be above .70. The minimum acceptable validity coefficient is generally set at .45 for a test to be used in guidance. A test with a validity coefficient of less than .45 has little practical value when used alone; but, when it is combined with other data, the validity of the combination may be higher with it than without it. Skill in the use of combined predictors is achieved through advanced training and experience in testing.

Validity coefficients as high as .90 are reported by some test makers who validate their tests by measuring the power of the test to differentiate between groups known to be different. To some extent such a test may be valid, but not to the extent indicated by the high validity coefficient. Furthermore, the high correlation coefficient does not establish the test as useful for some practical purpose. For example, a personality test for which a very high validity coefficient is reported may have some power for differentiating well-adjusted individuals from seriously maladjusted ones. But, as Darley [10] once said, the test "simply separates the two extreme groups in the same way that their fellow men have already separated them."

Reliability. Reliability shows the extent to which a test measures something consistently. That something may not be, however, that which the test is supposed to measure. High reliability may not indicate that a test is good, but low reliability does indicate that it is poor.

Because it is easier to determine the reliability than it is to determine the validity of a test, some manuals provide much more information on the reliability of the tests than on their validity. As a result, some test users may conclude that reliability is the most important characteristic of a test and that any test which is highly reliable may be considered a good one. This is not true. Validity is the first quality to be sought in a test, but reliability is a needed auxiliary.

Few authors of recently published tests use unqualified the terms "validity" and "reliability." Validity, as we have noted, is reported in terms of content, construct, concurrent, and/or predictive validity. The quality or kind of reliability is shown through the types of reliability coefficients reported. If reliability was established by administering the same

[10] John G. Darley, *Testing and Counseling in the High School Guidance Program,* p. 78. Chicago: Science Research Associates, Inc., 1943.

form of the test on two occasions, a coefficient of stability is reported. If reliability was established by administering parallel forms of the test in close succession, a coefficient of equivalence is reported. If administration of the second form was delayed, a coefficient of stability and equivalence was obtained. Coefficients of equivalence may also be obtained through use of certain statistical formulas developed by Kuder and Richardson and through the split-half and odd-even methods—administering a single test and scoring it in two parts. Coefficients of equivalence obtained through these methods—Kuder-Richardson, split-half and odd-even—are sometimes described as coefficients of internal consistency. They are not appropriate for speeded tests, that is, for tests that do not have liberal time limits. Information on other types of reliability is needed for such tests.

If a counselor wants to predict behavior over a long period of time, he seeks information on reliability obtained through retesting after a substantial interval—months or years. He needs to remember, however, that the longer the interval between the first administration and the re-test, the lower will be the reliability coefficient. Stability coefficients based on immediate retesting are higher than those based on delayed retesting because of variations produced by such factors as memory, health, interest, fatigue, and the like.

There is no single standard of reliability. There is, however, general agreement that we have enough good tests with reliability coefficients of .85 or higher for use of tests with lower reliability to be unnecessary in student personnel work. For use in counseling individual students, tests with reliability of .90 or more are needed.

The reliability standard for tests to be used with groups ordinarily need not be so high as for tests to be used with individuals, but at times group tests also need to have reliability coefficients of .90 or up. The more variable the group, the higher should be the coefficient. For example, the reliability coefficient of a test for use with students at more than one grade level should be higher (.90 or above) than that of a test for use with students at the same grade level (.85 or above).

Usability. A test must look valid to the person taking it. One of the early art appreciation tests, for example, is no longer very useful because it pictures clothes, household utensils, cars, and the like from the 1920s rather than from contemporary life. The items are outdated, and so the test does not look right to many students. Because it no longer has what is called "face validity," it is no longer usable.

A test must be usable in terms of practical considerations as well as validity and reliability. Hence, selection must be determined in part by the extent to which it can be used without undue expenditure of time, effort, and money. Practical considerations are especially important when funds are limited and tests are to be administered and scored by teachers. Tests that involve few materials, require simple directions to students and little supervision, are easy to mark and score, provide suitable inter-pretive aids, and have equivalent forms are the kind generally preferred.

Some tests are broken into many subtests, each with its own set of directions and time interval. The directions may be complex; and the intervals may vary, some being as short as one minute or less. When teachers are to administer the tests, both the giving of directions and the timing should be relatively simple. And the test manual should not only give the information needed but also give it in language that is sufficiently nontechnical to be easily understood by teachers, as well as psychologists.

DEVELOPMENT OF THE TEST PROGRAM

A Cooperative Project. The standardized test program should be planned in keeping with the needs and objectives of the particular school so that it may be integrated with the total school program and serve particular as well as general objectives. Because teachers, as well as counselors, should use the findings, all faculty members need to have an opportunity to share in defining the objectives and in deciding the types of tests to be used in seeking achievement of the objectives. Faculty understanding of the goals and faculty participation in planning ordinarily increase both the amount and the quality of faculty participation in carrying out the program. Hence, development of the program needs to be a cooperative undertaking rather than an administrative project.

The formulation of policy and the making of decisions with re-gard to such specifics as administering and scoring procedures should be made the responsibility of a group rather than of an individual—prin-cipal, guidance coordinator, head counselor, or the like. In a small school the group may well include all teachers. In a large school it may have to be limited to a portion of the faculty, but the committee should be repre-sentative of the total group. Obviously some committee members (de-sirably all) should have training in testing. At least one member should have the advanced training needed to provide leadership both in plan-ning the program and in providing inservice education in testing.

In all important matters the committee should seek faculty ap-proval before taking final action. Recommendations submitted to the faculty may be more readily accepted and supported than decisions handed down from above. Approval and cooperative support are wanted, if not actually needed, from all faculty members.

Scope. The kind of testing that can be done is limited not only by the funds available but also by the qualifications of the personnel. If the teachers are relatively inexperienced and untrained in testing, it is well to begin with a simple program of one or two types of tests. As the teach-ers gain understanding and skill, the program can be expanded. The quality of the program does not depend, however, upon the number of tests or of types of tests used.

The various recommendations offered in the literature regarding size or scope of the high school testing program are very similar. In general, it is recommended that the program include one or more scholastic aptitude tests (one at entry and one in late junior or early senior year), an achievement test battery, and a vocational interest inventory. Reading tests can be added when there is someone qualified to interpret the findings and to provide or direct remedial reading instruction. The inclusion of personality tests is not often recommended. The use of measures of special aptitudes, such as psychometer and artistic, is recommended only with special cases and only when counselors' education, time, and testing funds make use practical and appropriate.

The committee should carefully select the tests that it recommends to the faculty for inclusion in the program. Before making a recommendation, it should examine specimen sets and manuals of all tests being seriously considered, study other obtainable data, and consult available experts. For its own convenience, as well as for the information of others, the committee should summarize its findings in the form of evaluation reports on the tests studied. Suggestions for such analyses or evaluation reports are given by Cronbach,[11] Thorndike and Hagen,[12] and some others.

Sources of Information. The most easily accessible sources of information are probably current catalogs of the leading test publishers and distributing agencies. (These are listed at the end of this chapter.) Some other important resources are books on testing, test reviews in such professional journals as the *Journal of Counseling Psychology,* the *Journal of Consulting Psychology,* and *Educational and Psychological Measurement,* and such books as the *Mental Measurements Yearbooks* and the *Annual Review of Psychology.*

The several *Mental Measurements Yearbooks*[13] contain critical reviews of nearly all the tests available at the time of the Yearbook's publication. Reviews on each test are prepared by two or more specialists who do not always agree regarding the merits of a test. The potential test user will have to make his own judgments regarding the strengths and the weaknesses of a particular test for his purposes. The disagreement of the reviewers may create confusion and thereby make evaluation of a test difficult. At the same time, however, it calls attention to the fact that bias

---

[11] Cronbach, *op. cit.,* pp. 150–151.

[12] R. L. Thorndike and Elizabeth Hagen, *Measurement and Evaluation in Psychology and Education,* 2d ed., pp. 201–202. New York: John Wiley & Sons, Inc., 1961.

[13] The most recent volume: Oscar K. Buros (ed.), *The Fifth Mental Measurements Yearbook.* Highland Park, N.J.: The Gryphon Press, 1959.

can cause a reviewer to overlook or minimize some types of test defects and to belabor others.

Scheduling. Tests should be given at regular intervals rather than in some incidental manner according to the convenience of teachers or the desire of some administrative officer. Giving tests irregularly contributes no more to the making of growth studies of individuals than does changing tests frequently and without good reasons. The tests should be given according to some systematically recurring schedule, with particular tests scheduled in keeping with the testing purposes and student needs. If reading tests are given late in the spring rather than in the fall, some students may not receive remedial help sufficiently early in the year for them to feel that it is very helpful. Tests used to help senior high school students plan programs of study leading to graduation should be administered early during the tenth grade rather than late in the year. Tests used in helping seniors who are planning to go to college to decide on a type of college or a particular college are perhaps best given early in the senior year.

If a test is very long and is to be given in more than one session, the manual recommendations regarding number and length of sessions should be followed. Also, testing should be scheduled sufficiently far in advance to avoid as much as possible interfering with regular school activities. It should not be scheduled either the last day before or the first day after a vacation. Nor should tests be given immediately after a period of strenuous physical activity or at a time when testing is likely to be interrupted by announcements, fire drill, visitors, or the like.

Advanced Preparation. Desirably counselors are the ones to give tests to their counselees so that they may observe the students' reactions and use the opportunity for any precounseling orientation to interpretation and use of the findings. This is not always practical, however, in the public schools. Teachers may have to do most of the routine testing. Teachers selected for this function should be ones who accept the assignment willingly, realize the importance of following manual instructions carefully, and are interested in developing skill in testing. They should also be persons who find it easy to establish rapport with students. In group testing, as in individual testing, rapport is important. As Rothney [14] points out, it should approach as far as possible the rapport of the one-to-one counseling situation.

Testers need to prepare carefully in advance. They need not only to study the directions in the manual but also to practice giving the directions in a sufficiently loud voice, slowly and clearly, with the proper stress on key words and phrases. By pairing or forming teams, counselors and

[14] John W. M. Rothney et al., *Measurement for Guidance*, p. 101 New York: Harper & Row, Publishers, Incorporated, 1959.

teachers can help one another gain ease and develop skill through practice in taking and administering tests.

Proctors should be used when large groups are tested. They too need advanced instruction and practice. Their functions include not only distributing and collecting materials but also observing the group to give permissible help and to note and report unusual behavior. A proctor may need, for example, to point out to a student that he is placing his marks in the wrong column on the answer sheet. He may need to hand a pencil to another student. When he collects the papers, he may attach to one answer sheet a report stating that the student apparently marked the sheet without ever looking at the test booklet. The note attached to another student's answer sheet may report that this student seemed unduly anxious, that he constantly looked at his watch, that he gave a startled jump each time the tester said "Stop," even though the order was never given loudly or explosively.

If a counselor administers a test to a class group, he may wish to ask the class teacher to be the proctor. During testing he will refrain from conversing with the teacher and will discourage the teacher's writing on the board or doing anything else that may distract the students.

Advance preparation includes assembling and checking materials before the day of testing. In Super's [15] words:

> This involves preparing a list of items needed, from pencils to test blanks, and of the quantity to be provided; sorting the materials according to type and sequence in which they are to be used; and counting them out according to the number of subjects to be seated in each row and the number of rows in the room. This last step saves a great deal of time and confusion in handing out materials, and prevents the pocketing of excess copies of confidential test booklets.

Advance Orientation and Motivational Procedures. The goal is not to stimulate students to try to make the highest possible score. Stressing high scores may foster cheating and undesirable coaching. Also, it may create a crisis situation for some students, making them so anxious that they cannot do as well as they do ordinarily. The emphasis should be not upon competition but upon helping students want to use the opportunity afforded them through testing for gaining information that will be useful to both them and their counselors. The motivation that is most helpful to valid testing is, as Cronbach [16] emphasizes, "a desire on the part of the subject that the score be valid."

There should be group orientation to the testing. One or several days before the students take the tests, they should be told why the tests are being given and permitted to explore the situation through their ques-

[15] Super and Crites, *op. cit.*, p. 58.
[16] Cronbach, *op. cit.*, p. 56.

tions. If a student understands the purpose of testing and the importance to him personally of a valid score, he is likely to be motivated to give valid, reliable test responses. In an experimental study reported by Rothney,[17] oral explanations were supplemented by the following mimeographed statement distributed to the students as they entered the testing room.

> The tests and interviews which you are going to take, will help us to help you to find out the things that you can do best. Because of the competition which exists in the world of work today, it is important for you to find what your abilities are in order to develop them to your best possible advantage. As a result of all these tests and interviews we hope to be able to advise you about various kinds of work and study. It is also our purpose to aid you in learning more about your own strong points and to help you to make the best of your opportunities.

> We hope that you will do your best on the tests which are given to you. Remember that they have nothing to do with your school marks. You may now ask any questions about the work.

Because standardized tests generally include items that many students cannot answer correctly, students normally find taking such tests a frustrating experience. To help make frustration mild or tolerable rather than disintegrating, it is well to explain to the students that no one is expected to get every item right and that they can expect to do better on some tests than on others.

When students are to take machine-scorable tests for the first time, they should have advance practice in manipulating the answer sheets and in the proper marking of answers.

Administering Tests. In view of the extensive use that they make of test data in counseling, counselors have a professional obligation to do all that they can to have tests administered under proper conditions. The limitations of the findings are increased when students are tested in large numbers in such a place as auditorium, cafeteria, or cafetorium where students cannot write conveniently and the lighting and the ventilation may be poor. Some school people say that it is better to give tests in such places than in classrooms because in the large group situation the conditions are "standardized" in that they are the same for all. They overlook the fact that, while the conditions may be uniform for all students involved, they are not standard and may be uniformly poor rather than uniformly good.

Desirably, tests should be administered to relatively small groups in quiet, well-lighted, well-ventilated rooms where each student can be comfortably seated at a desk or table, have adequate writing space, and be sufficiently far from his neighbors for cheating not to be easy. Libraries

[17] John W. M. Rothney et al., *Guidance Practices and Results,* p. 73. New York: Harper & Row, Publishers, Incorporated. 1958.

and classrooms are ordinarily better testing rooms than are cafeterias or auditoriums.

Scoring. When very many tests are to be scored, the work should be done by machine if this is at all possible, because machine scoring usually means reduced cost and increased accuracy. Tests that are to be scored by hand are more likely to be scored accurately when the scoring directions are simple and clear, the scoring process is objective, the answer keys are complete, the scorers are *taught,* not just told, how to do their work, and their work is checked for accuracy. Even under these conditions there will very likely be some errors in scoring.

The first papers scored by a beginner should be checked at once to discover constant errors, that is, errors made continuously because of some misunderstanding of the scoring procedures. All other papers in the set should be checked also to detect variable errors. If it is not practical to have all papers checked by a second person, at least every fifth or sixth paper should be rescored. If many errors are found in any person's scoring, then, of course, all papers scored by that person should be checked by someone else. In all cases the totals for each section and for the whole test should be checked by another person.

If a school or school system does not have the clerical staff and other facilities needed, scoring is usually done by teachers. The practice is obviously not a good one in terms of economy if the teachers are paid salaries higher than those of clerks. Even if they are not, they may not be so efficient in this type of work as clerks, who may be able to do the job better and in less time. Some administrators justify the practice of using teachers as scoring clerks on the ground that teachers, by scoring the tests, gain an understanding of the difficulties, strengths, and weaknesses of individual students. These administrators, says Traxler,[18] confuse diagnosis and scoring. "It is reasonable to believe that both the diagnosis and the scoring will suffer if the teacher's attention is thus divided between two unrelated activities."

The practice of using students as test scorers is of doubtful worth and in some respects undesirable. Under such conditions the chances for errors in scoring are more likely increased than decreased. As Goldman [19] says, a school that cannot afford a near-foolproof scoring system cannot afford tests. When the test users are unable to assume a high degree of scoring accuracy, the tests become worthless if not actually dangerous.

Recording and Reporting Test Data. The test data should be recorded and thereby made available to teachers and counselors as soon as possible

---

[18] Arthur E. Traxler, *Techniques of Guidance,* rev. ed., p. 158. New York: Harper & Row, Publishers, Incorporated, 1957.
[19] Leo Goldman, *Using Tests in Counseling,* p. 308. New York: Appleton-Century-Crofts, Inc., 1961.

after the scoring is completed. On the official cumulative personnel records of the students and on the records sent to the counselors certain informa- tion items should always be given: (1) date test was given, (2) test title and form, (3) norms used, (4) raw scores, and (5) derived scores. If the test yields part scores and these are of sufficient reliability and practical impor- tance for guidance and counseling purposes, the raw scores and derived scores should be recorded for the subtests also.

While counselors should always find the official records readily available to them, most counselors wish to maintain files on their coun- selees. Therefore, they should receive test data as soon as possible after any tests have been administered to their counselees. The record sheets that the publishers ordinarily supply in packages of tests are useful for report- ing test results to both the counselors and the class teachers concerned. If these record sheets do not provide for inclusion of all items of information needed, mimeographed forms can be developed that do.

The test data should be reported to the students not too long after they are made available to teachers and counselors. Because the func- tions of reporting and interpreting test data are considered at some length two chapters later, no further attention is given to the subject here. Ade- quate provision for fulfillment of these two functions is an important part of the school's testing program. Unfortunately, in some schools it is a badly neglected part, and in some it is practically omitted.

NORMS

The numerical description of a student's test performance is termed a "raw score." By itself it is meaningless. The same raw score obtained by the same student on different tests or by different students on the same test can have very different meanings. A boy's score of 50 on an English test, for example, may be high, whereas his score of 50 on an algebra test may be very low. And the score of 50 on a science test may be above average for a ninth grader but definitely below average for a college freshman.

To have meaning, raw scores must be translated into derived scores or norms—age equivalents, IQ's, grade equivalents, percentile ranks, and standard scores. Test manuals usually contain norm tables. In selecting tests, counselors need to consider both the types of norms provided and the data given in the manual regarding them. Normative data are needed for groups comparable to the counselee's class group and the groups that he or she may be considering entering, such as college freshmen or first- year students in a nurses' training school. Hence, it is important that the manual supply information about the normative sample—size, extent to which it is representative of the population of which it is a part, age, sex, and educational or occupational status.

Some manuals report "national" norms. This description is not accurate. Such norms are national in a geographical sense only. They may represent different parts of the country but not different educational levels in all parts of the nation. No published test has been standardized on a sample representative of all socioeconomic groups at different educational levels in all parts of the nation.

It is important that the standardization sample be sufficiently representative of the group to be tested. A test standardized, for example, on students in a few large urban schools in one region may not be appropriate for use in a small rural school in a different region. Similarly, norms for a scholastic aptitude test established on freshmen in different types of colleges in various parts of the country are of limited value to a highly select college like Smith or Harvard.

Norms are needed that were established on a group comparable to the one to be tested. Also, norms should be reported for subgroups classified according to sex as well as educational level when such subgroups tend to earn significantly different average scores. The median scores in mechanical reasoning, for example, are generally higher for boys than for girls. The reverse is usually true for tests of clerical aptitude.

Norms show how a counselee's score compares to those of the normative group—whether high, low, average, above average, or below average. Norms are not, however, to be confused with standards. They show where individual students are, not where they should be. For instance, a student of high potential who has had better than average opportunity to learn may obtain a score that is average but no better. His test performance cannot be viewed as being up to standard. He shows only average performance, whereas he can be expected to do better than average.

Likewise, it is incorrect to assume that all students at a particular grade level should attain a score equivalent to the norm or mean for that grade. Fifty per cent of the standardization group obtained scores that fell below the mean. If the particular class group is weak in the abilities tested, more than 50 per cent of its scores may be expected to fall below the norm. On the other hand, if it is superior in the area covered by the test, the reverse can be expected.

Comparison of Norm Systems. The types of norms used most frequently are letter grades, age scores, grade equivalents, percentile ranks, and standard scores. While letter grades are employed in one widely used, highly respected psychological instrument—the Strong Vocational Interest Blanks, they are not used in many standardized tests.

Some intelligence tests use norms expressed in terms of mental ages and of intelligence quotients that are obtained by dividing the mental age by the chronological age and multiplying by 100. The use of MA's and ratio IQ's is not generally considered desirable beyond the elementary grades because the standard definition of mental age does not hold true at chronological ages beyond age thirteen or fourteen. Percentile scores and standard scores in the form of deviation IQ's are being increasingly used in place of ratio IQ's. The 1960 revision of the Stanford-Binet, for example, replaces ratio IQ's with deviation IQ's.

Grade placement scores are analogous to mental age scores. A mental age of 9–0, for example, represents the score made by the average nine-year-old. Similarly, a grade equivalent of 4.0 represents the score of the average beginning fourth grader. Grade scores are no more satisfactory for describing or reporting educational development than mental ages are for reporting mental development. And they are probably not so useful as percentile scores for helping teachers perceive the wide range of individual differences among members of a particular class group.

Moreover, some teachers at times misinterpret grade equivalents because of overlapping in the score distributions for students in consecutive grades. As Flanagan [20] points out, a fourth grader's score of 5.6 should not be interpreted as meaning that he has already mastered the contents of the fourth-grade and of the first half of the fifth-grade programs. It more likely means that he learned unusually well the materials covered in the first three grades.

Flanagan points out some other limitations of this type of norms: (1) Grade equivalents do not provide for growth during the summer vacation months, and age equivalents are based on the assumption that growth during the summer months is at approximately the same rate as during the school months. Both assumptions—no growth or same rate of growth—are extreme. The truth probably lies somewhere between them. (2) It is difficult to secure grade and age equivalents over a sufficiently wide range to cover the extremely high and low test scores. Derived scores to describe the very high and very low performances must be arrived at on the basis of arbitrary designations (perhaps based on observations) rather than through the usual procedures employed in setting up such equivalents. Hence, interpretation of extreme age scores or grade scores is difficult because they represent hypothetical medians, instead of the average scores that would be obtained if the test were administered to students at the corresponding age or grade levels. (3) The derived scores at the upper end of the range are for grades and ages at which the school subjects covered by the test are not usually taught, and so they are without direct meaning, as indicated above. (4) Grade and age equivalents rest on the assumption that from grade to grade instructional emphasis is continuous and constant in the various subject fields, which is rarely the case. Certain subjects, such as social studies, science, and literature, are taught formally in some grades but not in others.

Percentile scores or ranks and standard scores are the norms used

---

[20] John C. Flanagan, "Units, Scores and Norms," in E. F. Lindquist (ed.), *Educational Measurement*, pp. 695–763. Washington, D.C.: American Council on Education, 1951.

most frequently at the high school and college levels. Percentile scores are probably the most easily understood method of showing relative standing in all types of groups. They show relative standing along a scale of 100 intervals by indicating the per cent of cases that lie at and below the successive points on the scale. The student, for example, who has a percentile rank of 64 on a reading test performed as well as or better than 64 out of each 100 students in the standardization sample.

Percentile norms have one serious defect: The differences between the percentiles are not the same throughout the scale. They are smallest at the middle, tend to cluster about the midpoint, spread out toward the ends, and are largest at the two extremes. This inequality of differences is due to the facts that differences between individuals are most frequently narrow rather than wide and that with regard to almost any measurable trait or ability most individuals differ very little from the average of the general population. The percentile scores magnify small differences in the scores near the mean and minimize or reduce large differences in scores near the extremes. Consequently, a difference of only 2 points in the raw scores of two "average" persons may place one at the 54th percentile and the other at the 53d, whereas a difference as great as 10 points may place two other persons only 3 percentiles apart because both differ considerably from the average. The raw score of one may give him a percentile rank of 95; and that of the other, a percentile rank of 98.

Because of the inequality of percentile differences it is not correct to add or average percentile ranks. This fact may cause some teachers to question the accuracy of percentile scores for gross raw scores of tests that yield part scores. Since percentile scores cannot properly be averaged, the manual provides a table of norms for the gross scores along with the tables for the part scores.

Because standard scores are more difficult to interpret to persons with little knowledge of statistics, they are used less frequently than percentile scores even though they have many advantages. They can be added and averaged because, unlike percentile scores, they do not have the disadvantage of distorted values or inequality of interval differences. They are based on deviations from the mean and are directly comparable throughout the scale. Also, they have the advantage of permitting comparison among different kinds of measurements, such as school marks, grades on teacher-made examinations, and class rank, as well as scores on standardized tests. All such measurements can be uniformly expressed in terms of standard deviations from the mean.

Not all standard scores are expressed by the same method. Although they use different values for the mean and the standard deviation, they are logically the same. The most widely used system is that of T scores, which fixes the mean at 50 and the standard deviation value at 10. Figure 6 shows the commonly used standard score systems, the percentile equivalents, and their relation to the normal distribution.

Local Norms. The collection of local norms is an important part of the testing program, because interpretation of a student's performance in terms of local norms is sometimes more important than in terms of "national" norms. For example, a student who is earning only average marks in mathematics but is conscientiously doing his work may be confused by being told that his mathematics score on the Sequential Tests of Educational Progress is high unless he is also told that on the basis of the local norms his score is only average.

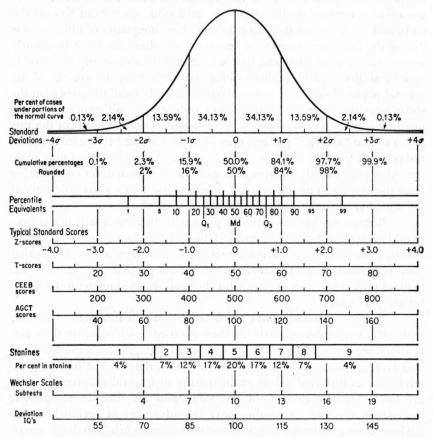

FIGURE 6   *Normal curve, percentiles, and standard scores.* (Harold G. Seashore, *Methods of Expressing Test Scores,* Test Service Bulletin no. 48. New York: The Psychological Corporation, 1955. Reproduced by permission of the publisher.)

Local norms have increased value when schools within the same system or schools with similar educational objectives and geographic location combine efforts in developing local norms. Such norms permit comparison of a student's scores with those of other groups within the community. They are useful, for example, in counseling junior high school students regarding choice of senior high school and high school curriculum. It is more helpful to tell a girl that she did as well on the scholastic aptitude test as the average sophomore in the foods program at Trade-Technical High School than to tell her that, according to the publisher's norms, she obtained a below-average score. A senior boy may find it useful to know that his score is above average when compared with the scores of last year's seniors now attending State College but only about average when compared with the scores earned by the ones admitted to the State Institute of Technology.

It is difficult to know how much significance should be attached to differences in scores obtained from independently developed tests of similar type because the norm groups and norms for the two tests are not the same. Local norms facilitate comparison when the norms for the two tests are collected on the same group. This does not mean, however, that a student can be expected to obtain the same derived score on both tests. Differences in the scores can be expected because of differences in the tests—differences in content, length, response categories, error of measurement, and the like. The elimination of one source of variance through the use of equivalent norms is, however, an important gain made possible by the use of local norms.

SOME ETHICAL RESPONSIBILITIES

In 1961 the American Personnel and Guidance Association published a statement dealing with ethical issues in counseling.[21] It is basically similar to the code of ethics of the American Psychological Association that was published in 1952 and later revised.[22] In the section on testing, the APGA code stresses that use of different tests requires different levels of competence and that it is the ethical responsibility of a counselor "to recognize the limits of his competence and to perform only those functions which fall within his preparation and competence."

Some other obligations stipulated in the APGA statement are (1) the "responsibility to provide adequate orientation or information to the examinee(s) so that the results of testing may be placed in proper perspective with other relevant factors"; (2) the obligation in statements to the public "to give accurate information and to avoid any false claims and misconceptions"; (3) the responsibility in selecting tests to consider both general and specific validity, reliability, and appropriateness of tests; (4) the responsibility to administer tests "under the same conditions which were established in their standardization"; and (5) the obligation not to endanger test security through acts that tend to invalidate test results,

[21] American Personnel and Guidance Association, "Ethical Standards," *Personnel and Guidance Journal*, 1961, 40:206–209.

[22] American Psychological Association, "Standards of Ethical Behavior for Psychologists," *American Psychologist*, 1959, 14:278–282.

such as giving information regarding test contents, coaching, or reproducing test materials.

The APA Committee on Ethical Standards has criticized the methods used by some representatives of test publishers in selling tests to schools. Some salesmen with little or no education in testing have assumed the roles of test specialists in advising school people who are also untrained in testing and, hence, not able to evaluate properly the advice received. In one of the Committee's reports the following illustration [23] of such objectionable practices is given: A school superintendent who knew little about testing and guidance asked a test salesman to help him plan a guidance program for his school. Thereupon the salesman (also little informed about guidance) drew up "a complete program" for the school by checking certain items in the catalog of the company that he represented. To help correct such situations, the committee has prepared a set of standards which contains, among others, the following principles:

> Tests and diagnostic aids should be released only to persons who can demonstrate that they have the knowledge and skill necessary for their effective use and interpretation. . . .
>
> Persons purchasing tests, assuming responsibility for testing programs, or distributing tests, should be governed by recognition of the fact that being qualified in one specialty does not necessarily result in being qualified in another specialty. . . . Being a psychiatrist, social worker, teacher, or school administrator, does not ipso facto make one a qualified user of projective techniques, intelligence tests, standardized achievement tests or other tests or aids often used by members of these professions. . . .
>
> The applicability of a test should be clearly defined in the manual in terms of the population on which it has been standardized. Limitations in its use should be clearly stated. Manuals should be considered factual expositions of what is known about a test and of its appropriate use, rather than as selling devices. Test names should reflect the professional nature of the test rather than popular appeal. . . .
>
> Psychological tests should be ordered for use or advertised on the basis of facts concerning the test's standardization and validation, as presented in the test manuals and in the professional literature, rather than on the basis of the test's title, author, publisher, or other evidences of authority. . . .
>
> Representatives and publishers of psychological tests who are not themselves highly trained in psychological or educational measurement should serve only as distributors of materials and takers of orders, not as consultants on testing problems. . . .
>
> Highly qualified psychologists may properly accept employment with test distributors to assist either publishers or clients with testing problems and programs. These consultants should by training, inclination, and

---

[23] APA Committee on Ethical Standards for Psychology, "Ethical Standards for the Distribution of Psychological Tests and Diagnostic Aids," *American Psychologist*, 1950, 5:620–626.

contact, work as measurement specialists. Their affiliation and sales function should be kept perfectly clear, and they should recognize and respond to the needs of their clients.

Professionally minded counselors share responsibility for helping to gain acceptance and support of these ethical controls. Acceptance and support of the APA and APGA ethical standards can do much to reduce some of the dissatisfaction currently being expressed in the press and on radio and television programs dealing with the school testing programs.[24]

SUMMARY

Tests are among the counselor's most useful aids in studying a student's abilities, interests, and adjustments and in helping him to understand himself. They are useful in the guidance and counseling of all students, not of the gifted and the retarded alone.

Tests yield information economically and in easily used forms. In general, the information is more accurate than that obtained through students' self-reports and teachers' observations. Test data are especially useful when the purposes are identification or classification, placement of students, and evaluation of progress in the regular curriculum or a special program.

Tests should be selected in keeping with specific purposes and should not be expected to serve purposes for which they were not designed. Selection should be preceded by careful study of the tests concerned through examination of specimen sets, manuals, and reviews given in such sources as the *Mental Measurement Yearbooks,* and through consultation with persons qualified to evaluate the tests being considered. Specific information should be sought on validity and reliability, administration and scoring procedures, norms available and conditions under which they were collected, and such practical matters as cost, face validity, quality of paper and print, and the like.

Because of their important relations with students and their important roles in using the test results, teachers and counselors should have as active a part as possible in the study and selection of tests and in the formulation of policy with regard to testing and the use of test data. Students should be adequately informed regarding the tests and sufficiently well oriented to the testing situation for them to be motivated to give valid responses. For the results to be of value, the tests must be properly administered under standard conditions and accurately scored and recorded.

To have meaning, raw scores must be translated into norms. The types of norms commonly used include IQ's, grade placement scores, per-

[24] One example: "A Rash of Testing in Schools: Is It Being Overdone?" *U.S. News & World Report,* June 15, 1959, pp. 44–46.

centile ranks, and standard scores. Standard scores are theoretically the preferred type, but their use in the secondary schools is not always practical because not all faculty members have the statistical knowledge needed for proper understanding and use. Hence, percentile scores are used more often than standard scores. Grade placement scores and ratio IQ's have a number of disadvantages. They are being increasingly replaced by percentile scores, at least in the secondary schools.

Norms are needed that were established on a group comparable to the one to be tested or to the group that the student is planning to join. For proper interpretation of the test data, local norms are often needed in addition to the publishers' norms.

Two professional organizations, the American Personnel and Guidance Association and the American Psychological Association, have published statements regarding the ethical responsibilities of counselors in the field of testing. Careful observance of the principles outlined in these statements can do much to help strengthen the usefulness of testing as a counseling technique.

MAJOR TEST PUBLISHERS

Bureau of Publications, Teachers College, Columbia University, New York 27, New York.

California Test Bureau, Del Monte Research Park, Monterey, California.

Consulting Psychologists Press, Inc., 577 College Avenue, Palo Alto, California.

Educational Test Bureau, 720 Washington Avenue, S.E., Minneapolis 14, Minnesota.

Educational Testing Service, 20 Nassau Street, Princeton, New Jersey, and 1947 Central Street, Berkeley, California.

Harcourt, Brace & World, Inc., 750 Third Avenue, New York 17, New York.

Houghton Mifflin Company, 1120 Avenue of The Americas, New York 36, New York.

Institute for Personality and Ability Testing, 1602 Coronado Drive, Champaign, Illinois.

The Psychological Corporation, 304 East 45th Street, New York 17, New York.

Science Research Associates, Inc., 259 East Erie Street, Chicago 11, Illinois.

Sheridan Supply Company, P. O. Box 837, Beverly Hills, California.

C. H. Stoelting Company, 424 North Homan Avenue, Chicago 24, Illinois.

Western Psychological Services, 12035 Wilshire Boulevard, Los Angeles 25, California.

REFERENCES

American Personnel and Guidance Association: "Ethical Standards," *Personnel and Guidance Journal,* 1961, 40:206–209.

American Psychological Association: "Technical Recommendations for Psychological Tests and Diagnostic Techniques," Supplement to *Psychological Bulletin,* 1954, 2(2):1–38.

————: "Standards of Ethical Behavior for Psychologists," *American Psychologist,* 1959, 14:278–282.

Anastasi, Anne: *Psychological Testing,* 2d ed., part I. New York: The Macmillan Company, 1961.

————: "Psychological Tests: Uses and Abuses," *Teachers College Record,* 1961, 62:389–393.

Bauernfeind, R. H.: "Are Sex Norms Necessary?" *Journal of Counseling Psychology,* 1956, 3:57–63.

Berdie, Ralph F.: "The State-wide Testing Programs," *Personnel and Guidance Journal,* 1954, 32:454–459.

Buros, Oscar K. (ed.): *The Fifth Mental Measurements Yearbook.* Highland Park, N.J.: The Gryphon Press, 1959.

Coleman, William: "Assisting Teachers in Using Test Results," *Personnel and Guidance Journal,* 1957, 36:38–40.

Cronbach, Lee J.: *Essentials of Psychological Testing,* 2d ed., part I. New York: Harper & Row, Publishers, Incorporated, 1960.

———— and Paul E. Meehl: "Construct Validity in Psychological Tests," *Psychological Bulletin,* 1955, 52:281–302.

Davis, Junius A.: "Non-apparent Limitations of Normative Data," *Personnel and Guidance Journal,* 1959, 37:656–659.

Eckerson, Louise O.: "Testing and Counseling: Three Letters," *School Life,* 1960, 43(1):10–13, 27–30.

Flanagan, John C., and John G. Darley: "Project Talent: The Identification and Utilization of Human Talents," *Personnel and Guidance Journal,* 1960, 38:504–505.

Froehlich, Clifford P., and Kenneth B. Hoyt: *Guidance Testing,* chap. 4. Chicago: Science Research Associates, Inc., 1959.

Goldman, Leo: *Using Tests in Counseling,* chaps. 1–6. New York: Appleton-Century-Crofts, Inc., 1961.

Kirk, Barbara A.: "Test Distributors and Our Needs," *Occupations,* 1951, 29:257–259.

Lindquist, E. F. (ed.): *Educational Measurement,* chaps. 1–4, 10, 14–18. Washington, D.C.: American Council on Education, 1951.

McLaughlin, Kenneth F. (ed.): *Understanding Testing: Purposes and Interpretations for Pupil Development.* Washington, D.C.: Government Printing Office, 1960.

Rothney, John W. M., et al.: *Measurement for Guidance.* New York: Harper & Row, Publishers, Incorporated, 1959.

Seashore, H. G. (ed.): *Methods of Expressing Test Scores,* Test Service Bulletin no. 48. New York: The Psychological Corporation, 1955.

Super, Donald E., and John O. Crites: *Appraising Vocational Fitness by Means of Psychological Tests,* rev. ed., chaps. 1–5. New York: Harper & Row, Publishers, Incorporated, 1962.

Thompson, Anton: "Test Giver's Self-inventory," *California Journal of Educational Research,* 1956, 7:67–71.

Thorndike, Robert L., and Elizabeth Hagen: *Measurement and Evaluation in*

Psychology and Education, 2d ed., chaps. 6–8. New York: John Wiley & Sons, Inc., 1961.

Traxler, Arthur E.: *Techniques of Guidance,* rev. ed., chaps. 9 and 10. New York: Harper & Row, Publishers, Incorporated, 1957.

Wesman, A. G.: *Better Than Chance,* Test Service Bulletin no. 45. New York: The Psychological Corporation, 1958.

Wickes, T. A., Jr.: "Examiner Influence in a Testing Situation," *Journal of Consulting Psychology,* 1956, 20:23–26.

Wolfe, Dael: "Diversity of Talent," *American Psychologist,* 1960, 15:535–545.

5

Tests of Ability
and Achievement

Certain kinds of tests, such as those of general ability and achievement, should be provided early in the guidance testing program and should be included for use with all students. Some other kinds, such as tests of special aptitudes, can be added later and may never be needed in a particular school.

TESTS OF SCHOLASTIC ABILITY

Tests of general mental ability are increasingly being referred to as tests of scholastic aptitude because they are based mainly on definitions of intelligence in terms of ability to succeed scholastically. Even as measures of scholastic ability they are, in the main, restricted to the measurement of certain aspects of abstract intelligence.

In general, abstract intelligence is the ability to understand ideas and the relationships among them. Since ideas are expressed by symbols, tests of intelligence commonly seek to measure the ability to comprehend and to use symbols. When the symbols used are words, the ability measured is referred to as "verbal ability." When the symbols used are numbers and such symbols as geometrical figures, the ability measured is referred to as "numerical" or "quantitative" ability. Success in school, as the schools are today, is ordinarily closely related to abstract intelligence; so such tests do serve to indicate roughly the educational level that may be attained by the individuals tested.

Intelligence tests are often validated against school marks or some similar index of school success. On the basis of such criteria they frequently show high validity because verbal ability is the greatest contributor to scholastic success as commonly measured in the schools today. Tests achieving this high validity, as Guilford[1] once pointed out, "may be the result of a vicious circle which has overstressed verbal ability in education." For more understanding on this point we need scholastic

[1] J. P. Guilford, in O. K. Buros (ed.), *The Third Mental Measurements Yearbook*, p. 323. New Brunswick, N.J.: Rutgers University Press, 1949.

aptitude tests that are more in line with other real or desired objectives of education—tests that measure insight, foresight, organization of ideas, and creative ability, as well as verbal ability. Such tests might not show as high validity in terms of the present criteria for scholastic proficiency, but their development and use might foster the improvement of education in terms of such criteria.

The Binet Scales. Some tests of general ability are designed for use with individuals only. The two outstanding examples are the Stanford-Binet and the Wechsler scales, one of which is ordinarily used when students are selected for placement in a special education or treatment program. These two tests are also of special importance because many group tests of general ability are validated against one or both of them. For competent use special training is needed. This training is specified for both counselors and school psychologists ín the credential requirements of some states.

A second revision of the Stanford-Binet was published in 1960 which combines in one form the best items of the two 1937 forms. The new L-M form is strengthened through a relocating and rescoring of some items, minor modifications to bring drawings of common articles up to date, and substitution of standard score IQ's for ratio IQ's. Also, standardization has been brought up to date.

The Stanford-Binet contains tests of memory, information, judgment, reasoning, and the ability to make adaptations in problem-solving tasks. These tests are grouped into age levels, ranging from age two to superior adult. They measure different abilities at different age levels. At the lower ages they measure mainly attention, discrimination, and judgment; at the higher levels, reasoning and verbal ability. At all levels, however, they call for skill in the use and the understanding of words and so are primarily measures of verbal ability. This emphasis upon verbal ability is increased in the 1960 revision, which strengthens its usefulness for predicting scholastic achievement in the schools as they are now constituted.

The Wechsler Scales. In 1939 the Wechsler-Bellevue scale was introduced for use with adolescents and adults. It was marked by two important innovations—use of separate verbal and performance IQ's and substitution of standard score IQ's for ratio IQ's. This scale is now replaced by the WISC (Wechsler Intelligence Scale for Children) for ages five to fifteen and the WAIS (Wechsler Adult Intelligence Scale) for persons over age fifteen. They are point scales rather than age scales. The items are grouped into subtests according to types and arranged within each subtest according to difficulty. In the Stanford-Binet test, an age scale, different types of tests are grouped into age levels; and all tests at any level are of approximately equivalent difficulty.

With minor exceptions the subtest patterns of the WISC and the WAIS are the same. The verbal scales include tests of information, comprehension, digit span (repeating numbers forward and backward), arithmetic reasoning, and vocabulary. The digit span test is optional in the WISC because of its low correlation with the overall performance.

The performance scales contain some tests that are taken from or modeled after other well-known performance tests of proved value. According to Cronbach,[2] the Wechsler scales contain the most important performance tests of today. They include digit symbol (code substitution which in the WISC is changed to coding of a simple message); picture completion (telling which part is missing from each picture in a series); block design (reproducing with colored cubes pictured designs that become increasingly complex); picture arrangement (rearranging pictures in their proper sequence); object assembly (assembling given pieces into a proper whole). A maze test is added as an optional test in the WISC.

Different abilities are measured by the verbal and performance scales. If a student's performance IQ is considerably higher than his verbal IQ, it may be because he has a hearing problem or language difficulties, because he has had limited educational opportunities, because his abilities lie along nonverbal lines, or because too much experience with failure in schoolwork has created an emotional resistance to verbal tasks. Such explanations do not, however, always apply. An adequate explanation has not been found for some students who apparently are not handicapped verbally or emotionally but do much better on the performance scale than on the verbal.

Nor is it easy to explain a student's earning a performance score that is much lower than his verbal score. A frequently used interpretation is that of "an emotional block." In some cases lack of interest, carelessness, undue haste or undue caution, and an artificially cultivated vocabulary producing an artificially high verbal score may be more plausible explanations.

Each subtest of the verbal and performance scales yields a raw score, which is translated into a standard score. The subtest standard scores are combined to produce a verbal IQ, a performance IQ, and a total IQ. As already stated, these are deviation or standard score IQ's, not ratio IQ's. Some counselors attach diagnostic significance to the subtest scores. This practice, however, is not warranted because the subtests are too short for their scores to be sufficiently reliable for diagnostic use.

Although the Wechsler and the Binet scales measure approximately the same abilities, their IQ's are not interchangeable. Moreover, they do not measure all ability or age levels equally well. The Wechsler scales, for example, do not measure very high or very low ability dependably; they do not discriminate in the extremes of the ability range as well as the

[2] Lee J. Cronbach, *Essentials of Psychological Testing*, 2d ed., p. 191. New York: Harper & Row, Publishers, Incorporated, 1960.

Binet does. Also, the WISC favors older children, whereas the Binet favors the younger ones. The WAIS is more appropriate than the Binet for adult testing because the Binet lacks sufficient ceiling for most superior adults and does not have the same appeal for adults that it has for children.

The Wechsler scales are easier to administer and to score than the Binet, which may explain why they are preferred by many guidance workers. Both instruments are in one sense standardized clinical interviews. In both the examiner has a chance to observe the subject's working methods and the qualitative aspects of his performance. He may gain some idea regarding the extent to which a student's test performance is affected by personality and emotional habits, such as self-criticalness, carelessness, willingness, excessive caution or haste, etc. Also, some subjects reveal their values and attitudes, as well as their emotional habits, through the test responses.

Single-score Group Tests. Group tests of general ability may be classed according to whether they yield a single score or separate verbal and non-verbal scores. Those that yield only one score or one IQ are sometimes referred to as "the old type of test" because the first intelligence tests (Binet and Binet-type scales) were of this kind.

The best group tests are as reliable as the Binet and Wechsler scales and may be used effectively in testing both individuals and groups. Although the group testing situation is not favorable for all subjects, for some it is better than the individual testing situation. The group situation has, in Super's [3] words, the advantages of "social stimulation, competition, the safety of numbers, the group example, and externally standardized conditions."

In student personnel work, group tests of scholastic aptitude are used chiefly for identifying slow learners and talented students for whom curriculum modifications seem needed, for appraising a student's chances at success in specific courses and curricula, for learning the extent to which a student is applying himself scholastically, and for determining the relative importance of deficiencies in background knowledge, mental ability, and lack of effort as the primary reasons for a student's academic failure. Such conclusions and decisions are not, or should not be, based on the test data alone. Other relevant evidences are also considered.

Some examples of the one-score group tests are briefly described below. All are appropriate for use at different educational levels. Most are not so satisfactory at the upper limits of their range of applicability as they are near the center of the range. A test that covers grades 10 through 13, for example, may discriminate more adequately among high school seniors than among college freshmen.

[3] Donald E. Super and John O. Crites, *Appraising Vocational Fitness by Means of Psychological Tests,* rev. ed., p. 80. New York: Harper & Row, Publishers, Incorporated, 1962.

The Otis tests (Harcourt, Brace & World, Inc.) are among the simplest and easiest and most economical to administer and to score of all tests of general ability. For purposes of predicting educational success they compare very favorably with other more intricate measures. There are two Otis tests in current use—the Quick-Scoring Test of Mental Ability and the Self-Administering Test of Mental Ability. The first is a revision of the second and is generally considered a better test because of certain improvements in its contents and scoring, but its norms are less adequate. Each test has equivalent forms that cover the intermediate grades, high school, and college. Much of the criticism expressed in the reviews is directed more against the insufficient information given on the test in its manual than is directed against the quality of the test itself.

The Kuhlman-Anderson Tests (Personnel Press, Inc.) contain batteries for all school grades, including the kindergarten, and for adults. The tests are arranged in nine booklets with ten tests each. They are relatively less dependent upon reading skill than most other group tests and offer a better balance of verbal, numerical, and spatial material than most other tests in their class. They are, however, much more difficult to administer and to score than the other tests. The timing is different for the various subtests, and at the lower levels some time intervals are as short as ten seconds. Research shows that, in comparison with others, these tests rank high in validity and reliability.

The Henmon-Nelson Test of Mental Ability (Houghton Mifflin Company) has been described by Shaffer [4] as a "scholarly example of the best in test construction, and as a remarkably efficient instrument for its length." It is an attractive test that provides two forms for its three batteries (grades 3 to 6, 6 to 9, 9 to 12). Administration is easy and requires only about thirty minutes. Scoring is by the Clapp-Young self-marking device (carbon-copy record), and so an answer sheet is not required. The validation criteria are scholastic achievement and scores on other commonly used tests of general mental ability. In content and standardization this test ranks with the best group tests and has the advantages of self-scoring and low cost.

The Pintner General Ability Tests (Harcourt, Brace & World, Inc.) have separate language and nonlanguage tests. The nonlanguage test is suitable for grades 4 to 9 and is a useful supplement to the verbal test at these grade levels. Cronbach [5] finds that the nonlanguage score adds more unique information to data normally available from achievement tests than does the Pintner Verbal Test or the usual one-score intelligence test. The verbal tests are not easy to administer but are generally rated among the best for school use. They have been subjected to careful statistical treatment, and information regarding the findings is given in the manual.

[4] L. F. Shaffer, in Oscar K. Buros (ed.), *The Fifth Mental Measurements Yearbook*, p. 473. Highland Park, N.J.: The Gryphon Press, 1959.
[5] Cronbach, *op. cit.*, p. 231.

The Terman-McNemar Test of Mental Ability (Harcourt, Brace & World, Inc.) is a revision of the Terman Group Test of Mental Ability, which was a standard intelligence test for many years. The arithmetical and numerical subtests contained in the old test have been dropped, making the new test primarily one of verbal ability. Hence, for certain purposes it would need to be supplemented with some measure of quantitative ability. It is a well-constructed, easily interpreted test.

The Ohio State University Psychological Test (Science Research Associates, Inc.) is designed for use with high school and college students and adults. It measures vocabulary and reading ability and has been found to predict college marks very well. The norms are based upon samples of adequate size but drawn mainly from one state. The reliabilities for its different forms have been found to be consistently high.

Group Tests with Separate Verbal and Nonverbal Scores. A second type of group test of general ability seeks to measure both general and special aspects of intelligence. These tests yield two part scores (verbal and non-verbal) and a total score. Some, such as the California Test of Mental Maturity, provide separate scores for the subtests that produce the two part scores. However, as in the case of the Wechsler scales, the subtests lack sufficient reliability for the subscores to have diagnostic value.

Because these tests yield separate verbal and nonverbal scores, some psychologists maintain that they have an advantage over the single-score tests in that they indicate the relative strength of a student's verbal and nonverbal abilities. Others doubt that the two "factors" measured by the two parts are independent variables. They question the use of three IQ's (verbal, nonverbal, and total). If the subtests are even quasi-independent, the total IQ, they say, is without meaning. Tests of this type are, however, being widely used; and their number is increasing.

The effectiveness of the verbal and nonverbal scores as differential predictors of success in particular academic courses has not yet been conclusively determined. Inconsistent findings have been reported, but English marks do seem to correlate more highly with the verbal scores than with the nonverbal or numerical scores. And the nonverbal scores have proved useful in calling attention to students who have good reasoning ability but are retarded in reading or verbal development.

Some tests in this group, such as the School and College Ability Tests, are primarily measures of general educational development. Others, such as the California Test of Mental Maturity and the Lorge-Thorndike Intelligence Tests, include reasoning tasks not taught directly in the schools. However, the scores of all mental ability tests reflect in large part the amount and nature of the subjects' schooling.

Three examples of the three-score type of test are the California Test of Mental Maturity, the Lorge-Thorndike Intelligence Tests, and the Cooperative School and College Ability Tests. The California Test of

Mental Maturity (California Test Bureau) is widely used and is generally rated a good test. Its format and standardization are good. The test comprises five series (preprimary, primary, elementary, junior high, secondary, and advanced) that contain a variety of items measuring memory, spatial relations, mathematical reasoning, logical reasoning, and verbal concepts. There is also a short form which can be given in a period ranging from twenty to fifty-three minutes according to the educational level at which used. The full form requires two periods of about forty-five minutes each.

The CTMM yields three IQ's—language, nonlanguage, and total. Consistent research evidence has not yet been provided to show the differences between the two part scores to be of practical significance. The back page of the test contains a "diagnostic profile" for the recording of subtest scores as well as the part scores. Although the manual states that the subscores are not reliable for diagnostic purposes, the profile encourages misuse. It leads some counselors and teachers to read significance into the subscore differences. Some reviewers of the CTMM also question the term "factor scores" as used in the manual. They protest the use of the term for other than an ability cluster located through factor analysis, a procedure not used with the CTMM.

The Lorge-Thorndike Intelligence Tests (Houghton Mifflin Company) provide tests for five levels ranging from kindergarten through grade 12. The tests for kindergarten through grade 3 are nonverbal. Above grade 3 the tests yield both verbal and nonverbal scores. Since the two scores correlate substantially, their differences may not be significant for many subjects. These tests are generally appraised as an excellent, well-constructed series, well adapted for use by teachers, as well as counselors. The lack of extravagant claims is noted and commended by several reviewers.

The Cooperative School and College Ability Tests (Educational Testing Service) comprise five levels covering grades 4 through 14. The SCAT series replaces the highly respected American Council on Education Psychological Examinations, which were among the first group tests to employ separate verbal and quantitative scores. The SCAT has two verbal sections that measure sentence understanding and word meanings and two numerical sections that measure numerical computation and problem solving.

The raw scores are changed into verbal and numerical converted scores that are serviceably equivalent for all levels. This makes possible a direct comparison of the scores from one educational level to those from another. Conversion scores are translated into percentile bands rather than percentile scores. This procedure helps the counselor to think of the scores as ranges rather than points and reminds him of the lack of precision in most test scores. With the SCAT, as with other two-part tests, the significance of the differences in the language and numerical scores is uncertain.

The SCAT represents a superior series of carefully developed, well-written, and well-standardized tests. The norms are satisfactory, and detailed instructions are given in the *Manual for Interpreting Scores*. Two other manuals are provided. One covers administration and scoring procedures, and the other presents the technical data. Because the tests are relatively new, the evidence regarding predictive validity is limited but promising.

"Culturally Fair" Tests. No truly "culture-free" tests can be developed because, as Anastasi [6] says, "persons do not react in a cultural vacuum." Some psychologists, however, believe that it is possible to develop a test that is "culturally fair." Davis,[7] for one, contends that our present intelligence tests are biased against lower-class children and that they are so constructed that their contents favor the middle-class child. Were their contents "culturally fair" to all students, he says, children of the lower socioeconomic groups would do as well on them as those from the upper classes.

Others also find ability test scores to correlate positively with social status but find an explanation in a difference in test motivation. Lower-class children are less highly motivated than upper-class children. Cronbach [8] is among those who question that the low test scores are due to any unfairness inherent in the tests. In his opinion, "the tests are unfair only if lower-class children do better in school than their test scores forecast. Investigations show just the contrary; when test scores are matched the middle-class children do somewhat better in school." He cites Turnbull's [9] study and adds that "if anything, the tests do not give the middle-class group enough advantage."

With Eells, Davis has attempted to develop a test which has content that is fair or common to all social classes within our culture. It is the Davis-Eells Games (Harcourt, Brace & World, Inc.) designed for use with grades 1 through 6. The contents deal with everyday situations and are presented pictorially. Some items represent humorous situations and have somewhat of a comic-strip appeal. No reading is required; the instructions are given orally. Despite its being less schoolish and abstract than most other mental ability tests, it does not seem to be any more free of cultural bias than are its competitors. Lower-class children do no better on it than on other tests.[10] Moreover, it has a lower reliability than most other tests

[6] Anne Anastasi, *Psychological Testing*, 2d ed., p. 256. New York: The Macmillan Company, 1961.

[7] Allison Davis, "Socioeconomic Influences upon Children's Learning," *Understanding the Child*, 1951, 20:10–16.

[8] Cronbach, *op. cit.*, p. 242.

[9] W. W. Turnbull, "Socio-economic Status and Predictive Test Scores," *Journal of Consulting Psychology*, 1951, 5:145–149.

[10] *See* William Coleman and Annie W. Ward, "A Comparison of Davis-Eells and Kuhlmann-Finch Scores of Children from High and Low Socio-economic Status," *Journal*

of general ability and is less effective in predicting academic success in the schools as they are now organized.

MULTIFACTOR TEST BATTERIES

Probably the most effective and economical measurement instrument so far developed for counseling purposes is the differential or multiple aptitude test battery. This type of test is based on research utilizing the statistical techniques of factor analysis and on evidence supporting the theoretical assumption that intelligence is not one aptitude or ability but is instead a constellation of aptitudes.

The tests that comprise a multifactor battery are designed to measure relatively independent abilities and to reveal significant differences in the score level within a subject's profile. The test makers hope that the pattern of abilities revealed by a subject's scores will indicate the courses, curricula, and occupational fields in which he can expect to find success. While these goals have not yet been reached, there is evidence that some progress is being made.

A number of multifactor test batteries are available for use in high schools and colleges, but attention is given here to only two because they are probably still, as described by Super [11] in 1957, the two that are "ready for use in counseling." They are the Differential Aptitude Tests (The Psychological Corporation) and the General Aptitude Test Battery (United States Employment Service). Both are based on long, careful, scientific research and are subjected to continuous study. The data gathered on the DAT, for example, are now so voluminous that they have had to be deposited with the American Documentation Institute in Washington.

The DAT has alternate forms which are well constructed and excellent in format, standardization, and validation. Its manual gives comprehensive information on validity, reliability, and research findings. Unfavorable as well as favorable findings are reported. The unusually strong manual is supplemented with a casebook [12] for counselors.

---

of Educational Psychology, 1955, 46:463–469; William L. Fowler, "A Comparative Analysis of Pupil Performance on Conventional and Culture-controlled Mental Tests," Yearbook of National Council on Measurements Used in Education, 1957, 14:8–19; Mary L. Love and Sylvia Beach, "Performance of Children on the Davis-Eells Games and Other Measures of Ability," Journal of Consulting Psychology, 1957, 21:29–32; Victor H. Noll, "Relation of Scores on Davis-Eells Test of General Intelligence to Social Status, School Achievement, and Other Intelligence Test Results," American Psychologist, 1958, 13:394.

[11] Donald E. Super, "The Multifactor Tests: A Summing Up," in Donald E. Super (ed.), The Use of Multifactor Tests in Guidance: A Reprint Series from the Personnel and Guidance Journal, p. 91. Washington, D.C.: American Personnel and Guidance Association, 1957.

[12] George K. Bennett et al., Counseling from Profiles: A Casebook for the Differential Aptitude Tests. New York: The Psychological Corporation, 1951.

The DAT provides a good foundation battery for measuring the abilities that ordinarily need to be considered in the counseling of secondary school students. It provides integrated tests of verbal reasoning, numerical ability, abstract reasoning, space relations, mechanical reasoning, clerical speed and accuracy, and language usage (spelling and sentences). Only the clerical is a speeded test. Administration of the total battery requires about three hours, but it need not be administered in one day. Several time schedules are suggested in the manual.

Norms have been developed for a combination of the verbal reasoning and numerical tests to provide a composite test that may serve as an overall predictor. It correlates well with other tests of scholastic ability. While the tests in the DAT scale measure relatively distinct abilities that are important in assessing a student's potentialities, there is considerable overlap in the tests. Their intercorrelations range from low to moderate, and so in a factorial sense they are not "pure" measures of the abilities tested.

Cautious interpretation of the significance of the differences in the scores is made easy by an arrangement of the profile chart which makes one inch of vertical distance equivalent to one standard deviation. If the distance between the two scores is one inch or more, it is assumed that the student is significantly stronger in one ability than in the other. If the distance is less than one inch, it is doubtful that he really differs in the two abilities.

The test is of limited effectiveness for differential prediction. The best of the verbally loaded, traditional type of intelligence tests predict academic performance about as well as does the DAT. In comparison with such tests the DAT is, as Super [13] has said, at least "a superior and somewhat refined intelligence test." The authors [14] summarize research data which show that in general its predictive effectiveness holds up very well with increasingly longer periods of time, which indicates that the test provides better than average assistance in long-range planning.

The tests of verbal reasoning, numerical ability, and language usage are good predictors of performance in English, mathematics, science, and social studies courses. The numerical ability and language tests give some help in forecasting progress in bookkeeping, and the clerical and spelling tests have been found to have predictive value in such courses as shorthand and typing. And certain studies show the tests of mechanical reasoning and space relations to predict marks fairly well in some shop courses. While the space relations test scores correlate positively with geometry marks, the numerical ability test is a better predictor in geometry courses.

[13] Super, "The Multifactor Tests: A Summing Up," p. 88.
[14] George K. Bennett et al., "The Differential Aptitude Tests: An Overview," in Super (ed.), *op. cit.*, pp. 12–15.

The predictive effectiveness of the tests varies from one situation to another. Failure to predict performance in specific courses as well in one situation as in another is in part a function of the differences in course content and in the reliability of the school marks. Also, as Cronbach [15] points out, "special abilities contribute little to prediction of overall grade averages, since no ability save verbal or numerical affects many courses." Tests of special abilities may prove to be better predictors in college and university courses than in high school.

The GATB makes it possible to measure a person's aptitudes with a short series of tests and to apply the findings to a wide range of occupations. In the words of Dvorak,[16] it is based on the assumption that "a large variety of tests can be boiled down to several factors and that a large variety of occupations can also be clustered into groups according to the similarities of abilities required" for success in them.

The GATB consists of eight paper-and-pencil tests and four apparatus tests that measure nine factors: general reasoning ability, verbal aptitude, numerical aptitude, spatial aptitude, form perception, clerical perception, motor coordination, finger dexterity, and manual dexterity. The apparatus tests are used for measuring finger and manual dexterities. Some of the tests are close adaptations of certain well-known single tests of special abilities, such as the Minnesota Rate of Manipulation and the Minnesota Clerical Test.

Not all the GATB tests are used for each occupation. Only those that have predictive value for the particular occupation may be used. Norms are expressed in terms of 22 occupational patterns. Each pattern shows the minimum or cutoff scores for the three aptitudes that are required or important for success in a cluster of similar occupations. To earn a qualifying score, a person must attain the minimum score on each of the three key aptitudes. The pattern that applies, for example, to the cluster of "laboratory science work and engineering and related work" consists of general reasoning with a minimum score of 125, numerical aptitude with a minimum score of 115, and spatial aptitude also with a minimum score of 115. Thus, interpretations or recommendations are made in terms of broad groups of occupations rather than individual jobs.

The GATB measures most of the occupationally significant aptitudes. It does not cover the special aptitudes of music and art. This test battery is provided mainly for use in the local branches of the state employment service but is available for use in secondary schools and colleges. Because of its extensive normative data for the skilled and semiskilled occupations, it is particularly useful in the counseling of high school students who are not college bound and who need help in planning or find-

[15] Cronbach, op. cit., p. 279.
[16] Beatrice J. Dvorak, "The General Aptitude Test Battery," in Super (ed.), op. cit., p. 22.

ing occupational training and beginning employment. In the opinion of Super and Crites,[17] "there is no doubt that this is the most adequately standardized and validated battery of tests now available for the vocational counseling and placement of inexperienced young persons and adults. The large and varied number of partly validated occupational aptitude patterns are equalled by no other battery."

MEASUREMENT OF OTHER SPECIAL APTITUDES

Appraisal of a student's performance in the fine arts is in general a better basis for judging his chances at success in the field than is appraisal of his performance on a test for aptitude in art or music. Such tests, however, do serve at times as the means of locating students who should be encouraged to explore their possible talent in the field. Then too, tests that are reasonably reliable measures of the functions in art or music that they are designed to measure have value when they indicate that an individual is not likely to profit to any great degree from further instruction because he lacks certain abilities required for success in the field.

Tests of Aptitude in Music. Probably the best-known and most widely used test of music aptitude is the Seashore Measures of Musical Talent (The Psychological Corporation). They are phonographically presented tests of six aspects of auditory discrimination: pitch, loudness, rhythm, time, timbre, and tonal memory. Their value for musical aptitude measurement is disputed. Some critics say that the tests are too analytical, that they analyze music to the point where little music remains. Much research has been reported, but the findings are conflicting.

A more recently developed test is the Drake Musical Aptitude Tests (Science Research Associates, Inc.), which measure musical memory and rhythm. In the memory test short piano melodies are presented two to seven times on phonograph records. The subject must tell whether the repeated melody is the same as in the first playing and whether changes are made in key, time, and notes. The rhythm test is essentially a test of ability to keep time. In the opinion of some reviewers, such as Lundin,[18] these tests are superior to the previously published tests of relative aptitude for general musical training. Administering is easy and scoring quick. Separate norms are provided for boys and girls for every three-year interval between ages seven and twenty-four.

The Wing Standardized Tests of Musical Intelligence, developed in England, have been generally appraised as very promising. They meas-

---

[17] Super and Crites, *Appraising Vocational Fitness by Means of Psychological Tests,* p. 338.

[18] Robert W. Lundin, in Buros (ed.), *The Fifth Mental Measurements Yearbook,* p. 379.

ure perception of musical relations and esthetic judgment through seven subtests of the ability to detect (1) number of notes in a single chord, (2) direction of change of one note in a repeated chord, (3) note changed in a repeated chord, (4) the better rhythmic pattern of two playings of the same piece, (5) the more appropriate of two harmonies for a melody, (6) the more appropriate pattern of dynamics for two performances of the same piece, and (7) the more appropriate phrasing of two renditions of the same piece.

Tests of Art Aptitude. Different art aptitude tests measure different abilities. The Meier Art Judgment Test (Bureau of Educational Research and Service, State University of Iowa) and the Graves Design Judgment Test (The Psychological Corporation) are essentially measures of esthetic judgment and appreciation. The items in the Meier test are pairs of pictures of art objects. One picture in each pair is distorted in some way. The subject must identify the better picture in each pair. In the Graves test the items are pairs of abstract designs. The subject must identify the pair member that violates some specified principle of design, such as unity, balance, proportion, or symmetry.

In contrast, the Horn Art Aptitude Inventory (C. H. Stoelting Company) attempts to measure ability to perform artistically. This test has two parts, the first of which measures dexterity, neatness, and aptness at quick sketching by having the subject draw 20 familiar objects. The second part tests originality by having the subject draw on cards, containing patterns of lines, pictures or sketches that incorporate the key lines. While this test provides useful clues regarding the presence or absence of certain basic abilities, it is criticized because it requires a certain amount of experience and training and because its scoring system penalizes deviation from the norms in technique and composition. It has been described as more a test of conformity than of originality.

Tests of Aptitude in the Professions. Tests have been devised for measuring aptitude in certain professions, such as law, medicine, engineering, and teaching. These tests are used mainly for screening candidates for admission to a college or university offering professional training. In some cases use of the test is restricted to the colleges and universities that have institution membership in a particular professional association.

Basically these tests are measures of general ability and achievement. Aptitude tests for medical students, for example, are tests of visual memory, memory for content, scientific vocabulary, comprehension of medical materials, logical reasoning, and ability for quantitative thinking. Tests of aptitude for the study of law measure accurate recall, reading comprehension of legal material, skill in logic, and reasoning by analogy and by analysis. In such tests the content is specialized. It is weighted with the types of materials and problems associated with medicine, law, engineering, or some other profession, in accordance with the intended use of the test.

Usually the criterion for the validity of professional aptitude tests is success in professional studies rather than success in the profession. The criterion is a narrow one but a useful one, for professional training is a hurdle that must be scaled before the profession can be entered. However, as already pointed out, success in professional studies has high validity as an immediate criterion but not necessarily as an ultimate one. Scholastic success coupled with low social adjustment may not lead to success in professional practice. Success in both professional training and professional practice requires high general intelligence, as well as the possession of certain special abilities. Information about a student's performance on a scholastic aptitude test or a differential aptitude battery, about his previous school achievement, and about his interest in the profession will together provide a fairly good index of a student's chance at being admitted to the professional training program of his choice.

ACHIEVEMENT TESTS

The distinction between tests of general ability and tests of achievement is not clear-cut. Both cover prior learning and bring into play abilities developed through standardized and unstandardized educational experiences. Both provide a basis for forecasting the quality of a subject's future performance in a new situation and for estimating the extent to which he will profit from training. In general, however, an achievement test is more useful than a test of general ability for evaluating learning that takes place under known and more or less controlled conditions.

Both ability and achievement tests provide only partial information and so need to be supplemented with relevant data from other reliable sources. The achievement test data, for example, need to be supplemented with observational data to determine whether the subject's test performance is his typical performance. A student may, for instance, attain a high score on a test of English usage but regularly misuse the language orally and in writing.

Content or curricular validity is very important in achievement tests. The test contents need to be representative of the course contents. Because content validity should be appraised in terms of the expected educational outcomes in a particular situation, some authors of educational achievement tests do not supply information on the content validity of their tests. Information regarding the content measured is needed, however, to help test users appraise relevance of the test to particular courses. Predictive validity becomes important when test data are to be used as a basis for selection or classification, as, for example, when class groups are to be sectioned into ability groups or when students are to be screened for scholarship awards or college admission.

Uses. Achievement tests are used for evaluation, placement, and selection. They are used in checking a student's progress during and at the close of training. The test data indicate whether a student is ready for the next stage in the educational program. They are useful in appraising a student's skills and knowledge and in diagnosing his disabilities. They help to identify students with special educational disabilities and in some cases provide clues regarding the reasons for emotional handicaps. The cause may lie, for example, in inappropriate educational placement or severe deficiency in some basic skill, such as reading. Combined with tests of general ability, achievement tests disclose which students are not making adequate progress in terms of expectancy rather than minimum standards. Used as aids in the evaluation of teaching, they may contribute to improved instruction and curriculum content.

Their use in the evaluation of teaching can, however, have undesirable as well as desirable outcomes. Use of standardized educational achievement tests may lead to excessive standardization and neglect of some important objectives. They may lead to an overemphasis on conformity and may cause individual differences in both teachers and students to be ignored. Spontaneity, creativity, and originality may thus be discouraged rather than fostered. Some achievement tests, for example, tend to measure primarily factual information and certain basic skills. They do not measure sufficiently well the student's skill in synthesis of materials, expression of ideas, application of principles, critical thinking, efficient work habits, creativity, and the like. A test can influence the goals and the methods of both teachers and students if preparation for the test becomes a major classroom objective.

Trends. Two trends in the development of educational achievement tests are clearly noticeable. First, there is a trend away from single tests of specific subjects, such as geometry and English history, toward batteries comprising tests of broad fields, such as mathematics, science, and social studies. Second, there is a trend toward decreased emphasis on factual information and a limited group of skills and increased emphasis upon comprehension, analysis, interpretation, appreciation, and attitudes.

For a time it was considered almost impossible to assess through objective tests achievement of outcomes in terms of expected behavior in applying principles, recognizing assumptions, drawing inferences from experimental data, judging the value of material for a given purpose, translating from one set of symbols to another, and the like. Such understandings and skills are more difficult to test and to teach than are facts. That intangibles as well as tangibles can be measured was demonstrated in two experimental programs carried out in the public schools—the Eight Year Study [19] of the Progressive Education Association and the Cooperative Study of Evaluation in General Education.[20]

The reports on these two studies show that definite progress was made in measuring understanding, ability to use information, and changes in attitudes and beliefs. Tests were developed that require students to generalize from data drawn from the sciences and the social studies, to use facts and principles in explaining scientific phenomena, to draw inferences from subject matter, and to apply generalizations to specific situations.

Some Examples. Almost all achievement tests for the elementary and junior high schools are in the form of overlapping batteries for different grades. Four well-known and widely used ones are the Iowa Tests of Basic Skills (Houghton Mifflin Company), Metropolitan Achievement Tests (Harcourt, Brace & World, Inc.), SRA Achievement Series (Science Research Associates, Inc.), and the Stanford Achievement Test (Harcourt, Brace & World, Inc.).

Two batteries cover the elementary and secondary grades and the first two years of college. One, the California Achievement Tests (California Test Bureau), yields scores in vocabulary and reading comprehension, arithmetic fundamentals and reasoning, and English mechanics and spelling. The CAT norms are obtained from the same norm group used in standardizing the CTMM, which facilitates comparison of a student with others of similar general ability. "Anticipated achievement charts," constructed in terms of grade placement, are provided in the manual for this purpose. See Figure 7. While the charts aid interpretation by providing a basis for appraising the relative progress of students at different ability levels, they cannot, of course, show the extent to which the needs of individual students are being met.

Diagnostic profiles are provided for the CAT, as for the CTMM. Frequent reference is made in the manual to the use of subtest scores for diagnostic analysis of a student's learning difficulties. The scores are not, however, sufficiently reliable for this purpose. Also, there is not enough evidence to show that the subtest categories represent separate factors.

The other series that extends through grade 14 is the Sequential Tests of Educational Progress (Educational Testing Service). It is generally considered an outstanding series and, in the opinion of Anastasi [21] and some other reviewers, represents content validation at its best. Although the STEP measures specific knowledge in particular subject areas,

[19] E. R. Smith, R. W. Tyler, et al., *Appraising and Recording Student Progress.* New York: Harper & Row, Publishers, Incorporated, 1942.

[20] P. L. Dressel and L. B. Mayhew, *General Education: Explorations in Evaluation.* Washington, D.C.: American Council on Education, 1954.

[21] Anastasi, *op. cit.*, p. 453.

it requires a deeper mastery than do most achievement tests and stresses the application of knowledge in the solving of new problems.

Three of the seven tests that make up the STEP measure mathematics, science, and social studies. The others measure communication skills. In addition to an essay test, there are three objective tests of reading comprehension, of "auding" or listening comprehension, and of the ability to judge and improve writing style. Five sample essays guide the scorer in his rating of a subject's product. While the use of an essay question is no new development, it is not a common practice. The inclusion of an auding test is a new development.

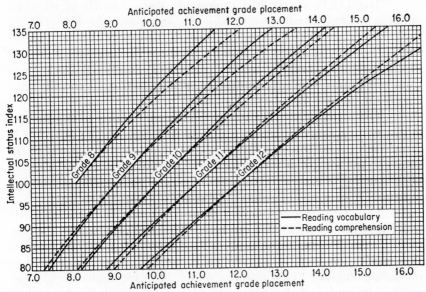

FIGURE 7 *Anticipated achievement chart for reading.* (Ernest W. Tiegs and Willis W. Clark, *Manual: California Achievement Tests,* Advanced Level, p. 52. Monterey, Calif.: California Test Bureau, 1957. Reproduced by permission of the publisher.)

Like the SCAT scores, the STEP scores are changed to converted scores and then translated into percentile bands rather than single percentile values. The bands cover approximately one standard error of measurement on either side of the corresponding percentile value. The manual contains considerable interpretive and explanatory material that is supplemented with new material as research makes it available.

The Iowa Tests of Educational Development (Science Research Associates, Inc.) were originally developed for the fall testing program of the Iowa high schools. They were developed to replace the subject examination program which, according to Lindquist,[22] was inadequate because of certain limitations: (1) failure to give information concerning

[22] E. F. Lindquist, "Some Criteria of an Effective High School Testing Program," in A. E. Traxler (ed.), *Measurements and Evaluation in the Improvement of Education,* pp. 17–33. Washington, D.C.: American Council on Education, 1951.

common traits or characteristics because all students did not take the same tests (enrolled in different courses, students took only the tests given in those courses); (2) failure to provide regularly evidence of achievement in particular areas (if, for example, a student was not enrolled any year in a social studies course, he was not examined that year in social studies); (3) undue emphasis upon the immediate objectives of a particular subject; (4) stress upon temporary outcomes as opposed to the more lasting ones; (5) neglect of the effects of out-of-class experiences, incidental learning, and self-education; and (6) failure to show relative improvement in growth in various areas.

The ITED battery is a compromise between tests of scholastic aptitude and tests of educational achievement in much the same way that the DAT and the GATB are compromises between tests of general ability and tests of special aptitudes. It is intended for use in grades 9 through 12 and designed to reveal individual patterns of educational development from year to year. It is well constructed, well normed, and generally rated among the best for secondary school use.

The battery includes a test of the student's ability to express himself in written English, tests of ability to interpret reading materials in three fields (social studies, natural science, and literature), a test of the ability to use sources of information, and tests of general vocabulary, of understanding of basic social concepts, of general background information in natural science, and of general mathematical reasoning ability.

The machine-scored answer sheet contains a "numeric grid" on which additional information can be recorded and processed by the computer system along with the answers. Such information may be recorded as identification data, age, grade point average, scores on other tests, previously obtained ITED scores, and quantified biographical and sociometric data, such as father's occupation and education level. A wealth of data can thus be made available for research studies of special importance to counselors.

The Cooperative Tests (Cooperative Test Division, Educational Testing Service) are another series which is generally held to be of superior quality. They are primarily tests of information and certain basic skills. In addition to separate tests in the major academic subject fields in high schools and colleges, the series includes the Cooperative General Achievement Tests, which measure general proficiency in the social studies, natural sciences, and mathematics. Each test has two parts. One measures understanding of terms and concepts; and the other, comprehension and interpretation of paragraphs, charts, and tables. One test that was developed for college students cuts across subject boundaries. It is the Cooperative General Culture Test.

The publishers of the Cooperative Tests also publish some of the instruments developed through the Eight Year Study and referred to above—an interpretation-of-data test for measuring ability to perceive relationships and to recognize limitations in data, tests of application of principles in science, a test of appreciation of literature, and a test of logical reasoning.

In spite of the improvements made in educational achievement tests, especially in batteries developed for use with high school students, strong criticisms continue to be made against them. The tests do not, the critics say, cover the course objectives or course contents sufficiently well; for example, they fail to cover the laboratory and field experiences which many courses provide. With all their defects, however, achievement tests are not without value. Not to include some of the best ones in the guidance testing program would be unwise. Not to use them cautiously and with full awareness of their limitations would be even more unwise.

While well-constructed teacher-made evaluation devices can generally yield better information than standardized achievement tests regarding the progress of the students in a particular class toward achievement of certain objectives, standardized achievement tests are useful aids for diagnosing a student's specific learning needs, for identifying his relative strengths and weaknesses, for studying his progress, and for predicting his success in particular curricula. In some colleges achievement tests are being used not only for selecting students and for guiding them in their choice of curricula and courses but also for placing students in refresher courses and in advanced courses. This practice helps to decrease the number of students who fail. By doing away with undesirable duplication it also helps to save time and to prevent boredom for some students.

College Entrance and Scholarship Examinations. The tests that are used in certain nationwide testing programs for screening applications for college admission and scholarships include tests of both achievement and scholastic aptitude. The examinations used by the College Entrance Board, for example, are the Scholastic Aptitude Test and the College Board Achievement Tests.

The SAT yields separate verbal and numerical scores, which are produced by five tests of vocabulary, verbal reasoning, quantitative reasoning, and knowledge of high school mathematics. It is essentially a measure of ability for academic tasks and has proved effective in estimating scholarship potential for college programs.

Some colleges that require applicants for admission to take the SAT also require them to take in addition three of the College Board Achievement Tests. Some specify which ones are to be taken. Altogether there are 13 tests that cover composition, intermediate and advanced mathematics, biology, chemistry, physics, social studies, and foreign languages, including Greek and Latin. They measure reasoning and problem-solving ability as well as the acquisition of information.

The Preliminary Scholastic Aptitude Test is another College Board examination. It is administered to tenth and eleventh graders who want to take it for practice as "preliminary candidates" for the SAT. It is also used in the guidance of college-bound students and in screening scholarship applicants. It replaces the Scholarship Qualifying Test that was used in many high schools before 1959.

The American College Testing Program is a relatively new program, which was initiated partly to serve colleges less selective than the ones served by the College Entrance Examination Board program. A large number of colleges now either require or recommend that their applicants for admission take the American College Test (Science Research Associates, Inc.).

The ACT is administered three times a year on a Saturday morning. It may be taken by any high school senior who registers in advance, pays a fee, and reports to one of the designated testing centers. It consists of four tests of about forty-five minutes in length that cover English, mathematics, social studies, and natural sciences.

In 1955 the privately financed, nonprofit National Merit Scholarship Program was organized by a group of citizens and certain professional and industrial organizations. This group provides scholarships to students who are selected through an examination that is administered each spring in all high schools applying for the test. Each school names two students who may take the test without paying a fee. As many others may take the examination who wish to do so, but they must pay a small fee. Those students who score sufficiently high on the examination taken in the spring may try to qualify for a scholarship by taking a second examination the following December. Because scholarships are assigned to the states on a proportional basis, it is possible for a scholarship recipient in one state to earn a lower test score than a rejectee in another state. Some rejectees, however, obtain scholarships because the names of high-ranking students are supplied to interested colleges and scholarship sponsors.

Prior to 1959 the test used in screening National Merit Scholarship applicants was the Scholarship Qualifying Test referred to above. Since 1958 it has been replaced by the National Merit Scholarship Qualifying Test prepared by Science Research Associates, Inc. This test is described by its publishers as a measure of educational development rather than of scholastic aptitude. It contains five subtests: English usage, mathematics usage, social studies reading, natural science reading, and word usage. These subtests closely parallel those of the Iowa Test of Educational Development, which is a broad measure of growth from grades 9 to 12. Some reviewers, such as Lennon,[23] question the desirability of having a test intended for use in identifying students in the upper end of the ability distribution resemble closely a test designed to serve a very different objective. Other reviewers are critical of the somewhat extravagant

[23] Roger T. Lennon, in Buros (ed.), *The Fifth Mental Measurements Yearbook*, p. 48.

claims made for the test in the manual and the "fact folder" used in publicizing the test.

SUMMARY

In secondary schools and colleges individual tests of mental ability, such as the Stanford-Binet and the Wechsler scales, are ordinarily used only with students considered for special placement or for special assistance in some other form. For reasons of economy and practicality group tests are used with most students. A good group test is about as reliable and as good a predictor of academic achievement as a comparable individual scale.

Several types of group tests of scholastic aptitude are available. Some yield a single score; some, separate verbal and numerical or nonverbal scores; and some, multiple scores on relatively distinct abilities. Of the multifactor test batteries, two are more important to counselors—the Differential Aptitude Tests and the General Aptitude Battery. The DAT forecasts performance very well in some academic courses and fairly well in some nonacademic courses.

The GATB measures more specialized abilities than the DAT. Neither battery contains tests of aptitude in music and art. Aptitude in these two areas is best appraised through actual performance. The art and music aptitude tests currently available measure a few simple functions involved in complex artistic performance. They are more measures of judgment and appreciation than of ability, and of conformity than of originality.

Tests of aptitude for the professions are basically tests of intelligence and of proficiency in the skills and knowledge stressed in preparing for the profession.

Tests of achievement in single subjects are still used, but less often today than formerly. Increased use is being made of survey batteries that measure achievement in broad areas. Stress is placed upon the need for tests that measure, in addition to factual information and a limited number of basic skills, the ability to make critical discriminations, to analyze and synthesize materials, to make inferences, to apply principles, to adapt learning in solving new problems, and to use certain work-study skills.

Some representative ability and achievement tests have been named and briefly described. Data from such tests, in combination with other relevant information, are used in counseling to help students appraise their progress, to understand their strengths and limitations, to set realistic goals, and to make sound, practical plans for achieving them.

REFERENCES

Anastasi, Anne: *Psychological Testing*, 2d ed., parts II and III. New York: The Macmillan Company, 1961.

Cronbach, Lee J.: *Essentials of Psychological Testing*, 2d ed., chaps. 7–8, 10–11, and 13. New York: Harper & Row, Publishers, Incorporated, 1960.

Dailey, J. T., and M. F. Shaycoft: *Types of Tests in Project Talent.* Washington, D.C.: Government Printing Office, 1961.

Droege, Robert C.: "G.A.T.B. Norms for Lower High School Grades," *Personnel and Guidance Journal*, 1960, 39:30–34.

Froehlich, Clifford P., and Kenneth B. Hoyt: *Guidance Testing*, chaps. 5–7. Chicago: Science Research Associates, Inc., 1959.

Katz, Martin R.: *Selecting an Achievement Test: Principles and Procedures.* Princeton, N.J.: Educational Testing Service, 1958.

Super, Donald E. (ed.): *The Use of Multifactor Tests in Guidance: A Reprint Series from the Personnel and Guidance Journal.* Washington, D.C.: American Personnel and Guidance Association, 1957.

―――― and John O. Crites: *Appraising Vocational Fitness by Means of Psychological Tests*, rev. ed., chaps. 5–7, 14–15. New York: Harper & Row, Publishers, Incorporated, 1962.

Thorndike, Robert L., and Elizabeth Hagen: *Measurement and Evaluation in Psychology and Education*, 2d ed., chaps. 9–11. New York: John Wiley & Sons, Inc., 1961.

6

Measures of Interest
and Personality

Interest and personality inventories are generally added to school testing programs after tests of scholastic ability and achievement are adopted. Interest inventories are ordinarily provided for use with most students, whereas personality inventories are generally used with only a limited number. In high schools and colleges these tests are generally administered to groups rather than given individually.

Vocational interest inventories are especially useful for providing a good starting point to serious discussion of vocational interests and goals. Such discussion can arouse strong interest in occupational choice, stimulate self-insight, and lead students to attempt objective appraisal of themselves, their plans, and their goals.

VOCATIONAL INTEREST AND ITS ASSESSMENT

Origin. A person's vocational interest is related to his general intelligence and special aptitudes and is determined in part by his environment and his opportunity to explore different kinds of activities. Super and Crites [1] have concluded on the basis of their review of the research that an adequate theory regarding the nature of interests "would recognize the fact of multiple causation, the principle of interaction, and the joint contribution of nature and nurture." Such a theory recognizes the significance of heredity, the role of experience, the relationships between aptitude and interest, and the "relationships between interests and the deeper layers of personality such as values, temperament, personality traits, and needs." They summarize as follows:

> Interests are the product of interaction between inherited neural and endocrine factors, on the one hand, and opportunity and social evaluation on the other. Some of the things a person does well as a result of aptitudes bring him the satisfaction of mastery or the approval of his com-

[1] Donald E. Super and John O. Crites, *Appraising Vocational Fitness by Means of Psychological Tests,* rev. ed., pp. 410–411. New York: Harper & Row, Publishers, Incorporated, 1962.

panions, and result in interests. Some of the things his associates do appeal to him and, through identification, he patterns his actions and his interests after them; if he fits the pattern reasonably well he remains in it, but if not, he must seek another identification and develop another self-concept and interest pattern. His needs and his mode of adjustment may cause him to seek certain satisfactions, but the means of achieving these satisfactions vary so much from one person, with one set of aptitudes and in one set of circumstances, to another person with other abilities and in another situation, that the prediction of interest patterns from needs and from modes of adjustment is hardly possible.

Stability of Claimed and Inventoried Vocational Interests. Super [2] defines interests in terms of the methods used to assess them. He describes them as expressed, manifest, inventoried, and tested interests.

Expressed interests are disclosed verbally. A boy, for example, says that he wants to be an aviator. This type of interest tends to change with age. In due course a boy s interest in being a policeman, fireman, or cowboy gives way to interest in being a professional ballplayer, aviator, or nuclear physicist. Not all persons, however, show change in interest with change in age. Some choose and enter into occupations for which they express strong preference throughout their lives, beginning with early childhood.

The expressed interests of children and adolescents are generally unstable. Their answers to direct questions regarding occupational interest tend to be unreliable, superficial, and unrealistic. Lack of information and experience makes it difficult for them not to think in terms of stereotypes.

Manifest interests are revealed through participation in particular activities. A boy may manifest an interest in aviation by collecting books on aviation, spending much time at the airport, seeking opportunities to talk with pilots about their flights, studying airplane models, and doing other such things. In general, the manifest interests of adolescents show little relationship to their measured interests and eventual choice of occupations.

An interest manifested during adolescence may be developed as an avocational interest during adulthood. A physician may regularly meet with other nonprofessional musicians for "orchestra practice." A college professor may slip away from his study to spend time restoring old furniture in his basement workshop. A printer may spend much of his leisure time studying and rehearsing his part in the next production of the "community players."

Inventoried interests are revealed through responses to questionnaires regarding one's likes and dislikes for certain activities. Different responses are assigned different weights which, when summarized statisti-

[2] Donald E. Super, *The Psychology of Careers: An Introduction to Vocational Development,* pp. 221–224. New York: Harper & Row, Publishers, Incorporated, 1957.

cally, reveal a subject's patterns of interests. It is with this type of interest that we are primarily concerned in this chapter.

The significance of inventoried interests varies with the maturity of the individual. There is reliable evidence that the inventoried interest patterns of adolescents are not so unstable as they are often believed to be. The strongest evidence probably comes from the work of Strong,[3] who found that the interest patterns of young people begin to resemble the interests of adults by age 14 or 15 and are fairly well crystallized by the end of the high school years. He found that at the age of 25 the individual "is largely what he is going to be and even at 20 years of age he has acquired pretty much the interests he will have throughout life." [4]

The changes that take place through exploratory experiences between ages 15 and 20 seem to be largely changes in the way of clarification, development, and elaboration. In the words of Super and Crites,[5] "for most persons, adolescent exploration is an awakening to something that is already there." Most high school students' interests are sufficiently stable to enable them to select between broad areas of training. During training and the subsequent experiences, they will modify their interests and make further decisions and choices affecting their careers. Thus the process of decision and choice will continue throughout their careers.

Tested interests are disclosed under controlled conditions. The boy who manifests an interest in aviation, for example, may be given a list of books from which to select two to read. If he selects books dealing with aviation rather than books dealing with forestry, veterinary medicine, printing, journalism, or some other occupation, his tested interest is in line with his manifest interest. Likewise, if on a test of occupational information he shows a knowledge of aviation that is more comprehensive, specific, and accurate than his knowledge of the other occupations covered by the test, his tested interest again agrees with his manifest interest. The research in the area of tested interests is so limited that relatively little is known regarding their stability and predictive value.

Choice a Continuous Process. The making of occupational choices is a continuous process. It is, as Super [6] says, a dynamic process involving a sequence of lesser decisions, "which brings about a progressive reduction of the number of alternatives open to the chooser." The process begins early in life and may continue long after the years of formal schooling. A professional man, for example, may decide during his middle years to

---

[3] E. K. Strong, Jr., *Vocational Interests of Men and Women*, pp. 278–279. Stanford, Calif.: Stanford University Press, 1943.

[4] *Ibid.*, p. 313.

[5] Super and Crites, *Appraising Vocational Fitness by Means of Psychological Tests*, p. 411.

[6] Donald E. Super and Phoebe L. Overstreet in collaboration with others, *The Vocational Maturity of Ninth-grade Boys*, p. 141. New York: Bureau of Publications, Teachers College, Columbia University, 1960.

change from practitioner to administrator. Similarly a skilled worker may decide to change his place of employment or even to move into a new field that offers promising opportunities for workers with his types of skills and experiences.

Interest is just one factor influencing choice or decision. Its role is primarily one of synthesis or compromise. Super gives this illustration: [7]

> A boy's interests may be like those of engineers, while his intelligence is not high enough for success in a college course or his funds are not sufficient for the extra years of schooling. He may, therefore, set his sights lower; he may become a mechanic or perhaps a crane operator. In this way, occupational choice is made in the *field* of greatest interest, while ability and opportunity (among other factors) determine the occupational *level* of the job choice within the field. In some instances the values of a subculture outweigh individual interests even in the selection of the vocational field.

The last point is well illustrated in the studies of McArthur,[8] who found that students from wealthy homes educated in certain private secondary schools tended to express occupational preferences in keeping with their families' wishes or expectations. Their expressed interests differed from the interests inventoried through the Strong Vocational Interest Blank. When a student's choice is thus determined by his subculture, there is little need, as Darley [9] says, for using a vocational interest inventory. All that the counselor needs to do is to ask the boy what he is going to be. The boy gives the right answer because choice is "totally predetermined by his entire environment." His subculture does not permit him to use the interest patterns that he reveals on the Strong Blank.

In junior and senior high schools interest inventories are useful mainly for helping students to think constructively about possible choices rather than for helping them to make specific decisions. In general, the vocational counseling offered students below the eleventh grade should be directed toward helping them to identify the various areas that they might want to explore. It involves helping the individual to become informed regarding the fields attracting his interest, helping him to recognize and appraise his personal and environmental resources, and helping him to perceive and understand the social and personal factors that he must reckon with in making his decisions. It is not, as Super [10] says,

[7] Donald Super et al., *Vocational Development: A Framework for Research,* p. 49. New York: Bureau of Publications, Teachers College, Columbia University, 1957. Italics in the original.

[8] Charles McArthur, "Long-term Validity of the Strong Interest Test in Two Subcultures," *Journal of Applied Psychology,* 1954, 38:346–353; Charles McArthur and Lucia B. Stevens, "The Validation of Expressed Interests as Compared with Inventoried Interests: A Fourteen Year Follow-up," *Journal of Applied Psychology,* 1955, 39:184–189.

[9] H. H. Gee and J. T. Cowles (eds.), *The Appraisal of Applicants for Medical Schools,* p. 26. Evanston, Ill.: Association of American Medical Colleges, 1957.

[10] Super and Overstreet, *The Vocational Maturity of Ninth-grade Boys,* p. 157.

"so much counseling concerning choice, as counseling to develop readiness for choice, to develop planfulness."

Once made, some choices and decisions can and will be modified in keeping with changing interests and opportunities. Other choices may be irreversible. Readiness and planfulness are obviously especially important to the making of the latter type of decision.

Strong Vocational Interest Blanks. A number of vocational interest inventories have been developed, but attention is given here to only two—the Strong Vocational Interest Blanks (Consulting Psychologists Press) and the Kuder Preference Record—Vocational (Science Research Associates, Inc.). These two are based upon extensive study and research and are commonly judged superior to the other vocational interest inventories currently available. They measure approximately the same general interests.

The Strong instrument probably represents the most successful approach to the measurement of vocational interests yet attempted. It is based on the assumption that a person who has the interest patterns typical of successful people in a given occupation will enjoy and find satisfaction in that occupation. Strong compared the inventory responses of successful members of different professional and business groups with those of men of similar age selected at random from the range of occupations ordinarily entered by college men.

The occupations covered by the SVIB are at and above the skilled level with the emphasis upon the managerial and professional occupations. Some criticism has been expressed because the reference group is not representative of the total population. Had, however, a more representative group been used, the discriminative value of the scales would have been reduced. The interests of individuals in the higher-level occupations differ so greatly from those of individuals in the lower categories that, were the latter included in the reference group, the differences between one high-level occupation and another would be obscured. At the higher levels job satisfaction is derived largely from an intrinsic liking for the work, whereas at the lower levels it is derived largely from such extrinsic factors as pay, job security, social contacts, and the like. As Anastasi [11] points out, workers in the semiskilled and unskilled occupations "seem to be as interchangeable with regard to interests as they are with regard to abilities."

The SVIB comprises eight parts that contain 400 items on vocational and avocational activities. The first five parts deal with occupations, school subjects, amusements, miscellaneous activities, and the peculiarities of people. The subject indicates his preferences by encircling letters that signify "like," "indifferent," and "dislike." In the other two

[11] Anne Anastasi, *Psychological Testing*, 2d ed., p. 531. New York: The Macmillan Company, 1961.

parts he ranks given activities according to his preferences, compares his interests in pairs of items, and rates his present abilities and characteristics.

The SVIB is an easy instrument to administer and has no time limit. The time required ranges from forty-five to ninety minutes. Scoring is intricate and tedious. To score it by hand requires several hours. Hence, the blanks are ordinarily sent to a scoring center where they can be scored electronically at high speed. The blanks are scored with different keys for different occupations. Forty-seven keys have been developed for the men's form and twenty-eight for the women's. New keys are developed as the data are collected for other occupations.

The raw scores can be translated into standard scores and letter grades, which show how closely a subject's responses resemble those given by the members of different groups. For example, a grade of A shows close resemblance. B+, B, and B— show lesser agreement. C+ and C indicate that the interests are most probably not similar. The scores have been found to be reasonably reliable for adolescents and adults.

In addition to the keys for single occupations, group keys have been developed for clusters of occupations that have been identified from correlations of the various key scores and corroborated through factor analysis. The groups for which such keys have been made available are as follows:

GROUP I.   Artist, psychologist, architect, physician, psychiatrist, osteopath, dentist, veterinarian
GROUP II.   Mathematician, physicist, chemist, engineer
GROUP III.   Production manager
GROUP IV.   Farmer, carpenter, forest-service man, aviator, printer, mathematics-science teacher, policeman, army officer
GROUP V.   YMCA physical director, personnel manager, public administrator, vocational counselor, physical therapist, social worker, social science teacher, business education teacher, school superintendent, minister
GROUP VI.   Musician, music teacher
GROUP VII.   Certified public accountant owner
GROUP VIII. Senior certified public accountant, accountant, office worker, credit manager, purchasing agent, banker, pharmacist, mortician
GROUP IX.   Sales manager, real estate salesman, life insurance salesman
GROUP X.   Advertising man, lawyer, author-journalist
GROUP XI.   President of manufacturing corporation

The blanks can also be scored with four other keys: (1) interest maturity, which differentiates between the interests of fifteen- and twenty-five-year-old men; (2) masculinity-femininity, which shows the degree to which the interests are characteristic of men or of women; (3) occupational level, which differentiates between the interests of laboring men and those of business and professional men; (4) specialization, which differentiates between the interests of specialists and generalists and differentiates specialists within some fields.

A student's blank can be scored for a single occupation; but, in general, it is best to score it with all or a number of the keys to show the patterning of his interests. The interest patterns revealed by the SVIB have been defined and explained by Darley [12] as follows:

> For an individual student, the *primary pattern* is the interest type within which he shows a preponderance (plurality or majority) of A and B+ scores on the specific occupational keys; the *secondary pattern* is the interest type within which he shows a preponderance of B+ and B scores; and the *tertiary pattern* is the interest type within which he shows a preponderance of B and B— scores in the specific occupational keys. Thus it would be possible for an individual to have a primary pattern in the "technical" interest type, a secondary pattern in the "business detail" interest type, and a tertiary pattern in the "welfare or uplift" type. It would also be possible for an individual to have no primary or secondary patterns, with a tertiary pattern in the "verbal" interest type.
>
> Notice that this procedure does *not* say that the *individual's* highest scores, even if they are only at the B level, become the primary pattern in his case. Known factors of maturity of interests, intensity of interests, and predictive value of interests preclude placing too much guidance weight on the lower interest test scores. An individual is judged to have a primary pattern *only* when a preponderance of A and B+ scores appears on the specific keys within an interest type.

Some students do not show clearly defined interest patterns. Darley and Hagenah,[13] for example, found in a sample of 1,000 university freshmen that 19.3 per cent showed no primary pattern and 26 per cent no secondary pattern. Forty-one per cent showed a single primary pattern and 30.3 per cent a double primary pattern. Since high school students are generally less mature than college students and have had fewer experiences in the activities represented by the SVIB options, a higher percentage of them can be expected to be without a primary pattern. Some individuals may never develop well-defined or strong interests. They must make their occupational decisions on the basis of other criteria, such as pay, working conditions, job security, social contacts, and the like.

Strong's technique for measuring vocational interests has proved more effective with men than with women. In the women's blank, interest in the home, as opposed to interest in a career, frequently outweighs occupational interest. Consequently, the value of the blank is reduced, ex-

[12] John G. Darley, *Clinical Aspects and Interpretation of the Strong Vocational Interest Blank*, p. 17. New York: The Psychological Corporation, 1941. Italics in the original.

[13] John G. Darley and Theda Hagenah, *Vocational Interest Measurement: Theory and Practice*, pp. 87–88. Minneapolis: The University of Minnesota Press, 1955.

cept with individuals who have definite career interests. For this reason Dickson [14] has recommended that the women's blank be used with caution and preferably with another vocational interest inventory, such as the Kuder.

The Strong blanks do not supply evidence regarding a subject's aptitudes. They show only the extent to which his interests correspond to the interests characteristic of the members of particular occupations. The assumptions implied in the use of the SVIB are that an individual is not likely to remain in a high-level occupation unless his interests resemble those of most members of that occupation, that he is more likely to remain when the work is interesting to him than when it is not, that interest in school subjects studied in preparation for a profession or semiprofession is not a sufficient basis for predicting success in the occupation, and that interests leading to job satisfaction at the beginning of one's career will continue to be related to job satisfaction at later times. Research findings tend to support these assumptions. They show the SVIB scores to be significant indices of interest patterns and reveal a significant relationship between the scores and such criteria as completion of professional training, satisfaction in an occupation, and vocational stability in terms of staying in the same occupation.

Kuder Preference Record—Vocational. The Kuder inventory (Science Research Associates, Inc.) represents a different approach to the measurement of interests. The items were formulated and tentatively grouped in descriptive scales on the basis of content validity or logical analysis of different occupational fields. Item analysis showed that the items tended to group in distinct clusters. Items in each cluster were found to have high consistency and to show low correlations with items in other coherent clusters. Items dealing with musical activities, for example, tended to cluster and to be relatively independent of other items. If a subject selected one, he tended to select the others also.

The items are presented in sets of three options worded in relatively simple language. The obvious vocational significance of the items is held at a minimum. The activities listed in one sample item are, for example, "collect autographs, collect coins, collect butterflies." The subject selects from each set the activity he likes most and the one he likes least. Thus all subjects express the same number of preferences and the same number of rejects or dislikes. The forced choice imposes a common frame of reference on all subjects and eliminates any tendency to select an unusually large number of items liked or not liked. It may also, however, eliminate or obscure some real differences in interests.

The Kuder reveals relative interest in a few general areas rather

<hr/>

[14] G. Schneidler Dickson, in Oscar K. Buros (ed.), *The Third Mental Measurements Yearbook,* p. 676. New Brunswick, N.J.: Rutgers University Press, 1949.

than interest in particular occupations. It covers ten broad fields: outdoor (agriculture, naturalistic), mechanical, computational, scientific, persuasive, artistic, literary, musical, social service, and clerical. Two sets of norms are provided—one for boys and girls and one for men and women. The scales are simple to administer, and the use of pin-punch answer pads makes scoring easy. Students can score their own tests, convert the scores into percentile ranks, and plot the results on profile sheets.

The manual aids interpretation by providing a "job chart" that shows the major specialities in each of the areas covered by the ten scales. The manual recommends that the job chart be checked for all areas in which the student earns significantly high and significantly low scores. Scores above the 75th percentile are considered significantly high and those below the 25th percentile significantly low. The significantly low areas need to be given consideration because, when the time comes for specific choice, the student may wish to eliminate from consideration occupations that involve much-disliked activities.

The scores may also be interpreted by combining the scale numbers for the two areas in which the student obtains his highest scores and then checking the job chart for the specialities listed for that particular number combination. The mechanical and persuasive scales, for example, are numbered 1 and 4 respectively. Among the occupations listed for the combination 1 and 4 are sales engineer, filling station manager, mine official, contractor, and salesperson of automotive and marine equipment, farm equipment, and general hardware.

Kuder and others have undertaken research to test the assumptions underlying the logical interpretations represented by the "job charts." In general, the findings support the interpretations. Tavris,[15] for example, studied 212 occupational profiles and found the stanine of mean scores for aviators to be 8 on the scientific and mechanical scales and the stanine of mean scores for civil engineers to be 7 on the mechanical and computational scales.

The Kuder scales are highly respected and widely used, particularly in secondary schools. Both the Kuder and the SVIB are subject to faking. When an interest inventory is used for the purpose of classification or selection, faking can be expected. When, however, the purpose is counseling, there seems to be little reason for faking unless counseling is confused with prescription by either the student or the counselor.

Predictive Efficiency. Vocational choice, success in training, and success on the job cannot be predicted on the basis of interest data alone. Ability

---

[15] E. C. Tavris, "D² as a Profile Similarity Measure of Kuder Scales," unpublished doctor's dissertation. Chicago: Illinois Institute of Technology, 1959. Reported in *Administrator's Manual: Kuder Preference Record—Vocational, Form C.* Chicago: Science Research Associates, Inc., 1960.

and opportunity to obtain any needed training also have to be considered by students in the planning of their future and by student personnel workers in the vocational counseling of students.

Interest inventory scores do not correlate very well with aptitude test scores. The correlations, for example, between DAT scores and Kuder scores show a significant, consistent relationship for only two pairings and for these two for boys only. The two pairings are DAT mechanical reasoning with Kuder mechanical interest and DAT mechanical reasoning with Kuder scientific interest.[16] For all other pairings, whether relevant or not, the relationships are low and nonsignificant.

Interest data alone are not very useful for appraising success in vocational training. Kelly and Fiske,[17] for example, found the correlations of the Strong scores with the ratings of trainees in clinical psychology to be generally low. Other investigators have reported similar findings for trainees in other occupational areas. Hence, a high interest score should be interpreted, in Cronbach's [18] words, "as indicating that *if* a person survives training and enters the occupation, he is likely to enjoy his work."

A fairly sound basis for predicting success and satisfaction may be obtained when interest data are combined with data regarding ability and opportunity to obtain any special training needed. Strong [19] compared the interest scores of several hundred former college students with the occupations in which they were engaged eighteen years later. He found that those who could finance college education tended to enter training programs that were in line with their inventoried interests, to complete the program if the interests were in harmony with abilities, and to enter occupations which provided outlets for interests, or, if they did not, to change to occupations that did.

Interest scores are more meaningful in terms of occupational choice for the professional and skilled occupations than for the lower categories. Strong [20] found in the study referred to above that in one sample an A rating in Engineer on the SVIB indicated one chance in three of the student's becoming an engineer, one in three of his entering a related occupation, and one in three of his entering an unrelated occupation. This, Cronbach [21] points out, is good predictive validity since a student may obtain several A's but can enter only one occupation.

[16] George K. Bennett, *Manual for the Differential Aptitude Tests*, 3d ed., p. 75. New York: The Psychological Corporation, 1959.

[17] E. L. Kelly and D. W. Fiske, *The Prediction of Performance in Clinical Psychology*. Ann Arbor, Mich.: University of Michigan Press, 1951.

[18] Lee J. Cronbach, *Essentials of Psychological Testing*, 2d ed., p. 427. New York: Harper & Row, Publishers, Incorporated, 1960.

[19] E. K. Strong, Jr., *Vocational Interests 18 Years after College*, chaps. 8–10. Minneapolis: The University of Minnesota Press, 1955.

[20] *Ibid.*, pp. 40–54.

[21] Cronbach, *op. cit.*, p. 423.

PERSONALITY MEASUREMENT

Measures of personality are often described as measures of typical performance because they disclose not what an individual can do but rather what he will do under certain conditions. Interest inventories are in a sense personality measures since they show the subject's preferences for particular types of activities, things, and people.

Personality measures may be roughly classed as (1) reports on the subject by others; (2) autobiographical and creative productions; (3) inventories and questionnaires answered by the subject; and (4) projective devices. Attention is not given here to the first two categories because they are dealt with in other chapters.

Projective Tests. In the projective test situation the subject responds freely to relatively unstructured stimuli. In doing so, he tends to structure the situation according to his own needs and thus unintentionally reveals some of his basic personality dynamics. The two best-known and probably most extensively used projective tests are the Rorschach [22] and Murray's Thematic Apperception Test.[23] In the Rorschach the subject is shown a series of inkblots and asked to tell what he sees in them. In the TAT he is shown a series of semistructured pictures and asked to make up stories about them. In other projective tests use is made of such unstructured or semistructured stimuli as drawings, toys, pictures of clouds, leaderless group discussion, modeling clay, finger paints, and incomplete sentences. Some psychologists find the projective techniques especially useful with young children and with individuals having language handicaps.

Most projective tests are complexly scored and interpreted, and some are very difficult to administer. To administer, score, and interpret them, a counselor needs comprehensive training of an advanced nature. Because projective tests are essentially clinical instruments, they should be employed only by counselors who have special training in their use, as well as broad training in counseling psychology.

One type of projective test, the open-end sentence,[24] is so easy to administer that it may be used by some workers who are not qualified to interpret the findings. A class group, for example, may be given sheets containing the beginnings of sentences and asked to complete the sen-

[22] Bruno Klopfer and D. M. Kelley, *The Rorschach Technique*. New York: Harcourt, Brace & World, Inc., 1942.

[23] H. A. Murray, *Thematic Apperception Test: Manual*. Cambridge, Mass.: Harvard University Press, 1943; H. A. Murray, "Thematic Apperception Test," in A. Weider (ed.), *Contributions toward Medical Psychology*, vol. II, pp. 636–649. New York: The Ronald Press Company, 1953.

[24] Amanda R. Rohde, *The Sentence Completion Method*. New York: The Ronald Press Company, 1957.

tences as rapidly as possible. Quick, spontaneous responses may be sought in the hope that the students will reveal attitudes, thoughts, and feelings which they might on second thought decide to withhold or disguise. The sheet might, for example, contain such items as the following:

I think that my father . . . .
When I am sad I . . . .
It makes me angry when . . . .
I like very much . . . .
I look forward to being grown-up because . . . .

Important information may be obtained on a student through the use of such a device. His responses may disclose some of his feelings toward himself and family members, his strong likes and dislikes, the sources of some of his joys, sorrows, anxieties, and so forth. In this type of personality test the student has some idea of the nature of the information that he is supplying and can avoid revelations that he does not wish to make. Hence, the open-end test may not be so hazardous as the TAT in the hands of an amateur; but it may be fully as hazardous if too much is read between the lines.

The scoring and interpretation of projective techniques are so highly subjective and their validity is so uncertain that some people doubt that they can be properly classed as tests. Others who see promise in them question their use in the school counseling program, at least for predictive purposes. Thorndike and Hagen,[25] for example, express their views as follows:

> In general, the conclusion on predictive validity at this time must apparently be that the Rorschach, and probably other projective tests, have some validity as predictors of psychiatric diagnoses, though just how much seems quite uncertain. For other practical criteria we must be more pessimistic. There appears to be no verified evidence that they have validity for any other practical outcome in the world of events.

Few high school counselors use projective tests like the Rorschach and the TAT because their functions do not include the making of psychiatric diagnoses. They do include, however, identifying students who may be in need of clinical help. For this purpose they ordinarily use such instruments as problem check lists and personality inventories.

Distortion of Responses. A student responds to a check list or inventory by checking an item or by indicating through underscoring or some other method that his answer is "Yes," "No," or "?" The validity of his responses depends largely on his ability to read or understand the items, his self-insight or ability to view himself objectively, and his willingness to answer truthfully. A subject may be able to read the item but may not understand it because of the abstractness or complexity of the concept in-

[25] Robert L. Thorndike and Elizabeth Hagen, *Measurement and Evaluation in Psychology and Education*, 2d ed., p. 439. New York: John Wiley & Sons, Inc., 1961.

olved. A student, for instance, who thinks of crises as things that lead to wars between nations or that create depressions may be uncertain regarding how he should mark the answer sheet for an item like "I shrink from facing a crisis." The addition of the words "or difficulty" may dissolve his confusion, or it may not.

The very length of a questionnaire may cause some students to lose interest and become bored as they grow weary. Even good readers run into difficulty with items employing very general or ambiguous terms. The item "I get angry easily" may, for example, be read differently by different students. To one "get angry" may mean to lose self-control; to another it may mean to experience annoyance or resentment. "Easily" may mean "often" to some, whereas to others it may be interpreted in terms of the amount of frustration that can be tolerated. Similarly, the item "I have strange and peculiar thoughts sometimes" may be to one boy an apt description of his daydreams of someday being a space traveler. To another it may seem to cover some of his thoughts regarding life and death, the present and the hereafter. To the author of the item it may have a wholly different meaning. The item can be read in different ways by different people.

Lack of self-insight may prevent a student from reporting his behavior, thoughts, and feelings correctly. Or response may be made in the light of a temporary situation or single incident rather than of typical behavior. A competent, self-confident girl, for instance, may mark "Yes" for the item "I am lacking in self-confidence" because she somewhat dreads being interviewed within a few days by a representative of the professional organization from which she is seeking a college scholarship.

The emotionally disturbed person finds it difficult to view himself objectively. A very shy girl may view her timidity as a lack of brashness and her withdrawing behavior as a becoming modesty. To live comfortably in her own skin, she may have to see herself thus. Moreover, she feels confirmed in this view if she hears her behavior so described by her overprotective parents. Even when self-insight is not lacking, dissatisfaction with self may cause responses to be distorted. The shy girl may actually see herself as others see her—shy, lacking in self-confidence, and withdrawn. She may be so unhappy with this picture that she wants others to see her differently. She selects her answers accordingly. The significance of such items as "I take an active part in social activities" and "I feel self-conscious when I have to recite before the class" seems so clear that she finds it very difficult not to fake her answers.

Distortion is not easy to control. Some inventory authors try to reduce it by wording items carefully and by placing constraint upon the responses through use of the forced-choice technique. The items from which a choice must be made are matched, for example, in terms of attractiveness or social desirability. Distortion is probably best controlled by administering the instrument in a permissive, nonthreatening situation. If a student feels that his responses will not be used against him in any way and if he sees the situation as giving him an opportunity to gain self-knowledge, he may want to give valid responses.

Problem Check Lists. Some inventories are in the form of check lists of problems. Perhaps the best-known and most widely used one is the Mooney Problem Check List (The Psychological Corporation). This inventory lists problems in 11 areas that include health and physical development, home and family, school or occupation, social and recreation, boy and girl relations, morals and religion, finances, etc. It is designed for use with students in grades 7 through 16 and with adults.

Two other inventories of individual student problems are the SRA Junior Inventory and the SRA Youth Inventory (Science Research Associates, Inc.). The first is designed for use with grades 4 through 8; and the second, for grades 7 through 12. They list problems, interests, and needs in social and emotional adjustment and in educational and vocational planning. Like the Junior Inventory, the revised Youth Inventory uses the strength-of-response method. If an item represents for the student "a big problem," he checks the largest of three response boxes. If it is a "middle-sized problem," he checks the middle-sized block, and he checks the smallest box if it is "a little problem." If it is "not a problem," he puts his check in a circle.

The Billet-Starr Youth Problems Inventory (Harcourt, Brace & World, Inc.) has two levels—one for grades 7 through 9 and the other for grades 11 and 12. They have 346 problems in common. The items are grouped into 11 areas, such as health, family life, school life, morality and religion, and boy-girl relations. The subject indicates whether an item represents one of his problems and, if so, whether it troubles him greatly or slightly.

These check lists are self-administering and furnish numerical scores. Scoring and profile analysis are, however, ordinarily not desirable. Examination of responses to particular items is generally more helpful than examination of the scores.

Check lists are useful for identifying some students who need or want help with their problems. They are even more useful as aids in preparing students for counseling or as springboards to discussions of personal problems in the group guidance or individual counseling situation. They help to focus talk on problems that the students are ready to discuss. Check lists are also valuable to the extent that they help teachers and counselors increase their understanding of the problems dealt with by students. Sometimes they disclose changes needed in particular school practices. They may show that some procedures, as well as some students, need to be singled out for special study.

Adjustment Inventories. Personality inventories are series of items that deal mainly with feelings about self, others, and environment; traits; interests; needs; adjustment; and overt behavior (acts of sympathy, aggression, etc.). A great many such scales are available today. The best of them provide qualified users with assistance in getting at aspects of personality and adjustment that are not easily and accurately observed. Thus they are helpful in locating students with adjustment problems, but their usefulness is limited by their uncertain validity. They have little predictive validity. Some show moderate concurrent validity in that they tend to separate normal people from the pathological. They may verify conclusions already reached on the basis of other evidence.

Most inventories yield part scores. Counselors need to guard against overinterpretation of these scores and should help students to avoid thinking that the subpart titles (dominance, sociability, responsibility, objectivity, etc.) are to be taken as well-defined, accurately measured personality characteristics and to be used accordingly in planning.

A "good" score cannot always be considered evidence of good adjustment. It may represent protective or defensive behavior on the part of a subject who cannot acknowledge or face his problems. A student who is aware of his difficulties and defects and is anxious that others not be aware of them too can obtain a good score by giving the "right" answers, which are clearly apparent in many instances. In this case a good score is evidence of a felt need to compensate for feelings of inferiority rather than evidence of good adjustment.

While a good score may not be indicative of good adjustment, a poor score is often evidence of maladjustment. Therefore, further study should be made of students who obtain unsatisfactory scores. However, not all will be found maladjusted. When a case does seem serious, referral should be made to a specialist qualified to use more refined diagnostic procedures and able to give the student, or to arrange for him to receive, the therapy indicated to be needed.

Unfortunately, some manuals of instructions for personality inventories encourage guidance workers to go beyond the limits of their training by suggesting the diagnosis and treatment of students shown by the tests to be cases of poorly integrated personality or persons with traits that might make for adjustment difficulties in certain situations. Most of the remedial suggestions offered are oversimplified. Some are of the pat-on-the-back-and-try-to-do-better type whereby the worker can pass the buck to the student by pointing out his flaws and then placing on his shoulders the burden of doing something about them. Teachers who follow such suggestions may not do the student any harm, but neither are they likely to do him any good. Some other recommendations offered in the manual-handbooks are inappropriate and may actually be dangerous. Teachers who follow them may do serious harm to some students. The advice given by Shaffer [26] in his review of one manual that offers recommendations for diagnosis and treatment may be good advice for readers of all such man-

[26] L. F. Shaffer, in Buros (ed.), *The Third Mental Measurements Yearbook*, p. 70.

uals to follow: "Those who have real professional training will not need a system. Those who lack psychological knowledge will help pupils more effectively by using simple human warmth and interest than by thumbing a handbook of oversimplified recipes."

Some Examples. Some personality inventories are in the form of preference records. Two examples are the Kuder Preference Record—Personal (Science Research Associates, Inc.) and the Edwards Personal Preference Record (The Psychological Corporation). In format the Kuder Personal Record is like the Kuder Vocational. From the three options offered in each item the student selects the one he likes best and the one he likes least. The options in each triad are designed to be equally desirable or attractive. The responses show preferences for engaging in personal and social activities, working with ideas, being active in groups, avoiding conflicts, directing others, and being in familiar and stable situations. This instrument is designed for use with high school and college students and adults.

The Edwards instrument is designed primarily for use in research and in the counseling of college students. It attempts to measure most of the manifest personality needs listed in Murray's *Explorations in Personality*.[27] Its scores are intended to show the relative importance of 14 key needs or motives—achievement, deference, order, exhibition, autonomy, affiliation, intraception, succorance, dominance, abasement, nurturance, change, endurance, and aggression. Each variable is paired twice with each of the others. There are 210 pairs in forced-choice format. The subject selects from each item the statement that is most characteristic of him. The options are matched in terms of social desirability to minimize any tendency to select face-saving or socially desirable responses.

The Gordon Personal Profile and the Gordon Personal Inventory (Harcourt, Brace & World, Inc.) are two short scales that can be used with grades 9 through 16 and adults. Each can be taken in fifteen minutes or less. The profile furnishes scores on ascendancy, responsibility, emotional stability, and sociability; the inventory, scores on cautiousness, original thinking, personal relations, and vigor. Both use the forced-choice technique. The subject selects from four phrases, two of which are complimentary and two uncomplimentary, the one that is most like him and the one that is least like him. An overall self-evaluation score may be obtained by totaling the number of items marked in a manner favorable to self.

The profile has been favorably received, largely for the following reasons: It is well constructed. Both internal and external validating procedures were used. The manual supplies better than average validity data, provides considerable research evidence, and offers conservative suggestions for interpretation. The reviewers do not accept, however, the manual

---

[27] Henry A. Murray et al., *Explorations in Personality*, pp. 144–145. New York: Oxford University Press, 1938.

statement that the profile can be used for meaningful interpretation of individual cases. The inventory was published three years after the profile. It has been less favorably received, largely because of the almost complete lack of validity data.

The Minnesota Multiphasic Personality Inventory (The Psychological Corporation) is the most workmanlike, elaborate, and thoroughly researched adjustment inventory developed to date. It is a refinement of the inventory technique and is commonly considered an improvement over other tests of its type. It is designed for use with abnormal subjects and for use in clinics rather than in schools and colleges. It has two forms, one for individual administration and one for group administration. Both are applicable to late adolescents and adults.

This instrument was constructed in an empirical manner similar to that used with the Strong Vocational Interest Blanks. In clinical work it is looked upon with as much respect as is the SVIB. It is not, however, the useful counseling tool that the SVIB is.

The MMPI contains over five hundred items that are answered with "T," "F," and "?" It yields scores on ten personality traits or patterns: hypochondriasis (excessive concern with bodily functions); depression (tendency to feel chronically depressed); hysteria (tendency to solve problems through physical symptoms, such as intestinal complaints, cramps, cardiac symptoms, etc.); psychopathic deviate (disregard for social pressures, lack of regard for others, inability to profit from experience, lack of deep emotional response); masculinity-femininity (interests characteristic of one sex or the other); paranoia (tendency to be oversensitive, suspicious, and to feel persecuted); psychasthenia (excessive fears or compulsive tendencies in thinking and acting); schizophrenia (tendency toward bizarre thought and behavior and tendency toward a private life not in harmony with reality); hypomania (tendency to overact and to flit from one thing to another); and social introversion (tendency to withdraw from social participation).

In addition there are four verification scales that yield scores labeled "?," "L," "F," and "K" scores. The ? or question score is the total number of items to which the subject responds with "?" The L or lie score is based upon a group of items that put the subject in a favorable light but which are normally not truthfully answered in the favorable direction. The F or validity score is based upon a group of items that were infrequently answered by the standardization group in the direction scored by the subject. A high F score indicates errors in scoring or carelessness, eccentricity, or deliberate malingering on the part of the subject. The K or correction score is based upon a group of particular items. A high K score indicates defensiveness or faking in a direction favorable to self. A low K score indicates excessive frankness and self-criticism or a deliberate attempt to give responses discreditable to self.

The amount of research carried out on the MMPI is voluminous.

It shows the instrument to be more valuable as a screening device than the average personality inventory but throws doubt on its validity or usefulness for individual diagnosis. The scoring and interpreting of the MMPI are intricate, elaborate, and time-consuming. For screening school and college students a simpler, shorter instrument is preferred. In the opinion of some reviewers, to use as detailed an inventory as the MMPI for such purpose is to send a man to do a boy's work. The MMPI may be profitably used after the rough screening has been done with some less elaborate instrument.

It should not, however, be used by counselors who do not have the advanced training in personality theory and appraisal needed for its proper use. Because administration is relatively easy, the MMPI has been adopted by some who have little understanding of the instrument and its interpretation. In their naïve interpretation of the scores, some users are mental health hazards to the students to whom they give the test. They seriously disturb students with their pseudoscientific talk of schizophrenia, paranoia, phobias, obsessions, and the like. They do not always heed the caution contained in the manual: "It should be continually kept in mind that the great majority of persons having deviant profiles are not, in the usual sense of the word, mentally ill, nor are they in need of psychological treatment. Having no more information about a person than that he has a deviant profile, one should always start with the assumption that the subject is operating within the normal range." [28]

The construction of other personality inventories has been strongly influenced by the MMPI. For example, the California Psychological Inventory (Consulting Psychologists Press) and the Minnesota Counseling Inventory (The Psychological Corporation) are derived largely from the MMPI. The CPI resembles the MMPI in contents and in the use of control scales. It contains 480 true-false items, 200 of which are adaptations of MMPI items. This test measures principally attitudes, interests, and traits that are considered important for effective social interaction, such as tolerance, flexibility, sociability, achievement via conformity, achievement via independence, and self-control. Eleven of the 18 scales are based on such external criteria as course marks, participation in extracurricular activities, prominence as a leader, and ratings for specific traits. Scores are recorded on an elaborate profile that is difficult to interpret because of the highly subjective procedures to be followed.

The CPI has been criticized because of its redundancy and the high correlations between many of its scales. It is also criticized because it uses value-loaded terms that may foster the idea of there being only one ideal personality. Cronbach,[29] for example, writes as follows:

[28] Reproduced by permission of the Psychological Corporation from the Manual for the *Minnesota Multi-phasic Personality Inventory*, p. 24. Copyright, 1943, 1951. The University of Minnesota. All rights reserved.

[29] Lee J. Cronbach, in O. K. Buros (ed.), *The Fifth Mental Measurements Yearbook*, pp. 98–99. Highland Park, N.J.: The Gryphon Press, 1959.

Such scale titles as Responsibility, Tolerance, and Socialization have a pronounced ethical overtone which suggests that low scores reflect faults, rather than symptoms of needs, skills, and cultural pressures. Because of this implicit conflict with modern views of personality, it would be deplorable if CPI profiles were interpreted by principals, teachers, parents, or students without guidance from a psychologically-trained person.... Further research may prove that the CPI patterns are richly significant. The reviewer's prejudices, however, lead him to prefer profiles describing the individual in psychological terms to profiles defined around complex social resultants, such as disciplinary problems, presence in numerous school activities, and high grades.

The Minnesota Counseling Inventory (The Psychological Corporation) contains 355 true-false items, many of which are reworded MMPI items. It gives nine scores, two of which are verification scores that check the subject's test-taking attitude. Three scores (family relations, social relations, and emotional stability) are intended to indicate areas in which the subject is making very good or very poor adjustment. The other four scores (conformity, adjustment to reality, mood, and leadership) are intended to show characteristic behavior in social groups and characteristic ways of meeting problems. The intercorrelations between the scales are substantial.

The MCI provides separate norms for boys and girls at two levels —grades 9 and 10 and grades 11 and 12. The manual gives explicit but conservative suggestions for interpretation. This instrument is classified by one reviewer [30] as "a serviceable instrument for counselors whose knowledge of test construction permits them to be aware of its limitations."

SUMMARY

A person's interests are determined by genetic factors, such as intelligence and endocrine balance, and personal-social-cultural learning. During childhood they tend to change with change in age. During adolescence, however, the process is more one of development, clarification, and elaboration than one of change. By adolescence a person's interests begin to resemble those of adults and are sufficiently stable to permit him to choose between broad fields of training.

Vocational choice is a dynamic process that continues throughout a person's career. Interest is only one factor determining the decisions involved in the choice process. Hence, in vocational counseling, interest data need to be supplemented with information regarding the subject's abilities and training opportunities. Interest is no substitute for ability, but ability without interest can mean limited job satisfaction.

The two most adequately validated and probably most widely used instruments for appraising vocational interests are the Strong Vocational

[30] Laurance F. Shaffer, in Buros (ed.), *The Fifth Mental Measurements Yearbook*, p. 158.

Interest Blanks and the Kuder Preference Record—Vocational. They measure approximately the same types of interests. The SVIB reveals interest patterns that distinguish specific occupations (largely business and professional). The Kuder identifies relative interest in ten broad areas. In taking the SVIB, the subject is free to impose his own standards, whereas, in taking the Kuder, he finds his freedom restricted by the forced-choice technique. Both instruments are sufficiently reliable for use with high school students. Faking is possible on both, but there is little reason for anticipating intentional faking when an interest inventory is used for guidance or counseling purposes.

Personality inventories are less useful than interest inventories as techniques for appraisal in counseling. There are hundreds of personality inventories currently available, the best of which have some value for identifying cases in need of special study and for bringing out leads to be explored in the group guidance or counseling situation.

Adjustment inventories should not be administered indiscriminately to all students. Teachers and counselors with limited training should use check lists like the Mooney and SRA instruments or simple descriptive inventories like the Kuder Personal. Only counselors with comprehensive training should use evaluative instruments like the Gordon Profile and the Minnesota Counseling Inventory. The Minnesota Multiphasic Personality Inventory is a clinical instrument. In general, its use by high school counselors is inappropriate.

The manuals for some inventories, such as the MCI, contain useful suggestions for interpretation and cautions against improper use. Some other manuals offer recommendations regarding individual diagnoses that are psychologically unsound. Unfortunately, not all counselors are prepared to distinguish the sound from the unsound.

Adequate validity has not yet been demonstrated for the personality inventories currently available for use by student personnel workers with no more than the basic training in counseling and personality theory. Some of the inventories seem to have substantial potential value, but all need further validation study to determine their practical usefulness in the counseling of students.

REFERENCES

Anastasi, Anne: *Psychological Testing*, 2d ed., part IV. New York: The Macmillan Company, 1961.

Cattell, Raymond B.: "What Is 'Objective' in Objective Personality Tests?" *Journal of Counseling Psychology*, 1958, 5:285–289.

Cronbach, Lee J.: *Essentials of Psychological Testing*, 2d ed., part III. New York: Harper & Row, Publishers, Incorporated, 1960.

Darley, John G., and Theda Hagenah: *Vocational Interest Measurement: Theory and Practice*. Minneapolis: The University of Minnesota Press, 1955.

Froehlich, C. P., and K. B. Hoyt: *Guidance Testing*, chaps. 9–10. Chicago: Science Research Associates, Inc., 1959.

Horst, Paul: "How Much Information on Test Results Should Be Given to Students: Views of a Research Psychologist," *Journal of Counseling Psychology*, 1959, 6:218–222.

Layton, Wilbur L.: *Counseling Use of the Strong Vocational Interest Blanks*. Minneapolis: The University of Minnesota Press, 1958.

Nachmann, Barbara: "Childhood Experience and Vocational Choice in Law, Dentistry, and Social Work," *Journal of Counseling Psychology*, 1960, 7:243–250.

Roe, Anne: "Early Determinants of Vocational Choice," *Journal of Counseling Psychology*, 1957, 4:212–217.

Rothney, John W. M., et al.: *Measurement for Guidance*, chap. 8. New York: Harper & Row, Publishers, Incorporated, 1959.

Singer, Stanley L., et al.: "Temperament Scores and Socioeconomic Status," *Journal of Counseling Psychology*, 1958, 5:281–284.

Stewart, Lawrence H.: "Interest Patterns of a Group of High Ability, High Achieving Students," *Journal of Counseling Psychology*, 1959, 6:132–139.

————: " 'Occupational Level' Scale of Children's Interests," *Educational and Psychological Measurement*, 1959, 19:401–410.

Stordahl, K. E.: "Permanence of Interests and Interest Maturity," *Journal of Applied Psychology*, 1954, 38:339–341.

Strong, E. K., Jr.: *Vocational Interests of Men and Women*. Stanford, Calif.: Stanford University Press, 1943.

————: *Vocational Interests 18 Years after College*. Minneapolis: The University of Minnesota Press, 1955.

Super, Donald E.: "Career Patterns as a Basis for Vocational Counseling," *Journal of Counseling Psychology*, 1954, 1:12–20.

———— et al.: *Vocational Development: A Framework for Research*. New York: Bureau of Publications, Teachers College, Columbia University, 1957.

———— and John O. Crites: *Appraising Vocational Fitness by Means of Psychological Tests*, rev. ed., chaps. 16–19. New York: Harper & Row, Publishers, Incorporated, 1962.

———— and Phoebe L. Overstreet: *The Vocational Maturity of Ninth-grade Boys*. New York: Bureau of Publications, Teachers College, Columbia University, 1960.

Thorndike, Robert L., and Elizabeth Hagen: *Measurement and Evaluation in Psychology and Education*, 2d ed., chaps. 12–13, 16. New York: John Wiley & Sons, Inc., 1961.

Tyler, Leona E.: "Development of 'Vocational Interests': The Organization of Likes and Dislikes in Ten-year-old Children," *Journal of Genetic Psychology*, 1955, 86:33–44.

Ullmann, Charles A.: "Teachers, Peers, and Tests as Predictors of Adjustment," *Journal of Educational Psychology*, 1957, 48:257–267.

7

Reporting and Interpreting Test Data

In general, test findings should be reported to students, teachers, and parents. The students are often the last persons informed of the results, whereas they should be among the first. Early in the development of school testing programs, certain leaders of the movement stressed the importance of sharing test data with students. Thorndike,[1] for example, stated that "the final justification for every testing regime rests in Mary Jones and John Smith, and it therefore behooves all persons who are making and giving tests to take them into partnership as soon and as completely as it is feasible."

The results are reported most often in the form of numerical scores, which many people do not know how to interpret correctly. The nonexpert is likely to interpret the scores too specifically or precisely.

PRECISE INTERPRETATION RARELY POSSIBLE

As stressed in an earlier chapter, a score is properly viewed as a range or band and not as a point. The width of the band is determined by the standard error of measurement, which shows the amount of fluctuation to be expected. For example, the standard error of the DAT mechanical reasoning scale for twelfth-grade boys is 4.8. If a senior boy attains a raw score of 44 in mechanical reasoning, the raw score band extends from 39 to 49. When these raw scores are converted into percentile scores, the band extends from the 25th to the 55th percentile. Here the counselor cannot say with certainty whether the test shows the boy to be average or low average in mechanical reasoning.

Percentiles throughout the middle range of the percentile distribution are more affected by the standard error than are those at either extreme of the scale. With many tests the standard error corresponds to 20 or more points in the middle of the percentile scale, and so there can be little certainty regarding the meaning of the score. Scores at the extremes of the scale are more meaningful. Had the senior boy, for example, made

[1] E. L. Thorndike, "Tests and Their Uses," *Teachers College Record*, 1924, 26:94.

a raw score of 65, the raw score range would be 60 to 70, which is a percentile score range of 95 to 99. The counselor would feel reasonably safe in assuming that the boy is high in mechanical reasoning ability.

The lower the reliability coefficient of a test or the higher its standard error, the more general must be the interpretation of the scores. If the test is of low reliability, the counselor can report only in very general terms, such as "about average" and "above average" or "below average." If the reliability is .90 or higher, he can use more specific terms, such as "high" or "very high" and "low" or "very low."

As Tyler [2] stresses, it is not sound counseling practice to tell a student who is at the 40th percentile on one test and at the 60th on another that he is below average on the first and above average on the second. The counselor does not know in which direction the chance errors have influ-

STANINE LEVEL	PERCENTAGE OF CASES	INTERPRETATION
9	4	High (4%)
8	7	Above average (19%)
7	12	
6	17	Average (54%)
5	20	
4	17	
3	12	Below average (19%)
2	7	
1	4	Low (4%)

FIGURE 8   *Meaning of stanines.*

enced the scores. They may have operated to bring down the first score and to bring up the second one. The only thing that the counselor can safely report is that the student is within the average range with respect to both traits or abilities. Similarly, in interpreting a percentile rank of 65 or one of 35, he cannot report anything more specific than that the score shows the student to be within the average range with respect to the ability measured.

Diagrams, such as the one shown in Figure 8, help teachers and counselors avoid the error of overspecificity and help them describe nu-

[2] Leona E. Tyler, *The Work of the Counselor*, 2d ed., pp. 114–115. New York: Appleton-Century-Crofts, Inc., 1961.

NAME CALDWELL, JOHN **BIRTHDATE** 2-14-33

YEAR	1944-1945	1945-1946	1946-1947	1947-1948	1948-1949	1949-1950
SCHOOL	MIDDLE RANCH		ESSEX PREPARATORY			
GRADE	7 7	8 8	9 9	10 10	11 11	12
MENTAL AGE	17-4	20-0				
CHRON. AGE	12	13	14	15	16	17

SUBJECTS, GRADES AND CREDITS

1944-1945

SUBJECT	FINAL
ENGLISH	C
ARITHMETIC	B+
SCIENCE	A
GEOG.	C
HISTORY	D

1945-1946

SUBJECT	FINAL	2ND SEM. FINAL
ENGLISH	C	
BEG. FRENCH		B
ARITHMETIC	A	
SCIENCE	B+	
SOC. ST.	B	

1946-1947

SUBJECT	FINAL
ENGLISH	B
FRENCH	B
LATIN	C-
ELEM. ALG.	A
BIOLOGY	B

1947-1948

SUBJECT	FINAL
ENGLISH	C+
FRENCH	C+
LATIN	B
INT. ALG.	B

1948-1949

SUBJECT	1ST SEM. FINAL	2ND SEM. FINAL
ENGLISH	C	C+
FRENCH	C+	B
PL. GEOM.	A	A
PHYSICS	A	A+
MOD. HIST.	C	C

1949-1950

SUBJECT	1ST SEM. FINAL
ENGLISH	C
FRENCH	B
TRIG.	A+
CHEM. (HONORS) (REVIEW)	A
AMER. HIST.	B

ACADEMIC APTITUDE

Year	TEST	SCORE M. A.	I. Q.	%ile
1944-1945	KUHLMANN-ANDERSON	17-4	149	91 / 95
1945-1946	KUHLMANN-ANDERSON	20-0	158	94 / 96
1946-1947	AMER. COUNCIL PSYCH. 1946 TOT.	108		87
	Q-SCORE	58		99
	L-SCORE	50		51
1947-1948	AMER. COUNCIL PSYCH. 1947 TOT.	115		78
	Q-SCORE	60		97
	L-SCORE	55		46
1948-1949	AMER. COUNCIL PSYCH. 1948 TOT.	135		86
	Q-SCORE	67		99
	L-SCORE	68		56
1949-1950	AMER. COUNCIL PSYCH. 1949 TOT.	156		95
	Q-SCORE	71		100
	L-SCORE	85		74

ACHIEVEMENT TEST SCORES AND PERCENTILES

1944-1945

TEST	SCORE E. A.	%ile
MET. ACH. ADV. C. TOT.	9.2	58
AV. READ.	9.7	65
AV. ARITH.	9.7	78
ENG.	9.3	64
LIT.	7.3	5
HIST.-CIV.	8.1	20
GEOG.	9.7	69
SPELL.	9.8	98

1945-1946

TEST	SCORE E. A.	%ile
MET. ACH. ADV. D. TOT.	10.2	75
AV. READ.	10.7	80
AV. ARITH.	10.4	88
ENG.	10.6	87
LIT.	8.4	7
HIST.-CIV.	10.7	71
GEOG.	9.1	40
SPELL.	10.6	96

1946-1947

TEST	SCORE E. A.	%ile
ENG. COOP. R		
A-MECH. OF EXP.	71	99
C1-READ. COMPR.	55	55
FR. COOP. Q ELEM. (GR. 9 1 YR.)	57	90
LAT. COOP. Q-ELEM. (ERB 1 YR.)	52	56
ELEM. ALG.-COOP. Q	72	88
BIOL. COOP. ERB-S	76 (RAW)	68

1947-1948

TEST	SCORE E. A.	%ile
ENG. COOP. S-TOT.	66	90
A-MECH. OF EXP.	68	95
B2-EFF. OF EXP.	66	90
C2-READ. COMPR.	61	72
FR. COOP. X-HIGH. SUB. TOT. (GR. 10 2 YRS.)	73	87
LAT. COOP. Y-HIGH. SUB. TOT. (GR. 10 2 YRS.)	64	90
INT. ALG. COOP. S	64	71

1948-1949

TEST	SCORE E. A.	%ile
ENG. COOP. Y-TOT.	68	88
A-MECH. OF EXP.	68	94
B2-EFF. OF EXP.	68	89
C2-READ. COMPR.	66	79
FR. COOP. S-HIGH. SUB. TOT. (GR. 11 3 YRS.)	86	93
PL. GEOM.-COOP. Y	72	95
PHYS. COOP. ERB-SX	56 (RAW)	86

FIGURE 9 *Filled-in portion of the ERB Cumulative Record Card.* (Arthur E. Traxler et al., *Introduction to Testing and the Use of Test Results in Public Schools,* p. 82. New York: Harper & Row, Publishers, Incorporated, 1953. Reproduced by permission of the publisher.)

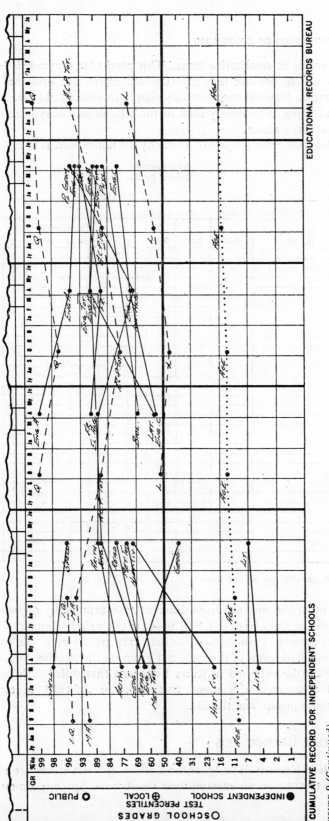

FIGURE 9 (*Continued*)

merical scores in qualitative terms. This particular diagram is based on stanines which, because they are standard scores, are preferred to percentile ranks. Stanines are relatively simple to understand and to apply. They are being increasingly used in the schools and may eventually replace percentile scores.

Another error frequently made by the nonexperts is to expect close

TEST RECORD
(Name of School)

Student _____ Date of birth _____

Date	Test name and form	Norm	Score	%ile	Percentile rank scale										
					0	10	20	30	40	50	60	70	80	90	100

FIGURE 10   *Sample test record form.*

agreement in the findings from different tests supposedly measuring the same abilities. Data from different tests are not strictly comparable. They may vary greatly. A student's scores may vary greatly even when they are from equivalent forms of the same test given on consecutive days. Greater variance can be expected in scores from tests that differ with respect to error of measurement, content, complexity or difficulty of tasks, test length, norm group, and the like.

SOME GRAPHIC AIDS

Cumulative Records. The manner in which the test scores are recorded can help teachers to understand their significance. Space is almost always provided on the cumulative record form for a tabulation of test data. Sometimes an analysis chart is also included. A chart that can be read easily and quickly helps to show the quality, amount, and consistency of the student's progress. When, however, the profile is crowded into too small a space, the record user finds it difficult to decipher explanatory phrases that are necessarily written in very small letters or to extricate quickly from the network of lines the information that he is seeking. Figure 9 illustrates the type of record that provides for both an analysis chart and a list of scores.

When blank cumulative folders are used instead of cards or printed folders, the test record should be kept on a separate form that is filed in the folder. Desirably the form should provide for both profile and tabulated entries. Even though the same information is given on the profile, the tabulated entries should be used for the sake of accuracy. To reduce clerical work, the titles of tests used regularly with all or most students may be printed or mimeographed on the form. The tests should be grouped according to type (scholastic aptitude, achievement, etc.), and sufficient space should be provided for adding data on other tests administered to some students only. If the form is to cover a three- or four-year period during which many tests are to be used, one side of the form may be used for reporting scholastic aptitude and achievement test data and the reverse side for reporting results from interest inventories and other types of tests. The use of both sides of one sheet or card will probably prove more convenient than the use of two sheets or cards. Figure 10 illustrates the general form for this type of test record.

Individual Test Profiles. To facilitate interpretation of test data, some publishers provide profile forms for tests that yield two or more scores. In some schools these forms are completed and filed in the students' cumulative folders. In some others they are sent to the stu-

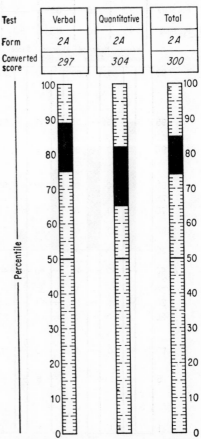

Test	Verbal	Quantitative	Total
Form	2A	2A	2A
Converted score	297	304	300

FIGURE 11 *School and College Ability Tests profile.* (Form reproduced by permission of the Educational Testing Service.)

dents' advisers or counselors, who file them in supplementary folders maintained for counseling purposes.

Figures 11 and 12 show two forms that have proved useful for helping both teachers and students to understand test results. The SCAT, as noted earlier, uses percentile bands instead of single scores. This not only helps the user to perceive the score as an estimate rather than an exact measure but also helps him to compare correctly the student's standings in the two abilities measured. If the bands overlap, there is no important difference. There is, for example, no important difference in the quantitative and verbal standings of the student whose profile is shown in Figure 11. The bands overlap.

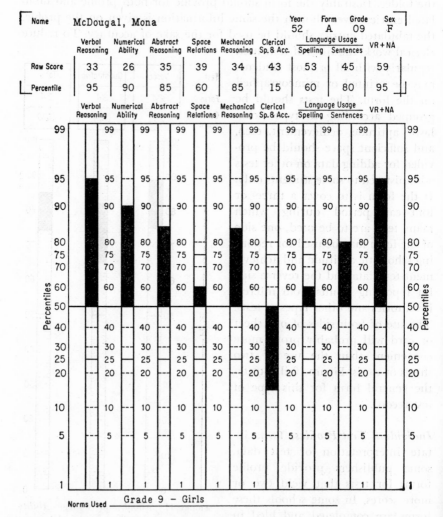

Name	McDougal, Mona								Year 52	Form A	Grade 09	Sex F
	Verbal Reasoning	Numerical Ability	Abstract Reasoning	Space Relations	Mechanical Reasoning	Clerical Sp. & Acc.	Language Usage Spelling	Sentences	VR + NA			
Raw Score	33	26	35	39	34	43	53	45	59			
Percentile	95	90	85	60	85	15	60	80	95			

Norms Used ____ Grade 9 – Girls

FIGURE 12   *Differential Aptitude Tests profile.* (G. K. Bennett et al., *Manual for the Differential Aptitude Tests,* 3d ed., p. 22. New York: The Psychological Corporation, 1959. Reproduced by permission of the Psychological Corporation.)

In the DAT Individual Report Form, shown in Figure 12, the bars are drawn upward and downward from the most meaningful reference point—the median. This profile permits the reader to note almost at a glance whether the subject's abilities are at about the same level or are highly differential. The form is so designed that in unreduced size, if the vertical distance between two scores is an inch or more, there is most likely a real difference in the scores. If the distance is between a half inch and one inch, the difference may or may not be important.

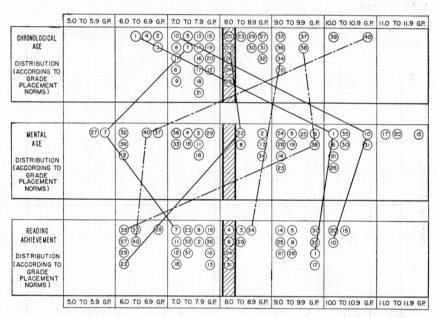

FIGURE 13 *Forty pupils, eighth grade.* (From a research report by Dr. Esther Grace Nolan. Reproduced by permission of the author and the Los Angeles County Superintendent of Schools.)

The profile in Figure 12 shows the clerical score to be significantly lower than all other scores and the verbal reasoning score to be significantly higher than the space relations, clerical, and spelling scores. The differences between the other scores are of uncertain importance. This profile shows the subject to be above average or high in verbal reasoning and numerical ability; average or better in abstract reasoning, mechanical reasoning, and sentences; average in space relations and spelling; and below average in clerical speed and accuracy.

Scattergrams. For showing the distribution of test scores, grade point averages, and the like for a particular group, scattergrams are more effective than lists or individual profiles. Figure 13, for example, shows how 40 eighth-grade students differ with regard to chronological age, mental age, and reading achievement. In each of the three sections of the diagram the 40 students are represented by circled numbers. Lines connect the circles that represent particular students to call attention to the differences in their three positions. Student number 10, for example, is in the first semester of the seventh grade on the basis of chronological age, in the second semester of the tenth grade on the basis of mental age, and in the first semester of the tenth grade on the basis of reading achievement. As is often the case, the youngest student (number 1) has a high grade placement for mental age and reading achievement, whereas the oldest student (number 40) has a low grade placement for mental age and reading achievement.

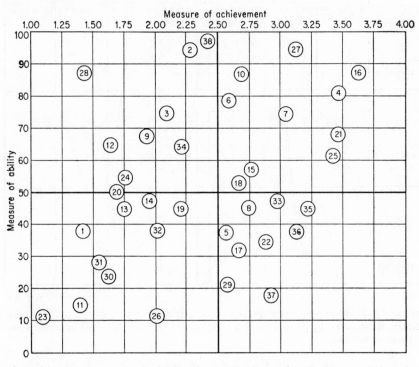

FIGURE 14   Scattergram. The measure of achievement is in terms of grade point averages for the semester. The measure of ability is in terms of percentile ranks on a scholastic aptitude test. The medians are for the total group of which the 38 students are a part.

Figure 14 shows another type of scattergram that reveals individual differences in ability and achievement among the members of a group and the relationship between ability and achievement for individuals. The circled numbers represent 38 students. The vertical scale shows percentile ranks on a scholastic aptitude test, and the horizontal scale shows grade point averages. The grade of A is given a value of 4.00, B a value of 3.00, C a value of 2.00, and D a value of 1.00. The scattergram shows, for example, that student number 24 has a percentile rank of 55 on the scholastic aptitude test and a grade point average of 1.75 for the semester.

The students in the upper right-hand quadrant are above average in both ability and achievement. Not all these students, however, are achieving to expectancy. Student number 10, for example, ranks higher in ability than in achievement. Nevertheless, we cannot conclude on the basis of the scattergram evidence alone that the students who are not achieving to expectancy should be expected to do better than they are now doing. The discrepancy between ability and achievement may not be due to lack of interest and effort. Moreover, some students who are doing very well should probably be encouraged not to do so well. Likewise, some who can do better should not be encouraged to do so. Student number 10, for example, may have to work after school and on weekends in order to help meet family expenses. To do better in school, he may have to devote to study some of the time now being given to sleep or to recreation.

Student number 27 is doing all right in school although he can apparently do much better. Some of his teachers may feel that he should be urged to seek grades of A. Others, better informed about this student's out-of-school life, may know that he has a number of interests of special value in terms of self-education and enrichment of personality. To make grades of A, he will have to give up certain hobbies and special activities. Some of his teachers may not believe A grades sufficiently important to warrant the sacrifice. Student number 25 is doing better in his schoolwork than student number 27. This may be good or not good. Numbers 25 and 35 may be giving too much time to schoolwork and too little time to socializing and to meeting such health needs as rest, sleep, and exercise.

The students in the upper left-hand quadrant are apparently not working to capacity, for they are not achieving to expectancy. Instead, however, of concluding promptly that these students are lazy and trying to decide the best way to jack them up, their teachers should delay conclusions and decisions until they analyze and diagnose these cases. These students are high in ability. They are definitely worth saving and should not be driven from school by pressure being brought to bear on them at a time when some may already be too hard-pressed. A study of these cases may show lack of interest and of effort to be the reason for low achievement on the part of some. In other cases it may show the reasons to be too heavy a program of study; excessive participation in extracurricular activities with the result of too little time and energy for classwork; lack of study time outside of school because of part-time employment, home responsibilities, or the like; poor background in the way of training for certain courses; bad health; unhappiness caused by personal or social maladjustment or worry over home problems; restlessness created by too much regimentation or other disliked conditions in the school, by indecision regarding vocational plans, by a future made insecure and uncertain by world conditions; or other causes.

The students in the lower right-hand quadrant, such as numbers 29 and 37, are achieving beyond expectancy. They may really be more able than the test scores indicate. The test results may be incorrect because of errors in scoring or recording or because the students were not in good "testing condition" the day they took the test. If a retest shows that the results of the first test are apparently correct, these students should also be made the subjects of special study. The study may show that high interest, well-organized efforts, and good study habits are helping to offset limitations in ability. Or it may show that the students are devoting too much time to schoolwork and too little time to recreation and other health needs.

Some students in the lower left-hand quadrant are low in both ability and achievement. The lack of achievement may be due to lack of interest and effort as well as to lack of ability. It may also be due to unhappiness and discouragement produced by inappropriate programs of study and inadequate instruction. Also, of course, it may be due to some of the same reasons considered above as the possible reasons for lack of achievement on the part of others who are more able than are these students.

The test scores and the grade averages may show what students can do and are doing, but they do not show why some students are not doing so well as expected. To get at the real causes and to secure correction of undesirable conditions, the teachers and counselors will need to observe the students, to interview them, to hold conferences about them, and, perhaps, to make extensive case studies of them.

Expectancy Tables. In expectancy tables test data are combined with data on subsequent performance to form experience tables like the one presented in Figure 15b. It provides a more definite explanation than can be given by lists. A counselor does not need much knowledge of statistics to construct an expectancy table. The simple steps involved are shown in Figures 15a and 15b, taken from an article by Wesman.

Figure 15a shows a grid along one side of which the test scores are indicated. The criterion-of-success data (scores in a rhetoric course) are shown along the top. A tally is placed for each student in the cell that shows vertically his test score and horizontally his criterion score. The student who obtained a DAT Sentences score of 62 and a rhetoric mark of B is tallied in the bold-outlined cell. The number in the right-hand corner of each cell represents the total number tallied in that cell. At the right of each row is recorded the total number tallied in that row and at the bottom of each column the total number tallied in that column.

In the left-hand half of Figure 15b the grid data are presented in organized form. In the right-hand half the frequency for each cell is converted into a per cent on the basis of the total number tallied in that row. The resulting expectancy table enables the user to answer with a reasonable degree of certainty such a question as "What is the probability that the student with a score of 65 will succeed in the rhetoric course?"

Grades in rhetoric

Scores on DAT sentence test	F	D	C	B	A	Totals
80-89					/ (1)	1
70-79				/ (1)	//// (4)	5
60-69			/// (3)	HH HH //// (14)	HH (5)	22
50-59			HH //// (9)	HH /// (8)	HH / (6)	23
40-49		/// (3)	HH HH /// (13)	HH / (6)		22
30-39	/ (1)	/// (3)	HH //// (9)	/// (3)		16
20-29	/ (1)	//// (4)	/// (3)			8
10-19		// (2)				2
0-9		/ (1)				1
	2	13	37	32	16	100

FIGURE 15a *Grid showing how students' marks in rhetoric and previously earned scores on DAT Sentence Test are tallied in the appropriate cells.* (A. G. Wesman, *Expectancy Tables: A Way of Interpreting Test Validity,* Test Service Bulletin no. 38. New York: The Psychological Corporation, 1949. Reproduced by permission of the publisher.)

Total No.	Number receiving each grade					Test scores	Per cent receiving each grade					Total per cent
	F	D	C	B	A		F	D	C	B	A	
1					1	80-89					100	100
5				1	4	70-79				20	80	100
22			3	14	5	60-69			14	63	23	100
23			9	8	6	50-59			39	35	26	100
22		3	13	6		40-49		14	59	27		100
16	1	3	9	3		30-39	6	19	56	19		100
8	1	4	3			20-29	13	50	37			100
2		2				10-19		100				100
1		1				0-9		100				100
100	2	13	37	32	16							

FIGURE 15b *Left-hand side shows frequencies that appear in the grid shown in Fig. 15a. The right-hand side shows these frequencies converted into per cents.* (A. G. Wesman, *Expectancy Tables: A Way of Interpreting Test Validity,* Test Service Bulletin no. 38. New York: The Psychological Corporation, 1949. Reproduced by permission of the publisher.)

The table then reads: of the 22 freshman girls who took a course in Rhetoric and had scored between 60 and 69 on the Sentences test, 23% (5 girls) earned a grade of A, 63% (14 girls) earned a B, and 14% (3 girls) earned a C. Not one of the girls whose score was in this group received a grade lower than C in Rhetoric. One might predict then that girls who take this course in future terms, and who have attained scores of 60 to 69 on the DAT Sentences test, will probably be better than average students, since all but 14% earned grades of A and B. Interpretations may be made in the same way for other test scores and individuals.[3]

McCabe [4] has reported the use made of expectancy tables in one high school for helping students to understand the predictive validity of test data. The scores earned by a group of students on the Terman-Mc-Nemar Test of Mental Ability were combined with the grade point averages earned by these students later as freshmen at the state university. Separate expectancy tables in the form of graphs were prepared for the students whose IQ scores fell within the three ranges of 100 to 120, 121 to 140, and above 140. Mimeographed copies were then given to the students currently enrolled in the school and planning to attend the state university. The graphs are reproduced in Figures 16a, 16b, and 16c.

A student did not receive copies of all three expectancy tables. He received only the graph for former students whose Terman-McNemar scores were similar to his. Also, the graphs did not show the range of test scores, as is done in the copies reproduced here. The counselors considered it best to omit this information from the students' copies because of certain common misconceptions regarding the IQ which are held by many students and parents. Information about high school grade point averages was also omitted from Graph I because no relationship was found between high school marks and subsequent college grade point averages for students in its IQ range. The high school students were told that the graphs do not apply to other colleges or universities.

According to McCabe, preparing the graphs was not costly. The data were already in the files because the state university regularly reports grades to the freshmen's high schools. Only about ten hours of work were needed to prepare the graphs. In Georgia the counselors have this work done for them and for practically all colleges in the state. In 1959 the regents of the state's university system published the first issue of a *Counselor's Guide*,[5] which was followed two years later by a *Supplement*.[6] These two publications enable a counselor to estimate a high school stu-

[3] Alexander G. Wesman, *Expectancy Tables: A Way of Interpreting Test Validity,* Test Service Bulletin no. 38. New York: The Psychological Corporation, 1949.

[4] George E. McCabe, "Test Interpretation in the High School Guidance Program," *Personnel and Guidance Journal,* 1957, 35:449–451.

[5] John R. Hills et al., *Counselor's Guide to Georgia Colleges.* Atlanta: Regents of the University System of Georgia, 1959.

[6] John R. Hills et al., *Supplement: Counselor's Guide to Georgia Colleges.* Atlanta: Regents of the University System of Georgia, 1961.

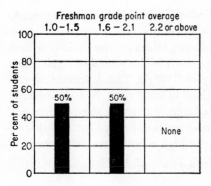

FIGURE 16*a* *Graph I for students whose IQ's were in the 100–120 range.* (G. E. McCabe, "Test Interpretation in the High School Guidance Program," *Personnel and Guidance Journal,* 1957, 35:450. Reproduced by permission of the publisher.)

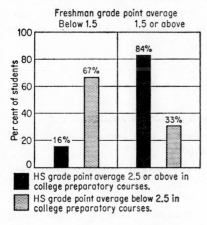

FIGURE 16*b* *Graph II for students whose IQ's were in the 121–140 range.* (G. E. McCabe, "Test Interpretation in the High School Guidance Program," *Personnel and Guidance Journal,* 1957, 35:450. Reproduced by permission of the publisher.)

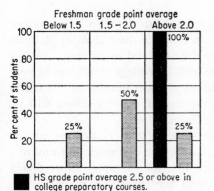

FIGURE 16*c* *Graph III for students whose IQ's were above 140.* (G. E. McCabe, "Test Interpretation in the High School Guidance Program," *Personnel and Guidance Journal,* 1957, 35:451. Reproduced by permission of the publisher.)

dent's freshman marks at a Georgia college from his high school marks and his scores on the Scholastic Aptitude Test.

The *Supplement* provides expectancy tables on the various schools or colleges within the larger institutions, such as the School of Agriculture or School of Business of the University of Georgia. This information permits the counselor to refine his predictions in some cases. Not all students, however, know which school within a large institution they prefer; and not all take the SAT because not all colleges require it. Worthwhile predictions can be made on the basis of the high school averages alone, but they are less specific or accurate than they might be if the other data were also available.

Both the *Guide* and the *Supplement* contain instructions for computing high school averages, for using the prediction tables, and for predicting on the basis of the high school marks alone. They also caution counselors to try to avoid making errors.[7]

> You are making an error if you:
>
> 1. Use a table or formula for a male student that was based on females, or vice versa.
>
> 2. Use a formula for one college with a table for another.
>
> 3. Try to compare colleges on the basis of their formulas, the sizes and ranges of their Index values, or their odds.
>
> 4. Try to evaluate the "quality" of a college or its programs on the basis of any of these data. . . .
>
> The data and tables are useful for one purpose only, to help students evaluate their scholastic prospects at the various Georgia colleges during their first year's study.

The College Entrance Examination Board[8] publishes a manual that enables counselors to help students estimate their chances of being admitted to some colleges that require the SAT and to estimate, if a student is admitted, how he will compare with his college classmates in aptitude and achievement. The second edition provides profiles on 205 CEEB member colleges located throughout the nation. Later editions will no doubt provide similar data on other colleges.

Expectancy tables are useful for showing that predictions can seldom be made on an individual basis, that they are best made in terms of a group. The expectancy table in Figure 15b, for example, shows that a counselor cannot tell a girl who has a DAT Sentences score of 26 that she will not be able to pass the rhetoric course at Kansas State Teachers College. If the counselor thinks that the girl needs to be cautioned regarding the difficulties that she may expect to encounter, he might say, "Students with scores like yours on the DAT Sentences scale find it difficult to earn

---

[7] *Ibid.*, p. vii.

[8] College Entrance Examination Board, *Manual of Freshman Class Profiles*, 2d ed. Princeton, N.J., and Berkeley, Calif.: Educational Testing Service, 1962.

a grade of C in freshman rhetoric at Kansas State—only about one out of three do it." He bears in mind that prediction of any criterion score is generally accompanied by a wide margin of error—that it is a probability statement.

INTERPRETING TEST DATA TO STUDENTS

Students need to know test results so that they may utilize the self-understanding achieved through such knowledge in selecting areas of concentration, planning exploratory experiences, accepting and appraising recommendations offered them at school and at home, setting and altering goals, and making plans to attain those goals.

Group Orientation. While the counseling situation has been improved in many schools through reductions in counselors' case loads, the number of clients assigned the average counselor is still too large for him to use counseling time for giving students individually information that can easily be provided in groups and that is needed by them for understanding the test data. Students can be given precounseling orientation to test interpretation in much the same way that they are prepared through group guidance for taking the tests. As explained elsewhere: [9]

> After the tests are taken (perhaps in the group-guidance class), the class is used to help the students understand and use the findings. The meanings of norms and percentile or standard scores are explained, and through wall charts or mimeographed copies the profile records of test data on John and Jane Doe are studied. Such group study helps the students to perceive the implications of test data for educational and vocational planning, to understand the usefulness and limitations of such data, to appreciate the significance, extent, and normalcy of individual differences and of variations in an individual's strengths. It helps many to give up false notions regarding absolute values of test scores and to perceive the absurdity of thinking in terms of one IQ.

The profile forms provided by the publishers for some tests, such as the DAT, SCAT, ITED, and Kuder, contain instructions and explanations for profiling and interpreting the scores. In some schools students record their own scores on the profiles in a class or group guidance situation. Each student, for example, may be given an ITED form and a slip on which are listed his nine scores and may then be instructed to make out his own profile.

The SCAT and STEP Student Report form is a four-page folder that describes the tests and tells in simple language what the various subtests measure. It contains the example given in Figure 17 to show students how to record their scores on the graphs provided for the various tests in-

[9] Jane Warters, *Group Guidance: Principles and Practices,* p. 234. New York: McGraw-Hill Book Company, Inc., 1960.

cluded in the SCAT and STEP scales. The example shows percentile bands for three of the seven tests in the STEP scale. It is accompanied by the following explanation: [10]

> The shaded areas for Mathematics and Social Studies overlap; there is no important difference in standings on these two tests. The same is true of Mathematics and Science. However, the shaded areas for Science and Social Studies do not overlap. The student is higher in Social Studies than in Science ability, as measured by these tests.

The DAT has two interpretive aids for students. One is the single-page Individual Report Form which contains, in addition to the graph, instructions for profiling the scores and for determining the significance of

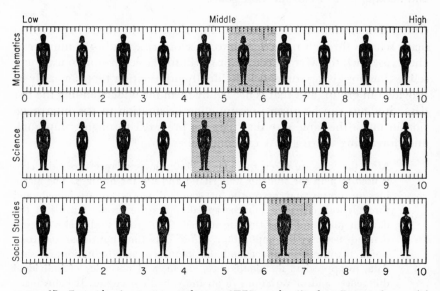

FIGURE 17   Example of report to student on STEP results. (Student Report: Sequential Tests of Educational Progress and School and College Ability Tests, p. 4. Princeton, N.J., and Berkeley, Calif.: Educational Testing Service, 1958.)

the differences between scores. The other is a six-page pamphlet entitled Your Aptitudes as Measured by the Differential Aptitude Tests, which explains the nature of aptitude and aptitude testing, describes the several abilities measured by the DAT, gives information regarding the limitations and usefulness of the scores for predictive purposes, and explains the expectancy tables provided to illustrate predictions using the DAT. Some students may be confused by both the amount and the technical nature of the material contained in the pamphlet. Others, no doubt, will find it interesting and very helpful.

[10] Student Report: Sequential Tests of Educational Progress and School and College Ability Tests, p. 4. Princeton, N.J., and Berkeley, Calif.: Educational Testing Service, 1958.

Some counselors prefer to have students fill out or first see their profiles in the counseling setting rather than in the group situation, particularly if the students are highly competitive and invidious comparisons are likely to be made. In the counseling situation the slow learner will not be hurt by belittling glances or comments, and the superior student can be encouraged to give serious thought to the responsibilities that accompany strength and still be free to feel and express pride in his strength. Precounseling orientation through group work can be very effective without the students' having their own test scores. Good use can be made of illustrative fictional cases or disguised cases of former students.

Even when students are informed of their specific test scores in the group situation, they need an opportunity to discuss them individually with their counselors. The group work serves as a preparation for counseling. It should not be used as a substitute.

The profiles prepared by the students themselves are generally the only written reports on tests results that should be given to students. If a school's overemphasis upon testing is not the reason for students' requesting written reports, overemphasis upon the part of students, parents, and teachers will very likely result from the routine issuing of such reports.

Use of Test Interpretation in Counseling. Questions are often raised regarding the desirability of the counselor's reporting specific scores to students. If through precounseling orientation the student understands the limitations as well as the meanings of the derived scores, little risk may be involved in supplying the numerical data. Ordinarily, however, such information is given only incidentally. The counselor usually talks not in terms of scores but in such terms as "high," "average," "somewhat lower than most others in the group," "not so high as you might expect in view of your ability," and the like.

More harm than good is likely to result from reporting to students and parents the specific IQ's, percentile ranks, or stanines attained on tests of general mental ability. Information about performances on such tests is best given in the form of general interpretation and only to the degree that the recipient can understand and accept it emotionally as well as intellectually. The interpretation should be woven into counseling conversations regarding educational achievement, plans for the future, and the like. These conversations are desirably held with the student over a period of time rather than concentrated into a single somewhat formal conference arranged specifically for this purpose. During the conferences the counselor tries to help the student explore his interests and appraise his strengths so that he may build plans that permit satisfaction of strong interests and development of talents.

When a high school senior asks his counselor, "How did I do on the intelligence test?" and "Did it show me good enough for college?" the counselor does not tell the student that the publishers' norms for high school seniors show that his total SCAT score gives him a percentile rank of 97. Instead, he tells him that he did well on the test and that the results indicate that he is indeed of college caliber. The counselor tries not to be judgmental in speech or attitude, but he does not always avoid the use of evaluative terms. The boy apparently wants to go to college, but his questions indicate that he may have some doubt regarding his ability to meet college academic requirements. Since the test data indicate that the boy is superior in scholastic aptitude, he should receive information that is sufficiently definite to enable him to perceive that, with respect to scholastic aptitude, plans for attending college are sound.

In reporting the results from any type of test, the worker ordinarily takes care not to indicate his own reaction through expressions of pleasure, disappointment, or the like. He is, however, sensitive to the student's reaction as shown through his expressions of satisfaction, dissatisfaction, disappointment, and the like. He tries to reflect the student's feelings through such remarks as "You are disappointed that your test score is not better than the average sophomore's?" or "You are pleased that you did very well on the test?" He encourages the student to express his feelings fully so that the student can gain the emotional release that may be needed before he can examine more or less objectively his aspirations and the reasons for his satisfaction or disappointment with the test findings.

The counselor may tell a sophomore girl whose percentile score on the Henmon-Nelson Test of Mental Ability is 75 that she attained a high average score on the test. He then encourages her to explore her strengths and weaknesses through study of her school marks and achievement test scores so that she may find out for herself that, if she puts her aptitudes to work, she can achieve satisfactorily in her classes.

He may tell another sophomore girl who has a percentile rank of 13 on the same test that her score is below that of the average sophomore. He then helps her to explore the situation through a study of her records so that he may help her to plan an appropriate program of studies and to perceive that she will have to work harder than many sophomores in order to succeed in her academic courses.

It is easier to report results from achievement tests than results from intelligence tests. Low performance on an achievement test can be blamed by the student or his parents on the schools or on other situational factors. It need not be seen as a reflection upon the student and his family. Hence, there may be less emotional involvement and thus more intellectual understanding, which may lead to acceptance in practice. Acceptance in practice may be shown through a modification of plans in keeping with apparent strengths and weaknesses.

In interpreting test results, the counselor should take care to compare the student with others of the same age or grade group rather than of some higher or lower group. It is more desirable, for example, to tell a freshman girl that she did better on a reading test than most freshmen than to tell her that she did as well as the average senior, and wiser to tell a senior girl that she did better than about one-fifth of the seniors than to tell her that her performance was equivalent to that of the average sophomore. And it is better to tell the parent of a fourteen-year-old boy that his son did as well as one-fourth of the fourteen-year-olds than to tell him that the boy has a mental age of thirteen.

The counselor avoids the use of technological terms and stresses the positive rather than the negative. He does not focus the discussion upon a student's lacks but instead upon the significance of the test data and past school achievement in the student's planning. He neither predicts nor prescribes. He does not, for example, tell a student who scored low on the DAT numerical ability, space relations, and mechanical reasoning scales that he should seriously consider sales work because he can never become an engineer. Through discussions of the test results, school achievement, and special likes and dislikes, the student may gradually change his self-concept and cease to aspire to play the role of a professional engineer. He may adapt himself to the requirements of the situation and decide that to become an engineer will require more time and effort than he can afford or is willing to give. When he perceives the situation more clearly, he may leave the conference room ready to explore other occupations in which he can satisfy his strong interest in mechanics and which are more in harmony with his pattern of abilities.

Instead of telling the student that he cannot succeed in the occupation of his choice, the counselor tries to help him to understand the probability of failure (as indicated in expectancy tables), to see what is involved in attaining such a goal, and to consider what special values and interests he hopes to achieve and to satisfy through his vocation. Under such conditions students are more likely to consider modifying plans in keeping with their real abilities and interests than they are when told that they should not make certain plans and should consider certain others. In the latter situation some students will persist in inappropriate plans partly because they resent being told what to do and being considered incompetent to attain their stated goals.

Suppose, some persons may ask, that a student clearly does not have sufficient ability to succeed in even the semiskilled work of the mechanic and yet he persists in planning "to work with machines"? Eventually this student may find it necessary to change his plans from repairing machines to working around machines. There are plenty of unskilled jobs that have to be done which make it possible for him to be around machines. If he is not able even to clean and oil the machines, he can sweep the floor of the machine shop or garage and do other unskilled jobs. Since there are places in the world of work for low-ability people, the low-ability student should leave a guidance conference in an optimistic as well as a thoughtful mood. He should gain hope as well as understanding from talking with his counselor.

In interpreting interest test data, it is best to talk first about the student's past experiences that have led him to express strong interest in certain areas. It is not wise to discuss specific occupations before helping the student to explore his understanding of himself and his past experiences. It is not helpful, as Darley and Hagenah [11] stress, to begin by telling a student that he has the same kind of interests as a school superintendent, lawyer, printer, or the like. While use of such statements is standard practice, it is not effective and is likely to lead into interpretive difficulties. Darley and Hagenah base this conclusion on such reasons as the following:

(1) If the student knows that he is wholly inexperienced in the jobs named, he may reject the statement. To overcome the student's resistance, the counselor has to give an involved explanation of the development of interest tests that may only confuse him. (2) Without such explanation, however, the student may conclude that he has both ability and interest in the areas named. (3) The student may resist or reject the statement for another reason—misconception of or dislike for the occupations named. He may, for example, hold uncomplimentary stereotypes about school superintendents and printers. (4) The counselor's opening statement may lead to premature consideration of such factors as salaries, prestige values, admission requirements, and the like "at the expense of the more important purpose of exploring the motivations, value systems, and insights from available past experiences of the student."

Moreover, such opening statements do not take into consideration the student's ability level and past achievement. They also fail to take into account possible cultural determinants of his choice and possible changes in measured interests. The direct reporting of interest test scores and the use of statements like "You have the same kind of interests as successful personnel managers or YMCA secretaries or school superintendents" are held less effective than some method like the following: [12]

> Suppose, in this hypothetical case, no reference is made to interest measurement until relatively late in the counseling process. Suppose, further, that the counselor permits the student to work through and verbalize the reasons for his three claimed choices. It may be that the student has done only superficial thinking about jobs, and this fact itself is important to know. But the counselor may also discover the specific factors leading to the choices: information (or misinformation) regarding salary scales and "overcrowded" or "undercrowded" fields and job duties; satisfactions expected from work; self-estimates of strengths and weaknesses; evidences of family pressure or tradition dictating certain choices; self-estimates of the aspirations and motives that are operative in the choices; and evidence about life experiences to this date that have shaped the choices.

If the counselor is well informed regarding occupations and understands interest types and the relations between interests and personality,

---

[11] John G. Darley and Theda Hagenah, *Vocational Interest Measurement: Theory and Practice*, pp. 195–202. Minneapolis: The University of Minnesota Press, 1955.
   [12] *Ibid.*, p. 197.

he may be able to gain through talking with the student information that indicates or contraindicates the claimed or measured interests.

Specifically, in the example we have cited, unhappy experiences or clearly poor performance in mathematics would contra-indicate the claimed choice of engineering. Participation in Hi-Y work and summer camp jobs might be found supportive of the measured social service patterns. A discussion of "executive work" as a pervasive problem of dealing with people might take it out of the claimed realm of business interests alone.[13]

When the counselor understands the student's thinking about the work world and his relations to it, he may then offer direct interpretation of the interest test results. He may discuss specific occupational titles as representative of the field(s) in which the student has expressed strong interest. He might say something like the following: [14]

"We can read the interest test you took to say that your basic interests seem to be those involved in helping people or in working with them in order to make their lot easier, rather than being engaged in impersonal, scientific activities, or in making a big fortune in business activities." In the discussion of this interpretation in terms of how the student has evaluated his experiences to date, the counselor may refer to specific occupational labels as *representatives* of the basic interest type or family. Thus he would say: "Basic interests like yours might find satisfaction in the job of personnel manager, for example." Here would follow a description of job duties, responsibilities, and training requirements of the occupational title. The counselor could go on to say: "These same interests could bring you satisfaction in the type of work that a Y.M.C.A. secretary does. So far as training is concerned, these two jobs—personnel manager or Y.M.C.A. secretary—require somewhat different types of abilities and aptitudes, as we can see in looking at the two training programs. Therefore, it becomes important next to get some estimate of your abilities and past achievement in related subjects to see how they might line up with the two training programs."

This type of interpretation opens discussion of the abilities needed for a wide range of jobs within specific fields and helps a student to examine more or less objectively the motives and personality needs that he seeks to satisfy through occupational choice.

In interpreting test data, the counselor gives counseling what Williamson [15] has described as a developmental thrust by emphasizing the future. In discussing test results with a student, he tries to help him "to anticipate the future by making his aspirations and potentialities come true—by so organizing his thinking about himself and his aspirations for his future development that he has a better likelihood of achiev-

---

[13] *Ibid.*, p. 198.

[14] *Ibid.*, pp. 198–199.

[15] E. G. Williamson, "Characteristics of the Counseling Relationship," paper read at the 1960 NDEA Summer Institute, University of Minnesota, Duluth Campus. (Mimeographed.)

ing his potential." The counselor assumes that knowledge of the test results will stimulate the student to want to make good use of his strengths: [16]

> But there are some difficulties in the application of such an assumption. For example, one of our tribal mores is that, being academically minded, we assume in a hazy way a high correlation between abilities and aspirations. That is, when we identify a high I.Q., we take it for granted that the individual wants to use it in highly motivated academic efforts. Such an assumption is not always justified. Nevertheless, sometimes we become indignant with the "loafing" high-ability student because we think that he "should use his ability." There is an implied moral imperative in our thinking. But we should not be startled, if some individuals respond, "I don't want to use my ability, then I'll have to work hard."

By avoiding the role of critic or judge and by not using test data as a spur or goad, the counselor may be able to help a student aspire to new roles—to cultivate the desire of becoming that which he is capable of becoming. A sympathetic relationship may do more to help him "to cultivate confidence in self and desire to become oneself than almost anything that the counselor says."

TWO EXAMPLES

These examples are not case studies. They illustrate mainly test interpretations offered a student during one school year or term.

Dentist or Farmer? Norman is a second-semester tenth grader in a senior high school. According to his cumulative record, his father is a dentist, his mother is a housewife, and both are college graduates. He is the younger of two children, the older being a girl who is a senior in the same school. Norman attended a local junior high school, where he earned A's and B's except for one C in social studies. He ranked 29 in the junior high school graduating class of 116. He is enrolled in the college preparatory curriculum. Last semester he received C's in all subjects except driver education, in which he earned a B. The cumulative record also contains the following test data expressed in percentile scores:

9th Grade	California Test of Mental Maturity	
	Language	95
	Nonlanguage	80
	Total	90

	California Achievement Tests	
	Reading vocabulary	99
	Reading comprehension	85
	Arithmetic reasoning	90

[16] *Ibid.*, p. 3.

Arithmetic fundamentals   95
Mechanics of English   99
Spelling   50

10th Grade   *Differential Aptitude Tests*

Verbal reasoning   80
Numerical ability   85
Abstract reasoning   95
Space relations   95
Mechanical reasoning   97
Clerical   60
Spelling   35
Sentences   90

Kuder Preference Record—Vocational

Outdoor   96
Mechanical   89
Computational   43
Scientific   83
Persuasive   8
Artistic   66
Literary   15
Musical   26
Social service   12
Clerical   57

Last semester Norman had two conferences with his counselor. One was initiated by him to learn how he had done on the tests taken early in the term, and the other was initiated by the counselor to help him check his program for the spring term. During the first conference the counselor told Norman that the DAT showed him to be about average in spelling and clerical speed and accuracy and that he ranged from above average to high in the other abilities measured by the test.

They discussed the facts that the DAT, like the CAT taken in the ninth grade, showed him least strong in spelling and that this could be improved through special effort. The boy said that he enjoyed reading but didn't "usually stop to look closely at the words." He also said that he disliked using the dictionary when writing letters or themes because it slowed his thinking. He decided, however, that writing in corrections after he had finished might be better than letting misspelled words stand uncorrected even though it made the paper "look messy." The counselor suggested that he might improve his themes by rewriting a first draft which could be written rapidly to get his thoughts on paper before any escaped him.

The counselor returned to the boy's statement about liking to read to encourage him to talk about the type of material enjoyed. Norman said that he liked to read adventure stories, particularly war stories, and books and magazines on farming and horticulture. He showed the counselor a bulletin on soil management for apple orchards that he had obtained from the U.S. Government Printing Office. When asked whether he did any gardening, he said he did very little at home because of the limited space but did a great deal during the summer months that he regularly spent with an uncle who had a farm in Oregon. He talked enthusiastically of his summer experiences and in particular of certain tasks that he had taken over in connection with the care of the pear and apple orchards. The counselor asked whether he had had any experience with mechanical farming. The boy said that his uncle had some farm machinery but was unwilling for him "to fool with it." He thought that the uncle would probably feel differently about this next summer, since he now has a car and does much of the repair work on it himself.

The boy abruptly cut short discussion of his agricultural and mechanical experiences by asking how he had done on the "other test." The counselor explained that it was a test of interests rather than of abilities and showed his interest to be significantly high in three broad fields—outdoor, mechanical, and scientific—and rather low in three others—persuasive, literary, and social service. The boy asked whether he had a graph of his interests like the ones they had studied in orientation class. When he was handed his profile and saw that the highest score was in outdoor, he seemed pleased. He asked whether "outdoor" meant farming. He was told that it included farming and was asked whether that was what he wanted to be. He said, "No," and added that he was going to be a dentist like his father. He said that, as his father had done, he was going to attend the dental school at the state university. When asked whether he knew the admissions requirements, he said that he did because in ninth-grade vocational civics he had had to prepare career books on two occupations. He had chosen dentistry and farming and thought that he knew "all about both."

Five weeks later during the program-checking conference, Norman again stated his intention of attending dental school. A program was planned for the remaining semesters that included the courses needed for admission as a predental student at the state university.

Two weeks after the beginning of the spring term Norman asked for a conference during which he expressed concern over his marks for the first semester—all C's except for a B in driver education. He said that he was afraid he would not be able to enter dental school unless his marks improved. He asked whether it was true that students were expected to have mostly A's and B's in the junior and senior years if they wanted to enter one of the professional schools of the state university. When the counselor confirmed this statement, Norman said that he would not mind too much being rejected but knew that it would upset his parents, particularly his father.

The counselor "wondered" what Norman might like to be if he could not be a dentist. After a long silence the boy said that he supposed he could always be a farmer "like Uncle John." During the ensuing conversation the boy said that he would not mind being a farmer, actually would "rather like it," but knew his parents would object because both had "snob ideas" that made them think more of doctors, dentists, and engineers than of nurses, farmers, and mechanics. He then told somewhat angrily of his sister's having once expressed a desire to be a nurse and of his father's talking her out of it by describing in detail some of the unpleasant tasks that nurses must perform. Norman said that he could not see that they were any worse than "poking around in other people's mouths" and having people breathe "their smelly breath right into your face." Then he said that he would actually prefer being a farmer to being a dentist but knew that his father would "never stand for it."

When the counselor asked whether he had ever talked the matter over with his father, the boy said that his father had no time to talk with him, that when the father was not working, he was out playing golf, but that he did seem to find time for his sister when she wanted to talk with him. The boy seemed reluctant to discuss the matter further. The counselor suggested that they have another conference the next week.

At this point the counselor was uncertain whether the boy's marks were declining because he was too unhappy or worried to concentrate on his studies or whether he was reluctant to earn marks sufficiently high to guarantee admission to the state university. He also wondered whether Norman actually rejected the idea of being a dentist because he really wanted to be a farmer or whether he was rejecting his father's goal for him because he felt that the father was neglecting or rejecting him.

The following week the boy opened the conversation by saying that he had been thinking about being a farmer instead of a dentist but, to be the kind of farmer he would like to be—"a really good scientific farmer," he would have to go to college. The best place, he thought, would be the school of agriculture at the state university. Hence, he still had the problem of how to improve his marks so that he could get into the state university. He seemed, however, less worried about the problem than the previous week. He told of studying with a friend for a geometry examination taken the previous day. Both thought it had helped, and both felt that they had done "all right" on the test.

The boy again said that he knew his parents would never consent to his going to college to study agriculture instead of dentistry. The counselor said that the program of study he had worked out in the fall would permit him to enter the lower division of the university, and that he did not actually have to reach a final decision regarding his lifework for at least another two years and perhaps could delay it even longer. He referred to the fact that the test data showed the boy well qualified to do college work and said that the immediate problem seemed to be one of getting better school marks. The boy said that he was already "working on it," had talked with two of his teachers, and planned to talk to the others about what they thought he needed to do to earn better grades. The counselor "hoped" that the boy would keep in touch with him and let him know how he was getting along. No date was set, however, for the next conference.

Since this conference the counselor has seen the boy twice outside the office and was able to talk with him briefly. Each time the boy seemed to be in good spirits. The last time he said that he thought he was doing better in all his subjects, and knew he would get better than a C in English at midterm because he had received A's in two book reports. He laughed as he told of writing one three times before he could get all his thoughts "nailed down" on paper.

This counselor did not do some things that many guidance people may think that he should have done. He did not check the Kuder findings by administering the SVIB. He did not think that the boy would find it easy to give valid responses at this time and so decided that use of the SVIB should be delayed until next year. The boy might use it now more for verifying his claimed interest in farming than for discovering his real interests. Neither did the counselor offer to talk with the father about Norman's apparently preferring dentistry to farming or his feeling that his father gives him too little time or attention.

Developing better father-son understanding is the boy's task, not the counselor's. Also, the family situation may not be as the boy describes or perceives it. The counselor can probably best help here by providing a counseling situation in which Norman can explore this problem, examine his role in its creation and correction, and try out in discussions with the counselor any ideas that he may have regarding solution.

The counselor believes that the boy has more to gain than to lose in delaying occupational choice and perhaps also in delaying telling his father that he does not want to be a dentist. Later, he may be able to discuss the matter more objectively than he can now. If, when he is a senior, he still feels that he does not want to be a dentist and wants to attend a school of agriculture, the father may give his views more serious consideration than he might now, if for no other reason than that Norman will be then more a man and less a boy than he is now.

There is also the possibility that by the time Norman is ready to enter college he may have adopted some of his parents' "snob ideas" regarding the prestige values of dentistry and farming. For that and other reasons he may then perceive dentistry as a highly desirable vocation and farming or horticulture as an interesting avocation. As he grows older, the dentistry interest may intensify, and the horticulture interest may wane. And, of course, the converse may occur with respect to vocational preference.

The counselor plans to see Norman more or less regularly. He hopes that the counseling sessions will help the boy clarify and define his interests and goals. He may not have him take the SVIB next year but may let him wait until the following year when he will routinely take it with the other seniors. By then they will know whether he has been able to achieve the grade point average needed for admission to college. The ITED and PSAT that he will take in his junior year will show whether he is gaining or losing ground in terms of scholastic aptitude. The SVIB will show the changes in his interests and the areas of intense interest.

The present picture seems more positive than negative. Norman's parents want him to go to college, and he wants to attend. He knows that he must improve his marks and seems sincere in professed intentions to try to do so. There is some evidence that he may be succeeding. He is uncertain regarding occupational choice and may be unhappy in his relations with his father. With change in age may come change in his attitudes and feelings, particularly if counseling provides him a chance to discuss periodically his goals and problems and to explore his thoughts and feelings regarding them.

Underachiever. Stanley entered senior high school as a junior at the beginning of the fall term. The registration card shows that his father is a carpenter and his mother a housewife. The record from his previous school, a four-year high school, shows an Otis IQ of 117 and marks of C's and D's in all courses except physical education, in which he made B's.

Four weeks after entering the present school he took the ITED with the other juniors and the DAT and the SVIB with the juniors and seniors who had enrolled with him as transfer students from other schools. Two weeks later he was told that he could see his counselor to learn the test results if he wished. He did not ask for a conference. His percentile scores were as follows:

Iowa Tests of Educational Development (see Figure 18)

Social studies background	73
Natural science background	75
Correctness of expression	21
Quantitative thinking	86
Reading—social studies	53
Reading—natural sciences	63
Reading—literature	44
General vocabulary	56
Composite score on tests 1–8	63
Use of sources	21

Differential Aptitude Tests (see Figure 19)

Verbal reasoning	80
Numerical ability	90
Abstract reasoning	85
Space relations	95
Mechanical reasoning	97

Clerical speed and accuracy   55
Spelling   15
Sentences   20

Strong Vocational Interest Blank for Men (see Figure 20)

Senior CPA   A
Accountant   A
Office worker   A
Engineer   B+
Chemist   B
Mathematician   B—

Stanley's midterm report showed B's in chemistry and physical education; C's in social studies, algebra, and mechanical drawing; and D in English. In December he received a note from his counselor asking him to see her the next day so that they might plan his program for future semesters. Stanley reported at the appointed time.

The counselor suggested that they look at his cumulative record to see what the tests showed before beginning work on his program. He agreed that this would be wise but did not seem very much interested. After briefly explaining what the DAT and ITED measure, the counselor said that both showed him to be above average in numerical ability and average or better in verbal ability, but weak in spelling and English mechanics. The DAT, she said, showed him average in clerical aptitude and high in mechanical reasoning and space relations.

When Stanley asked the counselor to tell him again about the mechanical reasoning test, she explained that it showed how well he understood the principles of physics as applied to everyday things and how well he understood the laws governing machinery, tools, and simple appliances. The boy said that he understood such things because he had had "quite a bit of experience using tools" through working in a garage and filling station. He said that he was trying to find a job like the one he had had in the community from which his family had moved during the summer. He also said that he hoped some day to own his own garage or filling station.

The counselor asked him whether he thought his numerical ability had also been developed in part through practical experience. The boy said that he doubted it because his work at the filling station had not involved much figuring; "that was done by machines." In the sixth and seventh grades he had served as assistant storekeeper while at the school camp, but the work had involved selling rather than account keeping. He agreed, however, that writing sales slips and making change had involved some computational work. Also, he had been earning his spending and clothes money for about four years and had his own bank account.

The counselor told him that some of the interests that he had expressed on the third test, the vocational interest test, might be expressed or satisfied through the type of work done by accountants and book-

Grade	1-Backgr'd soc. stud.		2-Backgr'd nat. sci.		3-Corr. of expression		4-Quant've thinking		5-Reading soc. stud.		6-Reading nat. sci.		7-Reading lit.		8-Gen'l. vocab.		Composite 1-8		9-Use of sources	
11	18	73	20	75	11	21	20	86	15	53	16	63	13	44	16	56	17	63	10	21
	Std.	%ile	Std.	%ile	Std.	%ile	Std.	%ile	Std.	%ile	Std.	%ile	Std.	%ile	Std.	%ile	Std.	%ile	Std.	%ile

IOWA TESTS OF EDUCATIONAL DEVELOPMENT — SRA *PRESSCORE*

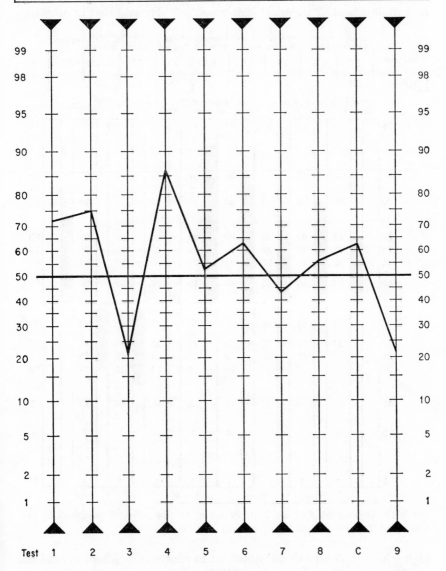

FIGURE 18 *Iowa Tests of Educational Development profile of Stanley Allen.* (Reproduced by permission of Science Research Associates, Inc.)

keepers. The boy rejected the implication, saying that he had no interest whatsoever in such work. He knew exactly what he wanted to do when he finished school—work in a garage or filling station and save his money until he had enough to start buying his own place. He gave an emphatic "No" in answer to the counselor's "You don't think you might like to go to a trade school or technical junior college?" He said that he wanted a

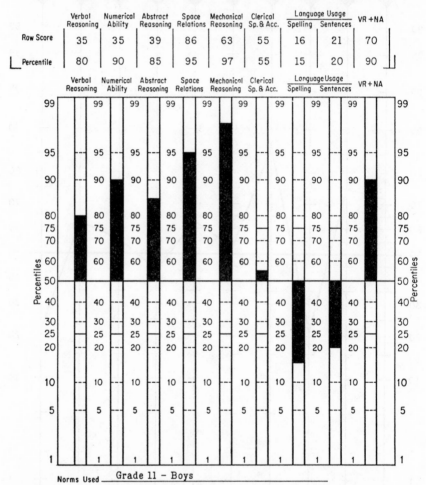

	Verbal Reasoning	Numerical Ability	Abstract Reasoning	Space Relations	Mechanical Reasoning	Clerical Sp. & Acc.	Language Usage Spelling	Sentences	VR +NA
Raw Score	35	35	39	86	63	55	16	21	70
Percentile	80	90	85	95	97	55	15	20	90

FIGURE 19 *Differential Aptitude Tests Profile of Stanley Allen.* (Reproduced by permission of The Psychological Corporation.)

high school diploma but did not want to continue in school beyond the twelfth grade. The conversation was then directed to program planning.

However, before Stanley left the conference room, the counselor picked up the two profiles shown in Figures 18 and 19 and handed them to him as she said, "I didn't show these to you when we were talking about the tests. You may like to see them." As he looked at them, she explained the scores in relation to the median. When he handed them back to her, he smiled and said, "I guess I am taller than I thought I was." She returned the smile but made no comment.

Now that Stanley knows that he is more capable academically than he thought he was, will he try to get better school marks? This is what the counselor and his teachers would like to see happen. He may, however,

Report on Vocational Interest Blank for Men

Group	Occupation	Raw Score	Standard Score	C (0–30)	B– (30–35)	B (35–40)	B+ (40–45)	A (45–65)
I	Artist							
	Psychologist							
	Architect							
	Physician							
	Psychiatrist							
	Osteopath							
	Dentist							
	Veterinarian							
II	Mathematician							
	Physicist							
	Chemist							
	Engineer							
III	Production Manager							
IV	Farmer							
	Carpenter							
	Forest Service Man							
	Aviator							
	Printer							
	Math. Sci. Teacher							
	Policeman							
	Army Officer							
V	Y.M.C.A. Phys. Dir.							
	Personnel Manager							
	Public Administrator							
	Vocational Counselor							
	Physical Therapist							
	Social Worker							
	Soc. Sci. Teacher							
	Bus. Educ. Teacher							
	School Supt.							
	Minister							
VI	Musician							
	Music Teacher							
VII	C.P.A. Owner							
VIII	Senior C.P.A.							
	Accountant							
	Office Worker							
	Credit Manager							
	Purchasing Agent							
	Banker							
	Pharmacist							
	Mortician							
IX	Sales Manager							
	Real Estate Slsmn.							
	Life Insurance Slsmn.							
X	Advertising Man							
	Lawyer							
	Author-Journalist							
XI	Pres., Mfg. Concern							
	Occupational Level							
	Specialization Level							
	Masculinity-Femininity			F				M
	Interest Maturity							

FIGURE 20   *SVIB profile for Stanley Allen.* (Reproduced by special permission from Strong Vocational Interest Blank by Edward K. Strong, Jr. Copyright 1945 by the Board of Trustees of the Leland Stanford Junior University.)

continue satisfied with grades just sufficiently high to ensure his getting a high school diploma, which he may value in much the same way that he might a union card.

In talking of his occupational goal, Stanley did not stress working in a garage or filling station as much as he did owning (or managing?) one. His expressed vocational interest may more support than contraindicate the inventoried interests. No doubt, the counselor will be interested in seeing what the SVIB that Stanley will take next year will show, but the boy may not be. He seems not at all uncertain regarding his occupational goal and so may have little interest in the test findings.

Illustrative Case Studies. The literature is rich in case studies that illustrate the use of test interpretation in counseling and that include follow-up and evaluation reports. Attention in particular is called to the cases described by Super and Crites,[17] Rothney and Roens,[18] and Goldman.[19] Transcriptions of portions of actual interviews in which test data are interpreted to clients are provided in books by Bordin,[20] Callis et al.,[21] Williamson,[22] and others.

SUMMARY

Test data should be interpreted to the students as early as possible after test administration. Numerical data are best used incidentally, and ordinarily only after the findings have been explained in general qualitative terms. Like counselors, students should perceive scores as bands rather than specific points along a scale.

Graphic presentations are useful in test interpretation. A profile shows the individual's standings on a number of scales. Scattergrams reveal individual differences in ability and achievement among the members of a particular group and the relationships between achievement and ability for individual members. Expectancy tables help to refine predictions regarding the individual's future performance.

The construction of expectancy tables may properly be regarded as part of the research for which counselors are responsible. The publishers of some tests, such as the SAT, provide probability data for some colleges.

[17] Donald E. Super, *The Psychology of Careers.* New York: Harper & Row, Publishers, Incorporated, 1957; Donald E. Super and John O. Crites, *Appraising Vocational Fitness by Means of Psychological Tests*, rev. ed., appendices A and B. New York: Harper & Row, Publishers, Incorporated, 1962.

[18] J. W. M. Rothney and B. A. Roens, *Guidance of American Youth: An Experimental Study*, chaps. 1–2. Cambridge, Mass.: Harvard University Press, 1950.

[19] Leo Goldman, *Using Tests in Counseling*, chap. 11. New York: Appleton-Century-Crofts, Inc., 1961.

[20] E. S. Bordin, *Psychological Counseling*, chap. 12. New York: Appleton-Century-Crofts, Inc., 1955.

[21] Robert Callis et al., *A Casebook of Counseling.* New York: Appleton-Century-Crofts, Inc., 1955.

[22] E. G. Williamson, *Counseling Adolescents,* appendix. New York: McGraw-Hill Book Company, Inc., 1950. Unfortunately, this book is out of print, but copies are available in many libraries.

It would be good if counselors in all states were provided expectancy tables, such as those provided by the regents of the Georgia state university system.

Test interpretation in counseling may be expedited and strengthened by students' being provided precounseling orientation through group work. However, even when students have an opportunity to study their own test profiles in the group situation, they should have a chance to discuss the test data with their counselors.

The counselor, in interpreting test results, focuses on the positive rather than the negative. He avoids the role of judge or critic. He tries to interpret the data in terms that the student can accept as well as understand so that he may examine his strengths and weaknesses as objectively as possible. Interpretation of the interest test findings best follows exploration and discussion of a student's abilities, academic achievement, and relevant experiences.

Two examples are given of test interpretation in counseling, and reference is made to illustrative case histories given in the literature.

REFERENCES

Bennett, George K., et al.: *Counseling from Profiles.* New York: The Psychological Corporation, 1951.

Bordin, E. S.: *Psychological Counseling,* chaps. 11–12. New York: Appleton-Century-Crofts, Inc., 1955.

———— and R. H. Bixler: "Test Selection: A Process of Counseling," *Educational and Psychological Measurement,* 1946, 6:361–374.

Dressel, P. L., and R. W. Matteson: "The Effect of Client Participation in Test Interpretation," *Educational and Psychological Measurement,* 1950, 10:693–706.

Durost, Walter N.: *How to Tell Parents about Standardized Test Results,* Test Service Notebook no. 26. New York: Harcourt, Brace & World, Inc., n.d.

Ebel, Robert L.: "How to Explain Standardized Test Scores to Your Parents," *School Management,* 1961, 5:61–64.

Goldman, Leo: *Using Tests in Counseling,* chaps. 11–16. New York: Appleton-Century-Crofts, Inc., 1961.

Herman, L. M., and M. L. Zeigler: "The Effectiveness of Interpreting Freshman Counseling-test Scores to Parents in a Group Situation," *Personnel and Guidance Journal,* 1961, 40:143–149.

Hills, J. R., et al.: "Admissions and Guidance Research in the University System of Georgia," *Personnel and Guidance Journal,* 1961, 39:452–457.

Kirk, Barbara: "Extra-measurement Use of Tests in Counseling," *Personnel and Guidance Journal,* 1961, 39:658–661.

————: "Individualizing of Test Interpretation," *Occupations,* 1952, 30:500–505.

McCabe, George E.: "How Substantial Is a Substantial Validity Coefficient?" *Personnel and Guidance Journal,* 1956, 34:340–344.

————: "Test Interpretation in the High School Guidance Program," *Personnel and Guidance Journal,* 1957, 35:449–451.

Ricks, James H., Jr.: *On Telling Parents about Test Results*, Test Service Bulletin no. 54. New York: The Psychological Corporation, 1959.

Rogers, L. A.: "Comparison of Two Kinds of Test Interpretation Interviews," *Journal of Counseling Psychology*, 1954, 1:224–231.

Rudikoff, Lynn C., and Barbara A. Kirk: "Test Interpretation in Counseling," *Journal of Counseling Psychology*, 1959, 6:223–228.

Super, Donald E.: "Vocational Adjustment in Terms of Role Theory," *Vocational Guidance Quarterly*, 1957, 5:139–141.

————: "The Preliminary Appraisal in Vocational Counseling," *Personnel and Guidance Journal*, 1957, 36:154–161.

———— and John O. Crites: *Appraising Vocational Fitness by Means of Psychological Tests*, rev. ed., chaps. 20–22 and appendices A and B. New York: Harper & Row, Publishers, Incorporated, 1962.

Tyler, Leona E.: *The Work of the Counselor*, 2d ed., chaps. 6 and 7. New York: Appleton-Century-Crofts, Inc., 1961.

8

Self-reports:
Personal Data and
Evaluation Questionnaires

In the final analysis, the student is the source of information secured about him through tests. Hence, broadly interpreted, the term "self-reports" covers some procedures previously considered. In this and the following chapters, however, discussion is limited to certain procedures used for securing reports written by the student in which he gives information about himself or appraises himself or evaluates some of his school experiences. Included in the discussion are the questionnaire, certain self-rating or self-inventory procedures, and some direct expressive materials, such as compositions, that yield autobiographical data.

Certain instruments discussed in the chapters on tests, such as the inventories designed for studying interests and personality traits, are questionnaires rather than tests if we accept Symonds's [1] method of differentiating the two. In a test, he states, the issue is whether a person can answer the questions, whereas in a questionnaire it is whether he will answer truthfully. The author of a test tries to make the questions sufficiently difficult to reveal the ability of the person taking the test, whereas the author of a questionnaire tries to make the questions so simple and easy that the respondent will understand and answer truthfully.

Further consideration will not be given in this chapter to the standardized questionnaire designed to measure interests, attitudes, and personality characteristics. In this and the following chapter we are concerned with (1) the questionnaire used to secure from the student information about his background and his plans for the future; (2) the evaluation questionnaire used to learn the student's reactions to instructional methods, course offerings, activity programs, guidance services, and the like; and (3) the follow-up questionnaire in which the former student reports on his postschool life and appraises the effectiveness of the school

[1] P. M. Symonds, *Diagnosing Personality and Conduct*, p. 122. New York: Appleton-Century-Crofts, Inc., 1931.

program in preparing him for his postschool life. Although the information obtained from these questionnaires is used along with data from other sources in studying and counseling individual students, these questionnaires are employed mainly for obtaining factual information and for ascertaining a student's opinion of himself and his school experiences rather than for scientific study of his personality.

PERSONAL DATA BLANK

Contents. The personal data blank is a questionnaire or set of open-end statements used to secure information from students regarding such

PERSONAL DATA SHEET

Date _____   Class of _____
Name _____   Boy _____ Girl _____
          Last   First   Middle
Home address _____   Phone number _____
              Street   City
Mailing address _____
Birthplace _____
              City   State
Date of birth _____ Age _____
          Month   Day   Year   Last birthday
School last attended _____
              Name of school   Location—city and state
Your religious preference _____
With whom do you live?   If you live with any person other than your
    Own parents _____   parents, give the following information:
    Father & stepmother_____
    Mother & stepfather_____   Name _____
    Guardian _____
    Relative _____   Residence address _____
    Other _____   Relationship to you _____ Phone number _____
Father's name _____   Mother's name _____
    Residence address _____   Residence address _____
    Phone number _____   Phone number _____
    Business address_____   Business address _____
    Phone number _____   Phone number _____
    Occupation _____   Occupation _____
    Birthplace _____   Birthplace _____
    Race _____   Race _____
    Nationality _____   Nationality _____
    Religious preference_____   Religious preference _____
    Is he an American citizen?_____   Is she an American citizen?_____
    Years completed in school _____   Years completed in school _____
    If father is not living,   If mother is not living,
        when did he die?_____   when did she die? _____
    Cause of death _____   Cause of death _____
Are your parents separated?_____   Divorced? _____
Do you have a step-   Do you have a step-
    father?   Yes___No___   mother?   Yes___No___
    Stepfather's name _____   Stepmother's name_____
    Residence address _____   Residence address _____
    Occupation _____   Occupation _____
    Phone number_____   Phone number _____
Brothers and sisters   Last school   School now
    Name   Age   grade completed   attending
_____
_____
_____
_____

FIGURE 21   *Huntington Beach (California) High School personal data form.*

REGISTRATION QUESTIONNAIRE

Name _____ Date _____

INTERESTS AND ACTIVITIES

In what do you get your best grades? _____
What is your favorite subject in school? _____
What honors have you received in or out of school? _____

Do you like to read? ____ What type of book? _____
What magazines do you have in your home? _____
What is your favorite recreation? _____ Hobby? _____
Do you play a musical instrument? _____ What? _____
Do you sing? _____ Do you take private lessons? _____
What activities do you enjoy most in school? _____

What clubs have you belonged to in school? (Indicate office held, if any) _____
What clubs have you belonged to outside of school? (Indicate office held, if any)

In what activities would you like to take part in high school? Check

Clubs _____	Art _____	Baseball ____	Please list
Public speaking _____	Acting _____	Basketball ____	other
School annual _____	Band _____	Football ____	_____
School paper _____	Orchestra _____	Swimming ____	_____
Student government ___	Vocal music ___	Tennis _____	_____
GAA _____		Track _____	_____

FUTURE SCHOOL AND VOCATIONAL PLANS

What are you planning to do when you finish high school: _____
    Go to junior college? __ Go to college? __ Armed Forces? _____
    Go to work? __ What kind? _____
Does your family want you to go to college? _____
Will you need to pay part of your expenses if you go to college? _____
All your expenses? _____
What occupations have you considered? _____

Do you have a part-time job _____ Do you have a work permit? _____

FIGURE 21   (continued)

items as identifying data and home information (name and age of student; home address and telephone number; names, occupations, and
business addresses of parents or guardians; names and ages of brothers
and sisters; other persons living in home and relationship to student);
health status; educational and vocational plans; most-liked and least-
liked subjects; work experiences; special interests and recreation activities; and experiences of special significance.

Figure 21 shows the personal data form used with ninth graders
at Huntington Beach (California) High School. It is short, simple, and
well organized and provides ample space for answers. This form has gone
through a number of revisions. In its previous forms it was much longer.
Some items, such as those regarding health and previous schools attended,
were dropped because this information is provided through other forms.
Some other items were dropped because the information given through
them was used so seldom that inclusion did not seem warranted.

Uses. The chief advantage of using this type of questionnaire is that it is
an easy way to obtain a great deal of information in a relatively short
time. Ordinarily, filling out the form requires no more than an hour, and

it can be done by a number of persons at the same time. The personal data blank is used mainly for (1) obtaining background information on new students, (2) bringing up to date certain factual information, and (3) securing some of the background information needed in providing a special service or in providing counseling through some special division of the school or school system.

To obtain background information needed immediately on new counselees, some counselors have these students fill out a personal data blank shortly after they enter the new school. The cumulative records from the previous schools are not always available. Even when they are, it may be a month or more before they are received and the information is posted on the cumulative record cards or filed in record folders to be kept on these students at the new school. In the meantime information may be needed at a time when it may not be easy or desirable to seek it from the student directly. A counselor, for example, wants information about a boy's home but does not wish to question him because he has heard that the boy's parents were recently divorced. If the counselor can obtain this information from a personal data blank, he can avoid making the boy uncomfortable by asking him about the home at this time.

In some schools, especially large ones, the counselors do not consider it practicable to try to secure such information through interviews. Actually, it is hardly possible if a counselor is assigned from 100 to 300 new students, as is often the case. Even when the number is as small as 75, it is difficult for a counselor to become acquainted with all his new counselees before the end of the first month. The questionnaire may be the only feasible means of obtaining the information needed.

Personal data blanks are often used for checking the accuracy of certain information and for bringing items up to date. The form can be so designed that the responses given by a student over a period of three or four years are made on the same blank. Such an arrangement increases the usefulness of the instrument for the counselor, especially during conferences or interviews. And it helps the student to fill out the form correctly. He need not wonder, for instance, what answers he gave the previous time or whether he began some activity before or after the last time he filled out the form.

The personal data questionnaire is commonly used in college or university counseling divisions or bureaus. The form used, for example, at the Counseling Bureau of the University of Minnesota yields considerable information about the student's background, present activities, plans for the future, and his attitudes toward self, plans, and his situation. Some understanding of how this questionnaire and the findings are used in counseling can be obtained by studying the case records contained in the appendix of Williamson's *Counseling Adolescents*.[2] Most of the rec-

[2] E. G. Williamson, *Counseling Adolescents*, pp. 285–536. New York: McGraw-Hill Book Company, Inc., 1950.

ords include the filled-in questionnaire. The questionnaire (entitled "Individual Record Form") used at the Counseling Center of the University of Oregon is reproduced in Tyler's *The Work of the Counselor*.[3]

Some personal data blanks include check lists of problems designed to help show the types of problems disturbing the students and to screen the students in need of special help. As stated in Chapter 6, perhaps the chief advantage gained from the use of problem lists, whether standardized or teacher-made, is their usefulness for increasing teachers' understanding of the problems that students must deal with. This usefulness, however, is dependent upon the insight and the frankness of the students.

Administration. Some counselors have individual students fill in the form immediately before or after one of their early conferences with the student. This is usually the procedure followed when the personal data blank is used in providing counseling of a specialized nature. Use of the questionnaire then becomes a part of the counseling process.

When the form is used as a routine procedure with all students, it is generally filled out in a group situation. It is better to administer it to small groups, such as homeroom groups or group guidance classes, than to large groups assembled in the auditorium, cafetorium, library, or other such place. For survey purposes the information obtained through the personal data blank administered to large groups is perhaps sufficiently reliable because, by the law of averages, errors tend to neutralize one another. The validity of the findings from the questionnaire may not be low for the total group, but for many individuals the results may have little validity. If, in using the questionnaire, the counselor is seeking information for use in the guidance of individuals, then administering the questionnaire in the large-group situation is not a good procedure.

Counselors are concerned with getting correct reports on individuals rather than with finding the average of a large number of answers. As Rothney and Roens [4] caution, they must be "aware of the danger of being misled by common generalizations which tend to make them think in terms of *group* characteristics at the time that they should be concerned about *particular* characteristics of the individual with whom they are to work."

The personal data form should not be used with groups of new students until they have been in the school sufficiently long to feel adjusted and at ease with the person who administers the questionnaire. This person should try to enlist student cooperation by explaining the form and letting the students discuss its purpose, the confidential nature

---

[3] Leona E. Tyler, *The Work of the Counselor*, 2d ed. New York: Appleton-Century-Crofts, Inc., 1961.

[4] John W. M. Rothney and Bert A. Roens, *Counseling the Individual Student*, p. 86. New York: Holt, Rinehart and Winston, Inc., 1949.

of their answers, and the use to be made of the findings by counselors and others. The more comfortable and secure the students feel in the situation, the more likely they are to give truthful comprehensive answers.

The students should not be led to believe that their responses will not be made known to others if they will be, even though this practice is not unusual and at times is described in the literature as a "justifiable subterfuge." Many boys and girls are too badly confused already by adults' contradictory behavior with respect to truth and honesty for counselors to increase their confusion by deliberately misrepresenting a situation which is as important to students as one in which they make confidential disclosures. The students should not be led to believe that only one person will read their answers if the blanks are to be made available to others. The best procedure is to give students full information on this point whether they ask for it or not, to explain why it is to their advantage to give the information requested, and then to do everything possible to ensure professional use of the results by all users.

Directions. Many personal data blanks contain an introductory section in which the purpose is explained and directions are given for filling in the form. The way in which the students are given the instructions, both orally and on the printed form, will determine in a large measure the way in which they will respond. Some introductory paragraphs seem well designed to secure cooperation. Others seem likely to arouse distrust and resistance. An example of the first type is found in the questionnaire used in the Plainfield (New Jersey) High School,[5] which begins as follows:

> To be of most assistance to you in planning your way through school, each one of your teachers would like to have a talk with you about your ambitions, interests, and activities. It would, of course, be ideal if some arrangement could be made whereby you could meet with all your teachers at one time; such an arrangement would conserve your time and theirs. But this is scarcely feasible when almost two thousand pupils are involved.
>
> The following questionnaire represents an attempt to find a substitute for an interview at which you and all your teachers talk over your plans. We expect you will give your fullest cooperation in answering these questions, and by so doing, helping us in our endeavors to help you.

The authors of a questionnaire that has been used at the El Monte (California) Union High School recognize the highly personal nature of some of the questions and so make it easy for students to withhold any information that they may not want to give. They instructed the students as follows:

> This questionnaire is for your counselors' information, in order that they may be more helpful to you and more understanding of your problems

[5] Reproduced in Arthur E. Traxler, *Techniques of Guidance*, rev. ed., p. 37 New York: Harper & Row, Publishers, Incorporated, 1957.

and needs. You need not reply to any questions which you may prefer not to answer.

The questionnaire reproduced in Figure 21 does not contain instructions. The directions are given orally. In some schools, as at Huntington Beach High School, the forms are administered in English classes shortly after the beginning of a new school year or term. Often (desirably always) the students are told that they may withhold information that they do not wish to give.

Sometimes filling out the form in English class can be related to the classwork without its being made an assignment. One teacher, for example, who is especially successful in winning student interest and cooperation, tells her students half seriously and half jokingly that we live in a "questionnaire age" and that they would do well, before reaching adulthood, to learn how to answer questionnaires and fill in forms accurately and efficiently. She shows them some forms that she has had to fill out, calls attention to the strong and weak points in their formats, and comments on the fact that the value of the information obtained from the best of them largely depends upon the willingness of the respondents to cooperate. She encourages the students to criticize construction of the personal data blank that they are given to answer and to discuss the worthwhileness of the purpose underlying its use.

In striking contrast to the two examples of written instructions given above is this paragraph that introduces another personal data blank: [6]

> Directions: Read every statement carefully before attempting an answer. Spend all the time necessary to complete your answers. Accuracy and neatness in writing is essential. Your handwriting will be rated, using the Ayres Handwriting Scale. Write small and use good English. You will not be given a second blank, so think through your answers before you write. This is very important, so do your very best.

Here the students are ordered, not asked. They are warned to watch their writing and to use good English. In answering this questionnaire, many will undoubtedly be so concerned over how they write that what they write may be of little value. The information regarding the use of the Ayres Handwriting Scale may well be omitted; for to some students, no doubt, it implies an ominous threat. A simple request that the student write clearly and neatly would probably produce a better sample of his handwriting as it ordinarily is as well as help him to write more freely and easily than he is likely to with the instructions as they now are. Also, some students will probably make fewer errors when told that another blank may be had if needed than when warned that they may have one

[6] Presented in C. E. Erickson (ed.), *A Basic Text for Guidance Workers*, p. 174. Englewood Cliffs, N.J.: Prentice-Hall, Inc., 1947. Reproduced by permission of the publishers.

blank and one only. On the whole, this type of introduction is likely to make students anxious, resentful, and inclined to give answers that are more in keeping with their best interests, as they understand them, than with the facts in the case.

Not a Substitute for Cumulative Records or Interviews. Early during a student's stay in a school the personal data blank may be the principal source of background information on him. Eventually, however, his cumulative record should contain comprehensive, reliable information obtained from a number of sources of which the personal data blank is only one. The questionnaire is a useful supplement to the cumulative record but not an adequate substitute for it.

The number of schools that use the introductory or "fact-finding interview" for securing personal data on incoming students is relatively small, but the number seems to be increasing. Because the interview is a flexible technique that can be adjusted to the individual case, more data— and more significant data—may be obtained on the individual through the interview than through questionnaires. The interview is generally the technique used when the students are also research subjects.

In the Wisconsin Counseling Study, for example, the first interviews were "introductory and exploratory in nature." The interviewers used a guide sheet that contained questions which, with the exception of the last one, are very similar to the questions in many personal data blanks. However, *"if the subject preferred to enlarge on any of his answers or wanted to talk about some other matter, the sheet was discarded completely,* and the information required to complete it was obtained at a later session." [7] The focus was on the student and those matters held important by him. The student did not have to limit his responses to items listed in the guide sheet, which read as follows: [8]

Interview Guide Sheet

Are you living at home with your father and mother?

What is your father's occupation?

How much education did he have?

Does your mother work? How much education did she have?

Did your mother work before she was married?

(Boy) Does your father want you to go on to the same kind of work he did?

(Girl) Does your mother expect you to do the same kind of work she did?

How many brothers and sisters do you have? How do you get along with them?

Is there anything special about the members of your family?

[7] John W. M. Rothney et al., *Guidance Practices and Results,* p. 75. New York: Harper & Row, Publishers, Incorporated, 1958. Italics in the original.

[8] *Ibid.,* pp. 75–76.

Have you ever discussed your school program with your parents?

Do you plan to stay in school until you graduate?

What plans for education or training do you have after you leave high school?

Have you made up your mind as to what occupation you are going to enter? What others are you considering?

Do both of your parents agree with your plans? If not, what do they suggest?

If you could do just as you pleased, what would you like to be doing five years from now?

If you could spend all of your time on one subject, which would it be?

If any subject could be dropped out of your high school program, which one would you like to see dropped?

What part-time or school vacation jobs have you had? How long?

What activities, other than school work, are you active in?

What do you do at home when you haven't any school work to do?

Is there anything about your health that keeps you from doing the things you like to do?

How do you get along with the other students in school? In your neighborhood? . . .

Do you think that the draft law will affect your educational or vocational plans?

If a counselor is able to hold conferences regularly with each of his counselees, and does not have so many that he cannot maintain contact with each through casual conversations and observations as well as through conferences with them and with others regarding them, he can obtain information that is vastly superior in quantity, quality, and relevancy to that ordinarily obtainable from a questionnaire. Under such conditions the questionnaire would not have to be a substitute for the interview, but neither would it be discarded. It could be used advantageously for obtaining valuable additional information and useful verifying data.

If rapport is good between the students and the person administering the questionnaire and if the questionnaire is carefully planned and well constructed, straightforward, full answers may be expected from most students. And if rapport is good between the student and his counselor, inaccurate, incomplete responses will usually be eventually detected. In time corrections will be made and the gaps filled in.

Interpretation of the Findings. For the information provided by a student's answers on a personal data blank to be most useful, its significance in the life of the student must be understood. To understand the real meaning of specific responses, a worker in many instances must already know something about the student, his home situation, and his cultural framework. Otherwise, the worker may misinterpret a response, over-rating or underrating its importance. A seventeen-year-old girl reports. for instance, on a questionnaire which she fills out at the beginning of a new school year that she is now working Saturdays and every day after school in a box factory owned by her uncle, in whose home she and her young brother have been living since the death of their parents some fifteen months ago. Anyone not informed regarding the home situation might think, on reading the girl's answers, that she has to work for her uncle to pay the cost of living in his home and might even wonder whether she is being exploited. Such thoughts do not occur to the girl's counselor, however, because she is informed. Instead, she notes as she reads the girl's answers, that the uncle and aunt are trying out a plan discussed the previous year as a possible solution to the problem of "how to keep the girl off the streets."

The aunt and uncle had been seriously disturbed by the problem, one that the aunt had tried to solve by giving up a good position to stay at home with the children. The plan did not work, however. The aunt stayed at home, but the girl did not. It was then that the uncle considered finding a job for her in his factory in the hope that it might give her something interesting to do. When the counselor talks with the girl, she finds that this plan seems to be working very well. The girl says that she works as a clerk in a supply room, is not always busy and so has time to study while at work, gets "regular wages," does not have to pay anything to her aunt, can use the money for clothes and the like, but wants to follow her uncle's advice to try to save something each month. Far from exploiting the girl, the uncle is trying very hard to help her meet some of the problems resulting from the unexpected death of both parents and a sudden change in home and school.

The information obtained from a questionnaire should always be interpreted in the light of information secured from other sources. For example, in answer to the questions "Do you have a separate room?" and "If not, with whom do you share your room?" one student answered "Yes" to the first question. Another answered "No" to the first one and "With my three brothers" to the second. These answers indicate that the first boy's home situation is better than that of the second boy, whereas the opposite is true. The first has a room that in the second boy's home would probably be used only as a storeroom because it would be considered too small and too poorly ventilated to be comfortable as a bedroom. The room that the second boy shares with his three brothers is a large attractive room with windows on three sides. It occupies the space usually given to two or more rooms. The "barracks," as the boys call this room, is the brothers' bedroom. They have elsewhere in the house ample space in which to play and study. While this example is somewhat extreme, it is not unusual. The misinterpretation that might follow from a comparison of the boys' answers by someone uninformed about the two homes is probably no greater than the misinterpretations actually made each day of the answers given by other students to other questions—misinterpretations made because the readers do not have sufficient background information to attach correct meanings to the students' answers.

The findings from the questionnaire should be used for the same purpose that any information gathered about a student should be used— to gain understanding of the student so that he may receive instruction and guidance in keeping with his needs and may be assisted in any way possible in his progress toward good development and maturity. The findings may be used specifically in different ways for achieving this general purpose. Some examples follow.

Each year a girl may give in answer to the question about vocational plans some vague response or may write "Undecided" or "Don't know yet." Or her responses given over a period of several years may vary widely, showing a lack of any consistent or definite interest. While this girl should not be pressed to come to a decision before she is ready to, she should be given help with her problem. The counselor can help the girl by encouraging her to talk about herself and the things she likes and dislikes and by trying to interest her in widening her range of occupational information through reading, looking at filmstrips on occupations, following certain radio and television programs, and doing other such things. The counselor may be able to help the girl to come to a better understanding of her assets and liabilities by going over the records with her and discussing the test findings and the data from questionnaires, autobiographical material, and other sources.

They may find an important clue in the questionnaire. The girl may, for example, consistently report home economics and art as the subjects liked best, which may indicate nothing more than a normal interest in a home career. If, however, the girl's school marks show that these specific interests seem to be accompanied by definite ability, the worker should try to interest the girl in learning more about the occupations or occupational fields in which she may be able to satisfy her interests in home economics and art and develop her abilities in these areas. The girl's answers to questions about work experience show that she has not had a chance to try out her interests and abilities, except at home and at school. It may be possible to arrange for her to obtain through work the exploratory experiences that she needs in order to find out whether she should make her interests in art, clothing, foods, home management, or the like vocational as well as avocational interests.

Another student's response to the question about free-time activities may show considerable participation in many different activities. Other evidence may indicate that his participation in extracurricular activities is excessive and may be interfering with his academic progress. The interview findings may reveal that the boy may be seeking through excessive participation in extracurricular activities some compensation for lack of success in academic work. In this case the counselor may be able to help the boy to work out an extracurricular program that will permit him to engage in satisfying free-time activities without jeopardizing his chance at success in classwork and at the same time may be able to help him to work out a curricular program that will permit him to have a better chance at academic success. By going over the boy's records with him and frankly discussing what they reveal, the counselor may help him to organize his efforts better and to think more clearly regarding his goals and interests than he may have done before.

The answer given by another boy to the same question on recreational interests and activities may show that he apparently does not have a hobby or special interest of any kind to serve as a balancing force or to fill any frustrating gaps in his life. The boy's response may provide an important clue or a completely false one. Further investigation may show that he has strong recreational interests which he cultivates enthusiastically but "just didn't bother to report." Or the investigation may show that he spends very little time in having fun because he thinks that "just having fun" is a waste of time and that he should always be doing something useful. The counselor may not be able to help this boy learn how to have fun and to be comfortable while doing so. Certain strong influences in his out-of-school life may prevent his ever being able to do so. Perhaps the counselor can help him by taking care never to show hostility toward students' having fun and by participating wholeheartedly with students in some of their fun-bringing activities. But this solution may be too simple and neat. Maybe the only way that the counselor can help the boy is by not doing anything and by preventing others as far as possible from doing anything that will cause him to feel uncomfortably different.

A student's reply to the question about vocational plans may show that his plans are not in harmony with his apparent pattern of abilities. As pointed out in Chapter 7, a counselor does not help such a student by telling him that he is aiming too high and then prescribing another objective for him. He may be able to help the boy, however, by encouraging him to discuss his plans and to examine the available evidence regarding his strengths and weaknesses so that the boy may perceive any contradictory patterns and study their significance.

The goals that some students report in their questionnaires are not, however, as unrealistic as the teachers of these students may think. Sometimes students and teachers use terms differently. In stating that he plans to be an engineer, a student may only mean that he wants to become an operator of a certain type of machine. He has every reason to believe that he can achieve this goal and knows that, when he does, his coworkers will usually refer to him as "the engineer." A teacher, however, may think that the boy wants to obtain a college degree in engineering. Some responses written on the questionnaires may be misunderstood by some readers until they are translated or interpreted by their authors.

A student's vocational objective may be more realistic than it seems to his teachers not only because the student and the teachers view the objective differently but also because actully the objective is not so much out of line with the student's abilities and talents as the teachers think. Dresden [9] gives a good example in her account of Delores, a high school student, who amused her teachers greatly when she indicated that she wanted to be a singer. The teachers knew that the girl was not even in the school chorus and that she had "made an IQ of 80 on an individual test." The girl did not think singing lessons necessary, and yet she wanted to be a singer. Apparently, however, she was not "all wrong." Dresden reports:

> "Do you think you can be a singer without taking lessons?"
>
> "Certainly—I am now! Don't tell anyone, because I'm not 16 yet so I haven't got a permit. Of course, I don't sing every night, and I don't get paid—but the manager always gives my mother some money."
>
> And so she told me about singing weekends for private parties in "small halls" back of taverns, and for weddings, offering continuous entertainment for the guests. She fairly sparkled as she told me of her triumphs, of the great demand for her talents, of the fun it was, and the money which her mother received.

Clearly, if a counselor is to interpret properly a student's responses on a questionnaire, he must have much more information about the student than he can secure through the questionnaire alone.

The questionnaire is an effective and safe tool only when used by workers scrupulously professional in their dealing with students. If the data are not used in a professional manner, some student might get hurt. Too many of us have witnessed a person's consulting some student's personal data blank in much the same way and for much the same reason that Mrs. Grundy may question her neighbor's children—to snoop. Students may not know that such actually occurs, but some suspect it. They feel justified in trying to protect themselves and their families by withholding information or by embroidering the facts.

IMPROVEMENT OF THE PERSONAL DATA FORM

The Need for Improvement. An examination of only a portion of the many questionnaires currently used for eliciting from students information about their backgrounds, plans, and various types of experiences makes one believe that the situation today with respect to student questionnaires is not very different from the much-protested questionnaire

---

[9] Katherine W. Dresden, "Vocational Choices of Secondary Pupils," *Occupations,* 1948, 27:104–106.

situation of 1927–1928 that led to an NEA investigation.[10] The NEA Research Division made an intensive follow-up study of 267 questionnaires on a variety of topics that were received by certain school superintendents during 1927–1928. The investigators found that many questionnaires made very small contributions, even to the ones circulating them. "No report of any kind could be obtained as to what happened to 64 of the 267. A considerable percentage of the questionnaires for which reports could be obtained were not . . . used in any way." If a similar investigation were made of the many questionnaires recently answered by students during a school year, it might be found that, like the questionnaires sent to the school administrators, some are worthwhile and are making first-rate contributions but many are not making any contribution of real value because the results are not used or because the questionnaires are badly handled, poorly prepared, and indefensibly time-consuming.

Some Guideposts. Authors of questionnaires generally find that the following guideposts mark the way to improved questionnaires.

1. *Limit the scope of the questionnaire.* To secure complete and truthful answers, the questionnaire should be as short as possible. It is generally better to use several short specialized questionnaires than one long questionnaire that seeks detailed information on many subjects. One boy, when about halfway through the task of filling out a very long personal data blank, wearily announced that he was tired of writing about himself. The other students, no doubt, felt the same way; and many, anxious to get the job over with, probably did not fill out the second half as carefully as they did the first.

Short questionnaires that deal with one or a few topics will, no doubt, yield better responses than the sections on the same topics contained in long questionnaires. It is very doubtful, for example, that the section on health as it usually appears in the long questionnaire produces much significant information on many students or that it is very useful for screening students in need of special attention. Besides, counselors should not have to secure this type of information on new students through a questionnaire. The students should be examined and questioned individually by a doctor or some other health specialist. If a questionnaire has to be the procedure used, a special committee, which includes the school nurse and some of the health education instructors, can develop a special questionnaire on health which will ask for pertinent facts and will yield information more valuable than that secured from a list of childhood diseases and a student's estimate of his health as "poor," "good," or "excellent."

Some authors of personal data blanks seem to confuse these in-

[10] "The Questionnaire," *Research Bulletin of the National Education Association,* 1930, 8:5–49.

struments with tests, for they include questions to which they surely know the answers. Included, for example, in the vocational section of one questionnaire are questions about the vocational virtues and vices; and in another the vocational section includes the question "How much training will be necessary to prepare for either of these occupations [the ones named as first and second choices]?" These are questions that the new student may properly expect to ask the counselor, instead of having them asked of him by the counselor.

Similarly some questionnaires and questionnaire sections on study habits seem designed more for testing or for pointing out the importance of certain matters than for securing information about the students' study habits. Since the information obtained from responses to questions on study habits is usually negligible, the time spent in asking students how they study might be better invested in teaching them how to study. Instead of using some teacher-made questionnaire on study procedures, it might be well to use some standardized questionnaire, such as the Brown-Holtzman Survey of Study Habits (The Psychological Corporation), the Wrenn Study Habits Inventory (Stanford University Press), or the study skills test of some achievement test battery, such as the Work-Study Skills Test of the SRA Achievement Series (Science Research Associates, Inc.) and the Study Skills Test of the Stanford Achievement Test (Harcourt, Brace & World, Inc.). A study habits inventory or study skills test may be used in much the same way that interest inventories are often used—to arouse interest and to start students to thinking seriously about the matter. The test serves as a springboard for discussions of the subject with a group or an individual.

The personal data blank is an analytical technique that should be used only for gathering information. It should not be used for the dual purpose of collecting data and of giving information or teaching by stressing the importance of certain matters through including questions about them.

2. *Eliminate questions which ask for information already available.* Unless there is doubt regarding its accuracy, information should not be sought that is already available. Like adults, young people dislike unnecessary duplication. Questions about grades repeated and courses failed are undesirable not only because such information is obtainable from cumulative records and hence the questions are little more than padding in a personal data blank, but also because they make some students feel uncomfortable or fearful. The new student who must list his past failures may fear that he is prejudicing his new teachers against him at the start and that some will give him lower marks than they might if they thought that he was a chronic success rather than a chronic failure in his previous school.

3. *Avoid using questions that suggest the answers, are incriminating, or reflect on others.* When questions suggest the answers, many stu-

dents give the answers suggested as "right." Self-interest and a desire to please dictate the responses that some students give to questions like the following:

Can you go out on school nights?

Do you listen to the radio while studying?

Do you have a regular bedtime?

Do you make an effort to give continued attention to speakers in class, assembly, and church?

Do you usually listen to at least one news broadcast every day?

Do you take pride in handing in neat, legible papers?

Some questionnaires contain items that many students are probably unwilling to answer for fear that an answer may boomerang. They are likely to consider it unwise to give honest answers to such questions as these:

Which subject do you dislike most?

Which is your easiest subject?

Do you usually get all the help you need from your teachers?

Are you afraid to ask your teachers for help?

Do you think of your teachers as friends?

Do you consider some school tasks assigned by your teachers a waste of time?

Such questions are more likely to be answered truthfully when given in an evaluation questionnaire which the students answer anonymously after they have completed the courses appraised than when given in an information blank which the students are asked to sign. Some, however, are even of doubtful value for inclusion in evaluation blanks. The inclusion of the last question, for example, may prevent some students from making a thoughtful objective appraisal and may cause some teachers to resist using an evaluation form that contains such a question.

4. *Avoid asking questions that may be embarrassing or that are highly personal.* Because personal data forms often contain questions that some students find embarrassing, students should be permitted to leave unanswered, if they wish, questions about religion, the education and occupations of their parents, home conditions, and the like.

One questionnaire, for example, contains a chart with spaces in which the student is to indicate the number of years each of his parents attended high school and college. Space is not provided, however, for showing education terminated below the high-school level; yet the parents of many students did not complete elementary school. If the student is embarrassed by his parents' limited education, he is likely to feel even more ashamed if the questionnaire indicates that teachers believe that all parents have at least some high school education.

Some students confronted with the problem of how to report their parents' education on a form which does not provide the spaces needed may solve it by awarding their parents high school diplomas and perhaps even giving them one or more years in college. In one school, teachers administering the questionnaire are instructed to try to guard against the students' tendency to conceal the real nature of their fathers' occupations by giving general occupational classifications, such as "salesman" or "factory worker." More specific information is certainly desirable, but it is not desirable that students be pressed to report more than they are willing to tell.

Information about the student's home conditions and his family's socioeconomic status is highly important and should be secured for every student if possible, but it is very doubtful that it should always be sought directly from the student. It is information that is best obtained through direct contact with the home rather than through direct questions. Much of it can be secured indirectly through observation, conferences with parents and students, and information obtained from other sources.[11]

Some questionnaire authors seem to hold the old storybook attitude toward stepparents, whereas many students hold attitudes of deep affection toward a stepfather or a stepmother. Some students do not like the way that the stepparent is pushed to one side in some questionnaires. Of the many questionnaires examined by the writer the Plainfield form is one of the few in which the stepparent is made equal to the parent whose place he takes. In it the same questions are asked about the stepparent as about the parent, and questions regarding the stepparents come immediately after the ones about the father and the mother. In some other forms questions about the stepparent are not even included in the section on family and home. They are given elsewhere and later, somewhat as an afterthought.

Many students fail to see value in certain questions concerning private matters. Others are antagonized because sometimes the questions are not asked with tact. One questionnaire, for example, contains the following questions that may be too blunt or personal for some students:

> Are you a ward of this state?
> Have you always lived with your parents?
> Do you like it there [home]?
> Do you enjoy entertaining friends in your home?
> Do you date with the opposite sex? If so, how often?

5. *Avoid making the questionnaire indefensibly long through inclusion of requests for information that is not essential or through use of*

---

[11] Ordinarily any questionnaire constructed for securing or recording information about the home, particularly socioeconomic data, should be prepared for use by staff members rather than for use with students. Such a form, called the Home Description Scale, was developed by Rothney and others for use in an elementary school. With a few modifications this scale or questionnaire can be made applicable for use in high schools. Rothney and Roens, *Counseling the Individual Student,* pp. 236–237.

questions that students will find difficult to answer because of lack of in-formation or understanding of the points covered.

Frequently questions are asked that some students find difficult to answer because they are not able to recall or to analyze their experiences sufficiently well. Symonds stressed this point, calling attention to the fact that students do not naturally observe their own habits or methods of work and that we should not assume that they have made observations of their conduct and are ready to answer our questions. "This form of retrospection, of looking back over one's behavior processes and recounting them," he said, "is a feat that requires special training." To make the point clear, Symonds gives a few simple questions on golf, such as "Does it bother you to have someone watch you drive?" and "How do you prepare for a match?" which some golfers would consider ridiculous. "The only golfer who stops to analyze his movements is the golf instructor or the professional who wants to write a book." [12]

Some students may consider ridiculous the questions given below. Others may consider them sensible but difficult to answer because they do not know how to answer them correctly. Rather than answer "I do not know" many will give answers which may approximate the truth or may be far from it. Here are the questions:

> How many hours a week do you spend in athletic activities? In non-athletic (extracurricular) activities?
>
> Why do you prefer the kind of athletics in which you take part?
>
> How long have you had each special interest?
>
> List the things you think you do better than most young people your age.
>
> Are you easily interrupted while studying?
>
> Do you often study hard and then forget what you have studied?
>
> Does difficulty with spelling keep you from doing as much writing as you would do otherwise?
>
> Do you have a good light on your work in all your classes? Please list rooms where the light is poor.

Students should not be asked the last question because many do not know the standard for a "good light." If the teachers believe that in some rooms the light is substandard, they should check and notify the proper authorities where improvement is needed. Since some forgetting follows practically all learning, some adults as well as some students would not know how to answer the question about forgetting after studying hard. Also, not many students really understand why they prefer certain activities or know whether, in comparison with others of their age, they have serious difficulty with spelling or are easily disturbed.

Some questionnaires are definitely overstuffed. Used as stuffing are

---

[12] From *Diagnosing Personality and Conduct* by Percival M. Symonds, p. 143. Copyright, 1931. The Century Company. Reprinted by permission of Appleton-Century-Crofts.

questions like "Do you have to be 'in the mood' to do your best work?" Adults generally enjoy their work more and work better when "in the mood" than when not; so they may assume that youngsters do too. Another question that may help to make a questionnaire indefensibly long is "Do you have common interests with your brothers? Explain." It is a rare student who does not have common interests with his brothers and sisters, and it is the student himself, perhaps, who should say "Explain." He may wonder whether the question refers to common interests in the family's welfare, in certain conditions in the home, and in the parents' affection or whether it refers to interest in the same TV programs, the same comics, the same hobbies, and the like.

When the question "How long do you study at home each night?" is followed by "Do you take books home to study each night?" the second question becomes a space filler. Also, why ask a student "Have you talked with anyone about your future plans? Who?" Of course, the student has talked with others unless there is something wrong with him or his home. We may assume that included among the persons with whom he has talked are his parents, brothers and sisters, and friends. The important question is "Has he talked with his counselor about his plans?" and that question should be put to the counselor, not the student.

6. *Do not control the students' answers too closely through the use of check lists and detailed questions.* Detailed questions do not always yield the comprehensive specific information that they are intended to produce.

Instead of asking such precise questions as "What poem, letter, or article have you written that has been published?" "Have you ever given a music recital?" "How many summers have you gone to camp?" "Which of the places on the following list have you visited?" it is better to ask the student to report what he did during particular summers, to tell about his special achievements and experiences, and to list the out-of-school groups and activities in which he participates. If sufficient space is provided on the form, more unusual experiences may be reported than are asked about in all the specific questions used on such topics. Moreover, experiences usually considered ordinary, such as spending a summer at home, may be reported by some boy or girl as an unusual experience. Furthermore, some students who do not have an opportunity to attend camps or to go elsewhere during the summer will report vacation experiences equally important in terms of developmental values, which are not covered by the questions generally asked about vacation experiences.

One Middle West school uses a questionnaire which gives, with the question on travel, a check list which includes all the continents except one, some foreign countries, and the various regions of this country, with instructions to check the places visited and to indicate age at the time of visit. The amount of time spent in the place is not asked, however. Although considerable space is given to this question, it is doubtful that it produces a clear picture of the travel experiences of most students in the school. Were the students asked simply to report their travel experiences, many would report trips to different parts of their own state and to some neighboring states. This is the type of travel experienced by most high school students. Not many are able to report travel in foreign countries. The check list, however, does not provide for reports on travel within the state and gives as much space to travel in foreign countries as to travel in the United States.

When answers are not controlled by detailed questions and check lists, students tend to report freely the experiences that they consider important. To help bring forth this type of information should be one of the principal contributions of the personal data blank.

7. *Try out the questionnaire in preliminary form,* preferably with individuals similar to the ones with whom the questionnaire is to be used, in order to determine whether every question asks what is intended, whether any is interpreted differently by different respondents, and whether any arouses resistance and antagonism.

THE EVALUATION QUESTIONNAIRE

The evaluation questionnaire is used to ascertain students' opinion of school offerings and practices in order to determine some of the changes needed for improving the educational program. This type of questionnaire may be used with members of a class to appraise the particular class situation (room conditions, student-teacher relations, skill and personality of the teacher, course content), or it may be used with all students in the school or a large portion of the student body, such as all freshmen or all seniors, in order to evaluate the total program or some phase of the program, such as instruction, guidance, or health services. To secure frank and comprehensive answers, the students are usually instructed not to sign the questionnaire.

Evaluation by a Class. The literature indicates that use of an evaluation questionnaire with class groups is a practice more frequently adopted in colleges than in high schools. Experience indicates that in both high schools and colleges use of evaluation questionnaires is most effective when use is optional and a teacher does not have to report the findings if he prefers not to do so. When results are reported on a voluntary basis, a teacher will probably be not only more willing to have students evaluate his classes but also better able to accept deserved criticism and sound recommendations, less disturbed by unwarranted criticism, and more willing to make modifications in keeping with the suggestions than he might be were he required to use the questionnaire and to report results or to hand over the forms to someone else to summarize and report.

When evaluation questionnaires are used upon administrative decree and the filled-in forms delivered to some administrative office, poor cooperation can be expected from at least some faculty members. Such procedures make even highly competent teachers feel insecure and probably make most teachers feel some resentment. Moreover, not-strong teachers can be expected to do all that they can to curry favor with students and to try to influence answers in other ways. Good teaching then may become subordinate to being popular with students.

The teacher who is sincerely interested in knowing the students' candid opinion of him as a teacher in order that he may improve his class procedures is usually able to help his students to approach the problem correctly and to evaluate objectively. Some teachers give the questionnaires to the students at the time of the last class session and ask them to return the answered forms after they receive their marks in the course. This procedure offers the important advantage of having the students know definitely that their statements will not affect their marks, but it has the disadvantage of increasing the possibility that some students will not return the questionnaires. For this reason many teachers have the questionnaires filled out during the last class period, assure the students that no attempt will be made to learn the identity of any respondent, and hope that the students will have faith in their integrity. If the students have found the teacher consistently aboveboard, they will trust him. If they have not always found him fair and straightforward, they will know how to protect themselves in their answers.

General questions followed by enough space for long answers will usually bring forth more helpful information than detailed questions like the following:

Are the assignments clear?

Is the work explained sufficiently well?

Does the teacher really enjoy young people?

Are the objectives of the course explained and followed?

Does he show thorough knowledge of his subject?

Better than such detailed questions are general questions like the following:

What did you like best about this course?

How do you think it could be improved?

What characteristics of the teacher do you like best?

What in the course have you enjoyed most (or found most helpful)?

What in the course have you enjoyed least (or found least helpful)?

The inclusion of specific questions about undesirable practices or objectionable personality characteristics of teachers antagonizes many teachers against the use of evaluation questionnaires. If students find certain teachers guilty of showing partiality, or of being inconsistent, dictatorial, or too lax, or if they consider some teachers not to be well-adjusted people or to be persons with annoying or offensive ways, they can express their feelings and make known their opinions in their answers to the general questions regarding things liked best and liked least, if they dare to criticize at all. Even the use of negative terms such as "dislike" should be avoided as well as questions like the following:

Are students given enough chance to talk?
Are students who disagree with the teacher made to feel uncomfortable?
Will the teacher admit he is wrong?
Is he basically a well-adjusted person?
Do you find the teacher a dictator?
Is he too personal?
Does he hold grudges?
Does he maintain an open mind?

Some evaluation questionnaires contain rating scales. The blank used at one university includes a scale that is somewhat like the following:

Directions: Answer question by placing check mark above answer that you think is correct.

In comparison with other courses has this one been

	?
more useful	about average	less useful

	?
more inter-esting	about average	less inter-esting

If you were considering another course taught by the same teacher, would his being the teacher be

	?
added reason for taking it	imma-terial	added reason for not tak-ing it

Evaluation of a Service or a Program. The evaluation questionnaire used with all students or with a large portion of the student body may be narrow in scope, covering only one phase of the school program, such as guidance or student activities. Or it may be very broad, covering the total program of administration, instruction, guidance, special services, and certain phases of student life.

A good example of the questionnaire used to evaluate a school's guidance program is the one used in the New York City survey by the Committee on Evaluation of Guidance. This questionnaire was used with the seniors in all high schools of the city.[13] It opened with a letter which asked the senior to help the Committee obtain "a picture of high school

---

[13] A copy of this questionnaire is given in F. M. Wilson, *Procedures in Evaluating a Guidance Program,* pp. 96–100. New York: Bureau of Publications, Teachers College, Columbia University, 1945.

life as the student sees it" and by so doing make it possible for the students who follow him in the school to benefit from his experiences and through his suggestions. The senior was asked to extend the scope of the questionnaire by giving on an added sheet further information and suggestions.

The New York City survey questionnaire was designed to secure information about various choices made by the seniors during their high school years, the persons (school and nonschool) whom they consulted in making these choices, satisfactions and dissatisfactions had from their school experiences and the particular faculty members who had helped and influenced them most. Since the students were told not to sign the questionnaires, information regarding previous schools attended, curriculum followed during high school, and certain other items, which ordinarily should not be sought through a signed form because obtainable elsewhere, was requested because needed for interpreting certain answers.

In the New York City survey blank the questions are simple and direct and more general than detailed. The senior is asked, for example, "What are the most important things that you have gained from high school?" "Could the school have helped you more?" and "What have been your main interests in school? Describe." Unlike many questionnaires of its type, it does not include check lists. Instead of being given a list of the principal student activities and told to check the ones in which he has taken part, the student is asked, "In what activities have you taken part for at least one full term?" Had a check list been used, some students, no doubt, would have checked activities in which they had not participated; and some probably would not have reported participation in activities not listed (because overlooked or because a subordinate part of one listed) even though they had been very active participants and even leaders in them.

The New York City questionnaire also includes a rating scale. The seniors are asked to indicate on a five-point scale ranging from "exceedingly satisfactory" through "exceedingly unsatisfactory" their estimate of the way in which the schools had met their needs with respect to development of personality, of good health habits, of reading habits and interests, of social behavior, and of social-mindedness; the general quality of teaching; the friendliness and helpfulness of the teachers; the information and advice received on further education and on vocations; training useful in getting a job and earning a living; and their all-round development and experience in school.

Preparation of the Form. The same rules given for preparing the personal data blank apply also to the evaluation questionnaire. Because the evaluation questionnaire is used for ascertaining opinion as well as facts, care should be taken to provide sufficient space for the answers and to word the questions in such a way that free expression is encouraged. Since the questionnaire is to be answered anonymously, the summaries of all answers to particular questions are often more used than the individual responses. Individual responses are not ignored, however, because, as in other types of writing, some individuals can analyze a situation better than others. The response of a particular individual may be more enlightening than the combined answers of all other respondents. Because, however, all answers should be tabulated and summary reports prepared, convenience of tabulating as well as convenience of answering needs to be kept in mind when the questionnaire blank is being prepared. Only one side of a page is used. Questions are numbered and subitems lettered so that the tabulator can identify each one quickly and easily. Also, it is well to arrange the blank so that, as far as possible, all or most answers will come to the same side of the page.

SUMMARY

The personal data blank is a useful device for securing background information on incoming students, particularly when a delay can be expected in obtaining cumulative record data from their previous schools. Even when the records are immediately available, the personal data blank may provide useful supplementary and verifying data. It is not, however, an acceptable substitute for the cumulative record or for the "get-acquainted interview."

The questionnaire needs to be administered with care. As with standardized tests, it is better to administer it to relatively small groups than to large ones. The purposes underlying its use and the confidential or nonconfidential nature of responses should be explained to the students. The instructions, oral and written, should be given in such a way that cooperation will be based on understanding rather than anxiety.

To interpret the findings correctly, a counselor may need to know much more about a student than is revealed by his personal data blank or cumulative record.

Short simple questionnaires seem better than long detailed ones. If the blank covers a number of different topics, care needs to be taken to avoid its becoming unnecessarily long through inclusion of irrelevant questions or requests for information already given and easily available. It is not wise to include questions that students find embarrassing or difficult to answer because of lack of information or understanding. General questions often yield more significant data than detailed questions or check lists. Testing a questionnaire through preliminary uses may show where improvement is needed before it is put into final form.

The same recommendations for the construction and administration of personal data blanks apply in general to the construction and administration of questionnaires used by students in evaluating a school program or particular aspects of the program. Permitting students to report anonymously helps many to report fully and truthfully. Making use of the questionnaire optional on the part of a teacher when it is his class that is being evaluated may help the teacher to accept deserved criticisms and to apply sound recommendations.

REFERENCES

Froehlich, Clifford P.: *Guidance Services in Schools*, 2d ed., pp. 186–192. New York: McGraw-Hill Book Company, Inc., 1958.

—— and Kenneth B. Hoyt: *Guidance Testing*, chap. 15. Chicago: Science Research Associates, Inc., 1959.

"The Questionnaire," *Research Bulletin of the National Education Association*, 1930, 8(1):5–49.

Rothney, John W. M., and Bert A. Roens: *Counseling the Individual Student*, chap. 5. New York: Holt, Rinehart and Winston, Inc., 1949.

Strang, Ruth: *Counseling Technics in College and Secondary School*, rev. ed. New York: Harper & Row, Publishers, Incorporated, 1949.

Symonds, Percival M.: *Diagnosing Personality and Conduct*, chap. 4. New York: Appleton-Century-Crofts, Inc., 1931.

Traxler, Arthur E.: *Techniques of Guidance*, rev. ed., chap. 4. New York: Harper & Row, Publishers, Incorporated, 1957.

9

Self-reports:
Follow-up Studies

Follow-up studies are made more often of graduates than of dropouts because they can be made much more easily. It is less difficult to obtain responses from graduates, and the questionnaire can be used reasonably well with them. The questionnaire alone is seldom effective for obtaining the information needed from a sufficient number of dropouts. It must be combined with the interview, a more difficult and expensive procedure.

PURPOSES AND VALUES

Purpose. Follow-up studies are ordinarily made for the twofold purpose of obtaining information about the postschool life of former students and their opinions of the general value, as well as the educational and vocational usefulness, of their school experiences. The studies need to be made, however, not only for the purposes of research and evaluation but also for the purpose of service—to discover and assist former students in need of further education and counseling.

For the purpose of service, the study made the year following a student's withdrawal or graduation is generally more important than the ones made two or more years later. It is during his first year away from school that the average young person has to contend with special problems and to make crucial educational and vocational decisions. For purposes of evaluation, however, the later follow-up surveys are probably more important than the one-year study. The person who has been out of school three or more years is ordinarily better able to appraise his school experiences in terms of intangible values and long-range objectives than the one who has very recently left school and still has more the point of view of the inexperienced youngster than of the adult.

The interest of high school counselors, teachers, and administrators in follow-up studies of students of particular schools has been in large part motivated and stimulated by the surveys that have been made of youth in relatively large areas by organizations not directly connected with particular schools. Some examples are the studies made by the

American Council on Education [1] and the Regents' Inquiry [2] in the 1930s, by the Child Labor Committee [3] and the Division of Labor Standards [4] of the U.S. Department of Labor in the 1940s, and by the Bureau of Labor Statistics [5] in the 1950s and the 1960s. These studies have called attention to the importance of a high school education, to the adjustment problems (occupational and otherwise) of boys and girls (graduates and dropouts), and to their evaluations (negative and positive) of their school experiences.

Value. Despite the limited reliability and validity of some findings, follow-up studies are useful in evaluating school programs. They have special values for counselors:

1. They show, among other things, how well the student personnel services are meeting student's needs and some of the changes needed in the guidance and counseling program.

2. They show the type of postschool guidance and counseling needed by many young people—the assistance that they need in changing from one job, occupation, college, or training program to another; in avoiding unemployment; in adjusting to new work conditions; in preparing for advancement; in dealing with causes of dissatisfaction; in solving problems of inadequate skill and training; and in planning and seeking further training. Counselors may not always be the best sources of help, but they need to be aware of the need for help and to do what they can to help make provision possible.

3. Follow-up studies help to keep counselors informed regarding training programs; the difficulties that young people encounter in moving from school to college, work, or military service and in assuming the responsibilities of marriage; the conditions and practices in the occupational world; and some of the special problems of the young worker with little or no occupational experience. They also help to keep counselors in touch with youth's world outside the school—with their interests and activities in general.

4. The studies yield information that may be used in counseling

[1] Howard M. Bell, *Youth Tell Their Story*. Washington, D.C.: American Council on Education, 1938.

[2] E. C. Eckert and T. O. Marshall, *When Youth Leaves School*. New York: McGraw-Hill Book Company, Inc., 1939.

[3] Harold J. Dillon, *Early School Leavers: A Major Educational Problem*. New York: Child Labor Committee, 1949.

[4] Elizabeth A. Johnson and Caroline E. Legg, *Hunting a Career*. Washington, D.C.: Government Printing Office, 1949.

[5] Margaret L. Plunkett and Naomi Riches, *School and Early Employment Experience of Youth: A Report on Seven Communities, 1952–57*. Washington, D.C.: Government Printing Office, 1960; Sophia Cooper, "Employment of June 1960 High School Graduates," *Monthly Labor Review*, 1961, 84:463–470; Jacob Schiffman, "Employment of High School Graduates and Dropouts in 1961," *Monthly Labor Review*, 1962, 85:502–509.

and group guidance work with boys and girls in school. For many students this information has a special significance because it comes from persons who are not far beyond them in age, whom they view more as peers than as "authorities," but whose words they tend to heed because they (the graduates or dropouts) have "just gone through it" and so can speak with the authority that comes with firsthand experience. In some group guidance classes summary reports on follow-up studies are very important resource materials.

Preferably a Cooperative Project. When follow-up studies are carried out according to a plan organized for all the schools in a town, city, district, or county, the work of canvassing the graduates and dropouts of a particular school, of studying and tabulating the replies, and of preparing the summary report is done by workers in that school. The survey instruments and procedures, however, which are recommended for use (often on an optional basis), are prepared and planned by a central group that is usually made up of representatives from various schools.

A cooperative follow-up plan organized at the community or county level has certain advantages over a plan whereby each school makes its own study more or less independently:

1. Participation in the work is increased because provision of consultation and advisory service helps to increase interest and to make the work easier than it would be otherwise.

2. Cooperative planning results in better procedures and more attractive instruments than would be used by some schools when acting alone. Arrangements, for example, are likely to be made for the use of printed form letters and questionnaires, which usually bring in more returns because they are ordinarily more attractive and more easily answered than are forms duplicated by some other means.

3. A composite report based on the summary reports from a number of schools provides an overall picture that will show, among other things, that offerings and activities which are good for students in one school may not be very good for students in another school in the same community and that in some schools the students are receiving a great deal in terms of certain services whereas the students in another school are receiving very little, not because of inadequacies in the persons providing the service, but because of inadequacies in provision for staff and facilities. In short, the composite picture helps to reveal differences in the needs of different groups of students in the same community and to show gaps in the overall program for provision of certain services. In some areas of service the minimum standards may be raised for all schools. The high standards achieved by some schools may encourage other schools to try to provide service above the minimum standards.

4. The cooperative plan adds weight to the findings, thus helping

to secure correction of certain conditions through action that must be taken or can be taken more effectively through the central office or by the school board than through action taken in a particular school.

5. Cooperatively organized follow-up studies attract public interest, help to secure public support for efforts toward improvement, and help to gain the assistance needed from nonschool groups. A community center, for example, was established in a Michigan town when the findings from a follow-up study of high school graduates showed that the young people in the community needed more opportunities for suitable recreation. When in another Michigan community, Kalamazoo, it became known that most of the students went from high school into industry and business, that during a six-year period only about 25 per cent of the graduates had gone to college, the chamber of commerce and certain other community organizations took action as follows: [6]

> ... set up a steering committee to work with the school authorities in developing adequate offerings and helpful relationships with the industries of the city. A training program in distributive occupations was established under the provisions of the Michigan State Plan for Vocational Education; an apprenticeship training program was introduced; a placement bureau was established for students; and a complete vocational survey was made to disclose the opportunities and demands of modern business.

FOLLOW-UP STUDIES OF GRADUATES

Studies in the Lower Schools. Very little follow-up work below the junior high school is reported in the literature. Such work seems carried out in the lower grades in an informal manner and most often through direct communication in the group situation. Arrangements are made for the former students (usually former kindergarteners or sixth-graders) to be brought back to their "old" school or classroom for something like a class reunion.

The students explore their former work and play areas, are served refreshments, reminisce regarding last year's experiences, and discuss their life in the new school or classroom. Usually their current, as well as their former, teachers are present so that they may gain knowledge and understanding that will enable them to help graduates of the lower school to make a good adjustment in the higher one.

Some school systems (apparently a minority) regularly follow up their junior high school graduates. The Providence Public Schools, for example, use the questionnaire shown in Figure 22 for learning how these

[6] D. E. Kitch and W. H. McCreary, *Guide for Making a Follow-up Study of School Drop-outs and Graduates,* California Guidance Bulletin 13. Sacramento: State Department of Education, January, 1950. (Mimeographed.)

students are getting along in senior high school and for giving them an opportunity to make suggestions to their junior and senior high school counselors.

The great majority of follow-up studies made below the college level are surveys of high school graduates. It is with this type of study that the remainder of this section is concerned.

PROVIDENCE PUBLIC SCHOOLS
JUNIOR HIGH SCHOOL FOLLOW–UP REPORT

1. My name is _____ Date _____
2. My address is _____
3. I was graduated from _____ Junior High School
4. My counselor (guidance teacher) there was _____
5. I am now attending _____ School in the
   _____ grade.
6. I have transferred from _____ High School to
   have not
   _____ High School during my high school course.
7. My present counselor is _____
8. I have taken the following subjects: 10B: _____

   _____

   10A: _____

   _____

9. The subject which interested me most was _____
10. The subjects in which I have failed in senior high school are:
    10B: _____
    10A: _____
11. The subjects which I have found most difficult in senior high school are:

12. If there are any suggestions about your work in either junior or senior high school which you think would help your junior high school counselor to prepare pupils better for the senior high schools, please write them below.

    _____

    _____

    _____

13. If there is any other message that you would like to send your junior high school counselor, there is room on the other side of this sheet for a personal note.

FIGURE 22   *Junior high school follow-up questionnaire.* (Used by special permission of the Superintendent of the Providence, Rhode Island, Public Schools.)

The One-year Study. The regular use of one-year follow-up studies helps schools to maintain contact with their graduates and to increase the possibility of their securing the kind of cooperation needed at the time of later follow-up studies. The former students are asked to report any changes in address and to tell what they are doing and where. They are urged to write letters in which they tell all about their lives since leaving school and their plans for the future.

The double-postcard type of questionnaire is commonly considered adequate for the one-year study. It is relatively inexpensive and usually produces the information needed for keeping the school's records up to date. Then when a more elaborate study is to be made, the graduates can be more easily located than would be possible had contact not been established during the year immediately after their departure. The postcard questionnaire was used in the one-year follow-up of the students who cooperated in the Wisconsin Counseling Study.[7] On one side of the card there was this message:

> We are still interested in you as we were when you were in high school. We want to know where everyone in your senior class is now and what he is doing. Will you let us know what *you* are doing by filling in the other part of this card, tearing it off, and dropping it in the mailbox?

On the other side of the card were these questions:

> What is your address? (street address and city)
> Name?
> Married girls give maiden name _____
> If you are working full time, what are you doing?
> If working, where do you work? (name of company)
> What do you actually do on the job?
> If working or not do you like what you are doing?
> What would you like to be doing in your *second* year out of high school?

The graduates who did not return the postcard received a second copy. Those who did not respond to the second inquiry were again sent the card, this time in a form letter that asked for their cooperation and provided socially acceptable excuses for the failure to respond, such excuses as "Maybe you lost the card. If you did, here is another" and "Maybe we didn't have your right address. If so, this card can be used now."

The first postcard brought returns from 56 per cent of the group. The second brought the cumulative response to 69 per cent, and the form letter with a third card raised it to 89 per cent. Handwritten letters sent to the remaining members brought the total to 95 per cent. As stressed by the research director,[8] in order for a follow-up study to give unbiased data, returns are needed from 100 per cent of the subjects. The goal of 100 per cent was achieved through visits to the last 5 per cent at their homes or places of employment.

Later Follow-up Studies. A longer questionnaire than can be contained on a postcard is needed for the study made two or more years after stu-

[7] John W. M. Rothney et al., *Guidance Practices and Results,* p. 145. New York: Harper & Row, Publishers, Incorporated, 1958.

[8] John W. M. Rothney and R. A. Mooren, "Sampling Problems in Follow-up Research," *Occupations,* 1952, 30:573–579.

dents graduate or leave school. To help secure a sufficiently large number of properly filled in questionnaires, the blank needs to be neat, easy to read and to answer, and as attractive as possible. It should be accompanied by a stamped addressed envelope and a letter that induces former students to give the time and effort needed for answering the entire form. The letter should sound warm and friendly.

To save time and money, a form letter is ordinarily used. The use of handwritten letters is neither practical nor sufficiently more productive than the form letter to justify the cost in time and money. That such greatly increased efforts to personalize follow-up procedures do not contribute significantly to the speed and quantity of the returns was another important finding in the Wisconsin Counseling Study.[9]

If the form letter is for use in a particular school, it can be personalized through reference to some important or interesting experience once shared by the members of the follow-up group and likely to be remembered by all, such as the "big game," the class-day party, commencement exercises, and the like, and through a request that each one return the questionnaire with a letter in which he tells all about himself. The letters that are prepared for use by a number of schools participating in follow-up studies according to some cooperative arrangement cannot be personalized as easily as letters prepared for use in only one school. For this reason some schools participating in cooperative studies use the recommended questionnaire blanks but devise their own form letters.

A good form letter for use in a number of schools can be prepared, however, which will bring the response wanted. It does not have to be a formal letter. It can be sincerely friendly in tone and can appeal strongly to a young person's feelings of school loyalty and of civic responsibility for contributing to the improvement of the public schools. Such a letter has been developed for use in the high schools and junior college of Chanute, Kan. This letter is the first page of a four-page pamphlet, the other three pages being used for the questionnaire shown in Figure 23. It reads as follows:

> The administration and faculty of the Chanute schools are eager to improve the school curriculum to fit the needs of the students. We know of no better way to acquire suggestions for this purpose than through the students who are graduating from the school system and are out in the field working. We feel that you have had, since you left school, many experiences which would aid us in providing future students with a better educational system. We are also eager to know how you are getting along and if we can be of some help to you. For this reason we are sending you this questionnaire.
>
> We have made the questions so that you can answer them by merely checking your response. However, if you desire to elaborate more fully,

[9] Robert A. Mooren and John W. M. Rothney, "Personalizing the Follow-up Study," *Personnel and Guidance Journal*, 1956, 34:409–412.

feel free to do so; in fact, we would appreciate your personal comments. If you have time, write us a few lines on the back of the questionnaire. Your answers will be treated confidentially, and your name will not be used in any way.

The Chanute schools are your schools. Your reaction to your school work and your experiences since graduation can be of real help in our enriching the curriculum and improving the schools for the youth of Chanute.

Will you sit down now, while you have this questionnaire before you, answer these questions, and return the form in the stamped envelope? We wish you the best of success in whatever your work may be.

Sincerely yours,

The procedures adopted for the follow-up study can probably be carried out more effectively by the former students' counselors than by others, provided, of course, that the counselors are interested and their case loads are sufficiently light to make follow-up work a practicable addition to their functions. Personal notes written by the counselors at the bottom of the form letters sent to their former counselees who fail to return the questionnaire may help to increase the number of returns to the second appeal and thus decrease the number of graduates to whom a third appeal must be made. Like the first, the follow-up letter should be cordial and one in which assistance is requested rather than demanded.

Like other questionnaire blanks, the follow-up form should be as short as possible and still provide sufficient space for the answers. Providing outline forms in which the answers may be written is a convenience for both the respondents and the persons who tabulate the responses. The question about work experience, for example, is generally followed by an outline form very much like the one used in the Chanute questionnaire. A similar chart can be provided for reporting further education which might be as follows:

Name of school	Course	Date entered	Date left	Reason for leaving

Some outlines provided for reporting work experience include spaces for salary. If the questionnaire is sent out by a placement bureau, a request for information about salary is desirable. Otherwise, it is probably better to omit the item. For some individuals the question may be embarrassing; to others it may seem too personal. Either embarrassment or annoyance may cause some not to return the form. If a former student is earning a salary that is above or below the average for the type of work

Name _____ Address _____

Directions: Check whenever possible the line of your choice; otherwise use a few words to answer the question. Your name will not be used in making reports on this inquiry.

I. MARITAL STATUS.

_____ Single   _____ Divorced   Date of Marriage

_____ Married   _____ Separated

II. SCHOOLS ATTENDED SINCE GRADUATION FROM HIGH SCHOOL.

Name of School	Dates of Attendance	Degrees Received

If you were just now completing high school and knew your own strengths and weaknesses as you now know them, what would you do? Check (X) below:

_____ a. Enter the same college that I did.

_____ b. Enroll in a junior college pre-professional course.

_____ c. Enroll in a course that could be completed in junior college.

_____ d. Enroll in a (different) liberal arts or denominational college.

_____ e. Enter a (different) large university.

_____ f. Take a different course in the same college.

_____ g. Not go to college at all.

_____ h. Enter the same work that I did.

_____ i. Enter a different kind of work.

_____ j. Enter some other type of school (specify).

_____ k. Other (specify) _____

III. WORK.

1. How much time elapsed between leaving high school or college and your first full-time job?

_____ Days   _____ Months   _____ Years

2. Please list the jobs you have held since you graduated. Include service in the Armed Forces.

Name of Firm (List present job first)	Address	Average Hrs. per Week	Weekly Earnings	Approx. Dates of Employment From To	Job Title or Duties

3. If you have left any full-time job, please check your reason below.

_____ a. Offered a better job.

_____ b. Disliked type of work.

_____ c. Needed at home.

_____ d. General economic conditions.

_____ e. Discharged from work.

_____ f. Moved with family.

_____ g. Married.

_____ h. Maternity.

_____ i. Disliked fellow workers.

_____ j. Continued education.

_____ k. Other (specify) _____

4. How did you secure your first full-time job?

_____ a. Personal letter.

_____ b. Letter of application.

_____ c. High school teacher, principal.

_____ d. Friends and relatives.

_____ e. College adviser.

_____ f. Employment agency.

_____ g. Advertise for job.

_____ h. Answer newspaper advertisements.

_____ i. Personal application.

_____ j. Other (specify) _____

FIGURE 23 *Questionnaire for former students at Chanute, Kansas, schools.*

5. Where did you get the training for your present job?

____ a. In school   ____ b. On job   ____ c. Elsewhere

Where? _____

6. Are you satisfied with your present job?

____ Yes ____ No   Why? _____

IV. CHOICE OF AN OCCUPATION.

1. Have you made a definite choice of an occupation? _____

a. If so, what is it? _____

b. Why have you chosen this occupation? _____

2. When did you decide on your present occupation?

____ a. Before entering high school.   ____ d. While on present job.

                                         ____ f. Still undecided.

____ b. During high school.   ____ g. Other (specify) _____

____ c. Following high school.

3. Where have you received help in planning for the occupation of your choice?

____ a. Friend.   ____ f. College adviser.

____ b. Relatives.   ____ g. Parents.

____ c. High school teacher.   ____ h. Reading.

____ d. Principal of high school. ____ i. Career conference.

                                   ____ j. Other (specify) _____

____ e. Adviser or homeroom teacher.

V. HIGH SCHOOL EDUCATION.

1. Do you think the courses you took were profitable for you?

____ Yes ____ No   Why not? _____

2. List in order of rank the three courses you took during your high school years which have been the most and the least valuable to you in your later training or work.

Most valuable: a. _____ b. _____ c. _____

Least valuable: a. _____ b. _____ c. _____

3. In what ways and to what extent did you obtain satisfactory training or experience while in high school? Use the following code to indicate your answers.

CODE: S — Highly satisfactory;   A — About average;   U — Unsatisfactory.

a. Information and advice on further education _____ S A U

b. Guidance and counsel on selection of the proper job for me _____ S A U

c. Training for the vocation in which I am now engaged ____ S A U

d. Development of effective health habits _____ S A U

e. Preparation for home and family living _____ S A U

f. Training for active participation in civic and community life _____ S A U

g. Development of high ideals and suitable moral code ____ S A U

h. Improvement in ability to undertake and proceed with new tasks _____ S A U

i. Development of ability to meet people easily _____ S A U

j. Preparation for further education _____ S A U

k. Training in supervising or directing the activities of others _____ S A U

l. Preparation in speaking and writing effectively _____ S A U

m. Stimulation of a desire to read and appreciate good literature _____ S A U

n. Development of a sound philosophy of life _____ S A U

o. Training for effective use of leisure time _____ S A U

p. Cultivation of a wholesome appreciation of work _____ S A U

q. Development of a broad understanding of social and economic problems _____ S A U

r. Stimulation of esthetic appreciation, particularly for good music and art _____ S A U

FIGURE 23   (continued)

4. Please give your evaluation of the extracurricular activities you participated in while in school.
Code:

1—Great value;   2—Some value;   3—Little value;   4—No value.

____ Basketball   ____ Kays   ____ Science Club
____ Track and field   ____ Golf or tennis   ____ GAA
____ School annual   ____ Plays   ____ FBLA
____ Y-Teens   ____ Football   ____ Others
____ Key Club   ____ Intramurals

5. What other subjects do you wish had been offered? _____

_____

_____

6. What help other than subjects offered could the high school have given you which it did not provide? _____

_____

_____

_____

VI. CONCERNING POST-HIGH SCHOOL SERVICES.

1. Should a school staff be interested in the post-high school problems of its graduates? ___ Yes___No
   If your answer to the question above is "Yes," answer items 2 and 3.

2. What are some of the post-high school problems that graduates need help in solving?

_____

_____

3. Which of the following would be of value to you?
   ____ a. Advisory council.   ____ e. Testing services.
   ____ b. College extension   ____ f. Trade courses.
        courses.   ____ g. Career night. (Occupations dis-
   ____ c. Library services.   cussed by leaders employed in the
   ____ d. Night classes.   occupations.)

FIGURE 23   (continued)

that he is doing, he may report this fact when he answers the questions regarding satisfactions and dissatisfactions in relation to work. Because most respondents want to show their former teachers that they are making good, many may be tempted to report better salaries than they are actually earning. A more accurate picture of the earnings of youth can usually be obtained through data from the state employment service than through data from follow-up questionnaires.

The use of check lists in follow-up questionnaires definitely facilitates the work of both the respondent and the person who tabulates the replies. It is much more difficult to summarize results from answers to general questions than the checks made on a list of items. The data from the replies to general questions are, however, probably more valid than the data from check lists. As Good [10] states:

The recipient comes to depend upon the list for suggestiveness and for a classification of his responses with the result that he is not so likely to write in additional items. In fact, items which the respondent might have

[10] From *Methods of Research,* by Carter V. Good and Douglas E. Scates, p. 613. Copyright, 1954. Appleton-Century-Crofts, Inc. Reprinted by permission of the publisher.

recorded, had there been no categories in the list, may be omitted when he checks a list either because the respondent considers the given list to be inclusive of all desired items or because he assumes an attitude of dependence on the list.

Yet the check list is a convenience for the respondent and, no doubt, helps to increase the number of returns. For such reasons check lists are generally used in follow-up questionnaires. They should always contain a final category of "other" so that the respondent is encouraged to expand the list to cover items that apply to him but are not given in the list. If the category of "other" is not included, some important answers may be omitted.

Increasing the Returns. In using evaluation questionnaires with students still in school, a faculty is not ordinarily concerned with the problem of how to secure enough returns because the forms are usually filled out at school. Thus replies are generally obtained from almost all students. In follow-up studies, however, the problem of obtaining enough returns can be a serious one. To secure an adequate quantity, the counselors need to know how to reach the former students to be canvassed, how to prepare a questionnaire that is reasonably easy to understand and answer and that is free from annoying or embarrassing questions, and how to compose a letter that will arouse interest and elicit the cooperation needed.

In many schools in which follow-up studies are a regular part of the guidance program, cooperation is sought from future alumni while they are still in school. In some, in order to maintain contact with the withdrawer as well as the graduate, students are told about the follow-up work during their first year in the school and are asked to keep in touch with the school should they find it necessary to leave school without graduating. In most cases, however, efforts to secure cooperation from present students are directed toward the seniors. In some cases the seniors are asked to notify their homeroom teachers or counselors the following year of any change in address and to report their new activities. Sometimes the seniors are given questionnaire blanks to fill out and return after a certain period of time.

In the Wisconsin Counseling Study the students filled out such a questionnaire, entitled Senior Report, one month before graduation. Five different forms were used according to the students' post-high school plans, but all opened with the following request: "Give the name and address of someone who will always know where you will be so that they can send mail to you."

In some schools the senior problems or group guidance class is asked to share responsibility for carrying out the follow-up study. The students may make suggestions regarding revisions in forms and procedures as well as share in the work of preparing the materials, sending out the questionnaires, typing copies of the summary report, and the like. Since individual replies are confidential, students cannot share in the work of tabulating and summarizing the responses. No doubt the seniors' sharing in the planning and the work helps to increase the returns for current studies and for later ones in which the seniors will be the respondents.

Because of changes in their addresses, some graduates do not receive the questionnaires. Information regarding the new addresses of some may be secured from family members whose addresses are known. The addresses of some others may be obtained through posting a list of "lost alumni" on school bulletin boards or through publication of such a list in the school and community newspapers. The use of local newspapers and telephone calls for learning the whereabouts of the graduates is easier when the graduating class and communities are small than when they are large. Ledvina,[11] for example, described the use of such methods for obtaining 100 per cent returns in a follow-up study of 136 members of three graduating classes of a rural high school.

Some graduates may have to be interviewed in order to secure their responses. The same questions are usually asked in the interview that are contained in the questionnaire. In both the questionnaire and the interview the respondents should be able to enlarge the questions and encouraged to give additional information.

Significance of the Findings. The significance of follow-up data depends largely upon the percentage of the returns. The fewer the returns, the less significant the findings. Ordinarily replies are received at first from little more than half the group. The returns are generally considered "good" when as many as two-thirds or three-fourths of the group finally reply. When only a portion of the group responds, the members replying usually represent chiefly the ones who have favorable reactions. They represent a biased sampling, and this fact must be considered in interpreting the findings.

To obtain an unbiased picture a return of 100 per cent is needed. Such a return does not, however, guarantee that the data are unbiased. The validity and reliability of data from follow-up questionnaires, like those from other self-report instruments, are often questionable. Many respondents, wishing to give a good account of themselves, withhold some facts and embroider others. In some cases there is intentional and gross misrepresentation. Personal problems lead other respondents to distort the facts or prevent their perceiving the facts correctly. Some report reactions based on majority opinion or hearsay rather than thoughtful, objective appraisal. Others tend to react in keeping with their postschool success, uncritically and incorrectly giving the school credit or blame for their success or lack of it. Some graduates respond indifferently, answer-

[11] L. M. Ledvina, "A 100 Per Cent Follow-up." *Personnel and Guidance Journal,* 1954, 33:90–93.

ing the questions carelessly and leaving some unanswered or incompletely answered.

By interviewing some respondents, the investigators can make a partial check on the reliability of the questionnaire answers. For example, in the New York City evaluation study (referred to in the preceding chapter) more than eight thousand students replied anonymously to a questionnaire filled out under uniform conditions in 47 schools. Fifty-two students were selected at random to be interviewed. Their questionnaires were held apart from the others so that the answers could be checked with the interview responses. In the interviews the students were asked the same questions asked in the questionnaire and in almost the same words.

Most reports on follow-up studies of students give only information regarding the respondents' educational and occupational status at the time of reply and their reactions to school experiences. Few contain information that makes possible comparison of the respondents' postschool status with school-period status. This type of information is usually provided, however, in reports on research studies, such as the Wisconsin study.[12]

Obviously a report that shows how many of the students who went to college ranked in the first, second, third, and fourth quarters, respectively, of their high school class, according to the findings from a test of scholastic aptitude, is more meaningful than a report that merely tells how many boys and how many girls attended college. And a report on a ten-year follow-up study of high school graduates which shows that most girls who ranked in the upper half of the group in terms of scholastic aptitude went on to college and from college into clerical work gives the reader far more to think about than it would if it merely stated that a certain percentage of the girls attended college and that a certain percentage of the girls were engaged in clerical work at the time of reply. Most readers of the second type of report would fail to see the girls who graduated from college among the young women employed as clerical workers.

Before a school can successfully make a follow-up study that gives a comparison of the status of the respondents during the school period with their status at the time of reply, the school must maintain cumulative records that provide the type of data needed. As Wrenn [13] has stated:

> If, for example, it should seem desirable to follow up the post-college civic or cultural activities of students who had participated in certain types of student activities, it would be essential to know the *quality* and *extent* of their student participation. This type of information could not well be gathered after they had left school. Too much dependence would have to be placed on retrospection, and this is known to place a serious limitation on the validity of the data. The study should be *planned and*

---

[12] Rothney et al., *Guidance Practices and Results*, chaps. 6–8.
[13] C. Gilbert Wrenn, *Student Personnel Work in College*, p. 494. New York: The Ronald Press Company, 1951. Italics in the original.

started while the subjects are still in school. A sharp distinction should be drawn between the follow-up subject's statement regarding present status and his reaction regarding what he *thought* he did or thought when he was a student. "Retrospective falsification" is a very real phenomenon.

SURVEY STUDIES OF DROPOUTS

A Large and Heterogeneous Group. The number of students who withdraw from school before graduating is decreasing but is still very large. According to one report of the Bureau of Labor Statistics,[14] some 350,000 quit school in 1960 in comparison to about 540,000 in 1950. Current trends indicate that about 7½ million boys and girls will enter the labor force in the 1960s without completing high school.

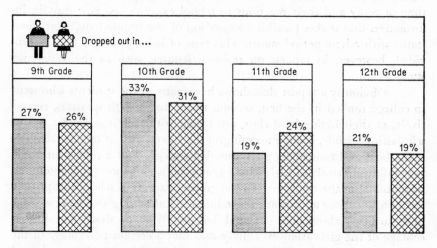

FIGURE 24   *Grade during which dropouts left school.* (Margaret L. Plunkett, *Highlights from a Study on the Early Employment Experience of Youth in Seven Communities 1952–1957,* p. 4. Washington, D.C.: Government Printing Office, 1961.)

The dropouts tend to stay in school longer today than ten years ago. While many leave school before age fourteen or fifteen, age sixteen is the most common age at which they withdraw. The largest drops occur in grades 9 and 10. Particularly disturbing for counselors is the fact that a considerable number withdraw during their senior year, presumably when they are in reach of graduation. Figure 24, for example, shows that one-fifth of the 10,000 students in seven moderately sized communities who quit school during a five-year period withdrew when in the twelfth grade.

The dropouts form a heterogeneous group. The numbers of boys and of girls who left school in 1960 were about equal. The dropouts include young people from all socioeconomic groups. They range from very

[14] Cooper, *op. cit.,* p. 467.

low to very high in mental ability. They include youth from rural, urban, and suburban areas. Contrary to popular opinion the dropout rate is higher in rural than in urban areas.

It is important to the welfare of both the individual and the nation that educable young people continue their education at least through high school. The individual who has less than a high school education is in an unfavorable economic position. His situation becomes increasingly serious as automation reduces the number of unskilled jobs. Hiring standards and employment trends underscore the importance of his staying in school. In 1960, for example, the Department of Labor listed 60 skills that were in short supply.[15] Every one of them required at least a high school education. A good number of the dropouts, had they stayed in school, might have become eligible for training programs in the skilled trades and found steady employment and job satisfaction.

The area and national surveys provide valuable information regarding the dropout situation in the nation as a whole and in some particular areas. What is true, however, of the nation as a whole or of another community may not be true of the local community. And what is true of one school in the community may not be true of another. Each school in each community needs to study its dropouts in order to understand its own situation and to increase its holding power.

Follow-up Procedures. Use of the questionnaire alone is generally not very effective in follow-up studies of dropouts. The percentage of returns is usually disappointingly low. The questionnaire seems most effective when used at the time that the student is withdrawing. Figure 25 shows a form that has been used for this purpose in one school.

When the follow-up study is made after the student has quit school, better results are obtained through use of the interview with or without the questionnaire than through use of the questionnaire alone. The same information is sought through both procedures. It generally includes personal data (name, address, employment status, marital status, length of time in the community, etc.), family status, present or last job, previous work experience, reasons for leaving school, family attitude toward education and school leaving, withdrawal procedures (parent-counselor conference, written consent of parent, advice sought, etc.), present feelings regarding the decision to withdraw, unemployment experience, union experience, vocational planning and preparation, job satisfactions and future plans, and suggestions or recommendations to the school.

The same general procedures are followed in preparing the questionnaire form and the interview guide sheet. Proposed items are carefully studied and selections made. A tentative list or form is prepared and submitted to consultants for appraisal. The form is then revised and tested

[15] Seymour L. Wolfbein, "Transition from School to Work: A Study of the School Leaver," *Personnel and Guidance Journal,* 1959, 38:105.

STUDY OF CURRENT DROPOUTS OF OXNARD UNION HIGH SCHOOL

Your answers will be considered confidential. They will be used for statistical purposes and for the improvement of the school program.

Name _____   Date _____

Age _____   Course: (Underline one)

Class _____   Business, College Preparatory,
General, Home Economics, or
Industrial

I. **Please** state very frankly the *real* reason or reasons why you are leaving school. Your honest answers will help us to improve the school.

_____

_____

_____

II. What do you plan to do after leaving school? (Check one)
1. _____ Work for pay full time
2. _____ Work for pay part time
3. _____ Marry
4. _____ Join Armed Forces
5. _____ Look for job
6. _____ Other (Please describe)

III. Please indicate by a check in the proper column how much this school has helped you in regard to each of the following:

	A great deal	Some	None
1. Getting along with other people			
2. Understanding yourself			
3. Selecting and getting a job			
4. Marriage and family life			
5. Thinking about personal problems			
6. Taking care of your health			
7. Taking part in civic and community affairs			
8. Using your spare time			
9. Using good English			
10. Using basic mathematics skills			
11. Using your money wisely			
12. Ability to read well			

IV. How could Oxnard Union High School have been more helpful to you?

_____

_____

V. What do you especially like about Oxnard Union High School?

_____

_____

VI. Can Oxnard Union High School be of further service to you? If so, explain:

_____

_____

FIGURE 25   *Questionnaire for dropouts.*

through actual use. It is again revised, and copies are prepared for use in the study.

Because many dropouts are reluctant to express themselves freely and frankly with school people, some investigators consider it unwise to use teachers or counselors as interviewers. They were not used, for example, in the Louisville study [16] or in the Child Labor Committee study.[17] However, they were used, along with other school people (vice-principals,

[16] Johnson and Legg, *op. cit.*
[17] Dillon, *op. cit.*

school social workers, attendance officers, etc.), in the studies made in Rochester [18] and Syracuse.[19] There the investigators decided that the disadvantages resulting from the interviewers' being school people were offset by the advantages gained through their knowledge of school conditions and extensive experience with young people. And the seven-community study (referred to above) was carried out in six communities [20] by colleges and universities under contract with the Bureau of Labor Statistics and in the seventh, Providence, R.I., by the public school system.

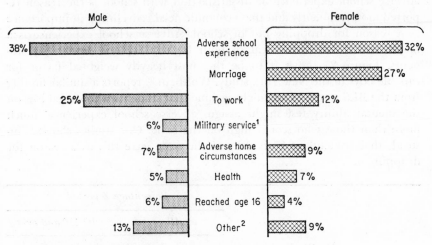

Based on interviews in 7 areas.
[1] This is understated since those in service at time of survey were not interviewed.
[2] Includes 3% of boys who gave marriage as a reason.

FIGURE 26   *Reasons for leaving school given by dropouts in the Bureau of Labor Statistics study in seven communities.* (Margaret L. Plunkett, *Highlights from a Study on the Early Employment Experience of Youth in Seven Communities 1952–1957,* p. 6. Washington, D.C.: Government Printing Office, 1961.)

Sometimes the dropouts are too many for all to be interviewed. When only a portion of the group is canvassed, it is important to use a representative sample. In the Syracuse study, for example, the subjects were students in grades 7 through 12 who dropped out during a seven-semester period. The sampling procedures were as follows: [21]

> The drop-outs' names and addresses were secured from the individual school records, arranged alphabetically by years or classes. Each fifth dropout was selected and his name and address were typed on a 3 × 5 card. Each sixth drop-out in the same group was selected as an alternate to be

[18] H. C. Seymour and C. E. Tremer, *We Left School a Year Ago.* Rochester, N.Y.: Rochester Public Schools, 1940.

[19] *Syracuse Youth Who Did Not Graduate.* Syracuse, N.Y.: Research Division of the Syracuse Board of Education, 1950.

[20] The six were Harrison County, W.Va.; Vanderburgh County, Ind.; Phoenix, Ariz.; Port Huron, Mich.; Saginaw, Mich.; and Utica, N.Y.

[21] *Syracuse Youth Who Did Not Graduate,* p. 11.

interviewed in the event that the fifth drop-out could not be located. This method of selection insured that all socio-economic groups and racial groups could be sampled in about the proportion that their children withdrew from the public secondary schools.

Reasons for Withdrawal. Figures 26 and 27 show the reasons for withdrawal given by dropouts in the BLS seven-community study and the New York Holding Power Project. Like other studies, these two show that adverse school experience or dissatisfaction with school is the reason reported most frequently and that economic need is declining in importance as a reason for dropping out of school. Adverse school experience is a major reason for withdrawal of both high-ability and low-ability students. Figure 27 shows it to be the most heavily weighted factor for capable boys in the New York study. Wolfbein [22] reports a similar finding from the BLS study: "One might assume that students who scored low on the mental ability test might assign 'adverse school experience' much more than those who scored high on the scale. Our studies showed, instead, that students at both ends of the scale gave this as a reason for dropping out."

	Percentage reported			
	All		IQ 110 and over	
Reason	Number	Per cent	Number	Per cent
Adverse school experience	386	46	20	39
Work	161	19	11	21.5
Marriage	118	14	11	21.5
Adverse home circumstances	85	10	4	8
Health	44	5	2	4
Military service	20	2	0	
Reached age 16	4	1	1	2
Other	22	3	2	4
Number in sample	840	100	51	100.0

FIGURE 27   *Reasons for leaving school given by dropouts in the New York State Holding Power Project.* [L. H. Woollatt, "Why Capable Students Drop out of High School," *Bulletin of the National Association of Secondary-school Principals,* 1961, 45(268):5.]

Marriage is increasingly reported as a major reason for girls' dropping out of school. In the New York study it is the most heavily weighted reason for capable girls. This study shows also that parental attitude is a significant factor for capable students, both boys and girls, and that subject failure and family need for financial help are less important factors for the more capable boys than the less capable ones.

[22] Wolfbein, *op. cit.,* p. 101.

Emotional problems may be a more common and more important reason for school withdrawal than the survey reports indicate. Many dropouts may not be aware of the nature, the severity, or the effects of their emotional difficulties. Some may be aware of them but may not report them or even perceive them as bearing on their decision to leave school. The studies of Lichter et al.,[23] and of others show emotional problems often to be the basic reason for dropping out of school.

In the demonstration project of Lichter et al., the subjects were 105 adolescents referred as potential dropouts to a counseling agency by the Chicago public schools. The clinical staff found severe emotional problems to be the major cause of these students' difficulties and the resultant school leaving.

No doubt, these adolescents' emotional problems continue to be interfering factors in their lives. Emotional problems that cause school maladjustment are likely to prevent occupational adjustment. The evidence? Dropouts have worse records than high school graduates "in terms of rates of unemployment, spells of unemployment, and the total time since leaving school spent as an unemployed worker." [24]

IDENTIFICATION AND RETENTION OF POTENTIAL DROPOUTS

Factors Contributing to Withdrawal. The studies show certain factors or characteristics to be associated closely with quitting school. On the basis of her summary of the literature, Lee [25] found that dropouts tend (1) to be from broken homes, (2) to have foreign-born parents, (3) to be of low intelligence—IQ below 85, (4) to be retarded two or more years in reading, (5) to be retarded two or more years in arithmetic, (6) to repeat grade or be passed on probation one or more semesters, (7) to be "behavior problems," (8) to have poor attendance records, (9) to have health problems, (10) to change home address six or more times during the period from kindergarten through ninth grade, (11) to change schools six or more times during the period from kindergarten through ninth grade, (12) to be overage for grade placement, and (13) to earn low marks. Some factors found in other lists but not given in Lee's summary are included in the form used in the New York Holding Power Project for identifying students "vulnerable to early school leaving." The form is shown in Figure 28.

School withdrawal cannot be predicted for individual students on the basis of these factors. Many students with the characteristics commonly associated with the dropouts stay in school. Lee, for example, studied the

[23] Solomon O. Lichter et al., *The Drop-outs: A Treatment Study of Intellectually Capable Students Who Drop out of High School*. New York: The Free Press of Glencoe, 1962.

[24] Wolfbein, *op. cit.*, p. 103.

[25] Margaret B. Lee, "Factors Associated with School Retention in a Group of Predicted Drop-outs," unpublished doctor's dissertation. Berkeley, Calif.: University of California, 1958.

ninth-grade cumulative records of 1,102 seniors in three San Francisco high schools. The ninth-grade record data showed 100 of these seniors to be "a typical group of dropouts," but they were still in school. What distinguished them from the ones who quit school? They liked school.

The presence of a number of the contributing factors in the life of a student cannot be considered indisputable evidence that he will drop out of school. It should alert teachers and counselors, however, to the fact that he is a potential dropout and that special efforts may be needed to counteract the factors possibly leading to withdrawal.

School Holding Power Study. The problems that culminate in withdrawal from school begin in the elementary grades. By the ninth grade, students who are highly vulnerable to school leaving can be identified fairly well.

A number of comprehensive studies have been carried out to determine the factors associated with school holding power, as well as the ones associated with early school leaving. One example is the New York Holding Power Project referred to above in which 89 school districts of the State of New York participated. Students who entered the seventh grade during 1954–1955 were followed through June, 1960. Some fifteen thousand students were involved. Annually an estimate was made of the disposition of all students in the project group toward school leaving, and specific efforts were made to hold in school the ones found to be vulnerable. Twice a year supervisors from the Bureau of Guidance of the State Department of Education visited the participating schools to provide assistance and to identify practices that seemed especially effective for increasing school holding power.

On the basis of the project findings, certain recommendations were made.[26] With regard to nonpromotions, for example, it was recommended that (1) reasons for nonpromotion and advantages of repetition be carefully explained to the nonpromoted students, (2) plans be made to prevent continued operation of the factors identified as causes of nonpromotion, (3) special support and encouragement be provided retarded students, and (4) the understanding and the cooperation of the nonpromoted students' parents be sought.

For early identification of potential dropouts it was recommended that (1) a comprehensive record be kept on each student, (2) the record be used as a basic resource in identifying potential dropouts, as well as in planning for the development of all students, (3) the records be regularly interpreted to parents, (4) case conferences be arranged for study of data on potential dropouts, (5) the "vulnerability rating scale" form shown in Figure 28 be completed regularly on all students and the results analyzed and studied, and (6) students with high vulnerable ratings be called to the

[26] *Holding Power Project,* Bulletin of the Bureau of Guidance. New York: State Department of Education, The University of the State of New York, n.d. (Dittoed.)

THE UNIVERSITY OF THE STATE OF NEW YORK
The State Education Department
Bureau of Guidance
Albany 1

Holding Power Project   *PUPIL HOLDING POWER DATA*
Form Number II
April, 1954

_____   _____

Teacher reporting   Date

Below are listed potential factors in early school leaving or retention. Only definitely negative and positive characteristics are shown; hence it may not be possible to check every item for each student. Items in Part I may be obtained from school records or observation by the person responsible for completing this form. Items in Part II should be a summary of the opinions of all teachers under whose supervision the pupil comes during the school year.

PART I

Last name	First	Initial		Age	Grade

FACTOR	VULNERABLE TO DROPPING OUT		FAVORABLE TO RETENTION	
a. AGE	Old for grade group (over 2 years)	—	At age for grade group	—
b. PHYSICAL SIZE	Small for age group	—	No size demarca-	
	Large for age group	—	tion	—
c. HEALTH	Frequently ill	—	Consistently good	
	Easily fatigues	—	health	—
d. PARTICIPATION IN SCHOOL ACTIVITIES	None	—	Planned and reasonable	—
e. PARTICIPATION IN OUT-OF-SCHOOL ACTIVITIES	None	—	Planned and reasonable	—
f. GRADE RETARDATION	One year or more retarded	—	At grade or above	—
g. FATHER'S OCCUPATION	Unskilled	—	Professional	—
	Semiskilled	—	Semiprofessional	—
			Managerial	—
h. EDUCATIONAL LEVEL ACHIEVED BY:				
FATHER	Grade 7 or below	—	Grade 10 or above	—
MOTHER	Grade 7 or below	—	Grade 10 or above	—

FIGURE 28 *Holding Power Project form for identifying students vulnerable to dropping out of school.* (*Holding Power Project,* Bulletin of the Bureau of Guidance. New York: State Department of Education, The University of the State of New York, n.d. Dittoed.)

215

FACTOR	VULNERABLE TO DROPPING OUT	FAVORABLE TO RETENTION
i. NUMBER OF CHILDREN IN FAMILY	Five or more ___	Three or less ___
j. SCHOOL-TO-SCHOOL TRANSFERS	Pattern of "jumping" from school to school ___	Few or no transfers ___
k. ATTENDANCE	Chronic absenteeism (20 days or more a year) ___	Seldom absent (10 days or less a year) ___
l. LEARNING RATE	Below 90 IQ ___	Above 100 IQ ___
m. ABILITY TO READ	Two years or more below grade level ___	At or above grade level ___
n. SCHOOL MARKS	Predominantly below C ___	Predominantly B or above ___

PART II

o. REACTIONS TO SCHOOL CONTROLS	Resents controls ___	Willingly accepts controls ___
p. ACCEPTANCE BY PUPILS	Not liked ___	Well liked ___
q. PARENTAL ATTITUDE TOWARD GRADUATION	Negative ___ Vacillating ___	Positive ___ United ___
r. PUPIL'S INTEREST IN SCHOOLWORK	Little or none ___	High ___
s. GENERAL ADJUSTMENT	Fair or poor ___	Good ___

Additional comments:

FIGURE 28   (continued)

attention of all staff members in contact with them and these students be given special study and help.

It was recommended also that the special demands of early marriage be made clear to girls vulnerable to early school leaving and that the increasing economic importance of high school graduation be explained to potential dropouts and their parents. Counseling contacts were to be established with potential school leavers as soon as they were identified and appropriate extraclass activities to be provided for them.

Factors Associated with Retention. The New York Holding Project showed some of the factors affecting school holding power to be class size, community type, school retention efforts, parental status, and educational appreciations. School holding power increases as school retention efforts, parental status, and educational appreciations increase. The holding power rates are much lower in metropolitan and small rural districts than in communities of intermediate size and location.

In a special report on the findings with respect to capable dropouts, Woollatt [27] suggests that "more leeway of action" may be needed by capable boys. They "may benefit by relaxation of rigid standards of control while in school" and may need kinds of activities that the school curriculum does not offer.

Lee [28] investigated the factors associated with school retention in a group of predicted dropouts who remained in school to graduate. The data obtained through the Illinois Inventory of Pupil Opinion and recorded interviews showed that the factors which markedly facilitated graduation for these predicted dropouts were (1) curricular flexibility, (2) individualized teaching, and (3) individualized consideration through counseling.

The responses of these predicted dropouts indicate that a student's participation in nonclass activities is somewhat a measure of his interest in school. Nonparticipants were referred to as "outsiders." According to Lee's subjects, when a student participates he feels that he belongs. When he feels that he belongs he takes school seriously. The students expressed approval of intramural sports programs, activity periods scheduled on school time, and teachers' showing interest in summer activities. They expressed appreciation for opportunities to engage in self-evaluation. Some were familiar with the contents of their cumulative records and reported this knowledge helpful.

Their expressions regarding favorable and unfavorable school experiences indicate that the practices which help to hold the high-risk students include clinical reading service, remedial laboratories in all subjects with outstanding students helping slow learners, small-group instruction, democratic classroom procedures, firm and consistent discipline, class trips, useful projects, experiments, teachers' planning individually with students, and a diversity of offerings.

Special Efforts to Increase Holding Power. The dropout studies show (1) that potential dropouts need to be identified early and given special counseling and/or psychological treatment, (2) that school and nonschool community resources for diagnosis and treatment of personality problems need to be increased, (3) that more special schools are needed to meet the needs

---

[27] Lorne H. Woollatt, "Why Capable Students Drop out of High School," *Bulletin of the National Association of Secondary-school Principals,* 1961, 45(268):8.

[28] Lee, *op. cit.*

of students not planning to go to college, and (4) that high school programs need to be expanded or readjusted to include some offerings not given now.

It is not always easy to identify the potential dropouts, and it is often difficult to hold those who are identified. Moreover, increasing a school's holding power is easier in some situations than in others. Providing sufficient diversity in class and nonclass activities, for example, may be easier in large schools than in small ones. Conversely, knowing students and working with them as individuals may be easier in small schools than in large ones.

Some programs for increasing school holding power are being carried out on a statewide basis. In Maryland a statewide study of dropouts is being made on a sampling basis. In Michigan the Committee on School Holding Power is working to stimulate interest in the dropout problem and to encourage local schools to try to reduce the number of dropouts through adequate provision for individual differences even if this involves the complete overhauling of some programs. Through its publications the Committee is keeping Michigan informed regarding the problem and specific efforts toward solution in order to arouse interest and to gain public support and assistance. The Committee plans to have eventually even the dropouts involved in the work.

In some communities fieldwork techniques are being used to gain the interest and the cooperation of parents. In a Maryland community a group of private citizens has initiated a home study program in an adjoining community where the dropout rate is unusually high. They have persuaded some parents to convert parts of their homes into classrooms for use by "parent helpers" or volunteer tutors in teaching the children at home. The tutors are college graduates. Each teaches one session weekly and serves as a helper to the parents concerned. "The students are assigned according to grade to a group which meets regularly four nights a week, each night at a different home and with a different parent helper." [29] An improvement in these children's attitudes and performances at school was soon noted by their teachers, many of whom confer regularly with the volunteer tutors.

New York City has an Early Identification and Prevention Program that extends through the third grade. It is directed toward reducing the incidence of school maladjustment and providing special help for gifted children. The program is carried out by teams. On each team there is a guidance counselor, a social worker, and a psychologist. Each team functions in cooperation with school personnel, parents, and other community agencies.

An experimental project has been undertaken in a Wisconsin elementary school to help culturally deprived kindergarten children overcome some of their initial disadvantages. In addition to the normal half-day kindergarten program, the project children are provided an additional

[29] "School Dropouts: Local Plans," NEA Journal, 1962, 51(5):60.

half day of instruction and activity to help them build "a background of experience and understanding, which can later lend meaning and motivation to learning to read." [30] The children have an abundance of experience with picture books, stories, television, and tape recorder. Twice a week they take field trips, such as hikes, fishing trips, and visits to museums, parks, farms, factories, and the like.

Many schools are using work-experience programs to hold potential dropouts in school. Some are also using them to help dropouts resume their education and to develop work skills and good work habits. Detroit, for example, has a Job Upgrading Program for dropouts between the ages of sixteen and twenty. In the morning the participants attend classes taught by special teachers. In the afternoon they fill community-subsidized jobs that provide them valuable work experience. When the project members "graduate," they are given help in finding full-time employment and follow-up service for six months.

A Ford Foundation grant helped to make possible the pilot Double-E (education-employment) Project initiated in 1961 by the Board of Education and a large department store in Chicago. Selected dropouts and potential dropouts (all teenagers) attended classes in a building near the store part of the time and filled regular jobs at the store part of the time. They received salaries and were eligible for most company benefits. When the one-year pilot program ended, six participants had completed or were shortly to complete the high school program through summer study and extension classes. More than half remained with the store as permanent full-time employees. "Those who left the store's employ went into military service, were married, or were ill." [31] The store decided to continue the program, and other Chicago companies joined the project.

Other communities are following different approaches in seeking solutions to the dropout problem. Different approaches are needed because what may work in one community may not work in another. Also, as stated in a report on the New York Holding Power Project,[32] no single procedure may have an appreciable or direct effect on the holding power rates of the school. "Only the summed attempts of all types seem to be positively related to changes in holding power." To alter substantially the dropout rate, support is needed in the school from all staff members and in the community from all agencies or groups able to help.

SUMMARY

Follow-up studies of graduates and of dropouts are becoming routine procedures in some high schools. The studies are especially valuable to counselors. They help them to appraise the strengths and weaknesses of the

---

[30] *Ibid.*, p. 7.

[31] "Work-study Plan Involves Total Education," *SRA Guidance Newsletter*, p. 2. Chicago: Science Research Associates, Inc., September, 1962.

[32] *Holding Power Project*, Bulletin of the Bureau of Guidance.

guidance program, to learn the types of postschool counseling and guidance needed by young people, and to keep informed regarding youth's world outside the school.

Making follow-up studies cooperative projects helps to improve survey procedures, to increase the percentage of returns, to foster community interest in the findings, and to strengthen organized efforts toward securing needed changes and improvements. A good form letter and an attractive, well-constructed questionnaire help to increase the number of returns. To obtain returns from all subjects, the questionnaire ordinarily needs to be supplemented by the interview. Enlisting the cooperation of students in school helps to expedite the work and to increase returns in the current study and in future studies that will involve the present students.

The validity and reliability of the findings are dependent upon the percentage of returns and the willingness and the ability of the respondents to give accurate, complete information. The significance of the data is increased when a comparison can be made of a subject's school-period status with his postschool status.

The number of dropouts is declining, and withdrawal tends to occur at a higher grade level than formerly. Yet the number is still very large. Dropouts form a heterogeneous group and include a substantial number of very capable students.

The research studies show the principal factors associated with school withdrawal to be limited intelligence, low achievement in reading and arithmetic, little or no participation in nonclass activities, poor health, emotional problems, broken homes, negative attitude of parents toward education, and early marriage of students. Marriage is increasingly given as a reason for girls' quitting school. Economic need seems to be declining in importance as a contributing factor. Adverse school experience is the major reason for the withdrawal of both low-ability and high-ability boys and girls.

The problems that culminate in withdrawal begin in the elementary grades. Hence, efforts to reduce the number of dropouts cannot be delayed until the high school years. The school factors shown by research to be associated with retention of potential dropouts are good interpersonal relations with other students and teachers, flexible curricula, democratic classroom practices, and individualized attention through counseling.

Some large-scale, long-term research investigations and experimental projects have been undertaken to provide increased knowledge regarding the nature and causes of the dropout problem and measures for effective solution. The work is being carried out at the state and local levels and involves school and nonschool people. The present indications are that only through combined efforts can any lasting solution be achieved.

REFERENCES

Arnholter, Ethelwynne G.: "School Persistence and Personality Factors," *Personnel and Guidance Journal,* 1956, 39:107–109.

Berston, H. M.: "The School Dropout Problem," *The Clearing House,* 1960, 35:207–210.

Byrne, Richard H.: "Beware the Stay-in-school Bandwagon," *Personnel and Guidance Journal,* 1958, 36:493–496.

Caravello, S. J.: "The Drop-out Problem," *High School Journal,* 1958, 41:335–340.

Cook, Edward S., Jr.: "An Analysis of Factors Related to Withdrawal from High School Prior to Graduation," *Journal of Educational Research,* 1956, 50:191–196.

Cooper, Sophia: "Employment of June 1960 High School Graduates," *Monthly Labor Review,* 1961, 84:463–470.

Davis, Donald A.: "An Experimental Study of Potential Dropouts," *Personnel and Guidance Journal,* 1962, 40:799–802.

Dice, L. Kathryn: "Unmet Needs of High School Students," *Education Leadership,* 1958, 16:169–175.

Dillon, Harold J.: *Early School Leavers: A Major Educational Problem.* New York: Child Labor Committee, 1949.

Dresher, Richard H.: "Seeds of Delinquency," *Personnel and Guidance Journal,* 1957, 35:595–598.

Epps, M. V., and W. C. Cottle: "Further Validation of a Dropout Scale," *Vocational Guidance Quarterly,* 1958–1959, 7:90–93.

Evraiff, William: "How 'Different' Are Our Drop-outs?" *Bulletin of the National Association of Secondary-school Principals,* 1957, 41(226):212–218.

Green, Donald A.: "School Drop-outs: A Matter of Philosophy," *Vocational Guidance Quarterly,* 1960–1961, 9:124–127.

Hermann, Lyndon, and W. C. Cottle: "An Inventory to Identify High School Dropouts," *Vocational Guidance Quarterly,* 1958, 6:122–123.

Lichter, S. O., et al.: *The Drop-outs: A Treatment Study of Intellectually Capable Students Who Drop out of High School.* New York: The Free Press of Glencoe, 1962.

Livingston, A. H.: "High School Graduates and Dropouts: A New Look at a Persistent Problem," *School Review,* 1958, 66:195–203.

Mooren, Robert A., and John W. M. Rothney: "Personalizing the Follow-up Study," *Personnel and Guidance Journal,* 1956, 34:409–412.

Murk, Virgil: "A Follow-up Study on Students Who Drop out of High School," *Bulletin of the National Association of Secondary-school Principals,* 1960, 44(262):73–75.

National Education Association: "High School Drop-outs: One in Every 3 Ninth-graders Fails to Finish High School," *National Education Association Research Bulletin,* 1960, 38:11–14.

Plunkett, Margaret L., and Naomi Riches: *School and Early Employment Experience of Youth: A Report on Seven Communities, 1952–57.* Washington, D.C.: Government Printing Office, 1960.

Research Division and Department of Classroom Teachers: *High-school Drop-outs: Discussion Pamphlet,* rev. ed. Washington, D.C.: National Education Association, 1959.

Roberts, Richard O., and John F. McGeever: "A Junior Occupational Program," *Bulletin of the National Association of Secondary-school Principals,* 1957, 41(232):43–47.

Rothney, John W. M., et al.: *Guidance Practices and Results,* chap. 4. New York: Harper & Row, Publishers, Incorporated, 1958.

Schiffman, Jacob: "Employment of High School Graduates and Dropouts in 1961," *Monthly Labor Review,* 1962, 85:502–509.

Segel, David: *Retention in High Schools in Large Cities.* Washington, D.C.: Government Printing Office, 1957.

Sorenson, Mourits A.: "Low Ability Dropouts versus Low Ability Graduates," *Personnel and Guidance Journal,* 1960, 39:144–145.

Tesseneer, R. A., and L. M. Tesseneer: "Review of the Literature on School Dropouts," *Bulletin of the National Association of Secondary-school Principals,* 1958, 42(288):141–153.

Thomas, Robert J.: "An Empirical Study of High School Drop-outs in Regard to Ten Possibly Related Factors," *Journal of Educational Sociology,* 1954, 28:11–18.

Wolfbein, S. L.: "Transition from School to Work: A Study of the School Leaver," *Personnel and Guidance Journal,* 1959, 38:98–105.

Woollatt, Lorne H.: "Why Capable Students Drop out of High School," *Bulletin of the National Association of Secondary-school Principals,* 1961, 45(268):1–8.

10

Self-reports: Self-appraisal and Autobiographical Material

SELF–ANALYSIS

Decreased Use. Much more attention was given in the early literature on student personnel work than is being given today to the instruments used for helping students to analyze themselves, such as score cards, self-rating scales, and questionnaires in which a student is asked to give an estimate of his abilities and to express his judgment regarding the extent to which he possesses certain traits and interests. In the earlier literature the emphasis was upon helping the student to understand himself by having him appraise his assets and liabilities and then report his findings. In the current literature it is upon helping him to acquire insight and self-understanding by providing him opportunities to discuss his problems and plans with a counselor or group of peers, to share in study of the information gathered on him, and to participate in evaluation of his progress.

Studies of self-ratings continue to substantiate the findings of earlier investigations by Hollingsworth, Allport, Hoffman, Shen, Adams, Hurlock, Conrad, and others: Self-ratings are low in validity and reliability. Superior individuals tend to underrate themselves; inferior ones, to overrate themselves. College students rate themselves more accurately than junior high school students rate themselves.

The continued reporting of such findings is no doubt one reason why less attention is given to self-rating in the recent literature than in earlier books by Brewer, Koos and Kefauver, Meyers, and others. Jones, for example, in the second edition of his *Principles of Guidance*[1] devoted some nine pages to the subject of "self-analysis blanks," reproduced Brewer's Vocational Score Card, and presented in part the elaborate blanks developed for the Boys' Work Division of the International Committee of the YMCA. In later editions, however, he does not even list the terms

[1] Arthur J. Jones, *Principles of Guidance*, 2d ed., pp. 182–192. New York: McGraw-Hill Book Company, Inc., 1934.

"self-analysis" and "rating scales" in the index nor refer to these instruments in the chapter on personality estimates and interest inventories.

A second reason for the decreased emphasis upon self-ratings may be the fact that counselors now realize that having a student admit (or informing him if he does not admit) that he is self-centered, shy, rude, or something else not desirable contributes little to correction. One shy, self-conscious girl may be fully aware of her shyness and readily admit it. Another may be equally aware of her self-consciousness but deny shyness and even rate herself as high in social adjustment and self-confidence. A counselor contributes little or nothing to the solution of either girl's problem by discussing with her the ratings that she has given herself with respect to social adjustment, leadership, and related characteristics. Such a discussion may only aggravate the problem for both girls.

To help either girl, the counselor may have to use a number of approaches. He may try to give help (1) through counseling that gives the girl a chance to think through her problem and consider some of the things that she can do about it; (2) through helping others (peers, teachers, parents, etc.) to understand the girl and accept her as she is; (3) through creating opportunities for her to have certain needed social (group) experiences; and (4) through helping her to progress from minor roles in simple activities to important ones in complex activities.

The process leading to self-understanding and self-initiated action on the part of such a girl may be a long, slow, tedious one. The solution achieved may, however, be more effective and lasting than any that can be attained merely through asking a girl whether she is shy always, generally, sometimes, or never, or through asking her whether she prefers to work with people or things; whether she would rather listen, take part in, or lead a discussion; and whether it bothers her to have people watch her while she works.

A third probable reason for decreased use of self-rating procedures is the increased use of standardized personality inventories in which the subject states his likes and dislikes, preferences, beliefs, and attitudes and tells how he feels or reacts in certain situations. The subject's responses on such a scale are used, however, by others, not by the subject, for appraising his social adjustment, interests, and the like.

Value. The chief value of self-ratings and self-descriptions is in their usefulness for showing how well a student understands himself. They may have some value for stimulating students seriously to consider their strengths and weaknesses, to give thought to some behavior characteristics commonly deemed important to success and happiness, and to see the need for correcting socially undesirable habits and developing acceptable behavior patterns.

One specialist [2] in vocational guidance recommends the practice of

[2] Gertrude Forrester, *Methods of Vocational Guidance,* rev. ed., p. 335. Boston: D. C. Heath and Company, 1951.

having students check themselves through use of the same scales that teachers use in rating them. She recommends that the student name some teacher for whom he has worked during the semester as the one to rate him and that he be the one to give the rating blank to the teacher. By finding it necessary to rate himself, the student, Forrester states, "may be brought face to face with his weaknesses with the result that he may take immediate steps to reduce them." The qualifications required of workers in various fields "will be brought home more forcibly" to the student if he asks the teacher to rate him. The teacher's evaluation of his personality traits can also be used "to stimulate him to take steps necessary for self-improvement." These are the reasons traditionally advanced in vocational guidance for the use of self-analysis blanks—to inform and motivate.

In the current literature less attention is given to the use of self-appraisal instruments for motivating students than to their use for helping a counselor to gain knowledge of a counselee's self-concept, the extent to which he understands and accepts himself, and the changes that occur through counseling in his perception of self and attitudes toward self.

The Traditional Type. Figure 29 illustrates the traditional type of self-ratings used largely for teaching or stressing the importance of certain characteristics and for motivating students toward improvement. It combines the check list with the graphic scale.

To what extent did you cooperate with the group in respect to the following:	Your opinion		Group opinion		Teacher's opinion	
	Satis-factory	Unsatis-factory	Satis-factory	Unsatis-factory	Satis-factory	Unsatis-factory
a. Punctuality at times on the trip						
b. Staying with the group						
c. Courtesy to others						
d. Paying attention to discussion and observation						
e. Encouraging other students in good conduct						

FIGURE 29   *Rating scale for student cooperation and social effectiveness. (Santa Barbara County Curriculum Guide for Teachers in the Secondary Schools, vol. 4, p. 68. Santa Barbara, Calif., 1941.)*

Self-rating devices are subject to the same limitations described in preceding chapters for personality inventories and rating scales in general. Like adults, students find it easier to rate themselves with respect to overt behavior than covert aspects of the self. A student, for example, can probably use fairly well a scale on which he indicates the extent of his participation in recreational activities by encircling one of five numbers. Five of the twenty items contained in one such scale are shown in Figure 30. The student will have difficulty, however, in rating himself in answering certain questions that appear on some other scales, such questions as "Do I have confidence in myself?" "Do I have emotional control?" "Do I depend on others?" and "Do I face reality?"

In using most self-rating forms of the traditional type, students cannot help knowing the most acceptable rating or response. Hence, many of these instruments are of little use for helping them to acquire self-understanding. Some may actually hamper growth toward understanding and acceptance of self. In providing some of the standards by which students appraise themselves, the schools, as Jersild [3] says, "in a relatively passive role," may reflect some of the unhealthy tendencies in our society.

Activities	None	Almost none	Some	Much	Very much	Points
1. Swimming	1	2	3	4	5	
2. Diving	1	2	3	4	5	
3. Canoeing, boating, and sailing	1	2	3	4	5	
4. Gymnastics, (circus) stunts	1	2	3	4	5	
5. Tumbling	1	2	3	4	5	

FIGURE 30　*Self-rating scale for pupil participation in recreational activities.* (T. K. Cureton et al., *The Measurement of Understanding in Physical Education,* Forty-fifth Yearbook of the National Society for the Study of Education, part I, p. 240. Chicago: The University of Chicago Press, 1946. Reproduced by permission of the Society.)

Through careless use of self-rating devices that stress conformity and control of the emotions, the schools may foster some unwholesome tendencies that Jersild underscores in reporting his inquiry into the role of the school in promoting self-understanding. The report is based in part upon data obtained from compositions written by some three thousand students in grade 4 through college on the topics of "What I like about myself" and "What I dislike about myself." In telling what they disliked about themselves, many students named characteristics or described behavior that indicates lack of poise or self-control. According to Jersild,[4] in emphasizing control or concealment of emotions, these students reflect the idea of control commonly stressed in the schools. They show the influence of training "designed to persuade them not to be emotional."

In evaluating themselves, students may at times be only "paying their respects to the kind of conformity that is expected of them." Their

[3] Arthur T. Jersild, *In Search of Self: An Evaluation of the Role of the School in Promoting Self-understanding,* p. 103. New York: Bureau of Publications, Teachers College, Columbia University, 1952.
[4] *Ibid.,* p. 37.

self-analyses may then show more a denial of self than an understanding of self.

As Appraisal Instrument in Counseling and Research. Self-ratings are used in counseling and research largely for gaining knowledge of a subject's perception of himself as he is and as he would like to be, of the discrepancy between his self-concept and ideal self, and of the changes in perception and acceptance of self that occur through counseling, remedial reading, speech therapy, or other special assistance. Self-rating techniques have been used for such purposes in some outstanding investigations. Here are three examples:

In the California Adolescent Growth Study a self-rating instrument, The Personal Social Inventory, was administered annually. Based in part upon tests developed by Rogers and Symonds and Jackson, it includes items like these: [5]

Read the sentences below, and the questions that follow them. If the answer to a question is "yes," put a check mark on "yes." If the answer is "no," put a mark on "no." If the true answer is somewhere between yes and no, put the mark where it will be most true.

B. is a big strong boy who can beat any of the other boys in a fight.

Am I just like him? | Yes | | | | | | | | | | No |

D. is the best ball player in the school.

Am I just like him? | Yes | | | | | | | | | | No |

K. has more girl friends than any of the other fellows.

Am I just like him? | Yes | | | | | | | | | | No |

The investigators found the chief value of this instrument to be in the possibility of studying significant agreements and disagreements among the individual items and in detailed comparison of self-report data with data from other sources. According to Jones, the inventory was the source that offered "the most clearly comparable evidence for successive years." The material collected over a seven-year period on one boy, for example, brought to light these tendencies: [6]

1. The acknowledgment, to a very unusual degree, of personal deficiencies.

2. The expression, on the other hand, of somewhat extravagant wishes to be outstanding in a wide range of personal characteristics.

3. The use of various protective devices, singly or in combination: fantasy, self-inflation, denial of emotional involvement, and, at critical times, the denial of deficiencies which at other times were freely admitted.

[5] From *Development in Adolescence* by Harold E. Jones. Copyright, 1943. D. Appleton-Century Co., Inc. Reprinted by permission of the publisher.
[6] *Ibid.,* p. 132.

A similar instrument was used in the California experimental study to develop a process for inschool screening of disturbed children. The elementary school inventory, *Thinking about Yourself,* has separate forms for boys and girls, whereas the secondary school inventory, *A Self Test,* does not. Each has two sections of 40 items each. The items are the same in both sections except that in Section I the subject indicates whether he wants to be like the person described and in Section II whether he thinks that he is like the description. The first two items of Section I of *A Self Test* are as follows: [7]

1. This person has many dreams. Do you want to be like this person?	YES	yes	no	NO	1.
2. This person dates a lot. Do you want to be like this person?	YES	yes	no	NO	2.

By encircling "YES," "yes," "no," or "NO," the student shows that his response means "Yes, indeed!" "Well, yes, perhaps," "I don't think so," or "No, no, a thousand times, no!" The instructions include the explanation that there are no right or wrong answers, that the subject will want to be like some of the people described and not want to be like others.

The Q-sort technique (described in Chap. 3) was used in the research studies in outcomes of personal counseling that were made at the University of Chicago and reported by Rogers and Dymond.[8] It was the only instrument used during, as well as before and after, therapy. Each subject was asked to sort 100 statements into nine piles, placing a specified number in each pile, thus forcing a normal distribution. The cards were sorted to "depict the self, the self-ideal, and the ordinary person." They were sorted before counseling began and after the seventh, twentieth, and each succeeding twenty interviews until counseling ended. Three items that represented good adjustment were as follows: [9]

> I make strong demands on myself.
>
> I often kick myself for the things I do.
>
> I have a warm emotional relationship with others.

Among the items indicating poor adjustment were these three:

> I put on a false front.
>
> I often feel humiliated.
>
> I have a feeling of hopelessness.

---

[7] Eli M. Bower and Nadine M. Lambert, *A Self Test.* Sacramento: California State Department of Education, 1962. Distributed for research use by Educational Testing Service, Princeton, N.J., and Los Angeles, Calif. Reproduced by permission of the publishers and the California State Department of Education.

[8] Carl R. Rogers and Rosalind F. Dymond (eds.), *Psychotherapy and Personality Change,* chap. 5. Chicago: The University of Chicago Press, 1954.

[9] *Ibid.,* p. 79.

An adjustment score was obtained for each subject by counting the number of "good adjustment" items he put in the "like me" piles and the number of "poor adjustment" items he put on the "unlike me" side of the scale. Analysis of the data showed that the members of the experimental group changed significantly over the therapy period. The females showed a significantly greater change in favor of increased adjustment than did the males.

The Q-sort procedure was used again between six and twelve months after therapy ended. Lasting improvement was indicated by the fact that the follow-up mean score for the experimental group was almost identical to this group's mean score immediately after therapy.

A number of investigations carried out at the secondary school level have been modeled after the University of Chicago studies. One example: Caplan [10] used the Q technique to study the changes after group counseling in the self-concepts of three experimental groups of adolescent "problem" boys. The boys sorted into a forced normal distribution 50 items describing various aspects of the self in school. The items were basically statements selected from student autobiographies. They included such statements as "get my work done on time" and "like school." The Q technique was used to measure the boys' self- and ideal-self concepts in school at the beginning and at the end of the one-semester experimental period. The data showed a significant change for the experimental group but not for the control group.

AUTOBIOGRAPHIES

Administration. Some schools routinely have new students write their life histories. Some have them write the autobiographies while they are still in the lower schools, where the students are encouraged to tell all about themselves because the papers will be sent to their future teachers and counselors.

Usually, however, the request for an autobiography is made in the new school and by the English teachers. With the students' knowledge and consent, the autobiographies are passed on to their counselors and eventually filed in the cumulative records or counseling folders. If the students' counselors are not strangers to them, the students will probably be as willing to have the papers read by them as by the English teachers. If, however, any students are reluctant for their autobiographies or other papers to be read by anyone other than the teachers for whom they are written, their wishes should of course be respected.

Sometimes the life histories are written in group guidance or social studies classes. Obviously the request for autobiographies should be made

---

[10] Stanley W. Caplan, "The Effect of Group Counseling on Junior High School Boys' Concepts of Themselves at School," *Journal of Counseling Psychology*, 1957, 4:124–128.

by only one person. A student should not have to write the story of his life several times during one school year. Once seems enough. Also, it is important that the request for autobiographies be delayed until new students have been in the school sufficiently long to feel at ease—at least two or three weeks. If a student is asked to write his autobiography at the very beginning of his stay in a new school, the natural desire to put his best foot forward may influence unduly the account of his past. The desire to make a good impression will, no doubt, influence the writings of some students as long as they are in the school. Nevertheless, as the students come to feel secure in the new situation and at home with other students and the teachers, many will feel free to be themselves and to report truthfully what they do and think. As shown by Shaffer's [11] study, rapport may not be essential for group administration in terms of the percentage of students who turn in autobiographies. However, it is probably very important in terms of the quality or significance of the material reported.

Writing the autobiography needs to be more than the writing of a composition that is assigned, begun, and completed all within one class period if the students are to find writing the autobiography an aid to self-understanding or to feel that achieving self-understanding is important. Desirably they should be given a week in which to write their life stories. More significant material is likely to be related if the students have time to think over the assignment than if they have to write their accounts on short notice. Moreover, giving students time in which to meditate and to decide what they will tell and how they will tell it aids self-evaluation as well as good writing. Planning and writing their life histories will help some students to clarify their feelings, attitudes, and goals and may even help them to perceive the reasons for some feelings and the causes of some conflicts. The effects of writing about oneself, as of talking about oneself, can be supportive, cathartic, and insightful.

While it is not usually desirable to ask a student to write his autobiography more than once during any school year, it is often desirable to ask the students when they become seniors to write their autobiographies again. Comparison of the second accounts with the first ones may disclose patterns of growth, gains made in social adjustment and emotional maturity, changes in interests and appreciations, increase in understanding of self and others, and general progress toward maturity. In the autobiographies written during their last year in a school many students tend to appraise both themselves and the school. The might-have-beens, should-have-beens, and could-have-beens as well as the actual achievements of both are sometimes listed. Both the school and the students may profit from this taking of stock.

[11] E. Evan Shaffer, Jr., "A Study of the Autobiography as a Secondary School Guidance Technique," unpublished doctor's dissertation. Los Angeles: University of California, 1953.

Structured versus Unstructured Reports. To make sure that the autobiographies include the factual information wanted, some counselors supply outlines in the form of questions or topics to be covered by the students in their reports. Others who use the technique more for gaining understanding of a student's inner world than for ascertaining facts regarding his outer world oppose any structuring of the report. To learn the events of a student's inner life—his wishes, aspirations, prejudices, frustrations, conflicts, hopes, and subjective impulses—it is important, they say, that the student give a relatively free-flowing account; that the report not be closely structured by a topical outline or specific questions.

For many students a general request that they write a full account of their lives, in which they just let their thoughts go, may be sufficient. For some, however, such instructions may be too vague. Something more definite may be needed. Furthermore, most (probably all) students find it helpful to have their attention directed to the two types of data wanted: (1) objective data regarding experiences in family, school, peer groups, neighborhood, church, and elsewhere in the community; and (2) subjective data regarding their sources of satisfactions, likes and dislikes, aspirations, values, and so forth. Group discussion of the instructions helps many students to understand the kind of autobiography wanted. Patterns or examples should not be offered, however, because they may serve to block or to mold expression rather than to free it.

An investigation made by Danielson and Rothney [12] as part of the Wisconsin Counseling Study was designed to determine the differential value of structured and unstructured autobiographies in terms of the degree to which each form suggests students' problems. Two matched groups, each composed of 78 high school juniors, wrote autobiographies. One group wrote structured and the other unstructured reports. Those who wrote without detailed directions were given the following guide: [13]

> The purpose of this assignment is to make you aware of the variety of things that influence us in our "growing up" and in developing plans for our future. Besides being an assignment in writing about a very interesting person, YOU, the autobiography will help you to decide "What kind of person am I?" "How did I get that way?" and "What do I hope to become?"
>
> Keep these three questions in mind and write freely about yourself. Include anything that you feel helped make you what you are. You will not be asked to read your autobiography in class nor will your teacher discuss it.
>
> You may begin writing during this period and then may complete the autobiography at home or in study periods, as you wish. The papers will be due two weeks from today.

[12] Paul J. Danielson and John W. M. Rothney, "The Student Autobiography: Structured or Unstructured?" *Personnel and Guidance Journal,* 1954, 33:30–33.

[13] John W. M. Rothney et al., *Guidance Practices and Results,* p. 97. New York: Harper & Row, Publishers, Incorporated, 1958. Capitalizations in the original.

The students who wrote structured reports were given a guide that contains the same opening paragraph as the guide shown above. It then continues as follows:

> The purpose of the questions listed below is to give you some ideas that will help you describe what makes YOU a person different from everyone else. Read them over carefully before you begin writing and keep them in mind as you write. Refer to them from time to time if necessary. DO NOT ANSWER THE QUESTIONS DIRECTLY BUT WEAVE THE IDEAS THEY GIVE YOU INTO THE PATTERN OF YOUR LIFE.

There follow 20 groups of questions under the three headings of (1) The Present—"What kind of person am I?" (2) The Past—"How did I get that way?" and (3) The Future—"What do I hope to become?" The first group of questions, for example, is as follows: [14]

> I. The Present—"What kind of person am I?"
> 1. How would you describe yourself to someone whom you have never seen? Would your friends describe you the same way? Are you the same person to your parents, to your teachers, to your friends, or at home, in class, on the sports field?

Analysis of the material showed neither method to be superior in eliciting clues about students' problems that would be helpful to counselors. No significant difference was found between the structured and the unstructured approaches in terms of the percentage of problems revealed in four areas—"financial," "socioemotional-personal," "vocational," and "personal appearance–physical health." However, the structured form seemed to elicit a significantly greater number of problems in the area of "education"; and the unstructured, in the area of "family relationship." Also, the structured form produced a significantly greater number of problems, which is not surprising since the outline provides many leads and suggestions.

The autobiographies [15] obtained in the Wisconsin study were of great value to the counselors. They "brought out a great deal of information and many suggestions, clues, and hints about the behavior and problems of the students that could not have been obtained in any other way." [16]

Interpretation. Perhaps it needs to be said again that data obtained on a student through the use of any technique usually have to be interpreted in the light of all information had on the subject. Hypotheses suggested by autobiographical data need to be substantiated by data from other sources. If they are not supported by other data, they must be modified or discarded.

[14] *Ibid.,* p. 98.
[15] A number are reproduced in John W. M. Rothney, *The High School Student: A Book of Cases.* New York: Holt, Rinehart and Winston, Inc., 1953.
[16] *Ibid.,* p. 15.

Frequently the meaning or significance of the material cannot be known without further knowledge of the autobiographer—knowledge gained by observation and through information secured from him and others. This point is illustrated in the "Story of Me" that one ten-year-old wrote: [17]

> I was born in Joplin. Then we moved to St. Louis then we moved to Kansas City and I started in Kindergarten, and on May day we moved to Brandon. Then we moved to Peoria. Then we moved to Springfield.

How should this report be interpreted? It tells us that during the ten years of his life the writer has lived in five different communities. It does not tell us what this frequent moving means to him. Does he feel uprooted and not identified with any particular place? Or does he feel pride in having moved so much? Does his not expressing any feelings in the report mean that he is so disturbed that he must gloss over his feelings or repress them? Or does he simply lack skill in communication? Or does he communicate quite well orally but not in writing? And does the autobiography represent facts or fantasy? Has someone whom the autobiographer knows lived in all these places, and he wishes that he had too? A great deal more needs to be known about this youngster before the meaning or implications of his life story can be understood.

Limitations and Advantages. Autobiographies have the same limitations with respect to validity and reliability that other self-reports have. The data cannot be accepted at face value. An unhappy, insecure student may seek escape or protection through fantasy, rationalization, identification, and other mechanisms. He may grossly misrepresent his experiences or distort their significance. Yet, as said before, the very inaccuracy of a student's report may be the counselor's most important clue regarding his problem.

However, checks by objective evidence often show seemingly apparent distortions to be factual accounts. Shaffer,[18] for example, found, when he subjected 18 suspected autobiographies to confirmatory checks, that 14 were honest representations. When the objective data (birth date, birthplace, number of siblings, etc.) reported in all the autobiographies studied were checked against the data given in school census reports, "the accuracy of reporting these facts exceeded 99 per cent."

The advantages of the autobiography outweigh its limitations. It is an economical, easily administered technique. It yields data that are useful in interpreting other data. It gives a longitudinal picture that helps teachers and counselors to view the student from his frame of reference. It presents him and his experiences from his point of view.

---

[17] Millie Almy, from materials prepared by Ruth Cunningham and Associates, *Ways of Studying Children: A Manual for Teachers,* p. 141. New York: Bureau of Publications, Teachers College, Columbia University, 1959.

[18] Shaffer, *op. cit.,* p. 296.

Writing his autobiography gives the student a chance to share in the appraisal process. It encourages him to review his past experiences and future goals and to consider just how he does feel about them. It may thereby help him to get a better perspective of himself—his past, his present, and his future.

Writing their life stories seems to help some students to develop insight regarding their need for counseling and may encourage some to seek it. Some report in their autobiographies sensitive, intimate material that they had previously been unable to disclose in the face-to-face situation.

THE DAILY RECORD

The daily record is another useful source of supplementary data. In using this technique, some counselors ask students to work out time budgets in which they show what they plan to do each hour of each day of the week. The students are expected to try out their plans and to revise them until they develop one that seems satisfactory for general use. Another procedure, and probably the one most frequently used, is to ask students to keep daily records in which they report what they do during each hour. They may be also asked to report in diary style their thoughts and feelings regarding the activities recorded.

Value. Even when the period covered is only a week, daily records are valuable for showing the general pattern of a student's life, the activities in which he customarily engages, and some of his special interests. And they may help some students perceive the importance of planning. As with autobiographies, fantasy and self-interest rather than truth may sometimes supply the basis for the report. Again, this fact (if known) may be a very important lead for the counselor.

The validity of the data from daily records kept at a counselor's request may depend largely on the quality of the student-counselor relationship. If relations are good and the student has found that counselors can accept the facts of student life undisturbed, that they do not feel compelled to point a moral or to label things "good" or "bad," they may accurately report how they spend their days and what they think while engaged in some of their activities. The records may provide new information. The new data may give new meaning to old data by bringing into focus some details overlooked or little noticed before.

Two Examples. Reading the reports of different students shows how very different the lives of some are from the lives of others. The difference is not usually so great as that indicated in the two following reports,[19] but neither is such great difference rare.

[19] Almy, *op. cit.,* p. 118.

Martha		Bertha	
5:30–6:00	sleep	5:30–6:00	get up, dress, clean room
6:00–6:30	sleep	6:00–6:30	clean washroom
6:30–7:00	sleep	6:30–7:00	clean washroom
7:00–7:30	sleep	7:00–7:30	eat breakfast, work in laundry
7:30–8:00	sleep	7:30–8:00	work in laundry
8:00–8:30	get up, dress, eat breakfast	8:00–8:30	work in laundry, get ready for school
8:30–9:00	read funnies, and go to school	8:30–9:00	go to school

The daily record was one of the analytical techniques used in the Study of Adolescents carried out by the Commission on Secondary School Curriculum in the 1930s. The following three-day record is from "the Case of Betty": [20]

Time	What I did	Remarks
Friday		
7:25	Woke up and went downstairs after getting dressed to meet the bus.	Was very sleepy
9:00	Had my Latin class—same as usual.	Was very bored
2:30	Left school with Ralph. We got a lift down the hill.	
3:30	I had my exercises and was on time for once.	
5:00	My piano lesson was a little late and I was rather tired. Didn't eat until late.	
8:00 10:00	After dinner I listened to the radio until I went to sleep.	Very sleepy
Saturday		
9:00	Woke up early because I had to have my hair done. The door bell woke me up.	Very tired
12:30	My hair was not dry when I went out. Arrived at my friend's house where we had lunch.	
2:30	After lunch went down town and had our pictures taken. We also did some shopping. We saw a movie. It was called "Private Worlds" and was rather good.	They are terrible
11:30	Got to bed.	

[20] From *The Adolescent Personality* by Peter Blos, pp. 46–47. Copyright, 1941. D. Appleton-Century Company, Inc. Reprinted by permission of the publisher.

Time	What I did	Remarks

Sunday

11:00 Woke up not so early and after getting dressed   Not so excited
       was told I was going on a picnic.

1:00   We left the house and met the other people we
       were going with. When we were half over the
       bridge it began to rain. We kept on anyway.

2:30   After eating dinner in the car and playing in
5:00   the rain we went home.   We were very
                                 hungry

5:30   I did my homework, listened to the radio, read
9:30   a little and went to bed.

Interpretation. Taken by itself, this diary is not without meaning. Combined with the rest of the material on Betty, it shows that she craves acceptance, attention, and love. It reveals a state of inner conflict in which divergent tendencies are at work and which leads unavoidably to defeat. According to the research report: [21]

> Betty's diary, which covers several days, is impressive by virtue of its monotony and the lack of personal coloring which prevails in the column "What I did." This is especially true in comparison with the diaries of others, and also with the remainder of Betty's own writings. The latter contrast reflects her twofold and widely divergent modes of experience: fantasy life versus daily personal routine. Listed in the diary is a sequence of facts, reported in such a way that school, piano lessons, radio, dinner, shopping, and picnic seem to happen to her as strange and impersonal incidents. They scarcely stimulate Betty to any remarks; it is as if they had not released in her any responses which might overcome her inertia sufficiently to be put down on paper. It is interesting to group all the remarks together. They read: "Was very sleepy. Was very bored. Very sleepy. Very tired. They are terrible. Not so excited. We were very hungry." All these remarks are negative; they express only unpleasant feelings or disappointments. This is very characteristic for Betty: the only sensations which she can remember are the unpleasant ones. This trend, expressed in some of her other writings as well, suggests that some unknown defeat or disappointment, hitherto unrecognized, has injured her self-confidence and optimism severely. This, of course, is speculation, expressed only in the search for a probable explanation. At least it does show how Betty's indifferent, diffident, and defeated attitude at school carries over into her entire daily life.

The research workers point out that this interpretation may be in part no more than speculation. Counselors need to be similarly cautious. Interpretations should be sought and hypotheses offered, but the hypotheses should be considered provisional and the speculative nature of the

[21] *Ibid.*, pp. 50–51. Reprinted by permission of the publisher.

interpretation acknowledged. Otherwise, justification is given for pro-tests, such as those made by Liebman,[22] who warns against the "amount of damage which may be accomplished by the salting and peppering of mean-ingless, yet impressive, words upon the records" of students by well-inten-tioned counselors, as in the following examples: "She is sometimes quiet and retiring which indicates that she is an introvert. She isn't particularly interested in associating with the members of her class which indicates that she is poorly adjusted. Her work of the last term is not commensurate with her ability which indicates that she is disinterested in school work."

It should also be noted that in her diary Betty failed to report on many hours and that she left out some details, such as the particular radio program listened to, which some counselors might like to know. The fact, however, that Betty kept her diary as she did may be more significant than the information omitted.

SOME OTHER WRITINGS

Not all the writings that students do for classes in English, social studies, and other subjects serve as sources of information about them. Little may be learned, for example, about a student from his descriptive theme on "Christmas in England during the Time of Addison and Steele" if the stu-dent leaves himself out of the picture. If, however, he puts himself into the picture through evaluative statements, identifications, and the like, as much may be learned about the student as about what he read in *The Spectator*. Likewise, if a student gives in a book report no more than a synopsis, little may be learned about the student through reading his book report. If, however, he writes a review in which he reports his reac-tions and tells what he considers significant in the book, much may be learned about him—his interests, philosophy, maturity level, and the like.

Essays, reviews of student-selected books, and themes written on such topics as "My Summer Experiences," "My Three Wishes," "Changes Needed in Hometown," and the like often yield important material. Poems give evidence of students' creative powers. Some also provide evi-dence of the writers' basic feelings—feelings of security or insecurity, of belongingness or loneliness, of hope or despair, of strength or helplessness. The motherless child, for example, was the theme of four poems written by Betty, the girl whose diary record is reproduced above. One poem, "The Lamb," contains these two lines: [23]

> "Now you are mine for you have left your mother,
> Little white lamb are you lonely?"

Another, "The Helpless Leaves," also deals with feelings of helplessness and loneliness.

[22] R. R. Liebman, "Let's Quit Being Amateur Psychiatrists," *Clearing House*, 1950, 25:217.

[23] From *The Adolescent Personality* by Peter Blos, pp. 68–69. Copyright, 1941. D. Appleton-Century Company, Inc. Reprinted by permission of the publisher.

They're helpless since they left the tree.
Our mother oak can't help us and here we lie.

. . . .

Here I lie helpless and about to die.

In striking contrast is a poem, "Sensations," written by one of the subjects in the Wisconsin study, a high school sophomore girl. The last stanza reads as follows: [24]

I look through my open window
And what do I feel?
The cooling touch of the playful breezes
And a delicate spray of rain on my face
And in my mind I feel secure
And at peace with the world.

The personal data contained in writings may be increased when students are encouraged to use classwork for exploring matters of special interest and concern to them individually. A good example is found in Murray's [25] report of a plan followed at Denver University in a basic communication class for providing students laboratory practice in communication and human relations skills. While sociodrama was the principal procedure used for giving help with problem situations, writing projects were used "to prime the class." One such project was, in part, as follows:

The class will be divided into pairs for the carrying on of correspondence. The correspondence between each pair may be carried on throughout the length of course or other specified time, or until a termination satisfactory to both students is achieved. Each member of the class may be a member of more than one pair if this is desired. Ordinarily a person should be paired with another person who has a widely different background. The following are examples of the sort of subjects about which correspondence might be carried on:

a. The problems of democracy in this school.

b. Your chief problems of communication and interpersonal relations.

c. The advantages and disadvantages of the vocations we (two) have selected.

Because in the past their letters may have been accepted with more understanding and tolerance (with respect to language usage in particular) than have been their compositions, some students write better on the same subject when writing letters than when writing themes. Knowing this, some teachers have students write letters about themselves, their

[24] Rothney et al., *Guidance Practices and Results*, p. 111.

[25] Elwood Murray, "Sociodrama and Psychodrama in the College Basic Communication Class," in Robert B. Haas (ed.), *Psychodrama and Sociodrama in American Education*, pp. 322–329. Beacon, N.Y.: Beacon House, Inc., 1949.

school, and community, instead of writing compositions on these subjects. Letters written under the usual conditions of personal correspondence ordinarily contain more biographical material than letters written as class assignments. A student may correspond with his counselor during the time that he is out of school because of vacation, illness, or some other reason. Some students write notes to their counselors while at school because they find it easier to say in writing than orally that which they wish to tell the counselor. In letters to adults whom they like and look upon as trustworthy friends, students often write as freely and fully of their activities, thoughts, and feelings as they sometimes do in diaries kept for their own reading only. Like diaries, such letters are confidential personal documents and must always be treated as such.

Ideally a summary should be prepared of the data obtained each year on a student through his writings and the summary filed in the counseling folder. The more background information counselors gather on their counselees, the better they can see them as "whole persons" and the better they may understand what can be expected of these persons. But they should not expect to achieve full understanding through analysis and diagnosis of such material. As Munroe [26] points out, there are no shortcuts to diagnosis by way of information on a student's background:

> For the present, at least, it does not seem possible to arrive at adequate hypotheses as to what to expect of a student on the basis of specific elements in her background. As teachers we lack both opportunity to uncover sufficient information and sufficient insight or skill to make use of the history we have in any systematic way. It is too easy to make snap judgments about students on the basis of some fragment of their history and a theoretical knowledge of current psychological interpretations. The way of true understanding is more painstaking and inclusive, more narrowly focused on the particular individual with whom we are dealing....
>
> To have learned to be cautious about making interpretations from isolated fragments of background data is a positive gain.

SUMMARY

The literature indicates decreased use of self-analysis procedures for self-appraisal and motivational purposes and increased use for studying the extent to which a subject understands and accepts himself and the changes that seem to occur in perception and acceptance of self during a period of special assistance through counseling or some other service. Examples are given of instruments used for both purposes.

The autobiography is often used in much the same way that the personal data blank is used for obtaining background information on in-

---

[26] Ruth Munroe, *Teaching the Individual*, pp. 150–151. New York: Columbia University Press, 1942.

coming students. It generally yields more information on the inner life or private aspects of personality than does the questionnaire. When students are provided outlines or guide sheets to use in writing their life histories, they tend to report a greater number of problems than when writing without such aids. The research of Danielson and Rothney shows that the structured approach elicits more education problems and the unstructured approach more problems in the area of family relationship but that in other areas neither approach seems superior to the other.

Time budgets and daily records provide information on the general patterns of students' lives, the activities customarily occupying their time, and some of their special interests. Essays, themes, book reviews, poems, letters, and other writings are also important sources of supplementary data. Such data need to be interpreted with caution. The counselor takes care not to read into the student's writings his own feelings, fears, hopes, aspirations, and sensitivities.

REFERENCES

Allport, Gordon W.: *The Use of Personal Documents in Psychological Science,* Bulletin 49. New York: Social Science Research Council, 1942.

Almy, Millie, from materials prepared by Ruth Cunningham and Associates: *Ways of Studying Children: A Manual for Teachers,* chap. 5. New York: Bureau of Publications, Teachers College, Columbia University, 1959.

Blos, Peter: *The Adolescent Personality,* pp. 53–58, 140–192, 209–213. New York: Appleton-Century-Crofts, Inc., 1941.

Danielson, Paul J., and John W. M. Rothney: "The Student Autobiography: Structured or Unstructured?" *Personnel and Guidance Journal,* 1954, 33:30–33.

Dinkmeyer, Don: "Reconsideration of the Autobiography," *Vocational Guidance Quarterly,* 1957, 6:9–11.

Jersild, Arthur T.: *In Search of Self: An Exploration of the Role of the School in Promoting Self-understanding.* New York: Bureau of Publications, Teachers College, Columbia University, 1952.

Magnuson, Henry W., et al.: *Evaluating Pupil Progress,* rev. ed., chap. 7. Sacramento: California State Department of Education, 1960.

Rothney, John W. M.: *The High School Student: A Book of Cases.* New York: Holt, Rinehart and Winston, Inc., 1953.

—— and Bert A. Roens: *Counseling the Individual Student,* chap. 3. New York: Holt, Rinehart and Winston, Inc., 1949.

—— et al.: *Guidance Practices and Results,* chap. 3. New York: Harper & Row, Publishers, Incorporated, 1958.

Shaffer, E. Evan, Jr.: "The Autobiography in Secondary School Counseling," *Personnel and Guidance Journal,* 1954, 32:395–398.

Strang, Ruth: *Counseling Technics in College and Secondary School,* rev. ed., chap. 4. New York: Harper & Row, Publishers, Incorporated, 1949.

Taba, Hilda, and Deborah Elkins: *With Focus on Human Relations,* chap. 1. Washington, D.C.: American Council on Education, 1950.

—— et al.: *Diagnosing Human Relations Needs,* chap. 2. Washington, D.C.: American Council on Education, 1951.

11

Analysis of the Individual's Position and Status within the Group

Through conferences and the use of various types of observation reports, counselors can learn something regarding the teacher's opinions of individual students. Through interviews and data from inventories, self-ratings, creative writings, and the like, they can learn something regarding a student's opinion of himself. Counselors also need to know the extent to which the student is accepted by his peers—his reputation among those of his own age and his position and status in classes, teams, clubs, and other peer groups.

The quantity and quality of a student's relations with other students determine in a large measure the quantity and quality of his various learnings—academic, social, and personal. Every group serves as a learning laboratory. The student learns best when he is comfortable in the group, when he feels that he belongs and is accepted, wanted, and appreciated. He is frustrated in learning when in a group where he feels more tolerated than enjoyed, not well accepted, unwanted, or rejected.

To help a student find a comfortable place in student life, the counselor needs to know not only the student's social needs but also the extent to which he influences others, his acceptance and rejection of others, others' acceptance and rejection of him, and his human relations values. He can obtain some of this information through observation and through reports from others. He can usually obtain, however, more accurate and comprehensive information through the use of sociometric methods that disclose the patterns of belonging within the peer groups of which the student is a member.

THE SOCIOMETRIC TEST

The sociometric techniques were devised by Moreno [1] and adapted by Jennings [2] for use in the classroom and other school situations. They are generally considered the most useful method yet developed for studying the social structure of a group and its patterns of interpersonal relations. Interest in the use of these techniques in the public schools was greatly stimulated by the American Council on Education three-year experimental study in intergroup education. It demonstrated the value of sociometry for promoting the emotional development and social adjustment of individual students.

The sociometric test consists of one or more questions that permit a student to reveal his personal feelings for others through his choice of the group members he wishes to be with in particular situations. The group is asked to name the ones whom they want to associate with for some common purpose. The members may be asked, for example, to name in the order of preference three students with whom they would like to play on a team or to work on a committee or to share a table at lunchtime.

Reality Value of Criteria. The situation for which wanted or unwanted associates are named is termed "the choice criterion." The research studies of Byrd [3] and others support the hypothesis stressed by Jennings [4] and supported by her own extensive research that the sociometric test is valid to the extent that the choice criterion has reality value for the subjects. The basis of choice must be real, not hypothetical. For the question asked to be a "true" sociometric test, a specific criterion, such as sitting near, rooming with, playing with, or working with others in a particular situation must be used and the group members must know that they will be grouped on the basis of their choices. Such questions as "Who are your best friends?" and "Whom would you like to have as a friend?" are actually not sociometric questions.

For the results to show the patterns of social relations in the group, the members must have confidence that their choices will be used for the purpose expressed; and the purpose must be one important to them. They are not likely to express choices in keeping with their real feelings unless they know that they are choosing for an actual situation of definite significance to them and believe that the group will be organized on the basis of their choices.

[1] J. L. Moreno (with Helen H. Jennings), *Who Shall Survive?* rev. ed. Beacon, N.Y.: Beacon House, Inc., 1953.

[2] Helen H. Jennings, *Sociometry in Group Relations*, 2d ed. Washington, D.C.: American Council on Education, 1959.

[3] Eugene Byrd, "A Study of Validity and Constancy of Choices in a Sociometric Test," *Sociometry*, 1951, 14:175–181.

[4] Helen H. Jennings, *Leadership and Isolation*, 2d. ed., chap. 1. New York: Longmans, Green & Co., Inc., 1950.

If, for example, a teacher, when first using the sociometric test with his class, makes the criterion "sitting in proximity," most of the students, wishing to sit near friends and perhaps not near certain other students, will express their real feelings. If this teacher, however, only asks the question because he wishes to find out which students are most liked and least liked by the others and if he does not change the seating arrangement in keeping with the test results, the students will lose confidence in both the teacher and the test. Should this teacher later use another sociometric question with the group, the results from the second test may be exceedingly low in validity. The students have good reason to doubt that they will be grouped as indicated.

Likewise, if the criterion for the sociometric question is "going to the movies," the validity of the results will be in keeping with the reality value of this question for the students. If they are told to name the three persons whom they prefer to go with to see a movie to be shown at school and if they know that the teacher is able to make their choices effective, the question has real significance for them. If, however, they are asked to name the persons whom they would like to go with to see a movie being shown in town and know that the teacher is not planning to invite them to a movie party but merely wants to know with whom they would like to go if they had the opportunity, some students will not name their real preferences because they do not think that they will ever have an opportunity to go to the movies with the students preferred.

For the criterion to have reality value, the students must know that they will be grouped on the basis of their choices and that this will be done shortly rather than at some vague indefinite time. When the choice criterion does not have reality value, the question is a quasi- or near-sociometric question rather than a true one. Sometimes regrouping is not possible or practical and so the near-sociometric question is used because it does have some diagnostic value. The use of quasi-sociometric questions may sometimes be necessary in research, but use should ordinarily be avoided in guidance, where the gathering of sociometric data is more a means than an end.

The sociometric test contributes to individual growth when it helps to improve the group climate. Participation in a group results in a gain or loss to individual growth in accordance with the emotional atmosphere in the group. Inadequate, discordant group life spells a loss in personality development. Harmonious, satisfying group life brings release of strengths and development of potentialities. Organizing or reorganizing a group on the basis of sociometric data improves intermember communication and understanding and thereby helps to create the type of group climate needed.

Administration. The validity of the data depends also in part upon how and when the sociometric test is administered. It should be used with groups small enough for the members to become well acquainted. It should be used only after they have been together sufficiently long to develop preferences and to establish rapport with the person administering the test. The word "test," however, is usually avoided because to many students it implies "right" and "wrong" answers. The question is asked informally and the choice criterion explained in clear, specific terms. The form is more easily illustrated than explained. The following statement, taken from Jennings,[5] was used with a high school social studies class:

> We are going to need committees to work on _____ and _____ problems. Each of you knows with whom you enjoy working most. These may be the same people with whom you work in other classes, or they may be different, so remember that we are talking about social studies. Put your name at the top of the page and numbers 1, 2, and 3 on lines below. Opposite "1" put the name of a boy or a girl with whom you would most like to work, after "2" your second choice, and after "3" your third. I will keep all of the choices in mind and arrange the committees so that everyone will be with one or more of the three people named. Remember, you may choose a boy or a girl who is absent today if you want to. Write down the last names as well as the first names so that I'll be sure to know whom you mean. As usual, we shall probably be working in these committees for about eight weeks, or until the Christmas holidays.
>
> Remember I said your committees will be so arranged that you will be with one or more of the boys or girls you choose. So it's best to keep your choices confidential. Since it's impossible to place every person so that he has all his choices, you will be with some who have chosen you and whom you may not have chosen. You wouldn't want such people to think you hadn't considered them when perhaps you would have chosen them for your committee if you'd had more than three choices.

The following statement from Northway [6] illustrates the test that contains several questions. It was used with a group of twelve- to sixteen-year-olds who were going to camp together.

> At camp, you like to do lots of things with other campers. In order to help the staff work out your groups we would like you to tell us which campers you would like best to do things with. We'd like to know who you would like to cabin with. We'd like to know who you would like to go on a canoe trip with, to be in your favorite activity with. When we know these things, we will try to work out the groups the way you'd like them to be.... So we are asking you to answer a few questions. One question is "Who of all the campers would you most like to go on a canoe trip with?" Put down the name of the camper you'd most like to go with you. Then the name of the camper you'd choose second and then the name of

---

[5] Jennings, *Sociometry in Group Relations*, pp. 15–16.
[6] Mary L. Northway, *A Primer of Sociometry*, p. 6. Toronto, Canada: University of Toronto Press, 1952.

the one you'd choose third. Another is "Who would you like to cabin with you?" Are there any questions? Be sure to fill in each space.

To facilitate administration of the test, mimeographed forms, such as the one shown in Figure 31, can be developed. An allowance of three to five choices is usually sufficient to show the individual's position in the group. Research indicates that permitting an unlimited number of choices apparently does not change the relative position of the group members. As summarized by Jennings,[7] "those individuals who attract the greater proportion of the choices on a basis of a small choice allowance, continue still to profit disproportionately under the larger choice allowance, and the number of individuals unchosen under the first condition is not substantially reduced under the second condition."

Name _____ Date _____	
Yes	No
1.	
2.	
3.	

FIGURE 31   *Answer form for sociometric question.*

At times it is desirable to explore the negative as well as the positive aspects of choice. It is best, however, to delay use of the negative question until the group members are accustomed to expressing preferences and feel comfortable in doing so. The negative question should be abandoned when its use creates discomfort or embarrassment. Positive choices for inclusion and negative choices against inclusion (rejections) should be given separately but may be given on the same slip or card.

Like the question for positive choices, the negative one should be given in an informal, direct, matter-of-fact manner and after it has been made clear that all responses will be kept confidential. Moreover, the question for negative choices should be carefully worded to avoid any implication of one student's being asked to pass judgment on another; and attention should be called to the two-way nature of negative feelings. Nothing should be said regarding the number of persons to be named or

[7] Jennings, *Leadership and Isolation*, p. 19.

the order in which they are to be written. The emphasis must be upon the situation rather than the rejection. The following illustrates the question for negative choice: [8]

> If there are any persons with whom you may feel especially uneasy or uncomfortable in the situation we are choosing for or if there is someone who, you think, may feel uncomfortable with you, write their names in the "No" column. If there is no one about whom you feel this way or who, you think, feels that way about you, leave the "No" side of the card blank. If I can arrange the groups to avoid putting these persons with you, I shall do so. Are there any questions?

Administration of the test question is most likely to be effective for obtaining accurate responses when the counselor or teacher takes care to observe seven points stressed by Jennings: [9]

> (1) To include the motivating elements in the introductory remarks, (2) to word the question so that children understand how the results are to be used, (3) to allow enough time, (4) to emphasize *any* boy or girl so as to approve in advance any direction the choice may take, (5) to present the test situation with interest and some enthusiasm, (6) to say how soon the arrangements based on the test can be made, and (7) to keep the whole procedure as casual as possible.

If a student feels secure in his relationship with the test administrator and feels certain that his responses will be kept confidential, he is more willing than he would be otherwise to make known his real preferences for and against his associates. The test results may then reveal preferences that some students are not willing to express overtly and so cannot be known through observation. A student, for example, in response to a sociometric question may name someone whose company he is unwilling to seek openly because of fear that the other person might not select him or timidity about approaching someone more popular than he or hesitancy created by difference in sex, race, religion, socioeconomic status, or the like.

Summarizing the Data. The choices may be summarized in tabular form, as is done in Figure 32. The names are listed along the top and in the same order down one or both sides of the chart. The rank orders of each member's choices are recorded in the row after his name in the proper columns under the names of the ones chosen. Assigning numbers to the members and writing the numbers in front of the names facilitate recording and reading of the chart. The number of choices received by each member is recorded at the bottom of the column under his name.

[8] Jane Warters, *Group Guidance: Principles and Practices,* p. 98. New York: McGraw-Hill Book Company, Inc., 1960.

[9] Helen H. Jennings, "Sociometric Grouping in Relation to Child Development," in Caroline M. Tryon (ed.), *Fostering Mental Health in Our Schools,* p. 206. Washington, D.C.: National Education Association, 1950.

Rejections are not shown on the chart pictured in Figure 32. They can be recorded, however, by writing R in the proper cell after the name of the rejector and under the name of the rejectee. Rejections are not totaled with the positive choices. They are added separately, labeled negative choices, and recorded below the positive totals.

The test data may be recorded or summarized graphically by means of a sociogram, as in Figure 33. Each sociogram pictures the choices for a particular situation and *is valid for that situation only*.

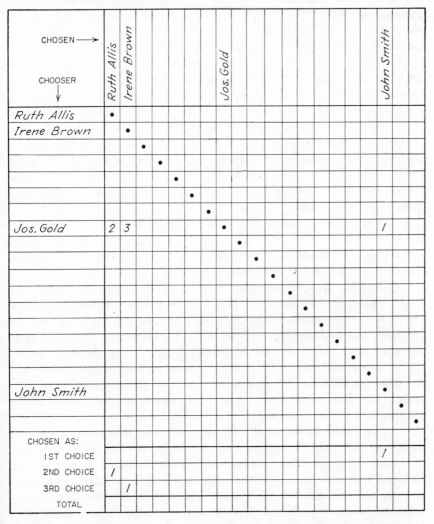

FIGURE 32   *Sociometric tabulation form. List names in the same order vertically and horizontally. Insert a "1," "2," "3," in the proper spaces to indicate the order of choices. Joseph Gold chooses John Smith first, Ruth Allis second, and Irene Brown third.* (Helen H. Jennings, *Sociometry in Group Relations*, 2d ed., p. 21. Washington, D.C.: American Council on Education, 1959. Reproduced by permission of the publisher.)

The procedures for constructing a sociogram are not standardized, but the ones used most often seem to be the following: Circles are drawn to represent girls and triangles to represent boys. Boys are grouped on one side and girls on the other to show the extent to which the students cross the sex line in their choices. Other subgroups can be separated similarly, as in Figure 34, to show the extent to which cultural, religious, socioeconomic differences or the like may be barriers to communication. In each such grouping the name of the person receiving the highest number of mentions is written in the center symbol. The names of the other members are written in the symbols beyond these in accordance with the number of choices received, the names of the unchosen and little-chosen members appearing in the symbols farthest from the center.

The choices between individuals are represented by lines drawn between the symbols, with the rank of each choice indicated by a number written at the base of the symbol representing the chooser. A one-way choice is shown by a line that ends in an arrow pointing to the symbol representing the chosen person. A mutual choice is shown by a line between two symbols with a small bar or circle in the middle and with or without arrows at both ends. One-way and mutual rejections are shown in the same way, but the lines are dotted or colored. Absent students are represented by dotted or colored symbols. Lines should bend to pass around intervening symbols; they should not pass through them.

The work of constructing sociograms can be reduced through the use of a mimeographed form that contains a sufficient number of circles and triangles for it to be used with groups of different sizes. The sociogram shown in Figure 33 is a filled-in mimeographed form.

Another type of sociogram is pictured in Figure 34. This is the target sociogram introduced by Northway.[10] Each of its four concentric circles represents one-fourth of the score points or the number of choices received. The names of the students in the lowest quarter of the group in terms of score points (explained below) are placed in the outer circle. The names of the ones in the highest quarter go in the center circle, and the names of others are placed in the other two circles according to their scores. The students are grouped according to sex, and the lines of choice are shown in the usual manner.

Vertical and horizontal lines may be drawn to separate subgroups according to ethnic or cultural background as well as according to sex. In Figure 34, for example, boys and girls are separated by the vertical line and Jews and Gentiles by the horizontal line. This sociogram shows a definite sex cleavage but no cultural cleavage. While the Jewish boys tend to choose other Jewish boys to a rather high degree, there is no cleavage between the Jewish and Gentile students.

The target sociogram clearly distinguishes the most-chosen from the

---

[10] Mary L. Northway, "A Method for Depicting Social Relationships Obtained by Sociometric Testing," *Sociometry*, 1940, 7:144–150.

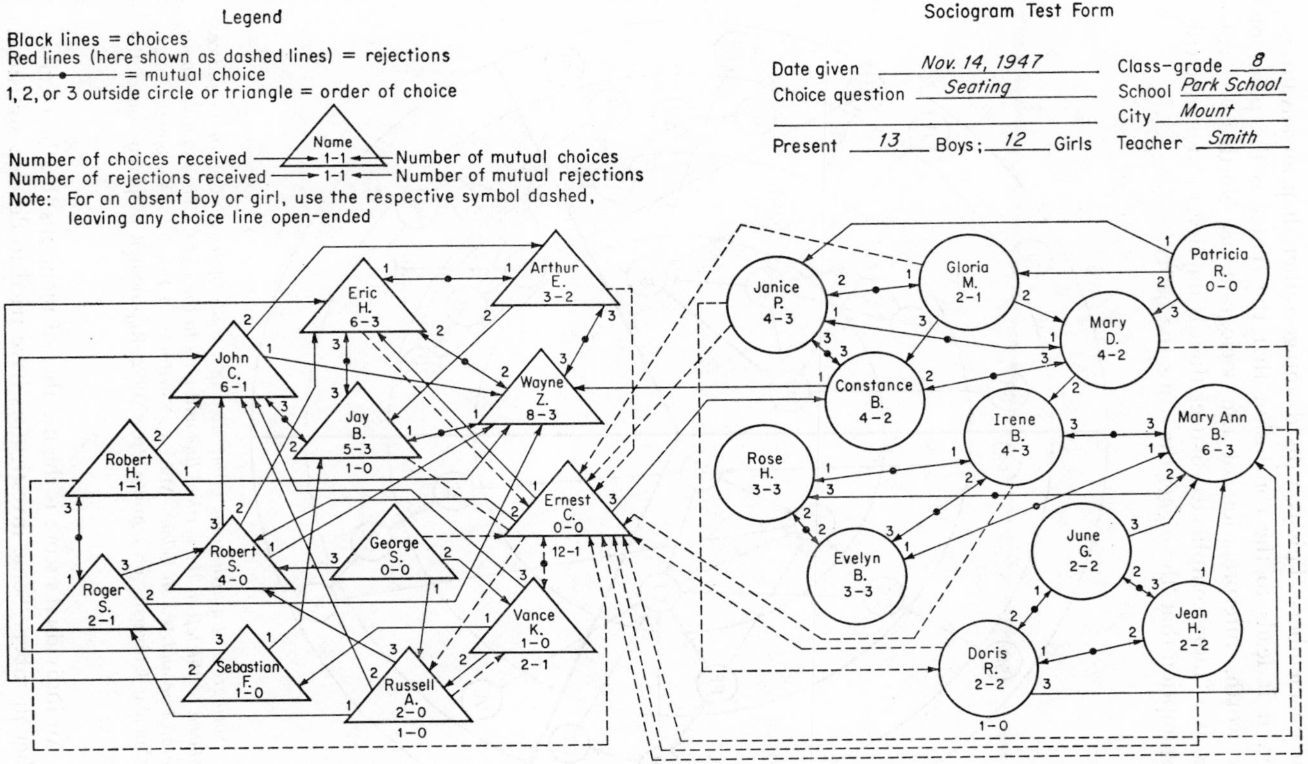

Sociogram Test Form

Legend

Black lines = choices
Red lines (here shown as dashed lines) = rejections
● ——— = mutual choice
1, 2, or 3 outside circle or triangle = order of choice

Name
Number of choices received ——— 1-1 Number of mutual choices
Number of rejections received ——— 1-1 Number of mutual rejections
Note: For an absent boy or girl, use the respective symbol dashed,
leaving any choice line open-ended

Date given _____ Nov. 14, 1947 _____ Class-grade _____ 8 _____
Choice question _____ Seating _____ School _____ Park School _____
                                    City _____ Mount _____
Present _____ 13 _____ Boys; _____ 12 _____ Girls   Teacher _____ Smith _____

FIGURE 33   Filled-in sociogram form, presenting graphically the choice patterns. Blank forms with empty circles and triangles may be mimeographed so that the teacher may fill in names and draw choice lines after the test has been given. (Hilda Taba et al., Diagnosing Human Relations Needs, p. 78. Washington, D.C.: American Council on Education, 1951. Reproduced by permission of the publisher.)

least-chosen members. This is a disadvantage rather than an advantage, however, if it leads to the conclusion that the center is the point of greatest worth. Interpretation of the sociogram, as Northway [11] emphasizes, is a "more complicated matter than is implied in the naive cultural assumption that 'the bigger the score, the better.' "

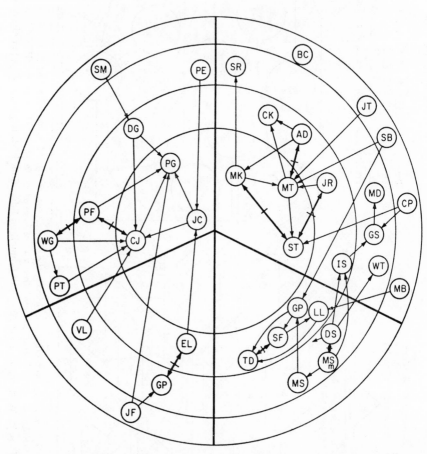

FIGURE 34   *Sociogram of a fifth-grade group used in a study of Jewish-Gentile prejudice. Boys are placed to the left of the vertical line and girls to the right. Gentile pupils above the horizontal line and Jewish below.* (Mary L. Northway, *A Primer of Sociometry*, p. 24. Toronto, Canada: University of Toronto Press, 1952. Reproduced by permission of the publisher.)

Scoring. An individual's score is the number of mentions that he receives from other members. Some investigators have tried to develop statistical procedures for weighting the choices, but without any significant success. The great amount of work involved in computing weighted scores does

[11] Northway, *A Primer of Sociometry*, pp. 34–35.

not seem warranted since, as Campbell,[12] Lindzey and Borgatta,[13] and others point out, experiential evidence shows such weighting to make little difference. Moreover, the significance of differences between first, second, and third choices is not yet determined.

A social-status index may be computed for the individual by dividing the number of choices that he receives by the number in the group minus one. However, a member of high social status is not necessarily strong in personal growth. Hence, the social-status index should not be considered a measure of mental health or inner growth. It may indicate primarily the extent to which the individual conforms to the group's mores or embodies values important to the group.

SOCIOMETRIC PATTERNS

Overchosen and Underchosen Members. The group member who is not chosen by anyone is described as an "isolate," although technically the term should be applied to only those who neither choose nor are chosen. The term "reject" may be used to describe any negatively chosen member, but ordinarily it refers only to the much-rejected person. Individuals who receive a disproportionately low number of mentions are described as "little chosen" or "underchosen"; and those who receive disproportionately high scores, as "stars," "leaders," or "overchosen." "Overchosen" seems the best term because it is easily related to the choice criterion— "overchosen for being on the same team" or "overchosen for being an associate on social studies committee."

The technical procedure suggested by Jennings [14] for determining underchosen and overchosen members is to classify as overchosen the ones whose scores fall one standard deviation above the mean score and as underchosen those whose scores fall one standard deviation below the mean. Because exact statistics are not needed in most nonresearch applications of sociometry, Taba [15] offers this nontechnical rule: "when more than one-fifth of the class [from 30 to 35 members] has five or more choices and a few have more than eight, then there is an unreasonable focusing on a few people and correspondingly more students with only one or no choices."

When students differentiate their choices in keeping with differ-

[12] D. T. Campbell, "A Rationale for Weighting First, Second, and Third Sociometric Choices," *Sociometry*, 1954, 17:242–243.

[13] Gardner Lindzey and E. F. Borgatta, "Sociometric Measurement," in Gardner Lindzey (ed.), *Handbook of Social Psychology*, vol. 1, p. 414. Reading, Mass.: Addison-Wesley Publishing Company, Inc., 1954.

[14] Jennings, *Leadership and Isolation*, p. 67.

[15] Hilda Taba et al., *Diagnosing Human Relations Needs*, p. 83. Washington, D.C.: American Council on Education, 1951.

ences in choice criteria, different individuals may be overchosen and underchosen in different situations. Some who are highly sought, for example, as playmates may not be highly sought as work partners. While there is usually some overlap in expressions of choices on contrasting criteria, being one standard deviation above the mean in one group may not mean the same as being one standard deviation above the mean in another.

Cliques and Cleavages. When there are small clusters bound closely together with mutual choices, cliques are indicated. As defined by Taba,[16] a clique is a small subgroup of three or more members each of whom chooses at least one person and is chosen by at least one other person (other than one he chooses) in the subgroup. A clique is described as "closed" when none of its members includes persons outside the subgroup among his choices. The clique is "open" when some member or members choose persons outside the clique. The sociogram pictured in Figure 34, for example, shows three cliques (one closed and two open) among the girls and one closed clique among the boys.

When a definite clique pattern is shown, antagonism or friction, as well as a general lack of cooperation in total-group activities, may be expected. When segments are shown cut off from the rest of the group or loosely joined to the rest by a few intermittent lines, cleavages are indicated. Short chains of one-way choices with little overlap in the links signify that the group members have not had sufficient opportunity to get acquainted. A shaggy picture with little focus shows a loose group structure and a lack of direction in group activity and indicates that, until the group members come to understand and to appreciate one another, little joint effort may be expected. In contrast, long lines or chains with much overlap in the links and a good number of reciprocated choices indicate a well-integrated social structure, good group spirit, and a spread of leadership—the result of good communication and wide understanding among the group members.

Reading the Sociogram. A study of Figure 33 shows some of the things that a sociogram can reveal about a group and its members. A good way to become quickly familiar with the general pattern of the group structure is to concentrate on a few individuals by following all the lines that lead to and from them. Because of the large number of broken lines (they show rejection) that lead to and from Ernest, attention is first attracted to this boy. Eleven rejection lines lead to Ernest, and three lead from him to others. No line of positive choice leads to him. Ernest's first preference is Eric, a well-chosen member of the group and one of the eleven who reject Ernest. His second choice is Robert S., another well-chosen boy; and

[16] *Ibid.*, p. 85.

his third choice is Constance, a well-chosen girl. (The sociogram cannot show why Ernest is unchosen or why he is strongly rejected. This information must be obtained from other sources.)

Turning to Vance, we note that he is chosen by only one person, George, an isolate. Vance's first choice is unchosen Sebastian. His second choice is average-chosen Russell, who rejects him. His third choice is John, who is overchosen and a member of the boys' closed clique. Vance is also rejected by Ernest, whose rejection he reciprocates.

Wayne's position in the group is in striking contrast to that of Vance. He is the most highly chosen class member and a part of the boys' clique. All three of his choices are reciprocated and in the same order as his. He receives five other mentions, four of which are first choices. He is chosen by overchosen, average-chosen, and little-chosen members. He is the only boy chosen by a girl. He is chosen by well-chosen Constance, the only girl chosen by a boy.

Moving over to the group of girls, we look at Patricia and Mary Ann, the least chosen and the most chosen among the girls. Patricia is the only girl unchosen. She names as her preferences three members of a four-girl subgroup. All three of Mary Ann's choices are reciprocated but not in the same order as made by her. She may be a strong link between two clusters or cliques, for she is the choice of three members of her own closed clique and is chosen by all three members of another clique. In a similar fashion we could follow the lines leading to and from all the other class members to learn the relative strength of their positions.

When we examine the sociogram as a whole, we note that there is a network of lines on both sides of the diagram, that the choices do not focus on a few members only but are fairly well distributed. On the whole, the picture seems to be a good one. Examining it more carefully, however, we see some weaknesses and two in particular: First, the class is divided into two segments—boys and girls. Only one girl chooses a boy, and only one boy chooses a girl. In each segment, then, there is only one member who serves as a link with the other segment; and one of these links, Ernest, has a very insecure position in the group. Although at the eighth-grade level boy-girl choices are normally few, the number here is definitely below average.

Second, the dominant pattern is that of pairs and subgroups. There is more pairing off (mutual choices) among the girls than among the boys —13 among the girls and 7 among the boys. More than half the class (16 members) belongs to a closed or a semiclosed group. There are three groups of girls and one group of boys that are bound closely together by mutual choices. The group of five boys (Arthur, Eric, Wayne, John, and Jay) and one group of girls (Rose, Evelyn, Irene, and Mary Ann) are self-contained cliques in that the members do not choose anyone outside their subgroups. The other two cliques of girls (Janice, Gloria, Mary,

Constance and June, Jean, Doris) are not closed groups because some members direct choices toward others not in their group and receive mentions from others outside their group.

There is more overlapping in the lines among the boys than among the girls, which indicates that more joint action may be expected from the boys than from the girls. The three clusters of girls are very loosely joined to one another. If there is antagonism or friction between the members of these three subgroups, there is a possibility not only that there may be little cooperation but also that one subgroup may try to block the interests of another.

In spite of the fact that the dominant pattern in this sociogram is one of pairs and subgroups, the sociogram yields evidence that there is good communication among the group members of each of the two main segments. First, there are few extremes. Only three members (Patricia, George, and Ernest) are unchosen, which is less than average. According to Taba's standard, the group shows no unreasonable focusing of choices. Four members (less than one-fifth of the group) receive more than five mentions each. No member receives more than eight choices; and only one member, Wayne, receives as many as eight. There are only two expressions of negative choice in addition to the negative choices received and expressed by Ernest.

Second, good communication is indicated by the long chains that, with some overlapping, connect the members within each segment. All the girls, for example, are on one or both of two long chains. Note the chain that begins at the top and runs from Patricia to Janice to Gloria to Constance to Mary to Irene to Rose to Evelyn and to Mary Ann, and the chain that begins at the bottom with Doris and runs to Jean to June to Mary Ann to Evelyn to Rose and to Irene. On the boys' side also there are several long chains, such as the one that runs from George to Vance to Russell to Robert S. to John to Jay to Eric to Arthur and to Wayne. In both segments (boys and girls) there are a number of chains that extend beyond three or four members. These chains indicate that the students have sufficient opportunity for contact with each other—at least with others of their own sex—and have an opportunity to influence one another through an exchange of ideas.

Learning the Reasons for Choices. The sociogram shows the choices, negative and positive, expressed by the group members; but it does not show why these choices are made. The sociogram in Figure 33, for example, cannot tell us why Ernest is unchosen and rejected or why he chooses and rejects certain students. We cannot assume that he is rejected by the other students because he is a very disagreeable person who does not try to get along with others or, noting that eight of the eleven who reject him are girls, assume that he likes to pick on girls or has "a bad reputation." Neither can we assume that the picture of strong rejection of Ernest given by this sociogram is one of long standing. It may be only a temporary one that reflects adult values rather than the values of the peer group. The rejection may not be based on any strong dislike for Ernest but may be the outgrowth of some special situation. If, for example, the sociometric question is used at the time of an exciting national election and the youngsters, like the adults, are engaged in heated political debates, and if Ernest and his family are staunch supporters of the Democrats in a community that is strongly Republican, Ernest may find himself for a time outside the pale. Once the election is over and life is back to normal, a new sociogram may show Ernest in his normal position in the group. All this, however, is supposition and nothing more. The picture given of Ernest's status may be the correct one. Without more information than we now have, any reason that we may offer in explanation of his being unchosen or of his being rejected can be no more than a guess. In place of guesses, we need hypotheses and conclusions based on valid, reliable information.

Here are only a few of the questions that we need to answer in order to interpret the picture given by the sociogram in Figure 33 but which we cannot answer on the basis of the data that we now have: What has caused the cleavage between boys and girls? School regulations? Classroom arrangements and procedures? Are the members of each subgroup of the same race or religion or from the same neighborhood or from the same lower school? Do the students who pair through mutual choices complement each other, or do they seek support from each other? In short, do the reciprocated choices represent dependencies? What have the highly chosen students in common? (They tend to choose one another.) What are the common characteristics and needs of the unchosen and little-chosen members? How is Ernest different from the others? Is his background so different that his personality is not understood? To these questions we could add others if we were the teacher of this class, because a sociogram usually raises many questions for a teacher by disclosing a number of things that he has not learned through observation and by giving increased significance to many of his observations.

Some understanding of the reasons for the preferences expressed may be gained through a study of the cumulative records and supplemental reports on the students concerned. More specific information, however, may be secured through the use of sociodrama, interviews, or written statements in answer to direct questions as to why the choices are made and why the persons chosen are important to the choosers or in answer to open questions, such as "What it takes to get along with the group" or "What I like most in my friends."

Because of the amount of time required, it is difficult to use sociodrama and interviews for learning the reasons for the choices made by all group members. It is ordinarily more convenient to ask students to state their reasons in writing, permitting them to write as fully or as concisely as they wish. The students should not feel called upon to justify or to defend their choices and should feel certain that their statements will be held confidential. The request for written statements should be so worded that "right" answers or value judgments are not implied. Taba [17] gives the following example:

> I wish you'd tell me how you happened to choose the people you did choose. When you use words like "nice" put down the specific things you mean or just add something he did so that it's clear what you mean. Write as fully as you can or wish. No one but me will see these papers.

Retesting. By using the same question repeatedly, a worker can study changes and trends in the organization of the group and the position of individual members. A test question repeated, however, shortly after its first use will not ordinarily yield much new significant information. The retest should be delayed until there is sufficient time for changes in feelings to become apparent. Since such changes do not occur rapidly, the time between tests based on the same criterion should be about seven or eight weeks.

A series of sociograms made on the same group and on the basis of the same criterion usually shows a similar overall pattern but reveals marked changes for some individuals. The sociograms for the retests generally show fewer rejections than is shown by the first sociogram because the groupings resulting from the first tests usually improve social relations sufficiently to lessen tensions in the group and thus decrease the need for scapegoats.

SOCIOMETRIC GROUPING

As soon as possible after a sociometric test has been administered, the data should be used in grouping the students for the particular purpose involved in their choosing. *Every member must be assigned to a group with at least one of his choices and as far as possible with the highest degree of choice expressed by him or the highest degree of his reciprocated choice.* A student should not be placed with those who reject him if this can be avoided. It cannot always be avoided. With almost half the class rejecting Ernest, for example, it may be difficult to assign him to a group that does not include any of those who reject him or whom he rejects and still have a strong committee of normal size.

Every possible effort is made to place each member with the ones he chooses and to whom presumably he will make the strongest response. When a student is placed with those toward whom he is drawn emotionally, he is generally found to behave more intelligently, to show more maturity, and to be more responsive to the needs and wishes of others than he might be otherwise.

[17] *Ibid.,* p. 90.

In grouping students sociometrically, the worker gives attention first to the preferences of the unchosen and little-chosen members. These individuals should be placed with their first choices and also, if possible, with one or more others chosen by them. When two students, one unchosen or little chosen and the other well chosen, name as their first choices the same person and only one of the two is to be placed with this person, the preferred position should ordinarily be given to the less secure member—the unchosen or little-chosen one.

In organizing work groups, such as class committees, skills, abilities, and temperaments as well as leadership need to be balanced. Each work group should include individuals who have the particular skills as well as the interest needed for carrying out the functions involved in the work.

When the sociogram shows serious cleavages on the basis of differences in sex, race, religion, family status, or the like, an effort should be made to bridge the gaps by placing minority and majority group members together. To do this, it is necessary to place some, perhaps many, students with their second or third choices because their first choices are usually members of their own groups. It is not wise, however, to place only one minority or majority group member with others who are not of his group. There should be at least one other, and preferably several, of his group with him. In this way the existing association patterns are not broken but are utilized for intermingling members of different subgroups. As the members of different subgroups or cliques function together for some common purpose, some, if not many, may become interested in the members of other subgroups and develop an understanding and appreciation of their ways and values. They may influence others to develop similar feelings and attitudes. In time the different subgroups may become integrated.

The data from one sociometric test are not to be used for grouping students for any situation other than the one covered by the test. A new question must be asked to ascertain preferences for a new situation, because a student may not choose as a preferred associate for one situation the person whom he names as his choice for another. As students mature, they come to see the value of special aptitudes and skills and of certain personality traits in particular situations. They learn to differentiate in their choices accordingly. Hence, to gain a comprehensive picture of the social relationships in a group as well as to aid personal development through sociometric groupings, a teacher needs to have his students select associates for a number of different situations, such as being on the same committee, going together on a field trip, sitting near others, and the like.

When sociograms that are made for the same group but on the basis of different criteria are very similar, it is because the students select the same associates for different functions. The sociograms indicate that the students have not had sufficient opportunity to interact on a personal basis. With increased opportunity to associate with others in accordance with their preferences, students grow in ability to select associates in accordance with the requirements of particular situations. The extent of overlap in sociograms based on contrasting criteria, such as associating in a work and in a play situation, is, in Jennings' [18] words, "an index of the extent to which the group life of the school as a whole is meeting the psychegroup needs" of students. The less extensive the amount of overlap, presumably the more suitable the group program is for helping students to mature socially by enabling them to participate in different kinds of group situations.

Grouping students on the basis of their preferences is only one step in improving the school's social climate. Other steps may also need to be taken to strengthen intermember and intergroup communication and understanding. Among other things, the values underlying the structure of interpersonal relations in the school may need to be studied. Are they supporting the isolation or rejection of some individuals or groups and the favored treatment of some others? Is bias or prejudice reflected in the allocation of marks, rewards, leadership roles; in the handling of discipline cases, etc.? Are there school practices (separate homerooms for boys and girls, for example) that foster development of cleavages and closed cliques? School policies, principles, and practices need to be continuously assessed for the human relations values that they support.

New content may need to be given to the school program and student life in order to broaden the scope of participation, to increase the number of active participants, and to widen access to belongingness and leadership. There may need to be increased education in interpersonal and intergroup relations in order to combat some outside environmental influences that make for prejudice, discrimination, cultural cleavages, narrow values, and rigid mores.

SOME RELATED PROCEDURES

Modified sociometric devices, such as near-sociometric questions, opinion tests, and social-distance scales, are easier than the sociometric test to administer and score and for that reason are probably more frequently used. In general, however, they are less helpful because they lack real-life motivation. But properly used they are not without value.

Near-sociometric Test. Reference has already been made to the use of quasi- or near-sociometric questions, which are used when use of true sociometric questions is not practical or appropriate. Some school people, however, employ the quasi-question when use of the true question is practical and desirable. They may substitute the near-sociometric question at times because they are unwilling to take on the extra work involved in

[18] Jennings, "Sociometric Grouping in Relation to Child Development," p. 223.

constructing sociograms and arranging sociometric groupings. The findings are often low in validity and reliability because many students (adolescents in particular) view the questions as prying or "nosy" and give answers that are more false than true.

The effectiveness of the near-sociometric test depends upon the students' willingness to answer truthfully. When they have confidence in the worker administering the test, are emotionally prepared for the question, and feel that their cooperating will help the group or them individually, near-sociometric questions may yield important data. It is difficult, however, to offer explanations for the use of such questions that are as readily accepted by adolescents as by younger students. There is no such difficulty in using the sociometric test. It requires little explanation. When the students are told that they will be grouped on the basis of their responses, the reason for asking the question is clearly evident. No pretending on the part of the students and little or no persuading on the part of the worker are required.

"Guess Who" Tests. The "Guess Who" test was developed by Hartshorne, May, and Maller for use in the Character Education Inquiry of the 1920s. It consists of 24 "word pictures," which describe "good" and "bad" attitudes and behavior. It includes such items as the following: [19]

> Here is someone who is always ready to play or work with the rest even when he (or she) can't have his own way.
> This one is always picking on others and annoying them.
> This is someone who controls his temper and never gets angry.

The student is told to read each statement carefully to see whether he can guess whom it is about and then to write in the spaces below it the name or names of the ones he thinks the statement fits. If he thinks that it describes himself, he writes his own name. If he thinks that it does not fit anyone in the group, he does not write any name. He turns in his report unsigned.

Hartshorne found that having the students sign such reports had a definite effect on the results. In one experiment, for example, he asked 117 students in three classes to list in rank order the three most-cooperative and the three least-cooperative students. The students did not sign their ballots, but these could be identified in another way. Shortly afterward they were asked to vote again and were told this time to sign their ballots. It was found that when the students signed their reports, 32 per cent of them cast a positive vote for themselves; when they did not sign, 74 per cent rated themselves positively.

In the California Adolescent Growth Study a modified form of the

[19] Hugh Hartshorne et al., *Studies in Service and Self-control.* New York: The Macmillan Company, 1929. Reproduced by permission of the publishers.

"Guess Who" test was used for the evaluation of adolescents by adolescents. Adopting the form of Hartshorne's test, Tryon [20] assembled in a test booklet 20 pairs of statements that represent the extremes of 20 traits. The first two statements, representing "restless" and "quiet," are as follows:

> Here is someone who finds it hard to sit still in class; he (or she) moves around in his (or her) seat or gets up and walks around.
>
> Here is someone who can work very quietly without moving around in his (or her) seat.

A positive score point is given the individual each time he is named for a positive trait and a negative point each time he is named for a negative trait. His total score is the algebraic sum of the score points. With a few modifications and a different scoring system the Tryon instrument was used by Cunningham [21] and her associates in their study of the group behavior of elementary and junior high school students.

Social-acceptance Scales. Some modified sociometric instruments are adaptations of one of the first scoring scales developed in social psychology—the Bogardus social-distance scale.[22] They are designed to show the degree to which each group member accepts every other member. A good example is the Classroom Social Distance Scale [23] that was used in the study reported by Cunningham and her coworkers and described as a "short cut in finding the place of the individual in the group." In using it, the student rates every member in the class, including himself if he wishes, on a five-interval scale. The intervals are defined as follows:

1. Would like to have him as one of my best friends.
2. Would like to have him in my group but not as a close friend.
3. Would like to be with him once in a while but not often or for a long time.
4. Don't mind his being in our group but I don't want to have anything to do with him.
5. Wish he weren't in our room.

This type of instrument is useful for revealing the range of interpersonal reactions in the group and the variability in an individual's choices when he can name an unlimited number of preferences. Its use,

[20] Caroline M. Tryon, *Evaluation of Adolescent Personality by Adolescents,* Monograph of the Society for Research in Child Development, vol. 4, no. 4. Washington, D.C.: National Research Council, 1939.

[21] Ruth Cunningham and Associates, *Understanding Group Behavior of Boys and Girls,* pp. 354–357, 419. New York: Bureau of Publications, Teachers College, Columbia University, 1951.

[22] E. S. Bogardus, "Measuring Social Distance," *Journal of Applied Sociology,* 1925, 9:299–308.

[23] Cunningham, *op. cit.,* pp. 171–174, 352, 401.

however, is somewhat hazardous because the students are passing judgment on one another. Hence, it should be used with caution and discarded whenever its use seems to create discomfort, embarrassment, or anxiety.

Combination of Methods. Some instruments represent a combination of one or more related procedures. One illustration is an instrument entitled *A Class Play* [24] that was used in the California study of emotionally handicapped children. It combines the guess-who technique with sociometric ratings. It contains six parts, each of which has the same 15 items. These items describe characters in the play and include such roles as "a person who is very smart," "a bully," "a mean, bossy sister," and "a person whom everyone likes."

In the first part, an adaptation of the guess-who technique, the student names the class members who, he thinks, are best suited for the different roles. In the other five parts he selects the two roles which he believes that (1) he would like to play "best of all," (2) others in the group would pick for him, (3) the teacher would give him, (4) his best friend would select for him, (5) he would most like to play should someday he become a movie or television actor.

SUMMARY

The sociometric test is generally considered the most useful procedure yet devised for studying the individual's position in the group and the social structure of the group. The validity of the test data depends upon the reality of the choice criterion, the extent to which the group members are acquainted with one another, and their confidence in the person asking the question(s).

The test results can be recorded on a chart or on a sociogram. The chart and sociogram reveal the choices made but not the reasons for the choices or the values underlying them. Such information has to be obtained through other means.

Repeated testing with different choice criteria helps students to learn to choose in keeping with the requirements of particular situations. Successive testing with the same criterion provides evidence of changes in the group's patterns and thereby gives evidence of the effectiveness of steps taken to strengthen intermember understanding and acceptance. The steps taken usually need to include, in addition to sociometric grouping, direct study of the human values underlying school practices and policies and a program in interpersonal and intergroup relations that

[24] Eli M. Bower and Nadine M. Lambert, *A Class Play.* Sacramento: California State Department of Education, 1962. Distributed for research use by Educational Testing Service, Princeton, N.J., and Berkeley, Calif.

helps students to develop enduring social values and to grow in perception and sensitivity.

Modified sociometric procedures, when properly used, can yield helpful information regarding the individual's status in the group. Some such procedures are near-sociometric tests, guess-who instruments, sociometric self-ratings, social-acceptance scales, and instruments that combine two or more related techniques.

The sociometric and related procedures help to sensitize teachers and counselors to interpersonal and intergroup difficulties among students. They often yield clues regarding modifications needed in school practices and policies in order to improve communication, understanding, and cooperation.

REFERENCES

Bonney, M. E.: "Sociometric Study of Agreement between Teacher Judgments and Student Choices in Regard to the Number of Friends Possessed by High School Students," *Sociometry*, 1947, 10:133–146.

———— and Johnny Powell: "Differences in Social Behavior between Sociometrically High and Sociometrically Low Children," *Journal of Educational Research*, 1954, 46:481–495.

Borgatta, E. F.: "A Diagnostic Note on the Construction of Sociograms and Action Diagrams," *Group Psychotherapy*, 1951, 3:300–308.

Criswell, J. H.: "Sociometric Measurement: Some Practical Advantages and New Developments," *Sociometry*, 1956, 18:639–647.

Cunningham, Ruth, and Associates: *Understanding Group Behavior of Boys and Girls*, chaps. 4–5. New York: Bureau of Publications, Teachers College, Columbia University, 1951.

DeLong, Arthur R.: "Values and Dangers of the Sociogram," *Understanding the Child*, 1957, 26:24–28.

Dimeen, Mary Ann, and Ralph Garry: "Effect of Sociometric Seating on a Classroom Cleavage," *Elementary School Journal*, 1956, 56:358–362.

Elkins, Deborah: "Some Factors Related to the Choice-status of Ninety Eighth-grade Children in a School Society," *Genetic Psychology Monographs*, 1958, 58:207–272.

Gronlund, Norman E.: "The Relative Ability of Home-room Teachers and Special-subject Teachers to Judge the Social Acceptability of Pre-adolescent Pupils," *Journal of Educational Research*, 1955, 48:381–391.

Jennings, Helen H.: *Leadership and Isolation*, 2d ed. New York: Longmans, Green & Co., Inc., 1950.

————: "Sociometric Grouping in Relation to Child Development," in Caroline M. Tryon (ed.), *Fostering Mental Health in Our Schools*. Washington, D.C.: National Education Association, 1950.

————: *Sociometry in Group Relations*, 2d ed. Washington, D.C.: American Council on Education, 1959.

Justman, Joseph, and J. W. Wrightstone: "Comparison of Three Methods of Measuring Pupil Status in the Classroom," *Educational and Psychological Measurement*, 1951, 11:362–367.

Laughlin, Frances: *The Peer Status of Sixth and Seventh Grade Children.* New York: Bureau of Publications, Teachers College, Columbia University, 1954.

Lloyd, R. Grann, et al.: "The Relationship between Academic Achievement and the Social Structure of the Classroom," *Rural Sociology,* 1956, 21:179–180.

Northway, Mary L.: *A Primer of Sociometry.* Toronto, Canada: University of Toronto Press, 1952.

—— and Lindsay Weld: "Children and Their Contemporaries: What Has Been Learned from Sociometric Studies," *Bulletin of the Institute of Child Study,* 1956, 18:8–16.

Taba, Hilda: *With Perspective on Human Relations.* Washington, D.C.: American Council on Education, 1955.

—— et al.: *Diagnosing Human Relations Needs.* Washington, D.C.: American Council on Education, 1951.

—— et al.: *Intergroup Education in Public Schools.* Washington, D.C.: American Council on Education, 1952.

12

Cumulative Personnel Records

The significant information gathered on a student through the use of observation, tests, inventories, questionnaires, case conferences, interviews, and the like should be assembled in a comprehensive summary form in an individual cumulative record. A cumulative record that provides a longitudinal view of the student is basic to the educative function and to the counseling function in particular. In the opinion of one writer,[1] it is the "strategic organizational device in the whole guidance program."

The counselor is vitally concerned with the establishment and proper maintenance of an adequate cumulative record system. The importance of the cumulative record in guidance and counseling is so obvious that many administrators look upon its maintenance as well as its use as being appropriately the duty of the counselor. Unfortunately, many counselors accept the clerical work as being properly a counseling task. For example, of the 242 counselors who participated in the American School Counselor Association Study[2] of the counseling functions, one-half indicated that clerical work, such as checking records, filing, and preparing transcripts, should be among the counselor's duties.

DEVELOPMENT OF THE MODERN CUMULATIVE RECORD

The modern cumulative record can be traced to both the early school records and a record developed for military personnel during the First World War. At the time that this country became involved in the war, a group of psychologists, headed by Scott and Bingham, were engaged in industrial research at the Carnegie Institute of Technology. They were seeking improved ways of selecting, training, and supervising salesmen. They were asked to leave this work to help develop improved methods for selecting, appraising, assigning, and training military personnel. When

[1] Arthur E. Traxler, *Techniques of Guidance*, rev. ed., p. 192. New York: Harper & Row, Publishers, Incorporated, 1957.

[2] C. Gilbert Wrenn, *The Counselor in a Changing World*, p. 194. Washington, D.C.: American Personnel and Guidance Association, 1962.

the war ended, many Army personnel directors took similar positions in industry. Some techniques and instruments developed for the Army were then adapted for use in industrial personnel work and later in student personnel work. The Army Qualification Card became a basic business instrument and may be viewed as a forerunner of a basic guidance technique—the cumulative personnel record.

However, school records existed long before the First World War. Some writers, such as Traxler [3] and Reed,[4] have traced development of the modern cumulative record from these early school records. Reed noted that the agitation for improvement of educational records in general coincided with the beginning of the organized guidance movement but found no relationship between the two. Like Traxler, she traced interest in the development of the modern cumulative personnel record to the 1928 work of the American Council on Education Committee on Personnel Methods which led to the development by B. D. Wood and E. L. Clark of four cumulative record forms—two folders (one for secondary schools and one for colleges) and two cards (one for elementary schools and one for elementary or secondary schools). Later these forms were revised.

The ACE and ERB Models. The original ACE folder is complex. Test scores, for example, are plotted by month and year on a gridiron chart, and much information is to be recorded elsewhere on the folder in a very limited amount of space. As a result, when the card is filled in, it is difficult to read quickly and easily because the information is crowded into too little space. In spite of such shortcomings, however, the ACE record form was generally considered excellent. Undoubtedly it did much to stimulate improvement of cumulative records by providing a model of high standards.

In 1933 the Educational Records Bureau published a simplified adaptation of the ACE form for secondary schools. The ERB form is a six-year record card, whereas the original ACE form is a five-year record folder. The ERB card provides for both a tabular and a graphic record of test data.[5] Comparable school marks may also be plotted on the graphic chart for test data.

In addition to identifying information, test results, school marks, and attendance items, the card provides for entries on discipline, home influences and cooperation, mental and emotional factors, physical health and athletic development, extracurricular activities and interests, notable accomplishments and experiences, educational plans, and personality ratings. The traits to be rated are not named on the card but are to be

---

[3] Traxler, *op. cit.*, p. 192.
[4] Anna Y. Reed, *Guidance and Personnel Services in Education*, p. 208. Ithaca, N.Y.: Cornell University Press, 1944.
[5] See Fig. 9.

determined by the faculty or administrators of the schools using the card. There is a section labeled "remarks" in which may be recorded other significant information, such as items regarding vocational plans and interests, not provided for elsewhere on the form.

Some schools adopted the ACE or ERB form without change. Some others adopted a modified version because they found that their teachers were not able to maintain and use effectively a record as comprehensive and elaborate as the model. Some, for example, adopted the ERB card without the graphic section. Some limited the test record to a tabulation of test results, probably because workers inexperienced in the use of graphs sometimes find it difficult to read test profiles, such as those contained in the ERB card and the original ACE forms. The schools that adopted the models *with alterations*, that modified them in keeping with the record needs of the schools and the faculty's readiness to use cumulative records, were, no doubt, more successful in using the ACE or ERB model than the schools that adopted the standard form without change.

In the early 1940s the ACE forms were revised. The revisions show the influence of the ERB card and of other simplified adaptations of the original ACE folder. They also show the influence of the Eight Year Study of the Progressive Education Association. This is not surprising, because the forms were revised under the chairmanship of Eugene R. Smith, director of the PEA experiment in evaluating and recording student progress.

The revised ACE folder for junior and senior high schools is a six-year record which includes the PEA behavior description scale with a few minor changes.[6] The influence of the PEA study is further shown in a decreased emphasis upon subjects, credits, and school marks. For each year five unclassified columns are provided for "analyses of development" in subject fields named at the left in a column labeled "academic achievement." The record form contains the suggestion that the headings for these columns might include "work habits, ability to think logically, mastery of techniques, oral and written communications, and some estimate of achievement." The objectives indicated by these headings were among those stressed in the Eight Year Study.

Half the test record section of the revised folder is used for tabulating test results under the general headings of "academic aptitude," "reading," "achievement and other tests." The other half is for "interpretation of test record and its relation to school achievement." For schools that wish a graphic record of test scores (one distinguishing feature of the original record form), an alternate form is provided that contains a graph, instead of the section for interpretation of test results.

[6] Described in Chap. 3.

USES AND USEFULNESS

The cumulative record serves both administrative and guidance purposes. In guidance the basic purpose is to provide a developmental picture that helps the counselor to understand the student, to assist the student in understanding himself, and to interpret him to teachers, parents, and others concerned with contributing to the student's improved development and with helping him to attain maximum self-understanding and self-direction.

To have practical value for this basic purpose, the cumulative record needs to give a full view of the student as a member of various groups, school and nonschool. The good record provides both a clear cross-sectional and a clear longitudinal view. It shows current status in different areas of growth and reveals developmental trends by showing status in different areas at different times. It reports significant experiences, indicates readiness for new experiences, and offers clues regarding routes to new goals. It indicates strengths and weaknesses and may disclose causes of some difficulties. It improves prediction by giving clues regarding future behavior.

The good cumulative record indirectly contributes to student growth by contributing to improved teaching. It indicates the degree to which certain objectives are being achieved. It focuses attention on an individual's characteristics and on individual differences within a group. When the record covers the student's whole history, it aids articulation by contributing to continuity. It provides the basic information that permits the teacher to get acquainted quickly with the student. As one state committee [7] on cumulative records reports, the average student has 45 different teachers from the time he enters school until he finishes junior college. Students whose families move often have many more. Also, a well-kept cumulative record prevents the loss of information that might otherwise be lost with changes of staff within the school.

The cumulative record provides the basic information needed in placement (educational and vocational). Also, it is the basic source for information requested by other schools and colleges and by nonschool agencies. It is useful in research work. It shows the extent to which certain objectives are being achieved and provides some of the data essential in carrying out follow-up studies. It serves such purposes well, however, only when it yields in meaningful form the data needed.

[7] State Committee on Cumulative Records, with the assistance of staff members of the California State Department of Education, *Handbook on California Cumulative Records*, p. 1. Sacramento: California State Department of Education, 1956.

RECORD CONTENTS

The Recommendations. The cumulative record contains both subjective and objective data. In general, it is recommended that it contain information on such items as the following:

1. Personal, identifying data, including photograph
2. Home and family data
3. School history and scholastic achievement data
4. Test data
5. Health and physical development
6. Personal and social development
7. Special aptitudes, interests, activities, experiences, and achievements
8. Educational and vocational plans
9. References to other sources of information

All these items, including identification data, may serve guidance as well as administrative objectives. To do so, however, the recording must be continuous, and the entries must be dated. Even though the material may be arranged according to time sequence, the length of the intervening periods cannot be known unless entries are dated. Behavior that is normal or relatively unimportant at one stage of development may be quite unusual at another stage.

If all the information covered by the items included in all lists of recommendations were given in the cumulative record for a specified student, that record would indeed give a comprehensive and meaningful picture of the student, provided, of course, that the information were correct. It is, however, unlikely that a cumulative record form will ever —or should ever—be developed that provides for all the types of information recommended for inclusion. It is unwise for any faculty group to make the development of such a form its objective.

Included in any school's records should be only the items that will actually be used in working with the students or in their behalf. In short, record development should be on the basis of what information is used and can be collected, not on the basis of what can be collected in terms of recommendations by the authorities. Over two decades ago Ruch and Segel [8] warned against overelaborate records, pointing out that "there is a human tendency to strive for completeness with the result that the volume of information recorded becomes so great that the significance of many basic facts may be lost."

The Situation. Too often that which is held good in education theory is not applied in practice, even though the practitioners and the theorists

---

[8] G. M. Ruch and David Segel, *Minimum Essentials of the Individual Inventory in Guidance,* Vocational Division Bulletin 202, p. 11. Washington, D.C.: Government Printing Office, 1940.

agree regarding the need for the practice. Sometimes the obstacle to action is no more than inertia. Sometimes it is lack of certain requirements, such as time or staff, which may or may not be due to lack of funds. At other times it is lack of skill and understanding, which is often due to lack of training. Whatever the reason, survey studies of the situation with respect to use of cumulative records commonly show that, in spite of general agreement regarding the importance of good personnel records, too many schools are without adequate cumulative records. It is encouraging, however, that studies of samplings of schools, such as those reported by Looby [9] and Kaczkowski,[10] show that the situation is improving.

The studies show that some schools have adopted good record forms but they are poorly maintained and/or poorly used. Stewart,[11] for example, in studying the records of a random sample of 20 junior and senior high schools, found that many teachers do not use the records at all and, of those who do, most fail to use them effectively. Administrators, teachers, and counselors reported the principal deterrents to use to be (1) lack of time, (2) inaccessibility of records, (3) incompleteness of information, (4) inaccuracies in entries, (5) reluctance to trust validity of record data, (6) unclear perception of purpose, and (7) insufficient training in use of records. Figure 35 indicates the relative importance of these deterrents to the three groups by showing the percentage of each that named the items.

Another investigator [12] found in a study of cumulative records in Ohio high schools that, despite its relationship to scholastic success, the section on social data (extracurricular activities, peer acceptance, etc.) was the least used part of the record. He found that the diagnostic function of the section on course marks was "definitely incapacitated" by failure to include supplementary information to show whether the marks were earned in a homogeneous or heterogeneous class situation, and the like. Rarely is such information included in the records, but others may agree with Green that "a realistic interpretation of the scholastic record" may depend upon a rather detailed description of the environments in which the marks are earned. Green also found the summary sections of the records to reflect a "tendency to look at subject matter and not at the learner."

Furthermore, the fact that certain items occur in the cumulative

[9] Arthur J. Looby, "An Inventory of Permanent Cumulative Pupil Record Systems in Selected Missouri School Districts," unpublished doctor's dissertation. Columbia, Mo.: University of Missouri, 1956; Dissertation Abstracts, 1956, 16(11):2064–2065.

[10] Henry R. Kaczkowski, "The Current Status of Cumulative Records," Vocational Guidance Quarterly, 1959, 4:211–213.

[11] Lawrence H. Stewart with Arthur D. Workman, Relationship of Selected Factors to Use and Maintenance of Cumulative Records. Berkeley, Calif.: School of Education, University of California, 1962. (Dittoed.)

[12] Donald A. Green, Cumulative Records in Ohio High Schools, pp. 5–9. Athens, Ohio: College of Education, Ohio University, 1960.

record forms adopted by a school cannot always be considered evidence that the type of information covered by the items is collected and recorded. An examination of cumulative records pulled at random from a school's record files may show that an excellent form has been adopted—perhaps one cited in the literature as a good example of some desirable development in cumulative records—but may also show that for most students it is an "empty form," except for the sections on educational achievement and attendance. Space is provided on the form for recording other types of information, but the information is not given.

Deterrents	Administrators' report on what deters teachers %	Teachers' report on what deters themselves %	Counselors' report on what deters themselves %
Lack of time	80.0	71.7	75.9
Inaccessibility of records	25.0	30.9	19.8
Incompleteness of information	50.0	37.4	59.4
Complexity of information	35.0	23.3	18.1
Inaccuracies in entries	10.0	15.2	25.3
Reluctance to trust validity	20.0	33.7	42.9
Unclear perception of purpose	45.0	20.3	11.0
Insufficient training in use	80.0	29.0	15.4
Lack of interest	(5.0)	15.4	(4.4)

FIGURE 35 *Principal deterrents to use of cumulative records.* (L. H. Stewart with A. D. Workman, *Relationship of Selected Factors to Use and Maintenance of Cumulative Records*, p. 18a. Berkeley, Calif.: School of Education, University of California, 1962. Reproduced by permission of the authors.)

This type of situation—*a good record form poorly maintained*—is found in schools where not only the record forms but also the guidance practitioners are among the best. Sometimes the practitioners, like some discouraged students, do not attempt to defend or to explain the situation. Some may simply say, "That's just the way it is," and refuse to say more. Others may say, "We do all we can and leave the rest undone. We can do more with the records if we leave some other things undone—like seeing students. We are not giving students enough time now, so it seems wrong to take time from students in order to give more time to paper work. We do not mean that we think the paper work is not important. We know it is, but we have to neglect something; so we neglect the records."

Sometimes the record examined as an example of a school's cumulative records is a folder, instead of a card. Often the folder is full of papers that contain a great deal of significant data about the student named on the record, but the material is not in usable form. To get information on a particular item, the examiner must go through many sheets and cards and check much unrelated material. Even when he does find the information, he is not sure that he has all the information or even the most important facts contained in the folder on the item in question. Once more an overburdened practitioner, fully aware of the importance of well-kept records, may not attempt defense of the situation.

Improvement through Clerical Aid and Automation. By providing clerical assistance and/or adopting modern methods of data processing, some schools are removing the obstacle to good records imposed by the great amount of paper work involved in record keeping. Some schools are increasing clerical help through the use of funds received under the National Defense Education Act. In 1960–1961, for example, $314,704 in NDEA funds was spent in California for the salaries of guidance clerks. This sum paid for the equivalent of 103 full-time clerical positions.[13] Once a school enjoys the advantages of adequate clerical help, no doubt it will try to find a way to continue having them when NDEA funds are no longer available.

Automatic and integrated data processing not only makes it possible for an increased amount of information to be communicated to counselors and teachers but also makes it possible for the data to reach them in time for effective use in working with students. Most of the essential information on students can be punched into cards. Field studies of data processing show that application is being made in the following areas:[14] testing, grade reporting, attendance accounting, preregistration information, programming, scheduling, postregistration changes, cumulative records, research, and statistics.

Efficient data processing in all such areas is important to counselors. Dropout statistics, for example, are an important by-product of application to attendance accounting. When a student withdraws from school, his attendance card can be coded with one or more of a large number of possible codes that show reason for withdrawal. Also, summary reports can be regularly produced by the machine. And mechanized duplication methods make it possible for up-to-date copies of cumulative records to be made available promptly to all who need them.

In most schools the cumulative record data are more quickly available to counselors than to teachers. Teachers have to make many im-

---

[13] "Highlights of Title V in California Districts, 1960–61," *California Guidance Newsletter,* 1961, 16(2):4.

[14] One example: Alvin Grossman, *A Report of a Study: Processing Pupil Personnel Data.* Sacramento: State Department of Education, 1962.

portant decisions without consulting records at the time that the data are needed. The environmental conditions are such that the sources of information have to be checked later. Since the situation has to be handled without delay, the check may not be made at all. In the future the teacher may be able to obtain information on a student at the time that it is needed through an automated system that involves use of a computer, information display, and console, or through use of some more modest system of mechanical or electromechanical display devices. In the development of such display systems the emphasis, according to Cogswell,[15] "will be focused on what kinds of information the counselors can make readily available to teachers for rapid information retrieval in the classroom, in what format should the information be displayed, and how can the information be updated effectively. The dependent variables will relate to how often the teachers use the information, the effect of the information on teaching behavior, and ultimately, the effect on student achievement."

Integrated data processing systems are being established on statewide, as well as district-wide, bases. In 1960 California used NDEA funds to initiate a statewide pilot study which has demonstrated that improved communication of student personnel data contributes to improved utilization of the data and thereby helps to improve counseling. School boards look favorably upon the programs because the results include economy, as well as an increased variety of data and a shortened interval between time of obtaining and time of reporting data. Also, professional-level employees need not be used for such nonprofessional duties as the manual posting, alphabetizing, and sorting of cards or slips.

Some counselors fear that the adoption of data processing systems may mean that the needs of students will at times be sacrificed to efficiency. This need not happen and will not occur if, as recommended by one state advisory committee,[16] the processing of student personnel records has comparable priority with the processing of any other data. "If the processing system is to provide an efficient service, the time of year, the speed of processing, and the form of the reports provided must meet the needs of the pupil personnel functions rather than being made available [only] when other business or administrative data are being processed." This committee also recommends that advisory planning committees include supervisors of student personnel services who can represent the professional needs and requirements for student personnel records and information.

Instead of subordinating the student to the machine, the data

[15] John F. Cogswell, The Systems Approach as a Heuristic Method in Educational Development: An Application to the Counseling Function, p. 6. Santa Monica, Calif.: System Development Corporation, March 5, 1962. (Mimeographed.)

[16] California State Advisory Committee on Integrated Data Processing, "The Feasibility of Establishing an Integrated Data Processing System for Pupil Personnel Records," Sacramento: California State Department of Education, April 11, 1962. (Mimeographed.)

processing system can increase the amount of counseling help he will receive. The guidance aspects of some functions may become as important as the administrative aspects. When mechanized, for example, preregistration, programming, scheduling, and postregistration may become more rather than less student-centered. Too often under traditional conditions, requests for changes in programs or schedules are refused, even though desirable, simply because of the clerical work involved in making the changes. When changes are made mechanically rather than manually, they can be made quickly and easily. Moreover, counselors have more time for conferences with students regarding requested and recommended changes. There can be an increase in counseling as well as in administrative efficiency.

TWO TRENDS AND SOME EXAMPLES

Toward Decreased Diversity. It is generally agreed that records are more likely to be properly kept and used when developed through cooperative planning and experimentation by the faculties concerned than when imposed by higher authorities. It is also agreed, however, that too much variation in the records of different schools and of different school systems may create obstacles to efficient use and exchange of records.

Much present diversity in school records within the same school systems is due to the fact that too often the various committees responsible for recommending or developing record forms work in isolation without trying to relate their work to that done by other committees within the same school system. To maintain the proper balance between similarity and diversity in records, workers at one level or in one school need to study and plan with workers at other levels and in other schools. Without such cooperation little coordination of efforts can be attained.

The adoption of system-wide and district-wide data processing programs will probably force the adoption of standardized items if not standardized record forms. One U.S. Office of Education specialist in educational records states that items which are combined from a number of sources "should be stated in standard terms and should be codable for automatic data processing." [17] Wide use of standardized, codable items would, in his opinion, result in these advantages:

> Greater comparability of information about pupils within various communities and States.
>
> Greater consistency in the kinds of information accompanying pupils who transfer from one school or school system to another.
>
> More accuracy in the summaries of information compiled by local, state, and national offices.

[17] John F. Putman, "Toward Improved Information about Pupils," *School Life,* 1962, 44(4):24.

A sounder basis for evaluating administrative, organizational, and teaching practices.

A greater quantity of significant information to guide local and state authorities in determining policy.

Easier and more reliable reporting to the public on the condition and progress of education.

More favorable conditions for research and use of research data.

The U.S. Office of Education has provided leadership in a cooperative project designed to help bring about agreement on terminology. In this project representatives of the American Personnel and Guidance Association and of nine other national organizations are developing a handbook of terms and definitions.

Another strong influence working for decreased diversity in record forms and more nearly uniform policies with respect to contents, transfer of records, and the like is the development of forms by state committees which are usually made available on an optional basis. When school people from different parts of the state participate in the development of record forms and arrangements are made for special study of the recommended forms at the local level, an increase in the number of schools that use cumulative records usually follows. The record forms adopted by the new users and the revisions of forms already in use are often adaptations of the form developed and recommended by the state committee.

California offers a good example of a state group's influence upon the records adopted by schools in various parts of the state. The cumulative record folder used in the Los Angeles City Schools, for example, is the state form with only minor modifications. The fact that California has a law that requires the maintenance of a cumulative record for each student "similar to that provided for by the form known as the California Cumulative Record" has no doubt done much to stimulate adoption of the state form.

The California Cumulative Record—Junior-Senior-Four Year High School Form [18] contains spaces inside a folder for identifying data, social security number, photograph, dates of entering and leaving, schools to which transferred, school marks, a check list of certain graduation requirements, and graduation date. On the front outer side are recorded test data, information regarding transmittal of the cumulative record or transcript of record data, "other follow-up," and "other notes." On the back outer side there are spaces for family and home information and "significant information" in terms of family and home relationships, attendance, health, maturation characteristics, accomplishments and honors,

[18] Copies of the California record forms can be purchased from A. Carlisle and Company, San Francisco.

interests and activities, educational and vocational plans, and referral to school services and/or community agencies.

There is a slightly smaller folder which can be inserted in the elementary or secondary school folder. It is used for recording the health data collected on the student from kindergarten through grade 14. It has spaces for data on immunization, screening tests, medical examinations, follow-up, health history, observations, and recommendations. The back outer side contains graphic charts on which growth can be plotted in terms of age, weight, and height. Separate charts are provided for boys and girls, on each of which printed lines show the medians and the upper and lower limits of the normal ranges for height and weight at different ages.

Toward Expanded Records. More high schools seem to use record folders than record cards. The printed folder has two advantages over the printed card: (1) it provides more space (four sides, instead of two), and (2) it can be used as a file folder for cards and sheets that contain additional material or material that cannot be easily summarized and recorded on the card or the printed folder. The printed folder that is used both as a file folder and a record form has, however, a serious disadvantage: Having to remove and to replace the folder contents, even for incidental use of information recorded on the inside of a printed folder, is at times very inconvenient. Also, it is difficult to read information recorded on the outside of a printed folder that is made unwieldy by many enclosures.

Because of the disadvantages encountered in using either a printed record folder or a card alone, some schools adopt the practice of using standard blank folders in which cumulative record cards can be filed along with other cards and sheets containing supplementary information. The sheet or card that contains the information wanted at a particular time may then be drawn from the folder and replaced without its being necessary to remove all material from the folder. Too often, however, so much material is placed in the folder, and the material is filed in such an unorganized fashion, that it is no more easy to obtain from this type of record the information needed than it is to get it from a printed folder.

Some schools that have adopted the combination of cumulative record and blank folder try to expedite use of the records by keeping the cards and folders in separate file cabinets. The cumulative record card, which generally contains the items of information used most often or used by the greatest number of staff members, is kept in one file. The folder, which contains supplementary information, is filed in another cabinet nearby so that record users may move from one file to the other without much inconvenience.

Some schools use record envelopes in which cards and sheets may be filed. The forms filed in the record envelope used in one Oklahoma school system, for example, provide a cumulative record from the kindergarten through the twelfth grade. Sometimes the contents are listed on the front of the envelope. Listed, for instance, on the record packet of a California junior high school are attendance card, cumulative record card, health card, report cards, stop clearance report, test records, transcripts, and reports by the vice-principal.

The practice of using separate jackets for different types of records, such as academic progress and health, and of filing the different records in different locations is definitely not recommended. Schools are attempting to consolidate records so that teachers and counselors do not have to lose time seeking the particular record needed at a particular time.

To provide more material than can be reported through use of a cumulative record card, folder, or envelope and to provide organized material that is systematically collected, some schools have adopted record booklets contained in binders that make easy the removal and addition of pages. Ordinarily the record booklet is a collection of record sheets arranged in some special order and fastened together in a standard file folder. This type of cumulative record seems to be more frequently used in elementary schools than in secondary schools or colleges.

Schools and colleges might do well to consider as possible models the cumulative service records maintained on the enlisted personnel in the Armed Forces. The record forms of the several branches of the military service are similar. Each is made up of 20 or more indexed, numbered standard pages stapled into heavy folders. The record can be easily expanded through the addition of other pages. The sheets contain printed items and provide ample space for recording the information.

While some military personnel make a life career of the service, the service period of the average enlisted man or woman is much shorter than the school career of the average student. Yet the cumulative records kept on students are in general sketchy and unsystematic in comparison with the ones maintained on the military personnel. Likewise, many hospitals, prisons, and other institutions maintain on their residents or charges records that are more comprehensive and better kept than those kept on students in the average school.

The use of record sheets assembled according to some plan and fastened in a binder or folder is not unusual with social workers, lawyers, physicians, clinical workers, and others trained to keep organized, comprehensive records on their clients. Counselors need similar records. They need records in which the material is systematically organized and in the same order for all students. The counselor needs to know, for example, that, if he turns to a particular section of a student's record he will find assembled there in chronological order and properly classified all test data on the student.

Similarly the counselor should be able to read information on the student's present or recent participation in nonclass school activities in relation to information on such participation in previous years. He should not have to go searching through the record for the information on earlier participation. Data on elementary school participation should precede data on junior high school participation, which should precede data on senior high participation.

The material should be organized in the same way in all records. A table of contents should be provided and the pages numbered. When the material on a particular subject or item requires more space than is provided, the record can be expanded through the insertion of additional pages at that point. The inserts are numbered consecutively with the page they follow as 23a, 23b, 23c, etc.

The story presented in a comprehensive record that is systematically organized has a higher degree of coherence and continuity than the one that must be pieced together by sorting loose sheets filed in an envelope or folder. Because it can be used more efficiently, this type of record is likely to be also used more often and more effectively than the type from which the user cannot quickly or easily extract the information needed and which yields little information because it provides little space for data recording.

DEVELOPMENT AND REVISION OF RECORD FORMS

The development of policy with regard to a school's cumulative records (objectives, form, maintenance, use, revision, etc.) should be as far as possible a cooperative project that involves administrators, counselors, teachers, and even guidance clerks. Lack of participation can lead to lack of understanding, and lack of understanding can lead to lack of use or ineffectual use.

The amount of participation permitted teachers seems determined largely by the size and administrative policy or organizational structure of the school. Stewart and Workman,[19] for example, found that teachers are more likely to be involved in policy development in "small schools where lines of communication are perhaps more open and direct and where staff relationships are not rigidly formal" than in schools where size and administrative policy foster a formal type of organization that lacks flexibility, restricts interaction, and does not permit equality of opportunity for participation. They also found that the teachers who reported participating in policy formation "expressed attitudes toward the records and uses of the records that could be considered more conducive to effec tive use of cumulative records than did those teachers who reported that they had not participated." Furthermore, this held true even in schools whose record policy was difficult to identify or seemed nonexistent. Teach-

---

[19] Stewart and Workman, *op. cit.*, pp. 15–16, 76.

ers' feeling that they have a chance to share in policy formation seems clearly to affect their attitudes toward records and their uses.

Ideally the record forms for a particular school should be developed by the faculty through group study and experimentation that are preceded by study or reexamination of the school's objectives and by formulation of a statement on general philosophy or policy regarding use of cumulative records. There is, however, a strong possibility that in the not very distant future few schools will have records that differ markedly from those of other schools within the same system. The adoption of automatic data processing programs on a district-wide or statewide basis will probably force adoption of uniform records, developed perhaps by groups representative of the schools involved.

If the trend is toward both comprehensive and uniform records, less attention will be given to Traxler's [20] recommendation that the records be sufficiently simple for the essential facts to be "grasped through a few moments of study by busy teachers and counselors who are not highly trained in interpreting records." The teachers, as well as the counselors, of the future will need to be equipped through professional education in the interpretation and the use of records. Inservice education will have to be provided for those whose preservice education is not adequate in this area. And the reading of records may no longer be viewed as something to be done on the run but may be held an important function for which sufficient time must be provided.

In the meantime, it is ordinarily desirable that a faculty start with simple forms that all members can use so that they may progress easily to use of more comprehensive and complex records. The faculty may want to study forms used in other schools. Copies of the ACE and ERB models may be obtained from the publishers. With some other forms they are reproduced in Traxler's [21] book. Sets of records may be borrowed from some state departments of education, and a sample set may be rented from the Educational Records Bureau.

In general, it is not desirable to try to secure through direct request copies of the record forms used in specific schools. The forms of certain schools have been so well publicized that the administrators of these schools receive a burdensome number of requests for copies. Some find that they cannot supply the copies requested. However, requests for information and assistance made to the state departments of education or to the U.S. Office of Education usually bring a prompt reply, and the help requested is given if possible.

Usable items that will actually be used are the ones to be included in the record forms adopted. The forms should be developed on the basis of information that will actually be used and can be collected rather than on the basis of information that should be collected according to some

[20] Traxler, *op. cit.*, p. 185.
[21] *Ibid.*, chap. 13.

recommendations. Each proposed entry should be appraised in terms of its possible contribution to the understanding of the interests, abilities, capacities, aptitudes, limitations, and needs of students.

There is need for research to determine the usefulness of particular types of information. Some items regularly contained in cumulative records may be less useful than it is generally believed. Other seldom-included items may prove very useful. For example, the father's occupation is usually recorded. This item may be more useful as a clue to the family's socioeconomic status than to the student's vocational interest. There is some evidence that with regard to the latter point the maternal grandparents' occupation may be more meaningful.[22] And a study by Ferreira and Oakes [23] shows very low or no relationship between father's occupation and various other variables, particularly in the areas of achievement and ability.

The research and statistics division of the Hawaii Department of Education is seeking a guide to usage of records through study of their actual use. Record users are asked to make an entry on a log provided for this purpose each time they consult a cumulative record. The form is placed in front of other materials in each record. See Figure 36. It is hoped that the log entries will show who uses the records, why, the kinds of information sought, and the like.

Adequate provision needs to be made for inservice education in the use of cumulative records. All that has been said in the preceding chapters regarding helping teachers to gain skill in using and interpreting test data, reporting and reading observation data, and the like, applies here.

Lectures and group discussions are probably the most frequently used inservice procedures. The record sections may be explained as teachers examine dittoed filled-in copies or the copy projected onto a screen. Questions are asked. The answers and lecture are discussed.

Sometimes practice exercises are added to focus discussion on the use of record data. In one school, for example, the group members were given copies of the records of four students. Discussion was then directed toward answering such questions as the following: Do the records show any of the students to need remedial instruction in a basic skill? What do the records indicate regarding the probability of the students' attaining their educational and vocational goals? Do the records indicate that any students need special assistance? If so, what clues does the record give regarding the nature of the problem and the type of help needed? What additional data need to be obtained? Does the record on one student yield clues regarding the reason for the recent drop in his marks?

[22] See Erik Erikson, *Childhood and Society,* chap. 8. New York: W. W. Norton & Company, Inc., 1950; Lawrence H. Stewart, "Mother-Son Identification and Vocational Interest," *Genetic Psychology Monographs,* 1959, 60(3):31–63.

[23] Joseph R. Ferreira and Phillip W. Oakes, "Automatic Data Processing: An Aid in Studying Pupil Characteristics," *California Journal of Educational Research,* 1960, 11(1):3–6.

In another school the critical-incident technique was used effectively. The project was developed in response to a request for help from two members of a committee on record revision. For several weeks teachers and counselors kept notes on their use of the cumulative records—why they were consulted and how profitable had been the consultation. At the end of that time they were asked to give the committee members concise written reports on (a) the incident in which record consulting had proved most helpful and (b) the incident in which it had proved least helpful. Group discussion of selected incidents and of the summary report on the types of information sought, found, not found, reported most useful, and reported least useful led to agreement on some recommendations for the deletion and the addition of items in the record forms.

Log

Date of reference	Check (✓)			Reason for Reference	Signature and position
	Parent conf.	Pupil conf.	Teacher conf.	Specify accession/deletion or comment	
SAMPLE: 9–12–62				Changed parent phone no.	

FIGURE 36 *Source data form for a cumulative records research study by Hawaii Department of Education, Research & Statistics.* (Reproduced by permission of the Department of Public Instruction, State of Hawaii.)

Inservice study of cumulative records can reveal that potential dropouts may be identified by the ninth grade or earlier. Inservice education that includes reports on findings from studies, such as the one reported by Lee,[24] and experimental projects like the New York Holding Power Project [25] helps to show that reliable predictions cannot be made on an individual basis. More important than use of the records for prediction is their use for identifying vulnerable students and ascertaining the type of help needed by these students.

[24] Margaret B. Lee, "Factors Associated with School Retention in a Group of Predicted Drop-outs," unpublished doctor's dissertation. Berkeley, Calif.: University of California, 1958.

[25] See Chap. 9.

Questions regarding certain practical details need to be considered before the first supply of record forms is prepared. What kind of paper or card stock should be used? How should columns and spaces be arranged? What color should the paper be? There will be general agreement on the answers to some such questions, but there will be different opinions on others. Most staff members will, no doubt, agree that all spacing should be such that eyestrain will be minimized and record reading made easy. Probably no one will question the desirability of an arrangement that permits presentation of cumulative data in time sequence so that developmental trends may be traced or will question the desirability of providing sufficient space for summary statements of the less objective data.

All will undoubtedly agree that paper stock should be flexible, durable, and of such quality as to take ink well; but perhaps not all will agree regarding the color. Some will agree that buff is better than white but will consider yellow better than buff. Some will want all forms to be of the same color whereas some others will want the different forms to be of different colors. In some cases the best answers can be easily determined through experimental use of mimeographed forms. In other cases the trial method cannot be used until after the records are adopted tentatively, and so tentative decisions must be reached through the discussion method.

The adoption of the cumulative record form agreed upon should be considered tentative. Rarely should more than a year's supply be ordered even though a larger order might bring some reduction in cost. Revisions should not be made hastily, but neither should changes needed for good reasons be delayed unnecessarily by the fact that a large supply of old forms must be used before new forms can be printed.

Revision, like the development of record forms, should be a cooperative undertaking. Revision should be based upon careful appraisal of the group's experiences with the records in use as well as upon further study of cumulative records in general. A revised form should not be adopted mainly because some staff members learned at summer school or at an institute that it is the latest thing in cumulative records. Only after the record forms adopted tentatively have been used sufficiently long for both their strong and weak points to be known should revision be considered, and only after careful study and extensive discussion should any proposed changes be made.

These principles and some of those given in the following sections apply, however, only where individual schools are permitted to develop their own record systems. As indicated above, automation may result in such schools being relatively few.

MAINTENANCE AND USE OF CUMULATIVE RECORDS

When a record form is agreed upon for tentative adoption, a bulletin of instructions should be prepared. This bulletin may be expanded into a manual or a handbook when more elaborate forms are adopted. Some handbooks contain statements regarding the importance of cumulative records, objectives served by them, policy, and cautions regarding their use, as well as instructions for filling out the forms.

Some definite general plan should be formulated for gathering, reporting, and recording the information to be contained in the cumulative records. While all faculty members should be responsible for reporting significant information that they obtain about students, certain individuals should be responsible for seeing that the minimum essentials of record data are gathered. To facilitate the reporting of certain types of information, forms other than the cumulative record forms may be developed. Supplementary report forms should be developed, however, ordinarily for the convenience of the reporters. Their use should probably be made optional.

Exasperated by too much red tape, some teachers may fail to report valuable information that they might report were they free to give it in their own way—orally or jotted down on paper found at hand at the time that they are free to make the report. It is very helpful to record clerks and to coordinators to have all reports turned in on a prescribed form; but, if the form requirement helps to lower the quality of some reports and to lessen the frequency of reporting by some teachers, the teachers should be instructed to report in their own way. Many, no doubt, will choose to use the forms adopted "for convenience in reporting" if the forms really do help to make reporting easy.

All teachers should share in the work of collecting and reporting information on students. Not all, however, should record information on cumulative record forms. Desirably only trained record clerks should make entries on these forms. Unless all the material in the record is recorded neatly and legibly, the reading of some records will be slow and difficult.

Cumulative records should reveal changes in specific items. In some schools it is the practice to type or to write in ink all items described as "permanent," such as parents' names, test results, school marks, and the like, and to record in pencil all items subject to change, such as home address and even vocational interest. In other schools all information recorded on a cumulative record form is typed or written in ink. Erasures are made in order to correct errors, not because of change in the information previously given. The second practice seems the desirable one.

The fact, for example, that a student may have several different home addresses during one year is important information that should have a permanent rather than a temporary place in his record. Changes in address made over a period of years may give some evidence regarding socioeconomic status of the family and may reveal change in status—improvement or decline. Information regarding changes in home address may also show that at certain times the student had to adjust to a change in neighborhood and, perhaps, in friendships. Changes in vocational interest are not unusual, but they are important and should be reported. Obviously, a cumulative record that shows the vocational interests expressed by a student throughout his school years is more useful to the counselor and to the student than a record that shows only the most recently expressed vocational interest.

Confidential material should not be put into cumulative records. Among the material that should not be contained in cumulative records is information of a confidential nature obtained during counseling or given by family member, doctor, nurse, or the like with the understanding that it be held confidential. Technical information that might be misinterpreted and information that might hurt a student were it to become common knowledge should not be contained in records available to all staff members. As a rule, for instance, the cumulative records are available to clerks and secretaries who may be trained to be discreet in the use of record information; but not all may be trained to understand and appreciate the significance of some types of information. Their misconceptions and prejudices based on their misunderstanding of record material can prove contagious and do harm to some students. Hence, some material should not be in the records available to them.

If some information is too technical or confidential to be included in the cumulative record but is available to teachers upon request, the folder should contain a statement that significant information on a certain point may be obtained from a specified person. This procedure helps to ensure the information's being given in a professional setting and only to professionally responsible persons, in keeping with their ability to use the information.

Teachers are professionally responsible persons. Many rightfully resent a counselor's autocratically withholding information on a student that is important to a teacher's understanding the student and working effectively with him. Counselors have a leadership responsibility for helping to prevent misuse of record data. They also have a leadership responsibility for helping teachers to gain skill in their use. They best fulfill this responsibility when they demonstrate faith in teachers' good intentions and show respect for their intelligence by sharing professional knowledge with them in a peer relationship, instead of telling or explaining in a teacher-pupil relationship. Some of the teachers interviewed by Stewart [26] and his coworkers reported feeling a lack of success in the use of cumulative records. They also felt that they were not trusted with information which the counselors retained. No doubt, such feelings explained why a large per cent of them said that they never used the records.

Withholding information is a poor way to combat teachers' using record data as a basis for gossip, rationalization, and the like. Using case conferences, consultation, and other inservice education procedures to

[26] Stewart and Workman, *op. cit.*, pp. 64–68.

help teachers acquire an understanding of the ethics involved and to gain skill in interpreting and utilizing record data serves as a preventive as well as a protective measure.

Cumulative records should be used by all faculty members, so they should be placed where all may use them easily. Counselors may want to have for their special use copies of the records on their counselees. In schools that have secretaries and/or modern duplicating facilities, the preparation of duplicate sets of records is not difficult. In other schools, however, duplicate sets are not usually possible because of the amount of extra work involved.

Efficient record keeping and effective use of records are aided by provision for record offices that, ideally, are centrally located, adequately staffed, well lighted, and sufficiently well provided with the equipment needed (file cabinets, tables, chairs, and the like), and that have inner offices or cubicles in which staff members may study records and use them in conferences with other persons.

The use of responsible record clerks (not students) and the adoption of regulations regarding use of the records and of the record office are aids to professional use of records and are means for preventing misuse. Providing such aids and trusting to the good judgment of other staff members will bring better results in the way of cooperative provision of record service than will displaying a dog-in-the-manger attitude and expressing a lack of confidence in the competence and professional integrity of coworkers.

To interpret the contents of a student's cumulative record to his parent or guardian is generally desirable. To let the parent inspect the record is rarely desirable. Recently there has been considerable debate regarding parents' rights to examine school records on their children. In California, for example, a strong effort was made to get a law passed that would require the schools to show the records to parents upon their request. The law enacted, however, does not require the schools to show the records but permits them to do so by stating that "during consultation between a certificated employee of a school district and a parent of a pupil, the cumulative record of that pupil may be made available to his parent for inspection." [27]

The position of the American Personnel and Guidance Association on this point is made clear in a formal statement on the use of student records, which contains, among others, the following items: [28]

> These rights and responsibilities [of parents to learn and know about their children's status in educational institutions] should be expressed in a manner which will be of the greatest value for the individual student being considered. Interpretation of a student's school record to his parents

[27] *California Administrative Code*, art. 9.1, sec. 80.3 of title 5.

[28] *The Use of Student Records*, pp. 1–2. Washington, D.C.: American Personnel and Guidance Association, June 1, 1961. (Mimeographed.) Italics in the original.

is a function that requires qualified professional personnel. Such records often contain some information which is confidential or technical in nature.

The best interests of the student are served when school records bearing upon parental questions concerning a student are *interpreted* by appropriate professional personnel, who are qualified: (a) to judge the validity of the information; (b) to determine how it may best be interpreted; and (c) to distinguish between that which should be regarded as confidential and that which may be disclosed to parents or other authorized school personnel.

Such interpretation may or may not include the actual display of record information. This decision is and must be part of the professional responsibility of appropriate school personnel and *not,* ultimately, the responsibility of the parent. The reasons for this are several: (a) the three statements in the preceding paragraph; and (b) the removal of any doubt among school personnel regarding the person with whom rests the ultimate decision as to any visual inspection of records. Failure to do so will almost certainly result in the reduction of information entered in school records. Any such reduction will work a very real disservice to the student.

It is, therefore, the position of the American Personnel and Guidance Association that the best interest of the student is served when school record information is interpreted by appropriate professional personnel. Any decision as to the display of such information for visual inspection by the parent or guardian must rest with the professional judgment of the appropriate school personnel.

TRANSFER OF CUMULATIVE RECORDS

Cumulative records should cover the entire span of the students' school careers. To be continuous, the records need to travel with the students from level to level and from school to school. Desirably a student's record should precede him to a new school. Otherwise, it should follow him as soon as possible. A number of states have laws which require that when a student transfers to another school district within the state his cumulative record, or a copy, *with entries brought up to date* be forwarded promptly to the new school district. The prompt transfer of records is particularly important in states like California, Florida, Hawaii, and Texas, in which many families are highly mobile. Before completing their education the children of such families may attend numerous schools. For this reason, one-half of the back side of the Hawaii cumulative record folder is devoted to "school withdrawals and transfers." Transcripts are photographed directly from the record, which is designed for use in kindergarten through grade 12.

When records are transferred to another school, the sending school should keep a record that shows to whom the records were sent and when. A summary of the important material in the records, instead of the records themselves, should be sent to the state employment service, prospective employers, or others who request and need such data for helping the former student or for working successfully with him.

THE CUMULATIVE RECORD AS A COUNSELING TOOL

A counselor should study the records on his counselees. Doing so not only makes it unnecessary for him to use interview time for obtaining from the student information contained in the records but also helps him to establish a good working relationship with the student. Many a student loses confidence in his counselor largely because each time he has a conference with the counselor, he must repeat information previously given during conferences, in questionnaires, or in some other way.

A counselor may think that, in asking a student certain questions, he is displaying a personal interest in him. The student, however, may consider the questions only evidence of lack of any real interest. The counselor who does not ask the student what he did last summer, which college he is planning to enter, or whether he has a weekend job this year but, instead, refers to the student's summer experiences, makes some remark about the college that the student wants to attend, or comments about the weekend job that the student now has shows interest by remembering just what the student has told him before or has reported about himself on the registration card or in some other way. The student then feels that he is important and that the counselor does not forget all about him as soon as he leaves the office.

The cumulative record helps the counselor to gain understanding of the student and his life situation and to perceive how that situation looks from the student's point of view. The record provides not only factual information regarding the student's abilities, interests, and achievements but also clues regarding his hopes and ambitions, his developmental needs, his difficulties, and the nature and some causes of those difficulties. By helping the counselor to understand the student and his needs, the record helps him to be accepting and responsive during the interview.

When not properly used as an adjunct to counseling, any technique can interfere with the counseling process. Misinterpreting record data and making unwarranted assumptions on their basis are among the pitfalls into which beginning counselors often stumble. Equally hazardous are the categorizing of students and the making of premature diagnoses. Record data regarding a student's aptitude test scores, family membership, home address, socioeconomic status, race, and the like should not, for example, lead a counselor to conclude that the student is a slow learner, a spoiled child of the idle rich, an unambitious lower-class child, a hardworking anxious-to-please minority group member, or the like.

However, in reading cumulative records, as in observing and

listening to students, a counselor does make inferences or tentative conclusions and constructs hypotheses based on the data. He considers these inferences and hypotheses tentative and is ready to revise them at any time. He continuously tests them with data independent of those on which they were founded.

The inferences based on the record data may or may not prove sound. Two examples: A senior girl seeks a conference with her counselor, saying she wants help with a problem. Before the interview the counselor reads the girl's record and, among other things, learns that the girl consistently earns high marks, that the test data indicate only average ability, that she wants to be a doctor, that her parents approve this goal, that an aunt, who is a doctor, wants to finance her medical education, and that the girl has twice taken the College Board Scholastic Aptitude Test and twice made low scores. The counselor hypothesizes that the girl is disturbed by the possibility of not being admitted to medical school.

Early in the interview the girl's remarks confirm the hypothesis. The counselor is able to help her express feelings of disappointment and hurt pride engendered by the SAT scores and her having already been rejected by two colleges on the basis of the scores. The counselor encourages the girl to look at other college possibilities. He mentions junior colleges and the possibility of shifting to a degree program at the end of the junior college career. He tries to help her consider other less demanding areas of the medical field by referring to degree programs in such areas as nursing, nursing education, physical therapy, and the like. The girl shows interest by asking for certain specific information. She says, however, that she wants to continue trying to get into a medical school but will talk with her aunt about some of the other possibilities. The counselor invites her to come back if she ever wants to discuss the matter further with him.

Examination of the girl's record before the interview enabled the counselor to equip himself with important facts and to formulate a tentative hypothesis which in this case proved valid. He would have discarded or modified the hypothesis, however, had the girl's talk not supported or confirmed it. Study of the record helped him to get ready for the interview in that it helped him to anticipate the girl's possible need for certain types of information and to be ready to answer her questions and to tell of other sources of information.

This same counselor is scheduled to see a junior girl the same day that he confers with the senior. Again he has a chance to read the student's record before interview time. The record tells him that the girl has high scholastic ability, is earning very good marks, wants to go to college but expects little financial help from her parents, who are divorced; that she and a younger brother live with the mother, who works as a bookkeeper; that she is very active in student life and currently is president of the girls' athletic association and vice-president of the junior class. The record also shows that the mother wants the girl to go to college and has talked with the dean of girls about her daughter's chances of obtaining a scholarship. The counselor hypothesizes that the "important matter" which the girl wants to talk about is a college scholarship.

During the interview, however, the girl refers only once to college. The "important matter" concerns her relations with her father. She and the brother are expected to spend every other school holiday period and one summer month with the father. Both dislike visiting the father. They feel, the girl says, that they can do nothing to please him and his "second wife"; and they resent his always "chopping" them down. The girl wants the counselor to help her find a summer job. "If I have a job and tell Dad I am trying to earn money for college, he won't ask me to give up my job to visit him. I think he won't. And he may not make Jack go without me. Jack throws the morning paper now and perhaps can get a job this summer bagging at one of the markets."

This student's record gave no clue regarding the problem that she wanted to discuss. Had the counselor maintained his assumption that she was worried about college and directed the conversation to this subject, the girl might never have brought up the sensitive and disturbing problem regarding her relationship with the father.

In reading cumulative records, a counselor looks for patterns and contradictions. He notes, for instance, that Jerry's record shows considerable participation in student activities up to last spring but for the past two semesters no participation in nonclass groups. He modifies his thinking on this observation, however, when on reading further he learns that Jerry has joined one of the area mountaineers' clubs. He knows that club activities include lectures, "blackboard sessions," and examinations, as well as weekend mountain climbing.

John's record shows that usually he is a homeroom officer or committee chairman. It also shows that sociometric data obtained in class situations usually show him little chosen or unchosen. The conflicting evidence causes the counselor to raise a number of questions: In putting John into office, are the other students honoring him or pushing him into jobs not wanted by others? Do the students choose their homeroom officers freely, or are "the eligibility requirements" such that officers are more teacher- than student-chosen? Is John well accepted in some situations but not in others? Do the sociometric data apply primarily to the latter?

Allen's record shows that his teachers think he shows little stick-to-itness, gives up too easily, and has a short interest span. It shows also that for two years he has been working in a neighborhood drugstore and his employer reports him highly reliable and responsible. Is Allen bored with school? Does he see little practical value in his studies? Is he giving so much time to the drugstore job that he is getting too little rest and recreation and so is restless and inattentive at school? Is it necessary for him to earn money? Is the need for money creating anxiety which makes the boy alert in the drugstore but apathetic in the classroom?

Do series of related items on a particular student's record indicate loss, gain, or little change over a period of time? Is the pattern one of marked change—positive or negative? Can clues regarding causes be found in other items, such as those on tests, home and family, health and physical development, social and emotional growth?

Does the record show contradictory evidence regarding achievement in particular areas? Does it show, for example, that the boy makes A's and B's in English some semesters and C's and D's other terms? Does he earn better grades with men teachers than with women? Are his English marks better in the fall semesters than in the spring, or vice versa? Does football seem to be a motivating or an interfering factor?

Studying relevant data from a number of sources; noting patterns, contradictions, and conflicts in the data; making inferences; differentiating inferences from observation; constructing and testing hypotheses through further observation and data gathering; conferring with others regarding possible analyses and diagnoses; and doing other such things are all a part of the counselor's functions. Hence, the cumulative record is a very useful adjunct to counseling when properly used.

STUDENT-KEPT CUMULATIVE RECORDS

Students are important sources of information for cumulative records, but they should not be used as sources of help in posting, handling, and filing the records. The official records should not be made freely available to them. Desirably, however, the data contained in a student's records are summarized and interpreted to him from time to time in keeping with his ability to understand and accept the information.

Some schools find that keeping unofficial records on themselves helps many students. They find that assembling and systematically recording significant data on himself may help a student to understand and accept himself, as well as help him to make realistic choices, plans, and decisions. Frequently this type of record is initiated in a group guidance situation, such as an orientation class or a core course. The order in which particular sections of the record are filled in may parallel the order in which certain subjects are taken up in the course. They commonly include such subjects as home and family, health, hobbies, study skills and study problems, educational and vocational plans, work experiences, and the like.

In its simplest form the record is a plan sheet on which the student gives identifying data; summarizes his educational history, work experiences, and educational and vocational plans; and lists according to semesters the courses that he has completed, is taking, and plans to take. In a study of the use of the plan sheet in one state, Malouf [29] found that it helps students to strengthen their planning, to become acquainted with

[29] Phelon Malouf, "The Plan Sheet: A Guidance Technique," *Personnel and Guidance Journal*, 1955, 33:451–455.

the school's resources, and "to gain added interest and motivation in their studies and activities, for as they look ahead they can see how present studies are related to future goals." He also found that many counselors consider the plan sheet a useful interview aid and registration guide.

In some schools the record is a plain folder in which the student may file such things as his autobiography, achievement and interest test profiles, list of subjects taken and marks earned, self-ratings, personal data sheet, and reports on hobbies, work experiences, travel, and the like. In some other schools the records are comprehensive booklets. The workbook type of record used in a number of California schools is an adaptation of earlier editions of the *Educational Guidance Record* developed for use in the senior high schools of the Los Angeles City Schools. The 1962 revision is a simplified, shorter edition. The explanation given on its title page includes the following: [30]

TO THE STUDENT:

The Educational Guidance Record is a workbook for you to use in making your educational and vocational plans. It will help you to know yourself; your achievements, interests, aptitudes, and personal characteristics. It will help you also to define your goals and plan the means of achieving them through education and the world of work.

The Record is intended to correlate with your studies in Tenth Grade Guidance. Following the completion of the guidance course, the booklet will be placed in your cumulative record in the counselor's office. You and the grade counselor will continue to use it during the eleventh and twelfth grades. When you leave school, the booklet can become your personal property.

The booklet has seven sections in which the student records information about his educational achievement in grades 8 through 12, personal characteristics, aptitudes, educational plans, vocational goals, and tentative decisions regarding post-high school plans. A similar instrument, *My Guidance Record,* has been developed for use in other secondary schools in Los Angeles County. It is based largely on the student-kept records developed for Hayward (California) High School,[31] Pasadena City Schools, and the Los Angeles City Schools.

SUMMARY

A cumulative personnel record is a comprehensive record that shows a student's progress and development in a number of areas over a period of time, desirably from the beginning of his school career until the time of

[30] *Educational Guidance Record for Senior High School Student Use.* Los Angeles: Los Angeles City School Districts, Evaluation and Research Section, 1962.
[31] The Hayward record form is described and reproduced in large part in Clifford P. Froehlich, *Guidance Services in Schools,* 2d ed., pp. 169–184. New York: McGraw-Hill Book Company, Inc., 1958.

graduation or withdrawal. A record that gives only information on courses taken, marks received, and standardized test scores is an academic record, not a cumulative personnel record.

The cumulative record varies in form from a single card to a relatively large collection of standard sheets assembled according to a plan, paginated, indexed, and fastened in a binder. The trend is toward more comprehensive and less diverse record forms.

Good cumulative records are essential in the instruction and guidance of students. A principal obstacle to the maintenance of good record systems is the tremendous amount of paper work required. Some schools are removing this obstacle by making increased and improved provision for guidance clerks and by adopting automatic data processing.

Integrated data processing is increasing the trend toward decreased diversity in record forms. Also, the increasing mobility of school populations makes it desirable that student personnel records be maintained with sufficient clarity and uniformity for records originating in one district to be meaningful and readily usable in other districts to which the students may transfer. There needs, however, to be sufficient diversity in forms and procedures for local needs and requirements to be met.

Cumulative records are confidential, professional records and so should be available to only professionally responsible staff members. Teachers who are without sufficient skill in the interpretation and utilization of record data and sufficient understanding of the ethics involved in their use should be given an opportunity to acquire such understanding and skill through inservice education. Cumulative records should not be available to students and parents, but their contents should be interpreted to them in keeping with their ability to understand and accept the information.

The cumulative record is a useful adjunct to counseling. It is misused when it leads to the categorizing of students and to premature diagnoses. The counselor makes inferences and formulates hypotheses on the basis of the record data, but he is cautious and flexible in doing so. He considers his hypotheses tentative and is alert to counterindicating, as well as supporting, evidence found in the records or elsewhere.

Student-kept records can help a student to gain understanding and acceptance of self, to make sound choices and realistic plans, and to improve his use of school resources. This type of record can also be used as a counseling tool, but it is not to be considered an adequate substitute for the official cumulative personnel record.

REFERENCES

Brewster, Royce E.: "The Cumulative Record," *School Life*, 1959, 42(1):16–17.
Cottle, William C., and N. M. Downie: *Procedures and Preparation for Counseling*, chap. 2. Englewood Cliffs, N.J.: Prentice-Hall, Inc., 1960.

Ferreira, Joseph R., and Phillip W. Oakes: "Automatic Data Processing: An Aid in Studying Pupil Characteristics," *California Journal of Educational Research,* 1960, 11(1):3–6.

Froehlich, Clifford P.: "Students Keep Their Cumulative Records," *The School Executive,* 1956, 76(2):54–56.

Green, Donald A.: *Cumulative Records in Ohio High Schools.* Athens, Ohio: College of Education, Ohio University, 1960.

Grossman, Alvin: *A Report of a Study: Processing Pupil Personnel Data.* Sacramento: California State Department of Education, 1962.

Hardee, Melvene D.: "Student Records and Reports: College and University," *Encyclopedia of Educational Research,* pp. 1433–1436. New York: The Macmillan Company, 1960.

Hoyt, Kenneth B.: "Study of the Effects of Teacher Knowledge of Pupil Characteristics on Pupil Achievement and Attitudes toward Classwork," *Journal of Educational Psychology,* 1955, 46:302–310.

Hurley, Neil: "Automation's Impact on Education," *Instruments and Automation,* 1956, 29:57–58.

Kaczkowski, Henry R.: "The Current Status of Cumulative Records," *Vocational Guidance Quarterly,* 1959, 4:211–213.

Looby, Arthur J.: "An Inventory of Permanent Cumulative Pupil Record Systems in Selected Missouri School Districts," unpublished doctor's dissertation. Columbia, Mo.: University of Missouri, 1956; *Dissertation Abstracts,* 1956, 16(11):2064–2065.

McLaughlin, Jack W., and John T. Shea: "California Teachers' Job Dissatisfactions," *California Journal of Educational Research,* 1960, 11:216–224.

Malouf, Phelon: "The Plan Sheet," *Personnel and Guidance Journal,* 1955, 33:451–455.

Martyn, Kenneth A.: "We Are Wasting the Counselor's Time," *California Journal of Secondary Education,* 1957, 32:439–441.

Stewart, Lawrence H.: "A Study of Critical Training Requirements for Teaching Success," *Journal of Educational Research,* 1956, 49:681–688.

Traxler, Arthur E.: *Techniques of Guidance,* rev. ed., chaps. 12–13. New York: Harper & Row, Publishers, Incorporated, 1957.

Tyler, Leona E.: *The Work of the Counselor,* 2d ed., chap. 5. New York: Appleton-Century-Crofts, Inc., 1961.

Williams, Frank E.: "The Importance of Records in the Guidance Program of the Small Secondary School," *The High School Journal,* 1957, 40:279–285.

Williams, H. M.: "Cumulative Record System Developed through Cooperative Group Work of Columbus Teachers and Administrators," *Nation's Schools,* 1952, 50(4):76–79.

13

The Case Study

The case study is the report on an intensive investigation of many important aspects of some unit—a person, a group, a community, an institution, or the like. We are concerned here only with the case study of the individual person. Two other terms, "case history" and "life history," are also used to describe this analytical and diagnostic tool.

Some writers, such as Strang [1] and Traxler,[2] make a distinction between the case history and the case study. They describe the case history as a synthesis of information made periodically, similar to but more detailed than that found in a good cumulative record. They describe the case study as an intensive analysis that includes interpretation and is focused upon the problems or adjustment difficulties of the subject. However, some other writers, such as Murray [3] and Thorne,[4] use the term "case history" to designate the "case study" as defined by Strang and Traxler, using it almost exclusively to describe the intensive analytical and diagnostic investigation in which interpretation has a large part and in which attention is focused upon factors contributing to the development of particular personality patterns and/or causing certain difficulties. In contrast, others, such as Shaffer and Shoben,[5] use the terms "case history" and "case study" interchangeably.

The term "life history" is most frequently used to describe the narrative account of a subject's life from birth to death. It relates a succession of behavior events and the subject's reactions to them. It furnishes a basis for analysis of the subject's typical behavior and prediction of future behavior, but the analysis and the forecast are not always made a part of the life history report. Some writers, such as Young,[6] use this third term syn-

---

[1] Ruth Strang, *Counseling Technics in College and Secondary School*, rev. ed., pp. 206–207. New York: Harper & Row, Publishers, Incorporated, 1949.

[2] Arthur E. Traxler, *Techniques of Guidance*, rev. ed., pp. 266–267. New York: Harper & Row, Publishers, Incorporated, 1957.

[3] H. A. Murray et al., *Explorations in Personality*. New York: Oxford University Press, 1938.

[4] F. C. Thorne, *Principles of Personality Counseling*, chap. 9. Brandon, Vt.: Journal of Clinical Psychology, 1950.

[5] L. F. Shaffer and E. J. Shoben, Jr., *The Psychology of Adjustment*, 2d ed., pp. 494–496. Boston: Houghton Mifflin Company, 1956.

[6] Kimball Young, *Personality and Problems of Adjustment*, 2d ed., chap. 11. New York: Appleton-Century-Crofts, Inc., 1952.

onymously with the other two. Some others, such as Dailey,[7] define it differently, yet use it interchangeably with "case history" and "case study." In general, the three terms describe the same technique—a comprehensive study of an individual.

By analyzing, synthesizing, and presenting in organized form data collected from different sources at different times, the counselor is able to develop a systematic full-length study of the subject, one that shows the continuum of his development and the interrelations of the many factors influencing his growth. A good case study shows the individual as a functioning totality. Not all case studies, however, provide the picture in the same way. Some open with a cross-sectional view of the subject at the time the study begins and move forward with the individual. Others are longitudinal studies that are somewhat historical in character, giving detailed information regarding family background and the subject's infancy and early childhood—information that is often gathered from parents and others rather than from the subject himself. And some other case studies are a combination of the historical and cross-sectional types, beginning with the subject at the current time and looking backward as they move forward with the subject.

Desirably, a case study is more than an expanded cumulative record. In addition to more detailed and comprehensive information than is usually included in even the best cumulative records, it contains interpretation, recommendations, and reports on follow-up work. When, however, the cumulative record is in the form of a folder or booklet that includes records or summaries of records from other schools and nonschool agencies, interview records, conference reports, summaries of anecdotal records, biographical material, recommendations, and the like, the distinction between the cumulative record and the case study may cease to be very clear.

USES AND USEFULNESS

Case studies may be made and used for different reasons. (1) They may be made for research purposes. (2) They may be made primarily to serve as a basis for diagnosis and treatment of special problems. (3) They may be made for study of nonproblem cases and solely for helping the subjects to achieve good development. (4) They may be made largely for instructional purposes—for helping others to understand individual students and to learn how to summarize and interpret data collected on students.

As a Research Method. To research workers the case study is useful both for gathering data and for reporting findings. The usefulness of the method for scientific investigation is limited, however, for the following

---

[7] C. A. Dailey, "The Life History Approach to Assessment," *Personnel and Guidance Journal,* 1958, 36:456–460; "The Life History as a Criterion of Assessment," *Journal of Counseling Psychology,* 1960, 7:20–23.

reasons: (1) Case-study procedures are not standardized. Case studies of the same person made by two investigators may differ in a number of important aspects. (2) There is a special problem with respect to sampling. Murray,[8] for example, in reporting an experimental study of fifty students, states that "there are so many varieties of human nature that there is little probability that fifty subjects chosen at random will constitute a fair sample of any much larger group." This statement no doubt applies to the number of subjects selected for any investigation. (3) The reliability and validity of case-study material cannot be checked to any great extent through use of statistical methods because the data used are in large part unstandardized and unmeasurable. Validity has to be checked by verifying information from one source against that from other sources and by checking inconsistencies in the subject's speech and behavior. Similarly, reliability must be checked by such internal evidence as accuracy of account and logical sequence. The chief source of reliability is, in Jones's [9] words, "the truthful and complete unfolding of pertinent data." This is difficult to check.

Despite such limitations, some investigators consider the case history method one of the most useful approaches to the study of personality. Murray,[10] for example, finds that "case studies are the proof of the pudding." The method has certain advantages, which Young [11] summarizes as follows:

> The defense of the life-history device has usually taken the form of pointing out that it provides a more or less continuous picture through time of the individual's narration and interpretation of his own experiences and often of that of others around him. It is said to be peculiarly valuable in providing a view of the inner life. It furnishes an account of past situations which gave rise to new meanings and new habits; that is, it gives information on the origins of subjective life as well as of overt conduct. In particular it indicates the place which crises have had in the development of new traits, attitudes, meanings, and habits. When prolonged interviews are used, such as are found in psychoanalysis, or other extensive clinical contacts, the method yields rich data respecting the operation of unconscious motivations, mental processes, and the specific effects of repression. It also helps to frame questions and hypotheses to be tested by further life-history analysis or by the application of experimental or statistical methods.
>
> More than this, this technique has possibilities for interpreting personality which the other methods, so far, have not given us; that is, it furnishes a framework for compiling relevant data about one individual, keeping

---

[8] Murray et al., op. cit., p. 730.
[9] Harold E. Jones, Development in Adolescence, p. 132. New York: Appleton-Century-Crofts, Inc., 1943.
[10] Murray et al., op. cit., p. 605.
[11] From Personality and Problems of Adjustment, 2d ed., by Kimball Young, p. 320. Copyright, 1952. Appleton-Century-Crofts, Inc. Reprinted by permission of the publisher.

attention upon both his common and his unique qualities. Within the context of the single person's life story, specific events in relation to other events and to external situations take on significant meaning. And, if we compare a series of such analyses of individuals, we may formulate some generalizations about both subjective life and overt conduct.

For Dailey [12] the life history or case study has a primary role in personality research. It provides not only a valuable source of data and a framework in which the data may be ordered but also "the ultimate criterion of truth for all assertions" about the subject. Other personality assessment methods, such as tests, are validated against case-study data.

The case-study method was used in certain important investigations of adolescence. In the study conducted by the Commission on Secondary School Curriculum, set up by the Progressive Education Association, the fundamental purpose was to gather material for a fuller understanding of adolescent personality. A staff, made up of educators, psychologists, psychiatrists, physicians, social workers, anthropologists, and others, collected material about ordinary students in typical school situations by using entire classes in private and public secondary schools and colleges in different parts of the country. To this group were added a limited number of older adolescents to serve as sources of information about the problems and responsibilities of postschool youth. The more than six hundred case studies made of these boys and girls provided the raw material for the study. This method was used because, according to Zachary,[13] it was decided that the intensive and many-faceted study of single cases could reveal most clearly the consistent trends underlying the apparent inconsistencies in adolescent behavior and could bring out the multiplicity of factors influencing the individual adolescent; thereby it could offer a sound basis for educational diagnosis and for judging the changes likely to result from educational action. Four cases of not-unusual adolescents are reproduced in full in one report.[14]

One report on the California Adolescent Growth Study is in the form of a single case study, which is a combination of the cross-sectional and longitudinal types of case histories. The author [15] describes it as a "montage" rather than a "single integrated picture" of the subject. It presents a series of views of an adolescent boy at home, at school, and in social group situations. It shows him as he is perceived by parents, teachers, peers, and self. It pictures his physical development; indicates his motor and mental abilities, interests, and attitudes; and provides the basis for an interpretive study of underlying tendencies in the realm of emotions and motivations. It gives a good picture of one boy and his struggle for maturity.

---

[12] Dailey, "The Life History as a Criterion of Assessment," p. 21.

[13] Caroline B. Zachary, Foreword, in *The Adolescent Personality* by Peter Blos, p. viii. Copyright, 1941. D. Appleton-Century Company, Inc.

[14] *Ibid.*

[15] Jones, *op. cit.*, p. 132.

In both the Harvard Guidance Study [16] and the Wisconsin Counseling Study [17] the basic research procedure was the longitudinal case study. Rothney, who directed both studies, emphasizes that life episodes cannot be studied as isolated parts, that a subject's life must be studied as a connected whole: [18]

> There appear to be no sudden delinquencies of the "model boy," no sudden failures or successes, no sudden breakdowns, no sudden attainment of readiness—perhaps no sudden insights. All of these seemingly sudden changes have seriatim and chronological order and though this order may be difficult to draw out it must be done if there is to be real understanding of present behavior and adequate prediction of future activity.

As a Basis for Diagnosis and Treatment. Not all psychologists agree regarding the value of the case-study method or the use of diagnosis in general. Some believe that an adequate case study is essential, that early in the counseling process detailed information should be sought more or less systematically from the client regarding his background and development and adjustment in different areas. Thorne,[19] for example, found that this procedure has definite benefits for both counselor and counselee. An adequate case study, according to Thorne, helps the counselor to perceive etiological relationships, to recognize illogical thinking and misinformation, and to differentiate between functional and organic complaints. The client derives satisfaction from the fact that a careful study is being made of his case. He experiences desensitization, catharsis, and abreaction in talking about his complaint, its history, his life, the significant people in his life, and his reactions to past experiences. As the details of his life history are reported and brought into perspective, the client begins to perceive causal relationships and to gain new insights regarding his problems and his ways of dealing with them.

Williamson [20] is another who stresses the importance of the case-study technique. He considers complete case data important to sound diagnosis and effective counseling. He recognizes, however, the difficulty and sometimes impracticality of elaborate case-study procedures in school and college situations. The counselor collects data on the case until he has sufficient relevant data for a valid diagnosis. "The point at which fact collecting stops is, of course, an arbitrary one dictated only by the counselor's judgment. As he collects these facts, the counselor reviews them to

[16] John W. M. Rothney and Bert A. Roens, *Guidance of American Youth: An Experimental Study.* Cambridge, Mass.: Harvard University Press, 1950.

[17] John W. M. Rothney et al., *Guidance Practices and Results.* New York: Harper & Row, Publishers, Incorporated, 1958.

[18] John W. M. Rothney and Bert A. Roens, *Counseling the Individual Student,* p. 58. New York: Holt, Rinehart and Winston, Inc., 1949.

[19] Thorne, *op. cit.,* p. 148.

[20] E. G. Williamson, *Counseling Adolescents,* p. 185. New York: McGraw-Hill Book Company, Inc., 1950.

'spot' a recurring theme, a unifying or consistent meaning, a valid diagnosis. When he perceives a diminishing relevancy of new facts, he makes a tentative summary."

For Increased Understanding. Case studies are especially useful for helping teachers to understand the factors that aid and hinder good development. They provide a practical way for applying the genetic point of view in guidance. Studies of "problem students," for example, show how such students become socially maladjusted. Continued study of the cases shows that changes in behavior and attitudes do not occur miraculously, that persistent, patient, careful, thoughtful efforts are required to help bring about desired changes.

Case studies are frequently made for the primary purpose of inservice education. They are useful means for explaining theoretical concepts through concrete example. They help teachers to increase their knowledge of the psychological processes and their understanding of critical issues involving emotions and motivations. The use of the technique for this purpose is discussed in the next chapter on the case conference, so no further attention is given to it here.

THE METHOD

Selecting the Subject. Probably no other technique is as useful as the case study for helping teachers and counselors to understand the complexities of students' lives. Even when the number of students assigned a counselor is so large that he has limited time for making case studies, he will find it well worthwhile to make at least one a year. If he regularly makes one a year and each year selects a different type of student, he will find the cumulative value of such study to be great. When all counselors in a particular school follow the practice of making at least one case study a year and of reporting the findings to the faculty, it may be well for them to decide together at the beginning of the year the specific students or types of students to be studied so that as far as possible these students may be representative of the total group.

Case studies should be made of average students, superior students, and well-adjusted students as well as of students who are retarded, delinquent, and maladjusted. Because problem students attract and generally require more attention than others, they are probably selected most often for intensive study. Special study should be made of them and special attention given to their cases, but other students should also be selected for special study.

Some counselors may make case studies of deviates only because many case histories reported in the literature by clinical workers are "interesting problem cases." Clinics are established for helping the seriously disturbed, and so the subjects of clinical studies can be expected to be individuals in need of special therapy. Schools, however, are established to serve all children and youth, all of whom have problems and some serious. Most are not "problem cases," and they need to be studied too.

School people are aware of the importance of superior students in the conservation of our human resources and are showing this awareness through increased interest in the study of such students. The secondary school principals, for example, who cooperated in the study by Rothney and Roens wished a large proportion of the experimental group to be superior students. In asking teachers to recommend students to be considered for selection, the principals directed attention to two groups of students—those of exceptionally high ability and those in need of special assistance—by instructing the teachers to use the following guides in making their recommendations: [21]

1. Children of exceptionally high achievement. (Note subject-field in which they excel.)

2. Children who show exceptionally high ability in Art.

3. Children who show exceptionally high ability in Music.

4. Children who show exceptional skill in practical arts or printing.

5. Children who are very persistent in striving for success.

6. Children who are trying very hard against great obstacles.

7. Children who constantly present behavior problems in class.

8. Children who do not seem to be able to do the work of the grade.

9. Children whose behavior makes them appear to be "Model."

10. Any other child you would like to see tested. Please give the reason.

Of the 129 students selected by the principals, 69 were listed as being superior and 60 as being in need of special help. Although no reason was given by the principals for weighting the group in favor of superior students, the investigators thought that it was done "in the belief that the usual guidance program overlooks the mentally superior child and otherwise gifted child." Later, however, it was found that actually the group was not weighted with superior students. "Among them were a number of very personable individuals who could get high marks but whose performance on tests was only mediocre." Some average students got into the group apparently by accident.

Counselors interested in systematizing the selection of subjects for study, and in gaining the cooperation of as many other counselors and teachers as possible, might ask the others to recommend students for study. Guides similar to the ones given above might be used to call attention to all types of students, instead of only two or three. If the counselors think that a particular group is being overlooked, attention can be focused upon the neglected students by having more studies made of them than of

[21] Rothney and Roens, *Guidance of American Youth*, pp. 109–110.

others. It is doubtful, however, that the case studies made during a particular year should ever be limited to studies of one type only.

Collecting the Data. As many relevant data should be collected from as many sources as possible. A number of procedures can be used. In the Wisconsin Counseling Study,[22] for example, data were collected through the use of tests, including projective techniques; interviews; conferences with parents, teachers, and others; questionnaires; autobiographies and other personal documents; membership lists; reports in school and community newspapers; and the like. Not all methods were employed for each subject, and the frequency and intensity with which a particular procedure was used varied from case to case.

The four cases reported by Blos[23] contain material from school records, observations, autobiographies, other self-expressive writings, conferences, and interviews. The material in Williamson's[24] illustrative cases was gathered largely through three procedures—tests, interviews, and an elaborate questionnaire that contains self-analysis material, as well as factual information items. The data for the case reported by Jones[25] were collected through physiological measurements, motor tests, intelligence and achievement tests, self-reports, photographic records, projective techniques, interviews, observations, and special devices for learning the opinions held of the subject by his associates.

Sometimes a case study is based primarily on material collected through the use of only one or two procedures, such as observation and interview. A collection of anecdotal records or interview reports is not, however, in itself a case study. To become a case study, the material must be synthesized, summarized, and interpreted in some organized form. (See Chap. 2.)

In the Harvard and Wisconsin studies specific criteria were developed to govern the data collecting process. The following is a brief summary of Rothney's[26] descriptions of these criteria:

CRITERION 1. *"Any datum about an individual that assists in the understanding of his behavior must be given due consideration."* Certain basic data are collected on all cases. Beyond that point the data collecting becomes an individual affair. The investigator looks for "what seems important to the particular individual he is studying even though it may be of no concern to any other member of the group."

The emphasis is upon the significance of an item rather than its frequency of occurrence. Rothney cites the case of an underachieving,

[22] Rothney et al., *Guidance Practices and Results,* chap. 3.

[23] Blos, *op. cit.*

[24] Williamson, *op. cit.*, pp. 285–356.

[25] Jones, *op. cit.*

[26] Rothney and Roens, *Counseling the Individual Student,* chap. 2; Rothney et al., *Guidance Practices and Results,* pp. 67–69.

superior-ability student with whom limited success was achieved in counseling until a particular datum was discovered: He was absorbed with weight lifting. "His daydreams were concerned with this activity, and his purposes were confused. He could not see how he could use this activity as a career, and he did not want to give it up." [27] Similarly, noting that a girl was the only student who wore overalls on all occasions led to the discovery that she was sensitive about pubescent changes in her body shape.

CRITERION 2. *"The culture in which the individual is reared must be thoroughly examined."* The investigator needs to learn the mores, economic pressures, and environmental forces influencing the life of a subject. Differences in student behavior are due to cultural as well as personal factors. Different students develop different standards and desires because they were reared in different cultures and so are subject to different stimulations and demands. "Delinquency is as natural in some areas of our culture as Sunday-school attendance is in others." [28]

CRITERION 3. *"Longitudinal data must be used in the study of the individual."* The subject needs to be studied over a sufficiently long period of time for the data to show his typical behavior, his consistency and variability with respect to certain characteristics, and the relationship between past experiences and current behavior: [29]

> The counselor who decides that there is no need to study the past, because it seems obvious that a boy's problem is caused, for example, by a recent personality clash with a particular teacher overlooks the fact that the boy may have met similar personalities before and may meet them again. What appears to be a casual incident or chance occurrence may be a phase of a long developmental pattern of response to such persons. Thus, the apparently simple remedy of removing him from the particular teacher's classroom may not be an effective means of preparing him for later meetings with foremen, employers, neighbors, or even marriage partner.

CRITERION 4. *"Conceptualization must be continuous as each separately evaluated datum is added to the study of the individual."* As data are gathered and evaluated, inferences can be drawn regarding the relationship between current behavior and past experiences, and tentative hypotheses can be reached regarding the conditions of instruction, guidance, counseling, or treatment that may contribute to good development.

There is no rule for knowing when sufficient information has been collected for making inferences or conclusions. All hypotheses need to be considered tentative since there is always the possibility that further data may not support them. New conceptualizations may require that the subject be counseled in a way quite different from that suggested by the previously obtained data.

[27] Rothney and Roens, *Counseling the Individual Student,* p. 51.
[28] *Ibid.,* p. 57.
[29] *Ibid.,* p. 60.

CRITERION 5. "*Any datum about an individual that is to be used in his counseling must be appraised in terms of its accuracy and economy.*" If more valid and reliable data can be obtained through use of the interview than through the questionnaire, then the questionnaire is not the most dependable or economical procedure to employ. It is difficult, however, to determine the validity and reliability of all sources of information, and it is difficult to weigh the probable outcomes of one method in comparison with others that may require less time.

The Scope. There is no standard outline for the case study. Some outlines recommended in the literature are more appropriate for use in clinics than in schools or colleges. In such outlines attention is given to some matters ordinarily not included in the case studies prepared by high school counselors. Among such items are those dealing with the circumstances of birth, matters regarding toilet training, and sexual development. Such items are important, and any information regarding them contained in the records received from the lower schools might well be included in the case study. Generally, however, unless the investigator (teacher or counselor) has special training in history taking and in interpreting such material, he may through his bungling embarrass the student and provoke criticism against himself and the school.

Given below is a list rather than an outline of the information items commonly included in case studies on students. No specific pattern is recommended with respect to order, emphasis, form, or the like. Not all factors listed will be investigated in every case. In general, however, as much specific information as possible should be sought on each. The sources of information should be reported. The items are as follows:

1. NAME OF WORKER AND DATE OF REPORT. If different parts are written at different times, each part should be dated.

2. IDENTIFYING DATA ON SUBJECT. Name, address, age, date and place of birth, race, and school grade. Adviser or counselor. General appearance of subject and impression made upon others.

3. PROBLEM (if study is made because subject seems in need of special assistance). Nature, onset, seriousness, frequency and duration (chronological order). Previous attempts to diagnose and eliminate difficulty. Feelings and attitude of subject toward problem. Opinions and attitudes of parents, teachers, and others, such as school nurse and doctor.

4. FAMILY. Name, age, sex, and educational attainment of family members living in home or closely associated with subject. Other persons, such as boarders, living in home but not of immediate family. Residential history of family (rural, small town, urban). Immigrant background if pertinent. (Less attention is given now than formerly to background information about grandparents and parents and subject's early childhood experiences unless such information has special significance.) Occupations of wage earners. Special health problems of any member. Religious affiliation(s). Apparent socioeconomic status. Special culture patterns. Nature of home life and quality of interpersonal rela-

tions. Subject's adjustment and special role in family. Attitudes of other members toward him. Method and amount of parental control.

5. PHYSICAL HEALTH DATA. Findings of medical examination(s). Growth characteristics, nutrition, and general health. Attitude of subject toward his health and appearance.

6. OBJECTIVE TEST DATA AND INTERPRETATION.

7. EDUCATIONAL HISTORY AND ACHIEVEMENT. Progress in past. Present status not only in terms of marks but also in terms of other objectives, such as appreciations, creative expression, good work habits, and the like. Attitude toward school. Special abilities and disabilities. Strong likes and dislikes with regard to school courses and activities. Educational plans and ambitions. Conduct problems, if any. Attitudes of teachers toward subject.

8. SOCIAL DEVELOPMENT. Sociability and adaptability. Companions and close associates. Rivalries. Group affiliations. Nature and extent of participation in groups. Acceptance by others. Status in various groups. Relations to neighbors and other adults in community. Social competence and confidence. Recreational interests and diversions. Recreational facilities. Special interests and accomplishments. Significant experiences. Civic participation in and out of school. Asocial tendencies. Court record if any.

9. EMOTIONAL DEVELOPMENT. General mental health. Predominant moods. Stability and excitability. Sense of self-confidence. Attitude toward self. Significant limitations. Symptoms of conflicts, such as tics, stuttering, tantrums, truancy, lying, stealing, etc.

10. WORK EXPERIENCE. Place and dates (from _____ to _____) of employment. Nature of work done. Attitude toward work.

11. VOCATIONAL PLANS AND AMBITIONS.

12. GENERAL APPRAISAL, INTERPRETATION, AND HYPOTHESES. The generalizations and conclusions should be developed from the data. The reporter takes care not to generalize from too few instances or from atypical instances. He considers his hypotheses tentative. He points to contraindications as well as calls attention to confirmatory data. He does not sort the data to prove particular points by bringing all supporting evidence into full view and discarding or covering up other evidence. Actually his purpose is not to prove any point but rather to see all parts of the picture and their interrelations so that he can analyze the complex pattern of the whole and perceive the underlying meanings and implications. He can never know that his interpretations and hypotheses are absolutely correct. He draws inferences on the basis of his best thinking and revises his interpretations and hypotheses as new evidence reveals the need for revision.

13. RECOMMENDATIONS. Treatment and follow-up are implied in every case study. In the case of students, treatment is probably more often developmental and preventive rather than, or as well as, corrective.

14. FOLLOW-UP REPORT(s). As long as the student is in school, the investigator periodically brings the study up to date by reporting additional information on the subject's development and the outcomes of efforts in his behalf. If the student is referred to someone for special assistance, reports from that person are incorporated in the report or appended to it.

The Form. The case study need not be written according to a particular form or a special style. Some investigators consider an informal, casual type of report preferable to a formal one. The length varies with the case and the purpose in making the study. It should not be overlong because much irrelevant material is included or because, as Jones [30] says, the reporter wanders around in the early life of the subject looking for the cause of maladjustment when the cause is quite recent. Yet, in general, it is better to report too much information than too little.

Whether long or short, written in a formal manner or in a free, descriptive, narrative style, the report should give as accurate and as objective an account and as complete and dynamic a picture of the subject as possible. The writer shuns loose generalizations and avoids the use of technical jargon. He tries to avoid such common sources of inaccuracies as errors in perception; falsification of memory; unconscious omissions; tendency to dramatize; projection of own ideas, attitudes, values, and the like into the report; inclination to give attention to unusual and striking incidents and to neglect the commonplace.

To interpret the subject's inner life as revealed in his creative writings and personal documents, speech, and behavior, the investigator must be able to identify himself sympathetically with the subject and still play the role of the critic who stands to one side to observe and to appraise. He must have the capacity for critical empathy. While reading the subject's writings, listening to him, and observing him, he tries to perceive things as the subject sees them. In interpreting, however, what he reads, sees, and hears, he resumes the role of the objective critic who is interested but not involved emotionally. At one moment he puts himself in the subject's situation, striving to feel as the subject feels. At another he is outside the situation, objectively appraising both the situation and the subject.

AN EXAMPLE

The following example is taken from a report on the Harvard Guidance Study. It is the case study of Nelson, a brilliant, physically vigorous, well-adjusted, and well-liked boy who accepted the limitations produced by his family's poverty. Consequently, he would probably never have continued his formal education beyond high school had he not received special assistance from his counselor. The investigators consider this boy's problems typical of those commonly encountered by gifted children whose families are not in the upper levels of the economic scale. Needless to say, we need to make case studies of more students like Nelson so that we may help such students to realize their superior potentialities.

In reading this case study, a teacher or counselor in the actual school situation would probably have at hand the boy's cumulative record as a source of additional information regarding names, addresses, test

[30] Jones, *op. cit.*, p. 166.

scores, course marks, and the like. Also, the present tense is ordinarily the basic tense used in writing case studies. This particular study is written in the past tense probably because it is part of a report on a completed investigation.

NELSON [31]

Nelson was referred to the guidance counselor in the eighth grade by the principal of a junior high school as a boy with very high ability and ambition who needed assistance in financing further education. His family was unable to provide any aid, and it appeared likely that his very high achievements and sense of responsibility could not be utilized to their fullest if he were forced to go to work as soon as he reached the legal age of school-leaving.

Interpretation of Test Record

Nelson made superior scores on every test administered to him over a five-year period. On the Stanford-Binet Test (old form) his I.Q. score was 145, and this appeared to approximate his true score. In the fields of reading, language, mathematics, spatial facility, and speed and accuracy as measured by a clerical test, he scored above the 85th percentile for five consecutive years. Although the scores on the personality schedule suggested some emotional maladjustment, no other evidence substantiated this finding. On the Strong Vocational Interest Blank for Men, he obtained an A rating in group I and group II, which might have indicated that his interests were most similar to chemists, engineers, mathematicians, architects, artists, dentists, and physicians. Other evidence indicated the same interest in occupations at a professional level.

Family Data

Nelson was the second of three children of American-born parents. His mother died when he was about four years old, and when he was six, his father remarried. There were no children from his father's second marriage. His father had been in very poor health since the first World War, and his earnings as a craftsman had been very meager. His stepmother, who was employed as a secretary, was the main support of the family. Nelson's older brother was attending a Midwestern college where he was considered to be an exceedingly brilliant student. A younger sister attended junior high school. She was not as successful as her brothers in academic work.

The home relationship between the parents and the children was excellent. Nelson's stepmother was very devoted to the children. She was very cooperative with the counselor, and she was a frequent visitor to his office.

[31] Reproduced by permission of the publishers from John Watson Murray Rothney and Bert A. Roens, *Guidance of American Youth: An Experimental Study*, pp. 16–21. Cambridge, Mass.: Harvard University Press, copyright, 1950, by the President and Fellows of Harvard College.

Health Data

Nelson was somewhat underweight according to the health records in the school, but he received excellent home care. His stepmother had been very careful about his diet and occasionally seemed somewhat oversolicitous about his physical condition. Routine school medical examinations did not reveal any physical defects or disabilities. A slight ocular disability was corrected adequately by glasses.

Leisure-time Activities

Nelson's major hobby was collecting phonograph records of classical music. His interest in music was strong. Whenever possible, he attended symphony concerts and seemed to gain a great deal of pleasure and satisfaction from them. Bicycling was a major interest which persisted throughout his secondary school years. He took several long bicycle trips through neighboring states.

Nelson was somewhat timid in social gatherings, and during his early high-school career, he avoided attending class dances and parties. In his senior year he sought such positions as ticket-taker at class dances so that he was not obliged to invite a girl. In discussing these activities with the counselor he attributed them to timidity in social functions, but the counselor believed that need for money played an important part in this lack of participation.

Work Experience

During the time that Nelson was in the ninth and tenth grades, he sold newspapers at a junction of the main traffic arteries leading out of town, and for a newsboy, his earnings were fairly large. He was markedly responsible in this job, and he carried on when others with less drive were unwilling to face disturbing circumstances. During the summers both he and his brother did sufficient odd-job work to pay for their own clothes and school expenses. After Nelson had entered the eleventh grade, he gave up his newspaper work because it interfered with school studies.

Vocational Choice

Grade 8 Science, probably engineering: This decision was probably influenced by his readings in science.

Grade 9 Same

Grade 10 Same

Grade 11 Science and teaching: Probably influenced by his success in chemistry and by his admiration for the chemistry teacher.

Grade 12 Same: The exactness of science appealed to him. He was considering teaching because of its security and immediate income after college graduation and because he thought he would like to work with young people.

PROGRESS OF COUNSELING

Nelson was a tall, thin, rangy, clean-cut boy with an engaging smile. During many interviews the counselor found him to be courteous, honest, straightforward, and attentive. He was one of the most conscientious pupils in the school in the matter of filling out questionnaires administered to him.

During the first interviews with him in the eighth grade the counselor saw immediately that Nelson would need help to continue his studies, and he discussed the problem of scholarship aid for further education. Nelson was told that his chances for such help were excellent if he did the school work of which he was capable. He was encouraged to do more than his regular class work in order to obtain as high marks as possible. With his cooperation, a school program for the ninth grade, which would not be too heavy in view of his newspaper work, was outlined. Science and engineering seemed to interest him as possible occupational choices, and the counselor gave him some general reading material covering these fields. During subsequent interviews these readings were discussed, and Nelson seemed to have a fairly good idea about what these vocations involved.

In the ninth grade, Nelson won a medal in a national contest for an essay on Graphic Arts. He had entered this contest without consulting his teachers or parents. The counselor made Nelson aware of the emphasis by colleges on "all-around boys," and worked out a program with him for participation in athletics and other extracurricular activities. As a result, Nelson campaigned for and won election as president of the Student Council, and he also became a member of the track team. He was very successful in all these activities. Although he was an all A student, he seemed to be popular with the other boys and was regarded more as a "regular fellow" than as a "sissy" or "teacher's pet."

In the tenth grade, Nelson and the counselor selected a program of only four subjects because it seemed desirable for the boy to do very well on these instead of carrying a heavier program with the lesser chance of keeping up his fine academic record. Later, when Nelson found that this load was too light, he decided to study Greek on his own.

Science still seemed to interest him a great deal, and his interest was further stimulated by his success in mathematics. Nelson and the counselor discussed several times the vocational possibilities for him in that field.

During the summer of this school year, Nelson worked with his brother. They cared for lawns in the community and their earnings were sufficient to keep them in clothes and to cover expenses for the following school year.

Shortly after Nelson entered the tenth grade, a long interview was held with his stepmother, at her request, concerning the problem of permitting Nelson to continue in the college-preparatory course. She thought that there was no prospect of financial help for college. She thought that he should take a course to prepare him for some immediate occupation, for she doubted that a partial scholarship would be sufficient to keep him in college. During this interview the counselor indicated that Nelson's chances for getting a substantial scholarship were very good. If this was not obtained, the alternative of having him work for a year after graduation from high school before going to college was considered. As a result of this interview, his stepmother decided that he should continue in the college course. Apparently, financial conditions at home were difficult because the counselor noted a very strong desire on Nelson's part to get out of school as soon as possible to earn money. He had strong feelings concerning his obligation to support the family, but the counselor pointed out that he probably could be of more help to his parents in the future if he obtained a college education.

With respect to extracurricular activities for this year, Nelson was confronted with the problem of studying piano or joining the debating club because he felt that there was not sufficient time for both. The pros and cons were discussed with him, and he made the choice of piano. When the decision had been made, he practiced one hour daily. He was able to obtain lessons free of charge from a friend. It was during this year that his interest in music increased greatly, and much of his leisure time was spent at concerts or in reading about music and musicians.

The summer following completion of the tenth grade he had a fairly extensive paper route and did odd jobs in the neighborhood.

When he returned to school in the fall, his morning and evening paper routes seemed to take too much time, and because he seemed to have sufficient money to carry him through the school year, he decided to discontinue them.

In discussing occupations with the counselor, he became somewhat discouraged about engineering because of what he considered to be the poor prospects in the field at that time. His interest in high-school teaching increased. He obtained a good deal of pleasure from his work in chemistry and became quite friendly with a chemistry teacher whom he admired.

After the midyear holiday of his eleventh school year, his stepmother became ill, and Nelson took over a number of the household duties. He did the cooking, washing, and ironing, as well as house-cleaning, so that he had very little time for homework or extracurricular activities. Except for his concern about his stepmother's health, he was as cheerful and good-natured as he always had been.

A summary of the counselor's information about Nelson, including marks, test scores, and evidence of his industry was sent to two local colleges with a query concerning the possibility of securing a scholarship after he had graduated. Both institutions indicated that his possibilities for scholarship aid were very good, and they expressed considerable interest in him.

During the summer, between the eleventh and twelfth grades, Nelson again sold papers and did odd jobs. This work again enabled him to pay for his clothing and save money for incidental expense during the following school year. At the beginning of the twelfth grade, the problem of continuing the paper route came up again, and after some discussion with the counselor, he dropped it. He estimated that he could make as much money by doing odd jobs that required less time.

The counselor encouraged Nelson to participate more in school activities, and he was elected Editor-in-Chief of the Year Book, a very responsible and highly important position. He also became a member of the varsity debating society and his performance in several debates was outstanding despite the fact that this was his first year of participation. The counselor encouraged him to join the Burroughs Newsboys Club, and he also became a member of a youth club in a church.

During the winter of his senior year, applications for scholarship were made to a number of leading universities and to outside agencies which offered college aid to needy students.

The latter part of Nelson's senior year was very trying because his stepmother became very much concerned about his chance to attend college. An indication of her state of mind at that time may be gleaned from her remark, "I would give my life to see that this boy goes through college." Her concern about Nelson became so distorted that the counselor found it necessary to have several interviews with her to alleviate her extreme anxiety and prevent a possible mental breakdown.

Nelson took the spring scholarship examinations administered by the College Entrance Examination Board, and he kept up his efforts to get high marks in his studies. During the spring of his senior year he was offered a tuition scholarship from the Midwestern college which his brother was attending. His parents were inclined to have him accept this scholarship and to supplement his resources by working for his board and room. The counselor reiterated that aid from one of the large universities would probably be forthcoming and that his vocational possibilities after graduation would probably be much better if he graduated from a larger university. Nelson and his parents finally decided to decline the scholarship, and shortly thereafter he was granted a National Scholarship from Harvard University for $800 annually. He was also granted a scholarship of $100 from his high school.

In view of Nelson's high performances and the fact that his college financial worries had been alleviated, the counselor predicted a successful college career and high achievement in any vocational pursuit which he chose.

ELEVEN YEARS AFTER INITIAL COUNSELING

Six years after Nelson had graduated from high school, the counselor obtained the following information in an interview with him.

At college Nelson received honor grades in all courses except a half-course in philosophy and a course in physics which was known to be exceedingly difficult. His work was good enough to permit acceleration, and he graduated in three and one-half years cum laude in electronic physics.

Following graduation he was deferred from military service and assigned to do some secret work in physics in a naval research project until the war ended. At that time, he continued his graduate work in physics, earned his master's degree, and received a generous fellowship which permitted him to carry on the work for his doctorate. Upon completion of that work in 1947, he planned to seek a university appointment which would enable him to do research in electronics.

Nelson married a girl whom he met at a church function, shortly after graduation. His parents were not particularly pleased about his marriage because they thought that it would handicap his efforts. His wife has, however, worked while he has been a graduate student, and has contributed much to his success. Nelson says that he is very happily married. His parents have been somewhat concerned about his independence since he has had sufficient financial support, but he has a strong feeling of responsibility toward his family, and both he and his wife have given some of their earnings to the family when they were in need.

The authors of this case study are fully aware that Nelson might have gone to college without any special assistance from his counselor or teachers. They know that the basic factors in the boy's earning a college degree are his abilities and his willingness to put them to good use, but they see the counselor's persistence as being also an important factor. They add: [32]

> The fact, however, that his parents urged him to change to a more practical course and the fact that he felt a strong obligation to make immediate contributions to the support of his family make it seem likely that he would have dropped into the commercial course to prepare himself for a job after he had completed high school. He would, therefore, not have had enough academic credits for college entrance if there had been a change in fortune, and would have found the work with less capable students lacking in challenge. In doing so he would have done as many others in public high schools have done, to their sorrow. The statistics . . . indicate that such persons are not happy about their vocational or social placements. . . .
>
> When we consider the particular case of Nelson there is very little reason to believe that his character was weakened by the assistance which the counselor provided. He sought information and advice, but he was intelligent enough to weigh carefully the information which he obtained. He did not lean upon the counselor, and when his share of the job of getting financial aid was outlined, he accepted it and put forth his best. With his abilities, his drive, his desire to learn, and his industry it seems that he might have been successful in almost anything that he undertook. If college can serve any young person, Nelson is the kind who should be served, and society cannot afford to neglect the potential contribution of a boy of his caliber. The counselors, who knew him for five full years, were convinced that this boy could be assisted without loss to him as an individual, and with gain to society. Not all of the students of superior ability who were studied could have received the same treatment as this lad without loss, but Nelson's rare combination of abilities, traits, and stamina were outstanding, and the counselor's actions appeared to have been thoroughly justified. Such students are too precious to ignore in the routine school procedures which schools without guidance services provide.

SUMMARY

The case study is a developmental approach to appraisal of the individual. Comprehensive information about the subject is gathered systematically

[32] *Ibid.*, pp. 21–22.

from as many reliable sources as possible. A variety of procedures is used in the data collecting. The findings are presented in a report that shows the continuum of development and the interrelations of the factors influencing growth and adjustment. The procedures used in gathering, recording, and interpreting the data are among the basic techniques of counseling and guidance.

The case study may be made for research purposes. It may be made primarily as a basis for diagnosis and treatment of some special problem. It may be made for study of some nonproblem case and solely for the purpose of helping the subject to achieve good development. Or it may be used largely for inservice education purposes—for helping teachers to gain skill in studying and understanding student behavior. In schools and colleges use of the method should not be limited to "problem cases." It should be used for studying the average and the gifted student as well as the retarded and the maladjusted.

A list is given of the information items commonly included in the case study. There is no standard style or form for the case report. It should be sufficiently comprehensive to reveal the subject's typical behavior and the past and current forces influencing his development. Generalizations, interpretations, recommendations, and follow-up reports are usually included in the case study. The reporter proceeds cautiously in generalizing regarding future developments because new data may not support his interpretations and hypotheses. He should be willing to seek new data and to revise his generalizations in keeping with new findings.

REFERENCES

Adams, James F.: *Problems in Counseling: A Case Study Approach.* New York: The Macmillan Company, 1962.

Blos, Peter: *The Adolescent Personality.* New York: Appleton-Century-Crofts, Inc., 1941.

Dailey, Charles A.: "The Life History Approach to Assessment," *Personnel and Guidance Journal,* 1958, 36:456–460.

———: "The Life History as a Criterion of Assessment," *Journal of Counseling Psychology,* 1960, 7:20–23.

Edelston, Harry: "Educational Failure with High Intelligence Quotient," *The Journal of Genetic Psychology,* 1950, 77:85–116.

Hahn, Milton E., and Malcolm S. MacLean: *Counseling Psychology,* 2d ed., chap. 9. New York: McGraw-Hill Book Company, Inc., 1955.

Jones, Harold E.: *Development in Adolescence.* New York: Appleton-Century-Crofts, Inc., 1943.

McDaniel, Henry B., et al.: *Readings in Guidance,* chap. 7. New York: Holt, Rinehart and Winston, Inc., 1959.

Murray, Henry A., et al.: *Explorations in Personality: A Clinical and Experimental Study of Fifty Men of College Age,* chap. 7. New York: Oxford University Press, 1938.

Rothney, John W. M.: *The High School Student: A Book of Cases.* New York: Holt, Rinehart and Winston, Inc., 1953.

——— and Bert A. Roens: *Counseling the Individual Student.* New York: Holt, Rinehart and Winston, Inc., 1949.

——— and ———: *Guidance of American Youth: An Experimental Study.* Cambridge, Mass.: Harvard University Press, 1950.

——— et al.: *Guidance Practices and Results.* New York: Harper & Row, Publishers, Incorporated, 1958.

Strang, Ruth: *Counseling Technics in College and Secondary School,* rev. ed., chap. 8. New York: Harper & Row, Publishers, Incorporated, 1949.

Traxler, Arthur E.: *Techniques of Guidance,* rev. ed., chap. 15. New York: Harper & Row, Publishers, Incorporated, 1957.

Williamson, E. G.: *Counseling Adolescents,* appendix. New York: McGraw-Hill Book Company, Inc., 1950.

14

The Case Conference

The case conference is one of the best methods for synthesizing and interpreting data gathered on a subject from different sources. As once defined by Fenton,[1] it is "a single though fairly long conference during which there is an orderly presentation of all the facts and points of view" on the case.

In general, three types of case conferences are held in schools and colleges. They are (1) the conference attended primarily by the staff members who are specialists in guidance and the related areas; (2) the conference attended by both specialists and nonspecialists and often arranged as much for the purpose of inservice education as for study of particular cases; and (3) the conference attended by a student, his counselor, and his parent(s).

The Guidance Staff Conference

The conference is primarily a guidance staff meeting when specialists in guidance, psychology, child welfare, social work, and health meet to consider the case of a student who seems in need of specialized assistance or of help beyond that available through teacher cooperation. The specialists study the records on the case, give and hear supplementary reports, and consider specific recommendations for working with the case. Teachers who have a special relationship with the student, such as homeroom teacher, coach, music teacher, or the like, are sometimes asked to participate in the conference. More often, however, statements are obtained from the student's teachers in advance and reported at the conference along with other information.

Because guidance specialists are usually well versed in conference procedures, little further attention is given here to this type of conference.

Case Conference for Nonspecialists

When the case conference is more than a staff meeting—when it is held for the purpose of providing inservice education for nonspecialists as

[1] Norman Fenton, *Mental Hygiene in School Practice*, p. 71. Stanford, Calif.: Stanford University Press, 1943.

313

well as for securing special study of a particular case—the conference participants desirably include all staff members who are directly concerned with the student or able to give pertinent information about him. Any staff member who is not actively involved in the case but who is interested in attending the conference is generally encouraged to do so.

When properly used, this type of conference almost invariably results in increased understanding and appreciation of students as unique individuals, in increased skill on the part of many participants, in increased awareness of the importance of the special services, and in better-organized efforts to secure an expanded program through increased personnel and improved working conditions. Some counselors and guidance directors who fully appreciate the value of the conference method abandon it because they find it almost impossible to schedule the conferences at a time when those who should attend can do so without too much inconvenience.

THE PROBLEM OF TIME

The case conference is comparatively little used partly because the method is not well known and partly because it is difficult to provide enough time for effective use of the technique. Ordinarily, when the conference method is first used, from one and a half to two hours are needed. As staff members become skilled in the technique, less time is needed. However, if interest and cooperation are strong, the time required will seldom be less than an hour.

The problem of providing enough time and of scheduling the conference at a suitable time is solved in various ways. The most common solution seems to be that of holding the conferences after school. This plan may work if the teachers are not asked to remain after school many afternoons and if all concerned with the case are free to attend, that is, if none has to be elsewhere to coach a team, to sponsor an activity group, or to take care of some other assignment. Serving tea or coffee, as Fenton and others suggest, may help to refresh the teachers and to make working two hours longer less difficult. If, however, the school day is frequently extended for afterschool work, serving tea or coffee may refresh the teachers but not lessen resentment sufficiently to make them feel interested or cooperative.

Some administrators and teachers dismiss this whole problem regarding time for special professional activities by stating firmly that attending meetings, participating in case conferences, helping with extracurricular activities, reading professional literature, and doing other such things are as much a part of a teacher's work as making lesson plans, teaching classes, and grading papers. This statement is true. It is also true, however, that, to be good teachers, teachers must not be drab, uninteresting people. To be alert and interesting people, as well as teachers interested in their work, they must have time to satisfy their normal needs for recreation, diversion, and rest.

When this problem of how to find time for professional meetings is put in the hands of the faculty, some faculties, like some administrators, can find no better solution than to schedule the meetings after school. But, because the plan is theirs and not one forced upon them, they may find it easier to accept than a similar plan imposed from above. One faculty group made the plan more acceptable than it had been previously by making it more definite. Operating as a committee of the whole, the teachers decided that one afternoon a week should regularly be reserved for professional activities and that other afterschool activities which might interfere with any member's taking part in the professional program were not to be scheduled for that day. The group also developed a plan for equalizing committee work because the members felt that a few were being asked to do too much and that the group resources were not being sufficiently well used.

The general plan agreed upon called for a meeting of the whole faculty one week, department meetings another week, committee meetings another week, and case conferences the fourth week. Desirably case conferences should be regularly held more often, but obviously once a month is better than never. Since the members of this faculty agreed that they would regularly devote two hours a week to professional meetings, all expected to participate in one of the two or three case conferences held on "conference day." At times some teachers were directly concerned with more than one case being considered on a particular day, even though a special effort was made to select for study on the same day students at different grade levels and in different curricula. The teachers were free to decide which conferences they would attend, but homeroom teachers were expected to attend all conferences on members of their homeroom groups. Conferences on two members of the same homeroom were never held on the same day.

In some schools case conferences are held in the morning before school. This plan has two disadvantages: The conferences are generally too short; and some faculty members cannot attend because of home routine, transportation needs of other family members, and the like. In some other schools the conferences are held on school time. In some they are scheduled during the lunch hour, which again usually means inadequate time. Moreover, a situation that involves a combination of eating and working is generally not an ideal one for effective conference work.

The best solution may be found in those schools that regularly schedule case conferences on school time and arrange for the teachers concerned to be relieved of classwork in order to participate in the conferences. In some schools conferences are rotationally scheduled at different periods so that a teacher need not be away from the same class too often. An effort is made to schedule a particular case at the hour which for most of the teachers involved is a "free period" (period used for work other than teaching). If it is important that a certain teacher attend a particular conference and he is scheduled to teach at the same hour, another teacher may take his class for him. Under this plan the time spent in a conference ordinarily cannot exceed the length of a class period.

INITIATING THE CASE CONFERENCE

Before the conference method is used, its purposes, principles, and procedures may well be considered by the faculty in advance. The effectiveness of the conferences can be determined in large part by the quality of the preliminary preparatory work.

Stress on Ethical Standards. In the preliminary stage attention needs to be given to the ethics involved. Too much stress cannot be placed upon the importance of keeping all conference proceedings and case material confidential, of reporting accurately and interpreting objectively, of being open-minded and ready to give thoughtful consideration to all recommendations even though all are not in keeping with one's own views, of keeping the discussion at the professional level and above the level of gossip and hearsay, and of keeping emotions under control.

Whatever is said, however, regarding professional behavior should be said in a way which makes it clear that every member is considered a responsible and reliable person; that violations of the rules of ethical conduct are not anticipated; that, in reminding the group members of the importance of observing the rules closely, the chairman is only exercising a routine precaution; and that he will repeat the reminder from time to time. Furthermore, he must take care to do so in the beginning until conference use has become routine. Thereafter whenever new members are present, the conference leader should remind the group of the confidential nature of all material presented at the meeting.

Use of Demonstrations. Demonstrations are sometimes used to help a faculty prepare for conference participation. The specialists with the help of some nonspecialists demonstrate the technique by using a real or hypothetical case. A real case probably arouses more interest but may not be so useful as a hypothetical one for helping the teachers learn to discuss a case objectively.

When the case is a real one, a teacher who has the student in class may be unable to accept, because he does not understand, some interpretations and recommendations offered by the specialists. He may feel that he knows the student better than they do, both out of school as well as in it. He may feel confident that the only reason "this boy acts that way" is that "he simply does not care and, like his father, just does not have any ambition." When the case is a hypothetical one, this teacher may not find it difficult to follow the specialist's line of thought and may agree with him in the main. After several hypothetical or disguised cases have been presented and discussed by the group, he may acquire sufficient general understanding regarding multiple causes, behavior symptoms, and the like to be able to apply the principles to the "unambitious boy" and to other students whose problems he tended to dismiss in the past with such loose generalizations as "lazy," "low IQ," "poor attitude," "inattention," "low-class home," etc.

Sometimes the demonstrations for orientation purposes are given in a school by staff members from some clinic or by specialists from some nearby university. Such demonstrations are helpful for some faculty members but may do others more harm than good. If the demonstration case is a complicated one and/or all demonstration participants are experts, some members may want to start at the level of the experts. They attempt to adopt the techniques and the terminology of the experts before they are ready to do so. Confusion and loss of interest may result. Also, some staff members, after observing a demonstration by experts, may feel somewhat as a fifth grader might if his art teacher placed an excellent drawing before his group and asked them to try to copy it. Knowing that his production would be far below the level of the artist's product, the fifth grader might feel that there was no use in trying to reproduce it.

Use of Case-study Instruments. Before attempting to use the conference method for study of real cases, some faculty groups first study or review, either as a total group or in small study groups, certain principles and techniques. They may, for example, practice interpreting test and record data in order to gain skill in recognizing pertinent items and significant patterns and in translating numerical data into qualitative terms.

Other faculty groups find such study more interesting and meaningful when they use case-study instruments that include exercises designed to help the user appraise his understanding of human behavior and development and evaluate his skill in drawing inferences, constructing hypotheses, and making diagnoses. A number of such instruments can be obtained commercially. One, *The Case of Mickey Murphy*,[2] is reproduced in full in a textbook edited by Erickson; [3] and two others, *The Case of Paul* and *The Case of Charles*,[4] are reproduced in a book of readings edited by McDaniel et al.[5]

Rothney's *The High School Student* [6] contains case studies of stu-

[2] W. R. Baller, *The Case of Mickey Murphy*. Lincoln, Nebr.: University of Nebraska Press, n.d.

[3] C. E. Erickson (ed.), *A Basic Text for Guidance Workers*, chap. 4. Englewood Cliffs, N.J.: Prentice-Hall, Inc., 1947.

[4] Published by the Bureau of Research and Service, Michigan College of Education, Michigan State University, East Lansing, n.d.

[5] H. B. McDaniel et al., *Readings in Guidance*, pp. 118–127. New York: Holt, Rinehart and Winston, Inc., 1959.

[6] John W. M. Rothney, *The High School Student: A Book of Cases*. New York: Holt, Rinehart and Winston, Inc., 1953.

dents at different levels of ability and achievement. Problems are presented, but solutions are not suggested, which makes the book especially
useful for group study when discussion is the method. The appendix of
another of Rothney's [7] books includes four case exercises in applying principles, identifying needs, interpreting data, evaluating treatment methods,
appraising need for referral, and doing other such things.

Group study of such case studies can help to increase teachers' understanding of student growth and development. It helps some to abandon the practice of explaining student behavior through such stereotypes
as "unhappy home life," "too much concerned with extracurricular activities," "is just plain lazy," "has not learned how to study," "should be
taking shop courses," "doesn't have the mental ability for the work," "is
preoccupied with sex interests," and so forth. When such explanations
are uncritically offered during the study of an actual case in the school
and the user of stereotyped explanations is asked the basis for his diagnosis, he can usually "remember" enough evidence on the spot. If, however, he offers his explanation during the study of a not-real case and the
only evidence is that contained in the printed or mimeographed material,
the teacher may find it difficult to justify his interpretation. When asked
the basis for a statement, he may find nothing in the case-study material
to support it. Others may call his attention to enough contradictory evidence for him to realize that his judgment was not based on reflective
thinking.

GENERAL PROCEDURES IN THE CASE CONFERENCE

In some schools teacher resistance to inservice education is sufficiently
strong for the use of demonstrations and small study groups to be unwise.
In such situations the conference technique is best introduced for the
same reason and in much the same way that it is adopted and used in a
social work agency or clinic: Some staff member wishes help with a particular case. He "draws on the best thinking" of his colleagues at a staff
session where they review his records on the case with him, appraise his
diagnosis, question him regarding plans for working with the case, and
offer their suggestions and recommendations.

This may be the best way for inexperienced conference participants
to become acquainted with the technique. If the conference time is used
efficiently and the worker seeking assistance finds the meeting helpful,
others may be motivated to seek conferences on some of their cases.

The Subject. If the conference is used primarily for helping colleagues
with particular cases, then the subject is a student whose case a teacher or
a counselor brings before the group either because he wants suggestions

[7] John W. M. Rothney and Bert A. Roens, *Counseling the Individual Student,*
pp. 338–355. New York: Holt, Rinehart and Winston, Inc., 1949.

or because he thinks that, if he shares with the others his information on the case, they will join him in special efforts to help the student. If the conferences are used largely for study purposes, then subjects should be selected in much the same way that they are selected for anecdotal reports and case studies. Because the number of students studied through the conference technique is necessarily small, only problem cases are selected in some schools.

While it is highly desirable to use the most effective procedures with cases requiring the greatest skill, it would be unfortunate never to hold conferences on average, superior, and other "nonproblem" students. To limit use of any technique to work with problem students strengthens certain false ideas regarding counseling and guidance that are already held by too many people, such as the idea that it is mainly work with problem students. To help develop a conception of it as work concerned with all students, an effort should be made to include all types of students in all parts of the program.

Moreover, if only maladjusted or problem students are considered at case conferences, being a "conference case" may stigmatize a student in some teachers' thinking. Also, should parents and students ever come to know that students are studied through the conference method and to know the type of students studied, then being a conference subject may be looked upon as a mark of disgrace. The use of case conferences should then probably be abandoned, because they can result in more harm than good for the students whom they are designed to help.

When the student selected for conference study is a "problem case," his case should not be so serious that little can be done for him at school with the help of teachers. Such cases are generally best studied by specialists. This is particularly true when rehabilitation in the school situation seems unlikely and referral to a nonschool agency may be the next best step.

Also, teachers find conference work more stimulating and the results more encouraging when the problems they study in conference groups are school-centered rather than home-centered. They may find (or feel) that they can do little to help a student whose problems are centered in the home and family situation. These cases are not to be wholly avoided in conference work, however. Through study of such cases teachers may learn how to help the students find compensating experiences at school and how they, the teachers, can serve as positive forces counteracting negative, even potentially destructive, influences in the home and the neighborhood.

The Participants and the Leader. The participants in a case conference desirably include all staff members working with the student, available specialists able to help with the case, and other interested faculty members. In order that discussion may be informal and easy, the group is small,

preferably 20 members or fewer. Attendance should not be compulsory.[8]
The spirit in which a participant attends a conference is more important than his presence there. If anyone is there under duress and not because he is sincerely interested in studying the case, perhaps it is better for him and for the student that he be elsewhere. Some harm may result from his being there. Not in sympathy with the conference idea, such workers may leave a conference feeling strongly opposed to all such "guidance nonsense"; and they may include the student as well as the program in their opposition. While they may never intentionally use in an unprofessional way the information obtained at the conference, they may project onto the hapless student the resentment felt toward the persons who, they believe, more or less forced them to attend the conference against their will.

Furthermore, if the conference is to provide a learning situation, the participants must be able to express their points of view freely and fully and must not feel obligated to adopt the viewpoint of another. A teacher's point of view may not be correct, but the change desired should result from growth through education rather than from fear or a desire "to please the authorities." Conflicts of personalities and clashes in points of views are not likely to be serious when the participants find the conference atmosphere permissive and the leader understanding and accepting. As Fenton [9] states:

> It is inconsistent with the purposes of the conference, for example, for anyone possessing legal or administrative powers, such as the superintendent or the health or attendance officer, to browbeat the others into accepting his recommendations or to insist stubbornly upon his point of view. The conference group exists primarily for the child's welfare. If one member must coerce or dominate the others to carry a point which he believes will help a child, the technique has failed of its purpose.

Ideally the conference leader or chairman should be a professionally trained counselor or psychologist; but, if the staff does not include such a specialist, use of the conference can still be successfully attempted. The members with some training in student personnel work can help those who are without training but interested in trying to understand and to help students as individuals. Together they can adopt the case conference in its least technical form and use it effectively for the purposes intended. By working together in the conference situation, most members

---

[8] While attendance at case conferences should be voluntary, it is necessary that all or almost all staff members attend as many of the demonstrations and preliminary discussion meetings as possible. Some authorities state that attendance at the initial meetings should be required even though they agree that ordinarily attendance should not be made compulsory.

[9] Fenton, *op. cit.*, p. 81. Reprinted with the permission of the author and the publishers, Stanford University Press.

will learn to deal more intelligently with students and will become more sensitive to students' needs and more aware of their own powers and fitness, as well as limitations, for helping to meet these needs. Some will be stimulated to undertake independent study and experimental use of other techniques, such as anecdotal reports and cumulative records.

The Special Report. There is no standard form for administration of the case conferences. The procedures sketched here are in general the ones reported as helpful by some counselors and guidance directors. All agreed regarding the importance of a full report being carefully prepared on the case in advance. Not all agreed, however, regarding the desirability of supplying the conference participants with copies or an abstract of the report before the conference.

Some workers believe that, if all participants receive copies of the report in advance, many may come to the conference with set ideas about the case. Others, however, think that the influence of any preconceived ideas will be minimized by the presentation of other ideas at the conference and believe that, if the participants have the basic data beforehand, they will give the case thoughtful attention and seek additional information. The second point of view is based on respect for the ability and integrity of coworkers, and so it seems more desirable than one based on reluctance to permit fellow teachers full participation. If the conference participants are to have a report before the conference, they should receive it a week, or at least several days, in advance. The report should open with a statement reminding the receiver that the report is confidential and cautioning him against letting any part of it be read by anyone else.

While the case conference is ordinarily used for focusing attention upon an individual, it can be used also for calling attention to the needs of a special group of students, such as the superior members among new students, the students who withdrew during the preceding term or year, the students of high scholastic ability who are not doing well in academic work, the students who show very high achievement in some areas but very low achievement in others, and the like. The report prepared in advance for this type of conference should contain thumbnail sketches on all members of the group, in which the most important data on each are summarized.

Because of the amount of work involved in preparing this type of report and the cost of mimeographing copies for all conference participants, such reports are often given orally or projected onto a screen. Use of mimeographed copies distributed at the beginning of the conference is preferred, however, because it facilitates discussion. It is difficult to remember specific items on different students when reports are given orally or projected onto a screen. When members have copies, they can easily refer to material on different students and note common and distinguishing factors in their cases. Better conference discussion and more appropriate recommendations are likely to result.

Synthesis and Diagnosis through Conference Discussion. To the material contained in the special report, prepared before the conference, other data are added systematically at the conference. First the person who collected the data for the special report summarizes all pertinent information obtained after the report was prepared. Then the other members report additional items that they consider relevant. When the report seems complete, the conference members discuss it, trying to determine the significant facts and to decide what needs to be done to aid development of the student concerned. As discussion proceeds, some members add information not given earlier because then not held important. Also, some things held important at the beginning begin to appear trivial when viewed in the light of the total report. Some interpretations and recommendations carefully thought out before the conference are not offered because they no longer seem appropriate.

As the members gain a more comprehensive and accurate picture of the student, they begin to see what they individually can do to help him gain some of the experiences needed. At times special action does not seem needed. Instead, all need to try to help the student utilize his personal and environmental resources. At other times special help is needed. Then recommendations are made regarding special action and the particular staff members to be made responsible for carrying out the recommendations. All recommendations should, of course, be put into effect as soon as possible, including the one for general assistance by all staff members.

If the services of a secretary are not available, some group member makes a record of conference findings and recommendations to be included in the student's cumulative record folder or booklet. Periodically special conferences or meetings are held at which follow-up reports on various cases are heard and the effectiveness of the recommendations previously made on these cases are appraised.

Students and Parents Usually Not Participants. Sometimes it is suggested that a student with a special problem, solution to which involves adjustment on the part of the school as well as of the student, discuss his problem in conference with his teachers, counselor, and others so that the group may consider various plans with him. This, of course, is the ideal situation—one in which the student, teachers, specialists, and the parents too, perhaps, pool efforts and resources in order that each may help dissolve the difficulty.

Usually, however, a student troubled by some special problem is so self-conscious and even frightened during the conference, despite all efforts to make him feel otherwise, that he is not able to participate construc-tively in the discussion. It is ordinarily better for him to discuss his prob-lem alone with his counselor rather than with a conference group. At the case conference the counselor can present the student's problem as it is seen by the student. Afterwards during his interviews with the student he can try to make good use of the conference findings and to carry out the recommendations agreed upon at the conference.

As the result of a case conference, an interview may be arranged with a student's parents in order to obtain the cooperation needed from the home. Usually parents are not invited to participate at a case confer-ence. As Fenton [10] points out, their presence inevitably limits the frank-ness and objectivity of the discussion. The case conference is part of the professional routine of the school, and parents do not expect to partici-pate. On the rare occasion when it does seem desirable to have one or both parents attend the conference, they should be present only part of the time. Some things are not easily discussed or should not be discussed in the presence of parents.

SOME POSSIBLE OUTCOMES

The most important of the possible outcomes of a case conference is in-crease in the participants' understanding and desire to play a helpful role in the lives of students. Most participants will leave a case conference with increased understanding and appreciation of the student studied, with greater awareness of the ways in which classroom conditions and instruc-tional methods contribute to good and bad adjustment, and with a desire to make better use of the facilities within their control for aiding develop-ment and for preventing or decreasing maladjustment in all students, not just the one studied at the conference.

Case conferences can help teachers function effectively in the class-room. They focus attention on student needs and show the importance of appraising a student in terms of his own growth and potential rather than some arbitrary standard. They stimulate teachers to try new ap-proaches to old problems. At case conferences ideas are sometimes ex-changed regarding instructional methods as well as guidance procedures.

Improved student-teacher relations may result from a teacher's conference participation if for no other reason than it gives the teacher a chance to ventilate negative feelings regarding the student. However, im-proved relations probably result more often from increased understand-ing than from reduced tension. Understanding is achieved as probable sources of difficulties and possible meanings of behavior symptoms are dis-cussed, as record data are properly interpreted and explained, and ques-tions and answers are exchanged. Controversial issues can be more freely

[10] *Ibid.*, p. 78.

discussed and opinions more frankly voiced in the conference than in a more structured setting.

Some participants may leave the conference fully aware for the first time of the fact that they must have comprehensive and accurate information about students if they are to know them as "whole students" or "total personalities." They perceive the bearing of certain factors in home and neighborhood environments upon a student's progress in school and see the importance of being informed about a student's out-of-school life. Some participants acquire new conceptions regarding their roles as teachers. Programs and procedures previously considered sound and good for all students may be seen as inadequate and possibly bad for some. If the conference case is a "discipline case," some participants may be less anxious at the close of the conference than at the beginning to have a student forced to conform. Their attention may have shifted from misbehavior and a need for punishment to maladjustment and a need for help. The central point in their thinking is no longer a disturbing student but the disturbing factors in a student's life.

Some participants gain professional knowledge and skill through conference participation. By sharing in the group thinking that leads to the group's conclusions and recommendations, they are able to decrease the number and the seriousness of errors in the interpretations and diagnoses that they make thereafter when working either alone or with the group. Group discussions help them to develop objective attitudes and to give up misconceptions regarding normal and abnormal behavior, the comparative significance of different educational objectives, and the relative importance of the various parts of the total program. The discussions help them to become more tolerant of different points of view and more critical of their own.

They find that others are more competent than they in some areas. They learn to draw upon the professional knowledge of others and thereby to increase and strengthen their own. Trained as well as untrained workers benefit in this way from conference participation. In an investigation reported by Murray,[11] for example, the conference method proved very useful for this reason. The method was used in its most technical form. The participants were highly trained specialists. Yet they found the chief advantage of the conference to be the minimizing of errors which arose from the participant's "personal viewpoint."

Through their conference experiences teachers may gain self-understanding and insight regarding some of their own behavior and feelings. They perceive that some of their problems are not unlike those of the students studied. Discussions of the students' problems help to dispel some of their anxieties. Actually a teacher may be indirectly talking about his own conflicts when discussing those of a student. At times the leader

---

[11] H. A. Murray et al., *Explorations in Personality*, p. 706. New York: Oxford University Press, 1938.

will recognize the roundabout approach to personal problems and will assist, not discourage, the teacher to use the conference in this way. Moreover, if the teacher reveals some reasons for his own feelings of inferiority and insecurity, it may be possible to help allay such feelings. Since the teacher's own personality enters into his handling of the students' problems, anything done to help the teacher may also help the students. Eventually the teacher may be able to separate his personal problems from those of the classroom and of the students.

Case conferences stimulate improvement of the guidance resources within the school. They show the need for the services of the specialists, such as nurse, speech therapist, expert in remedial reading, professionally trained counselors, and the like. Awareness of need may lead to efforts to secure adequate provision.

Case conferences also help to improve coordination of school and community resources. Counselors and teachers may begin to seek outside the school the special assistance needed by some students but not available within the school. They may succeed in interesting a citizen or a group in providing the help needed. A service group, for example, may agree to send to college some gifted student who should continue his education but whose family cannot afford to give him a college education. Sometimes the faculty find that the help needed is available upon request or upon the fulfillment of certain conditions easily met by the student, but neither the faculty nor the student before knew that it could be had for the asking.

SOME CAUTIONS

The good that results from the use of the conference method may not be so great or result so soon as some faculty members expect. Very little change may be noted in a student for a long time after the conference is held on him even though all who attended are trying very hard to carry out the recommendations made on the case. Rarely will change occur quickly or soon, so teachers must be patient and not expect rapid or early improvement. While the progress reported may not be great, ordinarily some progress can be expected. In the words of Fenton,[12] "investigations have indicated that, although seemingly miraculous improvement occurs rarely, complete failure is fortunately as infrequent."

Not all the progress reported may be real, especially with respect to academic progress. Some faculty members leave the conference room determined to help "the poor student" in every way they can. Helping him may be seen as passing him or raising his marks rather than as trying to modify instruction and environment so that the student may be able to achieve in keeping with his ability to do so. Actually the student may not be learning or adjusting any better than before; but, because he is

[12] Fenton, op. cit., p. 83.

receiving higher marks, progress is indicated. Then the student may be more confused than helped by the false evidence of progress. (This illustration is not to be construed as a defense of low and failing marks. Little defense can be offered for any marks—passing or failing, high or low—as given in the average high school or college today.)

Progress or improvement should be appraised in terms of the individual rather than in terms of some arbitrary standard. If, for instance, a student has been "acting in a childish manner" by losing his temper whenever thwarted and in other ways showing little self-control, progress should be reported when his temper outbursts become less violent and less frequent. The boy is learning to endure frustration; so he is progressing.

Improvement may not be consistently maintained. A student, for example, who has been negligent about completing his work and doing it on time may change and for a while show definite improvement with regard to punctuality and the quantity and quality of his work. Then he may slip back into his old ways. The relapse should not, however, be considered permanent. If the teachers are patient, the periods of backsliding may decrease in frequency and in duration.

The Student-Parent-Counselor Conference

Only rarely should a parent be invited to participate in a case conference on his child. There is, however, an important place for the conference attended by the student, his parent(s), and his counselor. When teachers are invited to join the group, it is at the request of the student or his parents. Otherwise, the teacher's being present may inhibit frank expression of feelings and opinions.

Many high school people are of the opinion that parent-teacher or parent-counselor conferences cannot be used as effectively in secondary schools as in elementary schools. Because adolescents, they say, seek independence from parents, they want to look after themselves at school and do not want parents, teachers, and counselors hovering over them protectively. Many adolescents, they believe, see the conferences as evidence of adults' lack of confidence in students' ability to get along on their own. The adolescent sees his parents, teachers, and counselors getting together just to check on him and to maintain their control. However, the findings from experimental use of the conferences in some high schools indicate that such thinking is based more on myth than on fact.

Some high schools are using the three-way conference for reporting student progress to parents in much the same way that the teacher-parent-pupil conference is used in elementary schools. They do not find students resisting the conferences. They find, instead, that many like having an opportunity to evaluate and interpret or explain their strengths, weaknesses, and progress. The students' appraisals and interpretations help parents and counselors to view goals and progress from the students' viewpoints. The conferences also strengthen school-home communication and thereby help parents and students to understand the school's objectives and programs and to perceive the ways in which different learning situations contribute to student growth.

Orientation Conferences. Many high school counselors use the student-parent-counselor conference only in crisis or emergency situations rather than routinely for developmental or counseling purposes. They appreciate, however, the value of conferences held with students and their parents for general orientation purposes before or shortly after the beginning of a new school year or term. Through such conferences they can help parents to become acquainted with the school's guidance services and to become involved in their children's educational and vocational planning. Many counselors find "back-to-school nights" and special PTA meetings to be inadequate orientation measures. They perceive the superiority of student-parent-counselor conferences but do not know how to provide the extra counseling time and secretarial assistance required. Some schools have solved this problem through use of funds made available under the provisions of the National Defense Education Act.

Examination of a limited number of reports on such NDEA projects indicates considerable agreement regarding the goals to be sought through orientation conferences. The objectives most frequently listed include the following: (1) to give the counselor an opportunity early to get acquainted with his new counselees and their parents and to give them a chance to know him; (2) to obtain information regarding the home and family; the student's aspirations, plans, special interests, strong likes and dislikes, and wanted school experiences; and the parents' aspirations and standards for the student; (3) to share with the student and his parents some of the information possessed by the school regarding the student's abilities and achievement (review and interpretation of cumulative record data) and to give information regarding the school's program (class and nonclass) and services, diploma requirements, and post-high school educational opportunities; (4) to help the student plan his program (class and nonclass) for the coming term and to make or review tentative long-range plans directed toward post-high school goals. Less frequently listed are such objectives as (1) to give information regarding group study and group counseling available to parents, (2) to motivate students to seek improvement in their work, and (3) to demonstrate to parents the value of the school's counseling program.

The basic purposes of establishing rapport and of gaining and giving helpful information are more likely to be achieved when the counselor's attitude is one of accepting, understanding, and caring or wanting to help than when the counselor uses the conference as a means of pressuring the student to "do better," or of forcing the student and his parents to consider data regarding the student's limitations in order to get them to abandon "unrealistic goals and plans." That the evidence regarding the student's limitations (if valid) needs to be examined is not disputed, but counseling leading to acceptance and use of the data cannot be telescoped into one session. Such counseling is a process, not an act.

Some reports indicate that college-bound students are better served through orientation conferences than others. If so, this is unfortunate. It is also unfortunate if the conferences are used to pressure able students who are not interested in going to college to change their minds. The conferences should be focused upon helping them to examine their strong interests and goals and to explore various ways of satisfying them. In the ensuing process the student may raise his sights and consider the possibility of developing his strengths through a college education. Or he may not. Moreover, he may not be setting his sights too low, and a college education may not be the best route to his goal.

In some schools the conferences are planned for all students and their parents. In others they are scheduled for new students only, and in some for only those students who are above average or superior in scholastic aptitude. The time provided for each conference session varies from about twenty minutes to an hour and a half or longer. In some schools the conferences are held during the summer months. In others they are scheduled throughout the school year on school time and in the evenings and on Saturdays. Some schools report holding them throughout the calendar year and at almost any time convenient to parents in order that as many parents as possible may take part.

Some schools aim at an attendance of 100 per cent, and some almost make it. The Huntington Beach (California) Union High School, for example, has used student-parent-counselor conferences systematically for years. It is not unusual for this school to report that more than 95 per cent of the parents participated during the preceding year. In general, schools report better attendance by parents of freshmen and sophomores than by parents of juniors and seniors. For example, one year the attendance record for Levittown (New York) Memorial High School showed the following: [13] 89 per cent of ninth-grade parents, 84 per cent of tenth-grade parents, 71 per cent of eleventh-grade parents, and 59 per cent of twelfth-grade parents. In over 75 per cent of the conferences both parents were present.

In some schools, such as Palm Springs (California) High School,[14] consultants are provided to help work out problems related to the counseling process. The counselors may also meet in workshop sessions with the consultants. Teachers are also an important resource. According to one symposium on use of the conferences in ten high schools, "it appears

[13] Gerald Pratt, "Counseling Parents and Pupil," *News Bulletin of New York State Counselors, 1958.* Reproduced in *California Guidance Newsletter,* 1958, 13(2):3–5.
[14] "A Brief Report of the Freshman Parent Conferences at Palm Springs High School," p. 1. (Mimeographed and undated.)

that teachers believe these conferences to be profitable in direct proportion to the extent to which they become involved in providing some of
the data used." [15]

A number of schools obtain follow-up statements from both students and parents regarding the worthwhileness of the conferences. In
some schools evaluation questionnaires are filled out immediately after
the conferences. In some others the report forms are mailed to the homes
at a later date in order to give students and parents a better chance, it is
hoped, to appraise the conferences objectively. Very favorable findings are
generally reported. That high school students are not opposed to the use
of student-parent-counselor conferences is indicated by such statements as
the following: [16]

"I found out where I was going."

"My conference with counselor and parent was definitely helpful."

"Now I don't have to worry about deciding on my own."

"It gave me a chance to express my feelings with someone with authority."

"Parents learned about school and understand me better also."

"I had a chance to talk with both my parents."

"I believe it was better for me to plan my schedule with my mother and
counselor there."

"I knew what I wanted to be, but I didn't know what I would like to take;
now I know what I *have* to take."

"I was more sure of what I would like to be."

Parents express their approval in statements like the following:

"We're closer now that we are aware of his interests, and we can talk
together."

"I feel that it (the conference) helped me understand my child better."

"We now discuss our problems openly."

"I was amazed at his ability to look ahead and plan his activities and to
discuss them intelligently with his counselor."

"Convinced me that my child is interested in his future."

". . . an interest in science—news to us!"

"Brought us closer to her—her interest in her future."

"Gave us a chance to see how our child selected his studies."

The evaluation reports of some counselors indicate that the conferences make them aware of the need for skill in interviewing and for an
abundance of educational and occupational information.

Orientation conferences often lead to follow-up conferences that
are focused on specific matters and that have preventive and develop-

[15] "Fact—Not Fad or Fancy," *California Guidance Newsletter*, 1958, 13(1):2.

[16] "A Brief Report of the Freshman Parent Conferences at Palm Springs High
School," pp. 3–5.

mental values. Without the initial or orientation conference, many such follow-up or counseling conferences might never take place.

A Neglected Resource. Too little use is made of parents as a counseling resource. As Berdie [17] has pointed out, many counselors show little understanding and sympathy for parents of their counselees. Like some psychologists, they tend to develop a "mother-blaming complex"—to trace students' problems "back directly to unwise, selfish, or emotionally unstable parents." The explanation of the "complex," Berdie says, may lie in the counselors' failure to resolve their own conflicts involving authority. Furthermore, they "may forget that parents are not authority figures because they choose to be, but rather because social mores, family traditions and customs, and individual emotional needs and drives force them into the authority role." [18]

The parent is a source of much pertinent information about the student's home and neighborhood life, his status in the family, interpersonal relations in the home, the student's nonschool interests and activities, and the nature and source of some of his difficulties. He can give valuable information on the student's developmental history—physical, intellectual, and emotional. He may know when the student started showing a strong preference for certain studies and a strong dislike of others. A parent's perception of the student may be very much in line with that reported by the teachers, or it may be quite different. The variance in perceptions may reflect considerable variance in the student's behavior at school and at home. This is important information that may not be easily obtained from other sources.

In other ways the parent is an important resource. He is able to modify home routine and environment in keeping with the student's needs. He can help the student secure and continue certain experiences, support him in his efforts to develop new behavior patterns, encourage him in seeking specific goals, and support him in the carrying out of plans.

Furthermore, counselors serve as sources of information and emotional support for parents, as well as for students. A parent may be disturbed by his child's motives and behavior. He may cease to be perturbed when he learns from the counselor that his son's or daughter's desires and behavior are typical of boys and girls of the same age. Conversely, the conference can help students perceive that parents are human too; that they need affection, approval, and understanding; that they have feelings that get hurt; and that on some matters they are better informed than students and even counselors. Thus the conference can serve as a means to

---

[17] Ralph F. Berdie, "The Counselor and the Parent," *Journal of Counseling Psychology,* 1955, 2:185–188.
[18] *Ibid.,* p. 186.

improved parent-child relations rather than as an unpleasant barrier to good relations.

In his anxiety to help his child grow up, the parent may give the student more independence than he can comfortably handle. The student may feel that he cannot assume as much responsibility for the management of his life as his parents are giving him. As one adolescent put it, he may want his parents "to ride herd on him" until he is ready to take over this responsibility. Until then he wants not only love and understanding and support but also control from his parents. Moreover, as Berdie says, "the student's need is not to achieve independence but rather to develop mature and appropriate dependencies. The student who seeks from his parent approval for every minor activity and reassurance in every dilemma is in no greater need of counseling than the student who is unable to obtain from his parent emotional support during periods of anxiety and a continuing feeling of being loved by his parents." [19]

In the three-way conference the parent and the student may come to see each other differently and learn new ways of dealing with one another. The counselor has to be sensitive to the needs of both. He works slowly and cautiously when there are signs of emotional conflict. A number of counseling conferences may be required before student and parent can fully express their feelings and explore the conflict sufficiently to develop insight regarding their roles in its creation and solution. The three-way counseling conference may help them learn new ways of communicating with, thinking about, and behaving toward one another. This type of student-parent-counselor conference is as important as the one arranged for orientation or information purposes. Usually it requires more skill on the part of the counselor.

SUMMARY

The case conference is an effective technique for synthesizing data from a number of sources. At the conference, specialists and nonspecialists pool information on a case and share in its interpretation, in identifying and bringing significant items together in a meaningful whole, and in formulating plans for developmental and corrective measures.

The sharing of information is not a haphazard affair. Summary statements of available data are prepared in advance, copies of which may be sent to the participants before the meeting. At the meeting supplementary information is added in a logical, orderly manner.

The case conference is a valuable inservice education technique. Its use may be preceded by demonstrations of conference procedures and by small group discussions of case-study instruments designed to help the user gain skill in interpreting data and in formulating and testing hy-

[19] *Ibid.*, p. 187.

potheses. Conference participation helps teachers to perceive the ways in which classroom conditions can affect, positively and negatively, the adjustment of students. It also helps them to make better use of school and community resources for fostering and strengthening good adjustment and for preventing and correcting maladjustment.

Conference discussions help the group members to augment their supply of professional knowledge and thereby reduce errors in their diagnoses and prognoses. Most participants come to a better understanding and acceptance of students through increased understanding of the nature and the sources of some students' difficulties, academic and otherwise. Some also come to a better understanding and acceptance of self and gain insight regarding some of their own emotional conflicts.

Including the student's parents among the case conference participants usually prevents free exchange of ideas and opinions and frank discussion of the case. The parent is, however, an important resource. His assistance can be utilized through the student-parent-counselor conference. This type of conference seems used most frequently for establishing good home-school relations and for gaining and giving information helpful to the student in his educational and vocational planning. It contributes to improved parent-child relations when it helps the student and the parent to understand each other and to develop more appropriate ways of dealing with one another.

REFERENCES

Berdie, Ralph F.: "The Counselor and the Parent," *Journal of Counseling Psychology,* 1955, 2:185–188.

Fenton, Norman: *Mental Hygiene in School Practice,* chap. 5. Stanford, Calif.: Stanford University Press, 1943.

Gilbert, William M.: "Training Faculty Counselors at the University of Illinois," in E. G. Williamson (ed.), *Trends in Student Personnel Work,* pp. 301–309. Minneapolis: The University of Minnesota Press, 1949.

Kurtz, John L.: "Learning to Interpret Child Behavior," *Educational Leadership,* 1950, 7:558–562.

McDaniel, H. B., et al.: *Readings in Guidance,* chap. 7. New York: Holt, Rinehart and Winston, Inc., 1959.

Rothney, John W. M.: *The High School Student: A Book of Cases.* New York: Holt, Rinehart and Winston, Inc., 1953.

Thompson, Jack, and Xarmen J. Finley: "An Evaluation of the Case Conference Method," *California Journal of Educational Research,* 1960, 11:87–93, 96.

15

Working with the Emotionally Handicapped

Counselors have an important role in work with students who are handi-capped mentally, physically, or educationally and with those who are talented or gifted. Leadership in such work is, however, usually assumed by some other specialist, such as the speech therapist, the physician, the school psychologist, the remedial education specialist, the curriculum co-ordinator, and the like. When the exceptional student has a social-emo-tional handicap, it is the counselor to whom high school teachers and administrators most frequently look for leadership. Hence, it is with this type of exceptional student that we are concerned in this chapter.

There is definite evidence that special assistance is being increas-ingly given to exceptional children. During one ten-year period, for ex-ample, the number of children enrolled in public school special educa-tion programs nearly doubled—from 378,000 in 1948 to 861,000 in 1958.[1] The rate of growth for this group was three times that of local public school elementary and secondary enrollments. The number of school systems reporting such programs in 1960 was more than five times the number reporting such programs in 1935. The most striking gains were in special education enrollment of the blind and the speech-impaired. The gains for the socially and emotionally maladjusted were substantial but far less striking than the gains for some others. See Figures 37 and 38.

MENTAL HEALTH CRITERIA AND MALADJUSTMENT SIGNS

The Goals. Biber [2] has extrapolated a set of mental health criteria from the contributions of certain educational, psychological, and social-political leaders. She describes the mental health goals as follows:

---

[1] Romaine P. Mackie and Patricia P. Robbins, *Exceptional Children and Youth. Special Education Enrollments in Public Day Schools*, pp. 4–5. Washington, D.C.: Gov ernment Printing Office, 1961.

[2] Barbara Biber, "Integration of Mental Health Principles in the School Setting," in Gerald Caplan (ed.), *Prevention of Mental Health Disorders in Children: Initial Explorations*, p. 326. New York: Basic Books, Inc., Publishers, 1961.

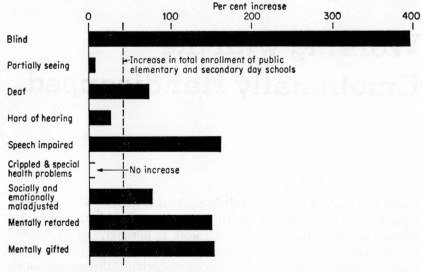

FIGURE 37   *Increase in special education enrollments.* (Romaine P. Mackie and Patricia P. Robbins, *Exceptional Children and Youth: Special Education Enrollments in Public Day Schools,* p. 5. Washington, D.C.: Government Printing Office, 1961.)

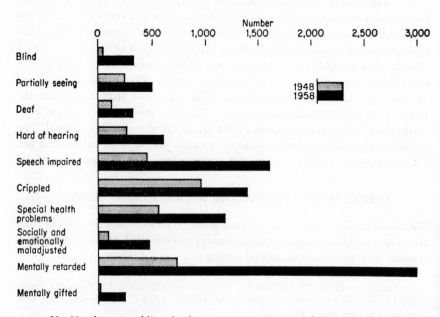

FIGURE 38   *Number of public school systems reporting special programs in each area of exceptionality.* (Romaine P. Mackie and Patricia P. Robbins, *Exceptional Children and Youth: Special Education Enrollments in Public Day Schools,* p. 7. Washington, D.C.: Government Printing Office, 1961.)

1. *Positive feeling toward the self:* sense of safety, competence, mastery; enjoyment of one's own powers as a sensing, feeling, thinking being; expectation that one's own capacities will find approximate fulfillment.

2. *Realistic perception of self and others:* differentiated knowledge of self available to scope and content of wishes and ambitions; capacity to see others in terms of their motivations, opinions, and conditioning life circumstances.

3. *Relatedness to people:* capacity to relate to others as individuals relatively free from group stereotyping; to develop and sustain relations of depth and warmth; to find a balanced, flexible way of interacting (join ideas, activities, etc.) with others while sustaining the core of one's own individuality (opinion, style, values, etc.).

4. *Relatedness to environment:* positive motivated connectedness with the contemporary world of processes and ideas; ability and drive to exercise capacities and skills in effective, responsible functioning; capacity to expand orbits of identification beyond realm of personal encounter.

5. *Independence:* freedom to undertake independent thinking, judging, acting; freedom from compulsion to submit or conform; adaptation governed by objective evaluation of situational demands and ultimate individual goals; capacity to accept position of dependence (take help) where insufficient knowledge, experience, or strength dictates it; balance between adaptation and need to sustain individual autonomy.

6. *Curiosity and creativity:* a sustained and deepened curiosity; drive to penetrate the unknown and to engage in directed search for resolution; to keep imaginative processes in vital condition and to be able to transform these into productive, creative reorganization of experience.

7. *Recovery and coping strength:* capacity to regain equilibrium in the face of trauma, frustration, and crisis; to corral and integrate available strength in the face of challenge and obstacle.

These goals do not represent optimal points. They are, instead, balance points or ranges of possible positive values. The ideal is not to function optimally in terms of all. Rather it is to maintain a proper balance among them. To function optimally in one can result in a too limited functioning in another. Full satisfaction of the need to sustain individual autonomy, for example, can interfere with the capacity to adapt to objectively evaluated situational demands. The approach to mental health is a multiple-criteria one. Parents and teachers aid development of healthy, stable personalities when they help boys and girls maintain a delicate balance between gratification and control of their basic needs.

Frustration. To overprotect young people from frustrations can inhibit their growth. Frustrations are a normal, natural part of life. They are required for growth and learning. They are unpleasant because they arouse tension, but it is this unpleasantness that drives the person to action—action that may be needed for removing obstacles to goals.

Frustrations are helpful when they stimulate learning. They are not helpful and may actually be harmful when they are too many and too severe. Individuals differ in the extent to which they require satisfaction of their basic needs and in the degree to which they can tolerate frustration of a want or need. Individuals who are exposed to stress in tolerable amounts throughout the various developmental stages build up a greater tolerance for stress and frustration than those who are overprotected. Good mental health is not secured by the removal of frustration.

Too severe frustration may be produced by such causes as physical difficulties and deformities (paralysis, defective vision or hearing, deformed hand, severe acne, ugliness, etc.); homes broken by voluntary or involuntary separation of parents, by divorce, or by death; family conflicts; shame because of some family member's failure to conform to the laws or the mores; lack of ability to succeed in school; unsympathetic and not-understanding parents; unsympathetic and not-understanding teachers, especially when parents are also not sympathetic and understanding.

The person who is too severely frustrated becomes so confused that he cannot find adequate ways to meet his basic needs. He cannot see in the possibilities for action a choice that will lead to his goal, and so he behaves in a nonoriented fashion. He resorts to frustrated behavior, which, as Segel [3] says, is terminal behavior—an end in itself rather than a means to an end. Although the behavior does not lead to need satisfaction, it may provide some relief from the tension created by frustration. The individual may resort to the behavior because of the satisfaction found in the behavior itself, not because it contributes to achievement of some goal.

While severely frustrated persons react in many different ways, they tend to follow behavior that can be roughly classed as aggression, regression, and fixation. The aggressive individual often gains relief from tension through his highly active behavior. At times he may even gain recognition or attention through it, but the behavior is not directed toward the end accidentally achieved.

Regressive behavior is withdrawal behavior. Feeling defeated, the individual no longer tries to attain his goal but withdraws from the struggle.

Fixated behavior is stereotyped behavior. The individual repeatedly behaves in a particular way even though the behavior does not help him to achieve his goal and may even lessen the chance of his ever attaining it. This type of behavior (automatic, repetitive, inflexible behavior) deprives the individual of the freedom and flexibility that he needs in order to learn from experience. It is not normal behavior because flexibility is the essence of normality.

[3] David Segel, *Frustration in Adolescent Youth,* U.S. Office of Education Bulletin no. 1, 1951, p. 25.

Signs of Maladjustment. Normality is a relative thing. The distinction between normal and abnormal behavior is not always clear. Many normal people are subject to the same kinds of deviations as are the abnormal. The chief difference is that the normal person suffers a less extensive and less severe emotional involvement than the abnormal person. The difference is primarily a matter of degree.

It is the person who is severely and persistently disturbed who is properly described as "emotionally handicapped." The normally emotionally disturbed individual should not be confused with the emotionally handicapped. Every person experiences emotional insecurity and most likely personality disorder at some time. Hence, most people display at times characteristics which might be described as neurotic. Furthermore, behavior that may be abnormal for one person may be normal for another. Behavior that is normal for a little child may be abnormal for a fourteen-year-old. Behavior that is not unusual for a sick person or for one who is not very intelligent may be very unusual on the part of a healthy, intelligent person.

The kinds of symptoms by which an individual reveals his disturbances are determined largely by his social or cultural environment. Behavior that is held abnormal in one culture may be viewed as normal in another. Hence, we must interpret desirable traits in the light of the types of responses a person may comfortably exhibit in his particular culture. Members of a certain social class, for example, frequently show affection by pommeling and cursing one another. This type of behavior on the part of a student from such a group is not indicative of maladjustment, but such behavior on the part of another student may indicate that all is not well with him. Or it may only mean that he has made friends with "the kids from the other side of town," likes them, and is trying to act as they do so that they will like him.

We must not be overeager to recognize signs of emotional instability. Normal persons suffer from minor mental deviations and reveal minor maladjustments through the same symptoms that are shown by the definitely pathological types. We should not interpret signs of minor deviations as evidence of serious abnormality or of incipient diseases. Nor should we be overready to interpret particular combinations of symptoms as indicating specific disorders. The symptomatology of one condition may not be unlike that of other conditions, including some benign ones.

Bower,[4] for example, in exploring the high school records of a group of schizophrenic patients in a mental hospital, found that during their high school years these patients had displayed such behavior characteristics as poor school adjustment in general, very little leadership ability, very low participation in student activities, lack of interest in

[4] Eli M. Bower et al., *High School Students Who Later Became Schizophrenic.* Sacramento: California State Department of Education, 1960.

girls, apathy, depression, carelessness, and perfectionism. Not all high school students, however, who exhibit a number of such characteristics later become schizophrenic.

From the foregoing it is clear that we cannot give a list of symptoms that consistently indicate maladjustment. We can only point to certain ones as possible indicators. Even though a symptom may be a sign of only transitory or minor maladjustment, it should be noted and its possible implications explored. Unfortunately, we may see some symptoms exhibited so often that we accept them as inevitable and fail to question their significance. All signs need to be noted; some may be danger signs.

Among the most easily read symptoms are failure to learn in keeping with ability to learn and concrete items of malbehavior, particularly aggressive malbehavior. Such behavior items include temper tantrums, resistance to authority, refusal to cooperate, bullying or hurting others, cruelty to animals, truancy, stealing, destroying property, cheating, lying, sex misconduct, and other forms of unruly behavior.

Not so easy to detect as the above-named symptoms are fears expressed through obsessions, compulsions, phobias, inhibitions, anxieties, and worries; emotional immaturity; extreme sensitiveness; great timidity; and daydreaming. Some daydreaming, however, is normal and desirable.

Not difficult to detect but often unnoticed are signs which indicate that a student has developed a low opinion of his own worth and is suffering from feelings of inferiority and insecurity. They include jealousy, insatiable craving for affection, self-centeredness, and seclusiveness. A student may be showing that he is socially and emotionally immature, or he may be revealing his doubt regarding his personal worth when he is too docile and too easily rebuked, when he shows that he is very much afraid of not being wanted, or when he asks too frequently for advice, instructions, or confirmation.

Nervous habits should be considered for their possible implications in terms of physical and mental health. These indicators include stuttering, facial tics and other muscle twitching, fingernail biting, thumbsucking, excessive restlessness while sitting, chronic fatigue, dizzy spells, frequent headaches, eyestrain, sleeplessness, and walking or talking while asleep. Such symptoms may be produced by physical causes or may be the student's reactions to some intolerable condition. In either case he needs help.

Torgerson's check list or behavior inventory (referred to in an earlier chapter) is useful for helping teachers to identify symptoms of withdrawal behavior, as well as those of aggression. In the section under "social behavior" 50 items are listed, of which the first 25 reflect aggressive behavior and the second 25 recessive or withdrawal behavior. These items are as follows: [5]

[5] Theodore L. Torgerson, *Studying Children: Diagnostic and Remedial Procedures in Teaching*, pp. 70–75. New York: Holt, Rinehart and Winston, Inc., 1947.

1. Angers easily
2. Temper tantrums
3. Uncooperative
4. Sex irregularities
5. Uncontrolled bladder or bowels
6. Enuresis (bed wetting)
7. Truancy, unexcused absences
8. Cheats
9. Resents correction
10. Destructive
11. Overcritical of others
12. Irresponsible
13. Impudent, defiant
14. Quarrelsome
15. Cruel to animals
16. Irritable
17. Belligerent, bossy
18. Bully
19. Vindictive
20. Steals
21. Dishonest, untruthful
22. Marked change in personality
23. Negativistic
24. Runs away from home
25. Seeks attention

26. Overconscientious
27. Emotionally inadequate
28. Procrastinates
29. Whines
30. Pessimistic
31. Suspicious
32. Plays by himself
33. Avoids others, unfriendly
34. Shunned by others
35. Over-religious
36. Daydreams, preoccupied
37. Plays with younger children
38. Physical coward
39. Selfish
40. Feigns illness
41. Too impulsive
42. Depressed
43. Overdependent
44. Sullen
45. Nervous tensions, tics
46. Bites fingernails
47. Fearful, timid, shy
48. Worries
49. Jealous
50. Cries easily

Screening. Whereas mentally retarded students are usually identified and screened for special assistance through individual psychological examinations administered by specialists, the socially and emotionally maladjusted are seldom screened so carefully. As a result, some capable students are classified as mentally retarded. They are so disturbed emotionally that they do poorly on tests and in classwork. Careful screening might reveal the real reason for their educational retardation.

The techniques used for screening the emotionally handicapped include sociometric procedures, group personality inventories, and observations reported through rating scales, anecdotal reports, and summary statements. However, regular, systematic use is not often reported. The usual practice is for a teacher to report a student's apparent need of assistance to the principal, counselor, or school psychologist. Decisions regarding which students should receive special help are then made largely on the basis of personal opinion and the availability of resources.

Some school systems are trying to improve the situation through research study in this area. During the 1950s, for example, two experimental programs were undertaken in California for the prevention of personality and behavior disorders in school children.[6] In both programs

---

[6] Eli M. Bower et al., *A Process for Early Identification of Emotionally Disturbed Children.* Sacramento: State Department of Education, 1958; Nadine M. Lambert and

the students who were given special help were systematically screened through the use of three rating instruments—teacher ratings, self-ratings, and peer ratings.[7] In one study individual psychological tests, administered by clinical psychologists, were also used in screening elementary school pupils.

The case conference is sometimes reported for screening purposes, particularly when several schools use the same special resources. Representatives of these schools periodically meet in conference to decide, on the basis of case-study data, which students are to receive special help.

PREVENTION THROUGH PROMOTION OF MENTAL HEALTH

Basic Requirements. Certain conditions are assumed essential for fostering mental health in the schools. Among them are (1) a school environment conducive to good emotional growth, (2) curriculum content and teaching methods congruent with the needs of students at successive stages of development, and (3) good student-teacher relations. Achievement of these conditions may be difficult because of obstacles encountered in the school, the community, and the culture.

Perhaps the greatest obstacle encountered in the school is the teacher who is inadequately prepared or insufficiently skilled to provide the type of education that contributes maximally to the development of integrating relationships. Teacher discouragement is another barrier. Many well-prepared, competent teachers are overwhelmed by having to play too many roles and the schools' having, as Bower[8] says, to educate "all the children of all the parents all the time."

The typical community expects its schools to educate all children enrolled in them and expects almost all children of certain ages to be enrolled. To provide programs and practices that are appropriate to the capacity, interests, drives, motivations, and developmental needs of all students, the schools have to perform a gigantic task. When a community expects its schools to set high standards for all students or to set approximately the same standards for all at the same grade level, the task becomes impossible.

Education that is appropriate for some students is inappropriate for others. Inappropriate education creates emotional problems. Emotional problems create learning difficulties. Learning difficulties often lead to failure and withdrawal from school.

Some boys' and girls' emotional problems stem from trouble in

---

Eli M. Bower, *Technical Report on In-school Screenings of Children with Emotional Handicaps*. Princeton, N.J.: Educational Testing Service, 1961.

[7] Two of the instruments are described in this book. One, *Thinking about Yourself*, is described in Chap. 3; and the other, *The Class Play*, in Chap. 11.

[8] Eli M. Bower, "Primary Prevention in a School Setting," in Caplan (ed.), *op. cit.*, p. 359.

the home. It may be a parent's way of dealing with the child or a parent's projecting onto the child his (or her) fears, hopes, or goals. Solution to the child's problem may seem to lie in intervention, but in our culture intervening in family matters is generally viewed as a violation of the rights to privacy. The state of affairs in the home has to be quite bad before school psychologists, counselors, social workers, or law officers may intervene to save a child from psychological or physical mistreatment.

Improving School Social Climate. Anything done to improve the classroom environment improves, of course, the social climate in the school at large. The faculty and staff assist further when they help students learn to respect and to enjoy different kinds of people and to accept individuals by virtue of their particular contributions rather than because of socioeconomic status, academic achievement, personal appearance, or the like. They do this through their own warm, friendly acceptance of different kinds of students and through encouraging a friendly give-and-take between student and student and between students and faculty.

The school atmosphere that is conducive to good personal development is one that is friendly and free of rivalry, hostility, and tension. Unfortunately, the nonclass activity program is at times a principal source of rivalry, frustration, and tension, whereas it should be a principal means for enriching school life and thereby helping to reduce tension. To fulfill its purposes, the program must be so planned and administered that opportunity for easy participation is afforded to students of low socioeconomic status, low IQ's, and little special talent as well as to students who come from the upper socioeconomic levels, who have high IQ's, and who are well endowed with special talents. The program should be student-centered rather than activity-centered. If it is, it will be evaluated in terms of its effects upon individuals rather than in terms of success in the activity—a game, dramatic or musical production, handicraft, or the like.

Recreation may not be able to do away with emotional handicaps or to cure delinquency, but it can do much to help prevent them. A free-time activity program, for example, can help the predelinquent to avoid developing the value system of the delinquent by providing him the status-gaining and ego-developing experiences that make it unnecessary for him to seek status in areas where adult restrictions are minimal and adult norms are ignored.

Providing students an opportunity to have hot lunches at a minimum cost in an uncrowded place is a boost to student morale. Providing students sufficient time to go through the cafeteria line, select their food, and eat unhurriedly is also important. Providing students a place in which to socialize after eating and before returning to class is to many students even more important. Many problems in the way of undesirable behavior that occur on and off the school grounds during lunch periods arise because students have nothing to do after eating except to stand around and wait to be summoned back to classes. They would like to dance, to play games, and to watch others dance and play while they chat with their friends; but in many schools students do not have a place in which to do such things or the minimum equipment needed. Shortening the lunch period until students have barely enough time to eat is not the answer, however. Including a lunchtime recreation program in the student activity program is a better answer.

Education in Human Relations. Much maladjustment is due to personal stress caused by faulty interpersonal relations. Hence, some schools provide for special education in human relations through units offered in "regular courses" or through courses organized specifically for this purpose. Such units and courses are designed to help students to understand themselves and others and to develop skill in interpersonal relations. Experience indicates that for the human relations class to be an effective means for promoting mental health, the focus has to be upon easy communication, democratic leadership, and an atmosphere of understanding and acceptance.

Some such human relations classes closely approach group counseling. In the Forest Hill Village project,[9] for example, students in grades 4 through 12 were given "a rather special experience" in free discussion. One hour a week under the leadership of a specially trained teacher the students could discuss anything they wished. The teacher opened each session with something like "Well, where shall we begin?"

> After that, the role of the teacher or staff member lay largely in listening, no matter whether the remark was ostensibly addressed from child to teacher or from child to child. Rare interventions would occur if one child's statement needed clarifying for another or if a summary of what had been said seemed to be necessary to dispel confusion. Sometimes, acting upon the expressed or inferred desire of the children, the teacher would note on the blackboard points that had been made. Otherwise, the teacher was to be as much as possible a warm and living presence, but interested only in watching a good game—a "good game" being one in which everybody got a chance to say whatever he wanted.... Under no circumstances was approval or disapproval of an act reported or of a statement made to be shown.[10]

SOME MEANS FOR SPECIAL ASSISTANCE

Counseling. In secondary schools and colleges, students who seem socially and emotionally maladjusted are usually referred first to a counselor. The counseling offered generally involves establishing an accepting, per-

---

[9] John A. Seeley, "The Forest Hill Village 'Human Relations Classes,'" *Personnel and Guidance Journal,* 1959, 37:424–434.

[10] *Ibid.,* p. 428.

missive relationship with the student to help him gain relief from tension through a ventilation of feelings. Talking about how he feels, what he wants, and why he feels and acts as he does may help him to understand his problem and perceive various courses open to him in relation to his goals or wants.

The manner in which a student is referred to a counselor may determine in a large measure the extent to which counseling will help him. It is not likely to be very helpful if the student is referred in a rejecting or a punitive manner as, for example, when he is sent to the counselor as a "discipline case." No threat should be made or implied. For instance, a student should not be given the choice of seeing a counselor or reporting to "detention study hall," as is frequently done in one high school. Nor should he be warned that he will have to drop a course unless he sees the counselor. When a student associates referral with punishment or rejection he becomes anxious or hostile and so may resist all efforts to help him.

Referral should not be made in a way that increases anxiety. To make a student feel that his case is serious can increase the burden of sensitiveness and anxiety that he may already be carrying. Nor should the person making the referral commit the counselor to specific action. He should not, for example, suggest that the student see the counselor "about taking some tests" or recommend that he ask the counselor "to take up" some matter with a parent or a teacher.

Referral should be warm and friendly. Instead of telling a student to see "a counselor," the person making the referral should suggest that he see a counselor mentioned by name or that he see one of two or three named. He would then do well to tell the student where the counselor may be found, explain that he (or she) is interested in helping students with their problems and is professionally educated and employed for this purpose. The teacher may further personalize the referral service by offering, if practical, to go with the student to the counselor's office to introduce the two, or by telephoning the counselor in the student's presence. Telephone referrals are not so easily made, however, in secondary schools as in colleges because of limited telephone facilities.

Emotionally handicapped students are among the most important counseling cases. They are also among the most difficult. They ordinarily require more counseling time than other counselees. If a case is so serious that it requires an inordinate amount of time or lies beyond the counselor's skill and understanding, the student should be referred to a mental health clinic (school or nonschool).

Group Counseling. Selected students may be given counseling in groups. The groups should be small (desirably from six to ten members) and balanced in terms of aggressive and passive members. The group may meet one, two, or three times a week.

In group counseling students receive acceptance, assurance, and support from one another, as well as from the counselor. They have a therapeutic effect on each other as they begin to identify with one another and to become increasingly aware of the similarities in their problems and concerns. As feelings of friendliness, freedom, and unity increase, tensions ease, negative feelings decline, and positive feelings gain strength.

Adolescents ordinarily talk easily together even when they are not very well acquainted. In expressing their views, they activate one another. At times they do not hesitate to break through one another's protective barriers. One, for example, will hoot good-naturedly at another's rationalization. A moment later he may flush but also grin when some member calls attention to one of his self-deceptions. Yet when participation becomes too difficult because talk bears too heavily on points that hurt, the student finds it easy to withdraw into his own thoughts. But he is not likely to take himself out of the situation. He does not go away but remains. Before long he may be again taking part even though he is only listening in silence.

The counselor's major function is to help create a friendly atmosphere in which the students can explore common problems and relationships. By listening attentively, he conveys understanding and acceptance and thereby helps the students to express their feelings and to air their worries and grievances. He aids catharsis and the development of insight by letting reassurance, analysis, and interpretation come from the group. Through occasional questions and comments he may aid clarification of feelings. By encouraging students to get things off their chests, he makes it easy for them to break through their anxieties. As the talk proceeds, the students will usually start taking down their ego defenses and may overcome their inhibitions and discuss things that they ordinarily find too embarrassing to talk about or that they had previously considered "forbidden topics."

As the discussion continues, the sharing widens and deepens. Information and ideas, as well as feelings and points of view, are shared. The talk tends to be experience-centered, and some members learn from the experience of the others. As the group counselees work out their feelings, explore their thoughts, and try out ideas together, some gain insight regarding their behavior. They begin to develop new attitudes and understandings, to perceive the nature of some of their problems, to accept responsibility for some consequences of their behavior, and to learn new ways of coping with some difficulties.

Adjustment Class. A student may be so disturbed and so disturbing to others that he must be taken from his regular class and put into the type of special group that is often called an "adjustment class." If the class is used largely for discipline purposes and is little more than a detention center, it obviously cannot function as a therapy group. Here we are concerned only with the use of the class for therapy or rehabilitation purposes. The adjustment class provides students a learning and therapeutic experience in a friendly environment that is sheltered from peer conflicts and the usual classroom pressures. The students receive instruction and guidance geared to their individual interests, motivations, and abilities. Group discussions and private talks with the teacher help them to resolve their conflicts and self-doubts and to gain understanding in some psychological areas.

In some elementary schools adjustment class work with students is accompanied by group work with their parents. In the Long Beach Unified School District, for example, parents participate through meetings held on school time every other week. These meetings are directed toward helping the parents to understand and appreciate themselves as well as to help them understand and appreciate the nature of child development and the roles that they play in their children's lives.

To fulfill well its functions, the class has to be small—eight to fifteen members. In some schools the number of students screened for such a class is so small that one group may serve two or more schools. In other schools the number of students in need of such placement may be so large that more than one class is needed. Students placed in the class should be able to profit from the experience. Unless the class is organized specifically for the mentally retarded, the members should be of normal intelligence and not so disturbed that they can be classed as incipient psychotics.

The teacher needs assistance from a mental health consultant, especially if he does not have special education in working with the emotionally disturbed. He should be carefully selected on the basis of interest in the work, ability to establish a therapeutic relationship with young people, skill in individualizing instruction, and ability to provide remedial instruction in the basic areas. He also needs to be able to direct a varied, flexible program.

The program provided in high schools that cooperated in the California experimental program with emotionally handicapped students is described in one report as follows: [11]

> [It] usually consists of functional, integrated units based on real life needs which incorporate experience in better use of language, mathematics, and other basic educational skills. Future employment, recreational, and human relations problems are also stressed. In addition, the special teacher may spend additional time with selected students in remedial work. The teacher attempts to find an educational anchor in each student from which he can sustain interest and perhaps broaden the student's educational horizon. The program is essentially aimed at improving the edu-

[11] Nadine Lambert et al., *The Emotionally Handicapped Child in the School: A Research Program in the Prevention of Personality and Behavior Disorders in Children.* Sacramento: California State Department of Education, 1959.

cational level of the student. The teacher's relationship to the mental health consultant and the psychological staff is essentially one of translating clinical insights about the emotional problems of students into classroom management and educational procedures.

Some interesting experimental work has been done with the special guidance class at the Washington Junior High School in Pasadena, Calif. Its unusual success is due to able teachers, skilled leadership, administrative support, and faculty cooperation based on faculty understanding and acceptance of the project.

Currently the program is more structured and the situation less permissive than when the class was first organized. The room continues to be equipped with comfortable chairs and tables; but radio, television, and record player have been removed. The students still find games on the shelves along with the reading materials, but they now find education games rather than play games.

The teacher accepts a student's not working, but he encourages students who seem inclined to work to translate such inclinations into action. The pressure to change, however, must come from the student, not the teacher. A newcomer finds that he may join students who are working or, if he prefers, he can do nothing. Some, on first entering the class, find pleasure in doing nothing more strenuous than kicking their heels in the air. They may look with pity and even scorn at the class members who are working alone or with the help of others. They smile broadly at the "regular students" who look in on them as they pass outside the windows on their way to gym.

Before long, however, what at first looked like a bit of paradise begins to look more like a bear trap. Being normal people, these students feel a strong drive toward normalcy and health. They know that they are not doing what boys and girls normally do at school. School is a work situation. Students go to school to study and to learn, not to pass the time loafing, talking, and laughing. They begin to feel pressure from within. The student who last week grinned at the window passers may now, when he hears the bell for classes to change, squat under a window where passersby cannot see him.

Because some students are in the group for only one period, the teacher several times a day has the students come together in a circle for ten or fifteen minutes of "group therapy"—unstructured discussion of problems, academic and personal. These group sessions help to strengthen the growing desire to be "regular students." When the inner pressure is sufficiently strong, a student may ask permission to get a textbook from his locker or to see a teacher about the classwork that he is missing. When he starts coming to the special class with books and assignments or in some other way shows that he is ready to start working, he finds that the teacher is ready and able to help him with his studies. The teacher encourages the students to turn in written assignments to the teachers whose classes they are missing. He knows that this helps to keep the students motivated and that it also strengthens a student's rapport with his teachers.

As the teacher helps the students with their studies, he tries to diagnose their learning difficulties. Many, he finds, need remedial instruction, particularly in reading and mathematics. He provides such instruction. Also, he regularly confers with the teachers of his class members so that, when a student returns to his regular class, he will not be so far behind the other students that he becomes discouraged and begins acting out his frustration in class.

A student is assigned to the special guidance class for a minimum period of two weeks, but this is too short a time for most students to receive the help needed. Most stay in the group from four to six weeks. During the 1960–1961 school year, for example, the average stay of the 32 students assigned to the group was twenty-nine days. All but four of these students returned to their regular classes before the end of the year. There was only one recidivist. He came back voluntarily.

That year the teacher was a man who believes strongly in early intervention. He feels that misbehavior in class may be evidence of severe frustration or a symptom of maladjustment. Because the school administration shares this view, ready consent was given to the teacher's request that students referred to the assistant principal for misconduct in class should be assigned to the special class on a temporary basis. The number of such referrals to the special group was sufficiently small to permit the group to stay within the limit set for it—12 students. Usually such a student needed to stay in the group only three or four days. Few of these "special assignees" were again referred to the assistant principal for misbehavior.

Activity Group Therapy. The group therapy techniques developed by Slavson [12] can be used in modified form in school settings. This was done, for example, in the Willowbrook School District (California).[13] Emotionally disturbed boys from four elementary schools were brought together once a week for a two-hour special class, called an "activity club." Third-, fourth-, and fifth-grade boys were selected so that every boy would have at least two years in the program before entering junior high school. The groups were balanced in terms of outgoing, aggressive children and passive, inhibited ones. Each club included Negroes, Mexicans, and Caucasians. They included educationally retarded students but not the mentally retarded.

[12] S. R. Slavson, *The Practice of Group Therapy.* New York: International Universities Press, Inc., 1947. The therapy method is represented in the film *Activity Group Therapy* (50 min.). New York: Columbia University Press, 1950.

[13] John W. Howe, "Special Part-time Classes for Emotionally Disturbed Children in a Regular Elementary School," *The School Counselor,* 1958, 5:26–33.

The club sessions were scheduled at the end of the school day so that hyperactive students would not have to adjust to classroom routine immediately after being in the highly permissive, almost laissez-faire club situation. The clubrooms were equipped with a one-way vision screen (set high in the wall and made to look like a ventilator covering), simple furnishings, games, woodworking tools, and such construction materials as scrap lumber, scrap sheet metal, clay, crayons, paper, and paints.

The three teachers who served as club leaders had special psychological training and counseling experience. They received consultative help from a psychiatrist furnished by the State Department of Mental Hygiene. They were highly permissive in their relations with the children and played very passive roles. They gave little or no direction, permitting the boys to select and structure their play activities as they wished. When, however, restlessness became high, the teachers did manipulate the situation by placing where the children could see them such semistructured materials as precut boards and copper sheets ready for tooling.

A careful study was made of each boy before and after the therapy experience. The teachers in charge of the club groups kept detailed records of their observations. The findings on the first experimental use of the activity groups showed, among other things, that the withdrawn boys had gained in confidence and activity and that the hyperactive ones had become less hostile and more inclined to express their aggressiveness in good-natured horseplay than in fighting. The boys' "regular teachers" reported similar behavior changes in the classroom.

Remedial Education. The emotionally handicapped child is extremely sensitive regarding his inadequacies. Often the inadequacies are in the basic skills and in particular the arithmetic and reading skills. The California study [14] of emotionally handicapped children, for example, showed that with respect to reading and arithmetic achievement "the higher the school grade, the greater the difference between the emotionally disturbed child and the rest of the class." Hence, helping emotionally handicapped students often involves providing remedial education. In the Pasadena project, described above, it was early discovered that the teacher assigned to the "social adjustment class" had to be someone skilled in remedial instruction.

Emotional problems are often the reasons for learning difficulties. As Rabinovitch [15] stresses, students faced with conflicts may be so preoccupied with their problems in the classroom that attention, concentra-

[14] Eli M. Bower, "A Process for Identifying Disturbed Children," in James F. Magary and John R. Eichorn (eds.), *The Exceptional Child: A Book of Readings*, p. 348. New York: Holt, Rinehart and Winston, Inc., 1960.

[15] Ralph D. Rabinovitch, "Reading and Learning Disabilities," in Silvano Arieti (ed.), *American Handbook of Psychiatry*, vol. I, pp. 860–862. New York: Basic Books, Inc., Publishers, 1959.

tion, and memory are seriously affected and impair learning. The student broods. His mind wanders. He cannot study. He may be too upset to assimilate what he is taught or to apply what he does assimilate. As he gets further and further behind in his classwork, he feels more and more inadequate. Depression may lead to inertia and withdrawal. The student may find himself caught in a vicious circle of emotional problems creating learning difficulties which in turn produce other emotional problems.

Reading is the most common area of difficulty for both secondary and elementary school students. According to Rabinovitch,[16] more than 10 per cent of the American students "are reading so inadequately for their grade placement that their total adjustment is impaired." Students who are seriously deficient in reading usually feel uncomfortably different. By the time a student who is seriously retarded in reading reaches high school, the cause of the retardation has most likely become obscure. It is difficult to determine whether his disability is organ-centered (visual defect, intellectual defect, cerebral disrhythmia) or school-centered (poor reading instruction) or child-centered (emotional problems) or family-centered (lack of interest and of good reading materials in the home). While the cause may be obscure, the fact of retardation is not. His teachers may consider his case hopeless. And he may feel that not being able to read in high school "is akin to being adrift in mid-Pacific without oar, sail, or motor." [17]

Because the emotional problems may result more from the secondary effects of being a nonreader than from the primary causes of the reading disability, the remedial reading teacher has to help the student with his emotional problems as well as help him to progress in reading. A frontal attack on the reading problem may, however, be the best approach because success in reading may help the student to function effectively as a person as well as help him to achieve scholastically. An oblique attack may have to be made on some factors inherent in the disability, such as poor interpersonal relations in the family. For example, a student may feel a strong need to be a poor reader in order to shame (punish) his parents who, he believes, love him only when he succeeds and rejects him when he fails.

MANIPULATING THE ENVIRONMENT

Sometimes an emotionally disturbed child is best helped through an environmental change. Therapy may involve a change in his teacher, study program, school, or even place of residence.

Change in Teachers. Some school workers believe that a student should never be permitted to change from one teacher to another, that he should

---

[16] *Ibid.,* p. 864.

[17] Lambert et al., *op. cit.,* p. 54.

be forced to get along with the ones to whom assigned. It is true that some students think of the counselor as someone who makes life easy for students by helping them to get out of trouble, to get around rules, and to avoid meeting disagreeable requirements. It is also true that some teachers do not really try to work with "difficult cases" and often ask that such students be taken out of their classes and put in the classes of other teachers who are willing to work with such students and may already have more than their share of "difficult cases." Counselors try to help such students and such teachers make better adjustments to the situations. At times, however, a change in teachers is desirable for the sake of the student or the teacher or both.

It is not likely that we shall ever have the utopian situation in which all teachers understand and accept all students. When assignments prove definitely faulty, we must recognize this fact and arrange a change in teachers in spite of the criticisms that may be expressed because of our doing so. In most schools there is at least one teacher who seems able to understand all boys and girls and able to bring out the best in the worst of them. In his homeroom and classes, "problem students" seem able to relax and willing to try to work. Usually such a teacher is willing to assume special responsibility for the instruction and guidance of difficult cases because he is genuinely interested in trying to help them. To change a student who is making a poor adjustment in school to the homeroom or class of such a teacher can be an important step in the treatment of the case.

Change in Program of Studies. Many students cease to be academic misfits or behavior problems when they change to programs of studies that are appropriate for their patterns of interests and abilities. A student may be following a program that is inappropriate because the work is too difficult for one of his ability, or because he does not have the needed background in the way of information and skills, or because the work is too easy and does not provide sufficient challenge, or because he has little interest in learning the things he is asked to learn. In short, the student cannot do the work, or he finds it uninteresting because too easy or because he "can't see any use in it."

Taking a slow learner out of an academic subject class and giving him another period of shopwork or her another period of home economics is not the way to provide an appropriate curriculum for slow learners. These students need to study English, civics, science, and mathematics also. Emphasis in such classes for slow learners should be, however, upon practical learning rather than theoretical knowledge and upon experiences closely related to homelife, civic activities, interpersonal relations, free-time activities, and job objectives. If the teachers cannot provide individualized instruction in their classes so that slow learners and students deficient in the basic skills are not pressed to move more rapidly than they are able, then remedial and practical courses in the major subject areas should be provided in addition to the "regular" ones.

Work experience programs help to meet the needs of both the low-interest and the low-ability students. They help to hold in school many boys and girls who might otherwise drop out because of failure in schoolwork, the desire or the need to earn money, or some similar reason. In some schools adjustment classes have been integrated with work experience programs. Dillon [18] once summarized the values of combining school and work as follows:

> The educational value of this type of work experience is not confined solely to actual skills acquired on the job but also includes the experience of accepting responsibility, or working with adults and, for some, of replacing a sense of failure with a sense of achievement and success. In many cases, the school work program provides the concrete situation in which the student can work out his social adjustment and prepares him to handle his problems more intelligently when he leaves school than does the usual school curriculum. Such programs offer a possibility of prolonging the period of education and, at the same time, of developing greater mental or social maturity where this is needed for the adjustment of the individual.

Change in Schools. Treatment of the academic misfit or some other case of maladjustment may be aided by a change in schools. If the change involves taking the student away from his best friends and the change is made against his will, the results may be more negative than positive. If the move is made to get him away from the detrimental influence of certain companions or away from other harmful forces that the student seems unable to combat, the move may be effective if combined with counseling and if a special effort is made to help him find a secure place in the new school as soon as possible. If the change is made because the new school offers the student a more appropriate curriculum or can provide him certain needed experiences that are not available in his present school and if the student understands the reason for the transfer, accepts it, and is willing to make the change, the move may have high value.

In the Los Angeles City Schools transfers are available for students who make very poor adjustment in high school—junior, senior, or four-year high school. A student may attend as many as two or three schools if changing schools seems to help him. If further assistance seems needed through a change of schools, the student may then be sent to one of the seven special schools. At the beginning it was decided that such schools should not be coeducational because the problems of many adolescents center around sex. Later, however, it was decided that some students might best work out their adjustment problems in a mixed group situa-

---

[18] Harold J. Dillon, *Work Experience in Secondary Education*, p. 89. New York: National Child Labor Committee, 1946.

tion, and so a coeducational special school was added to the three for boys and the three for girls.

These schools are designed to provide therapeutic environments and individualized programs for students who are seriously disturbed but nonpsychotic. If a student gives evidence of being mentally ill, he is referred to another agency for diagnosis, treatment, and placement. Although almost all students assigned to the special schools are of normal intelligence, most are seriously retarded academically. They have been under so much emotional pressure that apparently they have not been able to learn. Furthermore, some have been so frequently reprimanded, suspended, and punished in other ways for not learning and for trying to escape their school problems through truancy that they have developed a strong hatred for school and adult authority.

Hence, in the special schools the students experience considerably more permissiveness and freedom than students ordinarily know at school. They receive much special attention in the form of sympathy, understanding listening, recognition of effort, praise for achievement, remembrance of birthdays, occasional parties, and the like. In some instances the school may even have to take steps to see that proper provision is made for meeting a student's need for adequate food and clothing as well as his need for adequate attention and affection.

Classes are kept small (usually from 10 to 12 members), and there is considerable flexibility in both curriculum content and teaching methods. In general, the emphasis is upon remedial instruction and vocational courses. The content, however, is kept sufficiently similar to that of the programs to which the students will return for them to avoid feeling handicapped later in the regular school situation. A student is expected to stay in the special school for at least one semester. Some need to remain a year or longer in order to learn new ways of behaving, to develop new attitudes, and to assimilate new concepts.

Change in Place of Residence. Because a student's home situation is having an adverse effect upon his development or is depriving him of opportunity for good development, the transplanting of a student from one residence situation to another is desirable at times. Providing this type of treatment is, however, usually the function of social workers and nonschool agencies. Nevertheless, school people are sometimes directly or indirectly involved in its provision. The teachers are not few, for example, who have made places in their own homes for students who needed homes or a change in homes. Also, many students, through the help of some interested teacher or counselor, have moved into boarding homes so that they may finish school or live more normal and happy lives than is possible in their own homes.

At times arrangements are made for a student to live in a boarding home (where he works for room and board, usually) during the school days and at his own home during the weekends. Because of the location of his home or for some other reason, living full time in his own home does not permit him to participate sufficiently in student and community life or prevents his taking advantage of certain opportunities important to achievement of educational and vocational plans. In such cases the parents usually cooperate to make the two-home arrangement a successful one. They appreciate the advantages of the arrangement, want to do what seems best for their children, take pride in their children's ambitions and achievements, and share their hopes for the future.

In some other cases the boarding home arrangement is considered desirable because the students are not happy at home—the parents do not share their interest in further education and may even want them to quit school and go to work as soon as they are legally free to do so. The parents may be unwilling to help their children continue in school by helping them to meet the cost of clothes and supplies not provided by the state. They are willing for their children to live elsewhere because they think that they should earn their room and board, that it is a good experience for young people. They may wish their children to return home for the weekends because they want them to help at home, on the farm, or in some other work situation as well as because they are genuinely fond of their sons and daughters and want them at home part of the time. These parents do not reject their children, only their children's plans. They may reject the plans primarily because of their own experiences as young people.

Then there are the extreme cases—the students who are rejected, exploited, and even abused by their parents and the students whose homes are sources of psychological contagion. Helping these students through environmental treatment is generally the work of social service agencies and the courts, but school people are often instrumental in initiating such treatment as well as in helping to make it effective.

Environmental treatment may be employed in residence schools when arrangements are made for a student to move from one residence hall to another, from one part of a hall to another part, from one room to another room in the same part of the hall, from home to boarding home or residence hall, or vice versa. Sometimes a change in roommates is the only change needed in the environment.

TEACHER DEVELOPMENT

The emphasis in working with emotionally handicapped children is shifting from remediation or rehabilitation to early intervention and prevention. Hence, efforts are being directed toward helping teachers to increase their understanding of child development and behavior and of the scientific method of arriving at judgments regarding behavior.

Traditional inservice education procedures, such as workshops or institutes that feature talks by "visiting experts," are often replaced or supplemented with methods that put the teacher more in the role of active participant as speaker or contributor than of passive recipient or listener. Three such methods are the case conference, the child-study program, and mental health consultation. Because an earlier chapter is devoted to the case conference, it is not considered here.

Child-study Programs. The child-study programs are largely an outgrowth of a project begun in 1939 under the auspices of the Commission on Teacher Education of the American Council on Education. In this project 14 groups experimented with various ways of helping teachers learn to observe child behavior, to interpret it in terms of child-development principles, and to work out implications for classroom work.

Many current child-study programs are directly or indirectly sponsored by the Institute for Child Study of the University of Maryland under the leadership of Daniel A. Prescott, who was a leader in the Commission on Teacher Education project. The operational purpose of the program is development of clinically oriented teachers. As Prescott [19] says, the understanding needed by teachers to facilitate learning and good development does not require the depth of the psychotherapist's understanding, but it does require the kind of understanding that characterizes the clinical approach.

Participation in a study group is voluntary and the work informal and relatively unstructured. Groups range in size from 8 to 15 members. They generally meet two hours every other week throughout the school year. A group may be made up of teachers from the same school or from different schools. They may teach at the same or at different grade levels. The groups are usually organized in the spring so that during the summer the leaders may receive special help through leadership workshops. Special meetings are also provided for the leaders at other times during the year. Ordinarily a group is visited three times a year by a consultant from the University of Maryland.

Each member makes a careful longitudinal study of at least one student. He gathers his data from school records, conferences with teachers and parents, visits to the home and neighborhood, the student's creative productions (writings, artwork, craftwork, etc.) and observations of the student in as many different situations as possible. As he gathers his data, he notes recurring patterns of behavior and tries to formulate hypotheses regarding the reasons for certain developments. Periodically he reports to his group and submits for their criticism and evaluation some of his observation records, interpretations, and hypotheses. "Strong emphasis is given to the importance of living by a strict code of professional ethics

[19] Bernard Peck and Daniel A. Prescott, "The Program at the Institute for Child Study, the University of Maryland," *Personnel and Guidance Journal*, 1959, 37:115.

so that the confidential nature of the data compiled about each child will be preserved." [20]

Mental Health Consultation. In some schools teachers are able to consult someone more highly educated than they regarding the behavior of disturbed or disturbing students. The most common type of consultation is that in which a student is sent to a school psychologist or counselor for assessment and treatment. The consultant may or may not confer with the consultee (teacher). Too often, communication is very brief and only in the form of a short written report or memorandum. The teacher may have little opportunity to seek elaboration or to discuss specific points with the consultant.

Sometimes consultation involves collaboration. Then the consultant and the consultee work with the student concurrently. While they may work more or less independently, they share responsibility for study and treatment of the case. A student, for example, may go to the teacher for remedial reading and to the specialist for counseling. Good communication in this type of consultation is obviously very important.

In relatively recent years another type of consultation—mental health consultation—has been introduced in some schools. It is an interaction process in which teacher development is the primary goal. The consultant uses the professional relationship, as well as his professional knowledge, to help the teacher. This type of consultation is probably best known as developed at the Harvard School of Public Health and explained in the teachings of Caplan,[21] who describes the objective as follows:

> In the interaction the consultant attempts to help the consultee solve a mental health problem of his client or clients within the framework of his usual professional functioning. The process is designed so that while help is being given to the consultee in dealing with the presenting problem, he is also being educated in order that he will be able in the future to handle similar problems in the same or other clients in a more effective manner than in the past.

Caplan finds that different teachers and even different schools have characteristic "sore spots" to which they are excessively sensitive and which they handle with less than their usual skill. Hence, certain types of problems are repeatedly referred. The identity of the students changes, but the core problems are essentially the same. The main precipitating factor in the referral of these cases is the successive stimulation of the teacher's (or school's) "segmental problems": [22]

[20] *Ibid.*, p. 117.
[21] Gerald Caplan, *Concepts of Mental Health and Consultation*, p. 187. Washington, D.C.: Government Printing Office, 1959.
[22] *Ibid.*, p. 190.

In a school, for instance, objective examination of a "problem child" referred for consultation will often reveal no important disturbance in the child, who has to be labeled "troubling" to the teacher rather than "troubled" in himself. If the child is removed to another classroom and to a teacher who is not sensitive in that particular way, the difficulty will cease. In the absence of consultation, however, the first teacher will very often refer some other child with the same problem, either immediately or in the not too distant future.

Receiving emotional support through the professional relationship, as well as talking about the problem with a specialist, helps a teacher to view students' problems objectively. Sensitively aware of the personal implications of the discussion, the consultant does not take up the teacher's problems directly or explicitly. He talks about them only in relation to the student's problem.

Such corrective emotional experience may often lead to localized personality development. It may also have a stable carryover in the consultee's future professional functioning. So when he deals with clients with this particular difficulty, he may be able to use himself efficiently, instead of inefficiently. This enhanced use of the self is shown in successful cases by an increased human warmth and emotional closeness as well as by a more reality based perception in dealing with clients.[23]

In mental health consultation a member of one profession is trying to help members of another profession. It is a peer relationship between persons of different professions. When the consultant is a psychiatrist, he does not try to get the teacher to view a problem from a psychiatrist's point of view or to work out the solution in the way that a psychiatrist might. He seeks, instead, to use his background in the area of human relations to help the teacher make good use of his own background of educational experience in assisting students with their problems. The consultant knows that the solutions must be teacher solutions.

Caplan opposes a mental health consultant's directly helping a teacher with his personal problems. In his opinion, if a teacher's emotional problems are permitted to obtrude, the teacher becomes self-oriented rather than task-oriented. When the teacher tries to relate his problem to that of the student, the consultant shifts the focus back to the student by saying something like, "I am sure the fact that you once had a similar problem helps you to understand how the student may feel. But how can we help him? What do we know that can give us some clue regarding the most appropriate action?"

Not all mental health consultants agree with Caplan that consultation, whether with groups or individuals, should be kept focused on clients rather than consultees. The group procedures used, for example,

[23] *Ibid.*, p. 191.

in the Palos Verdes (Calif.) School District are not unlike those of group counseling: [24]

> The scope of the problem may be related to any aspect of the participant's job role. It may relate to authority figures, colleagues, subordinates, or to the consultee's own self-image in his role as a teacher, supervisor, consultant, or administrator. The other participants offer suggestions, and ask questions to elicit information which might serve to clarify the problem. The consultant asks only occasional questions to focus on some particular point.... The participants are assured that the contents of the sessions are confidential and cannot be used either to evaluate, promote, or remove from office any member of the group.

Usually persons from different authority levels do not work together in the same consultation group. Supervisors, for example, are excluded from teachers' groups. Groups are organized specifically for supervisors, for administrators, for counselors, etc.

It is generally agreed that the consultant should not be a part of the administrative hierarchy of the school. He should be perceived as an authority figure but on the basis of his professional competence, not hierarchical rank. Perceiving the consultant as an authority or a superego figure and yet finding him accepting, understanding, and sympathetic helps the consultee to reduce his feelings of guilt and inadequacy, which in turn helps to reduce his tension and to increase his effectiveness.

It should not be assumed that any mental health specialist is able to function effectively as a mental health consultant. The specialist not only needs to have an attitude of respect for members of other professions but also needs to have formal education in consultation work. The number of trained mental health consultants is relatively small, and so relatively few schools are providing this type of service as a means of strengthening teacher development.

SUMMARY

All people have certain basic personality needs; but they differ in the strength of these needs, in the ways in which they try to satisfy them, and in ability to tolerate thwarting of need satisfaction. To achieve and maintain good mental health, the individual has to achieve a proper balance between need gratification and need control.

Frustration is normal. Because it stimulates growth, it is also desirable. Children need to be exposed to frustration in tolerable amounts so that they will develop sufficient frustration tolerance to be able to take the stresses and strains of everyday living without becoming too disturbed. When a person experiences too much or too severe frustration, he may

[24] Ivy Mooring and Peter Guzvich, "Psychiatric Consultation Services in the Public School System," *California Journal of Elementary Education*, 1962, 31(1):40.

develop inadequate or undesirable adjustive patterns. The quality of his adjustment behavior determines in general the degree of his personal and social efficiency.

Normality is largely a matter of degree. Neurotic behavior is basically behavior that is unacceptable in a given culture at a given time. The same cause may produce different symptoms of maladjustment in different individuals, and different causes may produce the same or similar symptoms. The symptomatology of a disordered condition may not be unlike that of a benign condition. Some possible symptoms of maladjustment are failure to learn in keeping with ability to learn; malbehavior, such as rebellion against authority, destruction of property, and cruelty; excessive fears; extreme sensitiveness; seclusiveness; self-centeredness; nervous habits, such as stuttering, muscle twitching, and great restlessness. No symptom consistently indicates maladjustment, and a detected maladjustment may be minor or transitory. Some school people are more sensitive to aggressive behavior symptoms than to those of recessive behavior, whereas withdrawal more often than aggression may indicate maladjustment.

Many schools seek prevention of emotional handicaps through promotion of mental health. They seek, among other things, a school environment conducive to good emotional development and an education program that contributes maximally to development of integrating mechanisms and relationships.

The screening of emotionally handicapped students should be a systematic procedure. It should not be left to chance. Special assistance may be provided these students through counseling, group therapy, remedial instruction (particularly in reading), and manipulation of the environment. Indirectly they may be aided through strengthening teacher understanding of the nature and sources of mental health problems and by helping teachers to develop skill in working with troubled students.

The manner in which a student is referred for counseling helps to determine the extent to which he will benefit from counseling. The referral should be warm and friendly. It should provoke as little anxiety as possible.

The schools are the only social agency that works directly with all school-age children. The teacher is the key school person in identifying and preventing emotional handicaps. The average teacher is probably better equipped through psychological training than the average physician or minister for understanding child behavior and for appraising individual differences in developmental patterns. Anything that can be done to help teachers to become clinically oriented to the significance of specific behavior patterns contributes to the diminution of emotional handicaps in the nation's child population. Case conferences, child-study programs, and mental health consultation are being increasingly used for this purpose.

Mental health consultation is an interaction process that helps the teacher to develop insight into the nature and cause of students' mental health problems and to make effective use of personal and environmental resources in helping students solve such problems. Use is made of the professional peer relationship, as well as the consultant's professional knowledge. When a student's problem is associated with a problem in the teacher's life, the consultant may not deal with the teacher's problem directly. By dealing with it indirectly in relation to the student's problem, he may help the teacher to deal with the problem objectively.

REFERENCES

Bernard, Viola W.: "Teacher Education in Mental Health: From the Point of View of the Psychiatrist," in Morris Krugman (ed.), *Orthopsychiatry and the School*. New York: American Orthopsychiatry Association, 1958.

Blaine, G. B., et al.: *Emotional Problems of the Student*. New York: Appleton-Century-Crofts, Inc., 1961.

Blindman, A. J.: "Mental Health Consultation: Theory and Practice," *Journal of Consulting Psychology*, 1959, 23:473–482.

Bower, Eli M., et al.: *A Process for Early Identification of Emotionally Disturbed Children*. Sacramento: California State Department of Education, 1958.

────── et al.: *High School Students Who Later Became Schizophrenic*. Sacramento: California State Department of Education, 1960.

Bowman, Paul H.: "The Role of the Consultant as a Motivator of Action," *Mental Hygiene*, 1959, 43:105–110.

────── and others: *Mobilizing Community Resources for Youth: Identification and Treatment of Maladjusted, Delinquent, and Gifted Children*. Chicago: The University of Chicago Press, 1956.

Caplan, Gerald: *Concepts of Mental Health and Consultation*. Washington, D.C.: Government Printing Office, 1959.

Chanasky, N. M.: "Threat, Anxiety, and Reading Behavior," *Journal of Educational Research*, 1958, 51:333–340.

Cohen, Louis D.: *State Activities in Mental Health Education: A Survey of Nine Programs*. Washington, D.C.: Government Printing Office, 1961.

Cooper, Saul, et al.: "Classroom Screening for Emotional Disturbance," *American Psychologist*, 1959, 14:344.

Cumming, Elaine, and John Cumming: *Closed Ranks: An Experiment in Mental Health Education*. Cambridge, Mass.: Harvard University Press, 1957.

Daniels, E. M.: "Psychiatrists in the School," *N.E.A. Journal*, 1960, 49:11–12.

D'Evelyn, Katherine: *Meeting Children's Emotional Needs*. Englewood Cliffs, N.J.: Prentice-Hall, Inc., 1957.

Fabian, A. A.: "Reading Disability: An Index of Pathology," *American Journal of Orthopsychiatry*, 1955, 25:319–328.

Galdston, Iago: "The Trials of Normalcy," *Mental Hygiene*, 1957, 40:78–84.

Glidwell, John C. (ed.): "Mental Health in the Classroom," *Journal of Social Issues*, 1959, 15(1):1–62.

Hartzman, Jack: "Human Relations in the Classroom," *American Journal of Orthopsychiatry*, 1956, 26:633–642.

Jackson, Joseph: "The Effect of Classroom Organization and Guidance Practice upon the Personality Adjustment and Academic Growth of Students," *Journal of Genetic Psychology*, 1953, 83:139–170.

Jahoda, Marie: *Current Concepts of Positive Mental Health*. New York: Basic Books, Inc., Publishers, 1958.

Klein, Donald C.: "The Prevention of Mental Illness," *Mental Hygiene*, 1961, 45:101–109.

Kotinsky, Ruth, and J. W. Coleman: "Mental Health as an Educational Goal," *Teachers College Record*, 1955, 56:267–276.

Kubie, L. S.: "The Fundamental Nature of the Distinction between Normality and Neuroses," *Psychoanalytic Quarterly*, 1954, 23:166–170.

Lambert, Nadine, et al.: *The Emotionally Handicapped Child in the School: A Research Program in the Prevention of Personality and Behavior Disorders in Children*. Sacramento: California State Department of Education, 1959.

Lawson, Thomas O.: "Social Adjustment Classes," *Bulletin of the National Association of Secondary-school Principals*, 1959, 43(249):102–106.

Magary, James F., and John R. Eichorn (eds.): *The Exceptional Child: A Book of Readings*, part 8. New York: Holt, Rinehart and Winston, Inc., 1960.

O'Neal, Patricia, and L. N. Robbins: "The Relation of Childhood Behavior Problems to Adult Psychiatric Status: A 30-year Follow-up Study of 150 Subjects," *American Journal of Psychiatry*, 1958, 114:961–969.

Otto, Herbert A.: "The School Administrator's Mental Health," *Mental Hygiene*, 1961, 45:603–612.

Pellman, Maurine, and G. P. Liddle: "Programs for the Problem Child," *Phi Delta Kappa*, 1959, 40:174–178.

Schiffer, Mortimer: "A Therapeutic Play Group in a Public School," *Mental Hygiene*, 1957, 41:185–193.

Smith, M. B.: "Research Strategies toward a Conception of Mental Health," *American Psychologist*, 1959, 14:673–681.

Stranahan, Marion, et al.: "Group Treatment for Emotionally Disturbed and Potentially Delinquent Boys and Girls," *American Journal of Orthopsychiatry*, 1957, 27:518–527.

Taba, Hilda: *School Culture*. Washington, D.C.: American Council on Education, 1955.

Ullman, Charles A.: *Identification of Maladjusted School Children*, Public Health Monograph no. 7, Public Health Service Publication no. 211. Washington, D.C.: Government Printing Office, 1957.

16

Using Nonschool Community Resources

Counselors do well to strengthen and extend the school guidance work through the use of nonschool community agencies. Moreover, they do well to encourage workers in the other agencies to seek cooperation from the schools. A family welfare worker, for instance, in trying to help a student's family may need information or some other help from the school.

TYPES OF COMMUNITY AGENCIES

The community agencies and institutions that serve children and youth can be roughly grouped in two classes—(1) those whose functions are primarily developmental in nature and (2) those whose functions are mainly remedial or rehabilitative. In the first group belong the home, the school, the church, the Y, the neighborhood playground, the youth center, and the like. In the second belong the hospitals, the clinics, the welfare agencies, the probation division, and the like. The functions of none, however, may be exclusively of one type. A child or family welfare agency, for example, may sponsor some activities that are primarily developmental or preventive in nature, but in general it may focus its efforts on corrective work.

A more orthodox way of grouping community agencies is to classify them as public or tax-supported, as private or voluntary, and as proprietary or commercial. Public, tax-supported agencies are in general more highly structured than private agencies. For example, their eligibility requirements, as well as their budget and policies, may be more or less set by law. To the extent of their capacity they must ordinarily accept all applicants who meet the eligibility requirements.

Private, voluntary agencies are supported by contributions made to them directly or through some such organization as the Community Chest. They are organized to meet a need not met by the public agencies or to provide supplementary services. They may be nonsectarian, or they may be sponsored by religious groups, such as the Jewish, Catholic, Lutheran, and Seventh Day Adventist organizations.

In contrast to public agencies, private agencies may be quite flexible in policies and practices. Most, however, have codes and principles that set limitations on their procedures and services. The services may be limited, for example, to adolescents, to persons of low income, to the blind, to members of a particular religious faith, or the like. A private agency, however, can ordinarily free itself of such limitations more easilv than a public agency can. A person in need of help may, for example, not be able to receive service from a public agency if he has not resided in the community for a certain length of time. In the case of a private agency, however, urgent need may take precedence over rules. The private agency may extend service to an individual outside the group to which its service is expected to be limited, particularly if the service is not likely to be available elsewhere. It should be pointed out, however, that while the setting aside of rules and regulations is not so easy for a public as for a private agency, public agencies also make exceptions sometimes.

Commercial or proprietary agencies operate on a fee basis. Because they are dependent upon fees for maintenance, they may charge higher fees than do the public or community agencies. For the same reason they are generally open more evening and weekend hours than are the others.

Some school people seem to think that it is not professional or ethical to refer students to such agencies. Sometimes, however, the proprietary agencies are the best and perhaps only referral resources available. In more than a few communities, for instance, health cases can be referred only to physicians in private practice or to a proprietary hospital. Moreover, in many communities the demand for mental health service is far greater than can be met by the public and voluntary clinics. In these same communities there may be proprietary clinics that offer excellent service. We cannot assume that these physicians, psychiatrists, and hospital owners feel no community-wide interest or that they operate solely for their own benefit. Nor can we make such assumptions regarding workers in other agencies merely because the agencies are proprietary.

In making referrals to any agency, care of course must always be taken to determine as far as possible whether the agency is a responsible, reliable one and its workers are competent to provide the service offered. The fact that attention is focused here on the use of public and private agencies should not be interpreted as indicating lack of appreciation of the proprietary agency as a referral resource.

SOME OF THE NEEDS

Community agencies provide many kinds of help. They give financial aid and advisement. They help with problems of interpersonal relations. They provide protective intervention and care for unsupervised, neglected, or abused children and youth. They give medical care. They offer psychiatric services for persons who are seriously disturbed emotionally. They give legal aid, find employment for the unemployed, provide counseling and care for unwed mothers and mothers-to-be, wed and unwed. And they are sources of aid with many other matters. Because problems seldom occur singly, a number of agencies rather than one alone may become involved in the process of referral and treatment.

Financial Aid. The average counselor in any school year learns that a number of students have serious problems that can be resolved or lightened through financial aid. He may learn from one student that another student plans to leave school because his family desperately needs any money that he may be able to earn. A teacher may tell him of her great concern for some student who acts like "a tired little old man," who seldom smiles and seems weighed down by the burdens of the world. Later, in talking with the boy, the counselor may learn that the student is indeed heavily burdened, that he is sick with worry over his family's lack of funds and afraid that before long they "will be out in the street" because of long-overdue rent. And few counselors go through a school year without becoming aware of some students who seem to slip as quietly as possible in and out of school each day to avoid attracting attention to their shabby and perhaps even dirty clothing. The income of some student's family may be so low that living in a building with proper laundry, bathing, and toilet facilities is a luxury rather than a "standard necessity."

The basic resource for financial aid is usually the public welfare agency that is responsible for administering the programs of general assistance, child welfare, aid to dependent children, and the like. This agency also provides the casework service that may be needed to help the family increase its income or to manage present income better. When help from a public welfare agency is not available, short-term emergency relief may have to be sought from some private agency, church organization, or service group such as the Rotary, Kiwanis, and Zonta clubs.

Finding financial aid for students who wish to continue their education beyond high school is less difficult today than before the orbiting of Sputnik. Now it is relatively easy for an academically able boy or girl to obtain a scholarship. However, those who are no better than average scholastically but who also want a college education may find achievement of this goal difficult unless they live near a tax-supported college. If they must meet the cost of room and board, attainment of their objective may be difficult or impossible. Many deserve financial help in reaching their goal and may need a counselor's assistance in finding it.

Likewise, aid may be needed by students who want post-high school training to qualify as nurses, laboratory technicians, cosmetologists, and the like. The student whose family cannot pay the cost of such training no doubt feels as strongly frustrated as the student who wants a college education but cannot have it without financial help. Again, aid may be most likely obtained through appeal to individual citizens and to church or service groups.

Medical Care. Some school systems do not maintain dental and health clinics or offer special health services beyond the physical examinations routinely made of students from time to time. In such schools counselors may need to be particularly well informed regarding the services available through public health agencies, public and private clinics, hospitals, nursing services, and the like.

The students' needs for medical services are usually varied, frequently complex, and sometimes of an emergency nature. In emergency situations resulting from accident, heart attacks, or the like, the basic source of information and help is probably most often the public general hospital. Sometimes resuscitation help and ambulance service may be most quickly obtained from the fire department.

Mental Health Service. Few school systems can provide sufficient psychiatric or clinical service for all students in need of such help. Some students have to be referred to nonschool clinics and to physicians and psychiatrists in private practice.

When a student's emotional handicap or difficulties seem to stem from problems of family relations, it is often best first to consult a family casework agency. The student may not be eligible for clinical help or actually in need of such service. The specialized child guidance clinic with its interdisciplinary team of psychiatric social worker, psychologist, and psychiatrist usually restricts its services to children who are so seriously disturbed that they need intensive therapy. To refer to the clinic cases that can be served by a social caseworker or a physician is undesirably expensive. Also, it may deprive some children in need of specialized clinical help of the opportunity to obtain it.

In almost every community the number of children that the clinics are able to serve is probably only a fraction of the number who need clinical help. Hence, the best possible use should be made of the limited supply, but this is not always done. For example, a study [1] of 500 cases at the Los Angeles Child Guidance Clinic showed that only about one-fifth of the children referred to the clinic needed the services of the clinic team. At about the same time in the same community other investigators were finding that the number of children in need of clinic service far exceeded the available supply. They found that "referral to the clinics of cases other than emergencies is often an unproductive use of time." [2] Under such

[1] F. N. Anderson and H. C. Dean, *Some Aspects of Child Guidance Clinic Intake Policy and Practices*, Public Health Monograph no. 42, p. 13. Washington, D.C.: Government Printing Office, 1956.

[2] Wayne McMullen et al., *The Mental Health Survey of Los Angeles County 1957–1958*, pp. 6 and 11. Sacramento: Department of Mental Health, State of California, 1960.

conditions it is not surprising that a family or child welfare casework agency may become a kind of "catchall" agency for applicants not able to receive help elsewhere.

Protective Care and Intervention. Unsupervised, neglected, and abused children need someone to intervene for them. Counselors can sometimes influence parents to assume neglected responsibilities, or to seek assistance with their family problems, or to modify certain home practices. They may be able not only to inform parents regarding possible sources of help but also to influence them to seek such help voluntarily. When a student's parents are unwilling to do this and the student needs to be protected against neglect or abuse, the counselor may have to refer the case to some public agency with investigative functions, such as the probation department, the juvenile court, or the police. Obviously, the counselor must be able to supply factual information regarding the situation protested and/or the names of persons who can testify as observers of the situation.

Unfortunately, few communities provide protective services on a nonlegal basis. Referrals usually must be made to an investigative service of the law enforcement department. Because of the possible difficulties and unpleasantness involved, school people are generally reluctant to report delinquent parents. Also, judges are reluctant to take children from their parents if there is any chance of preserving the home. Hence, a bad situation may go uncorrected until family background and delinquency are so serious that they can no longer be ignored. Then correction may be very difficult and perhaps impossible.

Not all need for child placement stems from neglect or abuse. A student may be temporarily or permanently in need of home placement because of illness, accident, death, or some other disaster that disrupts family life. When in such instances referral cannot be made to a public welfare agency, help may be sought from a private one, such as a Jewish, Catholic, or Protestant agency, that can give direct help to the child and/or his parents or foster parents. Such referrals must be made skillfully so that the student's developing personality will be damaged as little as possible by the experience.

It is rarely desirable that a counselor make direct referral to an advertising foster home, even to one that is properly licensed and registered. Ordinarily it is better to use the casework services of a welfare agency whose functions include foster home placement and that has a staff member especially trained in this complex service.

Recreation Programs. In the average community, agencies other than the schools and the churches maintain activity programs for children and youth. While such programs usually focus on "character building" rather than reeducation or rehabilitation, they may serve both purposes. By helping a student to participate in the program at the Y, teen-age center, neighborhood playground, or the like, a counselor may help him develop wholesome, satisfying recreational interests and thereby help him avoid delinquent behavior.

Some group work programs are supervised by adult leaders trained to work with emotionally disturbed children and youth. And some agencies (relatively few) concentrate on case and group work with such clients. However, the majority of agencies offering recreational activity programs do not include small-group work specifically designed to provide individualized adjustment help to the group members. This type of service is not included in many programs where its provision seems natural, as, for example, in summer camp programs for children from substandard homes and for boys and girls who show delinquency tendencies.

Other Needs. A student may find learning difficult because he is too badly disturbed by family interpersonal problems. His family may need assistance from some agency able to help with problems stemming from personality conflicts, a family member's physical or mental handicap, marital discord, poor home management, and the like.

The problem of the unwed pregnant girl is an old one. In the past many counselors and deans of girls got rid of this problem by getting rid of the girl—by expelling her. Nowadays attention is more likely to be directed to possible ways of helping her. If needed, both financial aid and casework assistance may be obtained from a public welfare agency or a private organization, such as the Salvation Army, the Jewish Family Welfare Service, the Catholic Welfare Bureau, and the like. Upon request these agencies will usually initiate or assist in referral of the girl to other agencies, such as maternity homes and child placement or adoption agencies, when the services of these seem indicated also.

Some high schools provide placement service in part-time and full-time jobs. Many work in friendly cooperation with the state employment service, which provides vocational counseling as well as placement service to teenagers. Students may also receive counseling and occupational information at the local apprenticeship office of the state department of labor.

The state rehabilitation service is an invaluable source of help for students with handicaps resulting from illness or injury.

In the very small community, church societies, civic groups, and individual citizens are generally among the chief sources of help. A woman's club or a church group may give financial aid to "deserving students." At a luncheon meeting the members of a civic or service club may listen with pride to reports on the progress of the boys and/or girls whom they "have sent to college." The chamber of commerce or a group of merchants may donate and clear space for a baseball diamond, a tennis court, a football field, or some other type of playfield. The members of some other groups may sponsor scout troops, teen-age clubs, and the like;

provide them meeting places; and supervise their dances, parties, and out-
ings. The local dentist and physician may give free or low-cost service to
students who are unable to obtain it otherwise. A civic or a service club
may join forces with the chamber of commerce to provide high school
students information about job opportunities and to give placement service. And without the help of the local business, industrial, and professional people, the high school could not organize and maintain a cooperative work experience program.

ORGANIZED INFORMATION NEEDED

In some communities the referral resources are so varied and so many that
finding one's way in the network of agencies and procedures requires considerable time. Hence, counselors need to become adequately informed in
advance of need for their use. In other communities the very scarcity of
referral resources makes it necessary for the counselor to seek, in advance
of need, information about resources outside the community to which
referral is possible.

In large school systems there is usually a central office from which
counselors may secure information regarding referral resources and the
procedures to be followed in using them. In some the information bureau
is in the central guidance office, the health office, or the child welfare office.

Sometimes counselors assume that resources are lacking in some
areas, whereas this may not be true. The counselor may go a long time
before learning that certain resources are available. This is not likely to
occur, however, when the counselor has access to a directory or a descriptive listing of the various community agencies. Such directories typically
include, in addition to information about the name, address, telephone
number, and contact person of the agency, information about the types of
services offered, eligibility requirements, and routine referral procedures
during and outside office hours.

The preparation and distribution of such a directory are most
often the function of a central welfare planning council or bureau, which
may also provide free information and referral service to anyone seeking
it. The welfare information service of the Los Angeles Welfare Planning
Council, for example, maintains a card file on more than 6,500 services.
It publishes a comprehensive directory of the health, welfare, and recreational agencies in the community. The directory is regularly revised and
between revisions kept up to date through monthly reports on changes
and additions. An interagency committee has developed a referral process
manual to help make "responsible referrals" current practice. The following shows the type of information provided in the manual.[3]

[3] *Referral Process Manual*, pp. 57-58. Los Angeles: Welfare Planning Council,
Family and Adult Services Division, 1954.

PASADENA WELFARE BUREAU

301 City Hall, Pasadena 1

Telephone—SYcamore 2-6161

See Page 135—Health and Welfare Directory

Routine Process in Regular Office Hours

Before you pick up the phone

Office hours: Monday through Friday, 8 A.M. to 5 P.M.

Hours for telephone referrals—Monday through Friday, 8:30 A.M. to 12 noon; 1 P.M. to 4:30 P.M.

Exception—Tuesday, 9 A.M. to 10 A.M.

Emergencies—any time during regular office hours.

Contact persons: Regular referral—rotating intake worker.

Appeal or policy interpretation—director.

Information desired: Residence, problems presented, religious preference, identifying information.

When you get the agency

Procedure: Incoming calls are through the Pasadena City Hall switchboard.

Ask for Pasadena Welfare Bureau.

After this is achieved, the referring worker should ask to speak with the intake worker.

Clearance of agency records by caseworker will be done after discussion with referring worker.

If referral is accepted appointment can be arranged either through referring worker or directly by client.

Written referral slip is desired of referring agency.

Written summary is desired if referring agency has had more than initial contact with client.

Process outside Regular Office Hours

Time: Emergency referrals regarding Pasadena residents can be made after office hours, Saturday, Sunday and holidays.

Contact person: Pasadena Police Department, SYcamore 3-1121.

Procedure: Advise Police Department of nature of problem and identifying data. The referral worker will need to leave with the Police Department a phone number where she can be reached.

The Police Department will contact Pasadena Welfare Bureau agency person to follow through on request.

Financial assistance is granted on a limited and emergency basis.

Other emergency social service problems are met outside regular office hours. If necessary, follow-up or a referral is later made to the proper agency.
Follow-up or referral to the appropriate agency will be made by this agency when regular office hours are resumed.

Such manuals and directories are among the most useful sources of basic referral data. If a counselor does not have such aids because no community group has yet undertaken the task of preparing a directory, he might do well to urge the local association of guidance workers or counselors to take the initiative in getting the task done.

THE REFERRAL PROCESS

Many medical and mental health specialists are willing to cooperate as consultants and thereby contribute to prevention as well as to correction. Sometimes consulting a specialist regarding a problem or an incipient problem helps to prevent a referral becoming urgent and may even make it unnecessary. In many instances consultation should precede referral.

Case Conference Approach. Desirably a case conference is held before any referral action is taken, particularly if the case involves problems of school adjustment. Any staff member who can contribute information or can help strengthen understanding of the case should be encouraged to attend the conference. The group might well include, in addition to the student's counselor and teachers, the principal or vice-principal, nurse, school psychologist, and school social worker. Ideally a doctor should also be present, but this is not always possible.

The conference approach increases the possibility of referral to the most appropriate resource. It may also show that use of a nonschool resource is not appropriate because adequate use has not yet been made of school resources. The time spent in case conferences is profitably invested if it leads to more efficient use of both school and nonschool resources.

A useful by-product may be evaluation of school records on individual students. The conferences will usually disclose the general adequacies and inadequacies in the school's practices with regard to collecting and recording data. And they help to underscore the value of case studies, anecdotal records, reports on home visits, conferences with students and parents, and the like.

Designated Responsibility. If a student is to be referred to a nonschool resource, some school worker should be designated as the person to make the referral and to maintain contact with the agency. Confusion and conflict usually develop if more than one person tries to function as the contact person.

This does not mean that workers in the agency to which the student is referred should not consult with more than one school person regarding the case. Rather it means that responsibility for working with another agency should be centered in one person and that this person should be kept informed of any important new developments in the case at school. It may be desirable that the liaison person be also the one responsible for developing referral with the student and his parents. Most often the contact person is the principal, vice-principal, head counselor, school social worker, or, particularly in health cases, the school nurse. Some large school systems maintain a central referral bureau to serve all schools within the system.

Contacting and Working with the Agency. Before an agency is contacted, an effort should be made to ascertain whether another agency is working with the case. Through talks with the student or his parents it may be learned that some other agency has already been consulted. If so, then it should ordinarily be consulted before another is contacted. Perhaps referral should be made by this agency rather than by the school.

Disagreements and frustrations sometimes complicate referral. An agency may agree to accept emergency cases promptly, but there may be disagreement regarding the meanings of "promptly" and "emergency." Almost all agencies exclude some types of cases. One, for example, may exclude the mentally retarded; another may refuse a case that is not important in its training or research program.

The use of waiting periods is a common clinic practice that frustrates many school counselors. The majority of mental health clinics, for instance, use one or more waiting periods. They may have (1) a waiting period between application for admission and the intake interview, (2) one between acceptance and the beginning of diagnosis, and (3) one between diagnosis and the beginning of treatment. The length of a waiting period varies with clinics and cases. The longest is generally the one between acceptance and diagnosis.

Many clinical workers describe the waiting period between acceptance and diagnosis as a "cooling-off period" and apparently consider it a justifiable test of the client's motivation or real desire for help. They contend that it also helps to reduce the amount of time lost because of canceled appointments. Not all clinics, however, use waiting periods, and some clinical workers strongly oppose the practice. They find that it does not have therapeutic advantages and that it may reduce the therapeutic effects realized in the intake interview. A patient in need of help, for instance, may not return because during the long waiting period he builds up his defenses or loses his incentive or motivation for treatment. Moreover, cases not suitable for acceptance may be kept waiting too long before they learn that they must seek help elsewhere. While use of the waiting period is still widespread, dissatisfaction with it seems to be increasing. The directors of the clinics studied by McMullen,[4] for example, reported that they "believe prompt help is likely to be effective" and they "therefore deplore any waiting period."

Miracles should not be expected from a referral agency. Because change is slow and, when achieved, may not be lasting, it is often difficult to determine whether treatment in a particular case was worthwhile. Only partial success will be achieved in some cases and no success in others. The findings from a number of investigations show "full success" in only about 25 per cent of child guidance cases, "partial success" in about 50 per cent, and "failure" in approximately 25 per cent.[5]

Success may depend in large measure upon the cooperation obtained from the school. Among other things, the agency may need information beyond that obtained from referral and application forms and acquired during the intake interview. It seems, however, to be a matter of conscious policy on the part of most nonschool community agencies not to use the data available to them in the school records.

Counselors should not expect agency workers to share with the school people the information given in confidence by students at the agency. And, in giving information, counselors should take care to observe the ethical standards with regard to confidentiality of data set by the American Psychological Association and the American Personnel and Guidance Association. The information is given and discussed only for professional purposes and only with persons who are clearly concerned with the case. Any follow-up reports received from the agency are shared with the school people directly concerned with the case but in keeping with their ability to understand and to accept or use the information on a professional basis.

Developing Referral with Students and Parents. While the first step in contacting a referral resource may be taken by the counselor, application for service must come from the student or his parents. It is rarely wise to refer a student to a nonschool clinical agency without the parents' knowledge and consent. In some states such action is illegal.[6] Not to accept a child or an adolescent without the prior written consent of the parents is a ground rule with most clinics and hospitals. They have learned that success in treatment ordinarily depends upon the client's being willing to cooperate during the period of service. The consent statement provides

---

[4] McMullen et al., *op. cit.*, p. 6.

[5] Anderson and Dean, *op. cit.*, pp. 13–14.

[6] A recently enacted California law, for example, prohibits any school officer or employee from placing a public school pupil "in any public or private agency, institution, or place, outside of the pupil's school of attendance, for psychological treatment or psychiatric treatment, or both, unless the written prior consent of the parent or guardian to such placement and treatment is first obtained." *Education Code*, sec. 11804.

some evidence of the parents' wanting help and being willing to support the agency's efforts to provide the help needed by the child.

Because adolescents generally have more voice than younger children in decisions affecting their lives, many clinics accept only adolescents who come voluntarily—without excessive persuasion and coercion. Exceptions may be made, however, in the case of those who have serious behavior problems. Another person may have to take the initiative in such cases and may also have to see to it that the adolescent keeps his appointments.

While the initiative should ordinarily be taken by the student and his parents, a counselor or some other school person may have to give considerable help to students and parents who are ill, overly dependent, or seriously lacking in self-confidence. In some cases the school may even have to provide transportation and someone to accompany the student to the clinic, hospital, or other agency.

Sometimes developing referral is a smooth and easy process. A student and his parents, for instance, may offer little resistance and may cooperate fully when referral is being made for badly needed financial aid, medical help, or the like. The counselor's main problem may lie in determining the extent of need and in developing referral without doing damage to the student's self-esteem. Skillful counseling may be required for helping him feel that he is not being given aid "out of charity" but because he is worth helping and society has a stake in his future. It may help him to know that he can later repay through service to society.

When the student and his parents are willing to accept help, referral may be relatively simple. The counselor may make a telephone call in the student's presence, give him instructions regarding application, and offer any help that seems needed in filling out forms, finding out how to reach the place, and the like. A release-of-information permit may not be needed from the parents if the school does not have to give information beyond that provided on the forms signed by both parent and counselor or principal. Otherwise, it is best to obtain a signed consent statement for the release of information. If the student is an adult rather than a minor, obviously it is his consent rather than, or as well as, that of his parents which is needed.

In explaining the nature of the service offered by the referral resource, the counselor should not overlook or minimize its limits and limitations. Nor should he help the student to get around restrictions set by agency rules, policies, and procedures. He should not lead him to expect acts of magic and should avoid impressing or misleading him through the use of technical language.

Probably the most difficult type of referral is the one involving an emotional problem, such as problems of family relations and of personality disorder. The counselor needs to be able to work slowly and carefully. Hence, everything possible should be done to avoid making the referral an emergency or a crisis situation. Never should it be made an ultimatum situation where the student must accept referral or withdraw from school. If it is, the agency accepting referral may be so seriously handicapped at the start that it has little chance at success. A parent may docilely accept the ultimatum in the school office. In the agency office, however, he may be strongly resistant and even explosive. Moreover, parents may vent the resentment and ire provoked by such an ultimatum upon the student, thus worsening his problem.

The referral approach should be one of understanding, sympathy, and concern for helping the student. Instead of tying up treatment with permission to stay in school, the counselor explains to the student and his parents that the school staff feel that the student needs help and that they believe that he should receive assistance from outside experts who can give him the special help needed—help which the school people do not feel qualified to give.

There are times when counselors must act quickly and take emergency measures, but they are not so frequent as some seem to think. Some counselors are like parents who call in a doctor every time one of the children gets an ache or a pain. They always try to stop a crisis. They never try to help their children learn to live through crises. Likewise, some counselors want to refer to a specialist almost every student who comes to them with some disturbing problem. In the words of Arbuckle,[7] they are best described as "referral technicians" rather than as professional counselors.

Some counselors are overly quick to recommend referral because of their own insecurities and anxieties. A counselor may be afraid that he will be blamed if "something serious happens." To protect his own status, he wants to get the student off his hands and into the hands of an expert as quickly as possible. Another may feel impatient and even resentful because a student has not responded to his counseling efforts. Referral then takes on some of the aspects of punishment. Because the student did not follow the counselor's lead, he is now being sent to someone who will make him "straighten up" and "accept reality." Under such conditions the student may associate referral so strongly with rejection and punishment that he profits little from the help offered at the referral resource.

Referral should never be made a traumatic experience. Neither the student nor his parents, for example, should suddenly be confronted with the idea that the student *must* see a psychiatrist. "Something is wrong with your son (or daughter). We want you to take him (or her) to a clinic or a psychiatrist." Such statements may engender so much fear that the parents cannot think clearly and constructively about the situation. Extensive interviewing may be required to give the student and his parents time to realize that he needs more specialized assistance than the school

[7] Dugald S. Arbuckle, *Counseling: An Introduction*, p. 120. Boston: Allyn and Bacon, Inc., 1961.

can offer. They may need to do considerable thinking and talking about the problem before they can develop the needed insight regarding their roles in seeking correction. They may have to ventilate and explore their dreads and concerns, such as a fear of psychologists and psychiatrists, a fear of being stigmatized by the treatment experience, a fear of revealing too much and not having their revelations kept confidential, etc.

A counselor may strengthen a student or parent's resistance by implying that the student is neurotic or by saying that the student is in a bad way or that his case is urgent or that he must see a specialist before it is "too late." On the other hand he may help parents feel less resistant by showing that he realizes that the student is unhappy and the family worried, by telling them that he knows someone who may be able to help, by offering to arrange for the student to talk with this person if they want him to, and by adding that he thinks the student will value his contacts with this person and will find him very understanding and easy to talk to.

The wise counselor does not cite the experiences of other students who have had a similar experience and "come through with flying colors." Nor does he make reassuring speeches about the frequency of the incidence of emotional or mental disturbances. A student does not find it comforting or supporting to hear as one student did, according to McKinney,[8] that "all of us are a little crazy, and many of us would profit by seeing a psychologist" and so he should see Dr. X.

The parents' willing acceptance of referral is a necessity when their participation in treatment is needed. In many cases the parents need to participate because of their influence on their children's emotional development and their involvement in the problems and because of the children's needing parental support in order to sustain personality change.

A parent may be so emotionally involved in a son's or daughter's problem that he cannot acknowledge that any problem exists. To do so may mean to him admitting failure or defeat. If the parent believes that he has failed and that others think so too, he most likely feels hostile and defensive. He may have to criticize the school, the counselor, the teachers, and the child before he can begin to think less in terms of what the situation means to him and more in terms of its implication for his child. If in his feeling and thinking he can shift the focus from himself to his child, he may then be able to help the school to develop referral in such a way that the student will not see himself as being "dragged before a judge" but as being sent to someone who wants to help him.

If the parents reject the idea of referral, then plans for such action should ordinarily be abandoned or delayed. A counselor's understanding acceptance of the rejection may help the parents and the student to feel less defensive and confused and may thereby help them to work out a solution to the problem without outside assistance. Consultation may

[8] Fred McKinney, *Counseling for Personal Adjustment in Schools and Colleges*, p. 160. Boston: Houghton Mifflin Company, 1958.

prove a successful alternative. An outside specialist may be able to help the teachers and the counselors work with the student in the school situation more effectively than they could before.

Instead of the emergency growing worse, as feared or expected, it may begin to subside. Moreover, the parents and student, now feeling less anxious because feeling less pressured, may start to develop readiness for referral. They may later seek it on their own. The agency will then have a chance to give effective aid—perhaps effective largely because acceptable.

The primary objective in referral is to get the student to the person or persons believed to be able to help him. The objective is not to improve the school situation by getting rid of the student, although exclusion of a student is sometimes necessary for the sake of other students. In developing referral, a counselor wants to feel and to reveal an attitude of respect and confidence in the student's and parent's ability to cope with the problem situation. He does not wish them to feel that he wants to make their decisions or to direct their lives in any other way.

FAMILY GROUP THERAPY

Because adolescents commonly display rather ambivalent attitudes toward adults, it is difficult for a therapist to maintain with an adolescent the type of relationship needed for helping him to explore his difficulties and to work out effective solutions. For this reason group counseling and family therapy are frequently more helpful with adolescents than is the traditional type of individual-centered therapy.

The child's difficulty often is a symptom of disrupted family relations, usually of a breakdown in intrafamily communication. It is a result rather than a cause of family disruption, and the disturbing behavior may serve some purposes for the parent as well as for the child. Hence, the family, not the individual, is the unit treated. Children below age nine do not participate in the treatment session because they lack the needed ability in verbalization and abstract conceptualization. The therapist's overall function is to promote social interaction by facilitating communication within the family.

The parent's referral request represents a desire for change in the child. The first problem, according to Bell,[9] "is to translate this request for change in the individual into one for change in the family where it may be assumed change is needed. Such an assumption would not be foreign in the thinking of family members in most instances." The processes involved in promoting change develop through a series of overlapping phases, which, briefly summarized, are as follows:

1. ORIENTATION PHASE. The therapist arranges for an interview with the parents. He obtains information from them regarding the pre-

⁹ John E. Bell, "Recent Advances in Family Group Therapy," *Journal of Child Psychology and Psychiatry*, 1962, 3(1):9.

senting problem and then explains the therapy method. He explains that the whole family must be involved in treatment since the goal is better understanding and communication within the family. He describes his role as that of a referee or umpire, who will not give advice or impose solutions. His function is to see that everyone has an equal opportunity to express himself. However, at first, he explains, he will give more support to the children than to the parents in order to help the children gain confidence in expressing their feelings and opinions, particularly feelings and thoughts previously restricted from utterance in the family. He asks the parents to permit the children to do most of the talking at first and warns that they may vent strong negative feelings before their positive feelings begin to emerge. They will probably demand changes in family routine. Making the changes, as far as they are feasible, the therapist explains, will contribute to progress at the beginning; but it is the parents, not the therapist, who will decide whether any request for change should be granted.

2. CHILD-CENTERED PHASE. After the orientation interview with the parents, all treatment sessions are held with the whole family. The first conference sessions represent a warming-up period. Attention is focused on the children to help them feel safe in expressing their feelings, grievances, wants, and insights. "Normally the parents are discouraged from speaking so that their authority and hostility do not dominate the conference, thereby freezing the children." [10] The end of this phase is indicated when the children stop requesting changes. They are ready for a more spontaneous type of parent-child interaction.

The relationship involved in acceding to the children's wishes is not a normal parent-child interaction but is one contrived by the therapist for the needs of the children and of therapy. Although the requests made by the children may seem very important to them, they are not important in the overall pattern of family life.

3. PARENT-CHILD INTERACTION. The beginning of this phase is marked by a parent's taking the offensive, often by complaining about the behavior for which the child was originally referred. Verbal and emotional interchanges between child and parent follow. As other relationships in the family are explored, similar interchanges occur between other family members.

The therapist facilitates communication by maintaining a balance of opportunity for expression and by clarifying feelings. He reduces guilt about verbalizing certain aspects of intrafamily relations by encouraging such verbalizations. He promotes new evaluations of difficulties by directing attention to the motivating factors and by helping the family to explore the meaning of the child's symptomatic behavior and its responsibility for the development.

[10] John E. Bell, *Family Group Therapy*, p. 20. Washington, D.C.: Government Printing Office, 1961.

4. FATHER-MOTHER INTERACTION. As therapy progresses, discussion begins to focus on the father-mother interaction. Sometimes much of the father-mother interaction occurs outside the therapy conferences. At the family sessions the parents may refer to only the conclusions reached in the private discussions. They commonly assume that their conflicts are relevant to the children's problems. The therapist offers interpretations and encourages the other family members to express opinions regarding the reasons for the parents' behavior when in conflict.

5. SIBLING INTERACTION. By the time therapy has progressed to the stage where sibling interaction has increased, the therapist is playing a much less active role than at the beginning. The family is trying to empathize with one another and to understand the reasons for each other's behavior. They direct their remarks to one another rather than to the therapist, whom they may often ignore. In discussing their problems, they show much less tension and more rationality than in the early conferences.

6. TERMINAL PHASE. The principal features of this stage are the disappearance of many referral symptoms, laughter, reports of the family's doing things together, acceptance of a member's right to pursue special interests independently without interference from the others, the children's volunteering to do needed chores, and spontaneous expressions of satisfaction with improved family relations.

The family takes the initiative in terminating treatment. But, before therapy ends, the therapist summarizes the treatment features, discusses with the family some possible future steps, and lets the family know that, should treatment need to be resumed, it is available.

Participating in this type of therapy helps a family to reorder its relational processes. Through the ways in which its members relate to the therapist, the family learns that within the family there may be "(a) increased fluidity in communication; (b) greater flexibility in roles and functions; (c) greater discipline in the choice and forms of relationships." [11]

INTERAGENCY COOPERATION

The community agencies (this includes schools) are organized to meet many different needs. Some serve similar needs, and some serve the same individuals. Many workers in different types of agencies have similar training and employ similar techniques. All have the same general objective in terms of strengthening individual and community welfare. Only by working cooperatively can they best develop the community's resources for achieving their common and particular objectives.

Sometimes coordination of efforts is sought through more or less informal methods. The workers in the various agencies try to get ac-

[11] Bell, "Recent Advances in Family Group Therapy," p. 11.

quainted with one another and to learn more about each other's work. They visit the various agencies to gain firsthand information and to "get a feeling" for the work. They develop mutual respect and friendship as they meet periodically in interagency conferences to work on common problems and to share their work experiences.

Informal, relatively unstructured efforts at cooperation are often followed by systematic, well-organized attempts at coordination. The developments may include publications of directories that provide comprehensive information on each agency. Interagency meetings may be supplemented with case conferences held more or less regularly to help ensure the efficient use of all possible resources. And a central planning group may be established.

A highly developed plan for interagency cooperation usually provides for a community planning council or bureau made up of representatives from the different agencies. The functions of this council are, among others, (1) to promote group thinking and planning; (2) to develop high standards and increased efficiency; (3) to avoid misdirection and to reduce or eliminate duplication of efforts; (4) to provide the means for helpful exchange of information, ideas, and experiences; (5) to administer certain common services; (6) to make services readily available to all when needed; (7) to encourage and sponsor studies and projects involving different agencies; (8) to study community needs and to work for the prevention and elimination of conditions creating social problems; (9) to develop public understanding of community needs and to seek public support for agency programs; and (10) to relate local planning to state and national planning.

The development of planning councils seems generally to lead to increased use of the case conference approach. In Los Angeles County, for example, there are 47 planning councils, each of which has a professional group called the "case conference committee." Through the committee meetings professional workers get together to study specific cases and to interpret what is happening in particular problem areas. The Pasadena Case Conference Committee, for instance, is composed of three representatives of the City Schools (psychologist, school social worker, and counselor), representatives of the Welfare Association, the Family Service, the Pasadena Medical Association, the Bureau of Public Assistance, the Police Department, the Pasadena Boys' Club, the Catholic Welfare Bureau, the Child Guidance Clinic, the Community Planning Council, the California Youth Authority, the County Probation Department, and the Los Angeles Community Services.

This case conference committee is classified as a professional group because its participants are expected to function in a professional manner and to observe the ethical codes of their various professional organizations. The information shared during the conferences is held confidential because of its professional nature. Others sometimes find it difficult to ac-

cept this rule of confidentiality. A planning council member, for example, who represents a group like the chamber of commerce and is not
the council's representative on the case conference committee, may not
understand why all members of the planning council may not have access
to the minutes and other records of the case conference committee.

This committee has developed criteria for the selection of cases
to be presented to the group. The case must be one that makes possible
a psychosocial diagnosis. The conference attendants, in seeking an analysis, try to answer such questions as the following: What is the focal problem? How can we define it? How extensive is it? Why hasn't it yielded to
the usual techniques? How long has it been going on? Whom is it hurting?
How? What is basically wrong with this family? Is a crisis developing?
Do we have an appropriate referral resource? If not, how can we best live
with the problem and best help the young person to live with it? Can
any committee member provide guidelines from his experience? Do we
have suggestions for the member presenting the case?

As these questions indicate, cases are selected that give the group
a chance to study the management process and to learn how to distribute
responsibility. Some cases are new to only a few of the committee members because one or more agencies may have been working with the family
for years. Others are new to everyone except the persons presenting them
to the group. Some are marginal cases in terms of seriousness and duration. Others are hard-core cases.

Cases are selected that permit the sharing of information regarding situations that may suddenly demand attention. The representative of
a law enforcement agency, for instance, may report a case of believed
child neglect on which there is not yet sufficient evidence to document it
for court filing. He wants the others to know that at any time "something
is likely to pop" and so they all need to be alerted.

The primary values of the case conference form of interagency cooperation are probably early detection of problems, discovery of conditions predisposing to development of problems, and referral of such
conditions to the larger community through reports to planning and
legislative bodies that can take steps toward correction. An important
secondary value is the establishment of a stronger rapport among professional people than can ordinarily be developed through the usual
communication channels of letter and telephone.

Interagency cooperation helps a community to provide the auxiliary as well as the basic welfare services that it needs. It helps to expand
and to strengthen the overall program by stimulating extension of services and initiation of action in areas where services are lacking. By improving and increasing communication between professional groups, it
helps to increase the efficiency and effectiveness of the individual agency
programs.

SUMMARY

School guidance and counseling programs may be strengthened and extended through the appropriate use of nonschool community agencies—public, private, and proprietary. These agencies may prove important sources of special assistance for students with serious problems of health, finances, family relations, employment, post-high school education, and the like.

Referral is an expert aspect of counseling. To develop referral skillfully, the counselor needs ability to recognize and appraise student need for help, comprehensive, organized knowledge of available resources, skill in conversing with students and parents regarding problems and the possible need for specialized help, and ability to bring the outside expert into the picture without seeming to reject the student or his problem.

Participation in family group therapy may help the parents and other members perceive that the child's behavior is structured by intrafamily relations. Therapy may promote the changes needed for reordering the relationships.

The referral process varies with cases and resources. Each referral differs from the others. Each needs to be personalized. The counselor needs to allow sufficient time for the student and his parents to develop willingness to accept outside help. He should not pressure them to act promptly if they are unwilling. Nor should he encourage them to act at once by helping them to build extravagant expectations.

The counselor who lets the referral situation develop into one of crisis or emergency, who is overly anxious for immediate action, or who is too directive or authoritarian helps to strengthen resistance to referral. The counselor who is quiet and calm in his approach, who shows sympathetic understanding, and who is sensitively responsive to feelings helps to reduce resistance and to develop readiness for taking the initiative in arranging for outside help. If a counselor objectively accepts the parents' involvement in their child's problem and takes care not to identify himself with the child or either parent, tensions and anxieties may subside sufficiently for the parents to give the cooperation needed for working effectively with the student in both school and nonschool situations.

School counselors should share in efforts directed toward interagency cooperation and coordination. They may participate by helping to prepare classified directories, referral process manuals, and other such information aids. By attending interagency meetings, they may work with others for the efficient use of available resources. They may serve as school representatives on planning councils, case conference committees, and the like. They may be able to help create other opportunities for the various agencies to work together in augmenting and improving community welfare work in behalf of children and youth.

REFERENCES

Balser, B. H., et al.: "Preliminary Report of a Controlled Mental Health Workshop in a Public School System," *American Journal of Psychiatry*, 1955, 112:199–205.

———— et al.: "Further Report on Experimental Evaluation of Mental Hygiene Techniques in School and Community," *American Journal of Psychiatry*, 1957, 113:733–739.

Bell, John E.: *Family Group Therapy*. Washington, D.C.: Government Printing Office, 1961.

————: "Recent Advances in Family Group Therapy," *Journal of Child Psychology and Psychiatry*, 1962, 3(1):1–15.

Buxbaum, Joan: "Coordinating Private and Public Rehabilitation Services," *Personnel and Guidance Journal*, 1958, 37:139–142.

Family Casework in the Interest of Children. New York: Family Service Association of America, 1958.

Gibb, Jack R., and Ronald Lippitt (eds.): "Consulting with Groups and Organizations," *Journal of Social Issues*, 1959(2):1–67.

Goals and Methods in Public Assistance. New York: Social Casework, 1956.

Hoyt, Kenneth B., and John W. Loughary: "Acquaintance with and Use of Referral Sources by Iowa Secondary School Counselors," *Personnel and Guidance Journal*, 1958, 36:388–391.

Levitt, Eugene E.: "A Follow-up Evaluation of Cases Treated at a Community Child Guidance Clinic," *American Journal of Orthopsychiatry*, 1959, 29:337–349.

————: "The Results of Psychotherapy with Children: An Evaluation," *Journal of Consulting Psychology*, 1957, 21:189–196.

Mariner, Allen S., et al.: "Group Psychiatric Consultation with Public School Personnel: A Two-year Study," *Personnel and Guidance Journal*, 1961, 40:254–258.

Mass, Henry S.: "Psychiatric Clinic Services for Children: I. Unanswered Questions," *Social Service Review*, 1956, 30:276–288.

Peck, H. B., and Virginia Bellsmith: *Treatment of the Delinquent Adolescent: Group and Individual Therapy with Parent and Child*. New York: Family Service Association of America, 1954.

Polansky, Norman, and Jacob Kounin: "Clients' Reactions to Initial Interviews," *Human Relations*, 1956, 9:237–264.

Ramsery, Glenn V.: "The Referral Task in Counseling," *Personnel and Guidance Journal*, 1962, 40:443–447.

Robinson, Reginald, et al.: *Community Resources in Mental Health*. New York: Basic Books, Inc., Publishers, 1960.

Rosner, Joseph: "Therapy with 'Latchkey' Children," *American Journal of Orthopsychiatry*, 1957, 27:411–419.

Ross, Murray G.: *Community Organization: Theory and Principles*. New York: Harper & Row, Publishers, Incorporated, 1955.

Sanderson, Herbert: "What Is a Community Agency?" *Personnel and Guidance Journal*, 1955, 34:33–36.

Thomas, Edwin, et al.: "The Expected Behavior of a Potentially Helpful Person," *Human Relations*, 1955, 8:165–174.

Young, Leontine R.: *Out of Wedlock: A Study of the Problems of the Unmarried Mother and Her Child*. New York: McGraw-Hill Book Company, Inc., 1954.

17

Background to the Counseling Interview

SOME CHANGING CONCEPTS

Expanding Scope. In the 1920s and 1930s there was relatively little confusion regarding the meaning of the term "counseling" in student personnel work. It was generally described as the "heart" of the program and as the most technical and specialized service. It was rarely, if ever, confused with psychotherapy. The line between the two was clearly drawn, and counselors were repeatedly cautioned to stay on their side of the line.

Then as now, it was recognized that there are levels of counseling ranging from the casual, conversational type offered by teachers through the advisory service (largely information giving) of the nonspecialists (homeroom teachers, grade advisers, faculty advisers, and the like) to the service offered by professionally trained counselors. The work of even the specialists was, however, usually expected to be limited to helping students with educational, vocational, and "social" problems. Helping the emotionally disturbed boy or girl or helping students with personal and emotional problems was usually looked upon as the exclusive function of clinically and medically trained therapists.

During the 1940s and 1950s views regarding the functions and, hence, the education of school counselors changed considerably. It is now recognized that they must have, in Wrenn's [1] words, "a fairly high level of psychological sophistication" in their professional education because school counselors can no longer follow a hands-off policy with regard to helping students who are emotionally disturbed or who exhibit evidence of personality or behavior disorder. To leave all such counseling to the clinically and the medically trained is unrealistic in view of the limited supply of such specialists. Moreover, the professionally trained school counselor is better informed than such workers regarding the school situation and the particular age group served by the school.

The nation does not have enough medical and clinical specialists

[1] C. Gilbert Wrenn, "Status and Role of the School Counselor," *Personnel and Guidance Journal*, 1957, 36:179.

to meet the counseling needs of even a small fraction of its children and youth. In many communities the services of a clinical psychologist or a psychiatrist are not available. In communities where they are, almost invariably the demand far exceeds the supply. Los Angeles, for example, has a better than average supply of clinical psychologists and psychiatrists, yet a survey [2] of its mental health services showed that the "schools encounter a number of problems in making referrals." Among other things "they are deterred by the shortage of community treatment facilities and by the fact that many agencies have waiting lists." Too often when help finally becomes available, the child's case has become so serious that he cannot be easily helped and perhaps cannot be helped at all.

Most students have need of help with their emotional problems at some time. Today it is believed that those who seek it at school should be able to find it there. Many students who receive good emotional support from their parents prefer to go with some problems to their counselors rather than to parents because the counseling relationship is not the intimate relationship that ordinarily exists between parent and child. They expect the reaction of the counselor to differ from that of the parent. The fact that the relationship will not continue indefinitely, as well as the fact that the counselor, unlike the parent, is not emotionally involved in the matter, makes it easier for them to discuss some matters with counselors than with parents.

Increased Awareness of the Need for Professional Education. The growing practice of substituting the term "counseling psychologist" for "counselor" may help to bring about adequate provision for the type of preservice education needed today by school and college counselors. It may also help to do away with the practice of using as counselors persons who are not professionally prepared to fulfill the role. More and more counseling authorities are recommending that the preservice education of counselors be fully as comprehensive and intensive as that of clinical psychologists; that the provision for course work (theory and methods), internship, and supervised experience be equally strong for both groups.

School counselors need education that is sufficiently specialized to enable them not only to offer counseling at the level of the mental health specialist but also to work effectively with the medical and clinical specialists to whom they may make referrals. The chief difference in the professional education of counseling and clinical psychologists probably should be that the counselors' focuses upon work with people who are essentially normal. Their professional education needs, however, to include some work with the emotionally disturbed. Moreover, it should be at the same level as that offered clinical psychologists because, when re-

[2] *Los Angeles County Surveys Its Mental Health Services*, p. 33. Los Angeles: Welfare Planning Council, Los Angeles Region, 1960.

ferral resources are not available, counselors must work with the seriously disturbed. In short, the focus in their professional education should be upon the developmental and preventive aspects but without neglect of the remedial and therapeutic aspects of counseling.

Role of the Counselor. While complete agreement has not yet been reached regarding the various roles of the counselor, agreement outweighs disagreement. It is commonly considered, for example, undesirable for professionally educated counselors to give time to such clerical tasks as test scoring, data recording, and record filing.

There is still controversy regarding the counselor's role in discipline, but it is generally agreed that he should not be assigned roles that involve imposing penalties and forcing conformity. However, to divorce discipline and counseling seems equally undesirable to those, such as Williamson,[3] who perceive a student's misbehavior as evidence of his need for help in clarifying chaotic emotions, in developing new adjustive techniques, and in avoiding further wrongdoing. When counseling is not provided "discipline cases" for the purposes of rehabilitation, prevention, and development, the misbehaving student may substitute stronger misbehavior for counseling. As stated in the report of the Commission for Guidance in American Schools,[4] counselors are presumed to be aware of behavior and possible underlying causes. Hence, it is natural to expect them to work with students who are in difficulty. "This is quite different from making the counselor the school's disciplinary officer or even an adjunct to action that needs to be taken."

Increased awareness is being shown of two other roles stressed in the Commission's report. They are the role of consultant to parents, teachers, and administrators, as well as students, and the role of group worker. Increased attention is also being given to the counselor's social role, a role which Hobbs[5] would describe as that of social philosopher were this description not too pretentious. To fulfill this role, the counselor needs to be aware of what is happening in society and the effect of these happenings on the lives of individuals. He must be actively concerned with a number of social trends and issues that, as Hobbs says, "have traditionally been of relatively little import to him" so that he may "contribute to the development of a society in which the individual has maximum opportunities for fullest self-realization" and may help the student "in projecting a satisfactory life role in a complex and changing

---

[3] E. G. Williamson, "The Fusion of Discipline and Counseling in the Educative Process," *Personnel and Guidance Journal,* 1955, 34:74–79.

[4] C. Gilbert Wrenn, *The Counselor in a Changing World,* p. 147. Washington, D.C.: American Personnel and Guidance Association, 1962.

[5] Nicholas Hobbs, "The Compleat Counselor," *Personnel and Guidance Journal,* 1958, 36:597.

society." Fulfillment of the role involves being sensitive to cultural changes that affect student self-understanding and being sensitive to the characteristics of society that will mean most to the student. It may also involve being aware of those characteristics of society with which the student will be most in conflict.

Counseling and Psychotherapy. The psychological counseling offered in many schools and colleges cannot be easily differentiated from psychotherapy, although the problems dealt with in counseling are generally less severe than those dealt with in psychotherapy. In the opinion of some writers, distinctions in terms of problem severity or of techniques used are not sufficient to differentiate the two approaches. Other writers, however, do distinguish them. They stress that counseling, in contrast to psychotherapy, is concerned with people who are essentially normal, whereas psychotherapy is more concerned with the abnormal.

Counselors work at times with abnormal people, such as the mentally and physically handicapped. They deal, however, as Super [6] points out, with the normalities in the lives of these persons rather than with the abnormalities. Counseling, for example, may be directed toward helping a handicapped student make appropriate educational and vocational plans. Counseling is focused largely on the plans individuals have to make to play productive roles in their social environment. "Whether the person being helped with such planning is sick or well, abnormal or normal, is really irrelevant." [7]

In the opinion of some, such as Bordin,[8] the difference between counseling and psychotherapy is more quantitative than qualitative. The counselor, in contrast to the psychotherapist, establishes relatively short relationships with many persons rather than intensive, long relations with a few. This is mainly because the problems dealt with in counseling are more often reality problems (role problems in education, vocation, family, etc.) rather than problems of inner conflict. Hence, counseling is more often directed toward helping the individual to identify and develop his personal and environmental resources rather than toward helping him to reorganize his personality. The counselee may be a student, for example, who is not achieving his goals because he lacks certain skills or because he has chosen a program of studies that is not in keeping with his abilities, which he has misjudged.

[6] Donald E. Super, "Transition from Vocational Guidance to Counseling Psychology," *Journal of Counseling Psychology,* 1955, 2:2–9.

[7] Leona E. Tyler (chairman), *The Current Status of Counseling Psychology: A Report of a Special Committee of the Division of Counseling Psychology,* p. 6. Washington, D.C.: American Psychological Association, 1961. (Mimeographed.)

[8] E. S. Bordin, *Psychological Counseling,* p. 14. New York: Appleton-Century-Crofts, Inc., 1955.

THEORETICAL FRAMEWORK

A theoretical framework is needed for explaining what happens in the counseling relationship and for predicting and evaluating the outcomes. Different schools or systems of counseling reflect in varying degrees certain personality and behavior theories that have been developed largely within this century. The theories that seem to be exerting the greatest influence on current thinking regarding counseling are the psychoanalytic, field, organismic, phenomenological, and stimulus-response theories.

Psychoanalytic Theories

The psychoanalyst stresses psychological determinism. He views behavior as goal-directed. He sees the individual as continuously striving for satisfactions which his social world tends to restrict, redirect, or deny. He perceives the motivational forces in human behavior as being both conscious and unconscious, as being emotional in character, and as being biologically derived and/or culturally determined.

Freudian Theory. According to Freud, the founder of psychoanalysis, every individual has a certain amount of instinctual energy which is expressed through the two fundamental tendencies of sex and aggression, described as the life or love instinct and the death or destructive instinct. The life instinct, termed the libido, is expressed through primitive, biological, sexual impulses directed toward the external world of people and things and often revealed in strong self-preservative patterns. The destructive instinct may be expressed outwardly through overt aggression or turned inward through self-injury or self-punishment. As a result of internal or external pressure, it may be repressed and cause regression to primary levels of activity.

Repression and regression are central concepts in orthodox Freudian theory. The individual early comes to accept the reality principle: He learns that, to escape censure or punishment, he must adjust to the demands of others. He may adjust by pushing the unacceptable or forbidden impulses into the unconscious. This is repression. Or he may adjust by using a form of response which had adjustive efficiency at an earlier age but which is no longer effective or appropriate in the given situation. This is regression.

By constantly threatening to escape into consciousness, the repressed material creates anxiety, which is a vague, objectless sense of fear, dread, or foreboding. Learning the social mores often involves pain because punishment is a common method of external control. Hence, anxiety may be aroused by anticipation of pain in a new learning situation.

To cope with his anxieties, the individual develops such mechanisms as rationalization (giving "good" reasons for the real ones); projection (attributing to another person or thing the blame for one's own deficiencies or failures); displacement (directing toward one person or thing the feeling aroused by another); reaction formation (expressing an unwanted feeling, thought, or desire in some form other than the real one); retreat through shyness, day dreams, physical withdrawal, and the like; sublimation (substituting achievement of an acceptable goal or desire for an unacceptable one); and compensation (seeking superiority in one area to make up for inferiority in another). Both normal and abnormal people use these mechanisms. Use becomes neurotic when it is highly exaggerated, excessive, or stereotyped, that is, clung to in spite of the fact that use is inappropriate and not helpful in dealing with anxiety.

Freud stressed the genetic approach. He taught that the causes of all present behavior can be found in prior emotional experiences, that a person's significant adult psychological patterns are the products of his earlier adaptive experiences. He found the individual's personality dependent upon development through certain stages from birth to adulthood. He described these stages as fixed and universal. During infancy (approximately the first five years of life) the individual is controlled by the "pleasure principle." He seeks immediate and complete satisfaction of his wants and is mainly concerned with physical activities and sensuous satisfaction. He makes strong demands for love, care, and attention. His basic attachment is to the mother. The latency stage (roughly from the fifth to the twelfth year) is marked by repression, reaction formation, sublimation, and identification with the parent of the same sex. The third, the pubertal, stage is marked by sexual maturation and increased interest in erotic activities.

The classic psychoanalytic method utilizes free association (free-flowing, uninhibited talk) to help bring repressed material into consciousness and thereby to uncover early emotional traumata. Freud held that anything which comes to a client's mind is important because all mental processes are psychologically determined. He used transference to uncover the client's hidden (unconscious) goals. In transference the client displaces on the analyst the role of the parent or another person who has been the object of his ungratified wishes. By encouraging the outpouring of repressed feelings and desires and by interpreting the client's behavior and dreams, the analyst helps the client to bring into consciousness material from even deeper levels of repression.

One of Freud's colleagues, Carl Jung, developed his own theory of personality but within the Freudian framework. He too assumed the basic source of energy to be a generalized psychic force which he also termed the "libido," but he denied that the basic instinctual impulses to action are primarily sexual. He described the libido as tending to take one of two directions—(1) outward toward the external environment, resulting in development of the extravert type of person, and (2) inward toward the individual's subjective life patterns, resulting in the introvert type. While both directions are necessary, an individual tends to exhibit one more than the other and so can be typed accordingly.

Jung considered learning to express fully one's individuality ("individuation") to be essential to mental health. Individuation (sometimes termed "self-realization" or "self-actualization") stresses the uniqueness of human motives. This concept, the theory of personality types, and the introduction of the word association test for identifying neurotic complexes are among Jung's important contributions to psychoanalysis.

Neo-Freudian Theories. Some of Freud's followers developed new theories that are in part elaborations or extensions of his. They are frequently referred to as social psychologists because they stress the influence of social variables on personality development. Rejecting Freud's instinctivist position, they emphasize the social rather than the biological conditions of personality. They perceive anxiety as socially produced and underscore the concept of the creative self. Human nature, they say, is malleable; so is society. Through his inherent creative powers man can effect changes in himself and his society. Adler, Rank, Horney, Sullivan, and Fromm are some members of this group.

For Alfred Adler the basic motivating force was the "will to power" or the urge toward superiority. The helplessness and inadequacy experienced in infancy and childhood create in the individual a strong purposive impulsion toward some goal of perfect achievement. The individual early encounters frustration of this outgoing impulse or will to power. He finds that he must accommodate himself to the demands of others who are stronger than he. When this occurs, he experiences feelings of inferiority that cause him to develop compensatory patterns of behavior.

Emotional disturbances stem from difficulties in social adjustment. The individual who does not learn socially approved ways of dealing with his feelings of inferiority through compensation, sublimation, and the like may be caught in a vicious circle of inferiority feelings, ineffective compensatory acts, more social disapproval, more intense feelings of frustration and inferiority, and so on. Neurotic patterns result.

Each person develops a special life style which is relatively fixed before adolescence and which is revealed in the individual's typical ways of seeking goals associated with social approval and power. The determiners of the life style are social and constitutional in nature. Heredity endows the individual with certain abilities; the environment gives him certain impressions. The abilities, the impressions, and the way in which the individual experiences them or interprets his experiences are the bricks with which the individual creates or builds his attitude toward life—the attitude that determines his relations to the outside world.[9]

Otto Rank described the neurotic person as one who has not dis-charged through the beneficial catharsis of childhood the primal anxiety evoked by birth. Because birth creates the basic infantile need for shelter, safety, and someone to cling to, Rank saw in the birth trauma the proto-type of all situations arousing anxiety. He found that the neurotic needs a type of therapy that permits him to experience rebirth—to form a new ego ideal through progressive development of the will and the expression of individuality. He perceived psychotherapy as a socializing process di-rected toward helping the client exchange immature, dependent attitudes for attitudes of independence, responsibility, and initiative.

The therapist's chief function is to help the client discover and use his creative tendencies, to help him accept himself, develop self-con-fidence, and achieve creative adjustment. To be able to establish a rela-tion that has value in itself rather than merely as a means to an end, the therapist must genuinely respect the client and have faith in his capacity to "will"—to initiate and control constructive activity. Ex-periencing respect in his relations with the therapist helps the client learn to win respect in his relations with others.

Like Adler, Karen Horney stressed the importance of environ-mental and cultural factors in the development of behavior. She saw the individual's personality as evolving from his total childhood experiences and as being dynamic and not relatively fixed by adulthood. "All of us," she wrote, "retain the capacity to change, even to change in fundamental ways, as long as we live." [10]

She too perceived the basic anxiety as stemming from the child's helplessness and defenselessness. Because during childhood the individual cannot compete with those who are older, wiser, or stronger than he is, he early comes to see the world as "potentially menacing." In seeking safety in a threatening world, he is motivated by three fundamental tendencies: (1) to move toward others, a tendency that has its roots in love and the need to belong; (2) to move against others, a tendency that has its roots in a striving for power and prestige through aggression; and (3) to move away from others, a tendency that has its roots in self-concern. The neuroses are explained in terms of disturbances in these three funda-mental aspects of interpersonal relations. When, for example, the tend-ency followed is inappropriate to the situation or when a tendency be-comes fixated and is used compulsively, difficulty arises.

According to Harry Stack Sullivan, an individual's personality comes about through his dealing with the crises encountered in six de-velopmental stages—infancy, childhood, juvenile, preadolescence, adoles-

[9] Alfred Adler, "The Fundamental Views of Individual Psychology," Interna-tional Journal of Individual Psychology, 1935, 1:5.

[10] Karen Horney, Our Inner Conflicts, p. 242. New York: W. W. Norton & Com-pany, Inc., 1943.

cence, and maturity. The extent to which approbation and facilitation or disapproval and deprivation are experienced in early life, particularly in the home, determines whether the developing self is loving and appreciative or hostile and disparaging.

Like Freud, Sullivan considered anxiety to result from inner impulses that threaten one's relations with others. Unlike Freud, he found the wellsprings of anxiety not in the instincts, but in the habits or motives that the individual acquires in his social interactions, that is, acquires in striving to resolve conflicts between desire for satisfaction of biological needs and desire for security, culturally determined.

Anxiety is restrictive. It focuses attention selectively upon those aspects of personal interaction that bring approval or disapproval. Qualities that elicit acceptance and recognition are developed. Other potential tendencies are excluded or disassociated. Some tendencies that could increase the individual's capacity to handle future problem situations go unattended or are repressed. Thus anxiety interferes with learning and reduces the probability of foresightful planning.

Erich Fromm's analytic theory is based upon the conception of a disturbed relation of the self to society. Neurotic patterns are the result not only of social pressures that frustrate the expression of basic drives but also of new needs that are culturally produced. A society that emphasizes aggressive competition produces certain kinds of needs and personality difficulties. A society that emphasizes cooperation produces other kinds.

Man, says Fromm, has lost the security once found through a predetermined place in society. Today he experiences the loneliness that accompanies competition for status. The social structure of modern capitalistic society has brought him more freedom in that it has made him more self-reliant, independent, and critical. But with increased freedom man has become more isolated, alone, and afraid—more insecure. Seeking a new security, he may find "escape from freedom" in authoritarian structures that offer him certainty, group belongingness, and purpose but at the cost of self-reliance, freedom, and critical faculties.

Trends and Contributions. There is a clear trend in psychoanalytic theory away from stressing biological factors as the all-powerful determiners of human behavior to emphasizing social and cultural factors. Also today the focus tends to be upon the client's present condition rather than upon his past. Less stress is being placed on sexual needs and more on such needs and feelings as love, hostility, and ambivalence.

Psychoanalytic theory has made important contributions in the way of new emphases and relatively new concepts that were developed to describe the conscious and unconscious processes. These concepts have been adopted with somewhat altered meanings in other psychological theories. Such terms, for example, as "awareness" or "levels of awareness" are substituted for "the unconscious." The concept of the unconscious must be taken into account because, as Tyler [11] says, "while many psychologists do not like the notion of the unconscious as a part of the personality and while some have been able to dispense with the whole notion, most of us who are doing counseling constantly encounter what seems to be evidence for processes that occur without the subject's awareness."

Other psychoanalytic concepts that have infiltrated into psychology in general are those of the defense mechanisms, repression, and regression. Contributions in terms of emphases include the following: (1) Life is fundamentally a dynamic process, and man is striving, wishing, or purposive by nature. (2) The experiences of the early years of life have a special significance for personality development. (3) Life histories derived in interviews, systematic observation of child behavior and development, and study of regressive phenomena in normal and abnormal behavior are important sources of data on personality and behavior. (4) The interview is a social act. The quality of the counselor-client relationship and the client's perception of it are important factors in helping the client to become aware of his distorted behavior and in helping him to achieve spontaneity and rationality.

Psychoanalytic theorists have been severely criticized because of their failure or limited effort to test basic hypotheses through scientific research. It is recognized, however, that it is not easy to conduct experimental studies of psychoanalytic concepts because it is not easy to duplicate under controlled laboratory conditions the stresses and strains of everyday life.

Psychoanalytic theorists are charged with lack of clarity and explicitness. For example, the social psychologists, the critics say, stress that society molds its members but fail to tell how this is done. They are accused of believing in some sort of mystic elements which, if left to develop spontaneously, would lead to social adjustment. They are also criticized for holding too idealistic conceptions of man, for excessive use of reasoning by analogy, and for the use of pictorial, metaphorical language.

Despite such limitations, psychoanalytic theory is exerting a strong influence on psychological thinking. It is strongly reflected in the counseling literature, where personality and behavior are frequently described in psychoanalytic terms. Some counseling psychologists draw heavily on psychoanalytic theory because, as one [12] says, "it seems to offer a basis for explaining more of human behavior." And the teachings of Otto Rank is, according to Rogers,[13] "an important point of origin" for client-centered counseling.

[11] Leona E. Tyler, "Theoretical Principles Underlying the Counseling Process," *Journal of Counseling Psychology*, 1958, 5:5.

[12] Bordin, *op. cit.*, p. 127.

[13] Carl R. Rogers, *Client-centered Therapy*, p. 10. Boston: Houghton Mifflin Company, 1951.

Field Theory

Field theory was developed under the leadership of Kurt Lewin, who perceived behavior as the result of a dynamic force system that is in a constant state of change. According to this theory, the individual is a whole configuration of forces operating toward or away from an environment which also is a configuration of forces.

The environment is differentiated into the psychological and the objective. The first (termed "life space") includes the individual's needs, past experiences, potentialities to action, and the behavior possibilities perceived by him. The possibilities not perceived or not recognized by him are not a part of his psychological environment. They belong to the objective environment (termed "foreign hull of the life space"). Although not a part of the individual's life space, the objective environment is not without its influence or effect. A state's educational code, for example, may lie outside a boy's life space but affects it insofar as it helps to determine the quality of the instruction and guidance received by him at school.

Behavior is viewed from the frame of reference of the behaver. The forces directly producing his reactions are consciously experienced as restlessness or urges toward particular goals. They can be inferred by others from the presence of tension in the individual and from the movements he makes toward or away from objects and situations.

The individual's behavior is determined essentially by the value of the goal objects in his life space. This is the "principle of valence." Valences are determined by the kinds of needs that the objects reacted to fulfill for the individual—from the point of view of the individual. They are positive or negative in keeping with whether the objects meet his present needs or threaten him with harm or injury.

The course of an individual toward a goal may be through physical barriers, such as the distance a boy must run or the fence he must climb in order to retrieve a ball. Or it may be through psychological barriers, such as the prejudices a minority group member may have to overcome in order to become a public official in his community. Frustration of a need may lead to random or ill-directed activity. When frustration is chronic or overly severe, the most likely result is angry attack or fearful avoidance.

Lewin postulated two kinds of causation: (1) historical—previous events that cause a particular event to occur, such as events in the individual's home and school experience, and (2) systematic—relationships or properties of the individual's life space at the time the event occurs. Only systematic causation, Lewin said, is dealt with in scientific study and analyses. His insisting that behavior depends on the present rather than the past or the future has evoked strong criticism of his theory from psychologists who believe that prediction of future events requires a historical frame of reference.

While Lewin did not write about counseling problems directly, some of his writings on group dynamics, resolution of social conflicts, and reeducation indirectly bear on the subject. In these writings Lewin stressed that change in an individual's concepts, perceptions, and sentiments requires change in his culture or a new set of values from his point of view. This in turn requires, among other things, creation of an atmosphere of spontaneity and freedom of choice. "The objective sought will not be realized as long as the new set of values is not experienced by the individual as something freely chosen." If he complies from fear of punishment rather than from the dictates of his free will and conscience, reeducation will not be achieved. "Acceptance of the new set of values and beliefs cannot usually be brought about item by item" when the individual feels strongly loyal to the old values and hostile to the new.

> Arguments proceeding logically from one point to another may drive the individual into a corner. But as a rule he will find some way—if necessary a very illogical way—to retain his beliefs. No change of conviction on any specific point can be established in more than an ephemeral way so long as the individual has not given up his hostility to the new set of values as a whole, to the extent of having changed from hostility at least to open-mindedness.

> Step-by-step methods *are* very important in reeducation. These steps, however, have to be conceived as steps in a gradual change from hostility to friendliness in regard to the new system as a whole rather than as conversion of an individual one point at a time.[14]

Lewin stressed that "as a rule, the possession of correct knowledge does not suffice to rectify false perception" and that "change in sentiments do not necessarily follow changes in cognitive structures." Reeducation may be only at the level of verbal expression and never reach the level of conduct. Moreover, it may increase the discrepancy between the real self and the ideal self "and thus give the individual a bad conscience. Such a discrepancy leads to a state of high emotional tension but seldom to correct conduct. It may postpone transgressions but is likely to make transgressions more violent when they occur." [15]

Organismic Theory

Different versions of organismic theory are represented by Goldstein, Angyal, Maslow, and Lecky. In general, however, the basic features are as follows:

The organism consists of differentiated parts which are articulated in a unified whole. The individual is not a dual system of mind and

[14] Kurt Lewin (edited by Gertrude Weiss Lewin), *Resolving Social Conflicts*, p. 66. New York: Harper & Row, Publishers, Incorporated, 1948.

[15] *Ibid.*, p. 63.

body, nor does he function as a series of differentiated parts. The normal personality is an integrated, consistent, coherent unity. Disorganization is pathological and is usually produced by an oppressive or threatening environment or interorganic anomalies.

The unified whole can be analyzed by being differentiated into its constituent members, but a part abstracted from its whole cannot be studied as an isolated entity. What happens to the part affects the whole, but the laws that govern the whole cannot be found in the parts. The laws governing the functioning of the whole must be discovered before the functioning of any component part can be understood. An invalid's symptom, for example, cannot be explained as the result of an organic lesion or disease but must be considered a manifestation of the total organism. More can be learned about personality through intensive studies of individuals than through intensive studies of separate processes, such as perception and learning.

The sovereign motive that gives direction and unity to the individual's life is self-actualization. The individual continuously strives to realize his inherent potentialities for growth. Through the choices that he makes he in part determines or creates the self. Given a free choice, the normal person will most of the time choose that which is good for growth. His inner inherent nature is not "evil" or "bad"; it is "good" or neutral.

If the individual cannot control the environment, he adapts himself to it. He develops into a healthy, integrated personality in a favorable environment. An inadequate environment can limit his growth; a malignant one can cripple or destroy him.

Hall and Lindzey [16] describe organismic theory as being more of an attitude or frame of reference than a systematic behavior theory. There is little fault to find with it, they say, "because it is so universally accepted."

> Who is there in psychology today who is not a proponent of the main tenets of organismic theory that the whole is something other than the sum of its parts, that what happens to a part happens to the whole, and that there are no separate compartments within the organism? What psychologist believes that there is a mind which is separate from the body, a mind which obeys laws different from those pertaining to the body? Who believes that there are isolated events, insulated processes, detached functions? Very few if any psychologists subscribe any longer to an atomistic viewpoint. We are all organismic psychologists whatever else we may be.

Phenomenological Theory

The phenomenologists postulate a "phenomenal world" that is very much like Lewin's "life space." An individual's behavior is com-

[16] Calvin S. Hall and Gardner Lindzey, *Theories of Personality*, p. 329. New York: John Wiley & Sons, Inc., 1957.

pletely determined by everything experienced by him at the moment of action and by the way in which the events in the phenomenal field are perceived by him. Elements that are at a low level of awareness or "unconsciously perceived" come into awareness or consciousness when they are associated with a need. A man, for example, may pick up a nail file and use it to loosen a small screw when a screwdriver is not at hand. The nail file becomes differentiated from the figure-ground matrix and is perceived as a screwdriver rather than a file.

Reality for the individual is the phenomenal field as perceived and experienced by him, and his behavior is a product of the field as perceived at the moment of action. The field has stability but is not static. It changes with changes in the individual's needs and with changes in external conditions. Changing needs and changing alterations in the perceptual relations bring changes in behavior. A boy who "hates all grown-ups" needs adult assistance to get out of a bad situation resulting from his carelessness. He receives help from a teacher. The teacher previously perceived as "an old witch" is now seen as "a nice lady." Changes created in the field created by alterations in the perceptual relations bring changes in the boy's behavior.

Learning is change in the direction of increased differentiation in the phenomenal field (self, others, experiences, environment, etc.). Things first perceived by the individual as ground emerge into figure, and things previously seen as fixed are perceived as changeable. Learning is taking place in counseling, for example, when a girl begins to see herself not as "all bad" but with strengths and positive traits as well as weaknesses and negative traits, when she begins to differentiate childhood relations with parents from her relations with them as an adolescent or a young woman, when she perceives that a friend is overdemanding in some situations but generous and protective in others, etc.

The "phenomenal self" is that aspect of the private world which the individual refers to as "I" or "me." His "self-concept" is made up of those characteristics that he reacts to as the "real self" or the "real me." The self-concept may extend beyond the boundaries of the body to persons and things identified as parts of the self, such as parents or children, toy or house. A man may react, for example, to damage to his car as though it were damage to his body.

The basic motivation is to preserve and enhance the self. As Combs and Snygg [17] point out, the soldier facing a coming battle is not torn between a desire for self-destruction and a desire for self-preservation, as postulated by Freud.

> On the contrary, he is concerned solely with the adequacy of his phenomenal self. Although the situation will vary from individual to individ-

---

[17] A. W. Combs and Donald Snygg, *Individual Behavior*, 2d ed., p. 49. New York: Harper & Row, Publishers, Incorporated, 1959.

ual, it might roughly be described as follows: He may risk death on the one hand to *preserve* himself from becoming the kind of person who "lets his buddies down," and, on the other hand, to enhance his self-concept as being the kind of a person who is "one of the gang" or as brave as the others. Many of us place our physical selves in jeopardy to achieve a more adequate concept of ourselves.

Serious threat to the self-concept leads to adjustment difficulties. A situation that threatens one person may not threaten another. Possible failure in an examination creates tension for the boy who sees himself as a "good student" but not for the boy who knows he is a "poor student" and does not care. The individual may defend himself against danger to the phenomenal self by avoiding perceptions that threaten it or by perceiving threat all around him. A student with some particular adjustment difficulty, for example, may deny that he has a problem or may see his problem in every "case" that he hears about.

The individual with an adequate personality holds an essentially positive view of himself, that is, he sees himself as sufficiently adequate for dealing with life. He is able to take his negative aspects in stride. He has experienced sufficient acceptance by those around him (acceptance of people and events) to be able to accept himself and others. He is able to identify broadly and strongly with others. He feels a oneness with his fellows; he is sensitive to the feelings and attitudes of others. In contrast, the neurotic individual perceives himself in ways that are essentially negative. He cannot admit all aspects of his experience into the organization of his self-attitudes. He selects some perceptions for admission and denies admission to others.

Stimulus-response Theories

Because counseling is a process of learning and relearning, some counseling psychologists draw heavily on learning theories in which drive, cue, response, and reinforcement are basic concepts. A drive is defined as a strong stimulus that impels the individual to act and may be classified as primary or secondary. Primary drives are physiological in nature and include sex and aggression. Secondary drives are learned drives, such as fear and guilt. Cues are indicators that determine when and where the individual will act. Some cue examples are the sound of a bell, the smell of food or smoke, and the sight of a plane schedule.

Responses become learned or fixed if reinforced—rewarded. Responses that are not reinforced by reduction in the tension set up by the drive are weakened and may become extinct. Responses that reduce the drive are strengthened or reinforced. The reinforcement may be a primary reward, such as food that satisfies a physiological drive. Or it may be a secondary reward, such as praise, social status, belongingness, relief from anxiety, and the like.

Skinner [18] uses counseling to illustrate the operant conditioning principle: when a learner is reinforced for correct responses, he tends to make similar responses in the future. By not punishing (not showing shock, disapproval, or the like) and by listening attentively, the counselor reinforces the client's attempts to talk about his repressed and trouble-making behavior. "Free association (free of the punishment normally accorded illogical or excessive intraverbals) is encouraged by a permissive audience." [19]

Dollard and Miller [20] offer a detailed description of neobehavioral theory applied in psychotherapy. They perceive neurotic behavior as resulting from intense emotional conflict, such as that which occurs when fear motivates an avoidance response which conflicts with a goal-directed response. When the response toward a goal is halted because of fear, the fear is reduced. The avoiding behavior is thus reinforced, but the tension set up by the drive is not reduced. The individual again attempts a goal-approaching act. This again evokes fear, which causes the response toward the goal to be again halted. Because halting the response reduces the strong feeling of fear, the impulse toward the goal is repressed.

Although impulses to act are thus repressed, the unreduced drives remain strong. The individual is disturbed or preoccupied with thoughts motivated by them. Fear and unreduced drives cause him to develop neurotic symptoms in the form of phobias, obsessions, compulsions, and the like, which at the time of use may partly reduce fear and drive. In the long run, however, they reinforce them. Since repression keeps the individual from verbalizing his feelings, he cannot label or identify the causes of his neurotic symptoms.

In order that fear not be reinforced but be extinguished instead, therapy must provide a permissive type of situation that is the opposite of the punitive one in which fear, shame, and guilt were associated with certain words and generalized from them to thought. The therapist reinforces the client's response of talking while anxious by giving him his full, free, exclusive attention, by accepting and not condemning what he hears, by understanding and remembering, by not cross-questioning, by offering tentative rather than dogmatic interpretations, and by displaying calmness and sympathy. Talking freely helps the client to recover his lost memories and to lose his anxiety and fear. Extinction of fear helps him to become creative—to become "conscious of a new power in dealing with the world around him."

Through transference (transferring to the therapist strong emo-

---

[18] B. F. Skinner, *Science and Human Behavior*, chap. 24. New York: The Macmillan Company, 1953.

[19] B. F. Skinner, *Verbal Behavior*, p. 395. New York: Appleton-Century-Crofts, Inc., 1957.

[20] John Dollard and Neal E. Miller, *Personality and Psychotherapy*. New York: McGraw-Hill Book Company, Inc., 1950.

tional feelings learned in dealing with others) the client provides some information that he cannot give directly. Because some emotional responses transferred to the therapist have never been "labeled" by the client, he does not talk about them. He may not even be aware that he hates, fears, or pleads and so cannot label his reactions correctly; but the therapist can.

The client may acquire new verbal units (labels) in three ways: (1) He may hit on them himself when thinking aloud. The therapist silently verifies them. This is the preferred way. (2) He may acquire them through the therapist's selectively repeating things that he, the client, has said. This method is held advisable when the client gives evidence of being badly confused. (3) He may acquire them by rehearsal—by repeating or imitating statements made by the therapist. Traditionally this method is termed "interpretation." It has disadvantages and is used only when the client seems unable to help himself.

The lifting of repression and the learning of missing labels help the client to achieve the superior type of adaptive responses permitted by the higher thought processes. Restoring the higher mental processes in turn helps with further fear-reducing discrimination, foresight, hope, and adaptive planning.

The stimulus-response theory is an objective, experimental, functional approach to behavior. It is criticized for being atomistic, for overlooking the importance of the whole and the patterning of the parts, and for neglecting the subjective and intuitive aspects of behavior. The critics also point out that, while the heavy emphasis upon empirical research is approved, the considerable research reported deals only with animal behavior or narrow aspects of human behavior. In the words of Hall and Lindzey,[21] "as soon as the theory is applied to complex human behavior it is on all fours with other theories of personality, with *ad hoc* definitions, and reasoning by analogy, representing the rule rather than the exception."

Some Similarities

While there are marked differences in the five theories, there are also strong similarities; and the trend seems more toward agreement than disagreement. In all five theories the individual is seen as having to cope with ambivalences and conflicts that evoke anxiety. To understand how he acquires his anxieties, how he builds his defenses or develops his adjustive patterns, and how these patterns can be modified is a major concern in all approaches. All recognize, although in varying degrees, that motivation cannot be dealt with in terms of physical needs alone but must also be dealt with in terms of social motives—that the individual is molded by both biological forces and the expectancies and dynamic pat-

[21] Hall and Lindzey, *op. cit.*, p. 461.

terns of society. In all these theories increased emphasis is being placed on the psychological environment or world of experience as opposed to the physical environment or world of reality.

The relative importance of the conscious and unconscious determinants of behavior is disputed. There is less dispute, however, regarding the existence of unconscious motives than regarding the conditions under which they operate and the ways in which they operate. Reward or reinforcement, group membership, and early life experiences are generally considered behavior determinants. Disagreement focuses on whether they play major or minor roles. The theorists agree that the past influences present behavior if only through such factors as memories, ideas, and dispositions. They disagree regarding the best way to assess present behavior—through observing present behavior or through seeking detailed information regarding past events.

In all five approaches, counseling is viewed as a learning experience or developmental process. The process is explained in terms of such global experiences as maturation, individuation, and self-realization. It is assumed that the client brings to counseling problems associated with past experiences and that through the counseling experience he can learn to develop new adjustive patterns. Counseling is described as a process directed toward helping the client achieve change in needs, attitudes, and behavior.

While the methods differ, the basic tools are the same—the counseling talk and the counselor-client relationship. The psychoanalysts and the neobehaviorists emphasize more than do the phenomenologists the importance of interpretive cues, reinforcement, and manipulation of the counseling relationship. The phenomenologists focus more on motives and the organization of subjective, private experiences than on explanation of objective, observable events. But in all these theories recognition is accorded, with varying degrees of emphasis, to the importance of client motives and responses, internal experiences, communicable public events, counselor and client talk, counselor reinforcement (if only through attentive listening), an accepting and nonthreatening counseling relationship, the lifting of repression, and the freeing of growth forces.

PROFESSIONAL STANDARDS

Ethics. One mark of a professional group is that it has standards regarding professional responsibilities and ethical behavior. Some groups formally adopt and publish codes of ethics. In others the only systematic statements on the subject are the ones made by individual members in their presentations through the literature or at conferences and the like.[22]

---

[22] Two examples: Samuel Gluck et al., "A Proposed Code of Ethics for Counselors," *Occupations*, 1952, 30:484–490; C. Gilbert Wrenn, "The Ethics of Counseling," *Educational and Psychological Measurement*, 1952, 12:161–177.

The most influential codes in the field of counseling are undoubtedly the ones developed by the American Psychological Association [23] and the American Personnel and Guidance Association.[24] The second is basically similar to the first. Both deal with such matters as general responsibilities, competence, client welfare, confidentiality of counseling materials, and interprofessional relations.

Competence. An ethical counselor does not claim directly or imply indirectly professional competence beyond that which he actually possesses. If he lacks the competence needed in dealing with a particular case, he seeks consultation or makes referral to an appropriate resource.

A counselor needs to be competent in terms of personal as well as professional qualifications. Even the well-adjusted counselor needs to realize, as Patterson [25] says, that his needs, particularly his strong needs, affect his counseling and that professional education will help him to understand them and their effects on his work. A counselor's personal needs are likely to become interfering factors when he lacks sufficient sources of satisfaction outside the counseling situation. He is then tempted to use counseling relations for meeting his needs for recognition, prestige, self-aggrandizement, social companionship, and the like. For example, unaware of his motives, he may build up self-confidence by encouraging counselees to be dependent upon him. He may even use counseling to satisfy a need to teach which, in Patterson's [26] words, may include "a need or desire to be superior, to be dominant, to lead the client to the solution of his problems, or even to feel that the counselor must have the answers and should give them to the client."

Wrenn [27] also warns against "the tendency toward smugness and self-glorification" evoked by a client's dependence and gratitude. He cautions, moreover, against "the opposing danger of self-disparagement and discouragement because of the complexity of human behavior" and "the strain of indecision and uncertainty as to the most constructive course of action in dealing with a client." Because fatigue affects competence, a counselor should know his fatigue points and try to avoid counseling when he is too tired to function properly.

Confidentiality. The information obtained in counseling is confidential information that is discussed only for professional purposes and only with

[23] American Psychological Association, "Standards of Ethical Behavior for Psychologists," *American Psychologist*, 1959, 14:279–282.

[24] American Personnel and Guidance Association, "Ethical Standards," *Personnel and Guidance Journal*, 1961, 40:206–209.

[25] C. H. Patterson, *Counseling and Psychotherapy: Theory and Practice*, p. 47. New York: Harper & Row, Publishers, Incorporated, 1959.

[26] *Ibid.*, p. 50.

[27] C. Gilbert Wrenn, "The Fault, Dear Brutus—" *Educational and Psychological Measurement*, 1949, 9:360–378.

persons clearly concerned with the case. It is shared with others only when the others can be trusted to respect its confidential nature. In a case conference, for example, a counselor may report data obtained through counseling interviews; but all persons attending the conference should be so well trained in conference procedures that none will make the material a subject for conversation outside the conference or reveal any part of it to others. Also, a counselor may want to discuss interview material with some specialist, such as the school psychologist or the school doctor, whose assistance may be needed. Whenever possible and desirable (at times it may not seem desirable) the counselor should tell the student of his plan to consult others and seek his consent to such action.

A student may give the counselor information that the counselor thinks should be recorded and thereby made available to others. He should not record the information, however, without first obtaining the student's permission. In seeking permission, he may matter-of-factly explain that the information helps him to understand the student and his problem; that he thinks it may help others similarly and so he would like to record it but will not unless the student is willing. When the information is not likely to cause embarrassment or shame, the student will probably respect the counselor's motives, appreciate his interest, and readily agree to his recording the data where others, such as the homeroom teacher and class teachers, may share it. Should he refuse permission, then, of course, the information should not be so recorded. Once recorded, it should be looked upon as professional information and treated accordingly.

Obviously, a counseling interview should never be taped or recorded mechanically in some other way without the student's knowledge and consent. And when any counseling material is used in teaching or in writing, the identity of the persons involved should be completely obscured. Many people agree with Wrenn [28] that counseling material should not be so used without the permission of the counselee.

Students are sometimes thrown into a state of conflict by their having to choose between two courses of action, both of which seem wrong. Counselors experience similar conflicts. A student, for example, gives his counselor in strictest confidence information that the counselor may feel he should not keep secret. To violate the student's confidence and report the information may cause the counselee and others to believe that the counselor is not to be trusted. Not to report the information, however, may cause harm to the student or to others.

Each such problem must be solved by the counselor concerned in the way that he thinks best. Some counselors try to avoid facing such a dilemma by making it a rule "never to violate a student's confidence under any circumstances." Such a rule does not help the counselor to

[28] Wrenn, "The Ethics of Counseling," p. 171.

avoid the dilemma; it only changes the appearance of one of the horns. Instead of having to choose between violating the student's confidence and not reporting information that should be made known to others, the counselor has to choose between breaking his rule and not reporting information that should be made known.

Some counselors experience such conflicts when they learn of conditions that might be interpreted by the administrator or others as "calling for disciplinary action." Should, for instance, a counselor reveal to the dean, the principal, or some other authority what he has learned from a counselee regarding the prevalence of cheating or of homosexual activity among the members of a particular group of students? Some counselors would resolve this conflict by informing the proper authority of the condition but without revealing their source of information. If disciplinary action follows, it is not likely, however, that the counselee will be uncertain regarding the authority's source of information. Other counselors share the views of Tyler [29] regarding the proper answer to the question:

> My own answer would be "No." The risk that the counseling service could come to be regarded as an espionage agency is one which is too great to be taken, as it would rule out effective work from that time on. There are other channels through which knowledge of bad conditions can reach the authorities, and it is better that these channels be used. The counselee himself may decide to report the facts to the responsible officials. Another reason for the counselor to take no action himself is his realization that he is always working in the realm of attitudes and beliefs, not facts. What a client sees as homosexuality in his dormitory associates may only be a projection of his own desires. His belief that everyone else is cheating may be a rationalization of his own failure rather than an objective picture of what really occurs. As has been said before, the counselor is not in a position to sort out fact from fancy, and it is not important that he do so. It can only lead to confusion and complication if he drops this orientation.

If the counselor's position in the organization is such that his relationship with the counselee is not the confidential relationship normally expected, he should make his role clear to the counselee at the outset. A student may decide, for example, to keep silent about certain things if he knows that the man with whom he is talking is not only the boys' counselor but also chairman of the "discipline committee."

Counselors are sometimes asked by teachers, parents, and others what a student has talked about in general or has told the counselor regarding some matter in particular. Rarely is it necessary for the counselor to reveal confidential data. Suggestions and recommendations can be made to parent or teacher without violating confidences. While the coun-

[29] From *The Work of the Counselor*, 2d ed., by Leona E. Tyler, p. 98. Copyright © 1953, 1961. Appleton-Century-Crofts, Inc. Reprinted by permission of the publisher.

selor may need to take a firm stand against a parent's request for information, he cannot overlook the fact, as Bordin [30] points out, that the child
is not independent, legally, economically, or psychologically:

> Very rarely is it appropriate for the counselor to answer a parent's re-
> quest for information or guidance by saying only, "I do not think that I
> have any right to discuss this question with you." Where the counselor
> feels that he cannot or should not make any [disclosures or] recommenda-
> tions, perhaps because it is primarily a question of the child's attitude or
> because the major part of the difficulty is the parent's attitude, one that
> probably cannot be changed simply by recommending that it be changed,
> the counselor might respond, "Because a good deal of this situation can
> only be solved by your son's achievement of a deeper understanding of
> himself, I am afraid I cannot give you any concrete suggestions. Perhaps
> we would find it helpful if you can come in and talk it over."

When a counselor thinks it desirable to contact a counselee's
teacher or parents, he should usually first seek permission from the student. If he values competence and integrity more than he does expediency
and temporary success, he will abide by the student's wishes when permission is withheld unless doing so involves risk of "clear and imminent
danger" to the counselee or to others. When the student does give consent,
the counselor should bear in mind that the student may be glad for him
to "talk it over" with a parent or teacher because he welcomes the opportunity to shift to the counselor some of his own responsibility for correcting or improving the situation. Moreover, the counselor should consider
that the problem that the student is willing for him to talk over with a
third party may not be the real problem at all. To quote again from
Tyler: [31]

> To accept a boy's complaints about his mother's domination as the basis
> for his difficulties before the whole complex structure of interlocking at-
> titudes is made manifest may mean forfeiting whatever opportunity
> there may have been to change this structure. By the time it has been
> completely clarified, the boy himself may have handled the things that
> need to be changed without any necessity for the counselor's intervention.

There is no clear-cut rule to follow in such cases. The best one may
be the one offered by Tyler—"When in doubt, wait." Another good rule
may be, "Don't let the student feel betrayed or let down. Avoid working
behind his back."

Conflicting Loyalties. The counselor sometimes encounters basic conflicts
between a counselee's interests and those of society at large or of the

[30] From *Psychological Counseling* by Edward S. Bordin, p. 38. Copyright © 1955.
Appleton-Century-Crofts, Inc. Reprinted by permission of the publisher.
[31] From *The Work of the Counselor*, 2d ed., by Leona E. Tyler, p. 99. Copyright
© 1953, 1961. Appleton-Century-Crofts, Inc. Reprinted by permission of the publisher.

counselee's family or of the school, college, clinic, or agency in which the counselor is employed.

A counselor must use his best judgment in taking action to protect both society and the counselee. He does not want to take hasty or ill-considered action that might deprive a client of his liberty. On the other hand, neither does he wish not to report to the proper authorities if some serious crime may result from his failure to take such preventive action.

A counselor may feel that he has a professional obligation to contact some responsible family member who may be in a position to protect a counselee who is behaving in an impulsive, irresponsible manner with potentially dangerous consequences. A not-uncommon example is the teenager who is engaging in dangerous activities without the knowledge of his or her family. After tragedy strikes, the community might rightfully blame the counselor who knew of the situation but failed to take protective action by informing the family or the school authorities of the situation.

Responsibility to the Profession. The counselor encounters special problems of professional responsibility when a counselee seeks his opinion regarding the qualifications or actions of another counselor or teacher. He would then do well to heed Thorne's [32] instructions to clinical workers: "One professional man should never comment concerning the actions of another, since it is impossible to know the full details or reasons why a certain action was taken." In the reverse situation in which the counselor learns from a counselee of a colleague's presumably unethical behavior, the counselor may find it necessary "to take directive action to preserve the reputation of all concerned." Needless to say, such action should be taken in a professional manner.

Responsibility to Self. Counselors have a responsibility for safeguarding themselves against false accusation on the part of irresponsible persons. Those who handle serious types of cases will probably sooner or later find themselves in situations that threaten to compromise their reputations. In such situations it is wise to consult immediately colleagues or administrative superiors to explain the situation. The counselor's position is strengthened if he promptly assumes responsibility for reporting the alleged malpractice before the situation is generally publicized.

The counselor has an obligation to protect his professional reputation from damage by irresponsible or malicious persons. He should not, for example, hold conferences long after school hours when all others have left the building. Cautious counselors prefer to work in offices that have glass partitions that permit the occupants to be seen but not heard. To

[32] Frederick C. Thorne, *Principles of Personality Counseling*, pp. 67–68. Brandon, Vt.: Journal of Clinical Psychology, 1950.

some persons such precautions may seem absurd and unnecessary. To those who have had a bad experience or narrow escape, they seem sound.

The right to a private life is another of the counselor's rights that should be protected. In Patterson's [33] words, dependency, if encouraged, "leads to the client's placing demands on the counselor which interfere with his private activities. Such excessive demands should not be encouraged." Nor should a counselor become so involved in his work that away from the office he cannot keep from being preoccupied with his counselees' problems. He should not expect too much either of himself or his profession. He should not look for complete and miraculous cures. Otherwise, he should cease denying himself the right to engage in a satisfying occupation and seek another profession.

Adoption of the APA or any other code will not, as Wrenn [34] points out, solve a counselor's ethical problems with respect to his loyalties to clients and the corresponding loyalties to self, others, and profession. The conflict can be resolved only by recourse to the counselor's own value system, which should be characterized by the ethical, cultural, and social values of the mature person, not the warped concepts of the immature person.

SUMMARY

The scope of counseling offered in the secondary schools and colleges is expanding to include more than educational and vocational counseling. This makes necessary counselor education programs that are sufficiently broad in scope and specialized to qualify the counselor for assisting students with emotional problems of more than average complexity.

In both counseling and psychotherapy the practitioner is concerned with trying to aid personal growth. Because the techniques used in both fields are very similar, the line dividing the two is not always clear. The counselor, however, usually works with people who are essentially normal rather than abnormal, whose problems are more likely to stem from external rather than internal conflict, who must overcome barriers that are situational or environmental rather than—or as well as—emotional, and who may not need many or long contacts with the counselor.

The psychoanalytical, neobehavioral, and phenomenological theories have been briefly summarized. While these approaches to counseling differ regarding the sources of anxiety, the development of neurotic patterns, the therapist's role in helping a client to gain release from anxiety and to develop new adjustive patterns, and the relative importance of subjective and objective phenomena and of the cognitive and affective aspects of learning, they have much in common. In all of them, the practitioners employ similar techniques; and the theorists of one affiliation may borrow

---

[33] Patterson, *op. cit.*, pp. 41–42.
[34] Wrenn, "The Ethics of Counseling," pp. 174–177.

the concepts, principles, and language of another. The hypotheses of these theoretical groups are yet to be fully verified through research.

Counselors are bound by the ethical restrictions imposed on them by their own private value systems; by community, social, and moral expectations; by professional custom; and by the standards set by their professional organizations. The APA and APGA statements on ethical standards offer rules of conduct on such matters as competence, general responsibilities, relationships with client, client welfare, confidentiality of counseling materials, test interpretation, interprofessional relations, and ethical standards in teaching, writing, and research.

REFERENCES

American Personnel and Guidance Association: "Ethical Standards," *Personnel and Guidance Journal,* 1961, 40:206–209.

————: *Counselor Education: A Progress Report on Standards.* Washington, D.C.: The Association, 1962.

American Psychological Association: "Standards of Ethical Behavior for Psychologists," *American Psychologist,* 1959, 14:279–282.

————, Division of Counseling Psychology: *The Scope and Standards of Preparation in Psychology for School Counselors.* Washington, D.C.: The Association, 1961.

————, Division of Counseling and Guidance, Committee on Counselor Training: "Recommended Standards for Training of Counseling Psychologists at the Doctorate Level," *American Psychologist,* 1952, 7:175–181.

————, Division of Counseling Psychology, Committee on Definition: "Counseling Psychology as a Specialty," *American Psychologist,* 1956, 11:99–104.

Arbuckle, Dugald S.: "The Education of the School Counselor," *Journal of Counseling Psychology,* 1958, 5:58–62.

Bordin, E. S.: *Psychological Counseling,* chaps. 2 and 4. New York: Appleton-Century-Crofts, Inc., 1955.

Code of Ethics of the National Education Association of the United States. Washington, D.C.: National Education Association, 1952.

Dollard, John, and Neal E. Miller: *Personality and Psychotherapy.* New York: McGraw-Hill Book Company, Inc., 1950.

Durnall, E. J., Jr., J. F. Moynihan, and C. Gilbert Wrenn: "Symposium: The Counselor and His Religion," *Personnel and Guidance Journal,* 1958, 36:326–334.

Embree, R. B., Jr.: "The Use of Practicums and Internships in Counselor Training," *Educational and Psychological Measurement,* 1951, 11:752–760.

Fenichel, Otto: *The Psychoanalytic Theory of Neurosis.* New York: W. W. Norton & Company, Inc., 1945.

Freud, Sigmund: *Outline of Psychoanalysis.* New York: W. W. Norton & Company, Inc., 1949.

Fromm, Erich: *Man for Himself.* New York: Holt, Rinehart and Winston, Inc., 1947.

Horney, Karen: *Neurosis and Human Growth.* New York: W. W. Norton & Company, Inc., 1950.

Karpf, F. B.: *The Psychology and Psychotherapy of Otto Rank.* New York: Philosophical Library, Inc., 1953.

Lee, A. McC.: "Social Pressures and the Values of Psychologists," *American Psychologist,* 1954, 9:516–522.

Maslow, A. H.: *Motivation and Personality.* New York: Harper & Row, Publishers, Incorporated, 1954.

Mowrer, O. H.: *Learning Theory and Personality Dynamics.* New York: The Ronald Press Company, 1953.

Murphy, Gardner: "The Cultural Context of Guidance," *Personnel and Guidance Journal,* 1955, 34:4–9.

Patterson, C. H.: *Counseling the Emotionally Disturbed.* New York: Harper & Row, Publishers, Incorporated, 1958.

———: *Counseling and Psychotherapy: Theory and Practice,* parts I and II. New York: Harper & Row, Publishers, Incorporated, 1959.

Pepinsky, H. B., and P. N. Pepinsky: *Counseling: Theory and Practice,* chaps. 2–3. New York: The Ronald Press Company, 1954.

Rank, Otto: *Will Therapy and Truth and Reality.* New York: Alfred A. Knopf, Inc., 1945.

Schwebel, Milton: "Ethical Problems in Counseling," *Personnel and Guidance Journal,* 1955, 33:254–259.

———: "Why Unethical Practice?" *Journal of Counseling Psychology,* 1955, 2:122–128.

Shoben, E. J., Jr.: "New Frontiers in Theory," *Personnel and Guidance Journal,* 1953, 32:80–83.

———: "Theoretical Frames of Reference," in L. A. Pennington and I. A. Berg (eds.), *An Introduction to Clinical Psychology,* 2d ed., chap. 2. New York: The Ronald Press Company, 1954.

———: "Toward a Concept of the Normal Personality," *American Psychologist,* 1957, 12:183–189.

Super, D. E.: "Transition: From Vocational Guidance to Counseling Psychology," *Journal of Counseling Psychology,* 1955, 2:8–9.

Thorne, Frederick C.: *Principles of Personality Counseling,* chaps. 2 and 6. Brandon, Vt.: *Journal of Clinical Psychology,* 1950.

Tyler, Leona E.: "Theoretical Principles Underlying the Counseling Process," *Journal of Counseling Psychology,* 1958, 5:3–8.

Walker, D. E., and H. C. Peiffer: "The Goals of Counseling," *Journal of Counseling Psychology,* 1957, 4:204–209.

Wiskoff, Martin: "Ethical Standards and Divided Loyalties," *American Psychologist,* 1960, 15:656–660.

Wrenn, C. Gilbert: "The Ethics of Counseling," *Educational and Psychological Measurement,* 1952, 12:161–177.

———: "The Fault, Dear Brutus—" *Educational and Psychological Measurement,* 1949, 9:360–378.

———: "Philosophical and Psychological Bases of Personnel Services in Education," in Nelson B. Henry (ed.), *Personnel Services in Education,* Fifty-eighth Yearbook of the National Society for the Study of Education, part II, pp. 41–84. Chicago: The University of Chicago Press, 1959.

18

The Interview as a Counseling Tool

PURPOSES AND ADVANTAGES

Purposes. In this book we are concerned with the interview for guidance purposes only. The emphasis is upon its use for helping students in all areas of their lives—personal and social, as well as educational and vocational. The interviewee may be a student or his parent, guardian, teacher, friend, or someone else who is an influence or potential force in his life.

The purposes served by the interview are basically the same ones served by counseling in general. Some definitions of counseling are also definitions of the counseling interview. One such definition is given by Berdie [1] and reads as follows:

> Psychological counseling consists of listening and talking with an individual about those needs, characteristics, and behaviors which make him similar to or different from other persons with particular emphasis in the discussion on the rational meaning and emotional implications of these characteristics. The purpose of counseling is to assist persons to select goals and objectives and to discover means for obtaining these goals.

Advantages. Because of its complexity the interview is probably the most difficult counseling technique to master. In comparison with some others such as testing, it has the disadvantage of being highly subjective. It has, however, important advantages. During an interview, for example, a student may reveal thoughts, feelings, attitudes, preferences, hopes, and desires not easily identified by the counselor through use of observation or tests or readily disclosed by the student in questionnaires, autobiographical writings, and the like. Actually, until the student explores certain matters by talking about them with an interested, accepting adult, he may not be fully aware of just what he does think and feel regarding them. By talking things over, he comes to perceive or to understand how

---

[1] Ralph F. Berdie, "Counseling Principles and Presumptions," *Journal of Counseling Psychology*, 1959, 6:176.

he feels and what he thinks. Both he and the counselor can then see his life situation, problems, and pressing concerns more clearly than before.

Also, a student may reveal in an interview thoughts and feelings of which he is fully aware but has not been able to express because of shyness, fear, shame, guilt, or the like. In a nonthreatening interview situation he may find that he can hurdle the barriers to communication. Moreover, the student who is aware of his feelings and is willing, even anxious, to talk about them but usually has difficulty in expressing himself may find communication relatively easy with an understanding, accepting interviewer. Not only does he get help in finding the right words, but he also finds communication furthered through his facial expression, gestures, posture, tone and inflection of voice, sighs, groans, smiles, laughter, frowns, scowls, and the like. He does not have to rely wholly on words in trying to express his thoughts and feelings, and he can tell from the interviewer's face, words, and manner whether or not he is being understood.

THE COUNSELING RELATIONSHIP

The Determining Factor. Success in interviewing depends mainly upon the quality of the interaction between interviewer and interviewee—upon the quality of the relationship established between the two. The interviewer needs an ability that is basic in all good interpersonal relations— the ability to feel and to show respect, to experience and to express understanding, to develop and convey empathy. The major determining factor is not skill in technique or strategy. It is, instead, the interviewer's attitude toward people in general and the interviewee in particular and the private philosophy underlying that attitude.

A good counseling relationship is characterized by genuine interest and acceptance, understanding and respect, sincerity and honesty. It is perceived by the student as being a helping, not a manipulative, relationship.

Interest and Acceptance. It is not enough for the counselor to be interested in and to like students in general. It is important that he feel a genuine, special interest in the one being interviewed. Interest is a basis for liking. Special interest and liking may not be felt at first but develop as the counselor attends to the student's talk. The student gives clues or information that makes him stand out as an interesting human being. As interest grows, liking develops.

A counselor does not like all students equally well; but, if he honestly believes in the infinite worth and dignity of every human being, he finds that he can usually develop a liking for a student in spite of the student's inadequacies, idiosyncrasies, and foibles. This is acceptance. If the student feels that the counselor likes him and accepts him as he is, with all his weaknesses as well as his strengths, then he can use the counseling relationship for achieving understanding and acceptance of himself, for perceiving and realizing his potentialities, and for growing toward mature, creative patterns of behavior.

When a strong bond of mutual liking develops, the counselor may continue to be a strong influence in the student's life long after the interview ends. The formula is very simple: The student likes the counselor because he feels that the counselor likes him; and, because he likes the counselor, he wants to be like him. Needless to say, such a possibility places a heavy burden of responsibility on counselors. Because establishing a bond of mutual liking can result in the student's using him as a model, the counselor must exemplify in his everyday living the traits or characteristics that are important in aiding students in their efforts toward full development. This possibility is one reason why Williamson [2] describes the counselor himself as a counseling technique. As he says, the counselor's very style of living "is an extremely important and effective technique in counseling."

If a counselor finds that he cannot develop a liking for a student or that he actually dislikes him, he should arrange for another counselor to work with the student. If referral is not possible, then he must try to control his feelings and work with the student as best he can. Denying that he dislikes the student is no solution to the problem. Recognizing his feelings for what they really are, keeping them under control, and listening closely as the student talks, the counselor may, to his surprise, find his feelings of dislike diminishing and feelings of liking developing. Accepting our feelings for what they actually are and not pretending to feel something that we do not feel often effect a change. Rogers [3] explains this "curious paradox" as follows: "When I accept myself as I am, then I change. I believe that I have learned this from my clients as well as within my own experience—that we cannot change, we cannot move away from what we are, until we thoroughly *accept* what we are. Then change seems to come about almost unnoticed."

Acceptance involves permitting the student to talk on subjects of his choosing and to express his feelings fully. A student, for example, may verbally attack school and teachers or home and parents. By displaying a neutral interest, the counselor avoids making him feel not accepted or rejected. By making such noncommittal responses as "M-hm," "I see," and "Uh-hum," he avoids reinforcing or putting the student on the defensive. To disagree and to defend the ones attacked would make the student feel guilty. To agree might strengthen his negative feelings. Permitting him to express his hostility can help him to avoid acting out his antisocial tendencies. And the neutral interest and empathic listening can help re-

---

[2] E. G. Williamson, "The Counselor as Technique," *Personnel and Guidance Journal*, 1962, 41:108–111.

[3] Carl R. Rogers, "Lessons Learned in Counseling," in W. E. Dugan (ed.), *Counseling Points of View*, p. 16. Minneapolis: The University of Minnesota Press, 1959.

duce the intensity of the feelings sufficiently to enable the student to examine the situation more objectively.

Understanding and Respect. The counselor conveys interest through attentive listening. He conveys understanding through his responses. Responding to attitudes conveys greater understanding than responding to words only. For example, a tenth-grade girl, in discussing her academic difficulties, tells the counselor that she knows she is a poor reader and hates being called on to read aloud in any class because the other students always laugh at her halting reading. She will probably give only a faint "Yes" if the counselor's response is "You feel that you don't read as well as the other students?" She knows that the counselor is listening, but she may doubt that he understands the meaning of what she is telling him. She may feel more certain regarding his understanding her and may answer with a flow of words if his response is simply "And that hurts." Now she knows he heard her and that he understands not only that she is a poor reader but also that being a poor reader can mean humiliation and pain.

Understanding involves sympathetic listening if sympathy, like empathy, means the counselor's putting himself into the student's place emotionally and psychologically—seeing things from his frame of reference and understanding his purposes and the meanings of things for him. Understanding, however, does not involve sympathy if, as Tyler [4] stresses, sympathy means feeling sorry for the student or pitying him. Pity will not strengthen the student. It can weaken him.

Understanding involves empathic identification but not emotional identification. If, for example, a student tells how intensely he dislikes a teacher, the counselor strives to perceive the situation as the student perceives it and to experience the quality and intensity of his feelings. But it does not involve his actually sharing the feeling—his disliking the teacher. He experiences the student's feelings but does not make them his own.

The interviewee feels accepted when he feels respected. If a counselor respects the student, he is willing for him to be himself and to differ from others. He believes in his worth and dignity as an individual, in his capacity to make sound decisions, and in his desire to do so. He is hopeful and optimistic about the outcomes of the student's efforts to direct himself —to find solutions to his problems, to make plans for the future, to live a socially useful life as a responsible individual.

Respect involves faith and trust. It does not involve approval or disapproval. In the words of Brammer and Shostrom,[5] the counselor says in effect, "I neither approve nor disapprove of your behavior and atti-

---

[4] Leona E. Tyler, *The Work of the Counselor,* 2d ed., p. 54. New York: Appleton-Century-Crofts, Inc., 1961.

[5] Lawrence M. Brammer and Everett L. Shostrom, *Therapeutic Psychology: Fundamentals of Counseling and Psychotherapy,* p. 156. Englewood Cliffs, N.J.: Prentice-Hall, Inc., 1960.

tudes; but I deeply respect your right to feel as you please and to feel differently from me." He respects the student's right to be a separate person and to make his own decisions.

The counselor's displaying attitudes of acceptance and respect helps the student to develop a sense of self-respect and self-responsibility. Self-acceptance is based largely on being accepted and respected by others. To quote again from Brammer and Shostrom: [6] "The counselor's attitudes affect the interview climate which in turn influences the client's attitudes toward himself—attitudes of confidence, worth, and competence, for example."

Treating a student interviewee with courtesy and respect helps him to develop mature ways of thinking and acting—helps him to feel, think, and behave like an adult. Kidding and talking down to him can make him feel and, hence, act like a child. Joking and pleasantries are not out of order, but they should be used with students as with friends and co-workers. The interviewer may expect his students, like his colleagues, to resent remarks that sound too familiar or somewhat derogatory. In fact, he needs to be more considerate or cautious with students than with colleagues because adolescents and youth are likely to feel less secure and hence, to be more sensitive than adults.

Also, respect requires that communication be at the level of the student's emotional and intellectual development. A counselor does not use, for example, psychological terms or technical explanations that may be beyond his understanding. Nor does he expect a student to display restraint and understanding not ordinarily expected from one of his age and experience.

Honesty and Sincerity. Forthrightness and sincerity engender mutual understanding and respect and foster development of a helping relationship. When a counselor tries to be shrewd, to outguess or to outsmart a student, he shows lack of respect. When he is straightforward and honest in his approach, he shows respect and deals with the interviewee as, no doubt, he wants to be dealt with himself. Tricks and subterfuge put an interviewee on guard and can cause him deliberately to withhold information and even to falsify it or mislead the interviewer in other ways.

Even when lack of forthrightness is not motivated by a desire to trick the interviewee or to catch him off guard, it shows a basic lack of respect or faith and can evoke distrust on the part of the interviewee, who may decide that, to protect his interests, he should be reticent.

THE INTERVIEW A LEARNING EXPERIENCE

Not Standardized. There are no standardized interview procedures. Techniques are determined largely by the counselor's fundamental attitudes and theoretical training. Experimental research indicates that the person-

Ibid., p. 158.

ality and philosophy of the counselor and the quality of the counselor-client relationship are the major factors determining the effectiveness of counseling interviews. Counselors develop interview styles and patterns in keeping with their professional philosophy and their estimates of the needs of their clients. Those counselors who indiscriminately apply formulas and follow set procedures with all clients are most likely relatively untrained or charlatans.

Emotional and Intellectual Learning. Counseling is a learning experience. The counselor does not foster learning by lecturing or converting the interview session into a question and answer period. He does not use probing questions or prodding remarks to force the student to face himself squarely and accept the realities of life. It may be desirable that the student recognize and accept certain realities, but he may need time to accept the facts and to perceive their significance for him. He may not be able to learn them by listening no matter how often the counselor may point them out, but he may perceive them when he stumbles upon them in his own talking. To learn, he may have to do more talking than listening. To help him to learn, the counselor may have to do more listening than talking.

Much of the learning takes place outside the interview situation. The interview may only set the student on the path to learning. In schools and colleges the counseling cycles are often relatively brief. The counseling sessions with the average student are relatively few and intermittent.

The counselor helps the student use the interview for both emotional and intellectual learning by functioning as a facilitating and supporting agent rather than a manipulating one. In the past the emphasis was upon cognitive (intellectual) aspects of learning. Counseling was commonly described as proceeding through stages similar to the ones outlined by Dewey as the central steps in problem solving through reflective thinking. The conative or affect aspect of counseling was not always accepted. According to Williamson,[7] "a half century ago, emotions came into the [school] counseling relationship as a disturbance in the normal intellectual development of the individual. Indeed, the early literature of guidance deals with affect as something to quiet down so that it will not interrupt the development of the individual." Today it is generally recognized that both the conative and the cognitive aspects of learning are important, that neither should be overlooked or neglected.

The cognitive aspect of the counseling interaction is stressed more in counseling than in psychotherapy because in school counseling the average client is a normal individual seeking help in removing obstacles that are often more situational or environmental than emotional in na-

---

[7] E. G. Williamson, "Characteristics of the Counseling Relationship," in E. G. Kennedy (ed.), *Current Status and Future Trends in Student Personnel.* Pittsburg, Kan.: Kansas State College, 1961.

ture. Giving information and helping the student to strengthen his general understanding of human behavior are cognitive activities that many students want and expect in counseling. Some leaders, such as Williamson, consider it as unfortunate to underemphasize the rational aspects of counseling learning as it is to understress the emotional. Counseling, he says, should help the student learn to think logically, consistently, and constructively about himself, his relations, and his adjustments.

Under present secondary school conditions—many students but few counselors—the conative characteristics of the counseling interaction are probably the ones most often neglected. Too often a student is told and dismissed without being given a chance to tell or even to learn how he feels about what he is told. Hence, he may shortly have to go back or be summoned to be told again. If he were given an opportunity the first time to report and to explore his feelings he might not need to visit the counseling office as often as he does.

A primary goal of the interview may be to help the student change undesirable behavior patterns. Before change can take place, the student must feel sufficiently dissatisfied with his behavior to want to change and must feel that he is able to change. He may already be dissatisfied but lack confidence in his capacity to achieve and maintain new patterns. He may need help in feeling rather than in thinking his way through his problem.

Expressing his feelings clears the air and frees him to examine the bases for his concerns, worries, and problems. Expressing himself fully helps him to identify his feelings, important values, real interests, and goals. It helps him to understand himself as he is and as he wants to be. Talking uninhibitedly with the counselor may help him to recognize and accept his negative and ambivalent (contradictory) feelings as well as his positive feelings. He may learn that he can both like and dislike, love and hate the same things at the same time.

Talking freely with an understanding counselor in a nonthreatening situation helps the student to understand the feelings underlying his behavior and may help him to take responsibility for himself. For example, a student excluded from class because of an explosive outburst after a mild correction by the teacher may come to see that the behavior was caused not, as he had stated, by his intense dislike for the teacher but by fear of failure—by feelings of inadequacy produced by limited skill and lack of background knowledge in the subject. Perceiving the situation more clearly and objectively, he is in a better position to deal with his problem at the intellectual level. He can now direct his attention to finding out how to fill in the gaps in his knowledge and to gain the needed skills, to appraising his selection of course or curriculum, and to doing other such things.

Communication. The counselor's skill in communication helps to determine the quantity and the quality of the student's learning. In counseling, as in other interpersonal situations, the major barriers to communication are not listening, listening but not understanding, and the evaluative tendency—the tendency to judge, approve, or disapprove. As previously stated, these obstacles may be avoided by the counselor's trying to put himself into the student's place and by conveying understanding through responding to feelings as well as words. When the student accepts the counselor's responses as being accurate reflections of his feelings, the counselor knows that he is communicating understanding.

General rules cannot be offered; but some writers, such as Tyler and Brammer and Shostrom,[8] offer some helpful suggestions. Brammer and Shostrom caution against stereotypy—against stereotyped use of words and phrases. One example is the stereotyped use of "You feel. . . ." in opening statements reflecting feelings.

As Tyler [9] points out, the choice of words is important. A student may resent, "You were scared," but accept "You weren't sure you could do it." Another might vehemently deny that he was "emotionally disturbed" but readily admit that he was "confused" or "didn't know what to do." Should the counselor use terms rejected by the student, he quietly accepts the rejection and rewords his statement in keeping with the student's correction. Explaining or apologizing only increases the student's defensiveness.

The talk should be kept focused on the interviewee and his affairs. It is unwise to bring up one's own experiences or those of other counselees. The student may interpret the shift in focus as a shift in interest. When a student's remarks involve others, it is even wise, Tyler suggests, to respond to his side of the relationship rather than someone else's. If, for example, the student talks of a friend's rowdy behavior at a party, it is better to say, "You must have been embarrassed" than to comment on the possible reaction of the hostess or other guests or the meaning of the behavior to the behaver. If the student is concerned with the effects on the behaver or others, it is best to let him be the one to voice this concern.

Some writers include in their discussions of interview procedures suggestions for preventing a student's wasting time. They say, for example, that certain types of questions are useful for pulling a student back to the subject. But the point on which the counselor may try to focus discussion may not be the one of real concern to the student. It may be the one that he gives as his reason for seeking the conference but may not be the matter with which he really wants help. Experienced counselors know that an individual troubled by a matter that he finds embarrassing or difficult to talk about for some other reason is not likely to bring up this matter until he is reasonably sure that the counselor will understand or can be trusted to keep the conversation confidential. Hence, he may first talk about some "respectable" problem, such as choosing his lifework, selecting an elective, or joining a club. When he feels that it is safe for him to tell the counselor

[8] Brammer and Shostrom, *op. cit.*, p. 177.

[9] Tyler, *op. cit.*, pp. 30–31.

what is really troubling him, he begins to feel his way toward the real subject. If the counselor tries to direct the talk back to the first subject, the student may never get to the point.

It is often necessary for an interviewer to let a student ramble, not merely at first but at various points throughout the interview. Any questions asked by the counselor should be directed toward helping the student say what he wants to say. They should be such questions as "You think, perhaps . . . ?" and "Do you mean that you feel . . . ?" rather than "Now to get back to the subject. Did you say that you have always liked mathematics?" or "Why do you think chemistry would be better than physics?"

In communicating information obtained from tests, cumulative record, and the like, the counselor should not bore or confuse the student with long uninterrupted explanations. It is best to give the information in simple general terms and to pause periodically to let the student express his reaction and to ask for specific details or to request that a point be repeated or explained. If, for example, it is appropriate to report or to review the Differential Aptitude Test data contained in the cumulative record, the student may be confused by the counselor's reporting the subtest scores one by one and explaining in quantitative terms only. The student might not get a clear picture of the overall picture as he listens to the counselor say something like the following:

"Now, let's see. On the verbal reasoning test you made a score of 65, which means you did as well as or better than 65 out of every 100 of the students with whom you are being compared. On the numerical ability test your score is 10, which means that about 90 per cent of the norm group did better than you. On abstract reasoning your score is 45, which places you in about the middle of the group. On space relations you made 15, which is not much better than the numerical score. But on mechanical reasoning you do somewhat better. There you have a score of 45. On the clerical aptitude test you made 40, and on the language usage tests you do about equally well. On one, spelling, you have a score of 50; and on the other, sentence usage, you have a score of 55."

The information might be more meaningful to the student if the counselor would simplify his report and use qualitative terms primarily. He might follow his "Now, let's see" with something like the following: "The scores indicate that you are about average in language ability, abstract reasoning, mechanical reasoning, and clerical aptitude. They show from low-average to below-average performance on the numerical ability and space relations tests." The second sentence would be preceded by a pause and would not be given at this point if the student wished to explore the information offered in the first sentence. The discussion might lead him to ask for the information offered in the second sentence. He might ask, "How did I do on the math test—on the one where I worked with numbers?"

Similarly, educational and occupational information should be given in simple terms and in broken doses so that the student will find it easy to pick up information items and "handle" them as he sees fit. This type of communication gives him a chance to seek additional information and gives the counselor a chance to see whether he understands the information given and needs additional information.

Silence. The novice and the untrained counselor tend to find silence uncomfortable. They hasten to fill the conversational gaps and in so doing can hamper a client in his learning. A student's silence does not always reflect shyness, resistance, or anxiety. The student may need the time spent in silence for organizing his thinking, for finding words to express his thought or feeling, for reflecting on what he has just heard, for weighing what he has just said, or for relaxing. When disturbing feelings have just been expressed, the student may find relief in silence. Under the cover of silence he can reestablish control over his emotions and mend his defenses. He may need silence to look more closely at some insight just gained, to examine himself in a new light, to try to put some parts into a new whole. Without the silence he might not learn to see things differently.

A good counseling relationship helps to prevent long silences from becoming uncomfortable. At first, while such a relationship is being established, the counselor may need to give verbal support to help the student get started and to prevent his being made too uncomfortable by long silences. When, for example, silence has extended to the point that it becomes a barrier to communication, the counselor may help by commenting on the difficulty of getting on with the task of talking. He may say something like, "Sometimes it is hard to know where to begin. Take as much time as you wish to think about it, but it might help if you just start talking about yourself. Tell me anything you like." The student's response usually provides a starting point.

Much communication on the part of both counselor and student is nonverbal. The counselor must be as sensitive to the meanings of his own nonverbal methods of communication as he is to the student's. It does little good for him to assure the student in warm terms that he wants to help him if while he is talking he is looking through some papers on his desk or glances at the clock or, instead of sitting back in his chair in a relaxed manner, he sits upright, crossing and uncrossing his legs or grasping and ungrasping the arms of his chair. The average student will conclude that the counselor may want to help him but not much and that he wants him to get out of there as soon as possible. Likewise, the student will not believe what the counselor says if his facial expression and tone of voice contradict his words.

The basic communication skill is that of conveying understanding. It involves the use of more than words. It involves the total counselor—

facial expression, head movements, body posture, his sitting comfortably close or at a distance from the student, tone and inflection of voice, smiles, gestures, movements, and the like. Acceptance, understanding, respect, and sincerity can be communicated in many different ways.

GETTING STARTED

Some school people, intentionally or unintentionally, follow the practice of keeping a student waiting to learn the purpose of the interview. When the student is sent for and not told at once why he has been summoned, he is naturally curious. Unfortunately, under the usual conditions of student-teacher relations, he may also be anxious. He may then view the teacher, counselor, or administrator as a possible opponent rather than a friend. He may become defensive rather than cooperative. Not all interviewers, however, who employ the roundabout approach are trying to be cagey. They may be trying to put the student at ease. Such an approach is probably most likely used in interviews initiated by the worker but not scheduled routinely for advisement or counseling purposes.

For example, instead of explaining why he has arranged the conference, a counselor may first talk to the student about the weather, or ask him how he enjoyed the concert the evening before, or comment on some recent sports event won or lost by the school. One vice-principal in charge of guidance habitually uses this approach, as he explains, in order to help the student feel comfortable and to help the talk get off to a good start. Actually he makes some students feel uncomfortable. If, for instance, the student did not attend the concert, he may think that the vice-principal is indirectly reproaching him for not taking advantage of the cultural opportunities offered by his school or community. Even if the student did attend the concert, he may find such "small talk" annoying and wish that the adult would stop stalling and get to the point. He may wonder whether he delays explaining the conference so that he may "sneak up" on him and get him to "talk off-guard." If, however, on the basis of past experience, he knows that this is not the case, that the worker is only trying to be friendly, he may still prefer that time not be wasted in small talk. He wants to know what it is "all about" as quickly as possible.

Opening an interview by joking with the student, talking of some event supposedly of interest to him, relating some amusing incident, or discussing a gadget kept in the desk for such a purpose is a technique which is outdated but still used by some school counselors. It is not a very effective technique and becomes even less effective when stereotyped through routine use. It causes valuable time to be wasted.

Dressel,[10] for example, in a study involving recorded interviews,

[10] Paul L. Dressel, "Counseling Caprices," *Personnel and Guidance Journal*, 1954, 33:4.

found that from fifteen to twenty minutes were frequently spent in such conversations. He found that many interviews started out "with what might be considered a distinctly unprofessional approach involving entirely too much friendly exchange discussing nonessentials." Such use of interview time may depreciate in the student's thinking the value of the school's advisory or counseling service. If given a choice, many students would no doubt prefer that their interviewers be as forthright in their approach as is the counselor in these two examples. In the first one, the interview is initiated by an eleventh-grade boy and opens as follows:

STEVE: Are you busy, Mr. Moore?

COUNSELOR: (Looks up, smiles.) No, Steve. Would you like to pull up one of those chairs? (Steve brings a chair over to the desk.) How are you?

STEVE: All right. (Long pause.)

COUNSELOR: There is something you would like to talk about—

STEVE: Maybe I oughtn't to be taking up your time like this ... but I thought someone ... maybe you ... could help or tell me ... (hunches shoulders, takes a paper clip from desk, and pulls it apart).

COUNSELOR: Sometimes it is hard to find a place to start. Often the middle or the end is about as good a place as any.

STEVE: The end is best for me (speaks rapidly) because that's what it is for me. I busted another geometry test this morning— worse than the last time, and I really messed things up then.

COUNSELOR: You are afraid this means you will fail the course?

STEVE: Sure, I'll flunk it. No chance for me to pass it now. The folks say if I can't pass math, I can't go to ———— University ... that I'll have to stay home and go to junior college. Nobody wants to go there.

From the talk that follows the counselor learns that the boy feels that he has little status in his family and that he risks losing that little if he does not follow in the footsteps of his older brother, father, uncle, and paternal grandfather by becoming an alumnus of their alma mater. Some of his statements indicate that feelings of inferiority are preventing him from putting his aptitudes to work. Test data show him average or better in numerical ability. Toward the end of the conference the boy says that he intends to stay in the geometry class and get all he can out of it even though he feels certain that he will not pass the course and will have to repeat it in summer school.

In this next illustration of the direct approach in opening an interview it is the counselor who initiates the interview. The student is a ninth-grade boy.

COUNSELOR: Come in, Joe. I see you got my note (smiles). How are you?

JOE: All right, I guess.

COUNSELOR: Yesterday, I received this memo from Mr. Hamilton. He says that you won't dress for gym.

JOE: He said he was going to tell you.

COUNSELOR: Would you like to tell me about it too?

JOE: What's there to tell? (Raises his voice.) I wish he would stop talking and go ahead and flunk me or kick me out of class (scowls).

COUNSELOR: You feel you'd rather flunk than get into uniform ... but you are not very happy about it?

JOE: Naw, just mad.

COUNSELOR: Do you think you can tell me why?

JOE: Aw, you wouldn't understand.

COUNSELOR: You might try me (smiles).

Revealing mixed feelings of anger and shame, the boy tells in a stumbling fashion of losing his one gym uniform by leaving it on a bus, of not being able to replace it without asking his mother for money, and of not being willing to do this. Apparently until his father's recent illness and consequent loss of employment the family has had relatively few money problems but is now hard pressed financially. Pride and worry have caused the boy to handle the gym problem poorly. The counselor's inviting him to talk about the problem and his not pressuring him to justify or explain his behavior help the boy, as he might say, to get things off his chest. He finds that his problem is not beyond solution and that solution need not involve "taking charity" or making things more difficult for his mother.

A student personnel worker should, of course, open his interviews with a cordial greeting and some friendly remark, but he should quickly get to the point whenever he sends for a student or a parent, even when he must give him (or her) some unpleasant news, as when, for example, he must tell a father that his son will not graduate with his class or must tell a girl that she should go home because of some unfortunate occurrence there. When the interview is for the purpose of talking with a student about reported misbehavior, it is nearly always best for the interviewer to be straightforward—to say why he has summoned the student and then say something like "Would you like to tell me about it?"

At first the student may falsify and rationalize. If, however, in all his dealings with the counselor, he has found him to be sincere, frank, and consistent, he is likely to be more direct and honest than he would be if he thinks that the counselor is playing the role of a district attorney—trying to trick him into a confession. Friendly, courteous consideration and simple directness help him to speak frankly, to appraise the situation honestly, and to see what he can do about it. If counseling rather than court procedures are followed, both the worker and the student may come to understand why the student adopts certain behavior patterns. And the student may perceive other patterns as being more useful and more appropriate for achieving his purposes.

SOME AIDS TO SUCCESS

The counselor's effectiveness in interviewing increases if to the basic requirement (ability to interact empathically with others) he adds such important assets as maturity and emotional balance, objectivity and control of his biases, professional education, and a good reputation with students.

Reputation among Students. When an adviser or counselor has been in a school or college for some time, his reputation among the students may determine to a large measure the ease and speed with which he is able to establish good relations with incoming students. If the advisers or counselors are important people in student life and not just persons whom students see briefly on certain occasions, such as at registration time, a new student is very likely soon asked, "Whom did you get for your adviser?" If his reply evokes an "Oh, you will like him fine!" or "You surely did get a good break," then the way to adviser-student cooperation is opened. If, however, the comment is, "He's nice and a lot of fun but not much help," or "Be careful what you tell him," then the road to cooperation may be blocked before student and adviser meet. Obviously, development of good relations with the student's parents may be similarly obstructed.

To prevent communication with his advisees or counselees from being cut off or interfered with by other students, a worker needs to become known among students as someone who is warm, responsive, understanding, sincere, fair, consistent, *and competent.* It is not enough for him to be known as "a good guy." He must also become known as someone who "knows his stuff." Students have little respect for the counselor who offers the same explanations and solutions for all problems. They recognize the limitations of the untutored counselor who, in McKinney's [11] words, "adheres to a stock procedure—the employment of his own limited attitudes and skills irrespective of the counselee's needs." They respect the counselor who is able to help them in different ways with their different problems.

Personal Qualifications. A counselor's appearance in terms of dress and the like may be important because, as Robinson [12] says, it may be seen by the students as a symbol of maturity and ability. More important, however, is the level of maturity actually reached. The counselor needs to be a well-adjusted person who has achieved balance in his life, has developed insight regarding his own problems and conflicts, is able to live with them, and does not need to explore or refer to them during his interviews with students.

[11] Fred McKinney, *Counseling for Personal Adjustment*, p. 28. Boston: Houghton Mifflin Company, 1958.

[12] Francis P. Robinson, *Principles and Procedures in Student Counseling*, p. 43. New York: Harper & Row, Publishers, Incorporated, 1950.

The counselor who is handicapped by a lack of objectivity, who is not aware of his biases or is not able to control them, can be expected to show serious discrepancies and inaccuracies in his interview reports. If, for example, a teacher-counselor strongly disapproves of girls' appearing in public places dressed in shorts or jeans, his diagnoses and prognoses may be consistently more favorable for girls always seen "properly attired" than for girls often seen in "sloppy attire." His prejudice against girls' dressing like boys may influence the contents of his reports fully as much as does what he hears and observes during an interview. More than that, his prejudice prevents his establishing empathy with some students and thus renders him of little service to them.

The counselor who is not reasonably free of bias or is not able to control his prejudices tends to interpret an interviewee's remarks in keeping with these prejudices. The teacher-counselor, for instance, who generally thinks of Mexican-Americans as lazy and too easygoing, as being always willing to leave until tomorrow what should be done today, may accept Pedro Gonzalez's announcement that he plans to quit school as further evidence of the Mexican-American's lack of ambition and of failure to utilize his opportunities for advancement. Hence, he does not suggest to Pedro, as he did last week to Richard Gordon, that together they talk over his plan for withdrawal and consider its appropriateness for the future as well as the present. Were he to invite Pedro to sit down and reexamine his plan, he might learn, as he did with Richard, that the boy is very reluctant to leave school because dropping out means giving up a much cherished ambition, that it is the family's need for his help that makes withdrawal seem necessary rather than any desire for a chance to earn money so that he may have better clothes, buy a car, or the like.

The adviser was able to help Richard solve his problem and to stay in school. He might have given similar help to Pedro had his feelings toward the Josés, Pedros, and Jesuses in the school been as favorable or as free from bias as were his feelings toward the Thomases, Richards, and Harolds. In the case of Pedro, he did not even attempt to use the interview for eliciting and giving information that might have effected a change in both the boy's feelings and his plans. Not having encouraged the boy to talk, the adviser never learned that Pedro was not happy over having, as he thought, to quit school. The interview with Pedro was in no way interviewee-centered. Actually it is doubtful that the conversation with him should be even dubbed an interview.

Professional Education. To the strengths of personality the would-be successful interviewer needs to add the strengths acquired through professional training and supervised practice. The student who is served by a counselor who has the desired personal qualifications no doubt profits from his contacts with this person even though the worker may lack professional knowledge and skill. A mature, well-balanced adult can help young people with many of their problems but may not be able to help with some others that students rightly expect to take to counselors. Also, his efforts at times may be badly misdirected because more impulsive than systematic and objective.

The counselor needs to be well equipped with information about occupations, colleges, trade schools, apprenticeships, and the like. He also needs a broad, deep knowledge of people and human behavior. The knowledge of behavior dynamics that he may gain in the process of daily living is not enough. It must be supplemented by knowledge gained through professional study. Otherwise, he may accept at face value a boy's stating that he does not at all mind his parents' never permitting him to participate in afterschool activities or a girl's explaining that the only reason for her striving to be always at the head of her class is her strong thirst for knowledge. He may agree with a father that the man's son is an ingrate for not wanting to attend the college of the father's choice and prepare for a position in the family's business. The boy receives from the father everything that money can supply—car, fine clothes, generous allowance, etc.—and so should be more appreciative and more responsive to his father's wishes than he seems to be.

This same counselor may see in a young girl's anxiety never to go against the wishes of her parents only evidence of a happy homelife and an extraordinarily fine relationship between daughter and parents. He can be of little assistance to the girl and her parents in helping them to make the adjustment that all three may have to make before this girl can develop into a well-adjusted young woman. By praising the parents' too cautious watchfulness and by approving the daughter's unusual docility, he may help the parents to keep the girl a child and help the girl to slacken or even arrest her slow progress toward adulthood. The school counselor should be sufficiently well trained to be able to recognize undesirable emotional patterns. He should be able to see below the surface so that he will not unwittingly contribute to the strengthening or the continuance of undesirable patterns.

Lack of adequate education in psychology can handicap an interviewer. He may know, for example, that "behavior is caused" but not realize that he cannot always explain the cause in terms of his own way of life. He may know that differences in family backgrounds make for differences in student behavior but not know the behavior patterns, standards, values, expectations, and demands imposed by different social classes upon their members. Too many advisers expect all students and all parents to place the same value that they do upon certain standards of speech, dress, and behavior. Unthinkingly they tend to rate as less good, less important, or less worthy those who do not; or they tend to disapprove all behavior that conflicts with the standards of their own social group. They understand and accept better the students who follow their ways than those who do not. As a result, they may fail to establish good working relations with students and parents from socioeconomic groups other than their own—higher or lower.

Most counselors probably have learned to avoid, in their thinking about others, the stereotypes of race and religion. They know, for example, that not all Frenchmen are great lovers, not all Englishmen lack a sense of humor, not all Jews are money loving, and not all Presbyterians are cold. They laugh at such ideas because they consider them absurd, but many fail to recognize that some other generalizations that govern their thinking and behavior at times are also unfortunate and no less absurd.

At the end of the first day of school, for instance, a teacher-counselor may show her list of new advisees to another teacher and sadly call attention to the fact that she now has in her group Bill Jones, "another one of that Tom Jones's children who will be just like the others—completely impossible." It is the first day of school, and the counselor's contact with Bill was probably not five minutes long, but she has already typed Bill. In college this teacher-counselor studied courses in psychology, so she learned about individual differences. Yet she expects Bill to be just like his brothers and sisters, and she knows already that he is going to be completely impossible. Bill is not going to find it easy to establish rapport with his counselor, and at times this counselor may make it very difficult for him not to act "according to type."

There are other generalizations that make it difficult for some students to establish good working relations with some teachers and counselors and that interfere with their relations with other students if other students take their cues from teacher or counselor and reflect the attitudes of the adult in their behavior. The low-IQ student, the high-IQ student, the lazy boy, and the child from the broken home are a few examples. We have no right to assume that the boy or the girl from the broken home does not have satisfying emotional experiences; neither do we have a right to assume that the boy or the girl from the "good home"—the home not broken—does have such experiences. And by no manner of means can we assume that the low-IQ students cannot satisfy to a reasonable degree some of their strong vocational interests or cannot make important contributions to their groups, whether class group or some other. Then there is the girl with the bleached hair, the too bright lips, the low-cut blouse, and the too short skirt—is she an individual or a type? Is she adopting this standard of dress because she wishes to affiliate with the members of a particular group? Is she trying to affiliate with the members of that group because she has not been able to affiliate with the members of any other group? She must belong to some group or perish psychologically.

In short, to be able to use the interview for helping students with their many different problems, the counselor needs to have much specialized knowledge along with intelligent understanding of different types of groups and people. He needs to have the training that enables him to help students to achieve individualism while acquiring skills in social participation, to help them to make satisfactory peer-group adjustment while preparing for adult life, to help them to develop a moral sense and to attain moral maturity, as well as to help them to make good use of their educational opportunities and to find their places in the work world.

Interviewing is a science and an art that requires technical or professional knowledge of a high order. It requires the type of professional education recommended by the Commission on Guidance in American Schools.[13] Two recommendations are as follows:

> 1. That state certifying agencies for counselors and graduate faculties in counselor education specify that, in addition to essential professional courses and experiences, two other major cores be required in the counselor education curriculum; one major core is in the field of psychology, another in the social and other behavioral sciences, the two combined to represent a minimum of from one-third to one-half of the course work required for certification.

> 2. That the minimal two-year graduate program in counselor education include: (a) two major cores in psychology and the social sciences as described in Recommendation 1; (b) adequate orientation in educational philosophy and school curriculum patterns; (c) applied or professional courses ... to the extent of NOT MORE than one-fourth of the total graduate programs; (d) supervised experience in both counseling and planned group leadership to the extent of NOT LESS than one-fourth of the total graduate programs; (e) an introduction to the understanding and utilization of changing research concepts; (f) an introduction to the problems of ethical relationships and legal responsibilities in counseling.

CONDITIONS OF THE INTERVIEW

Setting. Some writers underscore the desirability of holding interviews in offices made attractive by comfortable chairs, flowers on the desk, drapes at the window, and the like. While an attractive office is desirable, it is not essential for good interviewing. The interviewer is more important than the place. A good interviewer can overcome inadequacies in the place through the attitude that he reveals toward the interviewee and his situation. If he is sincerely interested in helping the student and is ready to listen attentively and to try to understand, soon both he and the student have forgotten the place and are absorbed in the student's thoughts and feelings about his problem. If the interview is student-centered, it can be a good interview even though the chairs are hard, the desk is piled high with unfinished work, and the windows are dirty and curtainless. The physical environment is important, but more important is an emotional atmosphere of warmth, understanding, acceptance, and lack of pressure or coercion.

Some writers stress the importance of the location of the coun-

[13] C. Gilbert Wrenn, *The Counselor in a Changing World*, p. 161. Washington, D.C.: American Personnel and Guidance Association, 1962.

selor's office. Arbuckle,[14] for example, says that good counseling facilities "may be rendered ineffective by being placed cheek to jowl with the administrative offices. Students who may want to see a counselor to talk about their desire to bash the principal or perform some dastardly deed upon a teacher will naturally shy away if they see the offices together, assuming, reasonably enough, that there is a close connection between the people who are in the offices." Hence, Arbuckle would have the counseling offices away from the administrative offices and away from the flow of traffic.

Wide separation of administrative and counseling facilities may not be necessary or desirable, however, in schools where teachers and administrators, as well as counselors, accept and practice the personnel point of view and where the role of the counselor is well established in the thinking of students, teachers, administrators, and parents as being that of counselor in the true meaning of the term and is not confused with that of a punitive disciplinarian, "trouble shooter," or the like. Under such conditions there can be distinct advantages for students as well as faculty members if the distance to be traveled between administrative and counseling offices is not very great.

Privacy and Freedom from Interruptions. A comfortable setting may not be essential for a good interview, but privacy is. No matter how hard-pressed the counselor may be, he should try to conduct the interview in an unhurried manner. It is undesirable to delay seeing a student later than the appointed time, but it may be well to delay until pressing matters are taken care of and the worker is free to confer with the student uninterrupted. If he tries to attend to such matters during the conference, the student may feel that he should not be taking any of this busy person's time or that the counselor does not consider the student's affairs sufficiently important to require his undivided attention. He may depart without ever broaching the subject that caused him to seek the conference. The ideal of an uninterrupted interview is probably most frequently violated by telephone calls. If such interruptions are handled with tact and the student sees that the counselor sincerely attempts to moderate them, he understands and accepts such reality demands.

Interruptions by persons who want to say "just one word" can cause both parties in the interview not to use the time as well as they might were they not interrupted. That guidance is not equated with instruction in the thinking of some school people is clearly indicated by their not being so reluctant to interrupt an interview as they are to interrupt a class. Some teachers, who would be very much annoyed if others walked into their classrooms and interrupted teaching in order to ask for some bit of information or to make some other request, do not hesitate to open

[14] Dugald S. Arbuckle, *Counseling: An Introduction,* pp. 234–235. Boston: Allyn and Bacon, Inc., 1961.

the closed door of a conference room for such reasons even though they can see through the glass door or partition that counselor and student are engaged in a conference.

Time. Sufficient time is another ideal that is often violated. Much counseling offered in schools and colleges is of limited value because not enough time is allowed for the interviews. The time allotted to this service in some schools is no more than fifteen to twenty minutes a semester per student. The more active the student is in the conference, the longer the interview needs to be. Since the student should be a very active participant, such time allotments are exceedingly inadequate.

How can the time problem be solved? How can counselors have sufficient time for all their counselees, have time for follow-up work, and still have some time unscheduled for emergency cases? The best answer is probably the one suggested in the opening chapter of this book—reduce the counseling load to from 100 to 150 counselees per counselor, and do not assign to counselors functions that are not properly theirs. This situation already exists in some schools. The increased cost is justified since it can reduce the need for highly specialized treatment and/or institutional care of the emotionally handicapped and the delinquent. It should be added, however, that current provisions for the care and rehabilitation of the emotionally handicapped and the delinquent are far from adequate.

The amount of counseling time needed varies with students and the matters considered during the interviews. If, for example, the interview is held for the purpose of planning the program of studies for the next term, the time needed may vary from ten to sixty minutes. If the student is at the crossroads and cannot decide in which direction to turn, then an hour may be needed to help him define his problem, explore the alternatives, and come to a decision. On the other hand, if the student has reached a decision, the decision seems appropriate, and the counselor and the student have been working in close cooperation for some time, the time needed for filling in a form, verifying certain items, and checking the completed form may be less than ten minutes.

When establishing good working relations is considered a principal rather than an auxiliary use of the interview, the first interview will be scheduled soon after the student enters the school if not held before his entrance. If it is delayed until the student runs into some difficulty (fails a subject, breaks a rule, has trouble with other students or a teacher, and the like), the worker may not find it easy to establish the desired type of relation with the student or his parents.

Ideally the scheduling of interviews should not be left to chance, that is, scheduled only when a conference is requested by a student or when some special matter comes up. Under desired conditions every adviser or counselor sees each of his counselees early in the school year and at regular intervals thereafter. At the close of one interview he sets the time for the next one. Like some adults, some students may forget appointments made in advance and may regard a reminder as a friendly courtesy.

A counselor, in scheduling an interview initiated by him and not held routinely, should try to make the appointment for a time convenient to the student as well as to himself and should try to notify the student sufficiently far in advance. It does not contribute to good relations to decide to see a student during his "free period" on a certain day and not notify him until the morning of that day or even shortly before the interview hour. If the student has planned to use his "free hour" for some other purpose (and he has if he is a good manager), he may find having an interview then inconvenient and frustrating. As a result, he may not be very communicative or cooperative.

Interviews requested by students should be scheduled as soon as possible, and if possible, at the times requested by them. This is a chief reason why a counselor should not be overloaded. If he is, he may not be able to see a student until it is too late for him to be of any real help. In the meantime the difficulty may have become too great, or the student may no longer be willing to talk with the counselor even though he may still be in need of help and help is still possible.

SUMMARY

The interview is used in student personnel work for such general purposes as obtaining and giving information and for helping to bring about changes in attitudes and behavior. It is a highly subjective technique that can yield data not easily obtainable through such other techniques as tests, observations, and autobiographical writings. It is a valuable technique in the education and reeducation of students. In counseling it is the basic procedure.

The effectiveness of the counseling interview depends largely upon the extent to which it is interviewee-centered and upon the quality of the relationship established with the interviewee. The ideal relationship is one characterized by warmth, respect, forthrightness, acceptance, and empathy. The talk focuses upon the needs, feelings, values, and wants of the student rather than of the counselor.

The interviewer needs to be a well-adjusted, well-educated individual. He needs to be sufficiently at peace with himself to be able to avoid imposing his problems or conflicts on others. He needs the professional education that will give him a broad, deep understanding of human behavior and will equip him with the special skills and specialized knowledge required in helping a variety of students with a variety of problems.

The interview setting is of relatively little importance. The place selected should, however, provide privacy and a reasonable degree of freedom from interruptions. Ideally the conference time should be convenient to both counselor and student, and there should be sufficient time for the interview to be carried out in an unhurried manner. A worker's having to short-cut the interview process too often results in the talk never getting around to the subject that led the student to seek the conference.

REFERENCES

Arbuckle, Dugald S.: *Counseling: An Introduction.* Boston: Allyn and Bacon, Inc., 1961.

Barbara, D. A.: "The Value of Nonverbal Communication in Personality Understanding," *Journal of Nervous and Mental Disease,* 1956, 123:286–291.

Berdie, Ralph: "Counseling Principles and Presumptions," *Journal of Counseling Psychology,* 1959, 6:175–182.

Bordin, E. S.: *Psychological Counseling.* New York: Appleton-Century-Crofts, Inc., 1955.

Brammer, Lawrence M., and Everett L. Shostrom: *Therapeutic Psychology: Fundamentals of Counseling and Psychotherapy.* Englewood Cliffs, N.J.: Prentice-Hall, Inc., 1960.

Brams, Jerome M.: "Counselor Characteristics and Effective Communication in Counseling," *Journal of Counseling Psychology,* 1961, 8:25–30.

Callis, Robert, P. C. Polmantier, and E. C. Roeber: *A Casebook of Counseling.* New York: Appleton-Century-Crofts, Inc., 1955.

Davidian, Elizabeth V.: "Rapport and the Human Element," *Personnel and Guidance Journal,* 1955, 33:469–470.

Dement, Alice L.: "Good Students Want Counseling Too," *Journal of Counseling Psychology,* 1957, 4:113–118.

Foley, J. D.: "The Role of Counseling in Discipline," in E. G. Williamson (ed.), *Trends in Student Personnel Work,* pp. 201–212. Minneapolis: The University of Minnesota Press, 1949.

Hahn, Milton E., and Malcolm S. MacLean: *Counseling Psychology,* 2d ed., chap. 4. New York: McGraw-Hill Book Company, Inc., 1955.

Kahn, R. L., and C. F. Connell: *The Dynamics of Interviewing.* New York: John Wiley & Sons, Inc., 1958.

Kinzer, J. R.: "The Educated Counselor," *Journal of Counseling Psychology,* 1961, 8:14–16.

Krim, Elaine: "A Study in Nonverbal Communications: Expressive Movements during Interviews," *Smith College Studies in Social Work,* 1953, 24:41–80.

Lesser, William M.: "Counseling Progress and Empathic Understanding," *Journal of Counseling Psychology,* 1961, 8:330–336.

McKinney, Fred: *Counseling for Personal Adjustment,* chaps. 2, 9, and 11. Boston: Riverside Editions, Houghton Mifflin Company, 1958.

Parker, Clyde A.: "Empathy," *Personnel and Guidance Journal,* 1955, 34:89–93.

Peiffer, Herbert C., Jr., and Donald E. Walker: "The Disciplinary Interview," *Personnel and Guidance Journal,* 1957, 35:347–350.

Reik, Theodor: *Listening with the Third Ear.* New York: Farrar, Straus & Cudahy, Inc., 1949.

Rudikoff, Lynn C., and Barbara S. Kirk: "Goals of Counseling: Mobilizing the Counselee," *Journal of Counseling Psychology,* 1961, 8:243–249.

Tyler, Leona E.: *The Work of the Counselor*, 2d ed., New York: Appleton-Century-Crofts, Inc., 1961.

Walker, Donald E., and Herbert C. Peiffer, Jr.: "The Goals of Counseling," *Journal of Counseling Psychology*, 1957, 4:204–209.

Williams, John E.: "Changes in Self and Other Perceptions Following Brief Educational-Vocational Counseling," *Journal of Counseling Psychology*, 1962, 9:18–30.

Williamson, E. G.: "The Counselor as Technique," *Personnel and Guidance Journal*, 1962, 41:108–111.

Wrenn, C. Gilbert: "Some Emotional Factors in Counseling," in M. Eunice Hilton (ed.), *Guidance in the Age of Automation*, chap. 6. Syracuse, N.Y.: Syracuse University Press, 1957.

————: "The Self Concept in Counseling," *Journal of Counseling Psychology*, 1958, 5:104–108.

————: *The Counselor in a Changing World*. Washington, D.C.: American Personnel and Guidance Association, 1962.

19

Three Approaches to the Counseling Interview

The interview procedures followed by a particular counselor tend to follow a general pattern in accordance with his acceptance of the assumptions and principles of a specific counseling point of view. While the three approaches reviewed here—directive, client-centered, and eclectic—do not represent the only schools of counseling thought, they seem to be currently the ones best known and exerting the greatest influence on counseling practices in secondary schools and colleges. These three approaches are not so sharply differentiated today as they once were. Furthermore, as a counselor gains in experience, he finds that the differences in the various philosophical and theoretical frames of reference become somewhat blurred.

THE DIRECTIVE APPROACH

The approach commonly referred to as "directive" might be designated by some more appropriate term, such as "informative" or "counselor-centered." The term "directive" is retained here, however, because it is widely used and its use has been accepted and defended by some proponents of the method, such as the late Frederick Thorne.[1]

Those who adopt the directive approach perceive the school counselor as a master educator who helps students to solve their problems by consciously utilizing their intellectual resources. A major counseling goal is to help the student replace emotional, impulsive behavior with deliberate rational behavior. Release of feelings and acquisition of insight are held important but are not considered enough. In helping a student learn to solve his problems on a rational basis, the counselor does not assume an authoritarian, judgmental attitude. He avoids the use of such crude directive techniques as direct prohibitions, dictatorial prescriptions, and regulatory advice.

---

[1] Frederick Thorne, "Directive and Eclectic Personality Counseling," in J. L. McCary (ed.), *Six Approaches to Psychotherapy*, pp. 233–286. New York: Holt, Rinehart and Winston, Inc., 1955.

The counselor offers his specialized knowledge and experience as an aid to rational decision. He uses his skill in scientific diagnosis and interpretation of technical data to help the student find a shortcut to problem solutions without any premature settling of questions. Hence, many school people find directive counseling the most economical approach and consider it particularly appropriate in the counseling of students who are able but whose inexperience, youthful indiscretion, and optimism can lead them into making unrealistic choices and unsound decisions.

A counseling method can be fairly appraised only when used with skill. Directive counseling presupposes considerable skill acquired through extensive education and experience in psychology. It is assumed that the student consults the directive counselor with much the same attitude held when consulting his physician or dentist. He expects the professional relationship to be one of dominance through authority and prestige. He assumes that the counselor has the specialized knowledge required in making a scientific diagnosis, in helping him to determine the best course of action, and in assisting or directing him in following the course decided upon. It is the student, not the counselor, who makes the decisions. The counselor employs varying degrees of direction in helping students to arrive at sound decisions through the conscious use of intellectual resources. The need for direction is, in Thorne's [2] words, "inversely correlated with the person's potentialities for self-regulation." While in each case the counselor assumes the basic responsibility, he continuously encourages the student to take on increased responsibility for self-direction.

The concept of directiveness implies that the counselee needs help with some difficulty, that the counselor helps him discover what is the matter and what must be done, and that the counselor is able to help him get it done. The difficulties range from relatively simple educational and vocational choices to serious interpersonal conflicts. In helping students with their difficulties, the counselor uses tested scientific procedures that are based on the psychology of learning.

Some "directive" counseling offered in schools and colleges is ineffectual because it is little more than preaching, exhorting, or prescribing. When a counselor lacks professional education in the method, he can be expected to apply it incorrectly, inappropriately, and ineffectively. To take a teacher who is untrained in counseling out of the classroom, put him in a counseling office, give him the title of "counselor," and assign students to him as counselees is actually not much more absurd than to take a gas station attendant out of a filling station, put him in a medical office, give him a white coat and the title of "doctor," and send people to him as patients. The counselees and patients may find the ones consulted very agreeable persons with a pleasant desk-side manner, but they are not likely to find their services very helpful, and some may find them very

[2] *Ibid.*, 237.

harmful. A pleasant personality and an agreeable manner are no more adequate substitutes for professional knowledge and skill in the counseling office than in the medical office. Lack of skill stemming from lack of training may be concealed for some time in both situations. Once discovered, however, public confidence is lost. In medicine, removal of the untrained practitioner is more or less assured and ordinarily prompt. Unfortunately, the same is not true in counseling.

In schools and colleges directive counseling is commonly associated with the teachings of E. G. Williamson, who uses the term "counseling" in two ways. Sometimes he uses it broadly, making it synonymous with "guidance" and "student personnel work." [3] At other times, as in the two editions of his well-known book [4] on counseling, he uses it both to name a process and to designate one step (treatment) in that process.

The Counseling Relationship. Without minimizing the importance of technique, Williamson stresses the importance of a *human* relationship in counseling. To aid a student "to develop into full humanity," the relationship needs to have the following characteristics: [5]

It is highly individualized.

It is personalized through the counselor's striving to put himself into the student's place, "emotionally and psychologically, so as to understand him for purposes of assisting him."

It is a helping or service relationship but not solely problem-centered. It is as much for students without immediate problems to be solved as for those with problems. It is helpful for the normal student in anticipating his developmental stresses and strains and in helping him to realize his potentialities.

It has a future emphasis and thereby a developmental thrust. It helps the student anticipate the future by helping him to make his aspirations and potentialities come true—by so organizing his thinking about himself and his aspirations for his future development that he has a better likelihood of achieving his potential.

It is life-centered. Counseling is directed toward helping students to build their lives in a totality.

It is concerned with the identification of aspirations as well as with aptitudes. This is the emotional or affect aspect of the relationship. A sympathetic, highly emotionalized counseling relationship may do more than anything the counselor says to help the student cultivate self-confidence and a desire to develop his fullness of potentiality.

It assumes the "sovereignty of reason." Counseling is directed

[3] One example: E. G. Williamson, *Student Personnel Services in Colleges and Universities,* chap. 6. New York: McGraw-Hill Book Company, Inc., 1961.

[4] E. G. Williamson, *Counseling Adolescents.* New York: McGraw-Hill Book Company, Inc., 1950.

[5] E. G. Williamson, "Characteristics of the Counseling Relationship," in E. G. Kennedy (ed.), *Current Status and Future Trends in Student Personnel,* pp. 30–43. Pittsburg, Kan.: Kansas State College, 1961.

toward helping the student think rationally about himself and his life development.

It stresses the dignity and worth of the individual. A relationship based on respect and dignity helps the student to reach the conclusion, or at least the tentative hypothesis, that he is worthwhile. It "motivates him into his full potentiality."

Counseling Steps. Directive counseling, as described by Williamson, involves six steps. They are (1) analysis—collecting from a variety of sources the data needed for an adequate understanding of the student; (2) synthesis—summarizing and organizing the data so that they reveal the student's assets, liabilities, adjustments, and maladjustments; (3) diagnosis—formulating conclusions regarding the nature and the cause of the problems exhibited by the student; (4) prognosis—predicting the future development of the student's problem; (5) counseling—the counselor's taking steps with the student to bring about adjustment and readjustment for the student; and (6) follow-up—helping the student with new problems or with recurrences of the original problem and determining the effectiveness of the counseling provided him.

While Williamson stresses the importance of the gathering and recording of data, he warns that diagnostic activities must not "intrude between the counselor and student." [6] Testing and form filling are to be viewed only as means to an end. The focus is upon the counseling relationship rather than analytical and diagnostic techniques. "Without humaneness of relationship and without perception of the counselor as a kindly, sympathetic person who really does 'care' for students, without this kind of clearly defined, personal relationship, I doubt if we experience effective counseling, however many complete case histories we add to our files." Williamson describes the counseling interview "as a type of human relationship (warm, friendly, empathic), through which a person learns to perceive himself as he actually is and to live with and accept himself with all his faults and shortcomings as well as his positive capabilities and potentialities. Thus, his comprehension of himself is enlarged and made more accurate and useful." [7]

The fifth step—counseling—involves (a) assisting the student in self-appraisal—in identifying his interests, motives, and capabilities; (b) assisting the student to plan a course of action which utilizes the identified interests and capabilities, and assisting him "to develop a life style"; (c) utilizing "the interaction of efforts and successful progress as this progress produces more motivation for further effort." [8]

[6] E. G. Williamson, "Some Issues Underlying Counseling Theory and Practice," in W. E. Dugan (ed.), *Counseling Points of View*, pp. 1–2. Minneapolis: The University of Minnesota Press, 1959.

[7] E. G. Williamson, "Value Commitments and Counseling," *Teachers College Record*, 1961, 62:602–608.

[8] E. G. Williamson, "Counseling in Developing Self-confidence," *Personnel and Guidance Journal*, 1956, 34:398.

To help the student appraise himself—to develop "enlightened self-understanding," the counselor needs two types of data—self-perceived data and data from external appraisal. While the student is obviously the best source of certain kinds of information about himself, he does not always fully understand himself. He is "less than fully in possession of understanding about himself when he does not accurately perceive external appraisals of himself." [9] Hence, the counselor must translate into the student's language the technical facts made available by the counselor's analysis and diagnosis.

This translating, Williamson cautions, should not be carried, however, to the point of causing the student to think that both he and the counselor are "in the same state of ignorance" regarding the student's assets and liabilities. The counselor should maintain an attitude and bearing indicative of his professional background. The procedures to be followed in the interview at this point are described as follows: [10]

> In interpreting and translating the diagnosis and in explaining the evidence leading to that diagnosis, the counselor must make certain, as he proceeds, that the student is following him in the marshaling of the evidence leading to that diagnosis. The counselor proceeds no more rapidly in his explanation than the student can follow. The counselor does not enumerate in detail all the steps in his own diagnosing nor does he touch upon all evidence. He telescopes his own thinking, marshaling only that evidence which appears to be relevant to that diagnosis and to the desirable programs of action. This means that he mentions facts which point to, or from which he infers, his diagnosis and mentions, for purposes of persuasion, those liabilities which rule out certain lines of action.

The counselor presents his point of view with definiteness and tries to enlighten the student through exposition. He avoids a dogmatic position but displays an attitude of bringing knowledge, experience, and judgment to the assistance of the student: [11]

> On the other hand, the counselor does not at any time appear indecisive to the extent of permitting loss of confidence in the validity of his information. He maintains a varied and running discussion of the case data, constantly shifting his exposition and illustrations in terms of the student's verbal and facial reactions during the interview. In this way, the counselor seeks to arrive *cooperatively* at an interpretation of data and a program of training which will strike fire in the student's imagination and will result in a desire to achieve a goal which will be of lasting satisfaction because it is consonant with potentialities.

Williamson perceives counseling as a rational process in an affect context. It is directed not toward helping the student to become what he

[9] Williamson, "Some Issues Underlying Counseling Theory and Practice," p. 5.
[10] Williamson, *Counseling Adolescents*, p. 229.
[11] *Ibid.*, p. 231. Italics in the original.

wants to become but toward helping him to become what he *can* become. In Williamson's [12] words:

> It is a highly personalized teaching and learning process in which, some-times, the communication is not only oral but contextural and situa-tional as well. On some occasions, the relationship may be characterized as direct teaching through explicit explanations, suggestions of possible hypotheses, assistance in searching for relevant facts (aptitudes, inter-ests, motives, etc.) that illuminate the counselee's problems, and so on. On other occasions, the teaching method may be one of friendly, en-couraging listening. And, not infrequently, the counselee may use the carefully structured universe of the interview to "practice-teach" himself how to understand such a one as he is and how to attain maturity with such a repertoire of capabilities and motivations as he, the counselee, now is able to perceive himself to have. Such practice sessions permit him to stand off and look at himself in an objective manner—a perspective often difficult to produce except in the warm and rational ecology of inter-personal relationships with the counselor. After N number of such prac-tice sessions he may feel confident and ready to "go it alone," thus unify-ing and integrating within himself the counselor-counselee roles. That is, he then becomes his own teacher to an extent determined by his own potentialities and other controlling circumstances. And he thus ap-proximates a working integration sufficient for further development and satisfying in the consequent behavior results.

Value Orientation. Some of the most pressing developmental problems of students stem from the conflicting value systems to which they are ex-posed and from which they must choose in building a guiding philosophy of life. In Williamson's opinion, because counselors are educators, they cannot be neutral with respect to values. They are expected to try to in-fluence students in their social attitudes, outlooks, and behavior patterns. "Implicit in the philosophy of public education in this country are cer-tain moral standards, certain behavior patterns, rather loose fitting but still basic in our concept of what the schools should do in influencing individual lives." [13] Hence, the "imposition of values" is built into the counseling relationship: [14]

> I believe counselors are not in the business of aiding students to develop just any and all kinds of individuality for which they have potential. We are rather, as educators, in the business of helping students to become in-dividuals with some similar but not identical patterns of individuality. We are helping them avoid self-destructive and antisocial forms of in-dividuality, and to achieve, paradoxically, fullest freedom through effec-tive membership in groups, to achieve a community of individuals, inter-dependent, and with high social idealisms.

[12] E. G. Williamson, "Value Orientation in Counseling," *Personnel and Guidance Journal,* 1958, 36:522–523.
[13] Williamson, "Some Issues Underlying Counseling Theory and Practice," p. 6.
[14] *Ibid.,* p. 3.

The methods employed by the counselor in influencing the student regarding his value orientation do not include the crude techniques of scolding, admonishing, ordering, preaching, and the like. Nor do they include the propaganda method of arguing for particular values by expounding their virtues and advantages. Logical arguments may lead to intellectual acceptance, but they are not likely to "provide the student with a deeply meaningful learning experience which will have lasting effect." [15]

Desirably, the counselor applies the same methods in helping a student with his value problems that he uses in helping him with other developmental problems. He aids him to identify his motivations and techniques of living, to consider the role of values in his development and adjustments, to perceive the alternative value systems open to him for adoption, and to assess them in terms of their implications and consequences. When appropriate, he encourages the student to develop new behavior patterns as substitutes for patterns that are inadequate for satisfying moral and ethical motives.

This teaching or "imposition" of values does not involve violation of the right of self-determination. Such violation would be unethical. The counselor makes it clear to the student that, while he will help him review and appraise the options open to him, he will not deprive him of the right of independent choice. That the counselor's views will influence the choice can be expected. This is deemed desirable as long as the counselor's intentions are honorable. "We seek to influence, to help with moral intentions. We may do it awkwardly, but we do it the best way we know how" for the sake of the student's full development.[16]

Every counselor, no doubt, influences the values of students through his own values. He communicates his values through his ways of interacting with students and others, through his own techniques of living and life style, and even through his vocation. "Counselors are not usually associated with misbehavior and immorality. By their very form of association and by the context of their work and behavior they are clearly identified with certain value orientations." [17] They reveal their values in many ways and in so doing influence the value orientation of students, particularly of their counselees. Hence, Williamson sees the counselor himself as "an extremely important and effective technique in counseling." [18]

Williamson's views regarding counseling and discipline are consistent with his views regarding counseling and values. Because his con-

---

[15] Williamson, "Value Orientation in Counseling," p. 527.

[16] E. G. Williamson et al., "Counseling Theory and Techniques: A Panel Discussion," in Dugan (ed.), *op. cit.*, p. 32.

[17] E. G. Williamson, "The Meaning of Communication in Counseling," *Personnel and Guidance Journal*, 1959, 38:10.

[18] E. G. Williamson, "The Counselor as Technique," *Personnel and Guidance Journal*, 1962, 41:108.

cept of discipline includes acceptance of external authority, as well as self-regulation, he does not find counseling and discipline incompatible. In his opinion, counselors logically play a significant role in discipline. They are trained not only to identify subsurface causes underlying misbehavior but also to establish the type of relationship that permits students to ventilate feelings and reduce tensions that might otherwise function as barriers to learning how to get along with others and to becoming cooperative group members.

The counselor who uses counseling procedures in dealing with a misbehaving student may be still perceived by the student as an authority figure. The student may, however, perceive him as a benign, protective representative of authority and begin to modify his hostile attitudes toward all authority. Through the counseling relationship he may begin to cultivate "a new concept, one that all of us need to recognize, that external authority can be friendly, benign, and helpful to the individual as he strives to develop his individuality." [19]

EXAMPLE OF DIRECTIVE COUNSELING INTERVIEW

Unedited transcriptions of interviews or portions of interviews provide the best examples of interview procedures. Such transcriptions show, as edited reproductions and fictional examples cannot, the true tempo, the actual dialogue, and the development of the counseling process as it really occurs rather than as it is expected or believed to be. Unedited transcriptions show that sometimes the conversation proceeds slowly and haltingly rather than steadily and smoothly, that both the counselor and the client grope at times, and that statements by the counselor do not always bring forth the type of response expected from the client.

Some fictional examples of interviews give the beginning counselor false ideas regarding the pace and progress to be normally expected. Consequently, he may try to speed up the flow of talk and to force some responses or certain types of responses. By doing so, he impedes rather than aids the client's progress toward understanding himself and his problem. Also, if the worker finds his interviews very different from the "models," he may not estimate properly his own understanding of the interview or his success in its use. As a result, he may become unduly discouraged.

The examples given in this chapter are actual transcriptions of portions of interviews. In the following example for directive counseling the client is a college student whose basic problem is indecision regarding vocational choice but whose surface or immediate problem is school marks and study habits. The material is taken from one of the 12 cases given in the appendix of Williamson's *Counseling Adolescents*.[20]

[19] Williamson, "Counseling in Developing Self-confidence," p. 401.
[20] Pages 510–519.

S. I talked to Dean Peterson, and he said I should come and talk to you ... uh ... I want to try and find out what I could do to increase my ... I mean improve my record ... and I'd like to have some advice ...

C. You mean you're having trouble ... with ... studying?

S. Yes ... with my school exams ...

C. Uh huh. What seems to be the trouble ... can you ...

S. Well, uh ...

C. Tell me a little about it?

S. I don't know ... it seems ... I ... study ... I mean ... I ... do enough studying ... can't seem to uh ... make the grades ...

C. Uh huh.

S. Well, I have one difficulty in spelling ... I'm trying to overcome that ... taking the spelling lab ... this quarter ...

C. Uh huh.

S. And see if that will improve it ... affect it any ...

C. You don't think it's the time then ... you think you're studying enough ...

S. I think I'm studying enough, yes ... uh huh ... (pause). But uh ... I don't know if it's my study ... the way I study ... or what it is ...

C. Uh huh. Do you think you do a pretty good job of studying when you are studying with time limits?

S. Well, it seems to me ... I don't know I ... try to, but ... just doesn't seem to uh ... comprehend too much ...

C. Do you have some trouble understanding what you read?

S. Yes, uh huh. (long pause)

C. How about your reading uh ... from when you first learned how to read ... and so on ... have you uh ...

S. Well, uh ...

C. Been able to comprehend right along?

S. Well, not too much ... I took ... reading lab last quarter, too ... I'm ... I'm always a slow reader ...

C. You are very slow?

S. Uh huh. Then I took this reading lab fall and winter quarters. I think that ... helped me a lot.

C. You're talking about the reading lab over in the rhetoric uh ...

S. Yes.

C. Courses on the Ag Campus?

S. On the Ag Campus, yes.

C. Do you think anything happened there much that ... that has helped you?

S. Well, I ... I can read a little faster now ... and I seem to comprehend ...

C. Uh huh. You're not quite satisfied still ... with the way you do.

S. That's right.

C. Uh huh. Sometimes a problem like that is of long standing and you can't hope to build yourself up in a very short time ... when it is something that has been building up all through your school years. (long pause) Sometimes it's related to other things also ... I mean it

might not be just reading difficulty ... it might be a lack of interest
in your subject ...

S. Well, that might be ... because like ... now chemistry is giving me a
hard time. Then there is uh ... well, I don't know ... it shouldn't, like
some subjects, like in animal subjects ... animal husbandry ... subjects and on the Main Campus I should be interested in those ...

C. You just find that they aren't as interesting as you ...

S. That's right ...

C. As you think they should be. (long pause) Did uh ... Mr. Peterson
tell you anything about what we might do here? What we might talk
about?

S. No, he didn't. He said I should come over and talk to you ...

C. Uh huh. There are several possibilities ... what we might do ... one
might be to take some tests ... uh ... you've probably had quite a few
reading tests ... if you've been taking some of that work. It might be
that other tests, not just reading tests, would give us a picture there.
For example, an interest test. (pause) Have you ever had anything
like that?

S. Uh ... these uh ... aptitude tests uh ... and ... are those in the same
order or ...

C. Uh, yes. Some of them would be what I'm talking about ...

S. I ... took those in my senior year in high school.

C. Did you?

S. Uh huh.

C. Was that an interest test? (pause)

S. I don't know. I can't recall what they ... they called it ... an interest
test or what it was ...

C. Uh huh. (pause) We give many different kinds of tests ... and they
are sometimes lumped together and called aptitude tests ...

S. Oh, I see.

C. But each one might really be telling you something different about
yourself.

S. Uh huh.

C. One might give you an idea of your general ability to handle college
work. And another might give you an idea of your interests. Another
might give you an idea of your background in math and science ...
(pause) ... and it would be then a combination ... of all of those that
might be considered aptitude. Have you ever seen any test results for
yourself?

S. I uh ... not ... I haven't seen the results ... I think my IQ is ... it's
pretty low ... let's see, I talked to my high school superintendent. I
think he said it was 98 ... I think it was.

C. When was that?

S. That was my senior ... uh ... senior or sophomore year I took this
aptitude ...

C. Uh huh.

S. I mean, I've ... that doesn't mean too much ... does it?

C. You mean does that have any bearing on college?

S. Yes, and is it . . .

C. Well, we don't usually talk too much about IQ in terms of college work. We have some other tests that are designed to give you an idea of where you rank with college students . . . and they would perhaps be better. You've never seen how you came out on anything like that?

S. No, I haven't.

C. Would you like to look at your results? I think I have some here for you.

S. I . . . I would.

C. Do you remember taking that science test and the algebra test last September when you entered?

S. Uh huh. Yes, I do . . .

C. Those results might be the kind of thing that we're talking about. (pause) Here they are on the sheet here . . .

S. Uh huh.

C. In this column it indicates where you ranked . . . on a percentage basis . . . compared to entering agriculture freshmen. This number places you on a rank on a scale from 1 to 100.

S. Uh huh.

C. If you were then at the 50 on that, that would mean that you were right at the average.

S. Uh huh . . . (pause). So I'm below average . . .

C. The ranking there would be below average. (pause) Those tests, by the way, have been given to quite a few students over the years in that college and they have an idea of how you might be able to handle the work in that college from how you do on those tests.

S. Uh huh.

C. Scores . . . uh . . . (pause) . . . like this would be the kind of scores . . . that persons make who have difficulty in making a satisfactory record . . . in that college. (long pause) (Client sighs toward the end of pause.)

S. The answer, I mean, I always did have a hard time and it was through my high school and . . .

C. Uh huh. Do you find that you have that same sort of trouble in your college chemistry?

S. Yes, I think I do.

C. Uh huh. It's the same thing there . . .

S. Uh huh. (long pause) Uh . . . do you think that's because of the background . . . that I didn't have too uh . . . good a background in those subjects?

C. Well, yes. Either that or you didn't master it well . . .

S. Uh huh.

C. There are those two possibilities. (pause) You know there are all kinds of abilities and academic ability is just one kind of ability. It might be that you don't stand too well in that kind of ability. It may be that there are others for you. What sort of things do you think that you can do well?

S. You mean in subjects?

C. Or anything.

S. (Pause) Well, I don't know. (pause) I don't believe I understand what you mean.

C. That's a kind of hard question to answer. (pause) What I mean is are there things that you like to do better than school work or that you feel that you do better than school work?

S. Well, I mean there isn't much else . . . I mean, there's . . . I've lived on the farm all the time . . .

C. Uh huh. Do you like that kind of work?

S. Oh, yes . . . (pause) that's about the only work I ever did . . . I mean, it's . . . in fact, I know I like that . . .

C. Uh huh. What did you do?

S. Oh . . . just general farm work uh . . . all around the farm.

C. Like any of it better than any other part?

S. Oh, the machinery part I like better . . . tractors . . .

C. Did a lot of work on tractors?

S. Oh, yes, I have . . . (long pause).

C. That's an example of a kind of ability that's different from school work ability . . . mechanical skill . . .

S. Uh huh.

C. Working with machines and understanding them . . . it seems to be a very different kind of ability from academic or scholastic or college ability, we might say. (pause) Have you ever considered going into some kind of work that involves that sort of skill?

S. Well, like uh . . . certain mechanical work?

C. Uh huh.

S. I was . . . I uh . . . I haven't thought much about that but . . . like going to Dunwoody and taking up some mechanical courses . . . a person could do that . . .

C. You haven't considered it for yourself?

S. No, I haven't . . . like . . . I mean, I haven't written in there and asked for their bulletin or anything . . .

C. Uh huh. We have some tests here for that purpose too, tests that would give you a little better idea, maybe, of where you stand in that kind of aptitude or skill. They would be different from this kind of test that you've taken before. (pause) It might possibly be that you would like to do something on that order just to see where you stand and explore alternatives . . .

S. Uh huh.

C. To the course that you're in now . . . (pause).

S. I could do that . . . I might find this course I'm taking now . . . it's too hard . . . (laughs).

C. You're beginning to think that . . . that it may be too rough for you . . .

S. Yeah . . . I think so . . . (pause). I mean, I think I'll uh . . . transfer to something else . . . after the spring quarter is over . . .

C. What is your official status with the college now?

S. You mean my . . . honor point ratio? That's a .56 and I haven't raised it any . . .

C. Does that mean that you're on probation?

S. Yes, uh huh. (long pause)

C. Have you talked over any other possibilities with Mr. Peterson or any-body?

S. No, I haven't . . . no, I just saw him that one day and he said I should have an appointment up here. (pause)

C. Well, what we sometimes do is, as I said, start out with kind of test and then by talking with you about what alternatives look possible to you, then sometimes we can reach an answer on the thing as to what possibility would be best. (pause) You said that you had started think-ing about transferring to something else . . . what things have you con-sidered?

S. Well, uh . . . either . . . go to Dunwoody or else . . . uh . . . I've . . . talked to one of the students . . . his . . . his roommate . . . he took up mortuary science and I . . . I just had those two things in mind . . .

C. You haven't considered anything else or have you narrowed it down to these two things?

S. Well, uh . . . no, I just considered . . . I think those two . . .

C. Those are the only ones you've been thinking about at all. Do you have very much information about . . .

S. No, I haven't.

C. Those possibilities?

S. Not at the present, no.

C. Well, we have information about Dunwoody . . .

S. Uh huh.

C. In our files. We can give you a little idea of the courses that are avail-able there, and I think that we would suggest going and seeing the place and maybe talking . . .

S. Yes . . .

C. With them, in addition to looking over the bulletin. (pause)

S. Now this . . . mortuary science uh . . . that's a . . . just two years, isn't it?

C. It's a year in the General College . . .

S. General College and a year up here . . .

C. And then the mortuary science course in extension. Have you seen the bulletin on that?

S. No, I haven't uh . . . do you have it?

C. Yes. The General College bulletin gives the pre-mortuary science course.

S. Uh huh.

C. And then the mortuary science is written up in the Extension bulletin . . . (pause). Maybe we can look at them next time . . . I . . . don't locate them right now . . .

S. Yes . . . uh huh.

C. And if you would like, you could get them for yourself over at the Administration Building. Do you know where it is on this campus?

S. Yes, it's over there by the . . .

C. Ask at the information booth which is in the middle of the lobby.

S. Uh huh.

C. And you can get the bulletins that you wish there. You'd want the one for the General College . . .

S. Yes.

C. And the one for Extension. You may ask for others, too, by the time we get through talking.

S. Well, is that ... that ... mortuary science, is that ... is it as difficult as ... most of the other subjects?

C. You mean as in any other courses?

S. Yes.

C. At the University?

S. Uh huh.

C. Well, that's a problem that's kind of hard to say yes or no to, because it depends on you.

S. Uh huh.

C. The general idea is that it is not as difficult because it is not as long ...

S. Uh huh.

C. A course. (pause) But it would depend on you as to whether it would be difficult for you or not.

S. I mean ... that General College ... this one ... uh ... fellow ... his roommate ... he went to a teachers' college for a year and took up General College and then he transferred back up here. I guess he said he's finding it ... it isn't too difficult for him ... yet, we're two different people again ...

C. And different courses.

S. Uh huh. (pause)

C. Well, what would you like to do? Would you be interested in seeing what material we have on Dunwoody?

S. Yes, I would.

C. And would you like to maybe take one or two tests, and come back and talk about them later?

S. I think that's fine ... yes ...

C. I'll show you the ones that I have in mind ...

S. Uh huh.

C. They might be things like dexterity tests giving you an idea of how able you are using your hands, and mechanical comprehension ... that kind ...

S. Uh huh.

C. Of thing. Then perhaps an over-all interest test, and perhaps an over-all ability test. (long pause)

S. I think I'd like that choice ...

C. You think you'd like to do that?

S. Uh huh, I think so.

C. O.K. Then I'll check the card for those that we've been talking about.

S. Uh huh.

C. I wonder, would you be interested in a reading test? And maybe a study habits inventory while we're ...

S. Sure.

C. Doing it? I'm sure that this reading test is different from the one you take over there ... (pause). Are you classed as a freshman still?

S. Yes, uh huh ...

C. Then we'll put freshman on the card so you'll be compared to freshmen.

S. Uh huh.
C. Some of these are long and others are short...
S. Uh huh.
C. I can give you an idea of how long it will take you in all and then we can arrange when you might be able to come back.
S. Uh huh.

The counselor gives the student information regarding the amount of time required for testing, obtains from him information needed in arranging testing, and brings the interview to a close.

CLIENT–CENTERED COUNSELING

The second approach is generally referred to as "client-centered," but the term "nondirective" is sometimes used. The term "client-centered" may be no more appropriate for designating this second method than the term "directive" is for describing the first. To some it may imply that other counseling methods are not client-concerned, which is not the case at all.

This counseling approach is sometimes described as being as much a way of life as a counseling method because, to help the client realize his potentialities, the counselor himself must seek psychological maturity. He must be able to understand and to accept himself as he truly is, genuinely respect himself and others, and continuously strive to achieve his own potential growth.

The counselor provides a counseling atmosphere in which the client can fully explore his thoughts and feelings without fear of disapproval, criticism, or censure. He seeks to assume the client's frame of reference so that he may perceive the world as it is perceived by the client. His chief, if not only, source of data is the client himself.

The basic counseling objective is change or growth. The responsibility for change rests with the client, not the counselor; for change must come from within the client rather than from without. The client is seen as having the potential for growth and a natural tendency toward healthy growth. Hence, he is the one to determine the nature, the direction, and the rate of change. By functioning somewhat as a catalytic agent, the counselor helps the client to resolve his conflicts and to solve his difficulties by utilizing his resources for growth or self-actualization.

Like directive counseling, client-centered counseling, to be fairly appraised, must be used with skill. The counselor who adopts this approach without adequate education in its use may confuse lack of direction with lack of involvement. If so, he tends to play a highly passive role, trying to keep out of the client's way, so to speak. On the other hand, if he sees his role as being an active one, he may shift the focus from client to counselor as he subtly tries to direct the counseling process while pretending to let the client guide himself.

The historical origins of client-centered counseling are found in the teachings of Rank and Taft, but in this country client-centered counseling is most often associated with the name of Carl Rogers. Other strong advocates of the method, such as Arbuckle [21] and Patterson,[22] are clearly influenced by his teachings.

In the first systematic presentation of this theory Rogers [23] described client-centered counseling as a method used primarily with adolescents and adults. He described it largely as a process of verbal exchange, emphasized the development of verbal insight, and stressed the importance of the counselor's reflecting and clarifying the client's feelings. In his more recent writings it is the counselor's philosophy rather than his interview procedures that Rogers stresses. He describes the client-centered method as an approach to human relations that is applicable to a variety of activities of which counseling is only one. To achieve empathy (to assume the client's personal frame of reference) and to convey empathy are the counseling functions that he now underscores.

Central Hypotheses. While a comparison of the 1942 book with Rogers' more recent writings shows certain important shifts in emphasis, it also shows that his central hypotheses are essentially unchanged. Much empirical research has been and is being carried out to test the soundness of the hypotheses, which are as follows: [24]

> 1. The first hypothesis is that the individual has within himself the capacity, latent if not evident, to understand those aspects of himself and of his life which are causing him dissatisfaction, anxiety, or pain and the capacity and the tendency to reorganize himself and his relationship to life in the direction of self-actualization and maturity in such a way as to bring a greater degree of internal comfort.
>
> 2. This capacity will be released, and therapy or personal growth will be most facilitated, when the therapist can create a psychological climate characterized by (a) a genuine acceptance of the client as a person of unconditional worth; (b) a continuing, sensitive attempt to understand the existing feelings and communications of the client, as they seem to the client, without any effort to diagnose or alter those feelings; and (c) a continuing attempt to convey something of this empathic understanding to the client.
>
> 3. It is hypothesized that, in such an acceptant, understanding, and nonthreatening psychological atmosphere, the client will reorganize himself at both the conscious and the deeper levels of his personality in such a

---

[21] D. S. Arbuckle, *Counseling: An Introduction.* Boston: Allyn and Bacon, Inc., 1961.

[22] C. H. Patterson, *Counseling and Psychotherapy: Theory and Practice.* New York: Harper & Row, Publishers, Incorporated, 1959.

[23] Carl R. Rogers, *Counseling and Psychotherapy.* Boston: Houghton Mifflin Company, 1942.

[24] Carl R. Rogers and Rosalind P. Dymond (eds.), *Psychotherapy and Personality Change,* pp. 4–5. Chicago: The University of Chicago Press, 1954.

manner as to cope with life more constructively, more intelligently, and in a more socialized as well as a more satisfying way. More specifically it is hypothesized that the client will change in his perception of self, will become more understanding of self and others, more accepting of self and others, more creative, more adaptive, more self-directing and autonomous, more mature in his behavior, less defensive, and more tolerant of frustrations.

4. It is hypothesized that the therapeutic relationship is only one instance of interpersonal relationships and that the same lawfulness governs all such relationships. Thus, if the parent creates such a climate for his child, the child will become more self-directing, socialized, and mature; if the teacher creates such a climate for his class, the student will become a self-initiated learner, more original, more self-disciplined; if the administrator or executive creates such a climate for his organization, the staff will become more self-responsible, more creative, better able to adapt to new problems, more basically co-operative.

Rogers hypothesizes that various learnings or changes occur concomitantly with client-centered therapy. He cites research reports [25] which supply evidence that these sorts of changes occur: [26]

The person comes to see himself differently.

He accepts himself and his feelings more fully.

He becomes more self-confident and self-directing.

He becomes more the person he would like to be.

He becomes more flexible, less rigid, in his perceptions.

He adopts more realistic goals for himself.

He behaves in a more mature fashion.

He changes his maladjustive behaviors, even such a long-established one as chronic alcoholism.

He becomes more acceptant of others.

He becomes more open to the evidence, both to what is going on outside of himself, and to what is going on inside of himself.

He changes in his basic personality characteristics, in constructive ways.

Conditions of Learning. For client-centered counseling to facilitate significant learning, Rogers finds the following conditions to be essential: [27]

1. The client faces a situation which he perceives as a serious and meaningful problem but which he is not able to cope with successfully on his own. Although Rogers says that "the counseling process doesn't actually get under way until there is some desire for help," he recognizes that the school or college counselor may need to approach the student in-

---

[25] Carl R. Rogers, *Client-centered Therapy*. Boston: Houghton Mifflin Company, 1951; Rogers and Dymond (eds.), *op. cit.*

[26] Carl R. Rogers, *On Becoming a Person*, pp. 280–281. Boston: Houghton Mifflin Company, 1961.

[27] *Ibid.*, chap. 14.

stead of waiting for the student to approach him. The counselor should be forthright in his approach and not try to force his services upon the student.

> In the kind of situation that exists in a school setting, it would be far more appropriate for the counselor to express his own real feelings rather than try to maneuver a person into counseling. In other words, I can see the counselor quite readily going to a student and saying, "I would like you to know that the principal and a few of your teachers have come to me because they are very much concerned about you. So I feel concerned about you; and if there is anything I can do to be of help, I would be very glad to have you come in and see me, but I can't force you to help yourself. This is an offer and I want you to know that it is very real, and there it is." My guess is that whatever ensues, and it isn't at all certain that the student would then come in, the relationship would nevertheless be clear and real and open.[28]

2. In the counseling relationship the counselor must be a unified or integrated or congruent person. He must be what he really feels and not play a role or put up a facade. He must be as accepting of himself and his feelings as he is of the client. "He is freely, deeply, and acceptantly himself, with his actual experience of his feelings and reactions matched by an accurate awareness of these feelings and reactions as they occur and as they change." [29] The counseling process moves most rapidly when the counselor feels genuinely acceptant and understanding toward the client. But, if he does not feel that way, if he is "genuinely feeling something other than that, perhaps, it is better to be that than to meet the client's facade with a facade" of his own.[30]

If the counselor lets himself be himself, it is easier for him to accept himself as an imperfect person and to move toward becoming more nearly the type of person he wants to be. Rogers [31] says that "we cannot move away from what we are, until we thoroughly accept what we are. Then change seems to come about almost unnoticed." Furthermore, if a counselor can accept the fact that, for example, he is annoyed or bored by a student, he is more likely to be able to accept the student's feelings in response to his own. He can then accept the changed experience and the changed feelings which are likely to occur in both himself and the student.

3. The counselor achieves an attitude of unconditional positive regard for the client. He experiences a warm caring that is not possessive and that does not demand personal gratification. It is simply an "I care."

---

[28] Williamson et al., "Counseling Theory and Techniques: A Panel Discussion," in Dugan (ed.), *op. cit.*, p. 29.

[29] Rogers, *On Becoming a Person*, p. 283.

[30] Williamson et al., "Counseling Theory and Techniques: A Panel Discussion," p. 44.

[31] Rogers, "Lessons Learned in Counseling," in Dugan (ed.), *op. cit.*, p. 16.

It is not an "I care for you *if* you behave thus and so." It is complete acceptance—acceptance of both the negative and the positive feelings and expressions of the client and acceptance of him as a separate person with his own experiences and his own meanings for his experiences.

4. The counselor experiences empathy. Empathy is the sensing of the client's world as if it were one's own "but without ever losing the 'as if' quality." It involves sensing a client's anger, fear, or confusion without also being angry, afraid, or confused—without "getting bound up in it." Identification with the client is empathic identification, not emotional identification. The counselor never gives up his own identity as he tries to enter into the client's attitudes and private frame of reference.

5. The client perceives something of the counselor's acceptance and empathy and his congruence. It is not enough that the counselor achieve empathy; he must also convey it. That a counselor can communicate empathy, that he can help a client perceive that he is following his lead and getting "within his attitudes" is shown in these two excerpts from Lipkin's [32] account of the reactions of two of his clients.

> "During the interviews my psycologist [*sic*] took my views & thoughts and made them so that I could understand what was going on. He didn't conclude them but stated them back to me so I could draw my own conclusions. Things we talked about seemed clearer in my mind & organized it to an extent where now I belive [*sic*] I can think things out for myself."

> "I started to talk of the things that bothered me, and, at intervals, Mr. L. solidified my ramblings into a few clear concise words...."

Diagnosis. Rogers differs sharply from Williamson on three points—diagnosis, information giving, and the "imposition of values." He considers diagnosis the responsibility of the client, not the counselor. He sees counseling itself as a process of diagnosis but as a process that goes on in the experience of the client rather than in the thinking of the clinician.[33]

Even if the counselor knows what has brought about maladjustment in a client, Rogers doubts that he can use this knowledge effectively to help the client. Before the client can change his ways of acting, thinking, and feeling, he must change his perceptions. It must be a change that is experienced, not just verbalized or intellectualized. The forces that can bring about this change "reside primarily in the client and probably cannot come from outside." As the client experiences during counseling the inadequacies in his old ways of perceiving, he experiences new, more accurate, and more adequate perceptions and recognizes the significant relationships between these perceptions.

Rogers considers diagnosis in the form of evaluation by the coun-

[32] Stanley Lipkin, "The Client Evaluates Nondirective Psychotherapy," *Journal of Consulting Psychology,* 1948, 1:140, 145.

[33] Rogers, *Client-centered Therapy,* p. 223.

selor not only unnecessary but in some ways detrimental or unwise because it may increase dependent tendencies in the client and has the
long-range social implications of social control of the many by the few.
He endorses the use of tests and other measurement devices in gathering
data for research purposes but rejects them for counseling purposes. He
once explained his position as follows: "I think it [the gathering of data]
is extremely important, but I don't like to mix that external objective
view, which is a research measurement point of view, with what I think
is effective in the internal subjective experience. I don't think you help a
student because you have a folder of information on him; I think you
help because of a relationship." [34]

Information Giving. Rogers accepts information giving as a possible
counseling function when used for the following purposes: (1) The information is used to help clarify a choice. The client, for example, may
want to know how much training is required for a certain job. (2) Information is used to implement a decision. The client may decide not to
seek a job but, instead, to go to college. To carry out this decision he may
need information about particular colleges. (3) Information is used to
help the client discover his real problem. The client may want to take
tests and to read books about various vocations. After learning the test
results and securing information about certain occupations, he may discover that what he really wants to know is how to decide which vocation
he should plan to enter.

The counselor should not assume that the client's basic difficulty
stems from a lack of information: [35]

> It is true that some clients need only certain very specific information.
> Often they will be satisfied with reference to appropriate books or maga-
> zine sources that will tell them what they want to know. In most cases,
> however, the counselor can never be sure that this is all that is required
> unless he is convinced that the client has felt free to talk about anything
> he wished—whether related directly to his vocational or educational prob-
> lems or not. Any person may go to a book for information, but when he
> consults another person it is not always just pure information seeking.
> The meaning of the personal relationship must be assessed. What use is
> the client attempting to make of his relationship with the counselor? Per-
> haps he wants reassurance of a course of action he has chosen; perhaps he
> is afraid to make a decision by himself; perhaps he wants someone to side
> in with him against his parents' wishes. The point is that consulting an-
> other person for information is a much different action from consulting

[34] Williamson et al., "Counseling Theory and Techniques: A Panel Discussion,"
p. 36.

[35] Carl R. Rogers and J. L. Wallen, *Counseling with Returned Servicemen,* pp.
103–104. New York: McGraw-Hill Book Company, Inc., 1946.

a book. The counselor should be alert for signs that the person really wants something more than information from the counseling relation.

Development of Values. Rogers agrees with Williamson and others that the counselor cannot avoid having a value impact on his clients since his counseling philosophy reflects his basic philosophy of life. He strongly opposes, however, the counselor's teaching or imposing specific values or a particular value system or philosophy upon a client. He makes one exception, which he explains as follows: [36]

> I don't know by what right I, as counselor, have any earthly business imposing my plans, choices, or values on the person with whom I work. Yet there is one value, which, if held by the counselor, can become predominant in the situation without running into that philosophical difficulty; that is, if the counselor truly values the development of each separate individual, then he also values the self-directed development of that individual and that's a value I wouldn't hesitate to hold in a relationship with a client. It's a value which, from my point of view, I would see no harm in being present in the relationship. On the other hand, if it becomes something quite different, that I value being scholarly and he doesn't or I value a certain religious point of view and he doesn't, for example, then I think one can be strongly criticized, at least from the philosophical point of view, for imposing those values on the individual.

Counseling usually brings about changes in a client's value orientation. At the beginning the client may be living in keeping with what others think—in keeping with values introjected from the culture through the teachings of parents, friends, teachers, and the like. Gradually he begins to see that he is not being his true self but the self that he thinks others expect or require him to be. Not certain, however, just what he does think or what values he really holds important, he feels insecure and confused.

Feelings of insecurity and confusion decline as he learns that he can build a value system on the basis of evidence from his own experiences and that judgments thus arrived at are alterable—that they can be changed on the basis of new experiential evidence. Little by little he "finds that it is not only possible but satisfying and sound to accept the locus of evaluation as residing within himself. When this experience becomes internalized, values are no longer seen as fixed or threatening things." [37] In the beginning the client's thinking may run as follows: [38]

> "I should never be angry at anyone" (because my parents and church regard anger as wrong).

[36] Williamson et al., "Counseling Theory and Techniques: A Panel Discussion," p. 31.

[37] Rogers, *Client-centered Therapy,* p. 151.

[38] *Ibid.,* pp. 149, 151.

"I should be completely casual about sex behavior" (because my sophisticated friends have this attitude).

Toward the end of counseling his thinking may change to something like the following:

"I should be angry at a person when I deeply feel angry because this leaves less residual effect than bottling up the feeling and actually makes for a better and more realistic friendship."

"I accept my sexuality and value highly those expressions of it which result in long-range enhancement of self and others; I value less highly those expressions which give only transient satisfactions, or do not enhance self."

In allowing the client full freedom to feel and to be, client-centered therapy permits certain value directions to emerge. The client moves away from facades (defensiveness, putting up a front, etc.) and from doing things because he "ought to" or wants to please others to values based on his own experiences rather than introjected from others. His values are no longer held rigidly but are continuously changing with changes in experience and reactions. And his reactions become differentiated. He may, for instance, react differently to the same behavior in different persons because he perceives the differences in their circumstances, motives, and the like. He comes to trust himself, to find worth in his own reactions, and to value self-direction. Also, his valuing more and more involves past learnings and hypotheses regarding future consequences. To use an example from Rogers,[39] "it is not pleasant to express forthrightly my negative feelings to this person, but past experience indicates that it will be helpful to our relationship in the long run."

As the individual moves in the direction of valuing as a fluid, flexible process, he comes to value being open and sensitive to his own reactions, the reactions of others, and the realities of the world. He increasingly values sensitivity to and acceptance of others and develops a deep appreciation of close, fully communicative relationships with others. He exhibits "the rich, flexible, organismic, moment-by-moment, valuing process" which Rogers describes "as characteristic of the mature individual."[40]

EXAMPLE OF CLIENT–CENTERED COUNSELING INTERVIEW

The following example is taken from a film entitled *Client-centered Therapy*.[41] The interviewer is Dr. Carl R. Rogers. The client is a young

[39] Carl R. Rogers, "The Developing Values of the Growing Person," talk given at a conference held at the University of Florida, January 6, 1961. (Mimeographed.)

[40] *Ibid.*

[41] *Client-centered Therapy.* University Park, Pa.: The Psychological Cinema Register of the Pennsylvania State University.

woman, a graduate student, who came to the University of Chicago Counseling Center for assistance. The interview opens as follows:

S. I'm ahead of time.

C. When we talked the other day for a minute I certainly didn't give you an opportunity to say what really concerned you.

S. ... start from the beginning?

C. M-hm.

S. Well, the thing that precipitated my coming to you was the fact that this is my first year at Chicago, and I had a scholarship and then a fellowship during the year, and applied of course for one for next year, and didn't get it back. So now I'm forced to ... consider a job— what I would do if I couldn't get into teaching as I hope to do, what kind of a life I expect to lead and so on. And in so doing, I tried to take stock of ... social as well as vocational plans. And I decided it was about time I saw somebody about it.

C. It isn't only a question of what your academic plans would be, but quite a little broader than that, what really are you aiming for.

S. Yes. I think that as a matter of fact the academic angle will work out. Either I will go into teaching or if I can't get that, I'll go into secretarial work and then that will have to go a step at a time. But it seems to me that whatever I do, I've got to have satisfactory social adjustment and if I have that then the other doesn't matter so much.

C. M-hm. M-hm.

S. And I don't think that I do, and I don't think I'm going along in a direc—in a direction that's likely to lead me to much of anything in the next fifteen years, anyway. That's pretty late.

C. If I understand you there, you mean that if the kind of social adjustment you have now is projected just as it is into the future, then it isn't going to be what you want.

S. Well, it's partly that, it's partly also that I think that I've improved tremendously in the last ten years and I think I'll improve in the next ten, too. But after all, it's a pretty slow process when you're trying to work things out on your own and trying to work back and see why you do things the way you do. And I've never had training in psychology or anything similar to it. And I think that somebody can help me. And I think that if I had seen someone when I was twelve or sixteen, I'd be a lot better off than I am now.

C. So that really this is in the hope of kind of speeding up or improving the process that you're already trying to carry on by yourself ...

S. That's right. M-hm.

C. ... that brings you in.

S. I was quite an anti-social child, I think ... way back. It's not just something that I can trace to a beginning. I was put in nursery school in order to ... or in hopes that I would ... improve socially, so to speak, and that was at the age of three. Well, I can't remember much about that, but I was told that that was the reason. So apparently it was not something that just ... happened later. And that ... progressed. I had very few friends, one now and then. They'd be a friend to me and I'd be an acquaintance to them. Eith—... either they were queer people who didn't have friends or they were people who had other friends.

C. M-hm. So that for a good long time in your own feelings, and even longer if you can believe the reports of others, you haven't had the kind of relationship with friends that you'd like.

S. That's right. And here I'm on uncertain ground, but I don't think that the relationships I have had have been particularly normal in a ... if you can define normal; I don't know.

C. M-hm. Then it seems to you they're not ...

S. Certainly they're not satisfactory.

C. ... not satisfactory and not within the range of things that you'd really like.

S. That's right. And I feel I can get along fine now. I'm ... happy in what I'm doing and I usually can be happy in almost any job. But the people I know cease at the edge of the school, at the office, or whatever it may be, and as long as I've got my family to write to or to see occasionally, I've got a certain attachment outside. But after all, I have no intention of going back and living with my parents for the rest of my life. And in any case, they're likely to die before I do, and it seems to me that I had better start making provisions for that.

C. And the lack that you feel is in a meaningful kind of relationship that goes beyond just on-the-job kind of ...

S. I think so.

C. ... friendship. M-hm.

S. A normal give and take. I don't think I'd be particularly happy with mobs of people around, but it seems to me that there's something that I just don't have. And that goes for both boys and girls. Practically no ... arranged dates with either.

C. M-hm. You really sense that as a lack in yourself that you don't have the kind of contact you'd like either with fellows or girls.

S. That's right. And it's definitely in me. It's not them. Well I don't need to follow that out any further. It's obvious. (pause)

C. There's no question about that.

S. No. I don't think so.

I'd like to come back in for a moment to summarize the next three minutes of the interview, which are difficult to hear. She leaves the discussion of her social relationships and goes on to discuss how important it has been to her to be at the top. Losing the fellowship made her realize what she had known but never quite faced; that she is not a *really good* student, that she rates below the top. But along with and because of her social insecurity there has gone a determination to *be* at the top in her academic work. She realizes she has probably made her social situation worse by insisting that other people recognize that she is at the top. All this has meant that school has been the center and focus of her life.

S. ... And the school to me has been a center. After all, I've been going to school since the age of three. It's been the center of everything.

C. And you just wanted to be on the top in school, partly, you feel, because you weren't getting some of these other satisfactions that you would have liked.

S. Yes, I think so. But then that goes way back . . . I can remember arguing quite heatedly with a group of boys and girls in third grade. I was, also. Because I had been put into an experimental class and the experimental class consisted of ten third grade, and ten second grade students, and the same teacher. The idea being that they were advanced enough to do individual work; at least I assumed so at the time, and I still think so. But the other kids quite naturally were teasing us about being in, let's see . . . second grade. And to me it was quite . . . annoying that they shouldn't recognize that we were being experimented on.

C. You wanted the recognition that this was something special . . .

S. Yeah.

C. . . . and it really kinda hurt that they took it just the other way and felt you were really . . .

S. Yeah. Although I suspected that they were more teasing than anything else and I knew that, too, at the time. It made me kind of mad that I couldn't keep my mouth shut.

C. M-hm. You sort of wished you didn't have to defend your position to that degree.

S. I suppose so. I thought I was making kind of a fool of myself too; but it was very much an undercurrent. I may even be reading back my own ideas now into it. I can remember the scene, but after all, it's so long ago. But I al— . . . I've always had this feeling of trying to be different from other people and . . . then getting to the point where I realized that wasn't such a good idea and trying to reverse the process, which isn't at all easy.

C. M-hm. Do I understand there that there's really been then a shift in your own goal from wanting to be different to now really wishing you could be much like others? Is that what's implied there? . . . but finding that pretty difficult.

S. Well . . . yeah. In a way. Except that I . . . I still have this . . . can't quite give up the idea of being a little different. (laughing) That's what makes it so hard, I suppose. I want to keep on with my own peculiarities and at the same time I know that they're standing in my way of adapting sufficiently to other things, but . . . I think at least I recognize the difficulties.

C. M-hm. M-hm. But that . . . feels to you like something of a discrepancy, of wanting to be different and have your own uniqueness, and still wishing the other thing, too.

S. Well, yes, in a way. After all, the things that I have that . . . I've got a higher IQ than other people; there's no point in hiding it. But why stress it? That's the point. If I could just get so that it meant less to me.

C. M-hm. Why do *you* have to place such a value on it, hm?

S. Yeah. (pause) And that goes back too far too, because I think that partly my family's to blame for some of that; for starting it anyway. I

was certainly not uncooperative. But my father was always very interested that I was a bright child. He started to teach me duplicate bridge
at the age of six. And at the age of thirteen I quit. I couldn't stand
it any more....

She continues to give further details of her parent's attitude toward her
intelligence. It was always assumed that she would go to college, and that
she would get a Ph.D. It wasn't until she came to the University and was
asked her reasons for going into graduate work that she realized that she
had no reasons of her own. She then talks about some of the academic
decisions she has made, but at the point we cut back into the interview
she is returning to the attitude which she holds, that her standing in
school is so all-important.

S. ... so that, that really isn't so much the problem as simply the fact
    that... my standing was in the college groups, and the importance
    that school itself has for me is just too much, too important. It oc-
    cupies too much ... of my mind.
C. These other things are all right, but why you should value so highly
    a high standing in the group, and why school is so all important to
    you ...
S. M-hm.
C. ... that you don't like.
S. I ... I don't like it. I don't think it's correct. As I said, I've been getting
    along fine now. But when my family breaks up, after my mother and
    father are dead, if I don't marry, I've got to have something to tie to
    besides the job.
C. M-hm. The present you can stand quite comfortably, (S: M-hm) but
    it's the thought of the future that...
S. Yeah. I have ...
C. ... makes you think twice.
S. I think so. Well, I think that... life could be awful boring after your
    family has ... broken up. Old ... the older people that you know, too,
    or have some very close ties with. But after all that shouldn't be one's
    whole life either.
C. M-hm. You're really raising the question, aren't you, where are you
    going to live emotionally in the years to come. Is that...?
S. I think that's probably it. (long pause) I know the way, but how do
    I do it? And how!
C. M-hm. How does one reach the kind of goals that you'd like to have?
S. Yeah. And, too, I'm trying not to make a mess of it, and perhaps that's
    behind a lot of my trouble ... since it's hardly fair to expect other
    people to approach you if you don't approach these people first.
C. You feel as though you just haven't taken the steps that would lead to
    friendship, is that...?
S. That's right. (pause)
C. That's what you'd like to change.
S. M-hm. I think so....

In my judgment, there was a significant advance in the therapeutic process.
It was marked by the long pause. Up to this point she has been *explaining*

her problems, to *me*. But after the pause she begins to communicate with herself, and to express to *herself* some of her deeply puzzling feeling, "I know the way, but how do I do it? And how!" As she says this, and the sentences which follow, her voice and attitude are different. She is raising questions of herself, wondering within herself what she can do to get her mind and feelings "straightened out," as she goes on to say . . .

S. M-hm. I think so. It all focuses on the fact that next year I'll be doing something different. And if I can only get it straight in my mind, or at least have some idea of what I want—or partially straightened out, let's say—perhaps I can do something about it. I should think the change to . . . it's easier to try something when you just break clean through.

C. That here you're going to have a chance to do something of a different sort and . . . will you do it? And how should it be done? And so on. It's that kind of thing that . . .

S. Yeah. Except of course that I think I can work out tactics if I know just exactly what's in my own mind, and why I've been acting as I have for the past . . .

C. In other words, if you're really sure within yourself of . . . why you are the way you are, and what you want, then the rest wouldn't really trouble you.

S. I don't think so. After all, it's hardly . . . you don't consult someone to map out a plan of action to gain friends and influence people. Once you have the . . . emotional and . . . stability within yourself, then I think you go ahead on your own.

C. M-hm. The real problem lies in the uncertainty within yourself.

S. Yes. The problem . . . the problem is very definitely in my own reactions and so on. (pause)

C. And if you could deal with that, you'd feel quite comfortable about dealing with the tactics and strategy that the purpose might demand.

S. Yeah. Well, I think I would. After all, I've never done that so I can't tell. (pause)

C. Guess our time's about up for today. In regard to another interview, suppose I phone you.

S. All right.

C. And then we can arrange that (words lost).

S. All right.

C. Okay.

ECLECTIC COUNSELING

The eclectic counselor selects his interview procedures on the basis of their predicted effect upon the counselee rather than on the basis of some theoretical allegiance. He bases his counseling on concepts taken from a number of viewpoints rather than from one exclusively. When, for example, a counselor deliberately incorporates in his practice both directive and nondirective concepts, the result is eclecticism. This is not to be confused with trial-and-error counseling. The counselor does not try out various approaches until he happens to hit on one that works. Nor is it a procedure based on what Hilgard [42] describes as a general formula of "There's much good to be said on all sides." Such eclecticism (if it may be called eclecticism) is vague, superficial, and most probably opportunistic.

As Meehl [43] points out, the true eclectic, according to Webster's definition, strives to select that which he finds best in the various theories or systems. The selection might be made wholly on the basis of accumulated experience. In Meehl's opinion, a more effective approach might be to scan the theoretical offerings in the light of experience and try to bring about a more satisfactory conceptual unification through reformulations of principles selected from the various systems. Tyler [44] recommends that every counselor attempt to develop his own synthesis. The counselor "needs many different varieties of theoretical concept, but for his own confidence and peace of mind he needs to have them organized in some way." The cultivation or organization of one's individual theory is presumably a lifetime job.

Those who support the eclectic approach maintain that the counselor should not limit himself to one method but should vary his procedures in keeping with the needs of individual clients. Some agree with Thorne [45] that "the principal factor is not what method is used but rather the skill with which it is used." Outstanding representatives of the eclectic approach include Brammer and Shostrom, McKinney, Robinson, and Tyler. Space permits limited attention to be given to the views of only one—Leona E. Tyler. The following summary shows how she fuses directive and client-centered concepts in her eclectic approach.

To Tyler [46] it is essential that the counselor experience understanding and acceptance of the client and be able to communicate them to the client. Acceptance involves allowing clients to differ from one another in all sorts of ways. It involves realizing that each client's counseling experience is a complex pattern of striving, thinking, and feeling. It involves such simple things as hospitality—creating the right counseling atmosphere through office arrangement, avoidance of interruptions, and the like. It involves such complex things as skill in following a client's

[42] E. R. Hilgard, *Theories of Learning*, rev. ed., p. 13. New York: Appleton-Century-Crofts, Inc., 1960.

[43] Paul E. Meehl, Introduction, in L. M. Brammer and E. L. Shostrom, *Therapeutic Psychology: Fundamentals of Counseling and Psychotherapy*, p. xiv. Englewood Cliffs, N.J.: Prentice-Hall, Inc., 1960.

[44] Leona E. Tyler, "Theoretical Principles Underlying the Counseling Process," *Journal of Counseling Psychology*, 1958, 5:3–5.

[45] Frederick C. Thorne, *Principles of Personality Counseling: An Eclectic Approach*, p. 88. Brandon, Vt.: Journal of Clinical Psychology, 1950.

[46] Leona E. Tyler, *The Work of the Counselor*, 2d ed. New York: Appleton-Century-Crofts, Inc., 1961.

lead and in picking up clues to matters of interest or concern to him. And it involves being prepared to take whatever comes up without flinching, no matter how unexpected or unwelcome. But it does not involve approval or disapproval of the client's behavior or his personality.

As the foregoing indicates, Tyler stresses the counseling relationship rather than techniques. The relationship must be warm and friendly, based on confidence, respect, and sympathy, but not marred by pity. The counselor responds to attitudes rather than to words. He helps to open up the psychological realities in the client's situation by attentively following the client's train of thought and feeling. He never probes for hidden meanings.

The most common way in which a counselor assists a client is through aiding him to choose from the courses of action open to him. Hence, much counseling is oriented toward the making of choices and decisions. The counselor helps the client to survey the alternatives and to clarify for each both the possibilities and the limits—limits set by circumstances (family, financial, etc.), physical and psychological characteristics, past learnings, maturity, and experience.

By uncritically accepting a client's indecision, the counselor helps him to tolerate uncertainty and thereby avoid a premature or pseudodecision. He helps the client identify and examine possible reasons for his inability to reach a decision—reasons such as fear of failure, family pressure, equally attractive alternatives, conflicting attitudes toward a choice, etc.

The counselor helps the client to utilize his personal and environmental resources. When appropriate, he assists him to acquire new skills (dancing, improved reading skill, etc.) and new knowledge. The counselor has more information of various sorts than has the student. He is better informed, for example, regarding occupations and occupational opportunities, the meaning of test scores, treatment facilities, referral procedures, and the like. He brings such information into the interview as there is need for it. He takes care to give it in broken doses, so to speak, so that the client may have a chance to react to the information offered and through his responses to show whether he is understanding and assimilating it. Ordinarily this takes time, usually more than one interview.

The counselor utilizes all sources of relevant data regarding the client. Tyler accepts Williamson's concept of diagnosis as the whole comprehensive picture that the counselor develops of the client, including his strengths and weaknesses, interests and aptitudes, past experiences, and hopes for the future.[47] She accepts diagnosis as a crucial step in the educational and vocational counseling of students but opposes organizing counseling around diagnosis.

[47] *Ibid.*, pp. 61–64.

EXAMPLES OF THE ECLECTIC COUNSELING INTERVIEW

The two following examples are taken from Tyler's illustrations of the decision-making interview. In the first one a counselor is helping a college freshman plan his program of studies. It is as follows: [48]

JIM: Gee, I'm all mixed up. I certainly hope you can straighten me out.

ADVISER: Pretty confusing business, this registration. I expect you'll be glad when this week is over.

JIM: I sure will! (*He takes out his registration materials and spreads them out on the desk.*)

ADVISER: You know what the procedure is—what you are supposed to do with this blank and these cards?

JIM: Oh, yes. They told us that at the meeting last night. I'm supposed to put down the courses I'm going to take on this card. Then you sign it and I take it around to the departments the courses are in. It's deciding what to put down that bothers me. What do you think I should take?

ADVISER: Perhaps if you told me a little more about yourself—what your general plans are and what you want to get out of college—it would help us decide.

JIM: I've never really thought very much about it, I guess—just took things as they came in high school. I've done all right but haven't been too outstanding in anything. I suppose I've always assumed that I would go into business some day like my father. You probably know my father, Cuthbert and Harris, you know.

ADVISER: Of course. I don't think I've met your father, but I know the store. Is there some possibility then that you will go into your father's business with him?

JIM: Well, that's what he wants, of course, and I suppose that's what I'll do in the end. I probably ought to take a Business Administration course. The only trouble with that is that it says here in the catalog that you are required to take accounting before you can take anything else, and I don't know about that. The boys at the house say that's the hardest freshman course there is. They've got me scared. I'd hate to get some low grades the first term and have to drop out of college.

ADVISER: You want to be sure you don't do the wrong thing. You know probably that the placement test you took yesterday is supposed to tell you how you compare with other entering students in ability to handle college work.

JIM: I've got that score here on this other card they gave me. It says 5. What does 5 mean?

ADVISER: That is just an average rating. It means that there are just about

[48] From *The Work of the Counselor*, 2d ed., by Leona E. Tyler, pp. 190–191. Copyright © 1953, 1961. Appleton-Century-Crofts, Inc. Reprinted by permission of the publisher.

as many freshmen with lower scores than yours as there are with higher.

JIM: That's just about what I thought I'd get. But I was afraid maybe it might be lower. With that kind of score I ought to be able to do regular freshmen courses all right if I study, oughtn't I?

ADVISER: Surely. You're beginning to get a little more confidence about the whole thing!

JIM: Yes, I think I'll try the accounting after all. I'll just plan to spend a lot of time on it, especially this first term. These boys at the house that had it last year will probably be able to help me if I get stuck. What else do you think I should take?

ADVISER: (turning to the section of the catalog where general requirements are explained) The University decides some of these things for you. There is the English, the physical education, and the ROTC that everybody has to take. You might put those down and see what it adds up to. (Jim writes them on the card.)

JIM: It looks as though I could get in about two more things.

ADVISER: Did they explain these "group requirements" to you? In order to make sure that everybody who graduates has some broad liberal education, the University requires that you take at least one course in each of these groups: the humanities, science, and social science. Here is the list of courses you have to choose from.

JIM: How would it be if I took a history course this year? I've always liked history. I think I'll take this European History. I'd like to know something about that. (He counts up his credit hours.) I think I can take one more course, but I'd rather let the other group requirements go until next year. Do you suppose I could take some music? I'd like to go on with my clarinet lessons.

ADVISER: It sounds like a good idea. Well, that just about settles your program, doesn't it? I'll sign the card and then you can work out the times for all the classes from the time schedule yourself.

JIM: Thank you for all your help. I feel as if I were really getting started now.

ADVISER: You're more than welcome. You know where I am now, and I hope you'll come back any time you need my help. Good luck with the rest of your registration.

The second example is an excerpt from the third conference with a college sophomore girl regarding a career and a college major to correspond to it. It is as follows: [49]

CLIENT: I've been thinking and thinking about the possibilities we talked over last time, but I just can't make up my mind.

COUNSELOR: No single one of them seems exactly right?

CLIENT: The thing I keep coming back to is that my grades and the tests I took show that I get along better in social science than in anything else, and the natural, obvious thing is that I should be a social science teacher. There isn't any real argument against it either. I've looked up what the books say about the opportunities and they seem to be good. The sala-

[49] *Ibid.*, pp. 192–193. Reproduced by permission of the publisher.

ries are good now, too—higher than for anything else I could get a job doing. But somehow I just can't see myself as a teacher.

COUNSELOR: There's something about the role you'd be playing that just doesn't seem to fit you?

CLIENT: I don't know. Maybe it does fit. Maybe I'm just not being realistic about myself. I've been trying to figure out what it is about the job that I balk at. I like children and young people and have always gotten along fine with them. I don't think I'll have any trouble with discipline or anything. I never did in Girl Scouts or summer camp. It's more that I hate to settle down in a small town the way you have to do, at least the first job you get.

COUNSELOR: There are things about small-town life you don't like?

CLIENT: There certainly are! I grew up in one, you know. I know all about the narrowness and the smugness and the gossip. And as long as I can remember I've heard my mother complaining about it. She was a music teacher and wanted to go to New York to study voice. But she didn't have any money and decided to teach for a couple of years to save enough to get started in New York. Then of course she married my dad— he works at the First National Bank—and that was the end of all her plans. She's never even been to New York yet on a visit.

COUNSELOR: Your mother sort of got caught in a small-town life she hadn't planned for herself.

CLIENT: That's just it. I think she's always felt cheated. Between you and me, I don't think she has such a wonderful voice. She might not have gone very far with it if she had studied in New York. The family gets a little tired of hearing about what she has given up for us.

COUNSELOR: You're not completely in sympathy with your mother's attitude.

CLIENT: No, I'm not. And yet I seem to have been affected by it so that I'm afraid of being caught myself. I can see that I wouldn't need to be. You don't have to marry the cashier of the First National Bank unless you want to, and if you do want to—I probably would if he was like my dad—you shouldn't complain about the consequences. . . .

THE TREND?

The controversy regarding the relative effectiveness of directive and client-centered counseling is less sharp today than in the late 1940s and early 1950s. Also, there is considerably less tendency to exaggerate the differences in the two approaches. And there is a growing recognition, if not yet general acceptance, of the point of view that the choice of methods often depends on the counselor's personality. If, as Corsini [50] says, "we

[50] Raymond J. Corsini, *Methods of Group Psychotherapy*, p. 126. New York: McGraw-Hill Book Company, Inc., 1957.

accept the argument that the best method for any person is the one that accords with his own nature, and that a person can do his best work with a procedure that is natural for him, we may be freed of any hierarchy of values with respect to methods."

In general, this point of view seems to be endorsed by both Williamson and Rogers. According to Williamson,[51] "every effective counselor must develop his own style and his own theory, too." And Rogers [52] says that the wise counselor uses "those procedures which most nearly fit himself." He adds, however, that if the counselor is alert to the effects of the different procedures and the ways he expresses himself, he changes both his procedures and his attitudes.

Objective comparison of the counseling methods used by persons of different schools of thought shows that experience outweighs theoretical allegiance in determining how a person counsels. Fiedler,[53] for example, found that experienced counselors of different orientations agreed more highly with each other than with less experienced counselors in their own schools of thought. Similarly Strupp [54] found that experienced therapists of varying viewpoints differed less from one another in their counseling techniques than they did from little-experienced therapists of similar viewpoints. He concluded that "exclusive reliance on one technique appears to be a correlate of inexperience." [55] He found also that therapists' personality factors are more important in therapy than techniques.[56]

Wrenn [57] reports a study that supports the findings of Fiedler and Strupp. He used 13 interview situations in which it was thought that experienced counselors of different theoretical orientations would respond differently. On the basis of his findings, however, it was concluded that "theoretical orientation is of little influence in determining the manner in which experienced counselors respond."

[51] Williamson et al., "Counseling Theory and Techniques: A Panel Discussion," p. 42.

[52] Ibid.

[53] F. E. Fiedler, "A Comparison of Therapeutic Relationships in Psychoanalytic, Non-directive, and Adlerian Therapy," Journal of Consulting Psychology, 1950, 14:436–445.

[54] H. H. Strupp, "An Objective Comparison of Rogerian and Psychoanalytic Techniques," Journal of Consulting Psychology, 1955, 19:1–7; "Psychotherapeutic Technique, Professional Affiliation, and Experience Level," Journal of Consulting Psychology, 1955, 19:97–102.

[55] Strupp, "An Objective Comparison of Rogerian and Psychoanalytic Techniques," p. 7.

[56] H. H. Strupp, "Nature of Psychotherapist's Contribution to Treatment Process," Archives of General Psychiatry, 1960, 3:219–231; M. S. Wallach and H. H. Strupp, "Psychotherapists' Clinical Judgments and Attitudes toward Patients," Journal of Consulting Psychology, 1960, 24:316–323.

[57] Robert L. Wrenn, "Counselor Orientation: Theoretical or Situational?" Journal of Counseling Psychology, 1960, 7:40–45.

SUMMARY

Both directive and client-centered counseling are directed toward helping the client achieve development of his potentialities. In both the objective is change in terms of learning or growth. And in both approaches the quality of the counseling relationship is held more important than the interview technique. In directive counseling the role of the counselor is largely that of a master educator; in client-centered counseling it is largely that of a catalytic agent. The intellectual aspects of the counseling process are stressed more in directive counseling than in client-centered counseling, in which the feeling aspects of the process are stressed.

While the differences in directive and client-centered counseling are less marked today than in the 1940s, the two methods are still far apart with respect to three matters—diagnosis, information giving, and the teaching of values. All three are held important in directive counseling. In client-centered counseling, information giving is not rejected, but it is held of little importance or usefulness. Diagnosis is rejected as a function of the counselor; it is considered a function of the client. Similarly, the locus of evaluation is perceived as being in the client, not the counselor. The counselor does not strive to help the client cultivate specific values. Instead, he tries to help him to develop his capacity for direct evaluation on the basis of experience.

In eclectic counseling the contributions of various schools of thought are synthesized into a new or a somewhat different approach. A trend toward eclecticism seems indicated by an apparently widespread acceptance of the point of view that no one method is appropriate for all cases and that the counselor needs to be sufficiently versatile to be able to adapt his procedures in keeping with the best interests of the client and the requirements of the particular situation.

Research indicates that a counselor's counseling methods are as much determined by his personality as by his theoretical orientation.

REFERENCES

Arbuckle, Dugald S.: "Counseling: Philosophy or Science?" *Personnel and Guidance Journal,* 1960, 39:11–14.
———: *Counseling: An Introduction.* Boston: Allyn and Bacon, Inc., 1961.
——— and Angelo V. Boy: "Client-centered Therapy in Counseling Students with Behavior Problems," *Journal of Counseling Psychology,* 1961, 8:136–139.
Berdie, Ralph F.: "Counseling Principles and Presumptions," *Journal of Counseling Psychology,* 1959, 6:175–182.
———: "The Counselor and His Manpower Responsibilities," *Personnel and Guidance Journal,* 1960, 38:438–463.
Brammer, L. M., and E. L. Shostrom: *Therapeutic Psychology: Fundamentals of Counseling and Psychotherapy.* Englewood Cliffs, N.J.: Prentice-Hall, Inc., 1960.

Dugan, W. E. (ed.): *Counseling Points of View.* Minneapolis: The University of Minnesota Press, 1959.

Hobbs, Nicholas: "Client-centered Psychotherapy," in J. L. McCary (ed.), *Six Approaches to Psychotherapy,* chap. 1. New York: Holt, Rinehart and Winston, Inc., 1955.

———: "Sources of Gain in Psychotherapy," *American Psychologist,* 1962, 17:741–747.

Hoffman, Simon: "Diagnosis and Evaluation in Counseling," *Personnel and Guidance Journal,* 1959, 38:229–231.

Kirtner, W. L., and D. S. Cartwright: "Success and Failure in Client-centered Therapy as a Function of Initial Therapy Behavior," *Journal of Consulting Psychology,* 1958, 22:329–333.

McKinney, Fred: *Counseling for Personal Adjustment.* Boston: Houghton Mifflin Company, 1958.

Nachmann, Barbara: "Client Problems and Duration of Counseling," *Personnel and Guidance Journal,* 1960, 38:486–488.

Patterson, C. H.: "The Place of Values in Counseling and Psychotherapy," *Journal of Counseling Psychology,* 1958, 5:216–223.

———: *Counseling and Psychotherapy: Theory and Practice.* New York: Harper & Row, Publishers, Incorporated, 1959.

Pepinsky, H. B., and P. N. Pepinsky: *Counseling Theory and Practice.* New York: The Ronald Press Company, 1954.

Robinson, Francis P.: *Principles and Procedures in Student Counseling.* New York: Harper & Row, Publishers, Incorporated, 1950.

Rogers, Carl R.: *Counseling and Psychotherapy.* Boston: Houghton Mifflin Company, 1942.

———: *Client-centered Therapy.* Boston: Houghton Mifflin Company, 1951.

———: *On Becoming a Person.* Boston: Houghton Mifflin Company, 1961.

——— and Rosalind P. Dymond (eds.): *Psychotherapy and Personality Change.* Chicago: The University of Chicago Press, 1954.

Samler, Joseph: "Changes in Values: A Goal in Counseling," *Journal of Consulting Psychology,* 1960, 7:32–39.

Shoben, E. J., Jr.: "The Counselor's Theory as Personal Trait," *Personnel and Guidance Journal,* 1962, 40:617–621.

Snyder, W. U.: *Casebook of Nondirective Counseling.* Boston: Houghton Mifflin Company, 1952.

Strupp, H. H.: "An Objective Comparison of Rogerian and Psychoanalytic Techniques," *Journal of Consulting Psychology,* 1955, 19:1–7.

———: "Psychotherapeutic Technique, Professional Affiliation, and Experience Level," *Journal of Consulting Psychology,* 1955, 19:97–102.

———: "Nature of Psychotherapist's Contribution to Treatment Process," *Archives of General Psychiatry,* 1960, 3:219–231.

Thorne, F. C.: *Principles of Personality Counseling: An Eclectic Approach.* Brandon, Vt.: Journal of Clinical Psychology, 1950.

Tyler, Leona E.: "Theoretical Principles Underlying the Counseling Process," *Journal of Counseling Psychology,* 1958, 5:3–10.

———: "Controlling the Duration of Counseling," *Personnel and Guidance Journal,* 1960, 38:475–479.

———: *The Work of the Counselor,* 2d ed. New York: Appleton-Century-Crofts, Inc., 1961.

Wallach, M. S., and H. H. Strupp: "Psychotherapists' Clinical Judgments and Attitudes toward Patients," *Journal of Consulting Psychology,* 1960, 24:316–323.

Williamson, E. G.: *Counseling Adolescents.* New York: McGraw-Hill Book Company, Inc., 1950.

———: "The Fusion of Discipline and Counseling in the Educative Process," *Personnel and Guidance Journal,* 1955, 34:74–79.

———: "Counseling in Developing Self-confidence," *Personnel and Guidance Journal,* 1956, 34:398–404.

———: "Value Orientation in Counseling," *Personnel and Guidance Journal,* 1958, 36:520–528.

———: "The Meaning of Communication in Counseling," *Personnel and Guidance Journal,* 1959, 38:6–14.

———: "The Counselor as Technique," *Personnel and Guidance Journal,* 1962, 41:108–111.

Wrenn, C. Gilbert: "The Self Concept in Counseling," *Journal of Counseling Psychology,* 1958, 5:104–109.

Wrenn, Robert L.: "Counselor Orientation: Theoretical or Situational?" *Journal of Counseling Psychology,* 1960, 7:40–45.

Name Index

Adams, J. F., 311
Adler, Alfred, 389–390
Allport, G. W., 240
Almy, Millie, 40, 233–234, 240
Anastasi, Anne, 70, 89, 98, 106, 111, 117, 132
Anderson, F. N., 364, 371
Arbuckle, D. S., 18, 373, 407, 427, 430, 447, 465
Arieti, Silvana, 348
Arnholter, E. G., 221

Bales, R. F., 40
Baller, W. R., 317
Balser, B. H., 381
Barbara, D. A., 430
Barry, Ruth, 18
Bass, B. M., 40
Bauernfeind, R. H., 89
Beach, Sylvia, 99
Bell, H. M., 195
Bell, J. E., 375–377, 381
Bellsmith, Virginia, 381
Bennett, G. K., 99–100, 122, 140, 167
Berdie, R. F., 18, 89, 330–332, 409, 430, 465
Berg, I. A., 408
Bernard, V. W., 359
Berston, H. M., 221
Biber, Barbara, 334
Bieker, Helen, 33–34, 40
Bingham, W. V., 264
Bixler, R. H., 167
Blaine, G. B., 359
Blindman, A. J., 359
Blos, Peter, 235–238, 240, 300, 311
Bogardus, E. S., 260
Bonney, M. E., 262
Bordin, E. S., 166–167, 386, 392, 404, 407, 430
Borgatta, E. F., 251, 262
Bower, E. M., 228, 261, 337, 339–340, 348, 359
Bowles, F. H., 18
Bowman, P. H., 359
Boy, A. V., 465
Brammer, L. M., 412–413, 416, 430, 459, 465

Brams, J. M., 430
Brewster, R. E., 291
Buros, O. K., 75, 89, 91, 95, 110, 120, 127, 130
Buxbaum, Joan, 381
Byrd, Eugene, 242
Byrne, R. H., 221

Callis, Robert, 166, 430
Campbell, D. T., 251
Caplan, Gerald, 334
Caplan, S. W., 229, 355–356, 359
Caravello, S. J., 9, 221
Carle, R. F., 18
Carpenter, J. H., 46–47
Cartwright, D. S., 466
Cattel, R. B., 132
Chanasky, N. M., 359
Clothier, R. C., 43
Cogswell, J. F., 272
Cohen, L. D., 359
Coleman, J. W., 360
Coleman, William, 89, 98
Combs, A. W., 396
Conant, J. B., 5, 9
Connell, C. F., 430
Cook, E. S., Jr., 221
Cooper, Saul, 221
Cooper, Sophia, 195, 208, 221
Corsini, S. J., 463
Cottle, W. C., 221, 291
Cowles, J. T., 116
Criswell, J. H., 262
Crites, J. O., 66, 69, 71, 77, 89, 94, 102, 112–113, 115, 133, 166, 168
Cronbach, L. J., 60, 62, 69, 75, 77, 89, 93, 95, 101, 112, 122, 130, 132
Cumming, Elaine, 359
Cumming, John, 359
Cunningham, Ruth, 40, 233–234, 240, 260, 262

Dailey, C. A., 294, 296, 311
Dailey, J. T., 12
Daniels, E. M., 359
Danielson, P. J., 231, 240
Darley, J. G., 72, 89, 119, 132, 154–155

Davidian, E. V., 430
Davis, Allison, 98
Davis, D. A., 221
Davis, J. A., 89
Dean, H. C., 364, 371
DeLong, A. R., 262
Dement, A. L., 430
D'Evelyn, Katherine, 359
Dice, L. K., 221
Dickson, G. S., 120
Dillon, H. J., 195, 210, 221, 351
Dimeen, M. A., 262
Dinkmeyer, Don, 240
Dollard, John, 398, 407
Downie, N. M., 291
Dresden, K. W., 181
Dresher, R. H., 221
Dressel, P. L., 106, 167, 419
Droege, R. C., 112
Dugan, W. E., 425, 466
Durnall, E. J., Jr., 407
Durost, W. N., 167
Dvorak, B. J., 101
Dymond, R. F., 228, 447, 466

Ebel, R. L., 167
Eckerson, L. O., 89
Eckert, E. G., 195
Edelston, Harry, 311
Eichorn, J. R., 348, 360
Elkins, Deborah, 240, 262
Ellington, Mark, 40
Embree, R. B., Jr., 407
Epps, M. V., 221
Erickson, C. E., 175, 317
Erikson, Eric, 279
Evraiff, William, 221

Fabian, A. A., 359
Farwell, G. F., 18
Fenichel, Otto, 407
Fenton, Norman, 313, 320, 323, 325, 332
Ferreira, J. R., 279, 292
Fiedler, F. E., 464
Finley, X. J., 332
Fiske, D. W., 122
Flanagan, J. C., 82, 89
Foley, J. D., 430
Forrester, Gertrude, 224
Fowler, W. L., 99
Freeman, F. S., 46, 48, 62
Freud, Sigmund, 407
Froelich, C. P., 40, 62, 89, 112, 133, 193, 290, 292

Fromm, Erich, 389, 391, 407

Galdston, Iago, 359
Garry, Ralph, 262
Gee, H. H., 116
Gibb, J. R., 381
Gilbert, W. M., 332
Glidwell, J. C., 359
Gluck, Samuel, 460
Goldman, Leo, 79, 89, 166–167
Good, C. V., 204
Grant, C. W., 19
Green, D. A., 221, 269, 292
Greene, E. B., 55, 62
Gronlund, N. E., 262
Grossman, Alvin, 271, 292
Guilford, J. P., 59, 91
Guzvich, Peter, 357

Haas, R. B., 238
Hagen, Elizabeth, 41, 62, 75, 89, 112, 124, 133
Hagenah, Theda, 119, 132, 154–155
Haggerty, M. E., 44
Hahn, M. E., 311, 430
Hall, C. S., 395, 399
Hamalainen, A. E., 28, 35, 39
Hardee, M. D., 292
Hartshorne, Hugh, 49, 259–260
Hartzman, Jack, 359
Henry, N. B., 18, 408
Herman, L. M., 167
Hermann, Lyndon, 221
Hilgard, E. R., 459
Hill, G. E., 18
Hills, J. R., 146, 148, 167
Hilton, M. E., 431
Hobbs, Nicholas, 385, 466
Hoffman, Simon, 466
Horney, Karen, 389–390, 407
Horst, Paul, 133
Howe, J. W., 347
Hoyt, K. B., 40, 62, 89, 112, 133, 193, 292, 381
Hurley, Neil, 292
Hutson, P. W., 18

Jackson, Joseph, 359
Jahada, Marie, 360
Jarvie, L. L., 27, 33, 40
Jennings, H. H., 242, 244–247, 251, 258, 262
Jersild, A. T., 226, 240
Johnson, E. A., 195, 210
Jones, A. J., 223

Jones, H. E., 25, 31, 39–41, 44, 62, 227, 295–296, 300, 304, 311
Justman, Joseph, 262

Kaczkowski, H. B., 269, 296
Kahn, R. L., 430
Karpf, F. B., 408
Katz, M. R., 112
Kelley, D. M., 123
Kelly, E. L., 122
Kennedy, E. G., 414, 424
Kinzer, J. R., 430
Kirk, B. A., 89, 167, 168, 430
Kirtner, W. L., 466
Kitch, D. E., 197
Klein, D. C., 360
Klopfer, Bruno, 123
Kotinsky, Ruth, 360
Kounin, Jacob, 381
Krim, Elaine, 430
Krugman, Maurice, 359
Kubie, L. S., 360
Kurtz, J. L., 332

Lambert, Nadine, 228, 261, 340, 345, 349, 360
Laughlin, Frances, 263
Lawson, T. O., 360
Layton, W. L., 133
Ledvina, L. M., 206
Lee, A. McC., 408
Lee, M. B., 213, 217, 280
Legg, C. E., 195, 210
Lennon, R. T., 110
Lesser, W. M., 430
Levitt, E. E., 381
Lewin, Kurt, 393–395
Lichter, S. O., 213, 221
Liddle, G. P., 360
Liebman, R. R., 237
Lindquist, E. F., 89, 107
Lindzey, Gardner, 251, 395, 399
Lipkin, Stanley, 450
Lippitt, Ronald, 41, 381
Livingston, A. H., 221
Lloyd, R. G., 263
Lloyd-Jones, Esther, 2
Looby, A. J., 269, 292
Loughary, J. W., 381
Love, M. L., 99
Lundin, R. W., 102

McArthur, Charles, 116
McCabe, G. E., 146–147, 167

McCary, J. L., 432, 466
McCreary, W. H., 197
McDaniel, H. B., 311, 317, 332
McGeever, J. F., 222
Mackie, R. P., 334–335
McKinney, Fred, 374, 422, 430, 466
McLaughlin, J. W., 292
McLaughlin, K. F., 89
MacLean, M. S., 311, 430
McMullen, Wayne, 364, 371
Magary, J. F., 348, 360
Magnuson, H. W., 240
Malcolm, D. D., 18
Maller, J. B., 259
Malouf, Phelon, 289, 292
Mariner, A. S., 381
Marshall, T. O., 195
Martyn, K. A., 292
Maslow, A. H., 389, 408
Mass, H. S., 381
Mathewson, R. H., 12, 18
Matteson, R. W., 167
May, M. A., 259
Mayhew, L. B., 106
Meehl, P. E., 89, 459
Miller, C. H., 18
Miller, N. E., 398, 407
Mooren, R. A., 199–200, 221
Mooring, Ivy, 357
Moreno, J. L., 5–7, 242
Mowrer, O. H., 408
Moynihan, J. F., 407
Munroe, Ruth, 239
Murk, Vergil, 221
Murphy, Gardner, 18, 408
Murray, Elwood, 238
Murray, H. A., 123, 128, 293, 295, 311, 324

Nachmann, Barbara, 133, 466
Newcomb, T. M., 41
Newman, F. B., 31, 41, 44, 48, 56
Nolan, E. G., 141
Noll, V. H., 99
Northway, M. L., 244, 248, 250, 263

Oakes, P. W., 279, 292
O'Neal, Patricia, 360
Otto, H. A., 360
Overstreet, P. L., 115–116, 133

Parker, C. A., 430
Patterson, C. H., 401, 406, 408, 447, 466
Peck, Bernard, 354
Peck, H. B., 381

Peiffer, H. C., Jr., 408, 430–431
Pellman, Maurine, 360
Pennington, L. A., 408
Pepinsky, H. B., 408, 466
Pepinsky, P. N., 408, 466
Perlmutter, B. J., 18
Pierson, G. A., 19
Plunkett, M. L., 195, 221
Polansky, Norman, 381
Polmantier, P. C., 430
Powell, Johnny, 262
Pratt, Gerald, 328
Prescott, D. A., 21, 33, 37, 41, 354–355
Putman, J. F., 273

Rabinovitch, R. D., 348–349
Ramsery, G. V., 381
Randall, J. A., 21–26, 41
Rank, Otto, 389–390, 408
Reed, Anna Y., 265
Reik, Theodor, 430
Riches, Naomi, 195, 221
Ricks, J. H., Jr., 168
Robbins, L. N., 360
Robbins, P. P., 334–335
Roberts, R. O., 222
Robinson, F. P., 422, 466
Robinson, Reginald, 381
Roe, Anne, 133
Roeber, E. C., 430
Roens, B. A., 53, 62, 166, 173, 185, 193, 240, 297, 299–301, 305–310, 312, 318
Rogers, C. R., 19, 228, 392, 411, 447–458, 466
Rogers, L. A., 168
Rohde, A. R., 123
Rosner, Joseph, 381
Ross, M. G., 391
Rothney, J. W. M., 53–54, 63, 76, 78, 89, 133, 166, 173, 176, 185, 193, 199–200, 207, 221, 231–232, 238, 240, 297, 299–301, 305–310, 312, 317–318, 332
Ruch, G. M., 268
Rudikoff, L. C., 168, 430

Samler, Joseph, 466
Sanderson, Herbert, 382
Scates, D. E., 204
Schiffer, Mortimer, 360
Schiffman, Jacob, 222
Schwebel, Milton, 408
Scott, W. D., 41, 264–265
Seashore, H. G., 89
Seeley, J. A., 342

Segel, David, 222, 268, 336
Seymour, H. C., 211
Shaffer, E. E., Jr., 230, 233, 240
Shaffer, L. F., 95, 127, 131, 293
Shaycoft, M. F., 112
Shea, J. T., 292
Shoben, E. J., Jr., 293, 408, 466
Shostrom, E. L., 412–413, 416, 430, 459, 465
Singer, S. L., 133
Sisson, E. D., 62
Skinner, B. F., 398
Slavson, S. R., 347
Smith, E. R., 51–52, 62, 106, 266
Smith, H. M., 5
Smith, M. B., 360
Snyder, W. U., 466
Snygg, Donald, 396
Sorenson, M. A., 222
Stephenson, William, 53
Stevens, L. B., 116
Stewart, A. J., 19
Stewart, L. H., 133, 269–270, 277, 279, 283, 292
Stordahl, K. E., 133
Strang, Ruth, 62, 193, 240, 293, 312
Stranhan, Marion, 360
Strong, E. K., Jr., 115, 122, 133
Strupp, H. H., 464, 466–467
Sullivan, H. S., 389–391
Super, D. E., 66, 69, 71, 77, 89, 94, 99–100, 102, 112–116, 133, 166, 168, 386, 408
Symonds, P. M., 47, 57, 62, 169, 186, 193

Taba, Hilda, 240, 249, 251–252, 256, 263, 360
Tavris, E. C., 121
Tennyson, W. W., 19
Tesseneer, L. M., 222
Tesseneer, R. A., 222
Thomas, Edwin, 382
Thomas, R. J., 222
Thompson, Anton, 89
Thompson, Jack, 332
Thomson, G. M., 9–10
Thorndike, E. L., 57, 137
Thorndike, R. L., 41, 62, 75, 89, 112, 124, 133
Thorne, F. C., 293, 297, 405, 408, 432–433, 459, 466
Torgerson, T. L., 49, 62, 338
Traxler, A. E., 22, 27, 41, 62, 79, 90, 107, 136, 174, 193, 264–265, 278, 292–293, 312
Tremer, C. E., 211
Tryon, C. M., 33, 40, 246, 260

Turnbull, W. W., 98
Tyler, L. E., 133, 135, 168, 173, 386, 392, 403–404, 408, 412, 416, 431, 459–463, 466
Tyler, R. W., 51–52, 62, 106

Ullman, C. A., 133, 360

Walker, D. E., 408, 430–431
Wallach, M. S., 464, 467
Wallen, J. L., 451
Ward, A. W., 98
Warters, Jane, 19, 149, 246
Weider, Arthur, 123
Weld, Lindsay, 263
Wesman, A. G., 90, 145–146
White, Ralph, 41
Wickes, T. A., Jr., 90
Wilkins, W. D., 19
Williams, H. M., 292
Williams, J. E., 431

Williamson, E. G., 155–156, 166, 172, 297, 300, 312, 332, 385, 411, 414–415, 430–431, 434, 446, 449, 451–452, 464, 467
Wilson, F. M., 190
Wiskoff, Martin, 408
Wolf, Beverly, 18
Wolf, D. L., 19, 90
Wolfbein, S. L., 209, 212–213, 222
Wood, B. D., 265
Woollatt, L. H., 217, 222
Workman, A. D., 269–270, 277, 283
Wrenn, C. G., 5, 9, 12–14, 17, 19, 207, 264, 383, 385, 400–402, 406–408, 426, 431, 467
Wrenn, R. L., 464, 467
Wrightstone, J. W., 262

Young, Kimball, 293, 295
Young, L. R., 382

Zachary, C. B., 296
Zeigler, M. L., 167

Subject Index

Achievement tests, 104–111
Activity group therapy, 347–348
Adjustment class, 344–349, 351
Adjustment inventories, 126–131
American College Testing Program, 110
American Council on Education, Commission on Teacher Education, 21, 23, 28, 35, 38, 354
  Committee on Personnel Methods, 265
  cumulative record forms, 53, 265–266
  Personality Report, 49–51
American Personnel and Guidance Association, 85, 88, 274, 284–285, 371, 401, 407
American Psychological Association, Committee on Ethical Standards, 85–89, 371, 401, 406
  Committee on Test Standards, 70, 88
  Division of Counseling Psychology, 386, 407
American School Counselor Association, 264
Anecdotal records, 20–41
  advantages, 38–39
  desired characteristics, 30–35
  limitations, 39
  number, 27–28
  report form, 23
  summary, 35–37
  types, 21–27
Annual Review of Psychology, 75
Aptitude tests, scholastic, 91–100
  special, 102–104
Army Qualification Card, 265
Army Rating Scale, 43
Autobiographical materials, 229–239

Billett-Starr Youth Problems Inventory, 126
Binet intelligence scales, 92–94
Brown-Holtzman Survey of Study Habits, 183

California Achievement Tests, 106
California Adolescent Growth Study, 25, 44, 48, 55, 156–157, 227, 259, 296
California Psychological Inventory, 130

California Test of Mental Maturity, 96–98, 100, 156
Case conference, 11, 312–332, 340, 369, 378
  defined, 313–314
  initiating, 316–318
  outcomes, 323–326
  participants, 319–320, 322–323
  procedures, 318–323
Case study, 11, 14, 166, 235, 293–312, 317–318, 340
  contents, 302–303
  criteria, 300–302
  defined, 293–294
  example, 304–310
  procedures, 298–304
  use, 294–298
Chanute, Kansas, 200–204
Character Education Inquiry, 259
Child study programs, 20, 24, 354–355
Clerks, guidance, 126, 187, 191, 204, 358
Cliques, 252, 258
College Entrance Examination Board, 63, 109–110, 148
Commission on Guidance in American Schools, 11, 14, 365, 426
Commission on Secondary School Curriculum, 235, 296
Communication skills, 415–417
Community resources, cooperation with, 370, 372, 377–379
  information on, 367
  services, 362–367
  types, 361–362
Conferences, student-parent-counselor, 326–330
Confidentiality, 283–284, 355, 371, 374, 378, 401–404
Consultant, counselor as, 385
  mental health, 345, 348, 355–357, 369, 374
Cooperative General Achievement Tests, 108
Cooperative General Culture Test, 108
Cooperative Study of Evaluation in General Education, 106
Correlation coefficients, interpretation, 71–72

Counseling, changing concepts, 383–386
  client-centered, 446–448
  directive, 432–446
  eclectic, 458–463
  group, 229, 342–344
  a learning experience, 413–419, 448
  and psychotherapy, 386–387, 414–415
  relationship, 16–17, 410–413, 422, 434–435
  theoretical framework, 387–400
Counselor, case load, 4–8, 172, 201
  full-time versus part-time, 8–10
  personal qualifications, 422–423
  professional education, 8, 13, 384–385, 423–426
  role, 9, 264, 385–386
Counselor's Guide to Georgia Colleges, 140–141
Cumulative personnel records, 14, 37, 48, 136–139, 176, 207, 217, 255, 262–290, 369
  adjunct to counseling, 286–289
  contents, 268
  data processing, 271–273, 278
  development, 264–267, 277–281
  examples, 265–266, 278
  inservice study, 279–280, 283
  interpretation to parents, 284–285
  student-kept, 289–290
  transfer, 285–286
  trends, 273–277
  use, 267, 281–285

Daily record, 234–237
Davis-Eells Games, 98
Differential Aptitude Tests, 99–100, 122, 140–141, 149–150, 157, 161–162, 164, 417
Discipline, counselor's role, 385, 438–439
Drake Musical Aptitude Tests, 102
Dropouts, 208–219, 271
  identification, 213–216
  number, 208
  preventive measures, 217–219
  reasons for withdrawal, 212–214
  survey studies of, 209–213

Educational Policies Commission, 10–11, 36
Edwards Personal Preference Record, 128
Eight Year Study, 106, 108, 266
El Monte Union High School, 174–175
Emotionally handicapped children, assisting, 342–357

Emotionally handicapped children, identification, 339–340
  number, 334
  symptoms, 337–339
Environmental treatment, 349–353
ERB (Educational Records Bureau) Cumulative Record Card, 136–137, 265–266
Ethical standards, 85–89, 284, 354, 371, 378, 400–406
Evaluation questionnaire (*see* Questionnaire)

Family group therapy, 375–377
Field theory, 373–394
Follow-up studies, cooperative plan, 196–197
  of dropouts, 208–213
  of graduates, 197–208
  usefulness, 194–196, 392
Freudian theory, 387–392
Frustration, 335–336

General Aptitude Battery, 98, 100–101, 108
Gordon Personal Inventory, 128
Gordon Personal Profile, 128
Graves Design Judgment Test, 103
Group counseling (*see* Counseling)
Group guidance class, 6–9, 172, 288–290, 342
Guess-who technique, 259–260
Guidance program, basic principles, 10–15
  essentials, 2–4

Haggerty-Olson-Wickman Scales, 44–45, 46, 49
Harvard Guidance Study, 300, 304
Hawaii source data form, 280
Henmon-Nelson Test of Mental Ability, 95
Home Description Scale, 185*n*.
Horn Art Aptitude Test, 103
Huntington Beach High School, 170–171, 338

Inservice education, 279–280, 283, 298, 316–318, 353–357
Institute for Child Study, 21, 36–37, 354–355
Intelligence tests (*see* Aptitude tests)
Interests (*see* Vocational interests)
Interview, 176–177, 206–207, 209, 217, 255, 409–410
  desired conditions, 426–429

Interview, examples, 420–421, 439–446, 453–458, 461–463
  starting, 419–421
Iowa Tests, of Basic Skills, 106, 149
  of Educational Development, 107–108, 110, 161, 163

Kuder Preference Record—Personal, 128
Kuder Preference Record—Vocational, 117, 120–122, 128, 149, 157
Kuhlman-Anderson Intelligence Tests, 95

Lorge-Thorndike Intelligence Tests, 96–97
Los Angeles Child Guidance Clinic, 364
Los Angeles City Schools, 274, 290, 351
Los Angeles Welfare Planning Council, 367–369

Meier Art Judgment Test, 103
Mental health, criteria, 333–335
  promotion of, 340–342
Mental Measurements Yearbook, 75–76
Metropolitan Achievement Tests, 106
Minnesota Counseling Inventory, 130–131
Minnesota Multiphasic Personality Inventory, 129–131
Mooney Problem Check Lists, 126
Multifactor test batteries, 99–102

National Association of Secondary-school Principals, 47
National Defense Education Act, 63, 271–272, 327
National scholarship programs, 109–111
Nelson, case of, 305–310
New York City guidance evaluation study, 191, 207
New York Holding Power Project, 212, 214–216, 280
Normality, 336–337, 346
Norms (see Tests)

Observer, 37–38
Ohio State University Psychological Test, 96
Organismic theory, 394–395
Orientation course (see Group guidance class)
Otis Quick-scoring Test of Mental Ability, 95
Otis Self-administering Test of Mental Ability, 95

Oxnard Union High School, 210

Palm Springs High School, 328–330
Palos Verdes School District, 357
Parent, conferences with, 326–331
  developing referral with, 371–375
Pasadena Case Conference Committee, 378–379
Pasadena Welfare Board, 368–369
PEA (Progressive Education Association) Behavior Description Scale, 266
Personal data blank, administration, 173–176
  improvement, 181–188
  interpretation, 177–181
  usefulness, 170–173, 176, 182
Personality assessment, 123–131
Personality Record, 47–48
Personality Report, 49–51
Personnel records (see Cumulative personnel records)
Phenomenological theory, 395–397
Pintner General Ability Tests, 95
Plainfiéld High School, 22—23, 27, 174, 185
Projective techniques, 123–124
Providence Public Schools, 197
Psychoanalytic theory, 387–392
Psychotherapy (see Counseling)

Q-sort, 53, 228–229
Questionnaire, evaluation, 184, 188–192
  examples, 170–171, 198, 203–204, 210
  follow-up, 209–212
  personal data, 170–188

Rating scales, 42–62, 190–191, 340
  behavior description, 51–54
  check lists, 49–51
  criteria, 51, 53, 55
  graphic scales, 46–49
  guiding principles, 60–61
  improvement, 58–60
  limitations, 53–58
  ranking method, 45–46
Referral, 127, 342–343, 352, 355–356, 362–366, 369–370, 384, 401
Remedial education, 345–347
Rochester Athanaeum and Mechanics Institute, 21

Scattergram, 141–144
Scholastic Aptitude Test, 109–110
School and College Ability Tests, 96, 148

Seashore Measures of Musical Talent, 102
Self-analysis techniques, 224–229
Sequential Tests of Educational Progress,
106–107, 149–150
Social acceptance scales, 260–261
Social climate, school, 341–342
Sociodrama, 255
Sociogram, 248–250, 252–254
Sociometric grouping, 256–258
Sociometric test, administration, 243–246
criteria, 242–243, 256
interpreting results, 251–256
scoring, 250–256
summarizing data, 240–251
SRA (Science Research Associates),
Achievement Tests, 183
Junior Inventory, 126
Youth Inventory, 126
Stanford Achievement Tests, 183
Stanines, interpretation, 135
Stimulus-response theories, 397–399
Strong Vocational Interest Blanks, 116–
122, 129, 165
Student-kept records, 289–290
Student personnel point of view, 10–15
Study Habits Inventory, 183

Terman-McNemar Test of Mental Ability,
96, 146
Test data, interpreting, 68–69, 134, 138–
144, 149–166, 417
recording, 79–80, 137–140
Test program, development of, 74–80

Tests, of achievement, 104–111
administration, 78–79
advantages, 64–66
of aptitudes, 91–104
ethical issues, 85–87
limitations, 66–67
multifactor, 99–102
orientation to, 71–78
of personality, 123–127
preparation for, 76–78
reliability, 72–73, 135
scheduling, 76
selection, 69–73
uses, 99, 105, 113, 127
validity, 69–72, 91, 104–105, 121–122,
124–127
of vocational interests, 117–122
Time, need for adequate, 4–8, 269–271,
278, 314–316, 429
Time record (*see* Daily record)

Values, development in counseling, 437–
438, 452–453
Vocational choice, 115–117
Vocational interests, 113–122

Washington Junior High School, 346–347
Wechsler intelligence scales, 90–94
Wing Standardized Tests of Musical Intel-
ligence, 102
Wisconsin Counseling Study, 54, 176, 199–
200, 205–207, 231–232
Work experience program, 351, 367